Also in the Variorum Collected Studies Series:

BRENT D. SHAW
Environment and Society in Roman North Africa

MICHEL VAN ESBROECK
Aux origines de la Dormition de la Vierge
Etudes historiques sur les traditions orientales

HAN J.W. DRIJVERS
History and Religion in Late Antique Syria

R.A. MARKUS
Sacred and Secular
Studies on Augustine and Latin Christianity

W.H.C. FREND
Archaeology and History in the Study of Early Christianity

J.H.G.W. LIEBESCHUETZ
From Diocletian to the Arab Conquest
Change in the Late Roman Empire

FRANK M. CLOVER
The Late Roman West and the Vandals

SEBASTIAN BROCK
Syriac Perspectives on Late Antiquity

C.R. WHITTAKER
Land, City and Trade in the Roman Empire

LUISE ABRAMOWSKI
Formula and Context
Studies in Early Christian Thought

T.D. BARNES
Early Christianity and the Roman Empire

HENRY CHADWICK
Heresy and Orthodoxy in the Early Church

JOSEPH MÉLÈZE MODRZEJEWSKI
Statut personnel et liens de famille dans les droits de l'Antiquité

COLLECTED STUDIES SERIES

Rulers, Nomads, and Christians in Roman North Africa

TO SHAUNA

τὸν φρονεῖν βροτοὺς ὁδώσαντα
τῶι πάθει μάθος
θέντα κυρίως ἔχειν.
στάζει δ' ἀνθ' ὕπνου πρὸ καρδίας
μνησιπήμων πόνος καὶ παρ'
ἄκοντας ἦλθε σωφρονεῖν.

καὶ ἐξαλείψει πᾶν δάκρυον
ἐκ τῶν ὀφθαλμῶν αὐτῶν,
καὶ ὁ θάνατος οὐκ ἔσται ἔτι,
οὔτε πένθος οὔτε κραυγὴ
οὔτε πόνος οὐκ ἔσται ἔτι...

As true now as then...

Brent D. Shaw

Rulers, Nomads, and Christians
in Roman North Africa

VARIORUM
1995

This edition copyright © 1995 by Brent D. Shaw.

Published by VARIORUM
    Ashgate Publishing Limited
    Gower House, Croft Road,
    Aldershot, Hampshire GU11 3HR
    Great Britain

    Ashgate Publishing Company
    Old Post Road,
    Brookfield, Vermont 05036
    USA

ISBN 0-86078-490-8

British Library CIP Data
    Shaw, Brent D.
    Rulers, Nomads and Christians in Roman North Africa.
    (Variorum Collected Studies Series; CS497)
    I. Title. II. Series.
    939. 7

US Library of Congress CIP Data
    Shaw, Brent D.
    Rulers, Nomads and Christians in Roman NorthAfrica/Brent D. Shaw.
    p. cm. -- (Collected Studies Series; CS497).
    Includes bibliographical references and index.
    ISBN 0-86078-490-8 (alk. Paper)
    1. Africa, North--History--To 647. 2. Romans--Africa, North.
    I. Title. II. Series: Collected Studies; CS497.
    DT170. S54 1995   95-12456
    939' .7--dc20   CIP

The paper used in this publication meets the minimum requirements of the American National Standard for Information Sciences – Permanence of Paper for Printed Library Materials, ANSI Z39.48-1984. ∞ ™

Printed by Galliard (Printers) Ltd
    Great Yarmouth, Norfolk, Great Britain

COLLECTED STUDIES SERIES CS497

CONTENTS

Preface   vii–xi

PART ONE: ECONOMIC AND POLITICAL GEOGRAPHY

I   Rural markets in North Africa and the political economy of the Roman Empire   37–83
Antiquités africaines 17. Paris, 1981

II   The *undecemprimi* in Roman Africa   3–10
Museum Africum 2. Ibadan, 1973

III   The structure of local society in the early Maghrib: the elders   18–54
The Maghrib Review 16, London, 1991

IV   The Elder Pliny's African geography   424–471
Historia 30. Wiesbaden, 1981

V   The formation of Africa Proconsularis   369–380
Hermes 105. Wiesbaden, 1977

(In collaboration with Duncan Fishwick)

PART TWO: NOMADS

VI   'Eaters of flesh, drinkers of milk': the ancient Mediterranean ideology of the pastoral nomad   5–31
Ancient Society 13/14. Leuven, 1982/1983

VII   Fear and loathing: the nomad menace and Roman Africa   25–46
C.M. Wells (ed.), *Roman Africa/L'Afrique romaine. The 1980 Governor-General Vanier Lectures*, Revue de l'Université d'Ottawa 52. Ottawa, 1982

VIII   Autonomy and tribute: mountain and plain in Mauretania Tingitana   66–89
P. Baduel (ed.), *Desert et Montagne: Hommage à Jean Dresch*. Revue de l'Occident Musulman et de la Méditerranée 41–42. Aix-en-Provence, 1986

IX Soldiers and society: the army in Numidia 133–159
    Opus 2. Rome, 1983

PART THREE: AFRICAN CHRISTIANS

X   The elders of Christian Africa 207–226
    *P. Brind' Amour (ed.), Mélanges offerts à
    R.P. Etienne Gareau (numéro spéciale de Cahiers des
    études anciennes), Ottawa, Editions de l'Université
    d'Ottawa, 1982*

XI African Christianity: disputes, definitions, and 'Donatists' 5–34
    *M.R. Greenshields and T.A. Robinson (eds.), Orthodoxy
    and Heresy in Religious Movements: Discipline and
    Dissent. Lampeter: The Edwin Mellen Press, 1992*

Critical Bibliographical Addenda 1–22

Index 1–8

This volume contains xii + 338 pages

PREFACE

The eleven studies collected in this volume are intended both to supplement and complement those reproduced in *Environment and Society in Roman North Africa* (Variorum, 1995). They are part of my effort to describe and to analyze the modes by which the various peoples and regions of North Africa, between the Atlantic coast of Morocco and the hinterland of Tripolitania, became part of the Roman Empire. The essays are grouped under three general headings that reflect different aspects of the same problem: the mutation of African political and administrative institutions, the interaction between nomads and sedentarists in the process of the extension of Roman rule over the semi-arid and arid lands of the Maghrib, and, finally, the complex dynamic of cultural changes and continuities in the power conflicts that marked the Christianization of North Africa.

Unlike the studies reprinted in *Environment and Society*, these essays are less concerned with the interplay between the physical environment and human occupation—historical ecology—than they are with the cultural and economic institutions of the local society as it underwent the changes imposed upon it in the process of becoming part of a Roman Mediterranean order. The first group of the three series of studies, and the earliest in development, concentrated on what was the academic mainstream of historical analysis of the problem in the 1960s and early 1970s, namely the formal institutional aspects of the processes which at the time were usually lumped under the rubric of 'Romanization.' These studies attempted to resolve both the technical problems involved in the tempo and institutional developments entailed by the formation of the first Roman provinces in North Africa, including technical difficulties (that are still not wholly resolved) concerning the status of some of the critical primary sources used for analyzing these changes (chapters 2-5). Some of my earliest efforts in the field, however, were already devoted to the 'other side' of the same process—the mutation of indigenous instruments of governance under the impact of Roman rule (the *XIprimi* or 'Eleven Leading Men' and the councils of elders are exemplary instances).

The transitional and formative study reprinted in the present collection—the one that marked my passage from the analysis of formal political institutions to broader economic forces—is my analysis of the basic rhythmic institution of the rural periodic market. The aim of this study was to catch the social significance of an institution that simultaneously embodied the economic, cultural, political, and religious forces that coursed through the local societies of the ancient Maghrib (chapter 1). Even during the highest points of Roman power and rule in North Africa, the basic structure and function of the rural periodic markets revealed social institutions and behaviours that were monitored and controlled by the central state's authorities, and yet ones that continued to maintain their quite distinctive local character.

The critical nexus between social and economic forces that were deeply entrenched in local society, and yet which had to adapt and change to a dominant Roman social and political order—and be controlled by its agents—emphasized the need to study other sensitive 'barometric indicators' of change and order in local society. It was for this reason that my attention was drawn to the admittedly difficult and elusive subject of pastoral nomads, not only for whatever actual position they had in that social order, but also for the continual re-interpretation of the historical myths that they had provoked (chapters 6-9). In privileging their marginality as part of inquiry, the ideologies, ancient and modern (or, as is the fashion today, their 'discourses') had to be explicated—in addition to whatever actual problems of economic and military control pastoral nomads may or may not have posed (chapters 6-7). Clarification of the latter problem necessarily entailed a rethinking and renewed investigation of prevailing assumptions about the nature of 'the frontier' in North Africa.

An investigation of the Roman military frontiers in North Africa necessitated the reconsideration of matters as simple and basic as army recruiting practices (chapter 9), as well as the precise direction and material 'intent' of military constructions along the Saharan borderlands of the African provinces. The latter problem was one connected to an interpretive viewpoint that was more systematically elaborated in my Cambridge doctoral dissertation: that frontiers were zones of development in themselves, which have to be understood both as peculiar local communities in themselves and as the outer and final layer of defensive networks. These systems of roads, forts, and allied works were part of a frontier that not only extended into the desert periphery but was also a coalesced linear 'shoreline' of networks of roads and posts that policed the high plains of the North African hinterland. In this sense, the frontiers were intensely defended areas that simultaneously produced a local culture. The people who garrisoned the military establishments in these regions, and who inhabited them, were as much concerned with solidifying control over the immediate zone of 'the frontier' itself (especially its highland or mountain regions) as they were with maintaining a permanent barrier against any putative threats emanating from the Sahara desert. The domination of which these frontier zones were part was itself composed of a number of variables of which, for example, the imposition of tribute payments was but one. But tribute owed by 'barbarians' beyond the frontier was also multifunctional and variable, and was spread across a spectrum of actual or potential domination—not just up to the limit of the frontier, but well beyond it into so-called autonomous zones. It was this complex negotiated relationship that was investigated in one of the weakest and therefore most sensitively revealing sectors of the frontier in North Africa: the relationship between highland peoples and their leaders in the Middle Atlas mountains, and the Roman governors and military forces in the lowland plains of Mauretania Tingitana (chapter 8).

The fundamental cultural changes, and reinforcements of tradition, that followed on the Christianization of North Africa, as well as the massive and momentous social conflicts that came to be embodied in its religious divisions, offered a different perspective from which to sense and to describe the stress-lines as they were drawn into higher relief during an unusually well documented phase of North African history. The marvelously evocative and detailed sources that emerged from the rhetoric of this struggle enable the historian to trace the lineaments of minuscule and glacial changes which themselves amounted to an affirmation of the long-term social relations of most persons in rural settings—even after the addition of Christian churches. This convergence of tradition and change is reflected in the unusual predominance of elders in local ecclesiastical organization (chapter 10). The same densely disputatious texts also permit the historian to catch the changing alignments of the fundamental oppositions that rent local society. The extraordinarily detailed records of the quotidian talk—mundane conversation, bitter arguments, angry confrontations, and petty deceits—at the great Church Council held at Carthage in A.D. 411, therefore yield much more than a bare record of who was on what side, how many, and for what professed reasons. They also reveal how the lines of identification were drawn and maintained by different types of Africans, and they suggest the consequences that flowed from the angry words and postures for what that African identity was to become (chapter 11).

All of these studies, although perhaps somewhat disparate at first glance, share a common underlying historiographical concern: the existence of a peculiar historical laboratory in which specific problems of a given cultural history can be investigated with varying degrees of certainty and doubt—and perhaps thereby to contribute by small increments to a more general Mediterranean history of antiquity. This cultural history shares much in common with the problems of the imperialisms of the great European overseas empires of the early modern era, and with what have often been called the conceptions, and practices, of 'world empires' rather than 'world systems.' But the problems are even more complex and recalcitrant than this because the Roman empire was a coherent and contiguous domination of a great land mass. Moreover, some parts of the Roman empire were not well integrated with the political center of the state, while others were contributing to the formation of what might justifiably be labeled a quasi-national state. The investigations that are reproduced in this volume were written in an effort to try to answer questions concerning the nature of cultural change, political domination, and economic integration found in one region of this hybrid type of imperial state.

To place these contributions in the context of research done on the various subjects since they were first published, I have provided 'critical bibliographical addenda' at the end of this volume. In composing these additions, I have tended to be more fulsome in offering guidance to recent research on topics (e.g., prehistory of the Sahara, climate and environment) that might not be readily accessible to many readers of this volume, and where the amount and type of research is likely to make significant changes in our interpretation of the ancient Mediterranean. For the rest, I have tended to emphasize the arguments in the original publications that have proven to be the most contentious or which have raised critical objections—on which I have also attempted to offer some guidance to the reader.

I should like to thank the editors and publishers of the journals and books in which these articles were first published for their kind permission to reproduce them as part of this collection. In the process of making revisions and corrections to the originals and, especially, in conducting the research needed to compose the critical bibliographical addenda on new research done since my original publications, I had the advantage of using the marvelous holdings of the Library of the *Institute for Advanced Study* at Princeton. For the historian fortunate enough to be able to have access to it, the Library's extraordinary resources place at his disposal the very tools needed for the efficient and enjoyable completion of his task.

The first record of intellectual gratitude, however, must be assigned to my fellow research students at Cambridge University who, through the mid to late 1970s, shared in an unusual sodality, and who contributed to the lively discussions and debates that formed the questions and approaches that left their mark on almost all of the essays included in this volume. A further debt of thanks must be registered to Dick Whittaker and Joyce Reynolds. Dick Whittaker first provoked a deep and long-lasting interest in the history of North Africa, and has continued over these many years to raise iconoclastic questions relevant to the re-interpretation of that history, especially its military and economic aspects. Joyce Reynolds, to whom my debts were already acknowledged in the lead annotation of several of the articles reproduced in this collection, has that same thanks repeated here with the gratitude and warm affection properly due from a devoted student (though sometimes a querulous one) to a meticulous scholar and a humane teacher.

BRENT D. SHAW

Institute for Advanced Study
Princeton, New Jersey
March 1995

PUBLISHER'S NOTE

The articles in this volume, as in all others in the Collected Studies Series, have not been given a new, continuous pagination. In order to avoid confusion, and to facilitate their use where these same studies have been referred to elsewhere, the original pagination has been maintained wherever possible.

Each article has been given a Roman number in order of appearance, as listed in the Contents. This number is repeated in each page and is quoted in the index entries.

I

RURAL MARKETS IN NORTH AFRICA AND THE POLITICAL ECONOMY OF THE ROMAN EMPIRE

It has long been recognized that the study of the pre-Roman social structures of the ancient Maghrib is a necessary pendant to the understanding of the long-term process of the economic and political changes that followed upon the integration of North Africa within the Roman 'world system'*. In contrast with this admission, however, the balance of ancient North African studies is still tilted towards the urban centre and the upper political echelons of the Roman-African governing and land-owning elite. It is the purpose of this article to contribute to the fuller comprehension of one pre-Roman institution that was crucial to the function of social life in the rural regions of North Africa, both before and after the Roman conquest, namely, the rural periodic market.

The study of this institution is greatly facilitated by the plethora of excellent analyses of pre-modern marketing institutions produced in the last two decades [1]. The investigation seeks to extend the analysis beyond the institution itself into at least three major related areas of concern. First, it attempts to delineate the place of the rural periodic market within the broader economic and political development of North Africa in the Roman Empire, and especially its relationship to the dominant exploitative unit of the countryside, the large agricultural estate. Secondly, the relationship of this specific market *form*

---

* The author would like to thank Joyce M. Reynolds (Newnham College, Cambridge) and Mr. C.R. Whittaker (Churchill College, Cambridge) for their criticism of earlier drafts of this paper.

[1] The bibliography for early work on periodic markets can be found in FROHLICH (W.), *Das afrikanische Marktwesen*. Zeitschrift für Ethnologie, 72, 1940, p. 234-328. There was a 'lull' in market studies until the publication by BOHANNON (P.) and DALTON (G.), *Markets in Africa*. Evanston, Ill., Northwestern University Press, 1962 (African Studies, no. 5), and the paperback edition, *Markets in Africa : Eight Subsistence Economies in Transition*, New York, Anchor Books, 1965. A survey of more recent work can be found in LOCKWOOD (W.G.), *Periodic Markets : Source Materials on Markets and Fairs in Peasant Society*. Monticello, Ill., Nov. 1972 (Council of Planning Librarians, Exchange Bibliography no. 341) ; SMITH, (R.H.T.), *Periodic Markets in Africa, Asia, and Latin America*. Monticello, Ill., Sept. 1972 (*Ibid.*, no. 318) ; and BROMLEY (R.J.), *Periodic Markets, Daily Markets, and Fairs : A Bibliography*. Melbourne, 1974 (Monash Publications in Geography, no. 10) ; cf BROMLEY (R.J.), HODDER (B.W.), and SMITH (R.H.T.), *Market-Place Studies : A World Bibliography up to 1972*. London, S.O.A.S., 1974, and especially the valuable synoptic analysis of SMITH (C.A.), *Economics of Marketing Systems : Models from Economic Geography*. Annual Review of Anthropology 3, 1974, p. 167-201, which concentrates on work since Bohannon and Dalton (1965).

to market systems in general is studied, with an attempt to elucidate the nature of the separation between rural-local, centrifugal market systems and the large central market systems of town and domain. Lastly, the rôle of periodic markets in the process of urbanization is analyzed in order to illustrate the diverse potential of rural market systems with respect to town development and political control.

1. General Theories of Periodic Market Systems and the Berber Aswâq of the Contemporary Maghrib

There can be no doubt that the periodic market has been one of the central social institutions of the unurbanized rural regions of the Maghrib, at least from the beginnings of recorded history in North Africa until very recent, post-colonial times. The periodic meetings between the members of various ethnic groupings have been one of the most fundamental and enduring aspects of Maghribi society. But before considering the specific form which this type of rural market had in ancient and modern North Africa, some of the more common general characteristics of periodic market systems as delineated by an ever growing number of geographers and anthropologists should be examined first.

Periodic markets are primarily a rural phenomenon, a specific mode of centralised exchange and integration typical of many traditional societies. Even where they eventually become embedded in towns or villages, the clientele they are designed to serve is principally rural [1]. As their appellation indicates, it is above all a *time* frame that defines them; the peculiar periodicity or temporal cyclicality of the assembly is most characteristic of this type of market [2]. There is also a distinct tendency for periodic markets to build into mutually dependent *systems* of interconnected and non-competitive market-days and places. The nature of this systemic tendency, however, is not always well defined; that is to say, market days are not invariably mutually exclusive according to any 'law-like' principles [3]. Further, periodic markets are *centre-places* and are usually part of central-place systems; their place in the system is defined by a complex matrix of social and geographical factors. Where social boundaries are not in dominance and certain other conditions such as geographic isotropy are met, centre-places tend to build into various determinate geometric patterns (e.g. hexagons, rhomboids, and dendritic forms) depending on the predominant regional influences on communication (e.g. economic trade or ease of transpor-

---

[1] BOHANNON and DALTON, Markets in Africa, 2-14 ; MINTZ (S.), Peasant Markets, Scientific American, 203, 1960, p. 112-22 ; NASH (M.), in SHANIN (T.), ed., Peasant Societies. Harmondsworth, 1973, p. 161-77 ; HILL (P.), Notes on Traditional Market Authority and Market Periodicity in West Africa. Journal of African History, 7, 1966, p. 295-311, at p. 298 ; HODDER (B.W.), Periodic and Daily Markets in West Africa, (in) The Development of Indigenous Trade and Markets in West Africa. London, Oxford University Press, 1971, p. 347-58, at p. 350 ; see for the Maghrib : MIKESELL (M.), The Role of Tribal Markets in Morocco (Examples from the 'Northern Zone'). The Geographical Review, 48, 1958, p. 494-511, at p. 504-05 ; and TROIN (J.F.), Marchés ruraux et influences urbaines dans l'arrière-pays de Rabat. Revue de Géographie du Maroc, 7, 1965, p. 71-75.

[2] See BOHANNON and DALTON, Market in Africa, intro., and HODDER (1971) ; SMITH (R.H.T.), West African Market-Places : Temporal Periodicity and Locational Spacing (in) C. MEILLASSOUX (ed.), Indigenous Trade and Markets, 1971, p. 319-46, and The Synchronization of Periodic Markets. International Geography, 1, 1972, p. 591-93 ; WIRTH (E.), Zur Theorie periodischer Märkte aus der Sicht von Wirtschaftswissenschaften und Geographie. Erdkunde, 30.1, 1976, p. 10-15. The reasons for periodicity, as SMITH (1974) 81-86 points out, are not directly related to traders' itineraries or interests since the clientele is often both consumer and supplier at the same time (p. 84). This simple fact vitiates much of the analysis of e.g. WEBBER (M.J.) and SYMANSKI (R.), Periodic Markets : an economic location analysis. Economic Geography, 49, 1973, p. 213-37. The increase in the number and frequency of periodic markets is probably related more to the rise in the level of rural production (supply density) than to the level of consumer demand (pace FINLEY (M.I.),The Ancient Economy. Berkeley-London, University of California Press, 1973, p. 138, from B.J.L. Berry). Periodicity is, in fact, a simple attribute of certain types of central-place distribution systems, see SMITH (1974) 181.

[3] BROMLEY (R.J.), SYMANSKI (R.), and GOOD (C.M.), The Rationale of Periodic Markets. Annals, the Association of American Geographers, 65, 1975, p. 530-37 ; cf SMITH (1974) 167 ff. with emphasis on the systemic properties of periodic markets.

tation). These theoretical constructs, however, are only occasionally applicable to North Africa [1]. Lastly, periodic markets are *total institutions*, not simply economic markets in the narrow sense of the word, and so they are marked by a multiplicity of functions of which material exchange is only one [2].

With these general characteristics in mind, let us now turn to the modern counterpart of the ancient periodic market in North Africa, the rural *sûq*. Since the rural *sûq* (pl. *aswâq*) is situated in a similar geographical and social milieu, the patterns evident in its structure and function can be legitimately used as a comparative model or paradigm to elucidate certain aspects of its ancient precursor. Although I believe this proposition to be generally true, there are a number of caveats that the reader should note. First, most of the anthropological studies of the Maghribî rural *sûq* date from later colonial times, and therefore reflect conditions of a relatively modern North African society that is historically separated from that under Roman imperial aegis. One could stress numerous aspects of the great divide between the two societies, but three are particularly important for our purposes: the penetration of Islamic social structure, culture, law, and belief; the development of new forms of socio-political structures (e.g. different networks of cities and a 'feudal' régime in the countryside); and lastly the intrusion of modern colonial systems characterized by a significant immigrant movement of foreign colonists on to African lands. All three factors, as we shall see, left their imprint on the type of rural *sûq* observed by modern academic researchers. Another important caveat is that almost all available published reports on the structure and function of modern rural *aswâq* pertain to Berber communities in the mountain highlands of North Africa, principally the Middle Atlas and Rif of Morocco, and the Qabiliyya of northern Algeria. It might be claimed that these communities are in a more pristine state than lowland settlements and so reflect more accurately the ancient Berber society of Roman imperial times. Even if this were so, and it is only a guess, the comparative pattern would only hold true for the peculiar highland ecology and geography in which these markets have been studied. The rigidity and high degree of structural uniformity apparent in the organisation of these *aswâq* probably cannot be transferred willy-nilly to the lowland plains of the eastern Maghrib from which most of our information on their ancient counterparts is derived. Further, much of the comparative data has been provided by the efforts of a single sociologist, one Walter Fogg, a pupil of Eduard Westermarck, whose research methods, as one critic has remarked, were far from

---

[1] For the bibliography see BERRY (B.J.L.) and PRED (A.), *Central Place Studies, a Bibliography of Theory and Applications*. Philadelphia, 1965, and BERRY (B.J.L.), *The Geography of Market-Centres and Retail Distribution*. Englewood Cliffs, N.J., Prentice-Hall, 1967. Perhaps one of the best known and most successful applications of the theory is SKINNER (G.W.), *Marketing and Social Structure in Rural China*. Journal of Asian Studies, 24-25, 1964-65, p. 3-43, 195-228, and 363-99 (with reply by DONNITHORNE (A.) in vol. 25, 1965, p. 318-24) ; and for the Roman world: HODDER (I.) and HASSALL (M.), *The non-random spacing of Romano-British Walled Towns*. Man, n.s., 6, 1971, p. 391-407.

See further on application: SMITH (1971), (1972); with SYMANSKI (R.) and WEBBER (M.J.), *Complex Periodic Market Cycles*. Annals, the Association of American Geographers, 64, 1974, p. 203-13. SMITH (1974) 168-73 is an excellent survey of the conditions required for successful application of *CPT*, and its limitations.

In North Africa, the environmental conditions for settlement are so stringent, and isotropy so rare, that market sites, especially in the semi-arid zone, tend to be determined by the simple accessibility of water. There are some cases such as the High Plains of Numidia where such an approach might prove fruitful; for possible instances of centre-places in the region see BARADEZ (J.), *Vue aérienne de l'organisation romaine dans le Sud-Algérien : Fossatum Africae*. Paris, Arts et métiers graphiques, 1969, p. 227 and 260.

[2] See STANLEY (P.V.), *Ancient Greek Market Regulations and Controls*. PhD diss., Berkeley, University of California, 1976, p. 10-11 on the Athenian *agora* (cf Plato, *Legg.*, 817c); the Roman forum does not even call for comment; in general on substantivism see BOHANNON and DALTON, *Markets in Africa*, passim; for North Africa see ROBIN (N.), *Fetena Meriem (la guerre de Marie)*, RAf., 18, 1874, p. 161-70, at p. 163: «... certains *kanouns* prononçaient même des amendes contre ceux qui, sous le prétexte qu'ils n'avaient rien à vendre ni à acheter, ne se rendaient pas sur le marché de la tribu ». Cf HANOTEAU (A.) and LETOURNEUX (A.), *La Kabylie et les coutumes kabyles*. Paris, Imprimerie nationale, vol. 1, 1872 ; vols. 2-3, 1873, at 3, p. 77 f., and the articles by FOGG cited below.

FOGG (W.), *The Suq : A Study in the Human Geography of Morocco*. Geography, 17, 1932, p. 257-67, at p. 262; and MIKESELL (1958), 497.

ideal [1]. Nevertheless, one might justifiably hold that, as an heuristic methodology, the outline of the salient features of the modern-day rural *sûq* is a valuable tool in establishing a general model for our investigation.

The tribal market assemblies studied in the modern Maghrib vary greatly in size and frequency, but by far the most common type of periodic market is the weekly *sûq*, which numbers in the thousands [2]. Both its name (*sûq*: سوق، فى) < vb. *sawwaqa*: سَوَّقَ 'to market, to barter'), and the interval at which it takes place (once every seven days) bear the imprint of Islamic culture on the social structure of the countryside. The modern *sûq* is essentially a rural phenomenon that is characterised most not by its size or location, but by its peculiar periodicity and ephemeral existence. The sites of periodic assemblies, in their most basic form, usually lack any permanent marketing facilities — though sometimes the participating tribesmen may agree to mark the perimetre of the exchange area with a crude earthen wall topped by a row of cacti or jujube to serve as makeshift fencing. The market, therefore, is not defined by space (i.e. a strictly objectified place) but is specified by the dimension of *time*. The time dimension consists of a *market day* and the *duration of time* within the day itself that delineates the market proceedings. The actual duration of the market is surprisingly brief. Members of the tribe attending the market set out early on the designated day; they arrive by mid-morning and the market usually reaches a peak of activity about mid-day. By early afternoon people from the further destinations begin to leave, and well before sunset the site is completely deserted. The barren landscape shows few traces of the intense activity of only a few hours before [3].

Other than purely economic influences, there are two principal factors affecting the location of the *aswâq*: topography and the pattern of local social structure. Both factors underscore the essential liminality of the market and serve to emphasize the central function of the market as a type of communications link between various interfaces of local society that facilitates exchange between them. Insofar as geographical location is concerned, two main principles can be perceived: accessibility (i.e. communication) and diversity (i.e. exchange). The market is usually located close to a regularly used route connecting disparate zones: a high road, a route frequented by nomads or transhumant pastoralists, or a mountain pass. The site is within a day's return journey for those who trek to it, bearing in mind that the participants are often willing to trek long distance by foot in forbidding weather in order to attend. The general effective radius is about ten kilometres, and rarely in excess of thirty kilometres [4].

The other main geographical factor affecting location is the placement of important periodic markets on the frontier of zones of complementary production. Markets located at the juncture of two or more such zones tend to grow in importance because they facilitate a more permanent, large-scale exchange

---

[1] See articles by FOGG cited throughout; DAVIS (J.), *People of the Mediterranean : an Essay in Comparative Anthropology*. London, RKP, 1977, p. 17.

[2] BENET (F.), *Weekly Markets : their Importance for Research and Action*, (in) *Contributions to Mediterranean Sociology* (ed. J.G. Peristiany). Paris, Mouton, 1968, p. 163-66 ; BRUNSCHVIG (R.), *Coup d'œil sur l'histoire des foires à travers l'Islam*, (in) *Recueils de la Société Jean Bodin*, 5, « La Foire », Paris, 1953, p. 43-75, at 44-52 ; KINDERMANN (H.), *Al-Suḳ*, (in) *The Encyclopaedia of Islam*[2], Suppl., London, 1938, p. 213-14 ; for North Africa see SCHLITZ (H.), *Der marokkanische Souk*. Die Erde, 104, 1973, p. 320-35, and in the Middle Ages see Al-Bakri (trans. MacGuckin de Slane), Paris, Maissonneuve, 1965, p. 7, 36, 82, 135, 161-69 and 306, and Al-Idrisi (trans. de Goeje, Paris, 1866), p. 108, 111 etc.

[3] FOGG (1932) 260, and *Tribal Markets in Spanish Morocco*. Journal of the Royal African Society, 38, 1939, p. 322-26 (= 1939a), at p. 324 ; cf COON (C.), *Tribes of the Rif* (Harvard African Studies, no. 9). Harvard, Peabody Museum, 1937, pl. 2, 30, 31, and 32 ; see also *Encyclopédie coloniale et maritime* (ed. E. Guernier), *Tunisie*. Paris, 1949, pl. p. 195.

[4] BENET (F.), *Explosive Markets : the Berber Highlands*, (in) *Trade and Market in the Early Empires : Economies in History and Theory*, ed. K. Polanyi, C.M. Arensberg, H.W. Pearson, Glencoe, Ill., The Free Press, 1957, p. 188-217, at p 197 ; MIKESELL (1958) 497-98 ; TROIN (J.F.), *Observations sur les souks de la région d'Azrou et de Khenifra*, Revue de Géographie du Maroc, 3-4, 1963, p. 109-20, at p. 116 ; and FOGG (1932) 260-61.

commodities produced mainly in one of the two zones. The major frontiers of complementary production in the Maghrib with which we shall be concerned are two. First, the boundary between the mountain massifs and the valleys or plains which lie beneath them. The highlands are marked by a predominance of intensive garden farming, arboriculture, and summer transhumance, whereas the plains and valleys have a tendency to larger farm units with a predominance of cerealculture, winter transhumance, and pastoral nomadism. Second, there is the line between the *tell* and the semi-arid zone. The former is the domain of sedentary farming, usually intensive cerealculture, the latter a zone of irrigation or 'dry-farming' and nomadic pastoralism. Of course, there are many other micro-frontiers cross cutting each little geographical enclave in the Maghrib, but these are the two principal frontiers we should note for the following analysis [1].

But there is also the question of the determinant rôle of social structure. In regions, or times, in which political frontiers as defined by central states in the Maghrib have not been dominant, it is the structure of the local ethnic group or 'tribe' which is crucial in setting frontiers. In fact, one of the prime reasons for the remarkable persistence of the periodic *sûq* in the mountain highlands of North Africa lies in the complex structure of the Berber tribes which, in itself, tended to form a strong impediment to the development of the daily market place. Although villages or small towns may exist within the territory inhabited by a 'tribe', it is virtually impossible for permanent market places to be established in them because of the hostility of opposed tribal segments. The territorial hostility which is part of the system of 'segmentary opposition' discourages the members of one tribal group from traversing the territory of their neighbours. Because of the way in which segmentary opposition tends to lead to chequerboard patterns of alliances, hostile segments of the tribe are usually found in close proximity to one another. To facilitate some form of exchange within this social oxymoron, some neutral meeting place must be found between the juxtaposed hostile groups. Usually this forum is provided by the rural market which, for the reasons just outlined, must be placed in some neutral region between adjacent cantons, in a sort of 'no-man's land' separating feuding tribal segments [2].

Of course, the market site also obeys a number of other basic requirements, such as an adequate water supply. It also tends to be situated in a suitable topographical space. But requirements such as these are rather flexible — we must constantly bear in mind that the rural *sûq* is not a permanent market place and so its location can be shifted, within moderate distances, according to the needs of those who, by their attendance, virtually create the market [3]. Indeed, some of the physical requirements may seem mundane to mention, but in the fragile ecology of the Maghrib a factor such as water supply, which might be of variable influence in other environments and hence safely ignored by centre-place theorists, becomes crucial, even determinant, in the placing of market sites. In the Maghrib, where wadis flow at best for only a few days in the year, the water supply is usually provided by a perennial spring. The presence of this one element is, as we shall see, a constant element in the location of settlements and market sites in the ancient Maghrib.

2. The Urban Market Place and Rural Periodic Markets in the Ancient Mediterranean and North Africa

As a specific means of economic redistribution and integration, the ancient periodic market can be conceived as a distal point on a spectrum of marketing institutions that ends in the permanent market place at the centre of the Mediterranean town. But what specific type of redistribution does the periodic

---

[1] MIKESELL (1958), 498-99 ; FOGG (1932) 263 ; TROIN (1963) 109 f. ; cf LEVEAU (Ph.), Ant. Afr., 3, 1973, p. 188 for an ancient example.

[2] ROBIN (1874) 163 ; MIKESELL (1958) 498.

[3] FOGG (1932) 262.

market represent, within which wider networks of distribution is it engaged, and what are the modes of integration between the two ? To begin this inquiry, we might consider some of the salient characteristics of its opposite form: the permanent market place of the ancient Mediterranean city. As urban institutions, the Greek *agorā* (ἀγορά) and the Roman *forum* were marked out by the type of solid public edifices that symbolized the ancient city: temples, porticoes, record offices, paved plazas, legal and government centres, and permanent market facilities where various specialized urban traders and craftsmen managed their business on a day-to-day basis throughout the year. The major distribution networks in which these town markets were involved are:

1. markets which tied the immediate countryside to the urban core in a local system of distribution that provided the urban population with basic necessities;

2. much more rarely, and only in the case of some very large cities, there might be specialized markets serving as *entrepôts* for 'luxury' traffic or large-scale necessities, but not in the precise sense of trade for the city itself;

3. some urban centres had also absorbed the function of the rural periodic market in which case one day of the week of the urban market was set aside notionally as a service time for the rural population about the city;

4. urban markets which met the needs of internal commodity circulation within the town itself.

Only in cases two and four (and then only marginally) were urban markets tied into larger, extra-communal distribution networks. In theses instances the larger systems were limited to (a) specialized commodities being transferred or circulated through a series of urban and rural market places, and (b) high-level demand commodities (e.g. grain) controlled by the state.

The control of the urban market place was also a direct reflection of its complete integration within the structure of the antique city. Urban magistrates, almost invariably selected from local town élites, were held responsible for the policing and control of the market place, whether *agoranomoi* in the Greek city or *aediles* in the Roman town [1]. In the case of command commodities, sometimes urban officials were also set in charge of the actual market transactions [2]. The main defining characteristic of the urban market, therefore, was its permanency, a phenomenon mirrored materially in the building that surrounded the central plaza. Each of these was a reification of functions also inherent in the temporal market: the *basilica* or *hēliaia* (legal function), the *bouloterion* or *curia* (political function), and the temples (the sacred). The crucial difference is the process of objectification that signalled the inseparable connection between these 'market' functions and the Mediterranean town *and* their separation into distinct 'secular' institutions in their own right.

Not only physical construction (the concrete sphere), but also vocabulary (the mental-verbal) separated the polar expressions of these marketing institutions. The periodic market, whether it eventually became embedded in an urban centre or remained in the open countryside, was a purely rural institution designated *panēgyris* by the Greeks and *nundinae* by the Romans [3]. Its defining characteristics were the opposite of those of the urban market place: a crucial separation from urban centred institutions, a fully integrated, holistic structure that included diverse social functions, a freedom from formally impos-

---

[1] ROSTOVTZEFF (M.), *The Social and Economic History of the Hellenistic World*. Oxford, Clarendon Press, 1941, p. 451-54, 486, 952 ; *The Social and Economic History of the Roman Empire*², rev. P.M. Fraser. Oxford, Clarendon Press, 1957, p. 146-47 ; JONES (A.H.M.), *The Greek City*. Oxford, Clarendon Press, 1940 (repr. 1971), p. 215-17, 230-34, 240 ; STANLEY, *Greek Market Regulations*, chap. IV.B, p. 197-262 (on *agoranomoi*), 5.B-C, p. 264-316 (on harbour and grain officials).

[2] FINLEY, *The Ancient Economy*, p. 169-70 ; cf STANLEY, *Greek Market Regulations*, p. 237 f. for some examples.

[3] See LIDDELL & SCOTT, *Lexicon*, s.v. πανηγύρις from πᾶς and ἀγυρά (= ἀγορά), p. 16, 129. See ZIEHEN (L.), *Panegyris*. *RE* 18.3, 1949, coll. 581-83.

ed controls, a lack of permanency, and a predominance of non-formalist economic functions. The *panēgyris* (or *agorai koinai*) and the *nundinae* principally served the commodity exchange and communications needs of the countryside. As centres of communication, they were also places where issues of local leadership and repute were decided [1]. It is still a matter of dispute when the true urban market place emerged from the 'time market' in the history of the eastern Mediterranean, but at the origins of the Greek *polis* of the seventh-sixth centuries B.C., the *agorā* was still the communications centre of the countryside, a place where near-feudal lords dispensed judgements in return for 'gifts' [2]. The Homeric *agorā* was still a place of gathering, an assembly intended for discussion and debate (cf the verbs *agorazein*, *panagurizein*). Later, however, the *agorā* and the *astu* (the residential part of the city centred on the *akropolis*) were the component parts of the diptych of the classical city or *polis* [3]. The same process is discernible in the western Mediterranean where the tribal fair or market is the clear precursor to the urban *fora* of later times. The tribal assembly, it seems, was essentially a bundle of 'rights' protected by mutual consent. So, in rural pre-Roman Italy, the market or fair was the centre of integrated social life shared by hostile, warring Latin tribesmen. Here, under the umbrella of safe-conduct and neutrality, there could be certain guarantees of legal exchange (*ius commercii*),common religious ceremonies,and even assemblies for concerted political action [4].

The market *places* found in the *fora* of the towns and cities of the Roman period in North Africa are easily identified and studied from their architectural remains [5]. But in analyzing the evidence for the periodic market one must be careful, at least at the outset, to exclude from consideration these urban centred markets. The problem then remains: how are we to identify and study institutions that were so ephemeral and did not tend to leave any physical traces of their existence ? It is almost solely due to the fortuitous preservation and discovery of a series of Latin inscriptions erected at the sites of such periodic assemblies that we have any knowledge of them at all. Equally fortunate is the fact that the Romans, and the Africans who also employed Latin, carefully distinguished between the two types of market in their formal language. The permanent urban market located in the *forum* was designated by the terms *mercatus* or *macellum* [6]. Interestingly, both terms seem to be of Phoenician derivation, an indication that the concept of 'market' (as opposed to *agorā* or *forum*, meaning 'outdoor place of assembly') had a

---

[1] E.g. Hdt. 1.37.2, cf Luke 11.43 ; DE STE CROIX (G.E.M.), *The Origins of the Peloponnesian War*. London, Duckworth, 1972, append. 5, *Some Athenian Laws Affecting the Agora*, p. 399 ; cf STANLEY, *Greek Market Regulations*, 51-52.

[2] Hesiod, *Works and Days*, 22 f. ; see POLANYI (K.), *The Livelihood of Man*, ed. H.W. Pearson. New York-London, Academic Press, 1977, chap. 10, *Market Elements and Market Origins*, p. 123-42 and chap. 11.

[3] Cf Hdt. 1. 153-1-2 ; Eurip. *Orest*. 919 ; Demosth. *Or*. 17.17 ; cf Plato, *Rep*. 371 and *Legg*. 846d-849a, and Arist. *Pol*. 1331.a.30-64. STANLEY, *Greek Market Regulations*, 8-11 ; POLANYI, *Livelihood of Man*, chap. 12, *Local Markets : the Political Economy of the Polis and Agora*, p. 160-87.

[4] ALFOLDI (A.), *Early Rome and the Latins*. Ann Arbor, University of Michigan Press, 1971, 28 f., 40 f. ; cf Dion. Hal. 3.32.1-2, 8.58.1 ; Livy 1.30.5, 4.22.2, 6.22, 7.31.11 and 9.42.11.

[5] See the survey in ROMANELLI (P.), *Topografia e Archaeologia dell'Africa Romana* Enciclopedia Classica, sez. 3, vol. 10, t. 3, Torino, 1970, chap. 12, *Mercati*, p. 146-52 ; DEGRASSI (N.), *Il Mercato Romano di Leptis Magna, parte I*, QAI, 2, 1951, p. 27-70 ; CAGNAT (R.), *Le marché des Cosinii à Djemila*. C.R.A.I., 1915, p. 316-23 ; CHATELAIN (L.), Le *macellum de Mactaris*, M.E.F.R., 31, 1911, p. 349-63 ; and THOUVENOT (R.) and LHOUET (A.), *Le macellum (?) et les bâtiments voisins*. P.S.A.M., 9, 1951, p. 81-99 (at Banasa).

For the epigraphic evidence see C. 26.482 = *ILAfr*. 516 ; *ILAfr*. 523 = C. 26.530+26.533 (Thugga) ; C. 1406, cf 14.906 = *ILS* 6795 (Thignica, Hr. 'Aïn Tûnga) ; C. 12.353 (Turca, Hr. bû-Scha) ; *IRT* 294, 468 (*Lepcis Magna*), and *IL Afr*. 425 (*Utica*) for *tabernae*.

For literary evidence see Aug. *Confess*. 6.9; *Civ. Dei*, 16.8 ; Procop. *de Aedif*. 6.5.10, and Victor Vit., *Hist. Pers. Vand*. 2.13 (Carthage).

[6] SCHNEIDER (K.), *Macellum*. R.E. 14¹, 1928, col. 129-33 ; WYMER (G.), *Marktanlagen (römische)*. R.E. 14², 1930, col. 1876-80 ; LECLERCQ (H.), *Marché et foire*. DACL, 10.2, 1932, 1777-99 ; and HUVELIN (P.), *Essai historique sur le droit des marchés et des foires* Paris, A. Rousseau, 1897, p. 80 f.

distinctly Phoenico-Punic origin in the west [1]. Rural *times of exchange*, contrasted with the commercial town market, were designated by a *time* frame — the Latin word *nundinae* [2]. As is clear from the etymology of the word, derived from *novem* and *dies*, it referred to markets that took place on every ninth day, counting inclusively. The cycle was in fact one and the same as the archaic Italian eightday week [3]. Though such periodic markets are basically a rural phenomenon, when the full epigraphic evidence concerning specific *nundinae* first emerges from Italy, the *nundinae* had already been absorbed by urban centres. One of the known marketing cycles based on the tradition *nundinum* of eight days included the Campanian towns of Pompeii, Nuceria, Atella, Nola, Cumae, Puteoli, and Capua. The eighth city that completed the cycle was Rome itself, an inclusion that probably reflected the economic and political control of the central city later imposed on Campania [4]. But *nundinae* in towns are clearly a later developmental process for which there are good historical reasons (see. below pp. 64 f.). Otherwise, all literary information pertaining to *nundinae* in Italy indicates that they were a specifically rural institution. The ninth day was the one day of the week specially reserved for the inhabitants of the countryside; it was the one day when the peasants journeyed to the nearest town centre to exchange their produce, obtain necessities, and communicate information [5]. Although the term *nundinae* (and derivatives like *nundinari* and *nundinator*) did acquire broader semantic meanings (e.g. generally 'to market, to trade, marketeer') because of the dominance of urban markets, they retained their basic sense of periodicity and orientation to the countryside.

When the Romans and Italians came to North Africa as landowners and administrators in the decades and centuries after the final destruction of Carthage in 146 B.C., they applied this same distinctive terminology to the various types of marketing institutions they encountered in Africa. Latin inscriptions attesting the existence of *nundinae*, as opposed to *fora, macella* and *mercatus*, have been found throughout the countryside of the Maghrib, and it is primarily from this body of evidence that we can deduce something of the importance and function of this institution within the Roman system.

3. The Peculiarity of the North African Nundinae

Given the known continuity and strength of local institutions and social practices in the provincial regions of the Roman Empire, one would expect to find the persistence of African social forms even under the aegis of Roman administration. That the Latin term *nundinae* was applied by the Romans, or adapted by the Africans, to designate rural periodic markets in North Africa might be taken as a *prima facie* indication of the importation or adoption of an Italian institution. There is evidence, however, to show that this is definitely not the case. As stated above, the principal defining characteristic of the rural periodic market is its time framework, and the limits which this time system imposes on the system of markets

---

[1] DE MEYER (L.), *L'étymologie de macellum, marché*. A.C., 31, 1962, 148-52, and GABBA (E.), *Mercati e fiere nell'Italia romana*. S.C.O., 24, 1975, 141-60, at p. 145.

[2] BESNIER (M.), *Nundinae*. *Dar.-Sag.*, 4.1, 1904, p. 120-22, at p. 120 ; ERNOUT (A.) and MEILLET (A.), *Dictionnaire étymologique de la langue latine*⁴. Paris, 1959, s.v. 'novem', p. 447 : « adjectif composé de *novem+din* — 'qui a lieu tous les neuf jours' ». They understand the substantive *nundinae* to derive from a phrase such as *nundinae (feriae)* — though this is not universally accepted, see KROLL (W.), *Nundinae*. RE, 17², 1937, 1467-72, at col. 1467.

[3] On the archaic eight-day *nundinum*, see ERNOUT and MEILLET, *Dictionnaire étymplogique*⁴, *ibid.* ; Festus, *De verborum significatione* (ed. Lindsay), ss. 171, 181, 293 and below no. 139.

[4] DELLA CORTE (M.), *Scavi sulla Via dell'Abbondanza : epigrafi inedite*. Notizie degli scavi, 52, 1927, 89-116, at p. 98 = A.E., 1928 : 115 = *Inscr. Ital.*, 13.2, 1963, no. 53.

[5] Varro, *RR*, 2, pr., 1-2 : *Itaque annum ita (sc. maiores nostri) diviserunt, ut nonis modo diebus urbanas res usurparent, reliquis septem ut rura colerent*. Cf Columella, *RR*, 1. pr. 18 and Dion. Hal. 2.28.3; Pliny, *NH*, 18.3.13-14; Plut. *Quaest. Rom.*, 42 ; and Macrobius, *Sat.* 1.16.28-36.

or 'organic whole' to which each individual market belongs. Contemporary markets in the Berber highlands often function in such cyclic units. That is to say, periodic markets in any given tribal region do not ordinarily function independently of one another, but are arranged so as to form a single operating unit. The market days within each group develop so as to avoid clashes with nearby markets in the same unit. In this way the market days build into closely interwoven cycles of seven markets, one day of the week assigned to each market place. The unit thus formed can become the regular circuit for itinerant traders and tribesmen from the various segments concerned [1].

The marketing cycles found in the mountain highlands of the Maghrib in modern times are closely analogous to the ancient Italian *nundinae*. Both literary and epigraphic data confirm that the Italian periodic markets were held in strict sequential eight-day cycles, one cycle following the other in smooth uninterrupted order [2] (see fig. 4). Fortunately, the cycles of African *nundinae* can be computed from the information contained on several of the Latin inscriptions set up at the market sites (see charts 1-4). Unlike the Italian *nundinae* they are rather erratic, with a variation from twelve to eighteen days between one market day and the next, depending on the month in which the markets were held. Needless to say, this extremely peculiar 'periodicity' is not to be found in any region of the Roman Empire outside North Africa. In fact, no market system studied by any anthropologist or geographer has revealed such an erratic cycle and, for reasons we shall later discuss (see pp. 67 f.), market cycles based on non-periodic sequences must be ruled out as functionally and theoretically 'impossible'. The distortion perceptible in the African *nundinae* recorded in the Latin inscriptions, therefore, must be due to some external influence that has warped their original true periodicity. The most efficient explanation for this warping is the imposition of a Roman mode of time reckoning on an original African time-market system. And yet, whatever the new system employed for reckoning the African *nundinae* (i.e. either relative to the *ides* and the *kalends*, or relative to the *nones* and the *kalends*), there is absolute uniformity in the cycles of the African *nundinae* that can be computed (see charts 1-4) wherever they happen to be found, whatever their date, and whatever the different actual dates in the month on which the market days happen to fall. Moreover, our records, though not numerous, span more than two centuries in time and come from regions over five hundred kilometres removed from one another. This remarkable uniformity surely indicates an ancient institution that functioned as an integral part of rural society long before the Roman conquest and which persisted in the post-conquest period under a Latin label.

In considering periodic markets known from other parts of the Roman Empire, can one find any parallel in form to the African *nundinae*? One such market was held at *Aquae Iasae* in the *Ager Poetovionensis* in Upper Pannonia. After it had been destroyed by fire, the village of *Aquae Iasae* was rebuilt at the behest of the emperor Constantine. At the same time as the reconstruction of the town, the governor Valerius Catullinus supervised the establishment of regular market days. They were to be fixed at one week intervals, once every 'sun-day' throughout the year [3]. It seems probable that this new cycle, a seven-day period reflecting the influence of the cult of *Sol Invictus*, was an innovation that ignored the traditional market cycle previously in effect at *Aquae Iasae* [4]. But, as we shall see,

---

[1] HANOTEAU and LETOURNEUX, *La Kabylie et les coutumes kabyles*, vol. 2, p. 78 ; FOGG (1932) 260 ; BENET (1957) 197 ; and TROIN (1965) 72-73, with maps.

[2] Mac MULLEN (R.), *Market-Days in the Roman Empire*. Phoenix, 24, 1970, p. 333-41, at p. 339-41.

[3] *CIL* III, 4121 = *ILS* 704 (nr. Warasdin, Hungary), cf MOCSY (A.), *Pannonia*. Stuttgart, 1962, coll. 689-90 ; for the governor see *PLRE*, Catullinus (5), 188 and *fasti*, p. 1091 ; see further GORENC (M.) and VIKIC (B.), *Die Aquae Iasae und ihr Verhältniss zum Pannonischen Limes*. Quintus Congressus Internationalis limitis Romani Studiosorum, Acta et Dissertationes Archaeologicae, 3, Zagreb, 1963, p. 111-17.

[4] See MARBACH, *Sol (die orientalischen)*, *RE*, 5², 1927, coll. 406-13, and KUBITSCHEK (W.), *Grundriss der antiken Zeitrechnung*. Handbuch der Altertumswissenschaft, no. I,7, Munich, Beck, 1928, p. 33-39.

African markets were *not* held either according to the old Italian *nundinum* of eight days, or the novel Semitic 'week' of seven days that was becoming prevalent throughout the western Mediterranean by the late third century A.D. [1]. Rather, they took place twice a month at roughly biweekly intervals.

The African *nundinae*, as we have hypothesized above, must have been affected in their regular periodicity by the superimposition of the Roman system of time reckoning. Since the variation in the distortion engendered by the Roman system reduces to a mean cycle of fifteen days (15 ± 3), we must suspect that the markets were originally held either according to a twice monthly pattern of 15-day intervals, or according to 14-day cycles — i.e. twice each lunar month of 28 days. Given this hypothesis, it is perhaps interesting to note that the closest parallels to these periodic cycles are to be found in the Hellenistic East. One case are the markets in the village of Baitokaikê in Syria [2]. The periodic festivals (πανηγύρεις) held at the sanctuary of Zeus Baitokaikeus had their tax-free status confirmed by the emperor Augustus and later reconfirmed by the emperors Valerianus and Gallienus. The periodic festivals at Baitokaikê took place on two fixed dates: the fifteenth and the thirtieth day of each month. The origins of the periodic markets are very ancient, since it was either one of two Seleukid monarchs (Antiochos I, *regn.* 293-61 B.C., or Antiochos II, *regn.* 261-46 B.C.) who first granted the tax immunity [3]. Indeed, the practice of holding periodic markets twice every lunar month may have been a Semito-Hamitic social custom of great antiquity. It was even found in regions outside the Semitic orb in the East, as is demonstrated by the cycle of another periodic festival (πανηγύρις) held at Koulê in Lydia. A rescript from the governor of Asia, a certain Maximillianus (*gubern. c.* 260) to the Asiarch Domitius Rufus gave to the people (dêmos) on the estate of the 'Four Towers' (Τετραπυργία) permission to hold a fair on the fifteenth day of each month [4].

4. The Roman State and the Problem of Market Control

The Roman state administration, therefore, encountered in North Africa a peculiar local institution that was the analogue to similar periodic markets known in Italy and throughout the Empire. In all regions surrounding the Mediterranean under the aegis of the Roman state, these market festivals, numbering in the thousands, presented the administration with a common problem. [5] Since they were the customary point of assembly for otherwise dispersed rural populations, they formed a central node in a communications network that unified peasants, villagers, and nomadic pastoralists. As such the market has often been considered a potentially subversive institution in the eyes of political authority, whether

---

[1] KUBITSCHEK, *Antiken Zeitrechnung*, ss. 8, *Antiken Wochen*, p. 30 f. ; SAMUEL (A.E.), *Greek and Roman Chronology : Calendars and Years in Classical Antiquity*. Handbuch der Altertumswissenschaft, no. II.7, Munich, Beck, 1972, p. 18 ; widely known in the Latin west by the third century (cf Tibull. 1. 13.18 ; Dio 37.18 ; cf Gen. 29.27) ; known in Africa by the 2nd/3rd Cent., see *ILTun.* 710 (*Thuburbo Maius*).

[2] *CIL* III, 184 = Ditt. *OGIS*, 262 = *ILS* 540 = *IGLS* VII, 4028 (Hosn Soleiman = Baitokaikê, A.D. 253-59) = Abbott & Johnson, *MARE*, no. 147.

[3] SEYRIG (H.), *Antiquités syriennes, no. 48 : Aradus et Baetocaece.* Syria, 28, 1951, p. 191-206, at p. 202 = *Antiquités Syriennes*, 4, 1953, p. 172-85, at p. 181. See REY-COQUAIS (J.-P.), *Les privilèges de Baetocécé*. IGLS, 7, 1970, p. 54-67.

[4] *IGRR* IV, 1381 = *SEG* XIII, 518 (Koulê, Lydia) ; see KEIL (J.), *Ein Marktag in Maeonien*, (in) *Studies Presented to David Moore Robinson*, ed. G.E. Mylonas & D. Raymond, St. Louis, University of Missouri Press, 1953, p. 363-70 ; JONES, *The Greek City*, p. 260 ; and MAGIE (D.), *Roman Rule in Asia Minor*. Princeton, 1950, vol. 1, p. 449-50 (p. 1559, no. 8) ; for Maximillianus see *PLRE*, *Maimillianus (5)*, p. 575 and Domitius Rufus, *ibid.*, and *PIR*², D. 191 — though both publications mistakenly refer to him as 'Domninus'. It may reflect a Greek, or at least Athenian, practice of setting the periodic market day for the rural region surrounding a city one day of each month, see STANLEY, *Greek Market Regulations*, p. 53.

[5] MacMULLEN (1970) 333 *guesses* that three-quarters of all trade in the empire took place at such markets, a not implausible estimate.

ancient or modern. But the sheer number and diversity of rural periodic markets meant that they posed a particularly difficult problem of supervision and control; and yet the element of control was a necessary adjunct to the peaceful exploitation of the countryside.

Modern colonial authorities were most aware of the importance of the market and its potential danger. Since the periodic market was the one place where widely dispersed rural tribesmen could be observed in their collectivity, it became one of the most important keys to the control of the unurbanized countryside about its focal point. The significance of the *sûq* for political and military surveillance was manifest. Where villages, towns or cities existed, *they* became the administrative control centres for the rural district involved; where these urban centres were absent, the periodic market served in their stead. It was here that the colonial power located its 'propaganda' stations (*Bureaux de renseignements*), less to spread information favourable to its own position than to serve as a centre for discreet inquiry into tribal affairs [1]. Not all markets could be supervised easily or effectively *in situ* and so appropriate measures had to be taken to ensure that they remained harmless institutions. Where possible, market sites were moved forceably closer to zones of military control or, alternatively, forts or military camps were placed in proximity to the market site. Where these two options were not feasible, entirely new markets were created deep in zones firmly under the control of the colonial administration [2]. Concomitant with these moves, other measures were taken to tighten the grip of the colonial authority on the market place. The prime result of the intrusion of these formal controls into the local market was the confrontation and diminution of the indigenous market authority, usually the Berber holy man, and its replacement by external administrative officiers and local secular 'big men' who were held responsible for the conduct of the market participants [3].

As is well-known, the Roman state, as most other central states in antiquity, had an almost morbid fear of any unofficial assembly or association. But one manifestation of this fear in policy and legislation are the rigid controls and restrictions placed on any 'group' activity in the empire. Any collective activity, from the street gang to the formally organised corporate club, was usually designated by the term *collegium* — the best known examples of such organised behaviour being the craft associations found in the urban centres of the empire [4]. Of course, there is the classic case of the refusal by the emperor Trajan to sanction the organisation of a small fire brigade in the city of Nicomedia for fear of the possible dangerous political consequences of merely forming men into an organised group [5].

Given this general fear of assembly and since both the functions of 'assembly' and 'organisation' seen in *collegia* are also inherent in *nundinae*, it should come as no surprise that the right to hold periodic

---

[1] Fogg (1932) and Mikesell (1958) 510.

[2] Fogg (1932) 263, and his *The Economic Revolution in the Countryside of French Morocco*. Journal of the Royal African Society. 35. 1936, p. 123-29, at p. 126, (1939a) 324; and *Changes in the lay-out, characteristics and function of a Moroccan Tribal Market consequent on European Control*. Man, 41, 1941, p. 104-08, at p. 105.

[3] See Fogg (W.), *The Organization of a Moroccan Tribal Market*, American Anthropologist, 44, 1942, p. 47-61, at p. 58 and 61.

[4] Waltzing (J.P.), *Etude historique sur les corporations professionnelles chez les romains depuis les origines jusqu'à la chute de l'Empire d'Occident*, 4 vols. Louvain, C. Peeters librairie (repr. Bologna, Forni editore, 1968), vol. 1, 1895, p. 132-40; vol. 4, 1900, p. 581-83; Duff (P.W.), *Collegia : the Ius Coeundi*, chap. 4 (in) *Personality in Roman Private Law*, Cambridge, C.U.P., 1938, p. 95-128; cf *D*. 47.33.1 f., and *CIL* XIV, 2112.1; cf De Robertis (F.), *Il Diritto Associativo Romano*. Bari, Laterza, 1938, p. 195 f., 219 f., 247 f., and 269 f.

[5] Pliny, *Ep*. 10.33-34; cf Sherwin-White (A.N.), *The Letters of Pliny : A Historical and Social Commentary*. Oxford, Clarendon Press, 1966, 606-10; for other examples of imperial control of assembly at places of buying and selling see Suet, *Tib*., 38.2, 40.1; *Nero*, 16.2; Dio 60.6; cf Millar (F.), *The Emperor in the Roman World*. London, Duckworth, 1977, p. 178, no. 23.

markets, the *ius nundinandi*, was only to be obtained from the very highest level of state authority. In all the so-called 'senatorial' provinces of the empire, such as *Africa*, the request to hold periodic markets had to be filed with the consuls in Rome and permission had to be granted by the Senate [1]. In all other African provinces, as in all other so-called 'imperial' provinces, the applicant needed to get permission from the emperor himself. In all known cases, we may surmise the intermediary action of the provincial governor through whose agency the petition (*libellus*) of the applicant was passed on to the emperor who, if favourable, granted permission by means of a rescript to the original request [2]. In most provinces of the empire the grant was considered an imperial *beneficium* [3]. Upon receipt of permission, the applicant was then able formally to establish a periodic market (*nundinas constituit, instituit*) under official auspices [4]. The latter act also involved the participation of the provincial governor who supervised the terms of the implementation of the imperial rescript or *senatus consultum* [5].

It has been assumed that the power to grant the *ius nundinandi* in the 'senatorial' provinces, as with so many other powers, was gradually usurped by the emperor. But where we do have evidence concerning the establishment of markets in 'senatorial' provinces (e.g. Africa and Asia), there is no sign of imperial intervention. The only positive evidence that this power had become the monopoly of the emperor by the beginning of the third century is a statement made by the Severan jurist Herennius Modestinus which seems to suggest that all markets were sanctioned by the *princeps* alone [6]. But the phraseology of the passage in the *Digest* is ambiguous: it is possible that Modestinus is referring elliptically to those markets under the nominal control of the emperor and not any others. And in Africa the Senate maintained its jurisdiction in this matter, with no sign of diminution, at least till the reign of Antonius Pius (pp. 54 f.). In Asia there is no indication of direct imperial intervention in the text of Maximillianus' rescript to the Asiarch Domitius Rufus in the latter part of the third century (p. 45-46 above). Throughout, Italy was regarded as a 'senatorial' preserve, and so Claudius, ever the respectful 'constitutional' emperor, correctly sought permission from the consuls and the Senate to hold *nundinae* on his private estates in Italy [7]. Another such case is that of the senator Tiberius Claudius Sollers who submitted a request to the Senate to establish *nundinae* on his estate near Vicetia in northern Italy [8].

---

[1] See nos. 7 and 8 below.

[2] HUVELIN, *Droit des marchés*, 107-08 ; BESNIER (1904) 122 ; KROLL (1937) 1471 ; *D.* 50.11.1, cited in no. 6 below.

[3] MILLAR, *Emperor in the Roman World*, p. 350. The terms *beneficium* and *rescriptum* are used in *CJ* 4.60.1 cited in no. 2, p. 57 below, and in the 'Aïn Kerma inscription from North Africa, no. 2, p. 59 below.

[4] The terms used of establishing a market are *constituere* : 'Aïn Meshira (no. 1, p. 61), Aquae Iasae (no. 3, p. 45) ; *instituere* : Vicetia, Italy (no. 8 below), Casae (no. 1, p. 54 below), 'Aïn Melûk (no. 3, p. 62) ; and *habere* : Casae (no. 1, p. 54) and Rûffash (no. 1 p. 67), as well as *agere* : Castellum Tidditanorum (no. 3, p. 66). There does not seem to be any discernible difference in the terms employed.

[5] See 'Aïn Kerma (no. 2, p. 59) and Castellum Tidditanorum (no. 3, p. 66) in Africa, and Koulê (no. 4, p. 46) in Asia.

[6] In addition to BESNIER (1904) and KROLL (1937), see WILMANNS (G.), *S.C. de Nundinis Saltus Beguensis*. Eph. epigr. 2, 1875, p. 271-81 (with 'Scholia' of Th. Mommsen, p. 281-84), at p. 279 ; and SHERWIN-WHITE, *Letters of Pliny*, p. 319 ; MOMMSEN (Th.), *Römisches Staatsrecht*, 3 vols., Leipzig, 1874-87 ; II, p. 887, and III, p. 1181 and 1211. See now, MILLAR, *Emperor in the Roman World*, p. 350 — though the cases he cites do not prove the point.

For the Herennius passage see *D.* 50.11 (*de nundinis*) 1 : *Modestinus libro tertio regularum : Nundinis impetratis a principe non utendo qui meruit decenii tempore usum amittit.*

[7] Suet. *Claud.* 12.2 : *Ius nundinarum in privata praedia a consulibus petit* — in a passage retailing Claudius' virtues. See MILLAR, *Emperor in the Roman World*, p. 178.

[8] Pliny, *Ep.* 5.4 : *Vir praetorius Sollers a senatu petit ut sibi instituere nundinas in agris suis permitteretur*, cf *Ep.* 5.13 and SHERWIN-WHITE, *Letters of Pliny*, 318-20 and 339-43.

Ostensibly, this close supervision of markets enabled the authorities to establish set procedures for buying and selling. The laws on *nundinae* were also concerned with providing adequate protection for those travelling to and from the market place, and safety at the market site itself for the regular clientele. Both these measures were nominally instituted as part of an apparently benevolent concern for maintaining the freedom of the market. Nevertheless, the scarcely hidden implication of some of the legal texts is one of deep worry over the subversive potential of the market: the fear that the market might become more than just an innocent exchange of goods [1]. The fear, it must be admitted, was often justified. (see p. 69 f.).

5. The Markets of Pre-Roman Africa

Although there must have been thousands of periodic markets in the African countryside in pre-Roman times, there is little evidence from the period of the African kings to inform us of their 'pre-Roman' state. Archaeologists are sometimes able to suggest the location of a market site by correlating the factors of topography and material finds. A typical example would be the pre-Roman site on the ridge of Kef Smaar some eighteen kilometres ENE of Tiaret. The site is located strategically on the frontier of two distinct economic zones: with mountain arboriculture and dry-farming to the north, and the northern reaches of the High Plains of Algeria, principally a zone of pastoralism, immediately to the south. Kef Smaar is also located on a north-south route which, even to this day, has remained one of the most important roads into the *tell* followed each year by pastoral nomads on their trek to summer pastures. It is at this juncture that a small settlement was discovered that yielded fine quality Campanian 'B' ware in quantities unusual for a site so far inland [2]. Obviously Kef Smaar was an entrepôt for exchange between the Andalousian coast, via wadis Mina and Tiguiguest, to the interior. The main period of this trading activity involving the Campanian 'B' ware dates from the early second to the mid-first century B.C. [3]. But it seems probable that the site had long been a market centre for exchange between nomads and sedentarists, probably at annual fairs rather than hebdomadal markets. But details of the market's function, in the absence of any literary sources, elude us.

Another example from the regal period of such a regional market that must have had a periodic element is that found in the African town of Vaga (mod. Béja) in the Upper Bagradas river basin. Sallust, in the *Bellum Iugurthinum*, calls Vaga the 'forum rerum venalium totius regni maxume celebratum', and mentions the large number of Italian merchants who took advantage of its facilities as a centre-place

---

[1] HUVELIN, *Droit des marchés*, 113 f., citing *D.* 2.12 (*De feriis et dilationibus*) 3.2 (Ulpianus) : *Item in eum, qui quid nundinarum nomine adversus communem utilitatem acciperit, omne tempore ius dicitur*, cf GAUDEMET (J.), *L'Empire romain a-t-il connu des foires?*, (in) *Recueils de la Société Jean Bodin*, 5, *La Foire*, Paris, 1953, p. 25-42, at p. 39 f. ; presumably such fears were also at the root of the restriction of the 'contracted' right to ten years, see Herennius Modestinus in no. 6, p. 48 above.

Even more forceful is *Nov. Valent.* 15.5 (*De siliquarum exactionibus*), between 11 Sept. A.D. 444 and 18 Jan. 445 (= Haenel, *Nov. Theod.* 27.5), though the 'security' element is not so apparent because of the primary concern with the market as an instrument of taxation :

Sed haec, quae tam salubriter ordinamus, in omnibus provinciis atque urbibus una eademque volumus ratione servari : quod absque ullius erroris inpedimento explicabitur, si certae nundinae civitatibus earumque territoriis ordinentur. Iubemus enim et in oppidis et in regionibus certo loco ac tempore emendis atque vendendis rebus per honoratorum dispositionem nec non ordinum seu civium sub praesentia moderatoris provinciae manifesta definitione constitui. Nulli itaque mercatori praeter hanc observationem nisi ad designata loca temporibus praestitutis ad negotiationis suae species distrahendas passim licebit accedere, uti certa ratio emendi atque vendendi ibi constare possit, ubi nundinandi ius provincialium tractatu fuerit deputatum et id, quod praeberi supra statuimus, facilius eorum, qui praepositi fuerint, valeat diligentia reperire.

[2] CADENAT (P.), *Un établissement pré-romain dans la région de Tiaret (Oranie)*. Ant. Afr. 6, 1972, p. 29-58, at p. 56-57.

[3] CADENAT (1972) 57 on the market, p. 36-40 on the dates derived from pottery finds.

for the African kingdom [1]. Doubtless villages such as Vaga in the African kingdoms functioned as market centres, especially all those town specified in our literary sources as royal 'treasuries' (cf the modern *maghzen*) that were connected with the system of regal tribute. Alongside these town market-centres there were also the numerous periodic markets in the countryside; again this can only be argued from inference — such markets certainly did not emerge full-blown with the first Latin inscriptions that inform us of their existence, though we know virtually nothing of their specific function under the African kings.

Extrapolation from the data of the Roman period remains one of the most promising means of reconstructing the type and function of periodic markets in purely African contexts. One example of an indigenous market from the Roman period that illustrates the functioning of an African fair in a pre-Roman context is found in an inscription from the rural region of Hassawana, deep in the rugged foothills north of the Mejāna Plain, directly west of ancient Sitifis [2]. The fertile lands of the Mejāna Plain, whatever their previous type of development, were in the process of being incorporated into large imperial and private Roman estates in the first half of the second century. This process required the regularisation and definition of the estate lands vis-à-vis the members of the largest ethnic group in the region, the *Numidae*. Markers belonging to part of this operation, carried out in A.D. 137 by the governor of Mauretania Caesariensis, C. Petronius Celer, were found at al-Guerria on the western periphery of the Mejāna Plain [3]. The alignment of the boundary stones, running along the base of the mountain massif, seems to indicate that the Numidae were concentrated in the highland regions surrounding the Mejāna Plain, and that the mountains were regarded as their territorium or reserve. It is in the highlands to the north of the plain that the inscription mentioning the African market was found. Generally

---

[1] Sall. *Bell. Iug.* 47.1, *...oppidum Numidarum nomine Vaga, forum rerum venalium totius regni maxume celebratum, ubi et incolere et mercari consueverant Italici generis multi mortales...*
The is a rôle it has still had in modern times : see BONNIARD (F.), *La Tunisie du Nord, le Tell septentrional : étude de géographie régionale*, 2 vol. Paris, P. Geuthner, 1934, vol. 1, pt. V.1.4, *Les échanges. Les marchés*, p. 370-73, cf 135-42 and 427-28 : the Tuesday market centre for the region, the most important market centre of the northern Tell along with Mateur (anc. *Matera*). Note also the same distinction between the function of the local market and greater central market still existed in our day : « Aujourd'hui, ce sont les produits de Béja et des pays environnants qui alimentent le marché : miel et beurre en jarres, cire, peaux, laine en toisons, toutes sortes d'objets de sparterie en alfa, animaux... Béja est donc le type du grand marché agricole dans un pays riche. Les colons européens ne manquent pas d'y venir ; ils y traitent leurs affaires : vente de grains, achats d'engrais, de machines... » etc. — and that these two major functions co-existed with even more primitive marketing institutions in the region, see MONCHICOURT (Ch.), *La région du Haut Tell en Tunisie : Le Kef, Téboursouk, Maktar, Thala. Essai de monographie géographique*. Paris, 1929, p. 470 f.

[2] GSELL, *Atl. Arch.* f. 15 (Akbou) no. 73 ; Algeria 1 : 200.000 (Aumale) opp. no. 24 at M.tat el-Firane ; see GSELL (S.), *Recherches archéologiques en Algérie* (= *RAA*). Paris, 1893, p. 285-86 who lists the three most extensive ruins in the region as Kherbet-Guidra, Tassameurt, and Hassawana, cf GSELL (S.), *Les monuments antiques de l'Algérie* (= *MAA*), 2 vols. Paris, 1901, vol. 2, p. 211. The ruins of Hassawana cover approximately 13 ha.

[3] DESANGES (J.), *Catalogue des tribus africaines de l'antiquité classique à l'ouest du Nil*. Dakar, Université de Dakar, Faculté des lettres et sciences humaines, Publications de la section d'histoire, no. 4, 1962, p. 66-67 on the Numidae ; the boundary markers are C. 8813, 8814 = *ILS* 5960 ; on Celer see THOMASSON (B.E.), *Die Statthalter der römischen Provinzen Nordafrikas von Augustus bis Diocletianus*, 2 vols. Lund, 1960, vol. 2, p. 255 ; he was responsible for the delineation of boundaries between the *territorium* of the *civitas* of *Regiae* (mod. Arbal) and a *saltus* (C. 21.663 = *ILS* 5963, at er-Rahel, some 40 km west of Arbal), and it seems that he was varrying out similar operations in the Majāna Plain. For some of the estates affected, see C. 8811, cf 20.618 = *ILS* 5964 (Borj Majâna, nr. Satûr), and C. 8812 = *ILS* 5965 (Meris, nr. Majâna) : imperial estates of Trajanic and Hadrianic date established at the same time as the military colony at Sitifis, see FÉVRIER (P.-A.), *Inscriptions inédites relatives aux domaines de la région de Sétif. Mélanges d'archéologie et d'histoire offerts à A. Piganiol*, Paris, S.E.V.P.E.N., 1966, p. 217-28, at p. 220.

speaking, the use of Latin in the epigraphy of the Hassawana region does not antedate the Severan period and so it is most probable that the notice of the market post dated the Roman domain formation in the Mejāna Plain by about a century [1].

At the market site, the Africans erected the following inscription [2]:

*Nundina(s) / annu(as) quod / praecepit /
Iovis* (sic) *et Iu/ba et Genius // Vanisnesi /
quod precepe/runt Dii Ingi/rozoglezim*

Strictly speaking, the *nundinae* at Vanisnesus were not periodic markets of a hebdomadal type, but were annual fairs comparable to the great yearly festivals observed in present-day Morocco where large-scale trade takes place between incoming Saharan nomadic groups and local sedentarist populations. Such fairs are usually located, as at Kef Smaar, at the frontier between the Sahara and the *tell* [3]. Often such fairs are held on the anniversary date of an important saint and are therefore located close to a holy shrine. These annual markets last several days and attract thousands of participants, often from great distances [4]. Such a combination of annual trade that combines plain and mountain exchange, together with a religious celebration of some type would fit the context of the Hassawana inscription very well.

The significant feature of the market proclamation at Hassawana, apart from the faulty Latin, is the lack of any indication that permission had been sought from or was granted by the Roman provincial authorities. The fair appears to have been an autonomous institution with local holy powers and not the secular ruling authority creating and controlling the assembly. The *nundinae*, so we are informed, were established in response to the commands of certain divinities: Jupiter, Juba, the *Genius Vanisnesi*, and the *Dii Ingirozoglezim*. At first glance one might believe that a definite element of Roman influence is shown by the concession to Jupiter ('Iovis') of prime position as creator of the market and, inferentially, chief of the pantheon of deities envisaged by the proclamation. Although Jupiter is known as the patron deity of marketing in some places outside Africa, we must suspect that in this case 'Iovis' is a cover name for the African god Saturn [5]. Indeed, one can hardly doubt the cross identification of the two gods in our inscription when the deep imprint of Saturn worship upon tribesmen in the Hassawana region is

---

[1] In a region generally poor in epigraphic remains, both in numbers and quality, C. 8831, cf 20.631 (Sertei) of A.D. 211 is the earliest *dated* inscription. Nothing in the remaining inscriptions indicates a date before the end of the second century A.D.

[2] C. 20.627 = *ILS* 4490 = A.E., 1894 : 96 (Hassawana), marked by *hederae distinguentes*

[3] BERNARD (A.), *Le Maroc*, 8ᵉ éd. Paris, F. Alcan, 1932, p. 170 f. ; FOGG (1932) 257-58 (his type one) ; al-Bakri, 149, 185. For counterparts in the Roman Empire see GAUDEMET (1953), MACMULLEN (1970) 336, and SPERBER (D.), *Roman Palestine*. Ramat-Gan, 1974, p. 89, 232 no. 6 ; cf Strabo 13.629.

[4] BRUNSCHVIG (1953) 44-52 ; FOGG (1932) 258 ; BENET (1957) 197.

[5] For Jupiter as the patron deity of *nundinae* see Plut. *Quaest. Rom.* 42 ; Macrob. *Sat.* 1.16.30, and the dedication to *I(ovi) O(ptimo) M(aximo) / N(undinario)*, C. III, 3936 = 10.820 = *ILS* 7116, A.D. 238 (Siscia, Upper Pannonia).

See LEGLAY (M.), *Saturne africain, histoire* (= *SAH*). Paris, Editions E. de Boccard, 1966, p. 233-36 on the identification of the two gods. See also his *Saturne africain monuments, II ; Numidie-Maurétanies* (= *SAM*, II). Paris, CNRS, 1966, p. 310-11 = C. 9195 (*Rapidum*, A.D. 259), the collocation of Saturn and the *numen Iovis* by a Roman knight who was prefect of the *gens Masat...* ; *SAM* II.63 = C. 8246 = *ILS* 4477 (*Idicra*, 'Aziz-ben-Tellis), a dedication to three aspects of Saturn : *Nutrix, Iuppiter*, and *Tellus* ; and *SAM* II.268 = C. 8434, cf 20.340 (*Sitifis*, Sétif, A.D. 234), and cf C. 8432 and 3433 (A.D. 236).

For the total merging of the two deities see LEGLAY (M.), *Saturne africain monuments, I : Afrique proconsulaire* (= *SAM*, I), Paris, Arts et métiers graphiques, 1961, p. 336 = C. 16.523 = *ILAlg.* I.3006 (Hr. Rohban) ; 339 = C. 10.624 = *ILAlg.* I.3005 ; 348-49.43 = R.S.A.C., 55 (1923-24) 215-16 (Tébessa) ; 349.45 = *ILAlg.* I.3473 (Hr. Gûnfida).

Note that all 'equational' identifications are by Roman dedicants, all syncretistic identifications are by Africans.

considered [1]. At Kherbet-Guidra (anc. *Sertei*), for example, less than ten kilometres east of Hassawana, a *princeps* of the *Numidae* restored a temple, precinct, and altars dedicated to the god Saturn at his own expense [2].

After having invoked the head of the African pantheon, the tribesmen then mention the spirit of 'Juba'. This is almost certainly the apotheosis of Juba II, the African king who was one of the last to rule over this part of Mauretania. That he held a position only second in rank in the hierarchy of gods to Saturn over two centuries after his death is striking testimony to the continuing spiritual authority of African leadership amongst the *Numidae* [3]. Following on the list is the *Genius Vanisnesus* — the 'Spirit of Vanisnesus'. The question is: who or what is Vanisnesus? Possibly it is a place name, perhaps the site of the market itself. Certainly the veneration of the spirits of *loci* such as mountains, springs, rocks, caves, and even trees, was a common aspect of ancient African cultic practice [4]. But one cannot exclude the possibility that it might be the name of an individual and that it is the *genius* of a 'holy man' worshipped in connection with the fair. [5] In last place come the gods with the exotic name 'Ingirozoglezim', unknown save for this one instance. One cannot be absolutely certain about their function, but the analogy of the form of their name with other similar divine groups known from Africa (e.g. the *Dii Mauri*, *Dii Magifae*, *Dii Macni*, and the *Dii Gaetulorum*) argues that these are 'ethnic' or 'regional' deities of some type. Probably they are the local ethnic deities of the Numidae who inhabited the Hassawana region [6].

How did this hierarchy of Berber deities communicate their desire to establish markets to the tribesmen at Hassawana? The language of the inscription is explicit on this point: it states that they 'commanded' (*praecepit, preceperunt*) that this be done. By comparison with precisely the same terminology use in the Saturn cult (*praecepto, ex praecepto*) we know that these commands were commonly issued in a dream or vision [7]. Who might the ancient African recipient of such a dream have been at Hassawana?

---

[1] At nearby Hammâm-Guergûr (see LEGLAY, *SAM* II, 289.95) and at 'Aïn Roua (*SAM* II, 286-87.93) and at 'Azziz-ben-Tellis see BERTHIER (A.) and TAYEB (H.), *Une inscription à Saturne d'Azziz-ben-Tellis et la formule sub iugum intravit*, B.A.A., 4, 1970, p. 301-12.

[2] Sex. Victor, who was *dec(urio), pr(inceps) g(entis) N(umidarum)*, see LEGLAY, *SAM* II, 288.94 = C. 8826, cf 20.628 = A.E., 1946 : 92, *Sertei*, mod. Kherbet-Guidra, A.D. 247.

[3] TOUTAIN (J.), *Les cultes païens dans l'Empire romain*. Paris, Larose, 1917, t. III, ch. 1, *Les cultes africains*, p. 39-40 ; CAMPS (G.), *Aux origines de la Berbérie : Massinissa ou les débuts de l'histoire* = Libyca (Arch.-épigr.), 8, 1960, 279-87 ; BOUBE (J.), *Un nouveau portrait de Juba II découvert à Sala*. B.A.M., 6, 1966, p. 91-108, shows how his cult survived till the fifth century A.D. in Tingitana.

[4] For *genii loci* in Africa see Toutain, *Cultes païens*, p. 40-43 (cf C. 9014) ; GSELL (S.), *Histoire ancienne de l'Afrique du Nord* (= *HAAN*). Paris, Hachette, vol. 6, 1927, p. 132-35 ; Ch.-PICARD (G.), *Les Religions de l'Afrique romaine*. Paris, Plon, 1954, p. 4-5, 24-25. Cf *CIL*, *indices*, p. 224, and the following examples : of a mountain (*C.* 17.763 ; 14.588 = *ILS* 8723a, *Simitthus*, mod. Shemtû ; 9180, nr. *Auzia* ; 21.567, cf *ILS* 9241 note and *AE* 1948 : 208) ; of a river : *C.* 5884 = *ILS* 3906, cf *AE* 1942/43 : 31, *Sila* ; of a spring : *C.* 8926 = *ILS* 3924, *Saldae*, mod. Bejaïa. For *numina* of the market-place see Aug. *Ep.* 16-17 (A.D. 390).

[5] There is a Vannidensis presbyter known from the list of bishops of Caesariensis in A.D. 484, see MESNAGE (J.), *L'Afrique chrétienne : évêchés et ruines antiques d'après les manuscrits de Mgr Toulotte et les découvertes archéologiques les plus récentes*. Paris, 1912, p. 347, and MAIER (J.-L.), *L'épiscopat de l'Afrique romaine, vandale et byzantine*. Bibl. Helvetica Romano no. 11, Genève, 1973, p. 237 ; GSELL, *RAA*, p. 286 for the Christian basilica at Hassawana (see plan, fig. 103).

[6] See GSELL, *HAAN*, 6, 1927, p. 135-38, and CAMPS, *Massinissa*, p. 287 ; for the *Dii Mauri* see CAMPS (G.), *L'inscription de Béja et le problème des Dii Mauri*, R.A.f., 97, 1954, p. 233-60, and FENTRESS (E.), *Dii Mauri and Dii Patrii*. Latomus, 27, 1978, p. 507-16 ; *Dii Macni* : *C.* 8023 = 19981 = *ILS* 4136 (*Rusicade*) ; *Dii Magifae* : *C.* 16.749 = *ILS* 4493 = *ILAlg.* I. 2977 (Tinfadi/Hr. Mekkibes).

[7] LEGLAY, *SAH*, p. 27, 294, 304, 313, 336-41 ; cf Tert. *de Anim.* 57.10 ; Mela 1.46 ; Pliny, *NH*, 5.45 ; GSELL (S.), *Hérodote*. Alger, Jourdan, 1915, p. 184 ; see *ILAlg.* I.928 (Thagaste region), 1044 (Thagura), and *AE* 1906 : 122 (Dougga), for examples of this precise phraseology.

Significantly the inscription was discovered in the precinct of a Christian church erected, probably at a later date, at the market site. Could the communicant have been the counterpart of the modern-day Berber holy man? The possibility seems attractive, especially when we consider the crucial relationship between the holy and the secular control of markets in more recent times in North Africa.

When the fiercely independent and often bitterly hostile segments of a highland tribe meet on market day, it is practically impossible for any one of them to provide for secular order. An attempt by one chieftain or segment to exert control over the market immediately excites the suspicion and resentment of other tribesmen. Additionally, the great mutual hostility amongst the various factions of the *sûq* gives the market a potentially, explosive' quality; the slightest incident can lead to the dreaded *nefra'a* a blood-bath of internecine violence [1]. Fear of such uncontrollable violence leads to the imposition of extremely harsh communal penalties even against suspected violators of the 'peace of the market'. A more effective and reliable control can be provided by an 'unbiased' third party to the market, namely the *agguram* (pl. *igurramen*) or holy man whose magical powers (the blessing or *baraka* of Allah) not only ensure the peace of the market but also its economic prosperity. The holy men are able to serve this valuable function since they belong to 'holy lineages' that are independent of the secular tribal group networks. Being separate, they do not participate in the secular affairs of the ordinary tribesmen (e.g. feuds or wars) and are therefore in the position to act as middlemen and as spiritual mediators of *anaïa* or safe-passage on market day [2]. The actual presence of living holy men, however, is not necessary. The saint may have been dead for some time and it is the sheer aura of his power that emanates from his tomb and the power of his curse (*tagat*) against evil-doers, that is sufficient to enforce the sanctity and neutrality of the market held near his shrine [3]. The annual fair at Hassawana would seem to reflect this sort of situation, and indeed Herodotos (and other sources) do mention the connection between favoured holy persons in ancient Berber tribes and the reception of dreams and visions, as is suggested by the vocabulary of the inscription [4]. In fact, almost every aspect of the annual fair suggests a relative degree of political and social autonomy, a freedom from imposed external controls, which was doubtless fostered by its remote highland location.

6. Periodic Markets and the Domain System in North Africa

The very antithesis of tribal fairs of the type at Hassawana are the *nundinae* held in the lowland plains regions of the ancient Maghrib. In the case of these markets, the elements of political control and integration within a specific type of Roman economic network were the inverse of those of the *nundinae* at Vanisnesus. In the plains regions the great agricultural estates owned and operated by members of the Romano-African urban élites were the dominant form of centralised control of landed property.

---

[1] This is BENET's (1957) main thesis ; see also ROBIN (1874) 163 ; HANOTEAU and LETOURNEUX, *La Kabylie*, 3, 1873, p. 68 f., 303 ff. MONTAGNE (R.), *The Berbers : their Social and Political Organization*. London, Frank Cass, 1973 (trans. by D. Seddon of *La vie sociale et la vie politique des Berbères*, Paris, Société de l'Afrique française, 1931), p. 52 f. ; and UBACH (E.) and RACKOW (E.), *Sitte und Recht in Nordafrika* (Quellen zur ethnologischen Rechtsforschung von Nord-Afrika, Asien, und Australien, Band I). Stuttgart, 1923, p. 131-34 and 392-95.

[2] MONTAGNE (R.), *Les Berbères et le Makhzen dans le Sud du Maroc : Essai sur la transformation politique des Berbères sédentaires (groupe chleuh)*. Paris, Librairie F. Alcan, 1930, p. 251-53 ; MIKESELL (1958) 498 ; GELLNER (E.), *Political and religious organization of the Berbers of the Central High Atlas*, (in) *Arabs and Berbers : From Tribe to Nation in North Africa*, eds. E. Gellner & Ch. Micaud. London, Duckworth, 1972, p. 59-66, at p. 59-60.

[3] MONTAGNE, *Les Berbères et le Makhzen*, p. 261 ; FOGG (1932) 262, and his *Beliefs and Practices at, or in relation to, a Moroccan Tribal Market* (= 1940a), Folk-lore, 51, 1940, p. 132-38, and *A Moroccan Tribal Shrine and its Relation to a nearby Tribal Market* (= 1940c). Man, 40, 1940, p. 100-04 ; BENET (1957) 196, 200.

[4] Hdt. 4.172 ; GSELL, *HAAN*, 6, 1927, p. 168, 238, 243, cf. no. 4, p. 69 below.

There were, of course, many other types of units of agrarian exploitation and periodic markets attached to them that were outside the orb of the great estate. And yet, apart from the one inscription from Hassa wana, which does not refer to a true hebdomadal market, the only other epigraphic evidence concerning *nundinae* in Africa pertains to markets established by Roman landlords or by Roman provincial governor in towns. Even once the peculiar interests of the *domini* in having legally recognized markets established on their lands are taken into account, the odd distribution of the evidence is unexplained. Perhaps only Roman landlords cared to record the establishment of their estate markets. But the evidence as it stands might reflect some more profound socio-economic pattern. Amongst the alternative explanations might be a legalistic one: that is, that the imperial authority was primarily concerned with the control of *nundinae* attached to large-scale domains owned by wealthy and influential members of the central or municipal governing élites. Or the pattern might be explained by the virtual monopoly of legal markets as a benefit-right in the hands of either recognized municipal corporations or, in their lieu, of the large domain owner.

One of the best known examples of a domanial market is recorded in the earliest dated inscription concerning periodic markets in North Africa: the famous *Senatus consultum de nundinis Saltus Beguensis* [1]. The present day name of the site where the inscription was found, Henshir Begwâr preserves the designation for the region in which the market was located in antiquity, the *Regio Beguensis*. According to the regular procedure described above, the senator Lucilius Africanus, who owned a large estate in the district, made a formal application to the Senate to establish a periodic market on his property. The petition was submitted to the consuls through the agency of influential friends of his at Rome (... *desiderio amicorum Lucili Africani*, lines 12-13). The required legislation was presented to the Senate on the motion of the consuls, and the measure was passed by a formal vote of the house on the Ides of October, A.D. 138 (lines 5-9).

The location of the market itself would be sufficient cause for the state to be concerned about the granting of the *ius nundinandi*. Henshir Begwâr (anc. *Casae*) is situated at the base of a mountain ridge running south-west to north-east in the region midway between Thala and Sufetula (fig. 1). It is at the foot of J. Begwâr, the mid-section of the mountain named J. Duleb to the southwest and J. Tiwasha to the northeast. Directly southeast of the first ridge and parallel to it runs a second massif named J. Sem mama. If the considerable natural barriers imposed by the terrain are any indication, the southeastern

---

[1] C. 270 = 11.451 = Bruns, *Fontes*[7], 205 no. 61 = *FIRA* 1[2], no. 47 = Abbott & Johnson, *MARE*, no. 96 ; cf A.E. 1907 : 17 and *ILTun.* 396 (reproduced, in part, in Cagnat, *Cours 4*, pl. 12.1) ; see MERLIN (A.), *Observations sur le texte de Senatus Consultum Beguense.* C.R.A.I., 1906, p. 448-56 for the circumstances of the discovery of the stones by V. Guerin in 1860 and their removal to the Bardo in 1904).

S(enatus) C(onsultum) de nundinis Saltus Beguensis in t(erritorio) / Casensi. Descriptum et recognitum ex libro sen/tentiarum in Senatu dictarum, Kani Iuni Nigri, C(aii) Pompo/ni Camerini co(n)s(ulum), in quo scripta erant African iura et id / quod i(nfra) s(criptum) est. Idibus Oct(obribus) in Comitio 〈 rum 〉 in Curia Iul(ia) scribundo // adfuerunt Q Gargilius Q. f. Quir(ina tribu) Antiqus, Ti. Cl(audius) Ti. f. Pal(atina tribu) Severus, C. Oppius C. f. Vel(ina tribu) Severus C(aius) Herennius C. f. Pal(atina tribu) Caecilianus, M. Iul(ius) / M. f. Quir(ina tribu) Clarus, P. Cassius P. f Dexter q(uaestor), P(ublius) Nonius M. f. Ouf(entina tribu) Mac/rinus q(uaestor). In Senatu fuerunt CC[...] / S(enatus) C(onsultum) per discessionem fact(um) // quod P. Cassius Se/cundus, P. Delphinus Peregrinus Alfius Alen/nius Maximus Curtius Valerianus Proculus M. Nonius Muci/anus coss. verba fecerunt desiderio amicorum Lucili Africa/ni c(larissimi) v(iri), qu petunt ei permittatur in Provincia Afr(ica) regione // Beguensi, territorio Musulamiorum, ad Casas, nundinas / IIII non(as) Novembr(es) et XII k(alendas) Decembr(es) ex eo omnibus mensibus/IIII non(as) et XII k(alendas) sui cuiusq(ue) mensis ins-tituere habere, quid/fieri placeret, de ea re ita censuerunt/permittendum Lucilio Africano c(larissimo) v(iro) in Provincia Afric(a) // regione Beguensi, territorio Musulamiorum, ad Casas / nundinae IIII non(as) Novembr(es) et XII k(alendas) Decembr(es) sui cuiusq(ue) mensis in/stituere et habere eoque vicinis advenisq(ue) nundinandi / dumtaxat causa coire convenire sine iniuric et in//commodo cuiusquam liceat. Actum idibus Octobr(ibus) / P. Cassio Secundo, M. Nonio Muciano / Eodem exemplo / de eadem re duae tabellae signatae sunt : signatores / T. Fl(avi) Comini scrib(ae), C. Iuli Fortunati scrib(ae), M. Caesi Helv / Euhelpisti, Q. Metili Onesimi, C. Iuli Periblepti / L. Verati Philerotis, T. Flavi Crescentis.

frontier of Africanus' estate must have bordered the base of the first ridge. The ancient settlement of *Casae* (mod. Hr. Begwâr) was strategically located at the frontier of the domain itself, on the only pass which ran through both mountain masses and through which ran the only direct route connecting the towns of Thala and Sufetula [1].

Vast tracts of land both north and south of the mountain backbone of J. Tiwasha-Duleb were inhabited by peoples who identified themselves as belonging to the large ethnic group known as the *Musulamii*. It seems that *Casae* was probably the site of an ancient periodic market shared by various sub-tribes who considered themselves 'Musulamus', but principally it would seem, the group later identified in our sources as the *Beguenses* [2]. These markets would have been held at regular, twice monthly intervals, but, as with all markets in Roman Africa, they were adjusted to the Roman mode of time computation and were now held on the fourth day before the *nones* and the twelfth day before the *kalends* of each month (lines 15-16, 20-21). As the name of the place itself suggests, i.e. *Casae*, 'houses', probably there already existed a small African settlement at the location [3]. It seems probable that Africanus further encouraged the construction of some permanent marketing facilities at the site to solidify the function of the settlement as a centre-place connected with his domain [4].

In this particular case, however, there are a number of aspects to the granting of permission by the Senate that deserve further attention.

1. A relatively complete record of the formalities of the senatorial procedures along with the text of the decree was recorded on stone at the market site. In addition, some cautionary clauses appear to be stressed in the decree itself. Judged by 'normal' practice, both these actions were unusual.

2. Lucilius Africanus went much further than other landlords in his efforts to advertise his right to hold the *nundinae*. The rather lengthy S.C. was copied onto two separate stones, both of which were erected at the market site. This might have been dictated by reasons of architectural appearance; even so, the erection of dual copies of state decrees, though not unknown, is unusual [5].

3. The permission was sought and obtained at a rather late date. More than a century had passed since the Roman army had pacified the region and the régime of the large estate had become thoroughly entrenched.

There may be a hint as to the reason for these measures in a conventional phrase at the end of the S.C.: 'eoque vicinis advenisq(ue) nundinandi dumtaxat causa coire convenire sine iniuria et incommodo cuiusquam liceat' (lines 22-24). I say 'conventional' because such cautionary and restrictive clauses appear to have been a normal part of the legal controls established for all gatherings by the Roman State (e.g. the legislation on *collegia*). But the phrase does seem rather forceful: Lucilius is to allow persons to gather and congregate without obstruction or harm *only* so long as it is for the purpose of marketing. The statement certainly implies the reverse, namely that Musulamii would not be permitted to assemble *sine iniuria et incommodo* if there were any hint of trouble. Thus marketers were placed under the same

---

[1] Tunisia, 1 : 50.000, f. lxxvi (Djebel Semmama) ; GSELL, *Atl. arch.* f. 29 (Thala).

[2] DESANGES, *Catalogue des tribus* 117-21 ; on the Beguenses see *op. cit.* p. 83, citing Iulius Honorius, A. 48 = *GLM* (ed. Reise), p. 54.

[3] *Casae*, like *mappalia*, sometimes signified a collection of houses constituting a village ; see the lists in MESNAGE, *L'Afrique chrétienne*, 322, 444, and MAIER, *Episcopat*, 123-24.

[4] WILMANNS (1875) 271, citing the parallel of Mursa (*C. III*, 3288, Pannonia inferior).

[5] Compare ROUSSEL (P.) and DE VISSCHER (F.), *Les inscriptions du temple de Dmeir*. Syria, 23, 1942-43, p. 173-94, although since it is an official city inscription, it is not a precise parallel. MOMMSEN in WILMANNS (1875) 284 could think of no reason for the two copies except perhaps to avoid some sort of falsification.

stringent controls employed by the state in the *ius coeundi* imposed on *collegia* in general, clauses that restricted the right of assembly to precisely defined places and times, and solely for the legally permitted purposes of the association [1].

In considering the concern of the Senate in granting permission two factors can be connected: the presence of the market at a strategic location in the midst of Musulamian territory and the general political function of periodic markets in tribal social systems. At the periodic *sûq* of the Berber highlands the *jama'a* or council of elders meets under the aegis of the *shaykh* to conduct the common political business of the tribe. Legal matters are also dealt with under the auspices of experts in the customary law (*'urf*, *Kanûn*) who handle disputes amongst tribal members that have arisen since the last market day [2]. The market thus serves as a crucial link in the political power structure of the tribe; it is a place where the *amghar* or chieftain begins his ascendency, where, as a minor *shaykh* he spreads his patronage and extends his influence. It is the obvious venue for political contacts with other ethnic units, a place where chieftains can conclude alliances (*ribat*) with their neighbours [3]. Thus, no matter how difficult external powers have found the extrapolation of market control 'back' through the local social system, they have nevertheless felt compelled to make the attempt to curb this potentially dangerous stepping-stone to regional power [4].

A factor related to this general function of the market is the history of the pacification of the region in which the site of *Casae* was located. Roman military intervention in the region was marked by periods of considerable violence involving the Musulamii. The last of these reached the level of a regular war centred on the personality of the bandit-chief Tacfarinas. The local resistance involved contact with other, dispersed tribal units and market relations with them: the Mauri, the Cinithii, and above all, the Garamantes [5]. The Roman authorities must have been concerned with control of assembly as a vital adjunct to the policy of pacification, especially in view of the continued outbreaks of violence involving the Musulamii [6]. Certainly, we know that the Roman state imposed similar controls or bans on periodic markets in other sectors of the empire and its frontiers that were felt to be militarily sensitive, especially in the demilitarized zone on either side of the Danube [7]. And, in North Africa, the military forces of the legion were normally employed in the policing and surveillance of *nundinae* and *mercatus* [8]. Since

---

[1] WALTZING, *Corporations professionnelles*, 4, 1900, p. 581-83; DUFF (1938), 99, 119-22; cf *D*. 47.22.1.1; there are similar phrases in the decree of Valentinian and Valens cited in no. 2, p. 57, but in that case the injunction is specifically placed on the shoulders of the landlord, in a positive sense, to allow all comers to participate and not to interfere with them because of any personal reasons of his own (e.g.«...et commoneo privata exactione sectentur vel sub praetexta privati debiti aliquam ibidem concurrentibus molestiam possint inferre...»), whereas in the S.C. from Hr. Begwâr the warning is not directed as much towards the landlord as towards the marketers themselves — and further suggests that Africanus *did* have the right to obstruct them under certain conditions.

[2] See, generally, BOHANNON and DALTON, *Markets in Africa*, p. 22 ; FOGG (1932) 258 and (1942) in detail.

[3] MONTAGNE, *Les Berbères et le Makhzen*, 253, 261 ; BENET (1957) 195, 200-02.

[4] MINTZ (1960), 112 f. ; SILVERMANN (S.F.), *Some Cultural Correlates of the Cyclical Market*, (in) *Intermediate Societies, Social Mobility and Communication*, ed. V.F. Ray, Proceedings of the 1959 Annual Spring Meeting of the American Ethnological Society. Seattle, 1959, p. 31-36.

[5] BENABOU (M.), *La résistance africaine à la Romanisation*. Paris, F. Maspero, 1976, p. 75-84, and RACHET (M.), *Rome et les Berbères : un problème militaire d'Auguste à Dioclétien*. Bruxelles, Collection Latomus no. 110, 1970, p. 82-146 for general though unsatisfactory accounts of the conflict ; market connexions, see Tac. *Ann*. 4.23.2 and 4.13.

[6] See Dio 69.9.6 ; Suet. *Galba*, 7-8, and *C*. 9288 = 20.863 ; THOMASSON, *Statthalter*, II. 32-33.

[7] Dio 71.18, 71.19.2 ; see MOCSY (A.), *Pannonia and Upper Moesia*. London, RKP, 1974, p. 191, 193, and 197, cf Dio 72.11.2-3.

[8] *C*. 18.244 = *ILS* 2415 (*Lambaesis*), and A.E., 1914 : 234 (*Lambaesis*), cf CAGNAT (R.), J.R.S., 4, 1914, p. 142-46 ; DAVIS (R.W.), *The Daily Life of the Roman Soldier under the Principate*, *ANRW* 2.1, 1974, p. 299-338, x.4, *Supervision of Markets*, p. 326-27.

Lucilius Africanus was successful in his petition, however, we may surmise that the state now considered it safe to permit the establishment of legally recognized domanial markets in Musulamian territory.

If periodic assemblies were regarded by the authorities with fear or at least suspicion, the question must be posed: what factors encouraged the Roman landowners to overlook the negative aspects of the market and to petition the central government for permission to hold them? It has been suggested that there might be profits to be gained by the landlord who would collect market dues by levying tolls on the market transactions. There is no evidence to support such a view [1]. Additionally, the terms of an imperial edict issued by Valentinianus and Valens explicitly state that no *privatus* who has been granted the right to establish *mercatus* or *nundinae* is allowed to profit personally in any way from the market transactions, from the rental of market stalls, or from the imposition of market dues. Although the edict is of late date, its language strongly suggests that this had long been the standard ruling on the matter [2]. Naturally, laws of this type might imply that the opposite was regularly happening, though not legally. And it is this *legal* establishment of markets sought by the *domini* with which we are concerned.

Direct profits aside, however, there were other reasons why the founding and regulation of periodic markets would be regarded as a desireable adjunct to the organisation of their estates by Roman landlords. Probably one of the most immediate impulsions was inherent in the theoretical ideal of the estate as reflected in the dictum of the Elder Cato that the good landlord ought to be a seller but never, if possible, a buyer. Cato and other aristocratic writers after him were simply emphasizing the economic and social autonomy of the domain as an ideal economic formation [3]. By establishing periodic markets on his estate the landlord could ensure that all trading and marketing done by the *coloni* on his lands took place within the socioeconomic frame of the domain itself. At one stroke the landlord increased the isolation and dependence of his workforce, and also enhanced the *autarkeia* or economic self-sufficiency of the domain. And if, as seems demonstrable for all estate markets in Africa, the location of every domanial periodic assembly was at the periphery of the domain such a location would permit contact with external persons (e.g. itinerant peddlers, free peasant traders etc.) and yet restrict their influence and intrusion to the frontier of the domain.

Another benefit accruing to the landlord that can be perceived in the modern *sûq* is the function of the periodic market as a primitive labour exchange. In the countryside of the Maghrib agricultural labourers, including nomads on their annual sojourn in the north, have customarily congregated in gangs at local market places to offer their services for hire. It is to the periodic *sûq* that the indigenous peasant cultivator and the *colon* went to obtain surplus labour, especially at harvest [4]. The Roman landlord cannot have been ignorant of this convenient means of assuring a mechanism for the provision of extra labour for his domain. But whenever large numbers of workers gather at market sites, idling while waiting for employment, there is the ever present danger of violent unrest [5].

---

[1] BEAUDOIN (E.), *Les grands domaines dans l'Empire romain d'après des travaux récents*. Paris, Libr. Soc. lois..., 1899, p. 166-67 = *RHD*, sér. 3, 22, 1898, p. 87-88 ; SCHULTEN (A.), *Die römische Grundherrschaften : eine agrarhistorische Untersuchung*. Weimar, E. Felber, 1896, p. 112-15 ; BOISSIER (G.), *L'Afrique romaine*. Paris, 1895, p. 149.

[2] C.J., 4.60 (*De nundinis*) 1 : *Impp. Valentinianus et Valens AA. ad Probum PP.* (date ca. A.D. 368-75, see *Probus (5)*, *PLRE* p. 736).
Qui exercendorum mercatuum aut nundinarum licentia vel veterum indulto vel nostra auctoritate meruerunt, ita beneficio rescripti potiantur, ut nullum in mercatibus atque nundinis ex negotiatorum mercibus conveniant, vel in venaliciis aut locorum temporali quaestu et commodo privata exactione sectentur, vel sub praetextu privati debiti aliquam ibidem concurrentibus molestiam possint inferri.

[3] Cato, *De agri cult.* 2.7. ; cf FINLEY, *The Ancient Economy*, 109 f., and KULA (W.), *An Economic Theory of the Feudal System*. London, NLB, 1977, p. 50 f.

[4] FOGG (1936) 128, and (1942) 55.

[5] Cf the revealing parable in Matthew c. 20.

In addition to the concern with a reliable source of labour, there was yet another factor that incited the *dominus* to found a periodic market on his estate   This was the function of the domanial centre in the rent system, both government taxation and the dues and rents collected by the landlords themselves (the latter ultimately merging into the former system of state imposts). The *fundus-praedia* organisation headed by *vilici* and/or *procuratores* served not only the interests of the private owner, but often was the sole organisational mechanism available to the central state in the lieu of recognized urban corporations. Thus, in the vast expanses of the African countryside where no urban institutions existed, taxes were collected through the administrative structure of the domain. There is epigraphic evidence, such as the inscription from a domain in the Guert-Guessès Plain (southeastern Algeria) referring to the home farm as the place where *vectigalia locantur*, to subtantiate this view [1]. But the domain itself, often located in rural regions that lacked any obvious centre-places other than the home farm, required some institutional mechanism like the periodic market to assume the function of the town.

In more recent times, revenues stemming from taxation and dues levied at rural periodic markets have formed a not inconsiderable part of total colonial income. In fact, one of the principal reasons why colonial administrations became involved in market control was the importance of the market for taxation [2]. The plain fact is that the periodic market is the one place where scattered tribesmen, especially nomads, can be taxed with any degree of success. It was not at all uncommon for modern colonial powers to change the location solely for the convenience of the tax collector whose weekly rounds were announced in advance by the market crier [3]. The physical structure of the market place itself was often modified, defined, walled, and provided with gates to ensure that everyone paid market dues. In this way the colonial administration of predominantly rural regions could provide itself with up to a fifth of its total revenue [4]. It would be surprising, given the similarity of the problem, if the Roman administration did not employ comparable measures. Unfortunately, we have little direct evidence on the connection between tax and periodic market. We know that taxes of some sort (*proponenda*) were regularly collected at *nundinae* since Roman veterans were explicitly exempted from such imposts in a constitution issued by Constantine and Constantius [5]. There is also one Latin inscription from North Africa, unfortunately of unknown provenance, that associates the collection of taxes (*vectigal*) with *nundinae*, though it is so fragmentary that the specific rôle of the market in the taxation system is uncertain [6].

---

[1] A.E., 1894 : 84 = R.S.A.C., 28, 1893, p. 206, cf GSELL & GRAILLOT, M.E.F.R., 13, 1893, p. 470, no. 2 ; probably land rents, cf *C.* 20.578 and BROUGHTON (T.R.S.), *The Romanization of Africa Proconsularis*. Baltimore, Johns Hopkins Press (repr. New York, Greenwood Press, 1968), 1929, p. 161.

[2] HILL (1966) 309-10 ; MINTZ (1960) 120 ; historically this has been a rôle of periodic markets in North Africa, see e.g. St-HILAIRE (G.), *L'élevage en Afrique du Nord*. Paris, Challamel, 1919, p. 202 f., and BERNARD (A.) and LACROIX (N.), *L'évolution du nomadisme en l'Afrique du Nord*. Alger, Jourdan, 1906, p. 27, 209 ; and DESPOIS (J.), *Le Djebel Nefousa*. Paris, La Rose, 1937, p. 164.

[3] FOGG (1936) and (1942) 61.

[4] FOGG (1936) 126-28 on standardization ; (1939a) 325 and (1942) 56-57 on amounts ; cf (1941) 105) ; TROIN (1963) 111-13 : 90 % of taxation in local markets he studied was levied on animals and animal by-products ; cf MINTZ (1959) 22-23, and HILL (1966) 310.

[5] C.Th., 7.20 (*De veteranis*) 2.4, cf C.J., 26 (*De veteranis*) 1. (Date : A.D. 324, see *PLRE*, « Florianus (2) ») :
Constantius A. dixit : Iam nunc munificentia mea omnibus veteranis id esse concessum perspicuum sit, ne quis eorum in nullo munere civili neque in operibus publicis conveniatur neque in nulla conlatione neque a magistratibus neque vectigalibus. In quibuscumque nundinis interfuerint, nulla proponenda dare debebunt.

[6] *C.* 24.609 = A.E., 1893 : 56 (provenance probably Tunisia where the Comte Herisson found most other stones in this collection) ; cf HERON DE VILLEFOSSE (A.), *Inscriptions africaines au Musée d'Autun*. B.S.A.F., 1892, p. 214-16 ; for a photo. see MARCILLET-JAUBERT (J.), *Inscriptions latines d'Afrique du Nord au Musée d'Autun*. Mémoires de la Société Eduenne, n.s., 51.3, 1968, p. 226-32, at p. 232, no.

[c.6] LLL [c.10 / c. 4] PENSA [c.9 / c.3] NVS PRO[vinciales?]/PETVNT PROM [c.9] /SA VNA FOLLE[s c.7] // TRECENTA TRIG [inta c.4]/OCTAVIANVS PRO[curator?]/TABVL(is?) PROVINC(iae) TI(ngitanae?) [...]/TAT VECTIGALI LATE [...]/TIONE NVNDINA[s] // LATO FISCO A PROVINC[ialibus]/OCTO LIGNI PENSAS TRIA / OCTOGINTA QVATTUOR M[ilia]/PONDO QVINDECIM MILIA [.../...].

More precise information on the involvement of domanial markets with the taxation system is contained in an inscription from the estate of Munatius Flavianus, a municipal aristocrat from Cirta [1]. After the creation of the province of Numidia and the extension of the authority of the legate of *IIIa Augusta* over the Cirtan Federation, matters concerning periodic markets had to be referred to the emperor through his office. One such request was made in the late 270s or early 280s by one Munatius Flavianus who owned an estate at 'Aïn Kerma in the southwestern Constantine Plain (fig. 3). The markets at 'Aïn Kerma (anc. *Emadaucapensis*) had been established at a much earlier date, perhaps in the latter half of the second century, so that Munatius' *libellus* was not a request to found markets on his estate. The text of the inscription found at 'Aïn Kerma dates from some period after the grant of immunity from taxation that had been made by the emperor Probus in the 260s. The 'Aïn Kerma markets were held twice monthly on the fifth day before the *kalends* and the fifth day before the *ides* of each month [2]. 'Aïn Kerma exemplifies the type of liminal location for markets discussed above. It is situated in a strategic pass that pierces the massif of J. Tafrent, between J. Rherûr and J. Rokbat al-Jamal [3]. The pass, which permits access between the semi-arid zone to the south and the *tell* to the north, is guaranteed a year-round supply of water by the large perennial spring after which the site is named. The *vicus* constructed by the landlord near the spring dominates one of the most frequented routes in this region that connects the two diverse economic zones.

The markets on Munatius Flavianus' estate enjoyed the privilege of certain established exemptions (*nundinas... immunes*) from taxation. The precise nature of these exemptions becomes clear once it is realized that 'Aïn Kerma was located on one of the principal routes followed by nomadic pastoralists to their summer pastures north of J. Tafrent. Vast enclosures built by the local inhabitants in pre-Roman times were found in the pass close to the spring itself. The rough, dry-stone cattle pens attest a local pastoral economy that probably had wider connections with nomadic pastoralists to the south. Since modern patterns of nomadic movement through this region are a reliable guide to the routes followed in Roman times, the tribe passing through 'Aïn Kerma must have been the Nicibes from the Hodna Basin [4]. If so, there is good reason to believe that the *immunitas* granted to the markets at *Emadaucapensis* probably applied to animals driven north into the *tell* by way of the 'Aïn Kerma pass. The exemption, granted by the emperor Probus, was later interferred with since only a few years later the governor of Numidia, M. Aurelius Diogenes (*gubern. c.* 286) was compelled to intervene to reassure

---

[1] CHARBONNEL (N.) and DEMOUGIN (S.), *Un marché en Numidie au IIIe siècle après J.-C.*, R.H.D., 54, 1976, p. 559-68, esp. p. 561 f. for the Munatii at Cirta.

[2] First reported in a faulty version by CAGNAT (R.), *Découvertes épigraphiques des brigades topographiques de l'Algérie et de Tunisie en 1897*, B.C.T.H., 1898, p. 155-59, at p. 155 ; the best copy is that relayed by A. Joly to GSELL (S.), B.C.T.H., 1903, ccxi (incorrectly reported in A.E., 1903 : 243) ; location : see GSELL, *Atl. arch.* f. 17 (Constantine) no. 384, about 20 km SE of Tajananat (*ex* Saint-Donat).

Ex rescrip/*to Dei Probi* / *postulan*/*te Mun(atio) Flavia*/*no nundinas* // *Emadaucapens(es) immun*/[e]*s, V kal(endarum) et V idum cele*/*brandas, v(ir) p(erfectissimus)*/*p(raeses) P(rovinciae) N(umidiae), Aur(elius) Diogenes, benefi*/*cium datum sup*[l]*ere dignatus e**st*].

[3] See Algeria, 1 : 50.000, f. 119 (Saint-Donat) lit Suter (Y.), *Les cadastres anciens de la région de Saint-Donat*. Ant. afr., 7, 1973 (a part) : C.L. x = 305-306, y = 808-809 ; FERAUD (L.), *Monuments dits Celtiques de la Province de Constantine*, R.S.A.C., 8, 1864, 108-32 (= 1864a), p. 118, and his *Notice sur les Oulad-Abd-en-Nour*. R.S.A.C., 8, 1864 (= 1864b), p. 134-295, at p. 150.

[4] For other cases of market *immunitas* see the instance of Baitokaikê nos. 2-3, p. 46, and MIKHAILOV (G.), *IGBR*, 4, 2234, p. 198 f. ; on the nomadic routes see LANCEL (S.), *Suburbures et Nicibes: une inscription de Tigisis*, Libyca (Arch.-épigr.), 3, 1955, p. 289-98, and BERTHIER (A.), *Nicibes et Suburbures : nomades ou sédentaires ?* B.A.A., 3, 1968, p. 293-300, with DESPOIS (J.), *Le Hodna (Algérie)*. Paris, P.U.F., 1953, Publications de la Faculté des Lettres d'Alger, IIe sér., t. 24, p. 289-90 and map, fig. 30, cf FERAUD (1864a) 118. The phrase *nundinae celebrandae* in the inscription regarding *nundinae* on Munatius Flavianus 'estate finds an exact parallel in the African writer Apuleius' description (*Apol.* 23,9) of a crowded market on a rural domain.

the right of immunity according to the imperial rescript [1]. From the tariff list found at 'Aïn Zraïa to the south, we know that herds being driven to periodic markets across the southern frontier of Numidia were exempt from entrance levies (*pecora in nundinium* (sic) *immunia*) [2]. It is a fair guess that the *nundinae* at 'Aïn Kerma would continue to extend the privilege of this traditional immunity of the pastoral nomads' animals that passed north via *Diana Veteranorum* to the periodic markets of the north.

The clear implication of the case of the *Vicus Flavianus* at 'Aïn Kerma is that all *nundinae*, unless otherwise specially exempted, were integrated into the general taxation system for the collection of state levies [3]. Because of the permanence of the grant of *immunitas*, it has been argued that the taxes were only the lesser, indirect levies owed to the state such as imposts on purchases and sales, but not the *vectigal* or *tributum*, the major taxes assessed on land and *capita* [4]. Such an interpretation is substantiated in part by the type of immunity granted at Zaraï, but there can be no decisive argument based on the nature of the *immunitas* alone that would necessarily rule out the collection of *vectigal* and *tributum* as well. This interpretation must also account for the few inscriptions from North Africa where an explicit connection is made between *vectigal* and *nundinae*. Perhaps the answer is that the *vectigal* in these particular instances refers to private collections other than state taxes, although this is not certain from the sources themselves [5].

Taxation, however, is only one of the aspects of urban function filled by *nundinae*. It seems as though such markets generally substituted for the *civitas* wherever the large estate could not act as a suitable surrogate. Although it is clear that *nundinae* were replacing the antique city in some of its more important functions or were, as Isidorus puts it, *vice civitatis*, their function in the process of urban development is more ambiguous [6]. On the one hand, if the periodic market was successful in meeting all the commercial and social demands placed on it, then it tended to inhibit urban growth. On the other hand, it is well known that town development often took its impetus directly from the existence of market centres. It is this Janus-like potential of the market that warrants further examination [7].

From the evidence at our disposal, it appears that Roman *domini* attempted to encourage the latter course, that is, the establishment of periodic markets as precursors to, or correlates of, permanent urban settlements. Although the inscription recording the *nundinae* on the estate of Lucilius Africanus at *Casae* (p. 54) f.) makes no reference to any permanent centre, the archaeological survey of the site revealed the plan of a small trading centre with buildings whose ground plans resemble those of Roman *tabernae* [8]. In this case, it can only be surmised that there was a conscious effort to combine urban development with a newly established periodic market.

In other cases there is greater certainty. About twelve kilometres east of the *Vicus Flavianus* (above p. 58 f.), at 'Aïn Meshira in the southwestern Constantine Plain, one Antonia Saturnina founded a village

---

[1] Cf C. 2573-75 (*Lambaesis*) ; PALLU DE LESSERT (A.C.), *Fastes* II. 309-10 placed his governorship in A.D. 296-97, without confidence, referring to the arguments of GOYAU, M.E.F.R., 13, 1893, p. 274-75 ; STEIN, *PIR*², A. 1491 places him 'a 286 vel paulo post', followed by *PLRE*, *Diogenes (7)*, p. 256 and *fasti*, p. 1086.

[2] C. 4508 (*Zaraï*, Zraia, A.D. 202), see DARMON (J.P.), *Notes sur le Tarif de Zaraï*, C.T., 12, 1964, p. 6-23.

[3] CHARBONNEL and DEMOUGIN (1976) 559-61 who see this quite correctly.

[4] CHARBONNEL and DEMOUGIN (1976) 564-65.

[5] See above nos. 1 and 6, p. 58.

[6] Isid. *Etym.* 15.2.12.

[7] MacMULLEN (1970), and esp. GABBA (E.), *Urbanizzazione e rinnovamenti urbanistici nell'Italia centro-meridionale all I sec. a.C.*, S.C.O., 21, 1972, p. 73-112, for Italy. Cf FOGG (1932) 266 ; (1939a) 324 and pl. 2-4 ; (1941) 105 and (1942) 47 f., and TROIN (1963, 1965) for North Africa.

[8] See no. 4, p. 55.

(*vicus*) and established periodic markets that took place on the fifth day before the *kalends* and the fifth day before the *ides* of each month [1]. The site was at the epicentre of the *territorium* of the ethnic group of the *Suburbures*, just as in modern times 'Aïn Meshira was at the centre of the lands inhabited by the Awlad 'Abd-en-Nûr [2]. As mentioned above, this region is cut into two distinct economic zones by the massif of J. Tafrent which runs east to west, culminating in the heights of Rokbat al-Jamal (the "knee of the Camel"). The crest of J. Tafrent marks the boundary between the *tell* to the north and the more arid regions to the south. Communication between the two zones is afforded by a few passes which pierce the massif of Tafrent and that at 'Aïn Meshira is the most important of these. Thus the village founded by Antonia Saturnina was located not only on the frontier of two economic zones, but also dominated one of the most frequently used routes into the Constantine Plain.

The pass into the *tell* had long been one of importance as the 'pre-Roman' ruins all around 'Aïn Meshira attest. Two large drystone walls were built by the early African inhabitants of the site: one across the northern end of the pass and the other blocking the southern entrance [3]. These walls did not so much control entrance and exit points as they formed a cattle enclosure in the valley itself, a technique known from a host of other palaeo-Berber sites. As in those other instances, the walls also served as crude defensive barriers, enclosing the pastoralists' settlement and their main source of water, 'Aïn Meshira [4]. In Roman times, 'Aïn Meshira maintained its strategic importance, being the midway point on the military road that connected Diana Veteranorum and Cirta and the most abundant perennial source of water in the entire region. The control, both of trading by the Suburburi tribesmen and of the pastoral nomadic groups from the Hodna who passed through the region every year, must have been one of the principal motivations in founding the *nundinae* at 'Aïn Meshira. Indeed, the Roman army built a fort close to the spring itself and the Byzantines later rebuilt the fort on a larger scale and made it an integral part of their defensive line in this sector of the Numidian *limes* [5]. Thus we may note, even in antiquity, the close connection between military surveillance, the construction of fortifications, and a periodic market.

Antonia Saturnina was the wife of C. Arrius Pacatus, the wealthy senator from Cirta and builder of the magnificent *Balineum Pacatianum* in the city. He held numerous high posts in the Roman imperial administration, but perhaps most important for our analysis was his appointment to head a special grain commission when famine struck Italy in A.D. 166-67. In this capacity he organized a new African fleet to transport grain to Rome [6]. He was a logical choice considering the large landholdings of his family

---

[1] C. 8280, cf 20,077 = *ILS* 6869 ('Aïn Meshira). Gsell, *Atl. arch.* f. 17 (Constantine) no. 386 ; Algeria, 1 :50.000, f. 119 (Saint-Donat) about 25/30 km SE of al-Eulma (ex Saint Donat) : Soyer (J.), *op. cit.*, C.L. x : 307 ; y : 818-819. Originally reported by Benoit (Ch.), in B.A.H., c.r., 1888, lx.

Antonia L(ucii) f(ilia) Saturnina vicu(m) / et nundina(s) V kal(endas) et V idus sui / cuiusque mensi[s] constituit.
For Antonia Saturnina see C. 7032 = *ILAlg.* II.1, 616 (Cirta).

[2] Desanges, *Catalogue des tribus*, p. 135-36 ; Feraud (1864a) 115-16.

[3] Gsell, *MAA*, I, 10, 13 ; Feraud (1864a) 115-16.

[4] Feraud (1864a) 116-17 and pl. 21, plan, he saw a large number of these dry-stone enclosures south of the J. Tafrent Rokbat al-Jamal line (p. 118) ; cf (1864b) 140-50.

[5] Gsell (S.) and Graillot (H.), *Exploration archéologique dans le département de Constantine (Algérie) : ruines romaines au nord des Monts de Batna*. M.E.F.R., 14, 1894, p. 501-602 at p. 508 and 590, Diehl (Ch.), *L'Afrique byzantine : histoire de la domination byzantine en Afrique (533-709)*. Paris, 1896 (repr. B. Franklin, New York, 1970), 240-41 ; Feraud (1864a) 115.

[6] For the family see Groag's stemma in *PIR*² A. 214 (in need of revision) ; Antonia = *PIR*² A. 898 ; her husband, A 1102 ; for the baths see C. 7031 = *ILAlg.* II.615 (Cirta) and Gsell, *MAA*, I.229. On his career see HA, *Vita M. Aurel.* 10, 77 ; *Vita Commod.* 7.1, 11.1 ; Barnes (T.D.), *Tertullian*, Oxford Clarendon Press, 1971, p. 146-47 (Tert. *Scap.* 5.1), and Pavis d'Escurac (E.), *Réflexions sur la Classis Africana Commodiana*, (in) *Mélanges d'histoire ancienne offerts à William Seston*. Paris, Sorbonne, 1977, p. 397-408.

in Africa. One of Antonia Saturnina's nephews, C. Arrius Antoninus, owned an estate at Kaf Tazerût, between W. Rhummel and W. Endjas west of Cirta. And the name of an estate, the *Saltus Pacatensis* (**Bagatensis*) also reveals extensive holdings in the Qsar Mahajiba — al-Aria region east of the city [1]. Antonia's domain at 'Aïn Meshira was probably bounded by the great topographical barriers of the region and stretched northwards from the tellian slope of J. Rherûr to the mountain barriers of J. Shakba on the northwest and J. Tiffaltassîn on the northeast. If so, the market site is found, once again, on the geographic frontiers of the estate. At the site itself Antonia founded a village which she named the *Vicus Pacatensis* after her husband's family [2].

The phenomenon of the connexion between the establishment of the town and the periodic market is one which bears closer scrutiny, since Antonia Saturnina's action was not unique, even for the restricted area of the Cirtan Federation. Another landowner from Cirta, a certain Phosphorus, established *nundinae* and a *vicus* on his estate some fifty kilometres southeast of the city. The plains of this region are split into eastern and western halves by the mountain divide that extends from 'Aïn Trab in the north to Draa al-Qala'a in the south, a distance of about thirty kilometres. At the spring of 'Aïn Melûk (fig. 3), midway along the ridge, Phosphorus constructed a village which, as the centre of his domain and in a gesture of personal *grandeur*, he named after himself. He also established periodic markets in the village, though we are not informed of the frequency at which they took place [3]. Once again, the market site is situated on a geographic frontier, at the critical location of a perennial spring. It is also at the juncture of two distinct ecological zones: a zone of intensive irrigation culture along the mountain massif itself, dependent on a constant water supply from springs like 'Aïn Melûk, and the plains, a zone of dry-farming, on either side of the central dividing massif: the plain of 'Aïn Abid to the west and that of Tamlûka to the east [4]. As early as the reign of Vespasian, specially appointed imperial legates were delineating the frontiers between these agricultural populations and the in-coming pastoral nomads,

---

[1] *C*. 8241 = LECLERC (L.), *Une inscription du Kaf Tazrout*, R.S.A.C., 8, 1864, p. 74-77 ; Saltus Bagatensis: A.E. 1902 : 223 = R.S.A.C., 35, 1901, 190 = *ILAlg*. II.2, 4196.

[2] For the *Vicus Pacatensis* see MESNAGE, *L'Afrique chrétienne*, p. 327 and MAIER, *Episcopat*, p. 241 ; the location of the *vicus* and market at the edge of an estate was not, of course, a purely economic decision since the all-important perennial supply of water usually provided by a major spring which tended to be found at the base of a mountain ridge that formed the natural bounds of a given region.

[3] A.E., 1913 : 226 ('Aïn Melûk), cf PIQUET (M.), *Notice sur une inscription romaine et sur quelques vestiges romains trouvés dans la région de Canrobert et d'Aïn-Beïda*. R.S.A.C., 46, 1912, p. 283-85 ; CARCOPINO (J.), *Deux inscriptions du Département de Constantine récemment publiées*, II : *Inscription d'Aïn-Melouk*. B.C.T.H., 1914, p. 566-70 (of which the latter is by far the superior copy) ; and PIQUET (M.), *Découverte d'une inscription au douar d'Aïn-Melouk, Constantine*. B.C.T.H., 1916, cliv-clv, p. 62-69.

Caelesti Aeternae Aug(ustae) / aedem a solo cum pronao et co/lumnis et sedibus, Phosphorus / exstruxcit (sic) idemq(ue) dedic(avit). / Item, vicum, qui subiacet huic // templo, long (vac.) um 〉 CCCL cum / aedificiis omnibus et columnis / et porticibus, et arcus IIII / idem fecit, et nundinas insti/tuit. Qui vicus nomine ipsius // appellatur.

SCHTAERMAN (E.M.), *Die Krise der Sklavenhalterordnung in Western des römischen Reiches*. Berlin, Akademie Verlag, 1964, (trans. W. Seyfarth), p. 191, thinks that Phosphorus is the freedman agent of a landlord (i.e. a bailiff running the estate). Carcopino disagrees (referring to *CIL* XIV, 3440, cf THEILING (W.), *Der Hellenismus in Kleinafrika*. Leipzig and Berlin, 1911, p. 112) on the basis that there is no *prima facie* indication, other than his name, that he is a freedman. Staerman, however, might be correct, if the 'ipsius' of the inscription were taken to refer to the *dominus* rather than to Phosphorus himself.

[4] GSELL, *Atl. arch*. f. 18 (Souk Ahras) no. 163 ; Algeria, 1 : 50.000, f. 98 (Aïne Regada), immediately north of Bordj el Hadj Tahar, 6.3 km SW of Tamlûka (*ex*-Montcalm); CARCOPINO (J.), *Notes d'archéologie algérienne*, II : *Encore l'inscription d'Aïn-Melouk*. B.C.T.H., 1918, p. 232-37 correctly rejects TOUTAIN (J.), *Observations sur l'inscription d'Aïn-Melouk (Algérie)*. B.C.T.H., 1916, p. 62-69 that the dimensions indicated in the inscription refer to *centuriae* and hence mean an estate of 350 centuries in size (= 4.425 ha. or 44 km²). As seductive as the possibility of actually knowing the size of a domain would be, Carcopino is probably right in holding that the sign refers to a measurement of length, the *dupondius*, and indicates the size of the *vicus*, 350 *dupondii* square, or about 4 ha. in extent.

principally the *Nicibes*, from the Hodna Basin [1]. The markets at 'Aïn Melûk were ideally situated to facilitate contact between the local farmers, the *Suburbures Regiani* and the *Nattabutes*, and to provide surveillance over nomadic movements. It was located at the eastern exit of the one pass that provided easy access between the two plains, and close to the intersection of the two major trunk roads of the district. Through the pass itself ran the Roman road connecting Cirta and 'Aïn Beïda (anc. *Marcimeni*?), and as it emerged from the pass on the east it crossed the principal north-south route of the Tamlûka Plain, connecting 'Aïn Fakrûn in the south with W. Zenati in the north [2].

After Phosphorus had completed the construction of the *vicus* and the establishment of the periodic markets, he placed the settlement under the protection of the African goddess of fertility, *Dea Caelestis*. He built a temple to her on a small rise overlooking the village to the north. Though sometimes equated to the Roman Juno, Caelestis was in fact directly identified with the Punic Tanit and was venerated as the consort of Saturn [3]. The Africans saw her as the ruler of the heavens, the goddess of favourable weather and the protectress of the harvest. Tertullian called her *pollicitatrix pluviarum*: she who promises rain. At Cirta itself she was venerated as *Caelestis Sittiana*, though her cult appears to have been centred principally in the countryside. Antonius Philetus, a freedman who managed an estate belonging to C. Arrius Antoninus, one of Antonia Saturnina's nephews, constructed a temple to Caelestis on Arrius' domain at Kaf Tazerût [4]. Thus, there was from the inception of *vicus* and *nundinae* a set of associations of 'belief', though of a peculiar type. Although both Saturn and Caelestis can qualify as 'African' deities, in this context they appear as the sort of gods associated with the interests of the city and the urban-centred ruling classes. The education and cultural ties of these men bound them to a series of spirits that are indeed regional to Africa but not of the same general 'pantheon' as the market gods traditionally venerated by Africans who were not part of the imperial system (compare, for example, those at Hassawana). The distinction may seem subtle, but it is actually quite obvious and fundamental.

The question is: what were the principal forces motivating Roman landholders such as Antonia Saturnina and Phosphorus to establish *vici* in tandem with *nundinae* on their estates? Apart from the simple pride landowners would have as city-founders in miniature (*ktistoi/conditores*), there were some practical considerations in establishing these village-market complexes. Matters of taxation, labour, and administrative control have already been considered, but there remains the central factor of urban development itself. In founding a market system tied to the domain, it is arguable that the landlord was inhibiting true urban growth or, to put it differently, that he was ensuring that any town development that did ensue took place under his aegis, at a site of his choice, and was tied to permanent dependence on the home domain. One of the potential dangers that Roman *domini* had to face was the possibility of autonomous urban growth off or near the domain that might give rise to a parallel organizational structure independent of that on the domain.

One example of this type of phenomenon is reflected at 'Azziz-ben-Tellis (anc. *Idicra*?) in a dedication honouring a M. Aurelius Honoratianus, a *colonus Suburburus* who was styled *defensor gentis*. Presumably he was a patronal representative of fellow Suburburi tribesmen who laboured within the domanial structure

---

[1] See no. 4, p. 59

[2] PIQUET (1912) 283-84 ; CARCOPINO (1914) 566 ; DESANGES, *Catalogue des tribus*, p. 136 ; BOSCO (J.), R.S.A.C., 50, 1916, p. 202 = A.E., 1917-18 : 41, near 'Aïn Abid, Felix Nibilis, a *princeps* of the *Suburbures Regiani* ; for the roads in the region see CARCOPINO (1914) 569-70, and GSELL, *Atl. arch.* f. 18 (Souk Ahras) nos. 72, 82 and 157.

[3] TOUTAIN, *Les cultes païens*, p. 29-37 ; Ch.-PICARD, *Religions de l'Afrique romaine*, p. 105-17 ; cf AUDOLLENT (A.), *Carthage romaine*, Paris, 1901, p. 262-65 ; cf LEGLAY, *SAH*, p. 215-22 and p. 269 on the 'Aïn Melûk sanctuary.

[4] Tert. *Apol.* 23.6 (*ista ipsa virgo Caelestis pluviarum pollicitatrix*) ; cf C. 4635 = 16.810 = *CLE* 254 = *ILAlg.* II, 1, 807 (Cirta) for *Caelestis Sittiana* ; cf GSELL, *HAAN*, 4, 1927, 255 f., 262-63. On Philetus' domain see no. 1, p. 62.

(e.g. that of C. Arrius Antoninus nearby) and interceded with local landlords [1]. If Africans were freely allowed to form town governments they would then be able to represent themselves collectively against the force of the landlord and his agents, such as is already well-known from the village-centred organizations of *coloni* on imperial estates in the Upper Bagradas valley [2]. Of course, the very presence of large agricultural domains tends to discourage urban development; the existence of periodic markets only further strengthens the autonomy of the domain and impedes town growth. Indeed, it has been historically true of the Maghrib that the very success and durability of the rural periodic market has been one of the main hindrances to the urbanization of the countryside. Even till the late nineteenth century there was a 'vacuum', an absence of urban forms between the large towns on the one hand and the relatively empty countryside on the other — a gap filled neatly by the 'invisible' network of time-structures formed by the local market system. Only very gradually, like a photograph being developed, did the inherent potentialities of this system become reified in urban form [3].

It would be specious to argue that the ancient landlord was not perceptive enough to have an 'economic consciousness' of this effect of the periodic market. In Italy, in A.D. 105, the townsmen of Vicetia in northern Italy employed a number of legal advocates to plead their cause before the Senate to prevent a local senatorial landowner, Ti. Claudius Sollers, from establishing *nundinae* on his estate near the town. Clearly the citizens of Vicetia feared that the presence of markets on Sollers' estate would increase the self-sufficiency of the domain and would proportionately reduce the dependence of the *coloni* (e.g. in terms of market transactions) on the town. [4] And, in the fourth-century, Libanius could observe the same general process at work in the countryside around Antioch [5]. Insofar as the particular estates of Antonia Saturnina, Munatius Flavianus, and Phosphorus are concerned, we may note that the entire region of the south Cirtan Federation, a heartland of the great estate in Africa, is much less urbanized than the *sebakh* zone to the south [6]. Hence it seems only reasonable to suggest that the domanial economy, thus consciously linked to local periodic markets by landowners, was successful in inhibiting town development and in assisting the general interests of the land owning class.

7. Periodic Markets and Urban Centres in North Africa

It seems, then, that the function of the periodic market within the domanial system, insofar as urbanization is concerned, was largely negative. There seems to be little doubt that the landlord was not eager to increase the opportunities for outside communication for the *coloni* on his estate. The prevailing mentality was towards self-sufficiency in all aspects. In autonomous market systems, as we shall see below, a general characteristic of periodic markets is their sequential cyclicality — i.e. the ordering of

---

[1] *C.* 8270 = POULLE, R.S.A.C., 11, 1875, p. 417, cf HERON DE VILLEFOSSE, R.A., 31, 1876, p. 213 ('Azziz-ben-Tellis). *D.M.S. / M(arco) Aur(elio) Hono/ratiano Con/cessi filio, Subur/buri col(ono), dec(urioni) col(oniae) // Tutcensium, defen/sori gentis, viro / forti ac fidelissi/mo Aur(elius) Maximus / frater incom//parabili / v(ixit) a(nnis) LIII.*

For the location see MAIER, *Episcopat*, p. 220. The duties and social functions and rank of the *defensor gentis* must have been closely analogous to those of the *defensor civitatis*, see SEECK (O.), *Defensor civitatis*, *RE* 4², 1901, coll. 3365-71, esp. 2365.

[2] For the *magistri* on the Bagradas estates see *C.* 25902, 1. 31 (Hr. Mettish) : the *defensor*, Felix Annobalis Birzilni (filius), and *C.* 10570 (Sûq al-Khemîs). BROUGHTON, *Romanization*, p. 172 : « there is no evidence... of any *municipium* in *Africa Proconsularis* which developed out of the *vici* on a private or imperial estate. », a remark which is still true.

[3] FOGG (1932) 266 ; MIKESELL (1958) 494, 505-06 ; TROIN (1963 and 1965).

[4] See no. 8, p. 48.

[5] Lib. *Or.* 11.230.

[6] GSELL and GRAILLOT (1894) 589.

market days in order to avoid conflict with nearby markets. The supplemental tendency of periodicity then leads to the formation of market cycles. But this natural avoidance of temporal conflict is *not* to be found in the single instance where we can compare the marketing days on two neighbouring estates in Roman Africa: the markets on the domains of Antonia Saturnina and Munatius Flavianus. These two estate centres, only ca. 10 km apart, were ideally suited to be part of a sequential cycle of *nundinae* that would integrate the *coloni*. But we know from the precise dates on the respective inscriptions that the *nundinae* on these two domains were consciously set by the landlords on *precisely the same days* throughout the entire year [1]. The clashing synchronism could hardly be an accident, given the elaborate procedures initiated by the landlords or their agents to found the markets. The *domini*, it seems, were concerned with exchange and communication within the estate but, insofar as the *coloni* were concerned, not outside it. The reverse, of course, applied to themselves.

As a result of the imposition of the Roman administration on North Africa, the previously diverse and multifaceted system of pre-Roman *nundinae* entered a new economic network of control determined by the *praedia-fundus*. Where there once might have been numerous autonomous periodic markets functioning according to customary constraints, there was now just *one* single market tied closely to the domain. The pattern can be inferred from the data we have analysed above, and is confirmed by Festus when he describes the integral connection between *vici* and *nundinae* [2]. If this is so, we ought to establish not only a one-to-one correlation between agricultural domains and legal *nundinae*, but also a direct relationship between conscious incipient urbanization (e.g. *vici*) and the presence of periodic markets, so that the former will always suggest the existence of the latter. Such a model, in which periodic markets are tied to an estate economy, is quite atypical of traditional societies in which anthropologists have studied *nundinae*, but is entirely consistent with a model of the European feudal system where *nundinae* and estates were integral [3]. Perhaps this type of market formation is indicative of the typology of economy and society in Roman Africa as a whole.

The predominant influence affecting the control of *nundinae* in the unurbanized countryside was the economic régime of the large landed estate. Thus *nundinae* were tied to the internal economy of the domain, but *not* to the external sphere of large-scale trade and exchange between domains, and between agricultural estates and the central State. These are best viewed as two completely separate systems of exchange. As in the modern *aswâq*, which integrate small-scale peasant exchange with the petty dealings of the itinerant trader and craftsman, so the *nundinae* of Roman Africa remained the sphere of the trinket and utensil rather than that of large-scale agricultural transactions [4]. In terms of analysis of market systems, therefore, we have two separate and virtually independent marketing institutions: the regional, small scale market for the satisfaction of local needs alone, and the circuit of agricultural markets imposed and overlying these into which the domains and the towns are integrated. The question of the 'market' in this provincial area of the Roman empire, therefore, cannot be reduced to the extension of one market system over the entire region, but rather how one mega-market system (city-domain) is extended in such a way that one unit in it (the domain) comes to regulate, as an autonomous system in its own right, the hitherto unregulated and heterodox system of micro-markets in the region in which it is located. But

---

[1] Chart no. 2.

[2] Festus, *De verborum significatione*, 562.

[3] *Cambridge Economic History*, 1², p. 472 ; though from an early date the European feudal system showed other tendencies, see DUBY (G.), *L'économie rurale et la vie des campagnes dans l'Occident médiéval*. Aubier, Editions Montaigne, 1962 (Engl trans, C. Postan, *Rural Economy and Country Life in the Medieval West*. London, E. Arnold, 1968), p. 45, 132-33, and the warnings of BLOCH (M.), *Feudal Society*, I. London, RKP, 1965, p. 67.

[4] Apul. *Flor.* 9.26 ; cf FOGG (W.), *The Importance of Tribal Markets in the Commercial Life of the Countryside of North-West Morocco*. Africa, 12, 1939, p. 445-49.

the organization of the latter is in response to the demands of the domanial 'economy' and no more; it does *not* suggest any vital integration of the two systems into a functional whole. As far as can be discerned, the *nundinae* of the domain system and the larger 'state' market system remain functionally separate, the only relevance of the *nundinae* to the upper stratum of this two-system being that they are part of the economic operation of the successful domain which is then integrated into the larger market system.

Nundinae could, of course, be drawn into the ambit of the town rather than the domain, and it is in this latter context that their economic and political function is more difficult to define. Theoretically, a small village begins by belonging to a single marketing cycle. One day of the week is specified to serve the surrounding rural area. But as population density and the level of production rise, the town usually adds another market day by joining another marketing cycle. Finally, the point is reached in this process where the town has a series of marketing days throughout the week that are virtually indistinguishable from the permanent town market place. [1] This is the stage at which we find the *nundinae* in the epigraphic documents from first century Italy. Several cities in Campania (e.g. Pompeii, Capua, and Cumae) are known to have had two, three and even four different *nundinae* in the same week [2]. In North Africa our evidence on urban *nundinae* comes primarily from the small villages and towns (*castella*) surrounding Cirta. The evidence appears to come from the transitional stage from rural to urban during the first half of the third century when there was a tendency for these markets to be instituted in the town centres. Although the provincial governors authorized the new foundations, it is difficult to ascertain whether it was a deliberate coercive policy or simply a natural consequence of increasing urbanization. It must be borne in mind that these *castella* already were important centre-places with their own permanent *fora* that antedate the establishment of the periodic markets, perhaps by centuries.

In the reign of Alexander Severus, the governor Publius Iunianus Martialianus established periodic markets at *Castellum Tidditanorum* (fig. 3). The *nundinae* were to be held on the day before the *kalends* and the day before the ides of each month [3]. As stated above, this market is not to be confused with the permanent market of *forum* of Tiddis which was located in the northern section of the town. The *kardo*, which winds and twists its way south through the town, terminates in a spacious walled enclosure. The inscription proclaiming the *nundinae* was set up in the enclosure just inside the southern gate of the town [4]. A decade or two later the governor of Numidia, M. Aurelius Cominius Cassianus (*gubern.* 246-47) gave his permission for the establishment of *nundinae* at *Castellum Mastarense*, a small village

---

[1] HODDER (1971) 348 ; SYMANSKI and WEBBER (1974) 208 f.

[2] MACMULLEN (1970) 339-41, and map on 341, though he is clearly mistaken in his statement that : «... there is no logic to the order of the names. They do not arrange themselves in an orderly itinerary, nor do they follow a pattern of regular rotation, every eighth day». Obviously, each individual cycle *does* have a pattern ; to say that they have 'no logic' is to miss the essential point of the overlapping of discrete market cycles and the demographic implications of this process.

[3] LESCHI (L.), *Inscriptions du Castellum Tidditanorum*. R.S.A.C., 65, 1942, p. 154-83 = *Etudes d'épigraphie, d'archéologie et d'histoire africaines*. Paris, Arts et métiers graphiques, 1957, p. 145-59 = A.E., 1942-43 : 7 = *ILAlg*. II, 3604 (al-Kheneg) [...c. 14... D(omini) N(ostri) / i]nvic[tissimi Imp(eratoris) Caes(aris)] / M(arci) Aurel[i Severi Alex(andri) Pii / f]elicis Aug(usti) [et Iuliae / Mamaeae Aug(ustae) matris / Aug(usti) n(ostri) et castrorum et / Senatus et patriae to/tius(que) Domus Divinae] / nundinae agentur [in / C]astello Tidditan [or(um) / p]r(idie) kal(endas) et pr(idie) idus sui [cu/i]usque mensis ex auct(oritate) / [P(ublii) I]uli Iuniani Martia/[l]iani leg(ati) Aug(usti) pr(o) pr(aetore) c(larissimi) v(iri) / [c]o(n)s(ulis) amplissimi prae/[s]idis et patroni / nostri / d(ecreto) d(ecurionum).

For the location see GSELL, *Atl. arch.* f. 17 (Constantine) no. 89, about 16 km NNW of Cirta ; Martialianus' governorship can be placed sometime in the reign of Alexander Severus, see THOMASSON, *Statthalter*, II. 211-12.

[4] BERTHIER (A.), *Tiddis, antique Castellum Tidditanorum*. Alger, 1951, p. 31.

directly west of Cirta (fig. 3). These markets were to be held twice each month, on the third day before the *kalends* and the third day before the *ides* [1].

If one compares the dates assigned to the market at Castellum Mastarense with those allotted to Castellum Tidditanorum, only twelve kilometres to the north, it is arguable that they were deliberately set to provide continuity in the market days of the two villages and yet, at the same time, to avoid a clash between them. Perhaps all nine of the *castella* surrounding Cirta, and apparently attributed to the city, also had their market days so arranged, though the evidence for such a cycle is missing. It seems that where the large domain was not dominant, the policy followed by the Roman governors of Numidia was to attach independent rural periodic markets to established town sites. Since there was little to be gained in terms of domanial control of workers, trade and communication, there was no need to maintain a broken system of mutually exclusive market days. Such a pattern depended on the relative autonomy of urban growth over the domination of the large estate.

8. Rural Periodic Markets : Culture and Control

The two most important cultural correlates of the periodic market are the factor of periodic time regulation it gives to local society (a sense of secular integration) and the function of belief in market regulation. We have already seen (p. 45-46 above) how the Roman system of time-reckoning imposed on African markets utterly destroyed their periodicity. The effect this had on traditional African society can only be surmised, in large part because of the lack of evidence. But two major effects can be outlined with a fair degree of certainty. Firstly, so-called 'primitive' societies have two major modes of time-reckoning, cosmological and secular. The cosmologically generated time sequences are the day and the year, with the subdivisions of day and night, and the major agricultural seasons. The only other major time sequence within this system is the month, generated by the lunar cycle. But usually some shorter scale measure is required between the day on the one hand, and the month and year on the other. Usually this time scale is the 'week' which is culturally generated. In fact, in most societies the week is market time, and vice versa. *There is no artificial distinction made between the two : the 'week' is the market cycle.* One major effect of the intrusion of the Roman system upon the African was not only to throw the market system out of any regularity, but completely to destroy the local system of time computation [2].

A second effect, already alluded to above, was to adjust the *nundinae* to such an erratic schedule (for which a constant series of Roman computations and notices would be required) that it effectively destroyed

---

[1] C. 6357, cf 19.337 = *ILS* 6868 = POULLE (A.), *Les marchés des Beni-Ziad (Castellum Mastarense) et d'.Aïn-Mechira.* R.S.A.C., 17, 1875, p. 357-74, cf A.E., 1939 : 38 (Rûffash).

Nundinae ha[be]ntur hic in | Castello Mastarensi die | III kal(endarum) Septemb(rium) primarum | et die III idum septembrium | [s]ubsequentium et deinceps || suo quoque mense, ex per/missu | M(arci) Aureli Comini Cas/siani leg(ati) Aug(ustorum) duorum) pr(o)p_1 (actore) | e(larissimi) v(iri).

For the location see GSELL, *Atl. arch.* f. 17 (Constantine) no. 94, near the *dûar* of the Banû Ziad, 2 km south of Rûffash on the northern slope of J. Zuâwî, itself a spur of J. Shattaba, about 21 km west of Constantine. Cominius was governor in A.D. 246-47, see THOMASSON, *Statthalter*, II. 216-18.

[2] HILL (1966) 295 f. ; BOHANNON (P.), *Concepts of Time among the Tiv of Nigeria.* The Southwestern Journal of Anthropology, 9.3, 1953, p. 251-62 = (in) *Myth and Cosmos : Readings in Mythology and Symbolism*, ed. J. Middleton. American Museum Sourcebooks in Anthropology, New York, The Natural History Press, 1967, p. 315-29 ; and EVANS-PRITCHARD (E.E.), *The Nuer.* Oxford, O.U.P., 1940, p. 104-10, cf NILSSON (M.P.), *Primitive Time-Reckoning.* Skrifter utgivna av Humanistiska Vetenskapssamf, Lund, 1920. Official Roman computations in *Proconsularis* appear to have been made relative to the *kalends* and *nones*, see no. 1, p. 54, and *ILAfr.* 395 (Carthage), but relative to the *kalends* and *ides* in the other provinces. Cf SAMUEL, *Greek and Roman Chronology*, I.3, *Natural Units of Time*, p. 13-18, wrongly including the week.

the opportunity for African periodic markets to build into larger market cycles. The point is that wherever two markets were not in similar cycles, the fluctuation in market days, ranging from twelve to eighteen days at any time, made it virtually impossible to co-ordinate local cycles. What effect both these changes had on life is not ascertainable since, due to the extreme paucity of information, we can only guess at the importance of the social rôle played by *nundinae* in the daily activities of the African countryside where tribal institutions remained the backbone of society.

One indication of the pervasiveness of the institution in North African society is the relatively high incidence of the personal name '*Nundinarius*' ('marketer'). The name is not of Italian origin; it is not found in Italy except for three examples in the city of Rome. In the latter cases it even seems that the persons bearing the name were immigrants, one of whom is probably an African [1]. The Italian preferred to adopt the personal name 'Mercator', or some variation; 'Nundinarius' is of foreign coinage. There are over forty examples of the name known from Africa as opposed to only ca. fifteen from all the rest of the empire [2]. It seems probable, therefore, that this *cognomen*, like so many others in Africa, is merely a Latin translation, or equivalent, of an African name that had the same meaning. A survey of the Africans who bore the cognomen reveals that they all derive from the sector of local society least affected by the processes of imperial acculturation; only one managed to achieve municipal office, and he was the descendant of a veteran in a military colony [3]. Eight, possibly nine, who bear the cognomen also have the *nomen* 'Iulius' and are settled in towns that were centres of the *IIIa Augusta*, men like Iulius Nundinarius who erected the tombstone of his father Iulius Iubaeus at Ammaedara. It seems likely that these men were descendants of the Gaetuli who were enfranchised by Iulius Caesar and who formed one of the core recruiting elements of the legion in Africa [4]. Some men, even though they bear *tria nomina*, reveal their African background, like Ti. Claudius Nundinarius whose father Ti. Claudius Honoratus and mother Iulia Monnina are clearly of African origin [5]. Still others bear a purely African nomenclature, such as Nummu, Nundinari filius [6].

It is also possible that the name not only signified the predominance of this institution in Africa, but also a personal connection between the person bearing the name and the market itself. We must suspect that some of these names are 'doubles' that were not arbitrarily given at birth, but which were acquired artificially in later life by Africans who sought a Latin 'name' alongside their African one [7]. Certainly the four women who were named 'Nundinaria' may have acquired their names either by their constant presence at periodic markets or the actual operation of market stalls [8]. What is perhaps more

---

[1] No examples are known from Italy outside Rome, even in regions such as Campania where *nundinae* are *known* to have flourished. The possible African from Rome is *CIL* VI, 24.642, the other *ILCV* 3475a = Rossi, *Inscr. Christ. Urb. Romae*, 1, 1922, 367.

[2] See Chart 5 and KAJANTO (I.), *The Latin Cognomina*. Helsinki, 1965, 18, cf 221 f.

[3] Chart 5, no. 3 ; *Mascula* : probably a Trajanic military colony, see GASCOU (J.), *La politique municipale de l'Empire romain en Afrique proconsulaire de Trajan à Septime-Sévère*. Rome (Collection de l'Ecole française de Rome no. 8), 1972, p. 101-03.

[4] Chart 5, no. 8 is clearly originally from the Carthage region ; for the rest see nos. 3, 9, 17, 20, 29, 33, 37, and 38. Cf GASCOU (J.), *Inscriptions de Tébessa*. M.E.F.R., 81, 1969, ss. 4 : *Marius et les Gétules*, p. 555-68, and his *Le Cognomen Gaetulus, Gaetulicus en Afrique romaine*. M.E.F.R., 82, 1970, p. 723-36.

[5] Chart 5, no. 4 ; cf nos. 7, 15, and 25.

[6] Chart 5, no. 5.

[7] Latin names, as we know, were sometimes acquired in later life, and functioned alongside quite different African names, see *C.* 5209 = *ILAlg.* I, 137 and CAMPS, *Massinissa*, p. 152.

[8] Chart 5, nos. 14, 19, 32, 35, and 36 ; see the study by PFLAUM (H.-G.), *Remarques sur l'onomastique de Castellum Celtianum*, (in) *Carnuntina*, Römische Forschungen in Niederösterreich, hrsg. E. Swoboda, Bd. 3, Graz-Köln, 1956, p. 126-51, at p. 135 on *Nundinaria*.

suggestive is that the only deity explicitly recognized in any of the inscriptions concerning our 'Nundinarii' is Saturn. C. Silius Nundinarius from Calama erected a votive dedication to *Saturnus Augustus* [1]. Two men bearing the cognomen were actually priests of the deity: Pontilius Nundinarius, *sacerdos Saturni* at Thignica erected a votive stele to the god in the sacred *area* of the god in his town, and C. Iulius Nundinarius honoured the god at his temple at Sitifis [2]. Were these 'Nundinarii' perhaps connected with the market-place in their rôle as priests of Saturn? Bearing in mind that Jupiter-Saturn was considered to be the chief patron deity of the market at Hassawana, the suggestion is not without plausibility. Certainly many priests of Saturn are mentioned as performing duties that would naturally be construed as rites performed at market places [3]. And the sort of holy men like those mentioned by Herodotos among the Nasamones must have continued to function within the social structure of rural communities as a part of formal religion, whether pagan or Christian. But, if so, the peculiar absence of the figure of the 'holy man' during the Christian period is somewhat startling, since the African Christianity would seem to have provided an ideal milieu for the proliferation of such men [4].

Perhaps part of the explanation for the absence lies in the more highly integrated nature of African society — that is, just as in the unique brand of Islam found in the Maghrib, the holy-man or saint was bound up within the existing social and belief structure (e.g. Church) of the local community rather than being external to it. The priests of Saturn were certainly in this position, and there is no reason to doubt that, with the almost direct substitution of Christianity for the cult of Saturn, the Christian bishop filled an analogous function. The numerous bishops who came from places which were simply *vici* on large estates or villages that were simply centre-places of tribal *territoria* must have been the only local men of authority with any claim to neutrality who could serve as arbitrators in market affairs [5].

Indirect evidence of the involvement of bishops, priests, and deacons in rural markets can be found in the repeated warnings to them in the canons of the African Church, warnings which specifically caution them against any entanglement with the world of business and profit-making. If warnings of this sort were to have any meaning for the majority of bishops who came from small villages and hamlets in the African countryside, they must have assumed the rôle of periodic markets. As much is confirmed by a similar warning issued by the *Concilium Eliberitanum* to the Spanish Churches in A.D. 305 in almost precisely the same terms as the strictures published by the African Church. The Spanish order, however, is more specific and cautions bishops, priests, and deacons against attempting to reap profits from

---

[1] Chart 5, no. 6 ; cf LEGLAY, *SAM* I, 393.21 and pl. XIV.4.
[2] Chart 5, no. 8 and 13 ; LEGLAY, *SAM* I, 181.209, and *SAM* II, 278.25.
[3] C. 5304 = *ILAlg.* I, 189 ; C. 8452, 15.006.
[4] Hdt. 4.172 ; cf GSELL, *HAAN*, 6, 1927, p. 168, 238 and 243. FOGG (1940 a & b) *passim* ; cf BROWN (P.), *The Rise and Function of the Holy Man in Late Antiquity*. J.R.S., 61, 1971, p. 80-101 ; the *duces sanctorum* known from the fourth century are a close, but not exact parallel, see Optatus, *De schism. Donatist.* 3.4 and BRISSON (J.-P.), *Autonomisme et Christianisme dans l'Afrique romaine de Septime-Sévère à l'invasion Vandale*. Paris, 1958, p. 327, no. 1 and p. 345.
[5] For the rural bishopric see MAIER, *Episcopat*, p. 123-24, 240-42 (hamlets and estates), 122, 155, 166, 168-69, 180, and 190 (tribal centres). Cf DESANGES, *Catalogue des tribus*, p. 49-50 and 56. See Aug. *Ep.* 46, 65, 66, 96, 113-16, 125, 139, 149, 152 etc. for landlords as bishops ; cf LANCEL (S.), *Actes de la Conférence de Carthage en 411*, vol. 1, Paris, Editions du Cerf (Sources chrétiennes, no. 194), 1972, p. 134-43, and FREND (W.H.C.), *The Donatist Church : A Movement of Protest in Roman North Africa*, 2nd ed. Oxford, Clarendon Press 1971, p. 48-59.

The general importance of rural markets to the Christian community in North Africa can be seen in Aug. *Ep.* 46, and Tert. *Apol.* 42.2 : *Itaque non sine foro, non sine macello, non sine balneis, tabernis, officinis, stabulis, nundinis vestris, ceterisque commerciis eo habitamus in hoc saeculo*. And in the prohibitions against attending *nundinae* in connexion with certain religious observances : see C. 25.045, cf A.E., 1901 : 5 = A.E., 1924 : 86, cf *ILTun.* 1008 = *ILCV* 1003 (Carthage). See BICKEL (F.), *Protogamia : Zum Montanismus und Donatismus in Afrika*. Hermes, 58, 1923, p. 426-40.

activities at periodic markets (*nundinae*) [1]. Yet the strictures themselves suggest the opposite, and the fact that Christians involved in high-level power struggles in the Church also bore the name 'Nundinarius' (at Cirta) excites further suspicion [2]. In this context, certain remarks made by Cyprian concerning bishops and periodic markets assume greater significance. He speaks of bishops abandoning their proper clerical duties while they make the rounds of the *nundinae*, a pursuit that brought them not considerable profit [3]. Just as in the contemporary Maghrib, the distinction between the separate spheres of secular and sacred appears to have been blurred. The Berber holy man is not only blessed (*baraka*) by Allah, but also by material benefits that flow from his rôle as market mediator [4]. The Christian bishop, it would seem, performed a very similar functional role in the ancient society of the Maghrib.

The bishop was therefore involved in a local communications network that served, much as the modern rural *sûq*, to integrate life in the countryside. In the modern *sûq* the communications take place not only via informal exchanges between the tribesmen but also by more formal means such as political assemblies and the general use of a quasi-professional caste of market criers whose special task it is to announce 'news items' at the markets and to act as couriers between them [5]. All the integrated aspects of the African *nundinae* as modes of communication, exchange, trade, labour markets, religious venues, and as mechanisms of social control are perhaps best illustrated by events in the Numidian countryside in the mid-fourth century A.D.

In A.D. 347 two imperial commissioners, Paulus and Macarius, were appointed by the emperor Constans to investigate the rising tension between the African and Catholic churches. The two commissioners were frankly hostile to the position of the African Church and their presence in Africa provoked great resentment among the local populace, a resentment that turned to open resistance after the commissioners' 'investigation' became nothing less than full-fledged persecution, including the coercion and bribery of African Christians. As the imperial representatives approached the small *civitas* of Bagaï in southeastern Numidia, the local bishop, Donatus by name, was compelled to summon the forces of

---

[1] For the constant warnings in the African canons see MANSI (J.D.), *Sacrorum Conciliorum nova et amplissima Collectio*. Florence, 1760, V.iii, col. 147, xx. 6 (Council of Carthage, A.D. 348-49) ; col. 711, ss. 16 (*Codex Canonum ecclesiae Africae*, A.D. 391) ; col. 883, ss. 15-16 (Council of Carthage, A.D. 398, cf col. 947, ss. 14). A typical example is reprinted in JONKERS (E.J.), *Acta et symbola conciliorum quae quarta saecula habita sunt*. Leiden, 1954, p. 124-25 (ss. xviii) :

Item placuit, ut episcopi vel presbyteri et diaconi vel clerici non sint conductores neque ullo turpi el inhonesto negotio victum quaerant, quia respicere debeant scriptum esse : Nemo militans Deo implicat se negotiis saecularibus. (2 Tim. 2.4)

The strictures appear to have been ignored regularly, see Aug. *Ep*. 113-16. For the rules of the Spanish Council see JONKERS, *op. cit.*, 9, no. 19 (ss. 18) :

Episcopi, presbyteri et diacones de locis suis negotiandi causa non discedant ; nec circumeuntes provincias, quaestuosas nundinas sectantur.

[2] Chart 5, no. 40 (cf 39).

[3] Cyprian, *De lapsis*, 6 (A.D. 251 ; Migne, *PL*, 4, 484 = *CSEL*, 3.1, 1868, 240-41)

Episcopi plurimi... divina procuratione contempta, procurationes rerum saecularium fieri ; derelicta cathedra, plebe deserta, per alienas provincias oberrantes negotiantis quaestuosae nundinas aucupari ; esurientibus in ecclesia patribus, habere argentum largiter velle, fundos insidiosis fraudibus rapere, usuris multiplicantibus faenus augere.

[4] GELLNER (1972) 59-62.

[5] HANOTEAU and LETOURNEUX, *La Kabylie*, 2, 1873, 79-80 ; FOGG (1932) 262 and (1942) 54-55 ; on the hereditary nature of the position and its social status see COON, *Tribes of the Rif*, 92-95.

the local agricultural workers to his defence [1]. He called on the workers to assemble at a pre-arranged location by sending out criers to all the neighbouring rural centres and periodic markets: [2]

> Cum ad Bagaiensem civitatem proximarent (sc. Paulus et Macarius), tunc alter Donatus, sicut prima diximus, eiusdem civitatis episcopus... praecones per vicina loca et per omnes nundinas misit, circumcelliones -- agonisticos nuncupans -- ad praedictum locum ut concurrerent, invitavit.

The *praecones* dispatched by Donatus to all the surrounding *nundinae* bear a striking resemblance to the market criers known from the modern day *sûq*. It also can be deduced from this incident that gangs of labourers in the rural districts around Bagaï tended to gather at periodic markets, and Donatus knew that they could be contacted there through the agency of the market criers. That this was ordinarily the case is confirmed by yet another incident involving the *nundinae*. In this case we can see that the African (sc. so-called 'Donatist') Church did not have any greater degree of control over the violent excesses of itinerant labourers at the periodic markets, and that its response was no different from any other vested interest in late African society. Earlier, in A.D. 340, the bishops of the African churches had found it impossible to restrain the violence of agricultural workers in southeastern Numidia; finally, they were compelled to appeal to civil authority to restore order. Taurinus, the *Comes Africae*, responsed by sending in troops [3]:

> Tunc Taurinus... ire milites iussit armatum per nundinas, ubi circumcelliones furor vagari consueverat. In loco Octavensi occisi sunt plurimi, detruncati sunt multi, quorum corpora usque in hodiernum per dealbatas aras aut mensas potuerunt numerari.

The tragic truth of the rôle of periodic markets in the control of the countryside could hardly be put in plainer words. From the admittedly 'white' propaganda of Optatus of Milev we learn that rural workers *customarily* gathered at periodic markets; probably they were the ordinary points of assembly for the gangs of harvesters who roamed the countryside each summer in search of work [4]. But the *nundinae* also provided a natural channel of communication and action for agrarian workers in times of chronic unemployment and other such social disturbances. Here the agitation over social grievances reached a level that even frightened the local African clergy on whose side they were normally considered to be in sectarian battles [5]. The dead and mutilated at Locus Octavensis, murdered at the behest of the African Church but honoured by the peasantry as true martyrs, are brutal testimony to the transcendence of African social problems and institutions over Roman social forms and ideologies.

---

[1] On the events see FREND, *The Donatist Church*², 176 f., and TENGSTRÖM (E.), *Donatisten und Katholiken · soziale, wirtschaftliche und politische Aspekte einer nordafrikanischen Kirchenspaltung*. Göteborg, 1964, p. 40-41. For Bagaï (mod. Qsar Baghaï) see GSELL, *Atl. arch.* f. 20 (Aïn Beïda) no. 68 ; MESNAGE, *L'Afrique chrétienne*, 253, and MAIER, *Episcopat*, p. 110.

[2] Optatus, *De schism. Donatist.* 3.4 (Migne, *PL*, 11, 1006-09).

[3] Optatus, *ibid.*, for Taurinus see *PLRE, Taurinus*, p. 878-79, '*Comes Africae* before c. 345', cf *fasti*, p. 1117.

[4] "Nomadic" plains of Cirta because the nomads journeyed there for summer pastures, cf *C.* 11 824 = *ILS* 7457, lines 9-10 :

> Falcifera cum turma virum processerat arvis
> Seu Cirtae nomados seu Iovis arva petens,

in the famous 'Maktar Harvester' inscription.

[5] See Frend, *The Donatist Church*², 176 ; similar memorials were founded in connexion with the market at 'Aïn Meshira, see GSELL and GRAILLOT (1874) 591 (altar inscribed *memo/ria m/artur/ibus*).

So too a Quodvultdeus built a market in the countryside near a martyrs' shrine at Khanguet al-Hajâj (Cap Bon Peninsula), see GAUCKLER (P.), B.C.T.H., (1894) 232, no. 6, and MONCEAUX (P.), B.S.A.F., (1913), 178.

Compare the crucial rôle of rural markets, assembly, fairs, and rural labour unrest in HOBSBAWM (F.) and RUDE (G.), *Captain Swing*. Penguin, Harmondsworth, 1973, p. 35, 47, 158, and *passim*.

9. Conclusion : Rural Markets, Marketing Systems and « The Market »

In conclusion, we might make a few remarks on how the findings of this paper relate to the more general problem of 'the market' in the Roman Empire. Historically the problem has resolved itself into two opposing camps paralleling the 'substantivist-formalist' battle in anthropology. In the one camp, the line of scholars from Meyer to Roztovtzeff, and including the blunter Heichelheim, has pursued the direct application of the rules of classical and neo-classical economics to the ancient world. Opposed to this school of thought is the tradition extending from Weber and Hasebroek to Polanyi which has seen the economy as an 'instituted' process which, in the classic phrase, is 'embedded' in other determinant social institutions. To take a recent partisan of the latter tradition, Sir Moses Finley quotes the economic historian Eric Roll to the effect that an *economic system* (i.e. *the* economy) must be composed, at very least, of "an enormous conglomeration of markets". He then argues that such a conglomerate of (commodity) markets did not exist in antiquity, and hence the discovery of unitary economic 'laws' is not possible [1]. Of course, both sides in this debate are using the word 'market' in an entirely different, though not unrelated, sense from the one used in this paper. They are referring to the abstraction 'market' in the sense of "an exchange sphere of consumers and suppliers centred on a single good or service" (e.g. grain, slaves, or land) [2]. We, on the other hand, have been referring to an objective *institution*, even a place, within which such exchange activities take place. The problem is : how do the two concepts of 'market' relate to one another, if at all ?

The point of connection is that even abstract 'markets' require institutional forms in order to function. But their existence is only made possible (e.g. the 'real estate market', the 'automobile market') by the genesis of a number of institutions that effectively free the sphere of transactions from a concrete *place* (i.e. the market in the sense in which we have analyzed it in this paper) or *time*. Exchanges in the abstract market no longer need to be tied to objective places and times and can take place in a notional sphere ('the market') because there exist surrogate institutions such as banks, paper money, and credit which can stream economic exchanges around and past market places and directly join producer and consumer. But such institutions, surrogate to the market, either did not exist in antiquity or remained severely stunted in their growth, and hence 'markets' in the abstract sense could not, and did not, come into existence. Therefore, we are cast back, more than ever, upon the determinant rôle of institutional markets, both *places* and *times*, in the ancient economy. Lacking many 'markets' in the abstract sense, and certainly, as Finley states, any conglomerate of such markets, the extent of the ancient economy was effectively limited by the real potential of the concrete institutional markets, such as those described in this paper, to handle transactions. Some of the restraints are obvious. These markets are objectified, limited to specific times and places where concrete exchanges must take place. But there are also all the other impediments discussed in this paper: in such objective markets the mere physical constraints of geography and communication are far more determinant in the sphere of transactions than in abstract markets. So too, being reified, time and place markets are far more easily subject to political and social controls ; in fact, if the initial findings of this paper are any indication, Polanyi and his followers would be quite correct in maintaining that such institutional and social influences on these markets (and hence *the* market insofar as it existed) cannot be ignored. Then again, there is the demonstrated disjunction between what I have called the 'urban' and 'rural' market systems in North Africa. The real divide that separated these two transactional spheres meant that no continuous abstract 'market' could be formed between the major

---

[1] FINLEY, *The Ancient Economy*, 22 and 26. Cf POLANYI (K.), *The Great Transformation : the Political and Economic Origins of our Time*. Boston, Beacon Press ed., 1957, chaps. 4-6.

[2] The definition of the abstraction 'market' offered here is mine ; most of those offered by standard modern economics textbooks are too specific (speaking of 'commodities', 'buyers and sellers' and 'places') or too vague to be useful.

producers in a predominantly agrarian economy and the mass of the consumers in the towns, villages and cities. This was because there were actually two distinct sets of marketing institutions in the area of the Roman Empire under study. First, the 'urban' market places, not only encompassing the spectrum from the small village to the large city, but also the representative of the city in the countryside, the large domain. Secondly, there is the 'rural' system of institutional markets, extending from periodic markets and fairs in the open countryside to the towns and villages that have accreted around or absorbed such markets, as well as the village-market complexes serving the clientele on the domains themselves. What seems apparent, even at the narrowest interface between the two systems — i.e. in the *vicus-nundinae* complex on the domain or the small town market — is that the two are completely separate in a way which is not compatible with a 'conglomerate market' economy. There *was* a sort of permeable barrier between the two spheres across which market goods and services had to pass in order to become commodities in the only 'system' of markets that existed — that dominated by the city. But the process of passing out of the autarchic rural market system was not so much an economic as a political one, determined in the last instance by the social structure of the city and its ability to extend its systems of control over the countryside. It is within the context of this latter process that the control of the institutions of exchange and systems of communication were one of the most significant factors in the creation of rural stratification, a factor which must be set alongside the importance of the ownership of means of production in our analyses of Rome's African empire [1].

---

[1] As pointed out by SMITH (C A) in a most important set of papers : *Examining Stratification Systems through Peasant Marketing Arrangements : An Application of Some Models from Economic Geography*. Man, 10, 1975, p. 95-122, esp. p.116 1 and *A Rejoinder (to P. McDowell)*. Man 11, 1976, p. 278-81.

I

THE PERIODIC CYCLE OF AFRICAN MARKET DAYS

Chart n° 1. — The *nundinae* on the estate of Lucilius Africanus at Casae (Hr. Begwar) (fig. 1) ; the market days are set on the fourth day before the *nones* and the twelfth day before the *kalends* of each month.

Col. I Month	Col. II Dates	Col. III Days counted inclusively	Col. IV Interval between nundinae
Ianuarius	4		
	21	4 - 20	17
Februarius	2	21 - 1	12
	18	2 - 17	16
Martius	4	18 - 3	14
	21	4 - 20	17
Aprilis	2	21 - 1	12
	20	2 - 19	18
Maius	4	20 - 3	14
	21	4 - 20	17
Iunius	2	21 - 1	12
	20	2 - 19	18
Iulius	4	20 - 3	14
	2	4 - 20	18
Augustus	4	21 - 3	14
	21	4 - 20	17
September	2	21 - 1	12
	20	2 - 19	18
October	4	20 - 3	14
	21	4 - 20	18
November	2	21 - 1	12
	20	2 - 19	18
December	4	20 - 3	14
	21	4 - 20	17
(Ian.)	4	21 - 3	14)
			365 days

Chart n° 2. — The *nundinae* on the estates of Antonia Saturnina at Vicus Pacatensis ('Aïn Meshira) and of Flavius Munatius at Emadaucapensis ('Aïn Kerma) ; both sets of market days are set on the fifth day before the *kalends* and the fifth day before the *ides* of each month.

Col. I Month	Col. II Dates	Col. III Dates counted inclusively	Col. IV Interval between nundinae
Ianarius	11		
	28	11 - 27	17
Februarius	9	28 - 8	12
	25	9 - 24	16
Martius	11	25 - 10	14
	28	11 - 27	17
Aprilis	9	28 - 8	12
	27	9 - 26	18
Maius	11	27 - 10	14
	28	11 - 27	17
Iunius	9	28 - 8	12
	27	9 - 26	18
Iulius	11	27 - 10	14
	28	11 - 27	17
Augustus	11	28 - 10	14
	28	11 - 27	17
September	9	28 - 8	12
	27	9 - 26	18
October	11	27 - 10	14
	28	11 - 27	17
November	9	28 - 8	12
	27	9 - 26	18
December	11	27 - 10	14
	28	11 - 27	17
(Ian.)	11	28 - 10	14)
			365 days

Chart n° 3. — The *nundinae* in the town of Castellum Tidditanorum (al-Kheneg) (fig. 3) ; the market days are set one day before the *kalends* and one day before the *ides* of each month.

Col. I Month	Col. II Dates	Col. III Dates counted inclusively	Col. IV Interval between nundinae
Ianuarius	14		
	31	14 - 30	17
Februarius	12	31 - 11	12
	28	12 - 27	16
Martius	14	28 - 13	14
	31	14 - 30	17
Aprilis	12	31 - 11	12
	30	12 - 29	18
Maius	14	30 - 13	14
	31	14 - 30	17
Iunius	12	31 - 11	12
	30	12 - 29	18
Iulius	14	30 - 13	14
	31	14 - 30	17
Augustus	14	31 - 13	14
	31	14 - 30	17
September	12	31 - 11	12
	30	12 - 29	18
October	14	30 - 13	14
	31	14 - 30	17
November	12	31 - 11	12
	30	12 - 29	18
December	14	30 - 13	14
	31	14 - 30	17
(Ian.)	14	31 - 14	14)
			365 days

Chart n° 4. — The *nundinae* in the town of Castellum Mastarense (Rûffash) (fig. 3) ; the market days are set on the third day before the *kalends* and on the third day before the *ides* of each month.

Col. I Month	Col. II Dates	Col. III Dates counted inclusively	Col. IV Interval between nundinae
Ianuarius	13		
	30	13 - 29	17
Februarius	11	30 - 10	12
	27	11 - 26	16
Martius	13	27 - 12	14
	30	13 - 29	17
Aprilis	11	30 - 10	12
	29	11 - 28	18
Maius	13	29 - 12	14
	30	13 - 29	17
Iunius	11	30 - 10	12
	29	11 - 28	18
Iulius	13	29 - 12	14
	30	13 - 29	17
Augustus	13	30 - 12	14
	30	13 - 29	17
September	11	30 - 10	12
	29	11 - 28	18
October	13	29 - 12	14
	30	13 - 29	17
November	11	30 - 10	12
	29	11 - 28	18
December	13	29 - 12	14
	30	13 - 29	17
(Ian.)	13	30 - 12	14)
			365 days

Chart n° 5

The Cognomen Nundinarius

No.	Source	Name	Remarks
1.	*C.* 420 (AMMAEDARA, Haïdra)	Refrius Nundinarius	A tombstone erected by Refrius Nundinarius for his brother, Refrius Successus.
2.	*C.* 1916 = *ILAlg.* I. 3207 = Guichard, R.A.f., (1864) 277 (THEVESTE, Tébessa)	Q(uintus) Caecilius Nundinarius	A tombstone erected by Caecilius for his wife Calpurnia Victor[ia?]
3.	*C.* 2248 (MASCULA, Khenshela)	[- - - Iul(ius)] M(arci) f(ilius) Papir(ia tribu) Nundinarius	Tombstone. Aedile and duumvir quinquennalis at Mascula ; an *eques Romanus*. The whole family has Roman citizenship and bear regular Latin *tria nomina*
4.	*C.* 4734 = *ILAlg.* I. 2346 = Gsell, *RAA*, 404, no. 656 (MADAUROS, M'daurûsh)	Ti(berius) Claudius [Nu]ndinarius	Tombstone. The son of an African mother, Iulia Monnina, and father, Ti. Claudius Honoratus
5.	*C.* 5060 = *ILAlg.* I. 1797 (THUBURSICU NUMIDARUM, Khamissa)	Nundinarius	Nummu(s?), Nundinari(i) f(ilius)
6.	*C.* 5304 = *ILAlg.* I. 189 (CALAMA, Guelma)	C(aius) Silius Nundinarius	Dedication to the god Saturn
7.	*C.* 5620 (THIBILIS, Annûna)	[....]M [..]OLVS Nondinarius (*sic*)	Tombstone
8.	*C.* 8452 (SITIFIS, Sétif)	C(aius) Iul(ius) C(aii) fil(ius) Arn(ensi tribu) Nundinarius	Stele erected to the god Saturn by Iulius as priest of the deity
9.	*C.* 11598 (AMMAEDARA, Haïdra)	Iulius Nundinarius	Tombstone erected for his father Iulius Iubeus Fortunatus. All other Iulii in the family are also recorded
10.	*C.* 11686 (THALA, Thala)	A[ur]elius Nundina[r(ius)]	Tombstone
11.	*C.* 12041 line no. 7 (LIMISA, Hr. Bûja)	L(ucius) Sudius Nundin(a)r(ius)	A list of names, perhaps town councillors (?) ; 22 names are listed, all Africans.
12.	*C.* 12064 = Belenet, B.C.T.H., (1886) 204 (MUZUC, Hr. Khashûn)	N[un]dinar(ius?)	An official inscription of the early fourth century erected by the Municipium Muzucense

RURAL MARKETS IN NORTH AFRICA 77

No.	Source	Name	Remarks
13.	C. 15006 (THIGNICA, Hr. ʿAïn Tûnga)	[- - -] Pontilius Nundinarius	Dedication to the god Saturn by a priest, *sacerdos* ; from the great Saturn sanctuary at Thignica
14.	C. 15702 (UCUBI, Hr. Kaussat)	[P]omponia Nundinaria	Tombstone
15.	C.15941 = Esperandieu, B.A.H., 21 (1886) 195 no. 20 (SICCA VENERA, al-Kaf)	C(aius) Aurelius Nundimarius (*sic*)	Tombstone
16.	C. 16093 = Esperandieu, B.A.H., (c.r.) 19 (1884) lxxix, no. 15 = B.A.H., 21 (1886) 200, no. 78 (SICCA VENERIA, al-Kaf)	D(ecimus) Iunius Nundinarius	Tombstone
17.	C. 16970 = *ILAlg*. I. 650 (Guelaʿa bû-Atfan, Gsell, *Atl. arch.*, f. 18, no. 200)	Q(uintus) Iulius Nu[n]dinarius	Tombstone ; wife named Grania Saturnina. African symbolism : phallus and crescent moon in relief
18.	C. 17006 = *ILAlg*. I. 693 (Guelaʿa bû-Atfan)	Nu(n)dinari(u)s	Tombstone
19.	*Ibid.*	Ianuaria Nu(n)d(inaria)	Wife of no. 18
20.	C. 17096 = *ILAlg*. I. 808 (Hr. al-Hammâm/Hr. al-Menniâl : Gsell, *Atl. arch.*, f. 18, no. 208)	Iulius Nundinarius	Tombstone ; wife named Iuli(a) Vardali(a)
21.	C. 17108 = *ILAlg*. I. 825 (Hr. al Hammâm/Fej-Berkûsh)	Nundinarius	Tombstone
22.	C. 18536 = (4346) = Poulle, R.S.A.C., 19 (1875) 439 (CASAE region, near Medrasen)	Q(uintus) Nonius Nundinarius	Tombstone erected by his four sons
23.	C. 19025 = Bernelle, B.A.H. (c.r.) 25 (1891) viii, no. 1 (THIBILIS, Annûna)	M(arcus) Nundinarius	Tombstone
24.	C. 20214 = Scratchley, B.A.H., (c.r.) 24 (1889) xliii (CHOBA, Ziama)	M(arcus) Numis Nund(in)arius	Tombstone
25.	C. 20506 = Gsell, R.A.A., 247, no. 267 (Kherbet ʿAïn Sultân)	C(aius) Erenius (*sic*) Nundinarius	Tombstone

No.	Source	Name	Remarks
26.	C. 22252 and 22644 = Esperandieu, B.C.T.H., (1890) 476, no. 90 = Catalogue Musée Alaoui, 164, no. 147	Nundinarius	Terra cotta lamps stamped with the name of the workshop : ex offici(na) Nundinari(i)
27.	C. 22644 (243) (a) Delattre, Les missions catholiques, 1895, 10 (b) Delattre, R.T., 4 (1897) 25, no. 149 (c) Delattre, R.T., 4 (1897) 25, no. 158 (d) Delattre, R.T., 4 (1897) 25, n° 153 (KARTHAGO, Carthage ; a from the southwest flank of the Byrsa ; b-d from the amphitheatre) (e) Gauckler, B.C.T.H., (1897) 453, no. 291 (J. bû-Kornein, Saturn sanctuary)	Nundinari(i)	Terra cotta lamps with workshop marks
28.	C. 25663 = Toutain, M.E.F.R., 13 (1893) 467, no. 37 (SIMITTHUS, Shemtû)	L(ucius) Favonius Nundinarius	Tombstone
29.	C. 23784 = Toussaint, B.C.T.H., (1899) 224, no. 108 (Hr. Gammâma, near CHUSIRA, Kissera)	Iulius Nundin(ari)us	Tombstone
30	C. 27866 = ILAlg. I. 3192 (THEVESTE, Tébessa)	Ca[e]cilius Nundinarius	Tombstone erected for his brother, Q. Caecilius Felicior
31.	C. 28033 = ILAlg. I. 2860 = Carcopino, B.C.T.H., (1905) 243-44 (between Morsot and M'daûrûsh, 6 km from Clairfontaine on the left bank of the Mellègue ; see Gsell, Atl. arch., f. 28, nos. 224-25)	T(itus) Fl(avius) Nundina(rius)	Tombstone erected by this man for his niece. A veteranus whose family probably obtained citizenship under the Flavians as Roman auxiliaries
32.	Ibid.	Pet(ilia ?) Nundinaria	Niece of no. 31
33.	ILAlg. I. 1646 (THUBURSICU NUMIDARUM, Khamissa)	Nund[i]narius	Tombstone of his Iulius Cels[i]nus Nund[i]nari f(ilius)
34.	ILAlg. I. 2296 = Toussaint, B.C.T.H., (1896) 255 (MADAUROS, M'daûrûsh)	L(ucius) Caecilius Quir(ina tribu) Nundinarius	Tombstone
35.	ILAlg. II. 2238 (CASTELLUM CELTIANUM, al-Meraba or Kherba ; see Gsell, Atl. arch., f. 8, no. 91)	Arria C(aii) f(ilia) Nundinaria	Tombstone

No.	Source	Name	Remarks
36.	ILAlg. II. 2531 (CASTELLUM CELTIANUM, al-Meraba)	Clodia Nundinaria	Tombstone
37.	ILAfr. 177 = M.E.F.R., 32 (1912) 204 (Ht. al-Aouédi)	Iulius Nundinarius	Tombstone
38.	ILAfr. 479 = B.C.T.H., (1918) 169 (THUBURNICA, Hr. Sidi bel-Qassem)	C. Iulius Nundinarius	Tombstone
39.	ILTun. 201 = Leynaud, Les catacombes africaines [2], 1922, p. 296 = B.S.A.S., (1908) 140 (HADRUMETUM, Sûsa)	Nundin(ar)ius	Christian graffitus
40.	Migne, PL, 8, 728 (Gesta apud Zenophilum) ; cf Aug., Ep., 43.17 (A.D. 397) and Ep. 53.4 (CIRTA, COLONIA CONSTANTINA, Constantine)	Nundinarius	Christian deacon of the church at Cirta

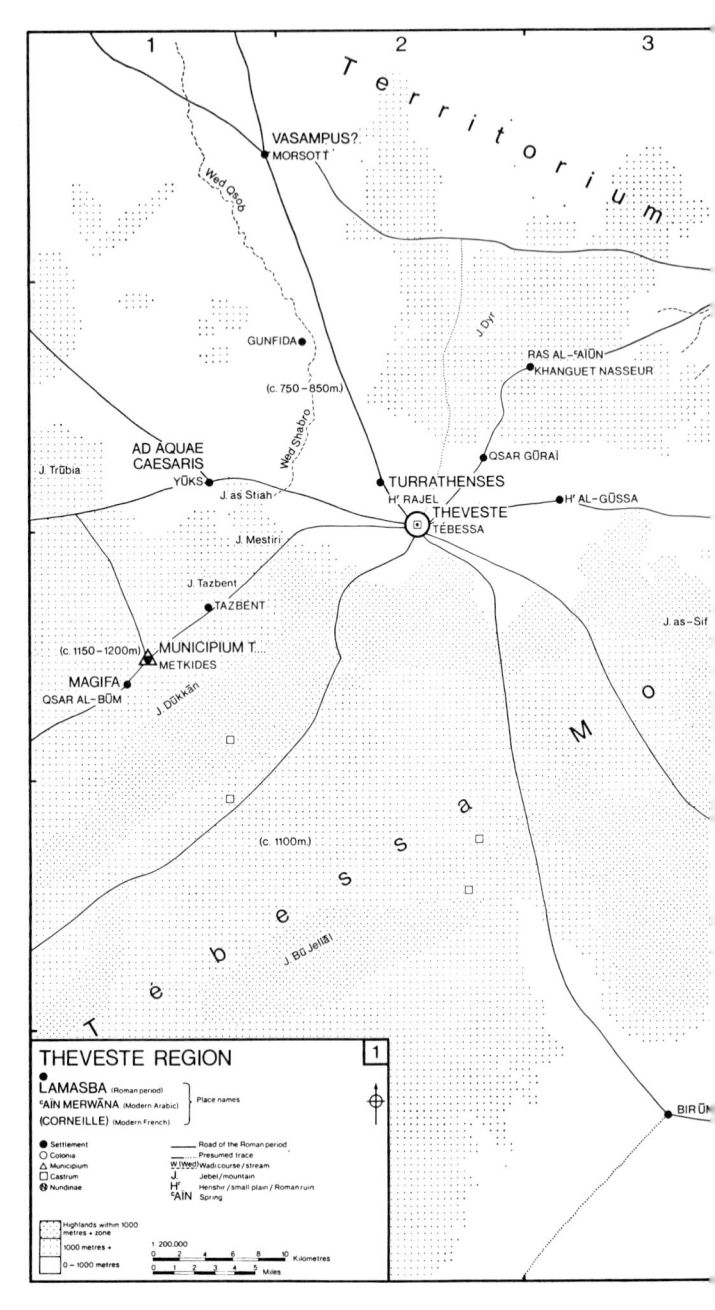

FIG. 1.

I

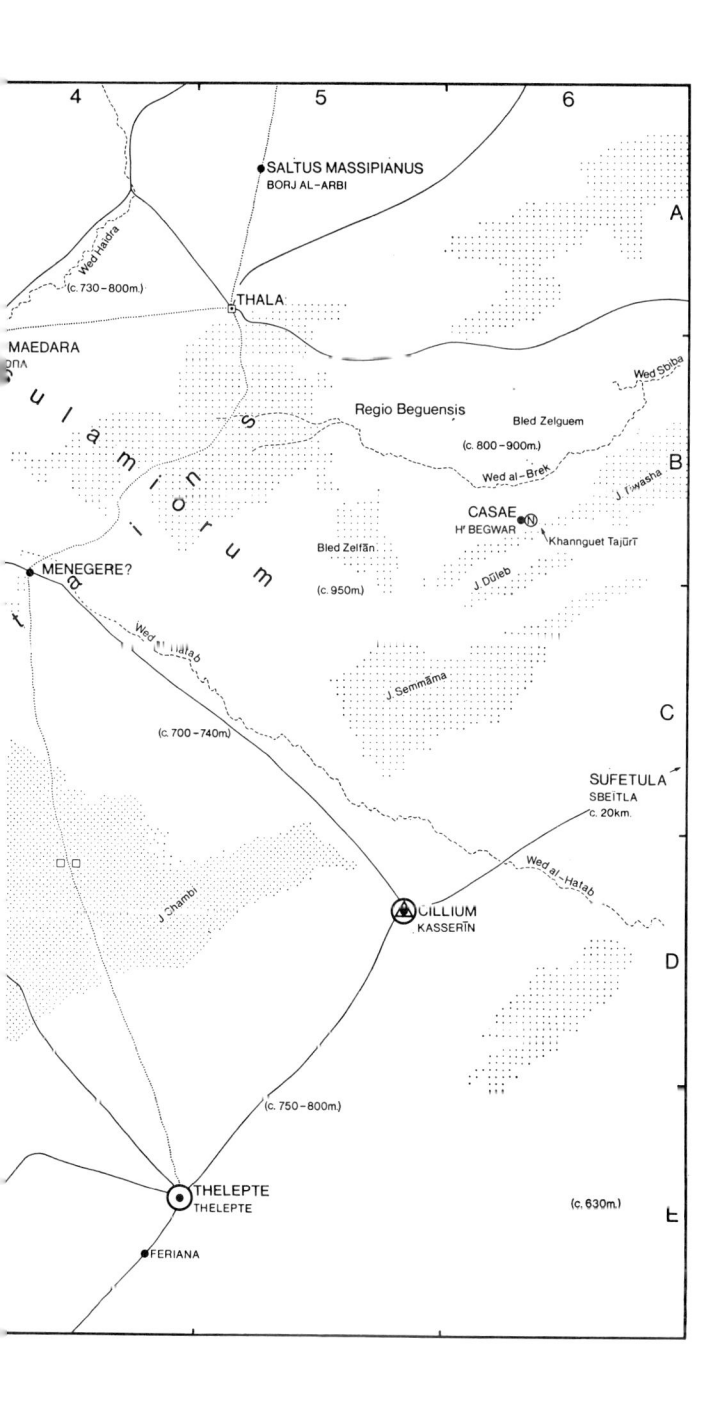

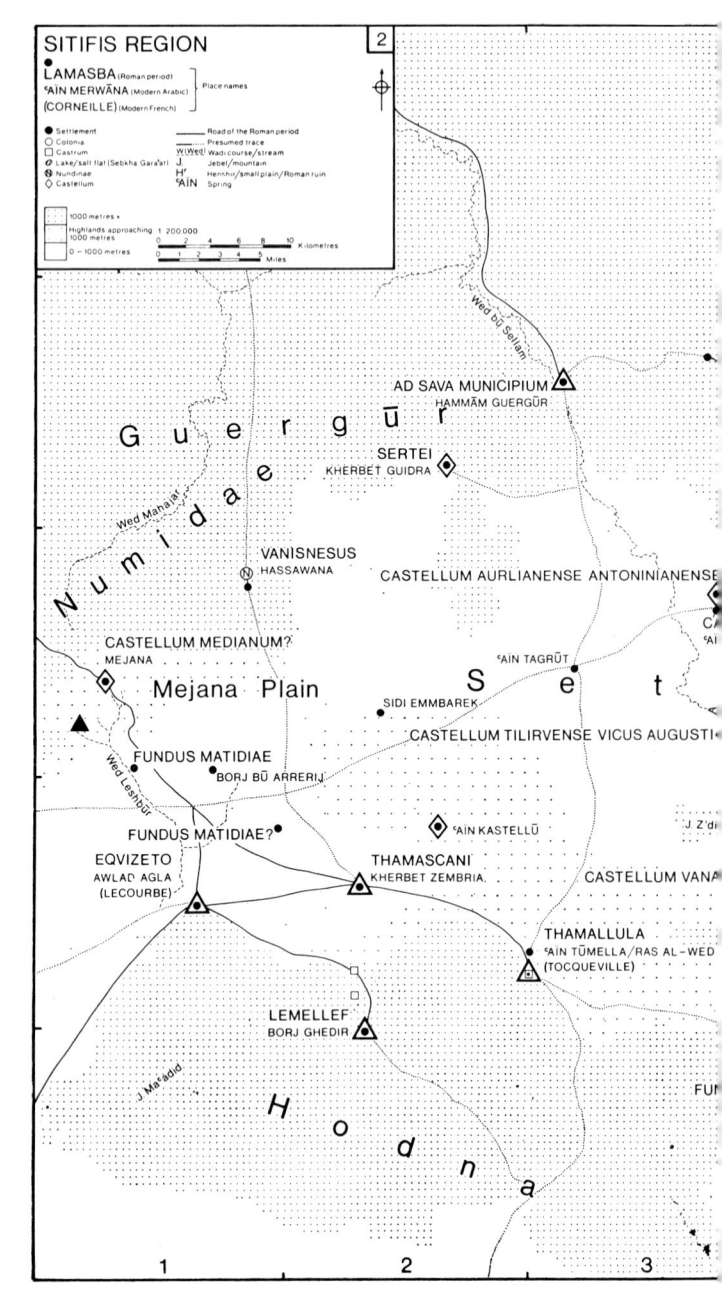

Fig. 2.

abor Mts.

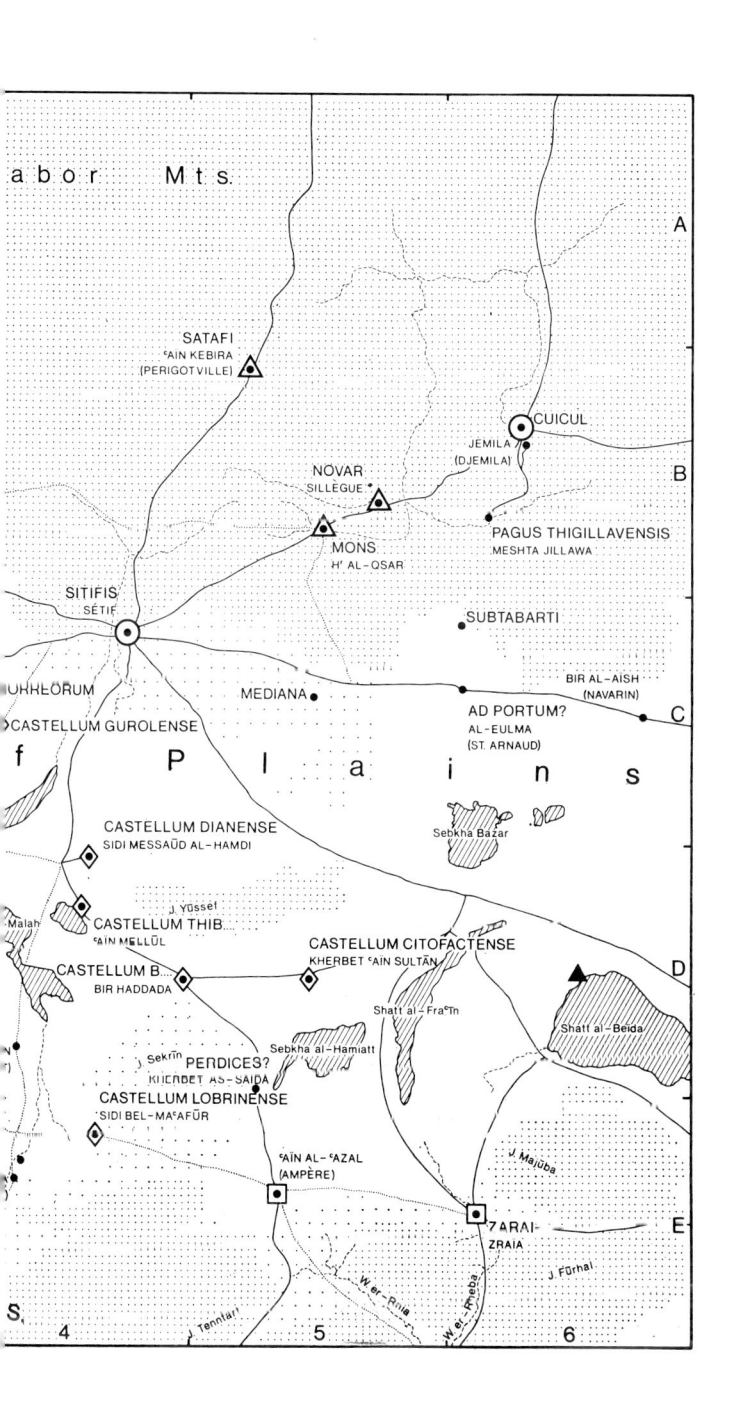

A

SATAFI
ᶜAIN KEBIRA
(PERIGOTVILLE)

CUICUL
JEMILA
(DJEMILA)
NOVAR
SILLÈGUE
B
MONS
H' AL-QSAR
PAGUS THIGILLAVENSIS
MESHTA JILLAWA

SITIFIS
SÉTIF
SUBTABARTI

UHHEORUM
MEDIANA
BIR AL-AISH
(NAVARIN)
CASTELLUM GUROLENSE
AD PORTUM?
AL-EULMA
(ST. ARNAUD)
C

f   P   l   a   i   n   s

CASTELLUM DIANENSE
SIDI MESSAŪD AL-HAMDI
Sebkha Bazar

J. Yūssef
CASTELLUM THIB.
ᶜAIN MELLŪL
CASTELLUM CITOFACTENSE
KHERBET ᶜAIN SULTĀN
CASTELLUM B.
BIR HADDADA
D
Shatt al-Fraᶜīn
Shatt al-Beida

Sekrīn PENDICES?
KHERBET AS-SAIDA
Sebkha al-Hamiatt
CASTELLUM LOBRINENSE
SIDI BEL-MAᶜAFŪR

ᶜAIN AL-ᶜAZAL
(AMPÈRE)
J. Majūba

ZARAI-
ZRAIA
E
J. Fūrhal

S
4
J. Tennlan
5
W. er-Rnia
W. er-Rheba
6

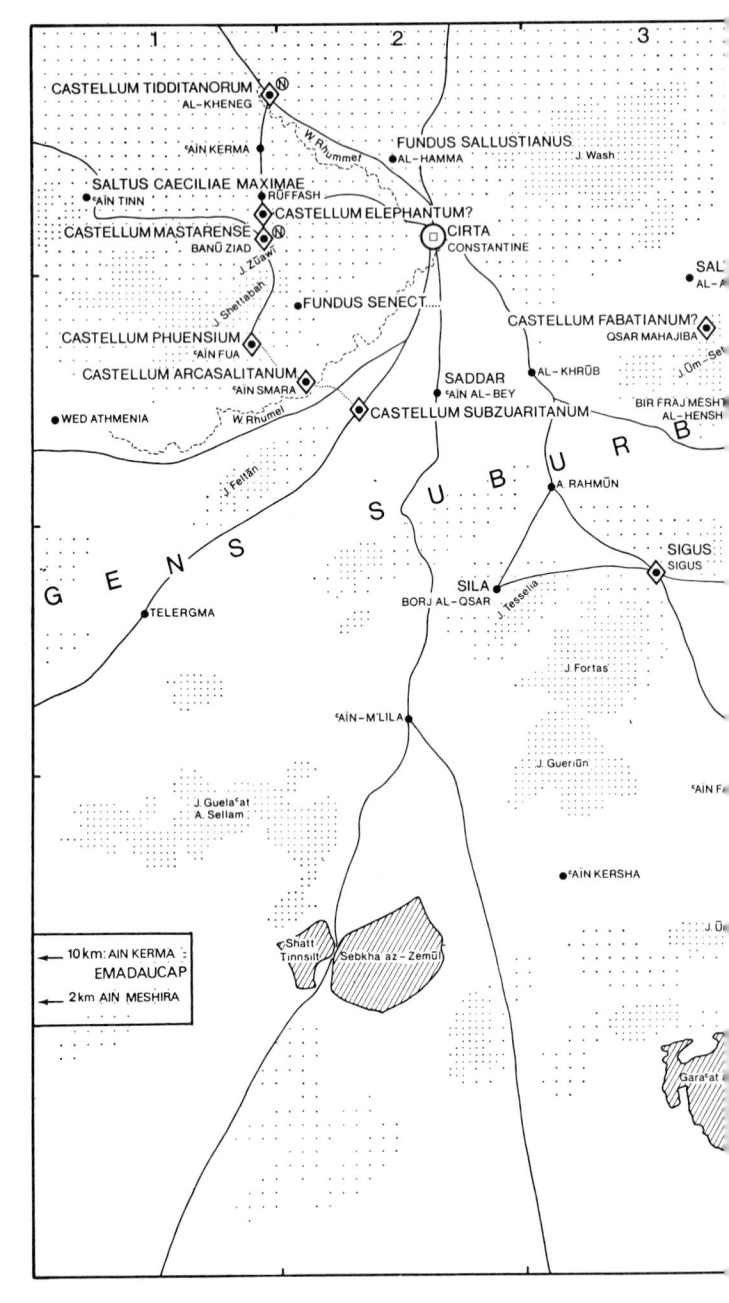

Fig. 3.

CIRTA AND ENVIRONS

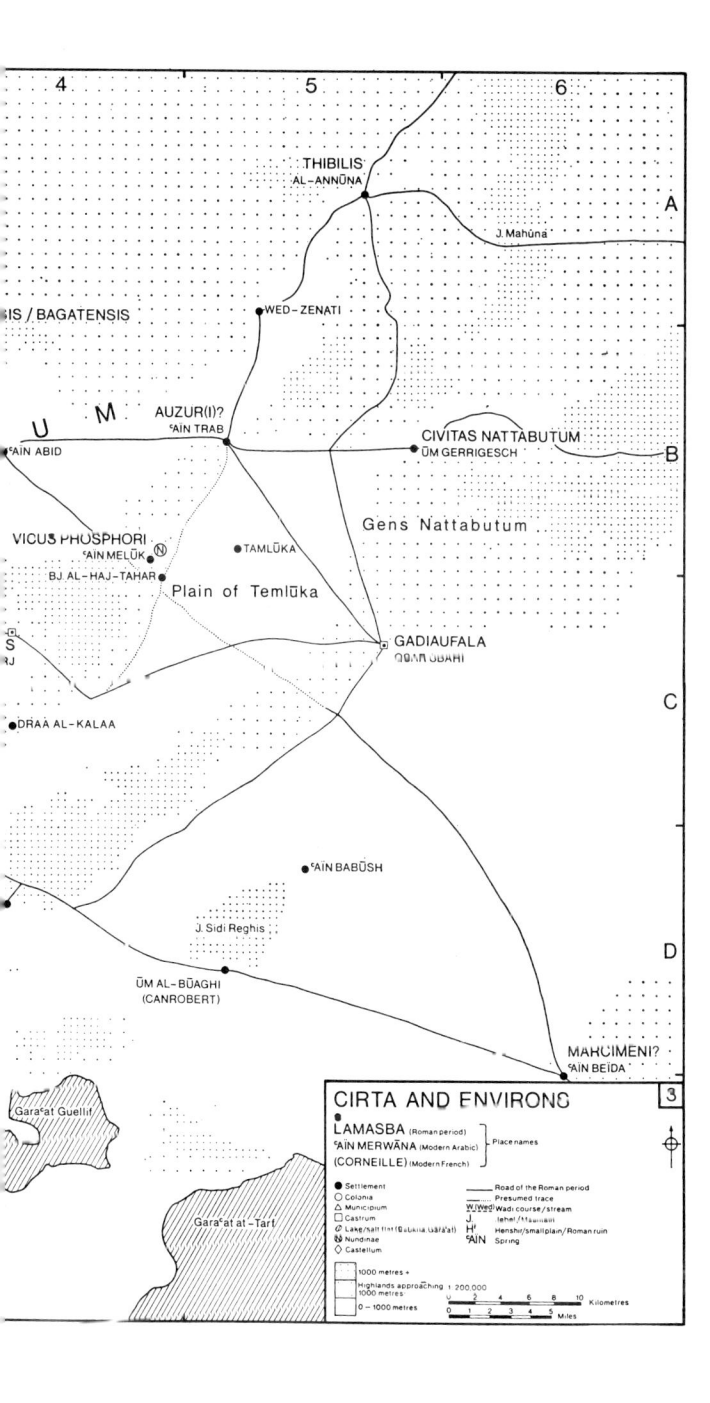

LAMASBA (Roman period)
ᶜAIN MERWĀNA (Modern Arabic) — Place names
(CORNEILLE) (Modern French)

- ● Settlement
- ○ Colonia
- △ Municipium
- □ Castrum
- ⌀ Lake/salt flat (Sebkha, Gara'at)
- ⓝ Nundinae
- ◊ Castellum

— Road of the Roman period
...... Presumed trace
W/Wed Wadi course/stream
J. Jabel/Mountain
H' Henshir/small plain/Roman ruin
ᶜAIN Spring

1000 metres +
Highlands approaching 1:200,000
1000 metres
0 – 1000 metres

Places visible on map:
- THIBILIS / AL-ANNŪNA
- J. Mahūna
- IS / BAGATENSIS
- WED-ZENATI
- AUZUR(I)? / ᶜAIN TRAB
- ᶜAIN ABID
- CIVITAS NATTABUTUM / ŪM GERRIGESCH
- VICUS PHOSPHORI / ᶜAIN MELŪK
- BJ. AL-HAJ-TAHAR
- TAMLŪKA
- Gens Nattabutum
- Plain of Temlūka
- GADIAUFALA / QAṢR ṢBAḤI
- DRĀA AL-KALAA
- ᶜAIN BABŪSH
- J. Sidi Reghis
- ŪM AL-BŪAGHI (CANROBERT)
- MARCIMENI? / ᶜAIN BEIDA
- Garaᶜat Guellif
- Garaᶜat at-Tarf

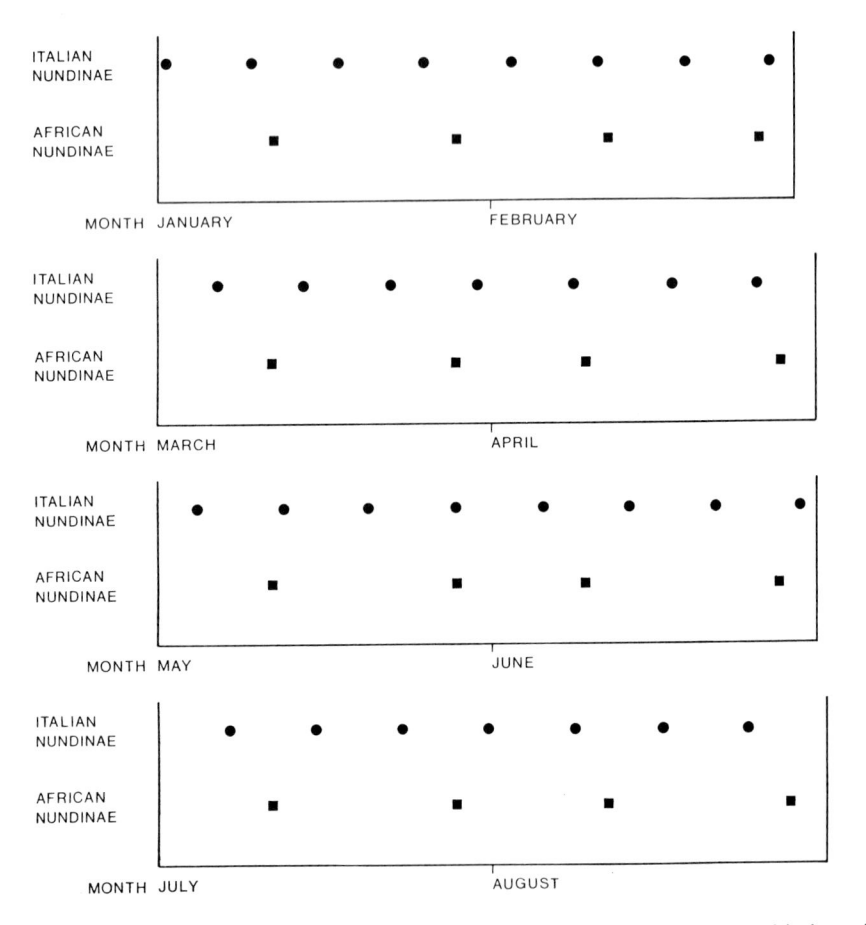

FIG. 4. — The sample period extends from January 1st to August 31st : the African cycle illustrated is the precise daily cycle for the VICUS PACATENSIS.

II

THE *UNDECEMPRIMI* IN ROMAN AFRICA

ANY ATTEMPT to unravel the relationship between African and Roman institutions in the Maghrib must include an analysis of those organisations which were indigenous to Africa. Further, this analysis should attempt to show in what way the indigenous institution related to the Roman development in North Africa, and what changes, if any, it underwent both in initial contact with Punic and Roman style administrations in the towns and in its final assimilation.

The *undecemprimi* undoubtedly represent one such indigenous institution, the analysis of which could give us some indication of the transformation of African organisations under Roman rule. The institution of the 'Eleven Leading-men' is relatively well attested in the Latin epigraphy of North Africa, but it is not to be found in any other part of the Roman Empire.[1] This fact alone certainly tends to confirm the local origin of the *undecemprimi*. Although the evidence for the 'Eleven' in Africa is limited to nine known cases, a close examination of each instance reveals at least a few facets (however conjectural) about their origin, function and development.

Eight of the nine instances of this institution are known from inscriptions found in the small towns in the region between the Upper Medjerda, its tributary the Oued Siliana, and the Oued Miliana (see map). Although few of these towns showed any great degree of Romanization and are therefore likely to have preserved older African institutions, it seems best to turn to the one remaining example for the best evidence concerning the origin of the 'Eleven'. The inscription comes from the colony of Cirta, far to the west, in Numidia:

M. Coculnio/ Sex(ti) fil(ius) Quir(ina)/ Quintilliano lato/ clavo exornato ab/ Imp(eratore) Caesare L. Septimio/ Severo Pertinace Augusto Pio/ Parthico Arabico Parthico/ Adiabenico post Flamonium et honores/ omnes quibus in Colonia Iulia/ Iuvenali Honoris et Virtutis Cirta/ patria sua functus est/ Florus Labaeonis fil(ius)/ Princeps et Undecim primus/ gentis Saboidum amico merenti/ de suo p[osuit ide]mq(ue) dedic(avit)/ l(oco) d(ato) d(ecreto) d(ecurionum).[2]

The inscription was set up as a dedication by Florus, chief of the Saboides, to a certain M. Coculnius Quintillianus, undoubtedly for some favour the latter had obtained either for the chief or the whole tribe while he was *triumvir* at Cirta.[3] The nomenclature of Florus ('son of Labaeo') reveals an Afro-Punic tradition still strong in the tribe itself, where even its head is still not profoundly affected by Roman influences. The inscription shows the 'Eleven' as an integral part of the ruling structure of an African tribe; more than likely, Florus was a member of the *undecemprimi* by virtue of his position as chief of the tribe.[4] The body of eleven men to which Florus belonged must have represented a sort of tribal council of notables close to the head of the tribe, acting in an advisory capacity. Thus, the inscription reveals that such an institution was still an active part of tribal government in the countryside near a highly Romanized center as late as the reign of Septimius Severus.

If we now turn to the other instances of the *undecemprimi* in the heartland of Africa Proconsularis, we should first examine the occurrence of the institution in those centers which showed the least progress in the Romanization of their local governments. This will allow us the opportunity of viewing the *undecemprimi* in an urban rather than a tribal context, and yet in a town milieu which was not dominated by Roman influence.

II

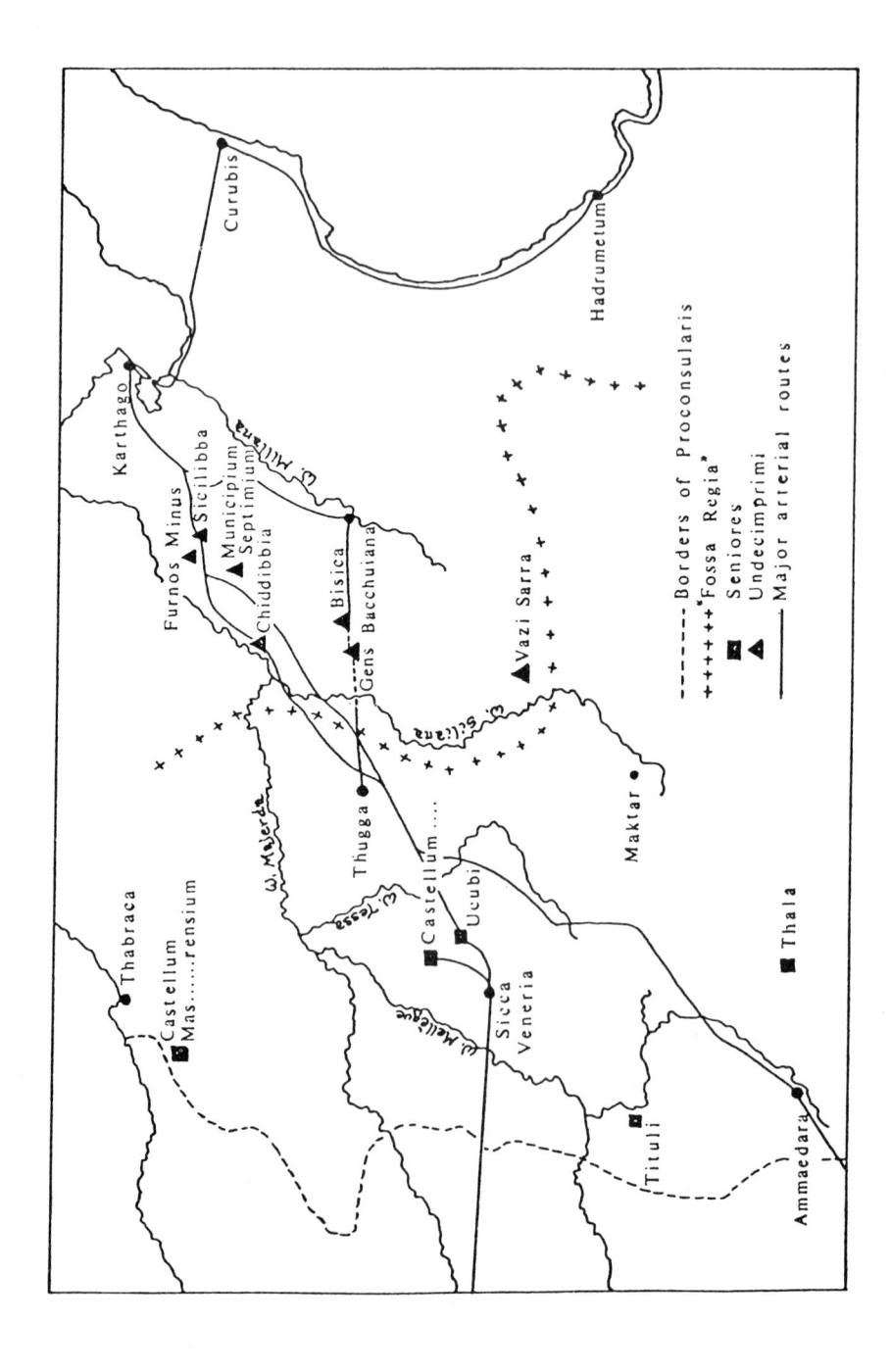

The small village of Biracsaccar remained a *castellum* even until the late fourth century A.D., and retained an Afro-Punic style civic administration with *sufetes* as the chief magistrates at least until the time of Antoninus Pius and probably beyond.[5] A funerary inscription from the town attests the existence of the 'Eleven', though not in the town itself.

Numeri/us Caesius/ Felicis f(ilius) ex/ XI primis Bisi(censis)/ pius vixit an(nis) LXXI/ [hic] situs est. O(ssa) t(ua) b(ene) q(uiescant), t(ibi) t(erra) l(evis) s(it).[6]

The floral decoration of the tombstone along with the crescent moon proclaims the African background of Numerius Caesius, as does his nomenclature. Numerius, though, apparently belonged to the *undecemprimi* of the near-by town of Bisica, some two miles away to the south. At Bisica itself additional proof is found of the *undecemprimi* mentioned in the inscription from Biracsaccar.

Zopyrus Tiro/nis f(ilius) Bisicensis/ ex XI primis/ vixit annis LXXXVIIII/ h(ic) s(itus) e(st)/ Ossa quieta precor/ Zopyri requiescant/ in urna et sit hum/us cineri non onerosa [precor]/O(ssa) t(ua) b(ene) [q(uiescant)]/ s(it) t(ibi) t(erra) l(evis).[7]

Once again, the African character of the nomenclature of Zopyrus, son of Tiro, tends to indicate that the African element is still strong in this town, and with it the probable maintenance of African institutions. Therefore, the inscription probably dates to some time before the grant of municipal status to the town.[8] The name Tiro is of Punic origin and occurs frequently in the neighbouring area, especially at Thugga.[9] But Zopyrus is a very unusual name; there is another instance at Bisica itself, in all likelihood the son of our Zopyrus:

Q. Caecilius Zop[y]ri fil(ius). . ./Pompeia Rogatula Rogatul(i) f(ilia) co[. . ./[10]

It should be noted that the son's name gives evidence of the growing Romanization of the town within his generation.

It is also important to note in these two examples that Zopyrus and Numerius Caesius do not seem to have held any other municipal offices. Their membership in the *undecemprimi* is unqualified in any way, leading one to suspect that both were permanent members of this organisation only. Also, the advanced age at which both men died (and the age to which they were *undecemprimi*), seventy-one and eighty-nine respectively, may imply that the organisation was filled on the basis of age and represented a small body of town elders. Since the *sufetes* at near-by Biracsaccar do not seem to have been *ex-officio* members of the 'Eleven' (as was the case with the *princeps* of the tribe) it may also be conjectured that in the transfer from tribal to civic organisation, the *undecemprimi* became separated from the main governing institutions of these small towns which tended to copy Punic models. If so, the *undecemprimi* were surviving as an African institution alongside the regular Punic-style administrations of the towns.

Such a transitional stage between tribe and Punic-style *civitas* can probably be seen in a town center just to the south-west of Bisica, at Gens Bacchuiana. This small village named after a tribe was undoubtedly the urban center of the rural area in which the tribe was located; as such it remained at the level of a *civitas* throughout its entire existence.[11] In the reign of Antoninus Pius, the town built and dedicated a temple to 'Achaian' Saturn for the well-being of the emperor.

Saturno Achaiae Aug(usto) sacr(um)/ pro sal(ute) Imp(eratoris) Caes(aris) Antonini Aug(usti) Pii p(atris) p(atriae)/ gens Bacchuiana templum sua pec(unia)

II

fecerunt id(emque) dedic(averunt)/ Candidus Balsamonis fil(ius) ex XI pr(imis) amplius spatium in quo templum fieret/ donavit.[12]
Candidus is surely an African, and his father a Punicized African who has taken the name Balsamon. The *undecemprimi* in this setting represent an urban institution, but one which has moved to the town directly from its tribal context. Since Candidus does not seem to be acting in an official capacity, but in a private role as benefactor in giving land to the town for the temple, it is difficult to infer much about the position of the *undecemprimi* of which he is a member. However, his undoubted wealth and high social position would tend to lead one to suspect that the 'Eleven' are more important in this context than in the Punic *civitates*. It may be conjectured that in the change from tribal to urban institution, the *undecemprimi* have remained the main governing body, and in lieu of a chieftain, have also become the chief magistrates of the town.

So far, we have surveyed the 'Eleven' in contexts in which the surrounding institutions have been entirely non-Roman (i.e. in a tribe and in three town centers all of which remained at the level of *civitates*). The question remains, what change, if any, did the *undecemprimi* undergo in towns where Romanization was a strong force?

At Furnos Minus, a town which became a *municipium* under Marcus Aurelius, an inscription of Severan date reveals some aspects of the 'Eleven' in Romanized communities.[13]

[Pro sal]ute Imp(eratoris) Caes(aris) M(arci) Aureli Severi Antonini Pii Felicis Aug(usti) Part(hici) max(imi) Brit(annici) max(imi) [po]ntif(icis) [max(imi) trib(unicia) pot(estate). .]/ imp(eratoris) III co(n)s(ulis) IIII p(atris) p(atriae) proco(n)s(ulis) et Iuliae Domnae Aug(ustae) Piae Felic(is) matris Aug(usti) et castror(um) et senat(us) et patr(iae) tot[iusqu(e) domus divinae]/ Sentius Felix Repostus ob honorem fili sui L(ucii) Senti Felicis Repostiani fl(amonii) p(er) p(etui) sive XI p[rimatus]/ et mag(isterii) non administrati sua pecunia fecit.[14]

In this case, the elder Repostus built some unspecified structure on his son's behalf in thanks for his gaining the office of *flamen perpetuus* or *undecemprimus* plus the office of *magister* which he did not fill. It can be seen from this inscription that the *undecemprimate* has now become a municipal office, and in this particular case there seems to be some close connection between it and the religious office of *flamen perpetuus*. Indeed, it seems (*pace* Broughton) that the two are meant to be taken as equivalent (*sive*).[15] Of course, as we shall soon see, this need not have been the case in all towns, and even in this instance the equation may not have reflected a legal fact but may have been merely a rough comparison, perhaps to elucidate the function or status of the new office of *flamen* in an African community which was gradually Romanizing its institutions. However, the religious overtones of the undecemprimate in the more Romanized towns seem to be confirmed by an examination of the four remaining cases.

At Henchir Debbik, to the south-west of Furnos Minus, we have further evidence for this:

Apollini Aug(usto) sacrum/ pro salute/ Imp(eratoris) Caes(aris) divi M(arci) Anto/nini Pii Germ(anici) Sarm(atici)/ fil(ii) divi Pii nep(otis) di/vi Hadr(iani) pronep(otis) [divi] Traian(i) abnep(otis) divi/ Nerva[e ad]nep(otis)/ M(arci) Aureli Commodi/ Antonini Aug(usti) Sar[m(atici)]/ Germ(anici) pont(ificis) max(imi) trib(unicia)/ potest(ate) VII imp(eratoris) IIII/ co(n)s(ulis) III p(atris) p(atriae)/ Q. Abonius I. fil(ius) Se/cundus ob honor(em)/ XI pr(imatus) quem ei ordo/ suus sponte decrevit/ s[t]atuam ex HS IIII mil(ibus)/ n(ummum) legitimis ampliata p/ecunia posuit et ob de/dicationem decurion[i/b]us sportulas et epulum/ [populo dedit l(oco) d(ato) d(ecreto) d(ecurionum)].[16]

Q. Abonius Secundus, though an African, reveals Roman influence in his nomenclature. The date of the dedication places it shortly before the time when the town became a *municipium* under the Severi.[17] In this case, the *undecemprimate* appears fully absorbed within the Romanized institutions of the town as a regular municipal office requiring a *summa honoraria* (4,000 sesterces 'legitimis').[18] The candidate for office has added more money to the required amount and has also bestowed the usual banquets for the town councillors and the people in order to demonstrate the depth of his gratitude. It can also be seen that Abonius received his office through a decree of the local town assembly. This process would fit the religious nature of the office since the major priesthoods, including the *flamen perpetuus*, were usually appointed on the authority of the town *ordo* whereas the other municipal offices were usually elective.

Far to the south, at Vazi Sarra, to the north-east of Mactar, comes the following inscription:

[P]ro salute Imp(eratoris) Caes(aris) divi Septimi Severi Pii Ara[b](ici) Adiabe[nic]i Parthici maximi Brit[an]nici maximi fil(ii) divi M(arci) Antonini Pii Germanici Sarmatici nepot(is) divi Antonini Pii/ pronepot(is) divi Hadriani abnep(otis) divi Traiani Parthici et divi Nervae adnepot(is) M(arci) Aureli Antonini Pii felicis Principis Iuventutis Augusti/ Parthici maximi Brittannici max(imi) Pont(ificis) max(imi) trib(unicia) potest(ate) XV imp(eratoris) II co(n)s(ulis) III p(atris) p(atriae) et Iuli[ae] Domnae Augustae Piae Felicis matris Aug(usti) et castrorum et senatus totiusq(ue) Domus Divinae/ P. Opstorius Saturninus fl(amen) p(erpetuus) sac(erdos) Merc(uri) cum patriae suae Vazitanae triplicata summa fl(amoni) p(erpetui) HS III m(illia) n(ummum) aedem Mercurio Sobrio pollicitus fuisset ampliata liberalitate eandem aedem/ cum pronao et ara fecit et ob dedicat(ionem) aepulum (*sic*) et gymnasium ded[it lo]c(o) dat(o) d(ecreto) d(ecurionum) idem(que) iam ant(e) hoc ob honorem XI pr(imatus) aedem Aesculapio Deo promissam bassil(icis) coherent(ibus) multiplicata pec(unia) fecit.[19]

P. Opstorius Saturninus, an African, had filled the office of *undecemprimus* before becoming priest of Mercury and *flamen perpetuus*. In this case, the municipal office fell in a line of priestly posts, but here the *undecemprimate* is clearly separated from the office of *flamen perpetuus*. Thus, though the office would seem to have a religious function, it is in no way to be regarded as an equivalent to the flaminate, at least in this community. However, at Henchir el-Aluin, near Sicilibba, a fragmentary inscription tends to reinforce the connection with the flaminate:

[Pro salute Imp(eratoris) Caes(aris) M(arci) Aureli Antonini Pii Fel(icis) Aug(usti) Parth(ici) max(imi) Brit(annici) max(imi)/ divi Nervae et] divi Traiani Parth(ici) abnep(otis) di[vi Hadriani adnep(otis) divi Antonini Pii/ pronep(otis) di]vi M(arci) Antonini Pii Germ(anici) Sarm(atici) nep(otis) divi [Severi Pii Arab(ici) Adiab(enici) Parth(ici) max(imi) Brit(annici)/ max(imi) f(ilii) ob] hon[or]em flam(onii) sive XI pr(imatus) Caledi Maxim[i.../...ex] HS IIII [mil(ibus) n(ummum) ded]it C. Cassius[...[20]

If the restoration of the inscription is correct, a certain C. Cassius is paying out a sum of money on behalf of Caledius Maximus who has obtained the office of *flamen or undecemprimus*. The same seems to be implied by another fragmentary inscription found at Chidibbia:

Iovi Optimo Ma/ximo Aug(usto) Sacr(um) P(ublius) Heren/[ni]us P(ublii) f(ilius) Felix [ob] spem/ XI primatus [prae]ter sum/mam [legitimam XI p] rimarii/ sua s[ponte . . . .] INDR/NI (?) [ob honor(em) f]lam(oni)/ siv[e XI pr(imatus) ex H]S IIII mil(ibus) n(ummum)/ [fac(iendum) curavit idemq(ue) de] dicavit/ l(oco) d(ato) d(ecreto) d(ecurionum).[21]

In this case, P. Herennius Felix is dispensing a large sum of money (even beyond what is required for a *summa honoraria*) in the hope of achieving appointment to the 'Eleven'; once again, if the inscription has been correctly restored, the office appears to be equated with the flaminate.

Of course, it is possible that the 'Eleven' had always been primarily a body whose concerns were mainly religious, but since the only indications that they had such a function come from Romanized towns where the institutions had become a municipal office, it seems best to turn to other possibilities. It seems more probable, on the basis of the evidence at our disposal, that the *undecemprimi* at their original tribal level represented a select group of elders about the tribal chieftain. As such, they should not be directly equated with the *seniores* also known from epigraphy in Roman Africa. Though this body also had a tribal origin, they represented a much more inclusive organisation than the *undecemprimi*; this is hardly surprising since one would expect the total number of elders (*seniores*) in a community to be a much larger number of men. In the case of the *seniores* this presumption is borne out by the epigraphic evidence.[22] Probably the *undecemprimi* originally were formed of a select body of elders forming an inner council around the tribal chieftain. As such it may be possible to identify them with a smaller group within the *seniores* found in the towns and known as the *principi seniores*.[23]

To sum up, it seems that the *undecemprimi* were gradually absorbed from their tribal surrounding into the urban environment of the towns. Initially they were maintained alongside the Punic-style civic governments in the small towns of Proconsularis where they formed a body of elders apart from the main administration of the town. Finally, in the gradual Romanization of these towns, the 'Eleven' were reduced to the status of a municipal office with only vestiges of religious powers left to them. All three stages in this evolution can be seen in different regions of North Africa in roughly the same period, at the end of the second and the beginning of the third century. In the tribe near Cirta they were a tribal council; at Bisica they represented an independent body of elders and at Vazi Sarra the *undecemprimate* had become a municipal priestly office. The gradual stages of development in the metamorphosis of this institution in turn mirror the differing degrees of Roman influence in the towns and countryside of North Africa.

NOTES

1. The only other example of an institution outside Africa which might be similar is the case of T. Iulius Festus at Nemausus in Gaul who was *XI vir: CIL* xii 3179 = *ILS* 2267. But *undecemvir* does not correspond to our terminology and does not seem to be related in any way to the African institution.
   Some scholars (cf. E. Cuq, *CRAI*, 1920, 340 f.) have attempted to connect the *undecemprimi* with the singular instance of a *decemprimus* from Africa. This is the case with Titius Faussanus who was *prior princeps civitatis ex decemprimis* at Altava (*AE* 1957:67) and perhaps includes Kal (*purnius*) Tacinus *decenvir* at Oppidum Novum (*CIL* viii 10945 cf. 21495). However, geography, time and context all separate this institution from that of the *undecemprimi* and P. Pouthier, 'Evolution municipal d'Altava aux IIIe et IVe siècles ap. J.C.', *MEFR*, 1956, 205-245 is quite correct in emphasizing the distinction between the two institutions (cf. esp. pp. 208-211).
2. *CIL* viii 7041(+19423) = *ILAlg.* ii 626 = *ILS* 6857; Cirta = Constantine; A.D. 195. For Coculnius cf. *CIL* viii 6993, 7042, 19508 (wife) and 19417 (*triumvir*).
3. For *principes* as the heads of tribes cf. T. Kotula, 'Les *principes gentis* et les *principes civitatis* en Afrique romaine', *Eos*, 55, 1955, 347-365. For the nomenclature of all of the *undecemprimi* mentioned in the paper (all are Afro-Punic) refer to L. A. Thompson, 'Some Observations on Personal Nomenclature in Roman Africa', *N&C*, 10, 1967-1968, 45-58.
4. This was also the conclusion drawn by J. Toutain, *Les cités romaines de la Tunisie*, Paris, 1896, 349 f.
5. Biracsaccar as *castellum* cf. *CIL* viii 23849; for the *sufetes* cf. *ibid.* 23876 (=12286) Antoninus Pius.
6. *CIL* viii 25853; Castellum Biracsaccarensium = Sidi Bou Medien; s.d.
7. *CIL* viii 12302 = *ILS* 6801/2; Bisica = Henchir Bijga; s.d.
8. Probably under Commodus or before under Antoninus Pius (*CIL* viii 12291 = *ILS* 1085. For a discussion cf. H.-G. Pflaum, 'La Romanisation de l'ancien territoire de la Carthage Punique à la lumière des découvertes épigraphiques récentes', *Ant. Afr.*, 4, 1970, 75-117, and esp. 90.
9. cf. *CIL* viii 26863, 26868 and 27082 (Thugga) and the P Caeilius (sic) Tiro at Sicca *CIL* viii 15949.
10. *CIL* viii 23885.
11. Though at least one other tribal center in Proconsularis rose to the status of a *municipium* under the Severi, the Gens Severiana: cf. *CIL* viii 883(+12386) = *ILS* 6816.
12. For the 'Achaian' Saturn see M. Leglay, *Saturne africain: histoire*, Paris, 1966, 123 and 235: an aspect of the African Saturn associated with the Greek Pluto. Also, Cl. Poinssot, 'Saturnus Achaiae (*CIL* viii 12331 = *ILS* 4440)', *Hommages à A. Grenier*. (Coll. Lat. 58, 1962, 1276-1291: perhaps a feature added to the god later in Roman times rather than a Hellenistic influence via Carthage (p. 1280, n. 4).
    For the inscription: *CIL* viii 12331 = *ILS* 4440; Gens Bacchuiana = Bu Djelida; Antoninus Pius, A.D. 139+
    M. Leglay in *Saturne africain: monuments*, t. 1, 124 remarks about the *undecemprimi*: '. . . c'est-à-dire des magistrats municipaux qui administraient les cités pérégrines au même titre que les sufetes'. This is possibly true of this inscription alone, but hardly applies to the *undecemprimi* as a whole.
    Ch. Clermont-Ganneau in *CRAI*, 1898, 362 wished to connect them with the Punic *Mazrah*, but actual proof of this connection is totally lacking even in the context of the Punic civitates.
13. *CIL* viii 25808b
14. *CIL* viii 25808; Furnos Minus = Henchir Msaadin; A.D. 213-217.
15. T.R.S. Broughton, *The Romanization of Africa Proconsularis*, Baltimore, Johns Hopkins, 1929, 182, n. 1.
16. *CIL* viii 14791 = *ILS* 6808; Municipium Septimium . — Henchir Debbik; A.D. 181. Pflaum, *art. cit.*, 91 remarks on an *undecemprimus*: '. . .c'est-à-dire il devenait un des onze magistrats superieurs.' which does not seem to be a possible interpretation for a Romanized community. He expresses a similar misconception on p. 89 where he states: 'Les *XI primi* sont l'equivalent de l'*ordo*. . .' which is only vaguely applicable to a tribal context and is certainly impossible in a Romanized community as is proven by this inscription where the *ordo* is specifically mentioned as a separate body involved in the appointment of Abonius to the office of *undecemprimus*.
17. *CIL* viii 14793
18. R. P. Duncan-Jones, 'Costs, Outlays and *Summae Honorariae* from Roman Africa', *PBSR*, 30, 1962, 68 and 103, no. 358: The examples cited in notes 20 and 21 should be added to the list.
19. *CIL* viii 12006 (cf. 12007); Vazi Sarra = Henchir Bez; A.D. 211.

20. *CIL* viii 14755; Henchir el-Aluin=2 to 3 miles from Sicilibba; Caracalla. The last line in the Corpus reads: ....] 1S 1111 [.....] IT C CASSIU[s... For the African name, cf. Iulia Fortunata Calediana at Aïn el Abid near Teboursouk, *CIL* viii 24440.
21. *CIL* viii 14875 (=1327); Chidibbia=Henchir Sluguia; s.d. Lines 5-6 in the Corpus read: S VAS [......] 1 INDR/NI [.........] NAM/SIV[....ex ii]S IIII ML N.
22. Broughton, *op.cit.*, 82-83; cf. at Thala: *CII seniores, AE* 1915:80 (A.D. 208).
23. *Principi seniores k(astelli)*=*CIL* viii 15721 (A.D. 213) Henchir Sidi Merzug near Sicca Veneria; cf. Gsell, *HAAN*, 5, 63-65 on the structure of the modern *djemaâ*.

III

THE STRUCTURE OF LOCAL SOCIETY IN THE EARLY MAGHRIB: THE ELDERS

THE interwoven structures of personal power formed by overlapping claims of kinship, friendship, patronage and neighbourliness (whether actual or fictive) represent some of the most important frameworks of social and economic interaction in rural north Africa of the Roman period. These structures may be reconstructed according to models suggested by a combination of comparative anthropological data and interpretations, and clues contained in the records surviving from antiquity. Contemporary ethnographic research does provide a range of social structures within which the African society of the Roman empire may be comprehended, but even the most careful use of the ideas of anthropology seems unable to penetrate the singular opaqueness of the ancient data. Moreover, a mere juxtaposition of modern anthropological parallels and a haphazard collection of facts from antiquity will not suffice. Certain *a priori* assumptions must be made about the functional structure of the whole society against which the ancient evidence might be tested. This methodology is open to serious question: the simple admission of a prior construct is usually construed as leading to simple tautology. To avoid this obvious pitfall, the model must be viable in its own right and then only used as a tool to assist in focusing our vision on a rather dim picture. The method is only acceptable insofar as it produces results which agree fully with the model and with the surviving evidence. However hazardous the methodology, it is preferable to a simple cataloguing of the available data and to the arbitrary slotting of discrete pieces of evidence from antiquity into convenient parallels offered by contemporary social theoreticians.

The contact between African societies and the expanding Latin cultural hegemony represented by the Roman state was necessarily marked by a broad spectrum of reactions. If any one element determining such reactions could be said to be evident in the rural societies of the Mediterranean, it would be the simple persistence of customary forms and the traditional forces inherent in them. This closed attitude established a certain intransigence to external influences of all types; whatever few foreign elements gained acceptance were mutated in their form and meaning in order to make sense and to function in the local context. Even in the urban environment of the towns and villages, the milieu most favourable to the transfer of such influences, African societies already had certain attitudes, represented externally in their social and political institutions, which frustrated the intrusion of a foreign culture. This internal momentum or inertia, set in counterpoise to external pressures, hindered an unimpeded interaction between the indigenous and the foreign. Even if com-

First published in *The Maghreb Review* 16, Nos. 1-2 (1991), pp. 18-54. Copyright © *The Maghreb Review* 1991.

munication between the two societies were restricted to purely administrative levels, there would still have to be a translation between the two. One society would still have to interpret its rules and meanings to the other to convey its intent; either that, or remould traditional institutions in its own image in order to make them functional.[1]

The nature of these interactions would probably be best assessed by a sympathetic observation of personal attitudes and the symbols, both abstract and tangible, that reflected the acceptance or rejection of outside influences as they pressed themselves upon local society. Such an analysis would reveal, in all its nuances and contradictions, the broader range of permutations of African societies at all their levels: the *interpretatio Africana*, so to speak, of things Roman.[2] Aside from a few periods and facets of society for which fuller accounts of social life are available, however, the analyst is confounded by the virtual absence of the range and depth of evidence required for a proper understanding of the processes of change in the material world of the Africans which eventually found expression in the structural 'levels' of their society. The great profusion of factual material ordinarily available to the modern sociologist has been denied the student of the African societies of the Roman Empire. The latter, therefore, is compelled to a far less satisfactory 'one dimensional' literary record represented, for example, by epigraphy. And this information, at best a discontinuous and haphazard sample of what once existed, is only amenable to certain cruder types of analyses and methodological approaches.

A possible working methodology would be one which would try to analyse the series of interlocking institutions which combined to form, so to speak, an 'external' aspect of the society. The reconstruction of this superficial aspect admittedly deals only with the very opaqueness to which we have alluded above and is certainly far less satisfying than an understanding of the real dynamic of African society. Although such an approach is a poor substitute for a sensitive appreciation of the interplay of the intricate social and psychological forces involved, the study of institutional change might provide some insight into the general orientation of African society. But since the rationale behind the constant transformation of the social and regional groups in the encounter tends to resolve itself into countless local and individual factors, any attempt at a sympathetic comprehension at this level will immediately find its path barred by the absence of pertinent data. Institutional analysis, on the other hand, offers some hope. In both 'tribe' and town, the metamorphosis of African social institutions under Roman impress is one 'barometric reading' by which the wider interaction between African and Roman might be estimated.

But where should the analysis begin? Where, *ex hypothesi*, should the nexus of African political life be placed? Comparative study of rural Mediterranean societies, 'tribal' structure in general, and contemporary Berber society in particular, tends to point to the existence of a set of permanent, integrated political institutions at the level of basic kinship units. Social integration in these units throughout the countryside is so diffuse, however, that attempts to grapple with it only exacerbate the problems rather than provide solutions. The functional elements of these social networks seem to gravitate towards the village milieu, so it seems that our analysis should be focused here before any assumptions are made about purely rural contexts. At first glance this 'ethnic' society appears to have had a definite hierarchy; hence the impulse to begin at the top and to analyse the institutional behaviour in sequential order. But that is deception itself. The pinnacle of the hierarchy, the 'first man' (*princeps*), is often little better than a first among equals, a leader who tends to emerge from the oligarchic ranks of society rather than to impose himself upon it. The point at which to begin our analysis, therefore, should be the traditional institutions which represented the fundamental social units from which larger and wider political power flowed. To comprehend the ebb and flow about the village administration is to perceive the balance upon which the political and social life of African communities was centred.

In societies as segmented and disintegrated as the various ethnic groups of ancient north Africa were, conciliar activity tends to take place at all component levels. We must therefore distinguish between the more permanent and institutionalized councils and those assemblies which had a more ephemeral existence. As Pomponius Mela observed, though somewhat crudely, there was probably a basic economic factor which affected the degree of permanency of political organizations in the ancient Maghrib. Economies which were sedentary to a full or partial extent (e.g., peasant farming, marginal pastoralism, or transhumant pastoralism) would tend to have had more permanent conciliar forms of political and social organization at the level of the extended household (*domus*) and the more extensive social blocks formed of these (*familiae*), whereas full or semi-nomads would have found it difficult to co-ordinate consistently such concentrated political integration beyond the unit of the extended family. Mela contrasts the internal differentiation of the cultivators into a commons (*vulgus*) and more eminent élite (*primores*) with the social organization of the nomads of the interior.[3] But this does not mean that the greatest ethnic identity, the so-called 'tribe' (as opposed to its smaller component segments), even ones with nomadic economies, *never* possessed a council which 'represented' all its constituent parts. The larger 'tribe' rarely had any real corporate unity (*qua* 'tribe') except in times of crisis, usually represented either by external military pressure or by a temporary impetus from within the 'tribe' to pursue a common objective (such as a campaign against a hostile neighbour). Thus councils can function at the 'tribal level,' but only as long as the crisis subsists which has provoked the group's temporary coalescence. These are also the sort of great 'tribal' councils attested among Germanic and Gallic ethnic groups. But it should be borne in mind that these types of assemblies were present in these societies at the times we hear of them for the specific reason we have just mentioned.[4] Such councils were also present around the African 'kings' of the second and first centuries B.C. precisely because the continued existence of the kingdoms over which they presided was to a large extent provoked by the unsettled conditions created by

III

21 THE STRUCTURE OF LOCAL SOCIETY IN THE EARLY MAGHRIB

the intervention of the Roman state, first against Carthage, and then against the interior of Africa itself. The ranks of *primores* about kings like Syphax seems to substantiate the existence of centralized councils at this early period.[5] Councils like these do not tend to form during the Roman period when activity at the higher collective levels was either sublimated or forcibly discontinued; but they do tend to reappear in the period of the later Empire when integrated action at the 'tribal level' became possible again.

The fullest record of elders or *patres* for this period of later antiquity is that found in Corippus' verse celebration of the exploits of the Byzantine general Iohannes Troglyta on campaign in north Africa in A.D. 546–548. Corippus employs the word *patres* in several senses, but all imply high rank, a senator, for example, whether imperial or municipal.[6] Thus Iohannes himself is the great benevolent leader, the *bonus pater*.[7] In an African context, the term signifies both ancestors and, more specifically, those responsible for 'tribal' actions. Bruten, the African leader, while lamenting the waning power of the *Gens Ilaguatan* and the *Austuri*, resolutely declares that the 'fathers' (*patres*) of the tribe will lead the defence against the attacking Byzantine general (5.178–80). Other passages show that Corippus had in mind a definable body of men within the ethnic unit, the *patres gentis*, who formed a 'tribal council, like that of the *Gens Astricum* (6.404–06). Corippus' lengthy evocation of the proceedings of the council held by the Africans (*Mauri*) on campaign against Iohannes is a stereotypical version of a 'barbarian' *concilium*. The assembly takes the form of a great open gathering. The Africans stand around their leader (*dux*) who, as prefect of the 'tribe', reports Iohannes' harsh terms (4. 333 f.)[8] From what follows it is clear that the *concilium*, not the chief, held the power to decide matters of war and peace (4.335–37). This seems to be an accurate reflection of the relationship between chief and council. The *proceres* or nobles of the 'tribe' who compose the concilium hold the ultimate right to direct the course of the affair for which they exist as a council, that is, to decide on the joint action to be taken by the 'tribe' in a conflict. According to Corippus' description, the debate hardly followed parliamentary rules of order (4.350–55). Though deliberately mocking in its exaggerated, and racist, caricature of the 'barbarian' characteristics of the assembly, the account no doubt comes close to what an outside observer accustomed to formal court procedure would have seen in such a meeting. After the initial reaction to the leader's announcement, the Roman legate dispatched by Iohannes to deliver his terms is permitted to address the assembly. The Africans listen to an admixture of open threats and the olive branch, then break into vigorous debate over the pronouncements of the envoy (4.393–403).

Corippus' vivid account of the *concilium* is hardly designed to elicit a favourable response from the Roman listener or to impress him with the 'civilized' behaviour of the tribesmen. It was no doubt calculated to reflect in emotive language and imagery the contemporary preconception of how 'barbarians' managed their affairs and is quite close in general outline to other descriptions of tribal councils from the same era.[9] Stripped of its ethnocentric prejudices, the account still has a ring of truth (as does much in Corippus) and seems to be basically accurate in its portrayal of the structure of the council and its procedure, considering that it is the perception of an outsider. Note the following: the *ad hoc* nature of the summons and response, the representative assembly of *proceres* from several *gentes*, the subordination of the chief (styled both *dux* and *praefectus*) to the will of the council, the role of the chief's personality and charisma, and lastly, the type of debate. All this fits well within a comparative framework for the understanding of the structure and functioning of such councils.[10] The mere existence of *concilia* of this type, however, should not obscure the fact that they were not the usual type of conciliar activity found in local society. Rather, councils at this level, that is of the full ethnic unit, would tend to exist only in crises which demanded concerted action by all the component segments which constituted 'the tribe'. As the instance illustrated, this was usually in a situation of warfare. But the very conditions which led to the creation of this larger council also prefigured its dissolution. Once the limited objective of victory was achieved or was no longer attainable such a council ceased to function.[11]

For the greater part of the history of north Africa in the Roman period the conditions did not exist which either created 'tribal' cohesion or permitted its existence within the sphere of hegemony of the central state. The norm of conciliar activity within African society remained centred at much lower levels of integration, in the *domus* (extended family), *familia*, or in the small village community, the focal point of communal life in the countryside. The important fact about 'tribal' *concilia* is that they simply did not exist under the conditions of *pax* enforced by the Roman state; at best they were a spontaneous expression of unity, usually at the outbreak of a war, and so cannot be regarded as truly institutional. The lack of such councils as a normal part of the political structure of rural ethnic groups and the fact that they ordinarily came into existence only at the onset of a crisis have significant implications. First, such observations suggest that 'tribes' only had *ad hoc* planning capacities and that a revolt would tend to be spontaneous in its origins. Combined military action of the whole 'tribe' would only tend to throw up its leadership after the initial stages of its unity; hence, the long-term planning of rebellions was an improbability. A purely internal affair, however, such as an intra-tribal conflict in mountain recesses far from central control could generate the type of unity and conciliar leadership which, if diverted from its internecine course, could create the concerted effort which could be of great danger to the plains. The very lack of systematic control over the mountain highlands, for example, meant that such unity and leadership could be generated internally, and with a spontaneity which would tend to catch plains settlements unawares. Any segmented society effectively beyond the observation of the state (e.g. nomads) would be capable of this cohesion. The hegemony of the state in the plains, attained by ensuring conditions of peace and order, would effectively hinder such an impetus towards

III

unification. The very presence of the central state guaranteed that the types of councils most typical of the towns and villages would be some structural level 'lower' than that of the whole 'tribe'.

1. Village councils in 'pre-Roman' Africa

It is unfortunate, though expected, that little evidence concerning village administration in Africa from the 'pre-Roman' period has survived.[12] The earliest references in classical sources which may refer to the precursors of town councils are to be found in Herodotos, though his information is so vague and imprecise that little of value can be derived from it. In a brief passage on the Nasamones, who inhabited the coastal regions of the Greater Syrtis, Herodotos mentions the 'men of power' of the tribe. Whether or not these *dunastei* were chieftains or a cohesive council of tribal nobles is unclear, though the former seems more probable.[13] In another passage Herodotos speaks of a common council held by the Psylli, neighbours of the Nasamones, before the tribe was obliterated in a sandstorm during an expedition they had undertaken against peoples to the south.[14] Herodotos indicates nothing beyond this elementary level of political organization, which probably reflects his own ignorance rather than any real lack of such institutions in the peoples whose customs he records. For rural society there is little else except for the broad analysis of the first-century geographer Pomponius Mela. He divides the inhabitants of the African countryside into two categories: the cultivators or peasant farmers in the Tell, and the pastoralists or nomads of the interior. The former, who lived in huts (*mapalia*), were socially and politically stratified into leaders (*primores*) and commoners (*vulgus*), whereas the nomads tended to lack such permanent differentiation. The *primores* were distinguished by their dress: they wore special cloaks, like the *sagum*, whilst the general populace were clad only in skins (*pelles*) of wild and domestic animals.[15] The *primores* could be chieftains, but the passage suggests a simpler division between the ordinary members of smaller ethnic units and a group of recognized leaders or elders who were marked by their social distinction and their honorific garb.[16]

The technical term *primores*, if it is such, is rather interesting since it is not the usual designation for elders or chieftains in North Africa, though it does occur a few times in the epigraphical record. But the instances are limited to the city of Altava (modern Hajar Rûm, ex-Lamoricière) in far western Mauretania Caesariensis. The *primores* are first recorded in the fourth century and appear to be the council in charge of the town. Yet the precise maner in which they functioned is not at all clear.[17] There appear to have been a secondary rank of councillors, called the *secundiores*, below the leading men of the village.[18] The head of the *primores* also seems to have been the director of an inner council of ten, and had the title *prior* or *princeps civitatis suae, ex decemprimis*.[19] The *decemprimi* we can only assume to have been a sort of inner or probouleutic council of which not all the *primores* were members. The terminology and organization are so idiosyncratic, however, that they cannot be taken to indicate much more than the situation at Altava in the fourth century. Only approximate parallels are known for the position of *prior* or 'leading citizen' as a quasi-official status.[20] The early references to *primores*, therefore, such as those in Mela, are tendentious and circumstantial; there can be little certainty about their precise significance for a study of social structure.

Considering the nature of the initial contacts between the Hellenistic and Roman worlds with that of the Africans, it is hardly surprising that the first unambiguous references to instititional elders come from an urban context. The earliest is contained in the narrative by Diodorus Siculus concerning a Carthaginian military sortie into the African hinterland in the mid-third century B.C. (ca. 247) led by the Punic commander Hanno.[21] During the course of this brief campaign, Hanno invested a town called 'The Hundred Gates' which is usually identified with the town later known as Theveste (modern Tébessa).[22] Though the account seems to have been elaborated somewhat, Polybius vouches for the historical veracity of the campaign mentioned by Diodorus. The manner in which Polybius refers to the village as 'in Africa' suggests that the town was in African lands outside the territory under direct Carthaginian control.[23] Diodorus states that after the town had been under siege for some time, it became clear to the inhabitants that to prolong the struggle against the besieging force was a hopeless prospect. As surrender seemed inevitable, the elders of Hekatompylos decided to approach Hanno to seek the most favourable terms that they could obtain. The incident as retailed by Diodorus is suffused with moral and ethical concepts proper to the Hellenistic world and it seems reasonable to question how much of the account can be regarded as an accurate reflection of African society.

We have a cross-check from almost the same period on the evidence provided by Diodorus. A few years before Hanno's expedition, another Carthaginian general, Hamilcar, had staged a similar raid into the African hinterland (in 254 B.C.). These two expeditions were presuambly part of the same process of Carthaginian expansion into the interior during the mid-third century. Orosius, who preserved the records of this campaign in this *Adversus paganos* (presumably from the lost books of Livy), states that the Punic commander imposed immense fines on the region in cattle and precious metals. The precise location of Hamilcar's punitive expedition is not specified in Orosius' text.[21] In fact, he seems to give contrary indications. He first speaks of regions well beyond the Carthaginian province in Africa (*Numidiam Mauretaniamque*), but in another phrase, perhaps a gloss by Orosius himself, he suggests that the mission was undertaken to punish Africans who had actively collaborated with Regulus, who had operated within Carthaginian territory during his expedition in 255. It seems preferable to follow the tradition which appears to derive directly from Livy and to view the operation as part of the larger Carthaginian attempt to expand her interests in the African hinterland and to connect it with the campaign waged by Hanno ca. 247. This, rather than punishment of those who too readily assisted

25 THE STRUCTURE OF LOCAL SOCIETY IN THE EARLY MAGHRIB

Regulus, was the motive behind the expedition into African territory. This would suggest a push to the southwest, towards the general region of Theveste. In his account of the earlier campaign led by Hamilcar, the late Roman historian, states that the Punic general made prisoners of the leading men of the peoples he conquered (*principes . . . omnium populorum*). The coincidence between the *presbuteroi* of Diodorus and the *principes* of Orosius is perhaps deceptive. The *principes populorum* appear to be the heads of tribal units not identified with any urban settlements. Perhaps it would be more accurate to see each of the leading men made prisoner by Hamilcar as a *princeps* of a defined *populus*. Probably they were not simply prisoners but hostages to be held responsible for the continued good behaviour of their respective peoples.[25]

The term *princeps* was also habitually used to designate village councillors. Livy refers to the leading men of the African centre of Cirta in 202 B.C. with precisely this term: *principes Cirtensium*.[26] As Massinissa advanced on the royal capital of his rival Syphax, with the permission of Scipio's *quaestor* C. Laelius he summoned these men to a conference (*conloquiam*) to discuss terms of surrender. It is clear from the context that these *principes* were in much the same situation as the *presbuteroi* of Theveste in 247. They were the *de facto* governing body of the town, perhaps a permanent royal council around Syphax. In the initial stages of the Jugurthine War (107 B.C.) a similar type of village council was involved in political machinations concerning the town of Vaga (modern Béja) in the upper Bagrada valley.[27] Appian expressly refers to the council as the administrative senate (*boulê*) of the town.[28] Whereas Sallust uses Latin terminology: *principes civitatis*. The gist of the incident in which they were involved centres round the decision by Jugurtha to renew the conflict. He sent envoys around to various towns and repeatedly to Vaga where the *principes* were constantly under pressure by his emissaries (*fatigati regis suppliciis*). Sallust distinguishes these men, the *nobilitas* of the town, from the commoners or *vulgus*.[29] The council made plans for an uprising against the Roman garrison which had been stationed in Vaga by Metellus. The insurrection was set for three days after the meeting of the *principes*, on a day which Sallust states was a festival day throughout all Africa (*quod is festus celebratusque per omnem Africam*).[30] Whether or not Carcopino's daring emendation of the text from *in diem dertium*, which he considered meaningless in the context, to *in diem [C]er[er]um* is to be accepted and the day identified with the great festival of *Tellus* and *Ceres* on the 13th of December, the event was clearly co-ordinated to coincide with a great public holiday of some sort when many inhabitants of the reigon would be flocking to Vaga, the principal market centre of the region.[31] According to Appian, when Metellus recaptured the town after the revolt he executed the entire village council which he held responsible for planning the insurrection. The accounts of both Sallust and Appian agree about the extent of contact between the village *nobilitas* and Jugurtha.

The account of Caesar's war with the Pompeiani in Africa (46 B.C.) also includes mention of the *principes civitatis*. Upon his arrival in Africa, few believed that Caesar had come to conduct the campaign in person. In order to ensure the maximum effect to be gained from his own presence, Caesar dispatched announcements to all the *civitates* to inform them of his arrival. The local 'big men' (*nobiles*) from each of these villages then made the journey to Caesar's camp undoubtedly to assess his potential for success and to forge personal bonds of clientage and friendship with him by which some advantage or protection for their community might be obtained.[32] According to the Caesarean version, because of Caesar's lack of troops he was compelled to stand by and watch as the forces of the Pompeiani systematically reduced the village communities in his immediate vicinity. Country estates (*villae*) were burned to the ground, rural tracts (*agri*) were laid waste, cattle were stolen, men were slaughtered, towns (*oppida*) and defensive towns (*castella*) were left in ruins, while their leading men were either executed or taken prisoner (*principes civitatum aut interfici aut in catenis teneri*).[33] The passage lists in detail the various types of rural communities found in the countryside in the hinterland of Hadrumetum (modern Susa) near which Caesar's camp was located. The governments of these peregrine *civitates* appear to be in the hands of local notables who were simply styled the *principes* or leading men of their communities. The use of the term *princeps* is of direct significance to an analysis of African society because the same word was also employed to designate a 'tribal chieftain.' As will be seen, the range of meaning covered by the term *princeps* was so wide that no connection is necessarily implied between the two institutions based solely on similarity of terminology. The presence of *principes* in these small rural communities (whether *civitates*, *oppida*, *castella*, or mere *loci*), however, does suggest that the power which was focussed on such urban centres typically expressed its political structure in terms of oligarchic councils. The leading men or *principes* were clearly distinguished from the undifferentiated commons, the *vulgus*. No governmental offices, elected or permanent leaders, or administrative hierarchy is mentioned in any of these contexts. On the contrary, the application of the same term, *princeps*, to designate both the 'tribal chief' and the town councillor or elder suggests a certain structural continuity between the two roles.

Although sparse, this evidence does give some idea of the type of administration common to the villages and hamlets of Africa in the pre-Roman era, before Roman municipal institutions were adopted by, or imposed on, many of these same *civitates* (e.g., Vaga, Theveste, Cirta). If such administrations were typical of the small urban centres of the rural districts surrounding them, then it seems probably that a similar sort of undifferentiated oligarchic government was also to be found in the countryside from which the urban agglomerations had been formed. In most cases the presence of councils of elders in the village was probably only the final stage in the incorporation of a rural/ethnic institution within an urban context.

III

27 THE STRUCTURE OF LOCAL SOCIETY IN THE EARLY MAGHRIB

2. The elders in Roman Africa

Because of the prolific epigraphical data covering the first three centuries of empire in North Africa, much more detailed information on the institution of elders as village councils is available for this period. Though the evidence is of a somewhat intractable official nature, careful analysis of the individual cases allows us to assess more accurately the relationship between this institution within the context of local, rural society on the one hand, and the pressures emanating from the Roman administration of nearby urban centres on the other.

Approximately two kilometers below the source of the spring of 'Aïn Majûba on the heights of J. M'zila, midway between Tébessa (anc. Theveste) and al-Kaf (anc. Sicca Veneria) lie the ruins of ancient Tituli. This small rural village was far removed from the major arterial routes of the region, and was also well isolated from the centres of Roman-style municipal government nearest to it.[34] Although the town was the *chef lieu* of a moderately prosperous agricultural plain and seems to have experienced some urban growth during the period with which we are concerned, Tituli remained at the administrative level of a peregrine *civitas* throughout its entire existence. Located in the heart of the semi-arid region of southern *Proconsularis*, it was in the middle of the *territorium* assigned to peoples belonging to the ethnic group of the Musulamii. The economy of the region was largely dependent on mixed farming near the J. M'zila foothills and dry-farming in the plains, though considerable areas of marginal land were probably occupied by pastoral nomads for at least part of the year. The plains extending to the east of Tituli appear to have been developed economically under the aegis of large private estates. Less than twenty kilometers east of the north-south ridge of J. Zaghalma–Kala'at as-Senâm (with Tituli at its northern tip), where the plains are cut by the valleys of W. Sarrath and its tributary W. Haïdra, was located the great domain known as the *Saltus Massipianus*.[35] The *Fundus Verrona*, on W. Sarrath, about twenty kilometres southeast of Tituli was yet another estate of this type.[36] In the regions closer to Tituli itself were similar domains such as that of C. Iunius Faustinus Postumianus, situated near Kala'at as-Senâm about ten kilometres directly south of Tituli. These estates would have been primarily devoted to the dry-farming of cereal crops. Hence the significance of the *sacerdos Cererum* at the small village of Hr. 'Aïn Kedim, just to the west of Thala.[37] The success of all these agrarian ventures was dependent upon the ability of the local inhabitants to exploit to the maximum what water resources were available. On the domain lands in the plains this meant full utilization of the late autumn and spring rains, as well as the run-off provided by the large wadis that drained the mountain highlands to the west. For the urban settlements along the mountain base, such as Tituli, the careful control of the only perennial supply of water, the nearby springs emerging from trap strata in the heights above the towns, was essential to their existence.

The village and immediate rural district about Tituli shared a common administration: that of the *Pagus Titulitanorum*. About the mid-second century, the inhabitants of the *pagus* pooled their resources to tap more effectively their one major water supply, the spring of 'Aïn Majûba. The project represented a rather considerable undertaking since a totally new system for ensuring a water supply for the village was to be built. A primary canal was constructed to draw off the spring water which then passed through a rock-cut tunnel by which it reached a primary cistern of modest dimensions. This cistern seems to have been intended as the reserve of potable water for the village. The water flowed from this cistern through a very long tunnel (forty-eight meters) hollowed out of solid rock and then emptied into a second, open-air basin. This latter reservoir was much larger than the cistern and probably provided a water supply for more general purposes.[38] The council of elders and the populace of the rural district of Tituli placed the following dedicatory inscription at the site of the large reservoir:[39]

>   Neptuno Aug(usto) sacr(um)
>   Seniores et Pleps (*sic*) Titulitan(orum)
>   aere conlato fontem c[um omni?]
>   opere a solo [fe]cerun[t] et dedi/[caver]unt
>   Tu[.]c[i?] f(ilius) Fel[ix?] Mag(ister)
>   P[a]g(i)

At first glance the dedication to Neptune, the lord of the ocean and the seas, may seem a little inappropriate to the context: the completion of a project concerned with the exploitation of a small mountain spring. But dedications of this sort to Neptune were a peculiar feature of African cult practices during the Roman period and appear to be a continuation of a traditional veneration of spirits of springs and streams, particularly the former. For much of the ancient Maghrib, the local spring (*'aïn*) was the sole source of a year-round supply of water, the only continuous supply of water upon which human communities could depend. Although the local spring might be supplemented by the excavation of wells or the construction of cisterns for water storage, it remained the one dependable source of water, especially in extended dry periods. Hence the degree of religious devotion attached to spirits of springs.[40] This close dependence of life on spring waters had no precise parallel in northern Mediterranean lands where the patron deities of streams and springs tended to be relatively minor spirits and *genii*. In North Africa, such a crucial element in the maintenance of local society could not be left to lesser deities. The adoption of Neptune, the most powerful of Roman water gods, as the guardian deity of running waters in regions of the hinterland, specifically springs, was a natural, if not predictable, translation. Neptune, in this peculiar role as the spirit of springs, is unknown in regions outside Africa, so the transition points to a phenomenon restricted to Africa itself.[41] The choice of Neptune indicates a particular type of Roman influence: the substitution of a Roman for an African form at the level of public proclamations which, being novel and formulaic, left few alternatives in reducing an unwritten cosmology to epigraphic form.

The paganal organization recorded in the official dedication has a tripartite internal division. The chief magistrate of the *pagus* was the *magister* who, to judge by his nomenclature, was a local African. *Magistri* as the heads of paganal governments are widely attested throughout Africa but, unfortunately, the types of administrations over which they presided are seldom specified. Possibly most indigenous *pagi* whose chief magistrates were *magistri* also possessed an administrative council of *seniores* who, along with the *magister*, formed the whole of the local government. Certainly there is nothing in our evidence which would prohibit the view that paganal organizations typically had this dual structure.[42] In addition to the *magister* there was a group of elders or *seniores* who represented the sole governing body of the *pagus*; no other municipal officers or magistrates are ever attested at Tituli. Further, a distinction was drawn between the body of elders and the rest of the citizenry of the town and rural district who were designated by the term *plebs*.[43] It is interesting to note that in a village of as modest a size as Tituli the elders were not an assembly of the free adult male family heads. If there was a sizeable enough body of citizens outside the *seniores* to deserve the appellation *plebs*, the elders were necessarily a more restricted group which did not include all the senior heads of family units within the *pagus*. The *plebs* would appear to have been a more inclusive body of the adult males of the region; that is, it did not just encompass young men as distinct from their elders (i.e., *iuniores* as opposed to *seniores*) but rather represented a crosssection of the young and old among the citizenry of the *pagus*. This, in turn, eliminates age as the sole criterion for membership in the *seniores*. The elders emerge as a more exclusive council whose members were selected according to criteria other than age and kinship, two factors which were no doubt very important in ascription to the *seniores*, though not the only ones.[44]

At this point it seems useful to recall the simple dichotomy observed in indigenous polities of the pre-Roman period. In those cases there was a contrast between the *principes/primores* who constituted a sort of village *nobilitas* and the 'commoners', the *vulgus*. If this distinction was real (and there is little reason to doubt the observations of the author of the *Bellum Africanum* at this basic level) it suggests that the village councils were to a certain extent closed and selfperpetuating, being made up of a number of men who traditionally represented the leadership of the village. Two principal factors would be inherent in the continued existence of such a local set of notables: the very strong influence of kinship and family, though probably not extending as far as an outright hereditary principal; and the importance of the economic basis of the power wielded by these *principes*. To a certain extent they must have been regarded as local big men because of their property interests, expressed primarily in terms of land and animals, which gave them the authority to speak for more members of the community than their own family.[45] In the absence of written regulations, membership was probably not precisely defined or delimited to a set number, so that wider membership would have been affected by other factors. Among these, the political power or patronage emanating from existing members of the council would have been most important. Other marginal factors which might influence membership would be personal charisma and sheer force of personality or oratorical ability which might set one of the *plebs* apart as a spokesman.[46]

The precise relationship between the three components of the paganal organization (the *plebs*, the *seniores*, and the *magister*), is not specified in the bare details of the Neptune dedication. Was the *magister*, for example, appointed from outside the *pagus* to provide a sort of external surveillance over its activities, or was he an integral part of the local government and community? Although procedures of the former type are well known for African *pagi* attributed to nearby urban centres where Roman municipal governments were firmly established, no such arrangement is evident at Tituli. Indeed the nomenclature for the magistrate, if correctly restored, would tend to indicate a man of local extraction.[47] Once the probability of an external appointee is ruled out, the fact emerges that the *magister*, in this case at least, was simply the highest ranking member of the *seniores* who had been co-opted from among them to be head of the *pagus*. As chief of the elders he was 'ex officio' the *magister pagi*. The office of *magister* was the normal acme of Roman paganal governments and was certainly *not* the term adopted by Africans to designate the leading or principal member of the elders. The use of the title *magister* at Tituli is almost certainly an example of the appropriation of terminology proper to a Roman model. In their own eyes, the African saw their council as equivalent to the typical Roman paganal administration: the nominal chief of the elders assumed the guise and role of *magister*, a titulary position which corresponded closely in structure and function to his own. In non-paganal (i.e., non-Roman) contexts the headman among the elders was probably styled simply *princeps*, just as all his colleagues were *principes* or *primores*. As we shall see, the ethnic headman, also a *princeps*, was traditionally little better than a temporarily appointed leader who emerged by consensus out of the ranks of the elders. On the Roman side of the ledger, the term *princeps*, like *senior*, was very general and self-descriptive and so represented the natural choice to be employed in this context. It accorded well with both indigenous and foreign tradition.[48] The very format of the dedication at Tituli, *seniores et pleps*, maintains a formulaic distinction between the elders and the people which, in itself, might be a slight indication of the broader context of change and adaptation in the African countryside. The spelling *pleps* in itself is a peculiarity which is probably to be ascribed to the influence of African dialect.[49] The people or *plebs* are rarely recognized in formal municipal decrees or dedications of this type. Cast in a format generally abandoned by Roman-type urban administrations in Africa by the mid-first century, the continued employment of the phrase here at a rather late date indicates both the recent adoption of Latin terminology and the persistence of traditional forms in local society.[50]

Another dedication from 'Aīn Majûba, dating to the last years of Commodus' reign, is in a fragmentary state; the title of the official body must be restored.[51] The restoration of *seniores* in the hiatus in the second line seems guaranteed by two factors: firstly, the official character of this imperial dedication made by the

31 THE STRUCTURE OF LOCAL SOCIETY IN THE EARLY MAGHRIB

local government. Since Tituli remained a *civitas*, it is reasonable to assume that the government was also peregrine. Secondly, the final verbs are plural (*fecerunt*, etc.) and their formulaic structure plus the genitive 'Titulitanorum' matches that of the dedication of the water project. Nevertheless, if we wish to maintain a reasonably balanced number of letters to the line in the restoration something must be omitted in line two and the obvious choice is the phrase *et plebs*. If this restoration is correct, it provides a *terminus ante quem* for the Neptune dedication, that is, a somewhat earlier date than the Commodan inscription above. In the interval the formality of referring to the *plebs* had simply been abandoned, a move which brought the format of the dedication more into line with the conventions of Roman municipal decrees of the time.

Another important group of inscriptions referring to elders in an entirely different context was found in the circle of *castella* surrounding the town of Sicca Veneria (modern al-Kaf), a centre of Roman municipal government with colonial status.[52] Three imperial dedications were found at the castellum of Ucubi (modern Hr. Kaussât) located about twenty kilometres northeast of al-Kaf. The earliest of these, a stereotypical dedication to Antoninus Pius made by the *seniores* of Ucubi, reveals little about the functions or composition of the elders except that, in the manner of a Roman municipal *ordo*, they collected the funds to erect the inscription and supervised its emplacement.[53] Since Ucubi remained at the level of a peregrine *civitas* and is never known to have developed any Roman magistracies, or an assembly of decurions, we can only presume that the elders represented the sole governing body of the town. The *seniores* at Ucubi had the same functional role and corporate identity as the *odo decurionum* in towns which had adopted the governmental structures of Roman municipalities. The striking difference between the two institutions as shown both at Ucubi and Tituli is the lack of any internal differentiation within the *seniores*. That is, no hierarchy or set of offices distinct from the general council is ever attested. There are none of the specialized governmental functions which one generally finds in Roman municipalities. At Ucubi, as elsewhere, the elders appear to have been an assembly without internal distinction. This implies a fundamentally different internal structure from that of the Roman *ordo* or official Roman *honores*. Specialized duties (i.e., juridical of the *duumviri*, financial of the *quaestor*, managerial of the *aediles*) were not formally distinguished, and, indeed, may not have existed at all. Town business was probably managed collectively, a feature which would effectively inhibit the internal development of the concept of offices as distinct from the individual.

A second imperial dedication (approximately a decade later in date) erected to the honour of Marcus Aurelius, reveals the continued presence of this traditional village council.[54] The *seniores Ucubitani* maintain the same place in the local social and political order as before with one important difference. In the dedication to Antoninus Pius the *seniores* appear to have made arrangements for the funding and erection of the monument without any external supervision. If the earlier inscription revealed the full range of political activity involved in the setting up of the dedication (that is, if no assumed involvement of external authority was omitted from the dedication) then there has been a genuine loss of autonomy in the village administration during the interim. In the decree honouring Marcus Aurelius, the entire procedure appears to have been superintended by two *duumviri quinquenniales* from Sicca Veneria: Mettius Secundus Memmianus and Publius Largius Numidicus. Moreover, the latter dedication was erected by the elders of Ucubi only *after* it had been approved by the passing of an official decree by the municipal senate at Sicca. The loss of local autonomy to the *ordo* at Sicca is confirmed by yet a third such venture undertaken by the *seniores* of Ucubi, a decree honouring Caracalla.[55] Although the elders of the *castellum* still manage the internal affairs of the village (in this case the collection of the funds and the erection of the dedication), they are second in rank to the decurions from Sicca. The decurions from the Roman colony clearly had an authority superior to that of the local council. As in the earlier dedication to Marcus Aurelius the whole procedure was sanctioned by a decree passed by the *ordo decurionum* at Sicca Veneria.

The subordination of the elders is a reflection of the special relationship between the Roman colony of Sicca Veneria and the *castella* which surrounded it. The very fact that these villages were placed under the guardianship of the colony shows that the Roman authorities (and the African ones before them) either did not believe that the local administrative institutions were competent to deal with local affairs in an efficient manner without some sort of supervision, or that such supervision was necessary because of the 'unreliability' of the communities concerned.[56] Considering the historical and geographical factors, the former would seem to have weighed more heavily in the decision to impose or continue external control over the local villages. In effect, the decurions and magistrates of the Roman colony were expected to exercise a trusteeship over the elders in the surrounding *castella* and villages, a paternalism no doubt meant in a positive sense to direct the elders' business along the lines established by the model of a Roman *ordo*.[57] Since the *castella* around Sicca were part of a general attribution of smaller centres to the colony, the direct supervision of the elders at Ucubi implies the same sort of governmental control over all of the *castella* so attributed. In these small villages, the traditional African institutions would have continued to function without great change from the pe-Roman into the Roman period. Political power was vested in village assemblies of elders who conducted local affairs by discussion and debate but, above all, by a constant struggle to obtain a *consensus* within which village affairs could operate, enabling village life to function with the least amount of internal conflict.[58]

The existence of an assembly of elders at yet another village attributed to Sicca, Hr. Sidi Merzûg (near Nibbûr) is further confirmation of the essential uniformity of traditional political organization throughout these *castella*. The *castellum* at Hr. Sidi Merzûg (whose ancient name we do not know) was located not far to the west of Ucubi, and only a slightly further distance north northeast of Sicca Veneria. At this site two inscriptions recording the formal activities of the elders were discovered. During the reign of Caracalla the town elders erected a dedicatory inscription honouring the powerful dowager empress Julia Domna.[59] Only a year before their neighbours at Ucubi took similar action, the elders of Hr. Sidi Merzûg set up a dedication to the emperor Caracalla himself.[60] The degree of supervision exercised by the colony of Sicca Veneria over the village of Hr. Sidi Merzûg, however, was of a different order from that at Ucubi. Unlike either Ucubi or Tituli, the *castellum* does not ever seem to have had elders who served as *magistri*, that is, as chief magistrates of the village and *pagus*. Instead, the director of village affairs was a resident outsider, a prefect (*praefectus*) who was appointed by the colony of Sicca as an overseer of the local administration. Men chosen to be *praefecti*, like the post-Constantinian *curatores rei publicae*, were members of the *ordo* at Sicca Veneria who had already had some role in local municipal administration. Such an achievement was a reflection not just of practical experience, but also of local power and prestige. One such prefect, C. Paccius Rogatus, had been both *duumvir* and *flamen perpetuus* at Sicca before he assumed the post of *praefectus kastelli* at Hr. Sidi Merzûg.[61] The bonds of patronage between the prefect and the village over which he was appointed were strong. When Paccius Rogatus died at the advanced age of seventy-eight, his burial was marked at the *castellum*. At Cirta, which had a similar system of attributed *castella* whose governments were directed by prefects from the central colony, the full title of the prefects, *praefecti iure dicundo*, indicates that they held supreme judicial power in the towns over which they were appointed, in the lieu of local chief magistrates who were the equivalent of *duumviri*.[62] The public nature of the appointment was reinforced not only by public proclamation but also, it seems, even by formal 'orders' issued from the central state in Rome. Such at least would seem to be the import of an inscription set up in the *castellum* announcing the appointment of one Publius Cornelius as *praefectus kastelli* (now in the guise of *curator*) along with notice of his imperial letter of instructions.[63] The presence of the prefect simultaneously removed part of the traditional authority wielded by the elders and directed local power towards a nearby imperial centre. The *praefectus* sent out from Sicca was therefore bound to upset the internal balance of village politics and to reduce the principal function of the council of elders and their ability to provide social consensus through the arbitration of local disputes.

It has been inferred from a mid-fourth century inscription from Hr. Sidi-Merzûg that the elders had assumed at least the outward trappings of a Roman *ordo* by this date, and that the town had begun to style itself a *res publica* in imitation of Roman municipalities. The complete lack of evidence for magistrates or decurions at any time in the known history of the *castellum*, however, casts grave doubt on such an hypothesis. The sole evidence for this supposed metamorphosis consists of the title of an imperial administrator who was called-*curator [re]i [p(ublicae) et] ordinis*.[64] The title *curator rei publicae*, however, is merely formulaic. The inclusion of the *rei publicae* does not signify anything peculiar about the status of the town over which the official was *curator*: it could have been a colony, a municipality, or any one of a number of types of peregrine *civitas*. There is no indication that the *castellum* itself had assumed the proud title of *res publica* as had many other peregrine towns, to reflect the spirit of assimilation to a Roman model of local government.[65] The term was merely a formulary part of the title of an externally appointed official: it was part of his definition, not theirs (see the case mentioned above). As for the phrase *et ordinis*, this too was of external coinage and did not necessarily entail the existence of a Roman-type *ordo* in the village. Again, it is clearly the case that the externally appointed official conceived his duties in this manner, as guardian of the town and its council. Nevertheless, the phrase *et ordinis* is unusual; there is no parallel in Africa for a *curator* regarding his duty as a trusteeship over an *ordo*, hence its particular significance for Hr. Sidi Merzûg.[66] Unlike the purely formulaic *rei publicae* in the curator's title, the *et ordinis* is perhaps a conscious addition indicating that the *curator* was replacing the position held earlier by the *praefecti* dispatched from Sicca. The phrase *et ordinis* does not mean that the elders had changed their structure, nor that the *curator* was trustee of the town (or mere formality in his title), but that his principal concern was to direct the local *ordo*, in this case the council of elders. If we accept the general proposition that post-Constantinian *curatores rei publicae* were usually municipal men who had filled some of the local *cursus honorum*, then this *curator* probably was dispatched from Sicca Veneria and his position was precisely that of the earlier *praefecti*.[67] Thus in the mid-fourth century the Roman authorities were still exercising an external control over the village council, no longer by means of a prefect from Sicca, but through the now common institution of the *curator rei publicae*.

Most *vici, oppida, castella*, and *civitates* in Africa, however, appear to have managed their local affairs with a minimum of outside interference. The arrangement whereby large towns of colonial status like Cirta and Sicca Veneria exercised a protectorate over surrounding African villages was an exception, not the rule. In fact, these two cases were probably the result of the peculiar historical circumstances which had led to the creation of two large urban centres outside the frontiers of the Roman province at an early stage of the Roman involvement in Africa. Presumably their relative isolation from the administrative structure of the Roman province encouraged the creation of quasi-state systems about the main urban centres in order to strengthen the corporate unity of their respective *territoria*. The process may also have been aided by the earlier existence of similar systems under the African kingdoms. These peculiar arrangements persisted after the incorporation of these regions into the greater African province of *Proconsularis*. The majority of village communities, however, were left to conduct their own affairs in the traditional manner without an excessive degree of direct external interference.

An example of an autonomous village administration of this type is found at the town of Thala, some sixty-five kilometers northeast of Tébessa. In the early years after the formation of *Proconsularis*, Thala was located on the frontier zone of the province, a region of frequent inter-tribal conflict involving police action by Roman military forces. Described by Sallust, surely in somewhat exaggerated terms, as an *oppidum magnum atque opulentum*, Thala was the 'treasury' or centre of a fiscal district controlled by Jugurtha. Ethnic groups in the region were presumably part of the *Thalai*, of which the town was the principal urban centre. The 'tribe', in turn, was probably part of the larger Musulamian group whose *territorium* extended over this region.[68] During the period of unrest associated with the brigand chief Tacfarinas, a small band of Roman veterans (*vexillum veteranorum, non amplius quingenti numero*) at Thala held off an attack by the rebel leader in A.D. 20.[69] As conditions in the region became more settled after the placement of the camp of *IIIa Augusta* at Ammaedara (modern Haïdra) some twenty kilometres to the west, the frontier was consolidated and moved further to the south and west. Thala lost any importance it might have had as a frontier post and became indistinguishable from other small towns in the region. Its relative lack of importance was reflected in a similar stagnation in its municipal status: Thala never rose above the rank of peregrine *civitas*. Nor is the town ever mentioned in any of the itineraries. The principal route traversing the region, from Ammaedara to Cillium, passed by Thala over twenty kilometres to the south, on the further side of the slopes of J. Buenó.[70] Located in the midst of the semi-arid zone, on the southern periphery of the *regio Musulamiorum*, Thala's economy was basically dependent on the herds of semi-nomads and marginal dry-farming. Even until the early decades of the twentieth century, Thala remained a small community essentially noted as a periodic market centre serving the local semi-nomadic tribesmen, the Awlad Fraïshish and the Awlad Majûr.[71]

The elders of Thala erected a dedicatory inscription to Caelestis Augusta, invoking the good will of the goddess on behalf of the continued well-being of the reigning emperor, Septimius Severus and his sons Geta and Caracalla.[72] Paid for by public funds, the dedication was completed and erected by the governing body of the town, the *seniores Thalae*. The phrase *cuncti seniores*, like the format of the rest of the dedication, faithfully copied one of the stylized expressions commonly employed by Roman municipalities, that is *cuncti decuriones*.[73] The dedication to *Dea Caelestis Augusta* is yet another indication that the honorific inscription, though conforming to the formalities of municipal dedications, was closely allied to a belief system which was rooted in African tradition. Caelestis, the consort of Saturn, was venerated by peasants and herders as the great sky goddess, the purveyor of rains, fertility, the success of harvest and herds. Her worship at Thala as at 'Aïn Melûk, far to the northwest, may indeed have been connected with the importance of the village as an indigenous market centre.[74] Significant for the transformation of the *seniores* within the Christianized milieu which was to supplant the pagan influences of Saturn and Caelestis was the fate of the great temple of Saturn in Thala. It was of both symbolic and real significance that the Christian basilica was built by reusing the very stones which at this period formed the temple to Saturn, the partner of Caelestis.[75]

Another, even more remote hamlet (the ancient name of which is unknown to us) located near Hr. 'Aïn Tella in the far western reaches of the Khoumirie has yielded further data on the general social and cultural milieu in which the *seniores* functioned. Hr. 'Aïn Tella is situated in the upper valley of W. al-Kabîr, in rough hills country isolated from the more open plains to the south. So far was this community removed from the nearest centres of urban development that it was perforce relatively free of any interference that might have emanated from larger towns.[76] The elders of this village set up a formal dedication to the Tetrarchs, in connection with their restoration of the local temple to Mercury.[77] The format, including the terminology employed to designate the village elder (*universi seniores*) parallels the usage of Roman municipal assemblies (i.e., *universi decuriones*), an imitation which indicates that the elders thought of themselves as closely analogous to the municipal senates of Roman towns. The chief magistrate of the village, a *magister*, whose name Fortunatianus indicates an African background, was restricted to an annual term of office (i.e., *anno Fortunatiani magistri*). The council itself took precedence over the *magister*, who is only mentioned to date the erection of the dedication. It is difficult to ascertain whether there was only one *magister* or if he was simply the eponymous magistrate, though the former seems more probable. The relationship of the council to the *magister*, therefore, was similar to that of the *seniores* at Tituli. There was one *magister*, a chief officer chosen for a term of one year from amongst the elders themselves. The *seniores* remained very much the locus of power, the decision-making body of which the *magister* was nominal head.

Probably the *curatores* mentioned in the dedication, Macidius(?) Primus and another or others unnamed, were also members of the elders chosen in an *ad hoc* manner for the specific purpose of direction this particular project of which they were the overseers. As in the dedication to Caelestis at Thala, the reconstruction of the temple of Mercury does not betoken any but superficial Roman influence. As befitted the rural economy of this particular region (a rugged, hilly area principally dependent on arboriculture and small-scale herding) the inhabitants venerated Mercury as Silvanus, the patron deity of forests, trees, garden terraces, and animals grazed in woodlands. Mercury-Silvanus was often featured in the coterie of gods surrounding Saturn and Caelestis, the chief deities of the African pantheon.[78] Since the rising hill slopes and narrow valleys about Hr. 'Aïn Tella have traditionally been devoted to the cultivation of the olive and the raising of small numbers of animals in the forested hillsides, the identification of Mercury-Silvanus with the patron deity of forests and his equation by the Africans to their protective spirit of trees and woods seems assured.[79]

The principal structural characteristic which marks all these traditional village councils is their lack of internal differentiation and all that such informal organization entails. This peculiar structural make-up of the councils had important significance for the potential development along the lines of Roman municipalities or their absorption within such a system. Comparison with an analogous village institution, the *undecimprimi*, will serve to highlight the differences between the informal governments of elders and more formal governmental systems in their reaction to Roman impress. Although there is a superficial resemblance between the *seniores* and *undecimprimi* (e.g., both were small village councils) there are several important characteristics which separate the two. Both terminology and geography distinguish the one from the other. Save for one instance at Cirta, all references in the epigraphical record attesting the existence of the Eleven are found within the *territorium* and *pertica* attributed to the Roman colony at Carthage. All known instances (again, save Cirta) are restricted to the lower valley of the Bagrada river basin, to the east of W. Siliana (see map on p. 55).[80] By contrast, all epigraphical data on *seniores* as village councils is concentrated further west, in the region usually designated by the hybrid term 'Proconsular Numidia', that is, the area bordered on the east by the *Fossa Regia* and on the west by the Cirtan Federation. Perhaps this distribution is merely the fortuitous result of epigraphic discoveries, but it does highlight the geographical isolation of the Eleven to the east in the heartland of *Proconsularis*. The clustering of the *XIprimi* in a region in such close proximity to Carthage must excite the suspicion that there is a connection between this sort of village council and political controls that once emanated from the Punic metropolis. This suspicion is further strengthened when we note the close proximity of the towns governed by *XIprimi* to the group of towns that maintained Punic-style administrations (i.e. with *sufetes* as chief magistrates) well into the Roman period.[81] At first glance one might believe the existence of an *XIprimus* in an ethnic context near Cirta to be a contradiction of this pattern. But Punic influences were deeply rooted in this city from the time it was one of the capital cities of Massinissa's kingdom of the Massyle.[82]

A second distinctive feature of the *XIprimi* is the pattern of their evolution. Originally the *XIprimi* were small village councils in peregrine *civitates* in the plains to the southwest of Carthage. Membership in these councils, however, gradually assumed the form of a Roman municipal office, the *undecimprimatus*. As with all municipal offices, it was gained by election and required the expenditure of an office benefaction, the *summa honoraria*.[83] The towns governed by the *XIprimi* reveal a similar impetus to adapt to Roman models of government and advance their municipal status. Five of the villages (possibly six) in which the Eleven represented the main administrative body rose in status from peregrine *civitates* to Roman *municipia* (that is, over half of the known total). One of these towns, Bisica Lucana (modern Hr. Bijga), achieved the status of a colony. Other villages which did not manage to advance their municipal status as far as these still show considerable development along Roman lines. Vazi Sarra (modern Hr. Bez), for example, possessed an *ordo* of decurions and a number of flaminates or priesthoods. Even the tribal capital of the Gens Bacchuiana (modern Bû Jelida) could boast a *sacerdos Cererum* (see Table on p. 56). The institution of the undecimprimate and the towns in which they were the governing body appear to have been very responsive and open to Roman influences. By their very structure, the institutional aspects of these village societies seem to have been arranged in such a way as to make the transition to Roman institutional life possible.

Though more widely attested in both epigraphy and the literary sources than the Eleven, the *seniores* reveal a quite different development. Whereas the Eleven gradually metamorphosized into Roman-style town administrations and eventually disappear from historical record (none are known after the Severan period), the *seniores*, as we shall see, not only survived until the last years of Roman Africa but continued to absorb massive new cultural forces such as Christianity. The *seniores* moulded these new forces to fit their world, and continued to function in the new milieu much as they had in the old. In complete contrast to communities governed by the Eleven, those headed by councils of elders reveal few signs of flexibility in adapting their local governments to fit Roman models. Not one of the villages where the epigraphic evidence attests *seniores* as the governing council raised its status above that of a peregrine *civitas*, or its organizational structure above that of a *castellum* or *pagus*. Save for one instance, Thala, there is no evidence of any nascent steps towards remodelling the councils along the lines of Roman municipal government, no mention of decurions, nor any Roman priesthoods. It is clear that communities governed by *seniores* were representative of the most basic element of African society, the last sector of the African community to respond to external pressure by internal change.

In large part this resistance to change was not so much part of a conscious policy as it was simply a structural inability of a social system arranged in such a different manner from the uniform institutional model of the Roman municipality as to be incapable of easy imitation. The elders closely mirrored, and were inextricably part of, indigenous society at all its levels, whereas the *XIprimi* were a uniform institution wherever they were found. The *seniores* were not as rigidly circumscribed. Informal extra-legal criteria seem to have determined membership (e.g., age, kinship, personal charisma, and influence), all of which made it difficult to define elders as a formalized institution. Since no concept of the office of elder separate from the individual was likely to have existed, the personal factor remained paramount in determining the limits of political behaviour. The elders and the communities over which they presided were closely interwoven social units, so much so that that separation of the two was functionally impossible. An organization composed of eleven men, on the other hand, is by definition tightly circumscribed and defined. The external characteristics of the Punicized undecimprimate, namely clear definition, consistency, uniformity and the concept of office, separated it from the loose, informal, and socially dependent and integrated nature of the elders. The transition of the XIprimate to a municipal office was a logical and possible development

A similar transition for a council of elders was more difficult and improbable. The simple lack of internal differentiation within the council made the tranformation to the concept of municipal office difficult. *Senior* does not easily translate into official terms. The *XIprimi* display the regional uniformity characteristic of a true institution. The elders, on the other hand, reflect the regional peculiarities of each village in which they happen to exist; they were what each small district and its economy required them to be. At Tituli they were part of an autonomous paganal organization headed by a *magister*. But the *castella* attributed to Sicca Veneria reveal no such internal stratification; this defect was overcome in different ways: either by the appointment of *praefecti* to oversee the local *ordo* (Hr. Sidi Merzûg) or by a sort of direct trusteeship exercised form the colony with the temporary presence of decurions in the village (Ucubi). Such diversity within the very restricted scope of our evidence more than adequately demonstrates a regional variation which accords with the geographical and social compartmentalization of the ancient Maghrib.

As for the actual mode of conciliar function, we know very little and only guesses can be made. One important clue is contained in an inscription from Thugga which mentions the town gates (*portae*) in the context of municipal decision making (*sententiis omnium portarum*).[84] The role of the 'gates' at Thugga immediately drew attention to Near Eastern parallels of assemblies of the town elders that were held at the gates of villages and town in the ancient near East.[85] Seston immediately latched on to this possibility as the sole context for understanding the Thugga inscription, and hence saw in it a direct Punic importation, an introduction from the 'constitution' of Punic Carthage.[86] That is a distinct possibility, but it is only one of several. We must remember that Thugga was a royal centre in the possession of Massinissa's grandfather and seized by the Carthaginian armies in the 240s or 230s B.C. It was retaken by Massinissa himself in the 170s or 160s B.C.[87] It was therefore under direct Punic rule for no more than a generation or two. And yet we find the *portae* mentioned as an entrenched municipal institution as late as the mid-first century A.D. Although there can be no doubt of Punic influence at Thugga (witness the *suffetes*), is there an alternative explanation for the *portae*? I believe so. The other obvious possibility is that the village 'gates' were the habitual meeting place of the elders and councils of pre-Roman Africa. The reasons are clear: namely that African society in its organization and structure provides an analogue to the type of situation in which the 'gates' function in ancient Near Eastern societies (e.g., no town-centred marked system or *fora*, and hence no gravitation of 'politics' to that centre). Not even orientalists have contended that the function of *portae* is unique to the ancient Near East; meetings are held at the gates for structural reasons that would remain true of all similar type societies. A clue to the continuity of the north African form is to be found in Masqueray's masterful survey of Berber highland communities. In his analysis of the village council (*jama'a*) he remarks that such assemblies were most often *situés à l'entrée même du village*.[88] Surely this is the more general context in which the significance of the *portae* in the 'constitution' of African Thugga is to be understood.

3. The elders in 'tribe' and town

Elders as a 'tribal' or village phenomenon are attested epigraphically in the Roman period principally in North Africa. Notices in the literary sources for regions outside Africa are exceedingly rare, though we must suspect that analogous institutions must have existed in many conservative Mediterranean communities north of the Mediterranean. The preceding sections have analysed the elders in Africa in the context of such village-centred rural communities during the African and Roman periods, but the peculiar role and continuity of the institution can also be seen to continue in an unbroken line into the later empire in the context of a Christianized African society.[89] A much more difficult task, however, is to place the elders within a consistent 'tribal' hierarchy and to trace their evolution in rural and urban contexts as this hierarchy underwent periods of change and integration.

There does exist a rather fragmentary and cryptic inscription from the Col de Fdoulès, a narrow pass some thirty kilometres southwest of the port of Jijil, the ancient colonial city of Igilgili, which has succeeded in baffling any of its would-be interpreters. The inscription was carved in very crude characters on a rock face above the pass which connects the parallel valleys of wadis Enja and Jinejin (or Missa) on the southern flank of the Babor (=Lesser Qabiliyya). In antiquity the Roman road from Milev in the interior to Igilgili on the coast passed very close to this site, though the pass itself was not a major route of communication. There are 'Roman' type ruins in both wadi valleys, and four kilometres south of the defile itself are concentrations of ruins which d'Yanville thought may have been a *castrum* (though this is not certain).[90] Whatever the context, the inscription is of a decidedly 'un-official' non-Roman character. Those who have reported it have only been able to make sense of small parts of it.[91] The conflicting readings reported in the *Corpus* and in the various journals are sufficient warning in themselves against drawing too detailed conclusion until a more accurate copy is available. Mindful of this caveat, however, we might hazard a few conjectural remarks about some phrases in this enigmatic inscription. Latin words can be discerned in the first half of the inscription but are more difficult to detect in the latter part; possibly the confusing array of letters is due simply to the lack of comprehension on the part of the copyists who were unable to decipher correctly the crude script on the rock face.[92] Words which could be Latin, or of Latin derivation, seem to appear sporadically in the second half of the text: for example, *adversus* (1. 5), *sit* (1. 6), *cessit, novio, victoria* (1. 7) and *[s]eptinnario* (? 1. 8), but they do not make any continuous sense. The overall impression is one of a language with only a marginal element of Latin, a sort of local patois including loan words from Latin to supplement its vocabulary.

The first line seems to mention a location (*in monti Muxpige?*) and a man, the subject of the inscription, whose name is lost to us who was *Rex gentis Ucutamani*. Presumably the *gens Ucutamani* were the ethnic group who inhabited this particular region of the Lesser Qabiliyya.[93] That he should style himself *rex* points to a substantial degree of autonomy and perhaps indicates that the inscription belongs to a rather late era when Berber kingdoms in mountain recesses such as this were beginning to reassert their independence from the Roman hegemony in the plains. That at least would also account for the poor script and the weak admixture of Latin in the local language. It is not possible to be very certain about the following three lines of the first half of the inscription. To construe the participle *continens* at the beginning of line three with its ostensible subject (*rex*, 1. 2) does not seem sensible. Given the loose or even non-grammatical structure of the whole, however, it might be logically taken with *gentis* (1. 2) or a now missing relative pronoun (1. 3) referring back to *gentis* (i.e., *quae... continens*). If this reconstruction is accepted, some meaning as follows might be discerned in the passage: the 'tribe' of the *Ucutamani* is thought of as containing or including all the component parts belonging to it (*continens omnes [h]onestos gentis*?). If this interpretation is correct, the elders or *seniores* in the fourth line would seem to be the councils of the *gentes* who were part of the larger 'tribe' of the *Ucutamani*. Their position *vis-à-vis* the 'king', however, is not at all clear, much less the strange phrase *egentes pane* which follows. We must be content with simply observing the juxtaposition of the institutions of the chief (*rex*) and elders (*seniores*) within the framework of the 'tribe' (*gens*); it would be unrealistic to force any further detail out of so doubtful a source.

Another difficult inscription from 'Aïn Qsar, the site of an African *castellum* or possibly *castrum* whose ancient name is unknown, might preserve the record of a council of elders in the last decades of the sixth century. 'Aïn Qsar is about eight kilometres northwest of an African settlement which was known as *Casae* and is the same distance directly west of the site of the great monument of the African regal period, the so-called Madrasan.[94] The text on the stone is divided into two vertical columns. The left side is an imperial dedication to Flavius Constantinus and Anastasia, and to the *magister militum* Vitalius. It records the construction of a *castellum* or *castrum*, or more likely the repair of the defences of such a settlement, by its inhabitants (*cives*) under the direction of Vitalius.[95] The right hand side of the stone records seventeen African names, one of which may be a personal name or title (*senior*) or the rubric at the head of a list of elders: *senior(es)*.[96] The latter would seem a probable interpretation given the context, that is, the list of men which follow are obviously the local inhabitants of the *castellum* and yet are a select body of men. The inscription is an imperial dedication erected by the *cives* of the *castellum* and it is quite clear that the locals listed on the right hand side of the stone were the men responsible for the erection of the inscription; in all probability they represented the local government of the *castellum*. The chief magistrate of the settlement was a *magister* under whose aegis the dedication was made (*Focas magister fecit*).

The elders at 'Aïn Qsar (the toponomy recalls the defensive importance of the place) are shown, by detail on the inscription, to be functioning fully within the Christian milieu of the late Empire and yet their structural make-up is precisely that of the village council of the pre-Christian period. Thus the elders or *seniores locorum*, like those councillors at 'Aïn Qsar, continued to be the typical village administration until the last years of the Roman domination in Africa. Not much later, the Islamization of North Africa brought about fundamental changes in culture, language, and religion, but there is no reason to believe that the force of Islam and the Arab presence wrought any more radical changes in the structure of social administration than had Christianity or the Roman presence. The changes in nomenclature in no way disguise, but rather affirm the essential continuity and conservative retention of social institutions in this rural society. The *princeps* and *primores* of a highly segmented rural society, the *magister* and *seniores* of the village milieu are effectively continued in the collective-assembly, *jama'a* and its members the *shiyûkh* and the *shaykh*. So too, the new terminology derived from the verb *jama'a* only served to reinforce the traditional concept of the assembly as an undifferentiated council which depended on the debate and social intercourse of members of equal status and, above all, the necessity for government by social *consensus*.

Perhaps more revealing of both the persistence and integration of tribal elders is the social structure found in the town of Gigthis, the principal urban centre of Cinithii, an ethnic group located in the regions inland of the Gulf of Gabès and the western shores of the Lesser Syrtis.[97] Although the great families of the tribe had long been subject to the influences of Mediterranean urban civilization because of their habitation of a town settlement at the vital juncture of the Lesser Syrtis and the Gulf of Gabès, Gigthis (modern Bû Ghara), the identity of the 'tribe' was still preserved in the urban milieu despite extensive integration with external social and political systems.[98] In the encounter between 'tribe' and town, however, the wider, more inclusive levels of 'tribal' organization naturally disintegrated so that only the smaller, more cohesive elements, closely bound by kinship such as the extended family and is dependent units, were likely to survive in symbiosis with the new institutional life adopted from the outside.[99] In the dedication by the elders of the 'house' of Servilia Serena to their *optima patrona*, is the term *domus*, in this context, used to designate a wider kinship unit, a house composed of a least one extended family unit and its clients? If *domus* were to be taken in its restricted sense, the limited number of elders in a nuclear family would surely not be such an anonymous corporate group. Then again, if they were literally the elders of Servilia Serena's narrow family group, the relationship between the two would probably have been one of natural respect from Servilia towards her elders. But since bonds of patronage are involved, the implication is that the *seniores* were distanced from Servilia by more than close kinship connexions; otherwise there would be no need to refer to a close blood relative with such a neutral term of subordination (i.e., *patrona*). In fact the dedication has hallmarks of social differentiation and stratification, of patronage, and also of corporate unity. That is to say, the group of *seniores* acted as a body within a definable kin group, the *domus*. Thus the *domus* would seem to be part of the segment to which Servilia Serena and her father, Caius Servilius Serenus, a Roman knight, were connected. The Servilii were one of the few great *domus* of the Cinithii in Gigthis. One of the others was the *domus* of her husband, C. Messius Pacatus, the family of the Messii.[100] The elders mentioned in the above inscription, however, belonged to Servilia's *domus*, not to that of her husband, and therefore continued to have a claim on her patronage in particular.

The text of the so-called *Tabula Banasitana* reveals the use of the term *domus* with precisely this meaning.[101] The *domus* was the basic kin unit in the structure of the 'tribe', within the *gens* and its subsegments, the *familiae*. The extended family and clients, the *domus*, was the unit to which the chief of the Zengrenses, Iulianus, belonged. In the Gigthis dedication to Servilia Serena, the *domus* was probably an 'ethnic' unit and not simply a 'family' in the narrower Roman sense. As we have stated above, Servilia's husband was a member of the Messii, another *domus* of the Cinithian tribe. One L. Memmius Pacatus, probably a close relative of his, though the precise degree of relationship cannot be determined, was also a leading man of the Cinithii.[102] A dedication was made to him by his fellow tribesmen, again to mark his outstanding patronage of the 'tribe'. The inscription specifies that Messius Pacatus was a *Cinithius* and that the dedication was made by the *Cinithii* to him *ob merita eius et singularem pietatem, quam nationi suae praestat*. The dedication establishes the critical links of patronage which existed between the urban dwelling 'families' and the wider ethnic unity of the 'tribe'. It also reveals that the whole tribe, the *Cinithii*, however diffuse, still maintained a corporate identity which individual members could somehow benefit by their patronage and who, by consciously striking connections with it in this way, could affirm their *pietas* towards the greater *natio*. The 'tribe', in turn, must have had some corporate being in order to make such a dedication (note the *pecunia sua* which implies at least a temporary financial structure) and conciliar activity of some sort. It seems that the family of the Messii Pacati, Punicized in the earlier urban stages of Gigthis' growth, later made the move to the new Roman political environment via the means of individual grants of Roman citizenship probably obtained under the Flavian emperors.[103] Despite the apparent limitations of their public activities to a sphere of urban politics as defined by the terms of Roman municipal government, and the advancement of several of their members to equestrian status (one was adlected by Hadrian to the panel of the five decuries at Rome), the *domus* of the Messii still maintained its identity as a unit within the 'tribe' of the Cinithii. The *seniores* of the *domus* of the Servilii were in all probability the elders of the extended household of the Servilii at Gigthis.

Whereas this case attests the presence of councils of elders at the basic level of the extended family, we need not doubt their presence in the superimposed levels of local social structure, such as the *familiae* of the *Tabula Banasitana* since the cryptic inscription from the Col de Fdoulès suggests their existence at the level of component peoples (*gentes*) of a larger ethnic unit (the *gens U-cutamani*). Corippus proved examples of the functioning of councils at the full 'tribal' level but, as we have pointed out, these elders were probably rather ephemeral. More significantly for the present case, the interrelationships between 'tribe' and urban centre at Gigthis indicates the continuity of parts of the tribal structure, that is *domus* and *seniores*, in the midst of a town where the urban aristocracy, itself derived from the 'tribe', actively and consciously pursued a policy of integration within the framework of Roman municipal government (while still maintaining their tribal identity and connections). It was one of the members of the *domus* of the Servilii, M. Servilius Draco Albucianus, who, after two embassies to Rome at his own expense, eventually succeeded in obtaining a grant of municipal status for Gigthis (i.e., *Latium maius*) from the emperor Antonius Pius.[104] 'Tribe' and town were not incompatible entities. Gigthis is one example, perhaps idiosyncratic of a certain response, of the way in which the two systems could relate to one another and remain closely interwoven, linked by the economic patronage of powerful and wealthy individuals.

But even more important is the general implication of this whole study. Although the information on the subject is scrappy in the extreme, the data's importance is surely significant in precisely inverse proportion to their number. If ever there was a case of 'tip of the iceberg' this must surely be it. There are a thousand or more centres in Africa of the Roman period of which we know at present that could be classified as villages or towns just within the Roman controlled zone. When smaller *castella*, *vici* and other settlements of only a few hectares in extent are added in one is clearly dealing with a number of settlements well over the one thousand mark, again for the Roman controlled regions alone. This computation does not include the 600–800 ethnic units ('tribes') known from the same region. Of this prolific village-centred society great emphasis is placed on the relatively small proportion of towns that had Roman-type institutions of municipal government (about two hundred) or those with some formal quasi-autonomous Roman governmental status, such as *colonia* or *municipium* (in the range 75–100). How were all the rest, that is to say by far the vast majority of villages and towns, governed? And how were an even greater number governed before the majority of the exceptions enumerated above assumed the formal regularities of Roman municipal administration in the first two centuries of our era?

Clearly a type of social and political structure such as that reflected in the term *seniores* (elders) was characteristic of most of the smaller centres amongst these (including such notionally large ones as Theveste) in the second and third centuries B.C. This type-organization is in fact identical with the political level of integration of the ethnic units (the so-called tribes) into which the countryside of Maghrib was divided. In more intensely developed and larger centres the conception of *seniors* or elders seems to have given way to a more general conception of 'leading men' (*primores*, *principes*, *primates* or equivalent term). The distinction seems to conceal a greater differentiation in power and wealth that produced a greater and more permanent separation between *seniores* or 'leading men' and the 'commons' or general populace (*plebs*, *populus*, *vulgus*) in

45 THE STRUCTURE OF LOCAL SOCIETY IN THE EARLY MAGHRIB

this village centred society.[105] The central point to be derived from this shift, historically, is that this is a bottom up development in African society that fed into the potential for the adoption of Roman municipal institutions. But the elders remained the bedrock institution of north African social and political life. in both numerical and temporal terms, through the Roman into the Islamic period. In any assessment of Roman imperialism along its southern frontiers. this critical fact must not be allowed to slip from view simply because of the grotesque imbalance between the data on the elders and *principes* on the one hand, and the Roman-style decurions and *ordines* on the other.

Notes

1. This essay is to be set within the wider discussion of the phenomenon of acculturation and political domination and resistance in the Roman world. For a synopsis see D.M. Pippidi, ed., *Assimilation et résistance à la culture gréco-romaine dans le monde ancien*, Paris, 1976. Some of the relevant analyses of local Mediterranean ethnic and political structures may be found in J. Pitt-Rivers, ed., *Mediterranean Countrymen: Essays in the Social Anthropology of the Mediterranean*, Paris-The Hague (1963), and J.G. Peristiany ed., *Contributions to Mediterranean Sociology: Mediterranean Rural Communities and Social Change*, Paris-The Hague, 1968. J. Davis, *People of the Mediterranean: An Essay in Comparative Mediterranean Anthropology*, London, 1977 is useful, especially for conceptions of domination and countervailing forces of 'egalitarianism'. There is also some interesting comparative material from sub-Saharan Africa. Those works I have found most useful are J. Tosh, *Clan Leaders and Colonial Chiefs in Lango*, Oxford, 1978; and, for the structure, power, and changes in bodies of elders, D.J. Parkin, *Palms, Wine, and Witnesses*, San Francisco, 1972, esp. chs. 3 and 8. This paper is pendant to two others written by myself: 'The *Undecimprimi* in Roman Africa', *Museum Africum* 2 (1973) 1–10, which deals with an African council analogous to elders in its structure; and another which treats the *seniores* in a later context: 'The Elders of Christian Africa', (in) P. Brind'amour ed., *Mélanges offerts à R.P. Etienne Gareau*, Ottawa. Editions de l'Université d'Ottawa=numéro spéciale de *Cahiers des études anciennes* (1982) 207–26. I would like to take this opportunity to thank both Joyce M. Reynolds (Newnham College, Cambridge) and Dr. R.G. Abrahams (Churchill College, Cambridge) for their criticisms of earlier drafts of this paper.
2. An approach which is perhaps best exemplified by the work of Jacques Berque on the early modern and modern Maghrib. It is especially apparent in his *French North Africa: the Maghrib Between two World Wars*, London, 1967 (transl. J. Stewart of *Le Maghrib entre deux guerres*, Paris, 1962).
3. Pomponius Mela 1.42; cf. A. Kuper, 'Council Structure and Decision Making', (in) A. Richards & A. Kuper eds., *Councils in Action*, Cambridge (1971) 13–28, at p. 16: 'The geographical, technological and economic bases of societies also set limits to the possibilities of council organization. . . . The force of these material circumstances may be deduced from the situation of the dispersed and semi-nomadic pastoral societies of Eastern Africa, which lack formal councils. In these societies decisions are made in *ad hoc* groups brought together by men of influence.'
4. I ought perhaps to make some remarks on the use of 'tribe' and 'tribal level'. Throughout this paper these terms will appear in quotation marks since I am fully cognizant of the problematical nature of their use to designate social units. This is not the place, however, to undertake an extended discussion of the problems concerning the conception of 'tribe' at the sort of length that would be required to do justice to the subject. I prefer alternative terms such as 'ethnic group', but 'tribe' will

suffice in the present context as long as it is clearly understood by the reader that this usage does not entail any colonialist assumptions surrounding the word. On *ad hoc* councils at the 'full tribal' level see, for example, the sort of tribal unity perceived by Caesar on campaign in Gaul and summarized in *BG*, 6.11-24 (his ethnographic survey); for an analysis see D. Nash, *The Celts of Central Gaul* . . . , DPhil Thesis, Oxford, 1975, 291-94; cf. E.A. Thompson, *The Early Germans*, Oxford (1965) 12 f., 32 f. and *The Visigoths in the Time of Ulfila*, Oxford (1966) 43-49; and S. Lewuillon, 'Histoire, société et lutte des classes en Gaule: une foedalité à la fin de la république et au début de l'empire', *ANRW* 2.4 (1975) 425-583, at 466 f., 521 f., 540 f. and 558 f.; though none of these cases offer precise parallels to the village-centred *seniores* as they developed in north Africa.
5. Livy 30.17.1; these are the same as the Greek *protoi* of Zonaras 9.13; cf. Eutrop. 3.20.4 on the same group of *nobiles*.
6. The text of Corippus used here is that of J. Diggle & F.R.D. Goodyear, *Flavii Cresconii Corippi Iohannidos Libri VIII*, Cambridge, 1970, an improvement over Partsch's text in *MGHaa* 3.2, Berlin (1879). On Iohannes' campaigns in Africa see D. Pringle, *The Defence of Byzantine Africa from Justinian to the Arab Conquest*, BAR International Series, 99 (i-ii), Oxford (1981), vol. 1, 74-76 and nn. 24-45, updating the classic account by C. Diehl, *L'Afrique byzantine: Histoire de la domination byzantine en Afrique (533-709)*, Paris (1896) 1.III.2, pp. 363-81. The term is used, e.g., of municipal senators at Carthage, cf. 3.280.
7. Iohannes as *pater*: 2:355, 3.294, 4.266, 564, 6.103, 326.
8. The term *proceres* has the same flexibility as *pater*. It is frequently employed to refer to officials at court, as well as to aristocrats at Carthage (*praef.*); on the phenomenon of indigenous *praefecti gentis*, especially in the later empire, see P. Leveau, 'L'Aile II des Thraces, la tribu des Mazices et les *Praefecti Gentis* en Afrique du Nord (A propos d'une inscription nouvelle d'*Oppidum Novum* et de la pénétration romaine dans la partie orientale des plaines du Chélif)', *Ant. Afr.* 7 (1973) 153-92, at 175-86, nos. 46 and 50-62; and C. Lepelley, 'La préfecture de tribu dans l'Afrique du Bas-Empire', (in) *Mélanges d'Histoire offerts à William Seston*, Paris (1974) 285-95.
9. Claudian, *De bello Pollentino sive Gothico*, 479-87 (= *MGHaa* 10.277) and Sidonius Apollinaris, *Panegyricus Avito Augusto*, 452-86 (= *MGHaa* 8.214-15); see also the commentary in C. Sanchez-Albornoz, *Estudios Visigodos*, Rome (1971) 159-60.
10. For a broader perspective see, e.g., the handbooks by L. Mair, *Primitive Government*, Harmondsworth rev. ed. (1964) 87-103, and M. Sahlins, *Tribesmen*, New Jersey (1968) 21-22; more specifically, see the introduction by Jack Goody to the collection edited by him entitled, *Succession to High Office*, Cambridge (1966) 1-56. On comparative studies of 'Berber' societies in modern-day north Africa see A. Hanoteau & A. Letourneux, *La Kabylie et les coutumes kabyles*, 3 vols., Paris, 1872-1873, II (1872), ch. 5, 'De la Thadjemaith ou Djemâa', 20-24; R. Montagne, *Les Berbères et le Makhzen dans le Sud du Maroc: Essai sur la transformation politique des Berbères sédentaires (groupe Chleuh)*, Paris (1930) 220 f., 224 f.; and his *The Berbers: Their Social and Political Organization*, transl. D. Seddon of *La vie sociale et la vie politique des Berbères*, Paris, Société de l'Afrique française, 1931, London (1973) 30 f.
11. Montagne (1930) 159-65, (1973) 31; see E. Gellner and C. Micaud eds., *Arabs and Berbers: From Tribe to Nation in North Africa*, London (1972) 62 f., 76 f., and 87 f.
12. The earliest record of councillors or elders as part of north African 'tribal' structure is probably to be found in Egyptian texts concerning the relations between the pharaohs and the 'Libyans' of the western desert. Ramses III (*regn.* c. 1195-1164 B.C.) had groups of 'ten men' brought before him, men who were nobles or councillors of the 'tribes' involved; see O. Bates, *The Eastern Libyans: An Essay*, London (1914) 114 (reprint: London, 1970).
13. Hdt. 2.32.2-3; cf. Strabo 17.3.25.

47 THE STRUCTURE OF LOCAL SOCIETY IN THE EARLY MAGHRIB

14. Hdt. 4.173; cf. S. Gsell, *Hérodate*, Alger (1915) 200–01.
15. Pomponius Mela 1.42; for the significance of the *sagum* as a sign of prestige and power in African society of the period see Procopius, *Bell.Vand.* 2.6.12 ad Corippus, *Ioh.* 2.134–35.
16. For the distinction of the cloak as a special garb of power in the modern day see Montagne (1930) 224–25.
17. J. Marcillet-Jaubert, *Les inscriptions d'Altava*, Aix-en-Provence (1968) 12–13, 59, no. 67 (A.D. 349–50); P. Pouthier, 'Evolution municipale d'Altava aux IIIe et IVe siècles ap. J.-C.', *MEFR* 68 (1956) 205–45, at 234 ff., and esp. P. Salama in *Libyca (Arch.-épigr.)* 2 (1954) 216.
18. Marcillet-Jaubert (1968) 38–39, no. 29 (A.D. 236) and 67–68, no. 83 (A.D. 362); cf. Pouthier (1956) 235.
19. Marcillet-Jaubert (1968) 169–70; Pouthier (1956) 209–12, 234; for comparative material cf. Montagne (1973) 30. Montagne reported the existence of small representative councils, usually a small 'senate' composed of about ten members who were headmen of each agnatic clan. Again (p. 47) he notes: 'In many regions one finds a representative body of ten notables sitting in the tribal council.' Of course, one must take the word 'representative' with caution.
20. Marcillet-Jaubert (1968) 169–70, no. 273 (Titius Faussanus, *prior civitatis*) and 190–91, no. 371 (Q. Sittius Maximus, *prior princeps civitatis suae*), cf. Pouthier (1956) 208–09. There is an approximate parallel in a man from Qsar M'duja (Byzacium) who was *prior omnium in civitate (Corpus Inscriptionum Latinarum*, Vol. VIII (henceforth = *CIL*) 23.662).
21. Diod. Sic. 24.10.2; on Hekatompylos see Diod. Sic. 4.18.1 where he states that the town was founded by Herakles in the waterless tracts of Africa. He also claims that it was of considerable size and had prospered until 'recently' when it had been captured by the Carthaginians.
22. F.C. Movers, *Die Phönizier*, 2.2, Berlin (1850) 119 identified it with Theveste. H. Dessau, 'Hekatompylos', *RE* 7.2 (1912) 2099 seems to concur; cf. G. Camps, *Aux origines de la Berberie: Massinissa ou les débuts de l'histoire* = *Libyca (Arch.-épigr.)* 8 (1960) 42–43 and 257. The identification is based on Jerome, *Comm. in Epist. ad Galat.*, 2.3.8–9 (Migne, *PL*, 26.354).
23. Polyb. 1.73.1; usually dated to ca. 247 B.C. See S. Gsell, *Histoire ancienne de l'Afrique du Nord* (henceforth, *HAAN*), vol. 2, *L'état carthaginois*, 2. ed., Paris (1921) 95–96 and 101, accepted by G. Charles-Picard, *Carthage*, transl. M. Kochan, London (1964) 199 and B.H. Warmington, *Carthage*, rev. ed., London (1969) 60. But F.W. Walbank notes arguments advanced by Thiel for a date after 247, *A Historical Commentary on Polybius*, vol. 1, Oxford (1957) 137.
24. Orosius, *Adv. pagan.* 4.9.9.
25. For examples of the Carthaginians taking hostages from African and Spanish tribesmen see Livy 28.34.9, 28.35.4, and 29.3.5.
26. Livy 30.12.8; cf. Gsell, *HAAN*, 5 (1927) 132.
27. Sall. *Bell. Iug.* 47.1.
28. App. *Numid.* fg. 3 (107 B.C.).
29. Sall. *Bell. Iug.* 66.2; cf. Gsell, *HAAN* 5 (1927) 132 and Camps (1960) 257.
30. Sall. *Bell. Iug.* 66.2–3; see J. Carcopino, 'Le culte des *Cereres* et les Numides', (in) *Aspects mystiques de la Rome antique*, Paris (1942) 13–37 = 'Salluste, le culte des "Cereres" et les Numides', *RH* 158 (1928) 1–18.
31. Sall. *Bell. Iug.* 47.1 and 29.1 *oppidum Iugurthae*, apparently an important centre for the exchange of grain produced in the region since L. Calpurnius Bestia sent his *quaestor* P. Sextius to the town to supervise the collection of grain supplies which Iugurtha had in store there (110 B.C.) Cf. *Bell. Iug.* 69.4 where Sallust calls Vaga *civitas magna et opulens*, perhaps exaggerating to highlight the magnitude of the Africans' perfidy.
32. Ps.-Caes. *Bell. Afr.* 26.1–2.

48

33. Ps.-Caes. *Bell. Afr.* 26.5; note that the same term is used of the leading men at Lepcis (97.1). T. Kotula, 'Les principes gentis et les principes civitatis en Afrique romaine', *Eos* 55 (1965)1 347–65 studied the concept of *princeps* as a 'tribal' chieftain and the supposed transition of the position to an urban office. At p. 347–48, n. 2 he notes the above examples but contends: 'De tous ces exemples il semble résulter que dans l'Afrique entière le pluriel *principes (civitatis)* désignait un groupe social défini et non les magistrates des cités.' I disagree in that for the small villages of Africa the two must have overlapped almost totally. In some cases (e.g., the *principes* of Lepcis referred to above) there can be little doubt that the leading men were tied to a formal municipal structure, and in other instances the *principes* represent at least a conciliar type of organization even if they did not hold formal offices. This was clearly Appian's understanding when he called the *principes* at Vaga *hê boulê*. Such a view seems to be justified by the *de facto*, if not *de iure*, power that the *principes* at Cirta held.
34. For the location see *CIL*, p. 2729; it is about 60 km SSW of Sicca Veneria, 20 km W of Althiburos, and 30 km north of Ammaedara. A bishopric was located in the town in later times, see J. Mesnage, *L'Afrique chrétienne. Evêchés et ruines antiques*, Paris (1912) 104, and J.L. Maier, *L'Episcopat de l'Afrique romaine, vandale et byzantine*, Neuchatel (1973) 46, nn. 80, 58, 200 and 226; *DACL* 9 (1930) 1276 s.v. 'Madjouba', and C. Saumagne, *Le Droit Latine et les cités romaines sous l'empire. Essais critiques*, Paris (1965) 110–11.
35. *CIL*, p. 73–76 and n. 587 (cf. 11735).
36. *Fundus Ver(rona)* at Hr. al-Hatba; a 'Donatist' bishopric was later located here, see Mesnage (1912) 83.
37. *CIL*, 597, 11763 (Kala'at as-Senûm); For the *sacerdos Cererum* see *CIL*, 580 = 11732 (Hr. 'Ain Kedim=Hr. al-Hammam).
38. A detailed description of the project can be found in P. Gauckler, *BSAF* (1897) 300–03.
39. *CIL*, 27828 = *ILS* 6805 = *AE* 1898:47 (see Gauckler, *BSAF* (1897) 301).
40. Contemporary parallels for this worship are detailed in E. Dermengham, *Le culte des saints dans l'Islam maghrebin*, 3rd ed., Paris (1954) 144–45, and L. Galand, 'Note à propos d'un génie Berbère', *JA* 252 (1964) 105–07 notes the case for continuity. The cult of Neptune in this connection is mentioned by Augustine, cf. *Ep*, 245, *Contra Cresc.* 3.78 (89), *Doctr. Christ.* 3.7.11, *Enar. in Psalm.* 145.6.12 and 183, and *Sermo.* 2.5.
41. In general see Gsell, *HAAN* 6 (1927) 132–40; G. Charles-Picard, *Les religions de l'Afrique antique*, Paris, Plon (1954) 6–10; J. Toutain, 'Les cultes africaines', (in) *Les cultes païennes dans l'Empire romaine*, vol. 3, Paris (1917) 15–11, at 372–78. The fullest treatment is by P. Petitmengin, 'Inscriptions de la région de Milev, pt. 4: Dédicace à Neptune', *MEFR* 79 (1967) 196–205. His map (200–01) shows the distribution of the cult of Neptune as the guardian deity of springs in north Africa.
42. P. Veyne, 'Deux inscriptions de Vina', *Karthago* 9 (1958) 89–117, at 103–09, and Petitmengin (1967) 193–95. There is nothing in the evidence to contradict this thesis; that is to say, wherever *magistri* are found in peregrine communities, no municipal assembly is attested. See Saumagne (1965) 110, who seems to believe this when he considers the existence of *seniores* to imply the existence of a *castellum*. Although I cannot share this view, I do believe that evidence of *magistri* may suggest the presence of *seniores* even where the latter are not directly attested.
43. For the use of the term *plebs* in north Africa compare the following instances: *CIL*, 1651 – 15883 (Sicca Veneria, end of the third century); 23022 (Hr. Salâh as-Sadîk, A.D. 159); 23822 = *ILAfr.* 210 (Saradi, Hr. Sahali); 23964 (=828) and 23965 (*Municipium Aurelium Commodianum* . . . , Hr. bu-Scha); 26276 (Uchi Maius, Hr. Duamis).
44. Hanoteau & Letourneux (1872–73) 20; A.R.P. Koller, 'La Jemâ berbère', *Civilisations* 4 (1954) 43–50 is too superficial to be of much use. J. Berque, *Structures*

III

49 THE STRUCTURE OF LOCAL SOCIETY IN THE EARLY MAGHRIB

sociales du Haut-Atlas, rev. & augm. ed., Paris (1978) 414, who emphasizes the non-institutional nature of membership and who stresses that these are not at all senates in our understanding of the word: 'Bien que le poids de l'âge, de le richesse, des alliances, toute comme celui de la parenté ou des prestiges d'ordre familial, compensant sa propension tumultuaire, ce n'est pas un "senate" ici, qui délibère, mais une foule.' See E. Gellner, 'Political and Religious Organization of the Berbers of the Central High Atlas', (in) Gellner & Micaud (1972) 59–66, as well as pp. 72 and 75–79 in the general work.

45. Montagne (1930) 218, 224–25, 269 f. and 300 f., and D.G. Jongmans, 'Politics on the Village Level', (in) J. Boissevain & J.C. Mitchell eds., *Network Analyses: Studies in Human Interaction*, Paris–The Hague (1973) 167–218, at pp. 171–74.
46. A. Richards, 'The Nature of the Problem', (in) A. Richards & A. Kuper eds. (1971) 1–12, at pp. 10–11.
47. A survey of the nomenclature at Tituli reveals that all are African: a certain [. . .]g Mger[a. .]us Felix and his sister Mgera Saturnin(a), *CIL*, 601; a Duda, 27836; a Faustus [.]stiabi fil(ius), 27837; and three *Iulii*, doubtless descendants of 'Gaetulian' tribesmen enfranchized by Marius or Caesar: Iulius Privatus, Iulia Donata (27838) and Iulia Fortunata (27839).
48. Gellner & Micaud (1972) 28, 30–31, 62–63, and 76–78; cf. Maier (1973) 146–64, 170–89, and 261–79, and M. Gluckman, *Politics, Law and Ritual in Tribal Society*, New York (1965) 155 ff.
49. A. Ernout & A. Meillet, *Dictionnaire étymologique de la langue latine*, 4. ed., Paris (1959–60) 513–14, s.v. 'plebs, pleps'. The consonantal shift 'b'–'p' is, however, rather common, see V. Väänänen, *Introduction au Latin vulgaire*, 2. ed., Paris (1967) 50 & 117.
50. The precise format *senatus populusque* (equivalent to *senatus et plebs*), copying the model of the city of Rome, is found regularly in the coastal cities of *Proconsularis* (e.g., Hippo Regius, Carthage, Curubis, Gigthis, and Lepcis Magna) at an early date (first century B.C.) when they began imitating Roman forms of government. But the formula was abandoned by the mid-first century A.D. in favour of the more regular *ordo, ordo decurionum* or *decuriones*.
51. *CIL*, 27832 (cf. Gauckler, *BSAF* (1897) 303, Tituli): Pro salute Imp(eratoris) Caesa[ris L(ucii) Aeli(i) Aurelii Com]/modi Aug(usti) Sarmatici G[erm(anici), seniores Tituli]/tanorum de suo feceru[nt et dedicaverunt].
52. Ucubi (Hr. Kaussât) is about 20 kilometres northeast of al-Kaf; it remained a *castellum* attributed to Sicca Veneria at least until A.D. 2144 (see *CIL*, 15669). On the attribution of these *castella* to Sicca Veneria see T.R.S. Broughton, *The Romanization of Africa Proconsularis*, Baltimore, 1929 (reprint: New York, 1968) 187 f.; on *adtributio* in general see U. Laffi, *Adtributio e contributio. Problemi del sistema politico-amministrativo dello stato romano*, Pisa (1966) 19–98. Surprisingly, he does not discuss the *castella* of Sicca, though he does deal with those attributed to Carthage, Maktar (?), and Cirta (81–86 and 135–48). See also Saumagne (1965) ch. IVb, a, 'Sicca et ses *castella*', 108–12.
53. *CIL*, 15666 = *ILS* 6806 (Ucubi, A.D. 150): '. . . seniores Ucu/bitani aere / conlato po/ /suerunt' (lines 13–16).
54. *CIL*, 15667 = *Eph. Epigr.* vii, 292 (Ucubi, A.D. 165): 'Seniores Ucu/bitani aere con/lato posuerunt / Mettius Secundus / Memmianus, P(ublius) Larg/ /ius Numidicus, II vir(i) / q(uin)q(uennales) dedicaverunt / d(ecreto) d(ecurionum)' (lines 6–13). The version in *CIL* reads Larcius, which is possible since there were Africans with this *nomen* adopted from A. Larcius Priscus, legate of *IIIa Augusta* under Trajan (see B.E. Thomasson, *Die Statthalter der römischen Provinzen Nordafrikas von Augustus bis Diocletianus*, 2 vols., Lund (1960) II. 164–65). But they are concentrated in Numidia and are mainly veterans. It seems more probable that the reading should be *G* rather than *C*; there were many *Largii* at Sicca to whom our man is probably related: e.g. C. Largius Cornelianus (*CIL*, 16102), Q. Largius P.f.

Quir(ina tribu) Maximus (16103) and T. Largius Numidicus (16104). See, however, R. Syme, 'Tacfarinas, the Musulamii and Thubursicu', ch. 9 (in) P.R. Coleman-Norton *et. al.* eds., *Studies in Roman Economic and Social History in Honour of A.C. Johnson*, Princeton (1951) 113–30 (= ch. 16 (in) E. Badian ed., *Roman Papers*, Oxford (1979) 218–30) at pp. 125–26. On the problem of autonomy of the *castella* at this time see Saumagne (1965) 108–09, at 109: 'On dirait que la *Colonia Sicca* résiste a une certaine tendance à l'autonomie qu'esquissent les *seniores* de l'année 155 lorsqu'ils prétendent faire seuls les frais par cotisation, d'un monument.'

55. *CIL*, 15669 = *Eph. epigr.* vii, 291 = *ILS* 6807 (Ucubi, A.D. 214): Decur[io(nes)] / Sic(censes) Ucubi morantes et seni/ /ores k(astelli) Ucubis aer[e] conl[a]t[o pos-uerunt] / d(ecreto) d(ecurionum) (lines 14–17). The sense of *morantes* suggests that certain decurions from Sicca were *resident* at Ucubi at least on a semi-permanent basis. Compare the following: *CIL*, 23125 (Vicus Haterianus, Hr. Zangru, A.D. 129); 14608 (Simitthus, Shemtu); 1641.

56. For comparative situations see J.F. Holleman, *Chief, Council and Commissioner. Some Problems of Government in Rhodesia*, Oxford (1969) 102 ff., and Gluckman (1965) 323–24.

57. Richards (1971) 9–10: colonial powers attempt to formalize the powers of the councils which are of functional use to them: 'Colonial authorities tended to place administrative functions *first*, but local councils saw their first priority to settle disputes.' That is to say, councils would spend 'inordinate' amounts of time (in the eyes of the colonial administrators, that is) discussing low priority, even trivial, matters simply to reach a consensus. Colonial officials tried to supervise the agenda so as to give a more 'logical' order of priority to business. The basic problem was that local councils did not see themselves as part of a larger system of local government tied in to a central authority; their horizons were bounded by the interests of their own community. Note especially Richards, p. 9: 'Colonial administrators . . . were not unnaturally impatient of large meetings which slowed down procedure . . . held up the type of discussion which they felt to be the proper tasks of local government councils. As time went on they began to try to streamline the procedure by fixing the personnel of councils whether by nomination or election.'

58. F.G. Bailey, 'Decisions by Consensus in Councils and Committees', (in) M. Banton ed., *Political Systems and the Distribution of Power*, New York–London (1965) 1–20. This excellent treatment analyses the basic reasons why councils of this type do no tend to divide on issues (e.g., by voting), but discuss matters at extreme length if necessary to reach unanimous assent. Essentially, councils function this way in 'face-to-face' communities because the members themselves function in multi-faceted roles in which they regularly encounter one another (e.g., as co-workers, religious celebrants, and marketers) so that consensus is all important to the continued function of the village community; see Kuper (1971) 9 f. for a refinement of Bailey's scheme.

59. On its location see *AAT*, f. 57 (Environs du Kef) n. 40. Direct contact with Sicca is barred by the large massif of J. Hadida. The ruins are on the deeply ravined north side of the mountain. Its organization as a *castellum*, its proximity to Sicca, and the enrolment of its citizens in the *tribu Quirina* (e.g. *CIL*, 15738, 15747) all guarantee its attribution to Sicca Veneria. For the inscription see *CIL*, 15722 (= 1616) = *ILS* 444 (Hr. Sidi Merzûg). Iulia Domna seems to have assumed this title (i.e., including *Mater Augusti*) under Caracalla (see *PIR*[2], I.663, p. 313) and *IRT* 404 (Lepcis Magna): *Iulia Aug(ustae) / piae felici / Matri Augus/ti et Castro/rum et Sena/ /tus et Par/triae, / seniores kast(elli) / pos(uerunt) et dedic(averunt)*.

60. *CIL*, 15721 (= 1615) (Hr. Sidi Merzûg, A.D. 213): . . . *opti/mo m[aximo]que / principi, seniores / k(astelli) posuer(unt) et ded(icaverunt)* (lines 7–10).

61. *CIL*, 15726 = *Eph. epigr.* v, 595 (Hr. Sidi Merzûg). He died at 78 and was buried at Hr. Sidi Merzûg (see Cagnat, *CRAI* (1882) 77). But Gsell, *HAAN*, 5 (1929) 65, n. 2 (reported in *ILAfr.* 1587) preferred the resolution *pr(a)ef(ectus) castel(lorum)*.

62. On *duoviri i.d.* and *praefecti i.d.* see W. Langhammer, *Die rechtliche und soziale Stellung der Magistratus municipales und der Decuriones*, Wiesbaden (1973) 62–64, and W. Simshauser, *Iuridici und Municipalgerichtsbarkeit in Italien* (in) *Münchener Beiträge zur Papyrusforschung und antiken Rechtsgeschichte*, 61 (1973) 85 ff.
63. *CIL*, 15724 (Hr. Sidi Merzûg).
64. *CIL*, 15723 (Hr. Sidi Merzûg, A.D. 360–61).
65. J. Gascou, 'L'emploi du terme *respublica* dans l'épigraphie latine d'Afrique', *MEFRA* 91 (1979) 383–98.
66. *CIL, indices*, pp. 185–86 and 283; in fact, the instance of *et ordinis* is unique.
67. C. Lucas, 'Notes on *Curatores Rei Publicae* of Roman Africa', *JRS* 30 (1940) 56–74; cf. *CTh* 12.1.20 (A.D. 331).
68. Sall. *Bell. Iug.* 75, refers to Thala's location as *in solitudines* and *in spatio millium quinquaginta loca arida atque vasta*. It was, however, one of the 'regal' towns of Iugurtha's kingdom *ubi plerique thesauri filiorum eius multus pueritiae cultus erat*. For the Thalai see Ptolemy 4.6.6 and H. Treidler, 'Thalai', *RE* 5.1 (1934) 1187. I cannot understand why J. Desanges, *Catalogue des tribus africaines de l'antiquité classique à l'ouest du Nil*, Dakar (1962) 238–39, following the order of citation in Ptolemy, would like to place them in the Grand Erg Oriental or the Fezzân.
69. Tac. *Ann.* 3.21. C. Courtois, 'La Thala de Salluste', *RSAC* 69 (1955–56) 57–69 refutes Gsell's argument (*HAAN* 5 (1927) 277 f. and 7 (1929) 208 f.) which seeks to distinguish between the Thala of Salust and that of Tacitus.
70. There are some bishops who later may have come from Thala, but none of the known instances are convincing, see Maier (1973) 213.
71. H. Treidler, 'Thala', *RE* 5.1 (1934) 1185–87, at col. 1187.
72. *AE* 1915: 15 = J. Martin, *BCTH* (1915) xxi, and *AE* 1915: 80 = A. Merlin, *BCTH* (1915) viii; *ILAfr.* 195 (Thala, between the second consulship of Geta, Jan. A.D. 209, and the death of Severus 11 Feb. A.D. 211). Cf. Gsell, *HAAN* 5 (1929) 65: *Deae Caelesti Aug(usae) sacrun* (sic) *[pro salute imperatorum Auggg(ustorum trium)] / L(ucii) Septimi Severi Pii Pertinacis [Aug(usti) et M(arci) Aureli Antonini Pii f(ilii) Aug(usti) et] / P(ublii) Septimi Severi [Getae] Caes(aris), bis co(n)s(ul) Au[g(usti) cun]cti seniores, sumpt(ibus) pub(licis) fecerunt e[t dedicaverunt]*.
73. *CIL, indices*, 280–81.
74. A. Audollent, *Carthage romaine*, Paris (1901) 262–65; Toutain (1917) 29–37; Charles-Picard (1954) 4–5, 24–25; and M. Leglay, *Saturne africain, histoire*, Paris (1966) 215–22, 356, and 403 (Thala); Caelestis was also the guardian deity of the periodic market centre constructed at 'Aïn Melûk, see B.D. Shaw, 'Rural Markets in North Africa and the Political Economy of the Roman Empire', *Ant. Afr.* 17 (1981) 37–83, at p. 63.
75. Mesnage (1912) 159, and *MEFR* (1902) 325; see esp. Leglay (1966) 187, and *Saturne africaine, monuments, I: Afrique proconsulaire*, Paris (1961) 229–30. The only dedication by a local priest is of Saturn, see Leglay (1966) 250, 402, and (1961) 301, n. 5.
76. For the location of Hr. 'Aïn Tella see *AAT* F. 19 (La Calle) n. 7: in the territory of the Awlad Masallam, on the trunk road from 'Aïn Draham to al-Kala (Fr. La Calle). It is situated on the Algero-Tunisian frontier, about 5 km NE of Rûm as-Sûq and about 15 km SE of al-Kala. Broughton (1929) 181 believed it to be a *castellum* (for which there is no evidence) attributed to Thabraca on the coast. There is no indication that this connection ever existed, and geography tells against it. Although a route inland from the coast up the valley of W. al-Kabîr exists, the massifs of J. Darâwî and J. Jadîda block the way east of the village to the defile. Al-Kala is much closer but access to it is barred by the (once) malarial swamp of Gara'at m'ta al-Hût.
77. *CIL*, 17327 = *Eph epigr.* vii, 422 (Hr. 'Aïn Tella, A.D. 293–305). For the dating see W. Seston, *Dioclétian et la Tetrarchie*, Paris (1946) 93, 120–21 (to be used with caution). Most (e.g., Gsell, *HAAN* 5 (1929) 64, n. 4) have accepted the *Corpus*' reading of the town's name as *Ma[. . . . . .]rensium* (1.6). But I have followed the readings of A. Papier, 'Inscriptions nouvelles de la Tunisie et de la province de

Constantine', *BAH* 22 (1886) 102–66, at pp. 107–14, n. 10 and pl. iii (photograph) as against the more speculative reading in the *Corpus*: Pro salute d(ominorum) n(ostrorum) quattuor) / Diocletiani et Maximiani perpetuorum /[A]ug(ustorum duorum) et Constanti et [Ma]ximiani nobilis/simorum Caes(arum duorum), tem-[pl]um Dei Mercuri /[v]etustate delaps[um c]ul[to ampl]issimo // universi sen[iore]s VV[. . . . . .]renuum (?) / sumptibus suis restituer[unt et de]dicaverunt / anno Fortunatiani Mag(istri), curatores / Macidius Primus [- - -].

78. Admiralty, *Tunisia*, London, Naval Intelligence Division (1945) 29–30, 91–93, and 308–10; J. Despois, *La Tunisie. Ses régions*, 2. ed., Paris (1967) 163–68, and *L'Afrique du Nord*, 3 ed., Paris (1964) 276–78. The traditional economy of the region is indicated by its name, Bilad az-Zaytûna: 'olive country'.
79. Mercury-Silvanus is often grouped together with Saturn and Caelestis, see the following examples: *CIL*, 8246–47 (Idicra, 'Azia ben-Tellis, with Saturn only) and 9195 (Rapidum, Sûr Juab). The identification with Silvanus is much closer in other instances: 2646 (on the southern slopes of J. Afia near Lambaesis), 11227 (scratched on a rock at J. Ras al-'Aïn deep in southern Tunisia) with the African name Maddsilacus; 23999 (J. Ust near Sutunurca); 26486 (Thugga) and *AE* 1928: 34 (Aradi), all in zones of hills and arboriculture, usually of olives See furthei Toutain (1917) 266–67; Leglay (1966) 242 45, and L. Chatelain, 'Le culte de Silvain en Afrique et l'inscription de la plaine de Sers (Tunisie)', *MEFR* 30 (1910) 77–97.
80. For the administrative district of Carthage see C. Poinssot, '*Immunitas perticae Carthaginiensium*', *CRAI* (1962) 55–76, and H.-G. Pflaum, 'La romanisation de l'ancien territoire de Carthage punique à la lumière des découvertes épigraphiques récentes', *Ant. Afr.* 4 (1970) 75–117 (reprinted in his *Scripta varia I: L'Afrique romaine*, Paris (1978) 300–44). For the *XIprimi* see Shaw (1973) 3–10.
81. Map and analysis of the clustering of *sufetes* in these towns in C. Poinssot, 'Suo et Sucubi', *Karthago* 10 (1959–60) 93–131.
82. Camps (1960) 176–79, 259–60, and 263–65; and A. Berthier and R. Charlier, *Le sanctuaire punique d'El-Hofra à Constantine*, vol. 1, Paris, (1955) 232–36.
83. Shaw (1973) 8–9.
84. *CIL*, 26517 (Thugga, A.D. 48–49): . . . *omnium portarum sententiis ornam(enta) / sufetis gratis decrevit* . . . (lines 11–12).
85. L. Homo, 'Les *suffetes* de Thugga d'après une inscription récemment découverte', *MEFR* 19 (1899) 296–306 (cf. *CRAI* (1899) 363, with the remarks by Berger), reported by the editors of *CIL*.
86. W. Seston, 'Remarques sur les institutions politiques et sociales de Carthage, d'après une inscription latine de Thugga', *CRAI* (1967) 218–22, and 'Des *portes* de Thugga à la "constitution" de Carthage', *RH* 237 (1967) 277–94. The Near Eastern data on assemblies of elders at the city gates are much more extensive than Seston seems to think (not limited to the handful of biblical parallels already adduced by Homo and Berger in 1899).
87. Camps (1960) 176 f., 236 f., and 256 f.
88. E. Masqueray, *Formation des cités chez les populations sédentaires de l'Algérie (Kabyles du Djurdjura, Chouïa de l'Aourâs, Béni Mezâb)*, Paris (1886) 38–83 (reprint: ed. Fanny Colonna, Aix-en-Provence, 1983), from which I would like to quote extensively in order to illustrate the parallel in situation and function. On pp. 45–47 he points out precisely the sort of probouleutic inner council type of elders alluded to above in his paper for Roman Africa. He later points out (p. 81) the location of these assemblies at the town gates ('à l'entrée même du village') and continues: 'A l'intérieur sont deux bancs, ou plutôt deux plates-formes d'allées, sur lesquelles on peut, non seulement s'asseoir, mais s'étendre. Une distance d'un mètre environ les sépare, formant couloir. Dans la plupart des autres villages, le djemâa n'est pas une maison, mais un tronçon de rue recouvert d'un toit, ou plutôt l'entrée même du village transformée en une porte profonde par laquelle on passe librement. A droit et à gauche sont encore de larges bancs d'allée, sur lesquels

III

53 THE STRUCTURE OF LOCAL SOCIETY IN THE EARLY MAGHRIB

l'Amîn, les Temman et les Oqqâl siégent face à face. Une des remarques qui m'ont le plus confirm dans l'opinion que les assemblées Kabyles ne sont jamais des *meeting* populaires, est précisément l'iquité relative de ces lieux de réunion. Il n'est pas de djemâa qui puisse contenir seulement la dixième partie d'une cité . . . [this seems to contradict the claim of democratic participation, but] . . . Cette contradiction disparait, si l'on considère que la salle de réunion est très largement ouverte sur une de ses faces ou à ses deux extrémités. L'Amîn et les gens les plus considérables y entrent et la tremplissent, mais la foule n'est pas exclue pour cela. Elle assiste y fort près à la déliberation; on discute sous ses yeux . . .', and (p. 83): 'C'est là plutôt une promulgation qu'un plébiscite. L'usage d'installer la djemâa près de la porte de la ville n'est-il pas aussi très remarquable? L'Amîn, les Temman et les Oqqâl sont des juges. Ils ont à décider des contestations entre citoyens et étrangers, et la prudence conseille de ne pas admettre l'étranger au coeur de la ville. Combien de souvenirs antiques cette observation peut évoquer!'. This is an amazing exclamation, since the Thugga inscription was not discovered until some thirteen years after Masqueray published his book. In fact, the whole significance of Masqueray's work in the development of European sociology has only come to be appreciated relatively recently, see E. Gellner, 'The Roots of Cohesion', *Man* n.s. 20 (1985) 142–55.
89. Shaw (1982) for the Christian context; for areas outside north Africa; Livy regularly uses *seniores* to denote a small village or 'tribal' council (e.g., 34.16.15, 38.55.1). See R. MacMullen, *Roman Social Relations*, New Haven (1974) 14, 23–27 and 81 ff. For different regional usages of the term see Livy 28.43.1, 30.21.6, 30.22.5, and 31.61.15. On its use in other institutional contexts in Africa see *CIL*, 2714 (Lambaesis, 230s A.D.).
90. Capt. d'Yanville, 'Sur l'inscription du Col de Fdoulès', *Ann. Const.* 3 (1856–57) 55–57, at p. 55, but cf. P. Leveau's studies of the mountain regions in *RHCM* 8 (1970) 7–21; *BCTH* n.s. 8 (1972) 3–26, *ib.* 10–11b (1977) 175–83; *MEFRA* 87 (1975) 857–71 and (1977) 257–311: many 'Roman' type constructions are, of course, built by local communities along Roman patterns.
91. *CIL*, 20216 (= 8379), cf. Heron de Villefosse, *AMS* 2 (1875) 442, n. 104, and the new edition by Cagnat in *BCTH* (1892) 489, n. 15. For the location see the report by Gsell, *Atl. arch.* f. 8 (Philippeville) no. 102: Col de Fdoulès, passage entre la vallée de l'oued Enndjas et celle de l'oued Djinedjène. Au lieu dit Souk el-Kédim, à environ 250 m au sud du col l'inscription lour texte de l'époque chrétienne (VIe ou VIIe siècle). For the historical and institutional context see G. Camps, 'Rex Gentium Maurorum et Romanorum. Recherches sur les royaumes de Maurétanie des VIe et VIIe siècles', *Ant. Afr.* 20 (1984) 183–218, 'Le Roi des Ucutamani', pp. 199–200.
92. I have followed Cagnat's reading because the editors of *CIL* have introduced arbitrary word divisions into the text which tend to give a misleading impression of the layout of the original. At the end of line four I have retained Villefosse's earlier reading. All editors accept the date of the inscription as 'Christian' or 'Byzantine', though the reasons for this escape me. If it is the 'cross' sign in line one, then there is little if no basis since the sign probably had no symbolic significance. If the presence of *seniores*, then, as argued here, they need not be an ecclesiastical body.
93. Desanges (1962) 71, cf. 57; see C. Courtois, *Les Vandales et l'Afrique*, Paris, 1955 (reprint: Darmstadt, 1964) 120, n. 2, and, by the same author, 'Ucutamani', *RE* 15.2 (1955) 553–54. The 'U' prefix means 'sons of' as in 'Aït (Berber) or 'Awlad (Arabic). The 'tribe' is probably to be identified with the *Koudamousioi* of Ptolemy 4.2.21, who still inhabited the region in the time of Ibn Khaldûn (see *Histoire des Berbères*, transl. MacG. de Slane, Paris, 1848, I, 291 f.).
94. *CIL*, 4354, cf. 18540 = *ILCV* 28 = O. Fiebiger & L. Schmidt, *Inschriftensammlung zur Geschichte der Ostgermanen* (= Denkschriften der Kaiserliche Akademie der Wissenschaften in Wien, Phil.-Hist. Kl. 60.3, Vienna, 1917, 45, n. 71) = Bücheler,

CLE, no. 795. Cf. the original reports by A. Cherbonneau, *RSAC* 6 (1862) 129 and A. Poulle, *RSAC* 13 (1869) 665.

95. The settlement may have been a *castrum* such as one of the many fortified settlements local Christian chieftains were erecting, *adiuvante Deo*, see *CIL*, 28000 = *ILCV* 800 (Hr. Za'aba, to the SE of Tébessa) and *CIL*, 14439 (Hr. Negaschia, 16 km NE of Vaga). For a discussion of the dating and historical context see *BSA* (1895) 170–71; Gsell. *MEFR* 15 (1895) 335–36, and Pringle (1981) I, 74–76 and nn. 24–45.

96. For *senior* as a personal name see Marcillet-Jaubert (1968) 36–37, n. 25 = *CIL*, 9892 (A.D. 318) where his interpretation *fili(i) senior<e>(s)* seems forced; it seems preferable to take *Seniori* as it stands as a dative with *patri* which follows; cf. *CIL*, 9106 (Auzia) and 21845 (Volubilis), and Shaw (1982) for the Christian context.

97. Desanges (1962) 86.

98. For the Punic period and influence see L.A. Constans, *NAMS* 14 (1916) 12–16, and the bilingual inscription *CIL*, 22726. For its municipal development see J. Gascou, *La politique municipale de l'empire romain en Afrique proconsulaire de Trajan à Septime-Sévère*, Rome (1972) 137–42; Saumagne (1965) ch. 5, 'La Latinité de Gightis, *Municipium Gightense* (sic)', 121–30, and L.A. Costans, 'Inscriptions de Gigthis (Tunisie)', *MEFR* 34 (1914) 267–86, at 269–71, n. 2.

99. *CIL*, 22741 (Gigthis).

100. Constans (1914) 279–81, n. 10 = *AE* 1915: 44 (Gigthis): *[Mem]io C(aii) f(ilio) Quir(ina tribu) / M[e]ssio Pacato / [fla]m(ini) p(er)p(etuo) omnib(us) / honorib(us) in pa/tria sua functo // optimo patrono / [f]ullones domus / eius*. A stemma of the *Servaei* can be found at *CIL*, 22734–35, p. 2298.

101. *AE* 1971: 534 (Banasa).

102. *CIL*, 22729 = *ILS* 9394 = *AE* 1908: 123 (based on P. Gauckler, 'Rapport sur des inscriptions latines découvertes en Tunisie de 1900 à 1905, I, Fouilles de Bougrara (Gigthis), épigraphie', *NAMS* 15 (1908) 283–330, at 319–20 n. 49), but I have followed Constans (1914) 278–79, n. 9, a copy which supersedes the above; cf. H.-G. Pflaum, 'les juges de cinq decuries originaires d'Afrique romaine', *Ant. Afr.* 2 (1968) 153–95, p. 163, n. 12: *L(ucio) Memmio Messio / L(ucii) (f(ilio) Quir(ina tribu) Pacatao flam(ini) / perpetuo divi Traia/ni, Chinithio, in quin/que decurias a divo // Hadriano adlecto / Chinithi(i) ob merita / eius et singula/rem pietatem, quam nationi suae prae//stat, sua pecuni/a posuerunt*.

103. Their grant of citizenship may be traced to Gaius Memmius Regulus (cos. ord. A.D. 63), though Thomasson (1960) does not mention him, there is a gap in the *fasti* from A.D. 73–76 where his governorship of *Proconsularis* could be placed. Or from P. Memmius Regulus, who held the military command of Numidia in the decade between A.D. 35–44, see Thomasson (1960) II.41. See Groag, 'Memmius(28)', *RE* 15.1 (1931) 625–26. The family did have connection with Gigthis: a[Q.] Memmius Pudens was patron of the town, see *CIL*, 22719; cf. Constans (1914) 282, n. 12. Gascou (1972) 140 gives the example of an individual who was admitted to the five decuries by Hadrian, one Servaeus Macer, probably a close relative of our Servilia Servaea (see *CIL*, 22699 and 22736).

104. *CIL*, 22737 = *ILTun.* 41; cf. Gascou (1972) 138–40. For a comparative instance of a clan-like *domus* in the region, see the 'house' of the Manilii Arelliorum (extending over six generations) at Hr. Guesiret to the south of Gigthis in the Matmata country (*CIL*, 22774). In speaking of 'tribe' and town in this way I do *not* mean to suggest that the identity and meaning to 'tribe' remains the same in an urban and a rural context. It probably does not: see the excellent study of D. Parkin, *Neighbours and Nationals in an African City Ward*, Berkeley (1969) esp. 182 ff.

105. Hinting at the sort of incipient domination of the factor of 'class' in society, as outlined for the Gauls by Nash (1975) and Lewuillon (1975) and Thompson (1965).

IV

THE ELDER PLINY'S AFRICAN GEOGRAPHY*

d. d. m. Leo Teutsch

Table of Contents

I. History of Research 424
II. The Text and its Composition 431
III. Historical Context of the Official Document 436
    1. Colonial Settlements of Caesar and Augustus. The Problem of *Africa vetus* and *Africa nova* 436
    2. The Six Colonies 438
        a. *Colonia Carthago Magnae in vestigiis Carthaginis* 438
        b. The Status of Cirta and Sicca 440
        c. Uthina and Thuburbo Minus 442
        d. The Case of Maxula 443
    3. *Oppidum Latinum Unum Uzalitanum* 444
    4. *Oppidum Stipendiarium unum Castris Corneliis* 445
IV. The Free Cities of Africa 445
V. *Oppida civium Romanorum* 449
VI. Political Significance of the Official Document 453

Appendices

A. Reconstruction of the Lists 456
B. *Oppidum liberum* 'Aves' 467

I. History of Research

Two decades have passed since the publication of Leo Teutsch's classic study of the towns and cities of North Africa under the Roman Republic.[1] His systematic and probing re-examination of orthodox interpretations of the status and history of African municipalities in their infancy, based on a critical rereading of the sources, marks a watershed in our understanding of Republican Africa. By carefully separating the facts from a tangle of modern hypotheses, Teutsch demolished ideas that had become hallowed by long acceptance.[2] No mere iconoclast, however, he established a basis for renewed

---

* I would like to thank C. R. Whittaker (Churchill College, Cambridge) for reading an earlier draft of this article and for making several valuable comments.

[1] L. Teutsch, *Das römische Städtewesen in Nordafrika in der Zeit von C. Gracchus bis zum Tode des Kaisers Augustus*, Berlin W. de Gruyter, 1962 (hencefort *Städtewesen*), published posthumously.

[2] Cf. his paper, "Gab es Doppelgemeinden im römischen Afrika?" *RIDA* 8 (1961) 281–356 which demolished the idea of the so-called 'double-communities', a concept which up to that time

inquiry into the early history of African municipal development and refocussed attention on the main problem confronting any new interpretation, namely, the question of the sources themselves. In particular he drew attention to the uncertainty surrounding our principal source, the Elder Pliny's geography of Africa (*Historia naturalis*, V. 1-30). He proffered a solution that clarified the main difficulties, but no consensus emerged in his favour. His death in an air crash in Turkey in 1962 not only robbed Roman history of an exacting and original scholar, but also cut short any possible *risposte* Teutsch could have made to his critics.

If it is true that *Quellenforschung* is unable to provide final answers to most of our historical problems, nevertheless, in the case of Pliny's geography a solution is critical to an understanding of the policies of the Roman state in North Africa in the late Republic. This is so because Pliny's information is almost the sole basis upon which are founded all modern analyses of the statuses of the various urban and ethnic communities that made up Rome's African *provincia*. Though doubts have been expressed concerning Teutsch's views, I believe that thorough re-examination of Pliny's text confirms his contention of an earlier date for Pliny's sources (that is, Caesarean rather than Augustan) and, on the whole, substantiates his other conclusions drawn from the premise of an earlier date. Nor is the question of the source material in Pliny and the formal community statuses of African towns an arid fine point of 'constitutional' government. Answers to this question reveal some rather significant trends in official Roman attitudes to the treatment of indigenous towns and peoples, attitudes shaped in the process of the extension of Roman political hegemony over provincial regions. The tempo and depth of political domination as well as the related administrative procedures, including the elements of tribute and taxation, are revealed in greater detail.

Apart from scanty epigraphical data, there are few valuable sources on the official statuses accorded towns in Africa generally – an observation that is particularly true of Africa in the late Republic. In fact, our sole literary source of any merit on African municipalities in the age of Caesar and Augustus is the information provided by the Elder Pliny in the fifth book of his Natural History. The core of Pliny's data is confined to a brief two-chapter survey that he appended to the main body of his African geography (*NH*, V, 29-30). This 'appendix' (as we shall refer to it henceforth) is obviously a copy of an 'official' list, reduced, as it is, to a simple catalogue of towns and their various statuses. Despite its great importance, or perhaps because of it, the 'official' document copied by Pliny has created more problems of exegesis than it has provided answers to conundrums it ought to have solved. The basic problem that has

had been a commonly accepted part of analysis of North African municipalities; see, for example, T. R. S. Broughton, *The Romanization of Africa Proconsularis*, Baltimore, Johns Hopkins Press, 1929, 48-49 (henceforth, *Romanization*).

barred confident use of the information in it is the question of the source Pliny used in compiling the appendix.[3] Until the problem of the date and nature of the source has been plainly resolved, the data contained in the lists cannot be used accurately, and many aspects of the early history of African municipal development will remain clouded in uncertainty.

In spite of more than a century of detailed research on the sources of Pliny's geography, and on this problem in particular, no decisive answer has yet emerged that commands general acceptance. The principal cause of the confusion is not inherent in the Plinian account. It is due to a simple lack of consistent critical inquiry and to the resigned acceptance of received ideas too cherished to be relinquished easily. Most of the initial answers to our inquiry, then, lie in a review of the historiography of the question itself. It is an object lesson in how yesterday's hypotheses became today's facts. In the formative article published on the question in 1877, Detlev Detlefsen suggested that the source of the crucial chapters in Book Five of the *Historia naturalis* relating to the status of African cities was a *formula provinciarum* which, he contended, had been composed, or at least included, as part of the 'World Map' of Agrippa. Therefore the *formula*, and also the relevant part of the fifth book of Pliny's geography, could be dated to the latter part of the reign of Augustus.[4] Otto Cuntz, in a dissertation published a decade later (1888), revised this assessment slightly by advancing arguments to demonstrate that the *formula* had been composed after 25 B.C. but before 12 B.C., the year of Agrippa's death. Cuntz also contended that the provincial survey was derived from an

---

[3] A few passages from one of the more recent synoptic works to appear on the African municipalities are sufficient to demonstrate the point; the author seems to despair of a solution.

Tant que ce problème des sources de Pline au livre V de *l'Histoire Naturelle* ne sera pas résolu, toutes les théories imprudemment échafaudées sur l'interprétation des données pliniennes risquent de s'effondrer.

and ...

... nous estimons le problème des sources de Pline au Ve livre de son *Histoire Naturelle* non résolu sinon insolvable ... Y a-t-il une source unique, ou des sources d'époque différente ... comme a tenté de le montrer L. Teutsch? On ne peut de toute façon l'utiliser sans d'infinies précautions.

J. Gascou, *La politique municipale romaine en Afrique proconsulaire de Trajan à Septime-Sévère*, Rome, B. E. F. A. R., 1972, 18 and 20, no. 1 (hereafter, *Politique municipale*). Poinssot reports that Quoniam provided him with persuasive, but as yet unpublished, arguments that the lists must be dated to just after Caesar's death and that they may even have been included in the dictator's papers; see C. Poinssot, "*Immunitas Perticae Carthaginiensium*", *CRAI* (1962) 55–76, at p. 67.

[4] D. Detlefsen, "Varro, Agrippa und Augustus als Quellenschriftsteller des Plinius", (in) *Commentationes philologas in honorem Theodori Mommseni scripserunt amici*, Berlin, Weidmann, 1877, 23ff. The first scholar to connect the administrative survey in Pliny's geography with Agrippa's map was F. Ritschl, "Die Vermessung des römischen Reiches unter Augustus, die Weltkarte des Agrippa und die Cosmographie des sogenannten Aethicius (Iulius Honorius)", *RhM* I (1842) 481–523.

official document included in the commentary accompanying the Map of Agrippa, but conceded that the list also contained some additions drawn from emendations made between 12 B.C. and 7 B.C., when Augustus finally published the map.[5] In a thesis on the cities of Roman Africa published in 1904, Wilhelm Barthel accepted that the source was an administrative list (*ein Verwaltungsbericht*) of Augustan date. Along with Kornemann, however, he noted some difficulties in accepting this solution, namely, the apparent incompleteness of the appendix recorded in Pliny. By the time Barthel was writing, the epigraphical evidence collected in the *Corpus Inscriptionum Latinarum* had appeared (evidence not easily accessible to earlier researchers) and it had become clear that certain colonies in Africa bearing the epithet 'Iulia' were missing from Pliny's African survey. Barthel sought to explain the discrepancy by claiming that the lists included only those towns that had been affected by some administrative change made personally by Augustus.[6] Why this should be so Barthel did not explain, but it is interesting to note that already at this early date the prevailing tendency among scholars was to retain the original hypothesis made by Detlefsen even if it was untenable, and to

---

[5] O. Cuntz, *De Augusto Plinii geographicorum auctore*, Diss., Bonn, 1888, 40–45; Cuntz later repeated much the same arguments in, "Agrippa und Augustus als Quellenschriftsteller des Plinius in den geographischen Büchern der *Naturalis Historia*", *Neue Jahrbücher für Philologie und Pädagogik: Jahrbuch für klassische Philologie* 17 (1890) 475 – 527. Cuntz's theory, which is at the root of all modern opinions on the subject, was simply founded on false premises and lack of good evidence. He had very inaccurate ideas about town status, and no epigraphic data beyond Vol. I of the *Corpus*. He dated the source after 36 B.C. (because of the status of Utica) and after 25 B.C. (because Numidia is apparently part of Africa), but before the reign of Tiberius because of the status of Hippo Regius. He held (p. 48) that the document dated to 8 B.C. when Augustus was censor, that it was a list prepared for census purposes, and that it was part of the *breviarium imperii* left by Augustus for Tiberius in A. D. 14. See J. J. Tierney, "The Map of Agrippa", *PRIA* 63, Sect. C, 4 (1963) 151–66 for one of the clearest explanations of the date, mode of composition, and purpose of the map. It was to be placed on the wall of the Porticus Vipsaniae which was still unfinished in 7 B.C. (Dio 55.8.4), but probably completed soon after this date. Detlefsen, in his *Ursprung, Einrichtung und Bedeutung der Erdkarte Agrippas* (Berlin, Weidmannsche Buchhandlung, 1906; Quellen und Forschungen zur alten Geschichte und Geographie, Hrsg. von W. Sieglin, Heft 13), held that there never existed a set of *commentarii* separate from the map itself, but rather that all information derived 'from Agrippa' actually came directly from the map. In his *Untersuchungen zu den geographischen Büchern des Plinius, I: Weltkarte des M. Agrippa*, Glückstadt, 1884 (Abhandlung zum Jahresbericht des Glückstadter Gymnasiums, 1884, Progr. nr. 254) he also showed that two later works, a *Demensuratio provinciarum* and the *Divisio orbis terrae* were both derived from a common source that described the map itself.

[6] W. Barthel, *Zur Geschichte der römischen Städte in Africa*, Diss., Greifswald, Druck von J. Abel, 1904, 27–37, esp. 33f. Barthel based his conclusion, in part, on Pliny's treatment of the towns and cities in *Italy* (*NH*, III, 6.46) though there is no reason to suppose that the Italian evidence was drawn from the same document as the African. He sought to explain the resulting conflicts in his theory by resorting to the concept of the 'double community' (pp. 20, 32) – accepted by Broughton, *Romanization*, 53.

attempt to revise or re-order the theory to accommodate new evidence that seemed to contradict its basic propositions.

Detlefsen himself returned to the problem in 1908 with a thorough investigation of all the work that had been done up to that time. He reaffirmed his belief that Pliny's source was a *formula provinciarum* included as part of Agrippa's Map. His analysis of similar provincial administrative surveys contained in the Natural History (which he believed to be derived from the same common source) led him to claim that the contents of the hypothetical *formula* reflected a situation towards the end of Augustus' reign. He therefore thought that the *formula* must date to some time *after* the completion of the Map of Agrippa by Augustus, that is, after 7 B.C., but sometime before Augustus' death in A. D. 14.[7] Until Teutsch tackled the problematic document in 1962, this final assessment by Detlefsen remained orthodoxy on the subject. Subsequent research on the African municipalities tended to accept that further investigation would not produce any new insight into the sources of the Plinian *Verwaltungsbericht*. The idea became fixed that Pliny's source for chapters twenty-nine and thirty of Book Five was an official list of provincial communities prepared in the latter part of Augustus' reign. Despite minor modifications depending on the individual scholar's viewpoint, this basic conclusion was repeated from work to work and gradually became entrenched as dogma. The obvious difficulties in interpreting the lists that kept recurring as a result of accepting a late Augustan date seemed neither to deter its continued use nor to raise doubts about the validity and basis of the original hypothesis.[8]

[7] His survey was contained in two articles: D. Detlefsen, *Die Geographie Afrikas bei Plinius und Mela und ihre Quellen*, and *Die formula provinciarum: eine Hauptquelle des Plinius*, pp. 1–62 and 63–104 respectively of Heft XIV in *Quellen und Forschungen zur alten Geschichte und Geographie* (hrsg. von W. Sieglin), Berlin, Weidmannsche Buchhandlung, 1908; see esp. p. 30f. and 88f.

[8] To list but some of those who accepted and repeated the findings of earlier research: E. Kornemann, "Die caesarische Kolonie Karthago und die Einführung römischer Gemeindeordnung in Africa", *Philologus* 60 (1901) 402-26 accepted Cuntz's dating, "Das Resultat der Thätigkeit beider liegt vor in der von Plinius ausgeschriebenen Reichsstatistik, die nach dem vortrefflichen Untersuchungen von Cuntz für Africa von Agrippa und zwar zwischen 729/25 und 742/12 hergestellt worden ist"; S. Gsell, *Histoire ancienne de l'Afrique du Nord* (hereafter *HAAN*), 8, Paris, Hachette, 1928, 159, 164, 168, 171, 198 and 201, and vol. 7 (1928) 40, no. 5 accepts Detlefsen's conclusions and frequently refers to, ". . . un document administratif du règne d'Auguste, copié par Pline l'Ancien"; Broughton, *Romanization*, 49, no. 9 also accepts Detlefsen's conclusions when he states that Pliny's information derives from a *periplous* with insertions and "a *formula Provinciae Africae* giving in some form the legal status of various African towns. Both sources are of Augustan date, and appear, unlike the account of Mauretania, to have been uncorrected by later information"; see p. 52f. where he finds refuge in "Pliny's known inexactitude elsewhere." L. Poinssot, "Macomades-Iunci", *MSAF* 81 (1944) 133-69, p. 130f. states that it came from a *formula provinciae* dating between 27-20 B.C., R. Chevallier, *MEFR* 69 (1958) 91 states, "Pline, qui utilise une statistique officielle de l'époque d'Auguste . . ."; and P.

But the hard question must be posed. What was the factual basis of the hypothesis first advanced by Detlefsen and Cuntz? The basic assumption made by these early analysts is that the source of the 'appendix' must be one of those mentioned by Pliny himself in the introduction to the *Historia naturalis*, and that of all the authors mentioned by him Agrippa and Varro were the most likely choices.[9] Agrippa seemed the logical alternative as the source of the 'appendix'; his map provided the ideal context for the sort of information contained in the survey. It is true, of course, that Varro and Agrippa were most probably the authorities that were personally consulted by Pliny in the composition of his work, and that Varro is excluded as the likely source of the 'appendix' because of his early date. But it is hardly necessary that the material contained in either of these authors had a *terminus post quem* with the publication of their respective works, or that the information in Agrippa was an accurate reflection of the contemporary situation in Africa between 7 B.C. and A.D. 14. Hence the fundamental supposition made by Detlefsen and Cuntz was very weak and, further, was never put to the test by subsequent researchers.

The young German historian Leo Teutsch, after a careful analysis of the Plinian lists on Africa, came to the conclusion that the source was of an earlier date than had hitherto been supposed. He based his case primarily on one of the *oppida libera* mentioned in chapter thirty of the survey, a town called *Vagense aliud* in the list in order to distinguish it from another centre of the same name in the Bagradas river valley.[10] According to Teutsch this town should be identified with the Vaga that was destroyed by the forces of the African king Juba I in 46 B.C.[11] Since it appears in the list of *oppida libera*, he argued that the entire list of free cities (and therefore probably that of the *oppida civium Romanorum* as well) probably dated to some time *before* the

---

Romanelli, "Note storico-geografiche relative all'Africa al tempo di Augusto, II: La statistica Pliniana delle città Africane e la sua interpretazione", *RAL*, ser. 8 (1950) 481–89, who accepts Barthel's conclusions- a position that he repeats in his *Storia delle Province Romane dell'Africa*, Rome, "L'Erma" di Bretschneider, 1959 (henceforth, *Storia*) esp. 189, no. 1, "... un documento pure dell'età di Augusto ma piu tardo della carta di Agrippa..." (i. e., Detlefsen's argument), and p. 208, "... noi abbiamo la trascrizione di un documento amministrativo dell tempo di Augusto, nel quale dovevano essere annotati i provvedimenti presi dall' imperatore nei riguardi dello stato delle città della provincia sotto l'aspetto amministrativo". (i. e., Barthel). More recently, see P. A. Brunt, *Italian Manpower, 225 B. C. - A. D. 14*, Oxford, Clarendon Press, 1971, append. no. 13, "Pliny on Africa", 581–83.

[9] See pp. 17–18 of the Teubner edition, *C. Plinius Secundus, Naturalis Historia*, vol. 1, ed. L. Ian and C. Mayhoff, Leipzig, Teubner, 1967 – the text I have used throughout.

[10] Teutsch, *Städtewesen*, 34–37; see the riposte by Gascou, *Politique municipale*, 17, no. 5. See no. 13 in the list of *oppida civium Romanorum* and no. 16 in the list of the *oppida libera* in Appendix A.

[11] On its destruction by Caesar see *Bell. Afr.*. 74; Strabo 17.3.12; Teutsch, *Städtewesen*, 35 – 42 locates the site of the latter Vaga just to the southeast of modern Jammal.

destruction of Vaga in late 46 B.C.[12] He further maintained that the compiler of the lists was neither Agrippa nor any other Augustan source, but an ". . .unbekannter, der über die schon vor Caesar's Krieg in Afrika bestehenden Städte des römischen Afrika schrieb."[13] The redating of the Plinian lists enabled Teutsch to make better sense of the numerous vexatious problems that had been created artificially by an Augustan dating, notably the 'problem' of the *oppida civium Romanorum*. Nevertheless, Teutsch's early dating of the lists and, following on that, his solutions of related problems came under heavy criticism. The only substantial objection to his thesis seems to be the lack of uncontrovertable evidence that would clinch the identification of the *Vagense aliud* mentioned by Pliny with the site destroyed by Juba I in 46.[14] In spite of the transparent feebleness of the whole counter-attack (based on this one case alone, rather than Teutsch's whole argument) the forces of reaction seem to have won the day in defence of a nineteenth century interpretation of the Augustan date and a rejection of Teutsch's theory.

I believe that a closer re-examination of the *whole* of Book Five of the *Historia naturalis* and a careful structural breakdown of the text, along with a consideration of the known history of the era, will show that Teutsch is right. The investigation will reveal that the example of *Vagense aliud* is not the only discrepancy in the orthodox interpretation, but that the rot runs much deeper — in fact, through the whole nineteenth century edifice of exegesis. This is the sort of detailed investigation that Teutsch never had the opportunity to perform in his own defence and, in broad terms, it justifies his earlier date and most of his conclusions.

---

[12] Teutsch, *Städtewesen*, 37, "Hiernach läßt sich das Alter der von Plinius bei der Abfassung seiner Liste der *oppida libera* benutzten Quelle, — wahrscheinlich sogar einer älteren Quelle, die der des Plinius zugrunde lag, bestimmen. Der *terminus ante quem* für die Entstehung dieser Urquelle dürfte demnach das Jahr 46 v. Chr. sein."

[13] Teutsch, *Städtewesen*, 93; cf. L. Foucher, *CT* 8 (1960) 11–17.

[14] See H. H. Abdul-Wahab, "Le 'Vaga' du *Bellum Africanum*", *CT* 8 (1960) 19–23 on the profusion of 'Vagas' in Tunisia. This type of criticism was first voiced by F. Vittinghoff, "Zur vorcaesarischen Siedlungs- und Städtepolitik in Nordafrika: Bemerkungen zu den 'Städtelisten' des Plinius (n. h. V)", (in) *Corolla Memoriae Erich Swoboda Dedicata* (Römische Forschungen in Niederösterreich, Bd. V), Graz-Köln, Böhlau (1966) 225–33, esp. p. 230–32; L. Foucher, "La localisation de la ville de *Vaga* mentionée dans le *Bellum Africum*", (in) *Mélanges d'archéologie et d'histoire offerts à A. Piganiol*, ed. R. Chevallier, Paris, S. E. V. P. E. N. (1966) vol 2, 1205–10 has the same argument, but he also admits that the town might have been reconstructed after the war. The latter argument, though not necessary, is plausible and is emphasized by Gascou, *Politique municipale*, 17, no. 5.

II. The Text and its Composition

Before turning to a consideration of the date and source of the Plinian 'appendix', it seems best for the sake of context to review briefly the salient passages from Book Five relating to town status in Africa (see Append. A). To facilitate the interpretation of the two crucial chapters, we must consider the sources of information and methods of composition used by Pliny in the first twenty-eight chapters of Book Five. In short, the geography of Africa as written by Pliny falls into the same tradition as the writing of much 'history' in antiquity, as well as its main components, geography and ethnography. With very disparate and fragmented sources at their disposal most ancient historians had to make a selection of 'topics' and to construct an artificial whole out of them. The *logos*-style construction of ancient historians and its highly structured matrix have not yet been investigated in the detail they merit, but Pliny's geography of Africa is, to put it unkindly, a classic example of the cruder 'scissors-and-paste' method typical of the less skilled and subtle schools of history. Or, as Sallman has expressed it in more favourable terms, Pliny's

Chart 1: *Detlefsen's Identification of the Sources for Pliny's Geography of Africa* (Book V, of the *Historia Naturalis*)[*]

Chapter	Source
1	Varro
2−4	A *periplous* with additions from a *formula provinciarum* and earlier sources
4	Cornelius Nepos
5	A *periplous* with additions from a *formula provinciarum*
6−7	*Celebrati auctores* mentioned by Pliny in the introduction
8	Hanno
9−10	Polybios with additions from Agrippa
11−13	Contemporary information culled by Pliny
14−15	Suetonius Paulinus
16	Juba
17−21	*Periplous* with additions from a *formula provinciarum*
21	Agrippa
22−28	Varro and a *periplous* with additions from Polybios
26	Agrippa and an account left by Cornelius Balbus
28	Callimachus
29−30	A *formula provinciae Africae*

[*] Detlefsen (1908) 59−60, cf. no. 7.

geography exhibits a *Mosaikstil* type of composition. Pliny, in short, resorted to excerpting whole passages *en bloc* from several sources. He then rewrote and knit them together into a rather loosely joined whole.[15] The result is a haphazard collection of facts that can only be useful to the modern historian if he is able to isolate the 'bloc' in which each statement or discrete fact is embedded, and to identify the source behind each separate statement.

By correlating the sources mentioned by Pliny in the course of his narrative with the sources listed in the introduction to Book Five, Detlefsen was able to identify most of the authorities used by Pliny in the writing of his geography of Africa. His conclusions are summarized in Chart I. Not all these sources need concern us here, since a check of the distribution of the cities in the outline of Pliny's geography shows that his information on the statuses of African towns is concentrated in certain sections (*i. e.*, chapters 2, 5, 19–21, 22–25 and 27). Detlefsen specifies a *periplous* as the main source for these chapters. The sole exception seems to be the province of Mauretania Tingitana (the extreme northwestern sector of modern day Morocco) in which case Pliny appears to have had a near contemporary source on inland urban centres, perhaps a *formula provinciae*.[16] But the *periplous* must be of a rather earlier date (*i. e.*, pre-Claudian) since his knowledge of hinterland towns of mid-first century Mauretania is already defective. Pliny is able to give the correct status for Claudian foundations along the coast, but is ignorant of contemporary statuses for inland centres. For example, he does not know of the existence of a *municipium* at Volubilis, but merely lists the city as an *oppidum*.[17]

Pliny's dependence on the *periplous* for town and city status explains why he is well informed on all Vespasian's municipal grants and settlements in the

[15] On Pliny's methods see K. G. Sallman, *Die Geographie des älteren Plinius in ihrem Verhältnis zu Varro: Versuch einer Quellenanalyse* (in) *Untersuchungen zur antiken Literatur und Geschichte*, hrsg. von H. Dörrie & P. Moraux, Bd. 11, Berlin (1971) 27–34; Mommsen rightly saw this a century earlier when he called Pliny a 'liederlichen Compilator' (*Römische Staatsrecht*³, III, 1, 684).

[16] For Babba and Banasa see Pliny, *NH*, 5.5: "Ab Lixo X̄L̄ in mediterraneo altera Augusti colonia est Babba, Iulia Campestris appellata, et tertia Banasa L̄X̄X̄V̄ p., Valentia cognominata." This *formula* must be rather early in date since the colony of Zulil (*NH*, 5.2: "Ab eo X̄X̄V̄ in ora oceani colonia Augusti Iulia Constantia Zulil, regum dicioni exempta et iura in Baeticam petere iussa.") is spoken of as exempt from the jurisdiction of the African king, which must be a situation obtaining only before the end of the reign of Ptolemy in A. D. 40 (cf. Gsell, *HAAN* 8 (1929) 201f.).

[17] Cf. Pliny, *NH*, 5.2: "Oppida fuere Lissa et Cottae ultra columnas Herculis, nunc est Tingi, quondam ab Antaeo conditum, postea a Claudio Caesare, cum coloniam faceret, appellatum Traducta Iulia ... Ab ea X̄X̄X̄V̄ colonia a Claudio Caesare facta Lixos ..."; *NH*, 5.20: "Promunturium Apollinis oppidumque ibi celeberrimum Caesarea, ante vocitatum Iol, Iubae regia a Divo Claudio coloniae iure donata; eiusdem iussu deductis veteranis Oppidum Novum et Latio dato Tipasa ... Rusucurium civitate honoratum a Claudio ..."; on Volubilis (*NH*, 5.5) we read, "Ab ea X̄X̄X̄V̄ Volubilis oppidum ...", whereas by the time of Claudius it had become a *municipium* (see *ILMar.* 116).

coastal centres of the Mauretanias but is ignorant of any of his municipal grants to towns in the interior of Numidia.[18] There is another observable deduction that can be made from Pliny's state of knowledge: the *periplous* only covered the coastal towns of the Mauretanias and not any centres to the east of these provinces. Pliny has nothing of note to say about the coastal cities of Numidia (*i. e.*, the Cirtan Federation or western Proconsularis).[19] His actual knowledge of coastal city statuses to the east of the frontier of Mauretania (the Wed al-Kabir) clearly shows that he no longer has the *periplous* at his disposal and must now rely on whatever information he can glean from the official lists (our 'appendix') that he appended to the end of his geography. He must plunder the lists to flesh out his account of the regions of western Proconsularis.[20]

We may sum up the argument thus far. Insofar as city status is concerned, the main text of Pliny's African geography (*NH*, V, 1-28) depended on the

[18] Pliny does know of Icosium, "... itemque a Vespasiano imperatore eodem munere donatum Icosium" (*NH*, 5.20) but does not even mention the Flavian colonies at Ammaedara (mod. Haîdra, C. 308, cf. 302) or Madauros (mod. M'daûrûsh, *ILAlg.* I, 2152). Flavian *municipia* may be found at Bulla Regia (mod. Hammâm Darrajii, *ILAfr.* 458; *AE* 1964: 177; cf. P. Quoniam, *Karthago* 11 (1961-62) 5f.), Mascula (mod. Khenshela, C. 1/222, 22302, very questionable), Sufetula (mod. Sbeïtla, *ILAfr.* 136; C. 23222-25), and Cillium (mod. Kassrin, based on the large number of Flavii amongst the citizenry: C. 23207; L. Poinssot, *BCTH* (1934) xiii f.; Romanelli, *Storia*, 294; Broughton, *Romanization*, 101f.). On all these see T. Kotula, "A propos d'une inscription reconstituée de *Bulla Regia* (Hammam-Darradji). Quelques municipes 'mystérieux' de l'Afrique proconsulaire", *MEFR* 79.1 (1967) 207–20. He doubts the case of Cillium since like nearby Thelepte most of its citizens are enrolled in *tribu Papiria*; hence he prefers Trajan as the benefactor. All these municipalities have been 'mystérieux' to modern scholars simply because Pliny does not mention them (as he does Icosium on the coast) and we depend on epigraphic data alone to reconstruct their civic history.

[19] That is to say, Chullu, Rusicade, Hippo Regius and Thabraca are all merely noted as *oppida* (Pliny, *NH*, 5.22) without further comment about their status. Exactly the opposite is true of the Mauretanias where virtually every town status is specified. Out of the twenty-two coastal sites mentioned in the Mauretanias, only three are left uncommented (Sala, *NH*, 5.5; Russadir, 5.9, 19, and Siga, 5.19), but this is not surprising since all of them were still peregrine *civitates* at the time Pliny was writing.

[20] A survey of the major coastal sites to the east of the River Amsaga in his own time would have included the following:
1. Chullu – an Augustan colony (*C.* 6710-11; 6958, 7094-98; 7123, 7125, 8210).
2. Rusicade – an Augustan colony (*C.* 6710-11, 7124, 7969).
3. Hippo Regius – probably an Augustan *municipium*, and a later Flavian colony (*AE* 1958: 141-42; 276; 1960: 104; cf. *II Alg.* I, 109; all of very difficult interpretation, see Gascou, *Politique municipale*, 35 and Kotula (1967) 217, with Teutsch, *Städtewesen*, 163-64 and Vittinghoff (1966) 115).
4. Thabraca – an Augustan colony (*ILAlg.* I, 109 = *ILS* 59/a; cf. *AE* 1959: 77; Teutsch, *Städtewesen*, 162-63; Guey & Pernette, *Karthago* 9 (1958) 79-88 and nos.; Gascou, *Politique municipale*, 23-24).
5. Hippo Diarrhytus – either a Caesarean colony (Gsell, *HAAN* 8 (1929) 179-80) or Augustan (Teutsch, *Städtewesen*, 93, 112-14, 160-62; and Gascou, *Politique municipale*, 21, 24; both based on *C.* 24317, cf. 1206, 14333).

following sources. First, for the Mauretanias he used a *periplous* as his basic source, but he was able to update it occasionally with more current information. Even in this case, however, he was at the mercy of his sources: some cities are assigned a correct contemporary status, while others are wildly anachronistic. Secondly, for regions *east* of the Mauretanias Pliny apparently had *no source other than the administrative survey appended to the end of his geography of Africa*. Again, he was at the mercy of this latter source alone, and he excerpted from it freely to fill out his account of the geography of Proconsularis but made no attempt to update the information. The latter point is most important to note. There is not the slightest whit of evidence to show that Pliny was ever concerned with presenting a coherent contemporary analysis in his geography. He did not compare one source with another in order to correct conflicting reports, nor did he update all his information. He merely collated everything he had at his disposal pell-mell; it is our task to disentangle the strands of his sources. Lastly, for all regions east of the Amsaga River (the western border of the Cirtan federation, called the Ampsaga by Pliny) it is clear that the administrative 'appendix' was his *only source* for city statuses, and hence the importance of determining its date and purpose. But equally, since he has drawn upon the 'appendix' to compose the main body of his geography, we have the opportunity to reconstruct the lists as they originally appeared, a task which, of all modern historians, only Teutsch attempted.

We may now turn to the administrative document itself, as contained in chapters twenty-nine and thirty of Book Five. After having completed his account of the geography of Africa (*NH*, V, 1–28) Pliny appended to it an official survey containing references to various town statuses (principally *coloniae, oppida libera*, and *oppida civium Romanorum*) and related information pertaining to various land-tax administrative units important to the Roman government, including *nationes* or 'tribes'. Unlike his geography of Africa as a whole, however, the survey only covers the area between the River Amsaga (present day Wed al-Kabir) and the so-called *Arae Philaenorum* (*NH*, V, 29–30). These two points were respectively the eastern and western termini of the greater Roman province in Africa, including the Cirtan Federation.[21] The reason why Pliny chose to insert the administrative document at this point in his narrative, before continuing the geography of Africa further to the east

---

Pliny knows of the status of none of these cities. He does not even refer to Hippo Regius and Hippo Diarrhytus, and merely calls Chullu and Rusicade *oppida*, and Thabraca an *oppidum civium Romanorum*.

[21] The survey covered the regions between the Amsaga and the Arae Philaenorum, as Pliny himself states (*NH*, 5.29), but as Gsell notes (*HAAN* 8 (1929) 164, no. 2), the coastal measurement of the old province of Africa (580 miles = 858 km) would only cover the range between the Amsaga and the Gulf of Gabès.

(*i. e.*, to include Cyrenaica) is obvious. The document was already available to him intact and rather than break it down and use its information piecemeal (which he could not do in any event because of his ignorance concerning most of its contents) he decided to include the bulk of the document *en bloc* as an appendix to the main body of his narrative. Of course, Pliny did have the entire document before himself during the 'composition' of his geography and even a cursory glance reveals that he drew on it occasionally to supplement his narrative, especially for information pertaining to the few important urban centres in Africa known to him from other sources. When he appended the document, therefore, Pliny did at least take the trouble *to delete from it the few towns and cities he had already mentioned in his main narrative*. Thus, whereas the text of the 'appendix' states that there are fifteen *oppida civium Romanorum*, only thirteen are actually named since Pliny has deleted Thabraca and Utica which he had excerpted and placed in the main account (at chaps. 22 and 23). The same observation is also true of the thirty declared *oppida libera* in the 'appendix'. Pliny names eighteen; the other twelve are easily retrieved from the main text once Pliny's method of composition has been recognized. Keeping these observations in mind, and remembering that the original document included only towns between the Amsaga River and the 'Altars of the Philaeni', it is possible to reconstruct the lists as they originally stood (see Append. A).

Even a superficial examination of the names of the towns that Pliny excerpted from the lists will show that they are cities that were commonly known at the time, whereas those he left untouched are usually obscure centres, in all likelihood unknown to Pliny as many of them are still unknown to us. Rather than discard this unused information Pliny decided to retain what remained of the lists as an 'appendix' to his main account, a procedure that explains both the apparent incompleteness of the lists as they now stand and the rationale behind their inclusion. The implications of this preliminary analysis of Pliny's composition of the geography and the 'appendix' for the reliability of his writings as a coherent whole are fairly harsh. The author was only as accurate as each fragment of source material he inserted into the composition. Although knowledge commonly available to him at the time he was writing flatly contradicted much of what he put into the geography, there is no indication that this caused him to hesitate to include anachronistic materials in one great *potpourri*. The questions can now be posed: what was the original administrative document, what were its official connections, and what date and purpose can be ascribed to its composition?

III. Historical Context of the Official Document

Contrary to now common belief, the internal evidence of the official lists clearly points to a pre-Augustan date. This conclusion is confirmed by a detailed examination of the known historical context of early municipal development in Africa. On balance, the whole argument indicates a date between 46 and 44 B. C.

III.1. Colonial Settlements of Caesar and Augustus. The Problem of Africa vetus and Africa nova

In his main narrative (*HN*, V, 1–28) the Elder Pliny is clearly aware of the existence of Augustan colonies in Africa.[22] Yet the lists in the appendix do *not* recognize any of Augustus' settlements in *Africa proconsularis*. A few examples will suffice. It is well known that Simitthus (mod. Shamtū) was an Augustan colony, and yet the lists cite it merely as an *oppidum civium Romanorum*.[23] Thabraca is another Augustan colony listed merely as an *oppidum civium Romanorum*.[24] *It is most improbable, therefore, that these lists could have been composed in the latter part of Augustus' reign if the compiler did not even know of the existence of a single Augustan colonial settlement in Africa.* And if the identification of Absuritanum with Assuras is correct, then there is yet another example of an Augustan colony of which the lists are ignorant.[25] But there is more evidence. An indication of an even earlier *terminus ante quem* for the list is provided by the list of *oppida libera*. The towns of Clupea and Curubis were almost certainly granted colonial status by Caesar, and yet both are still listed merely as free towns.[26] Carpis is another Caesarean colony in the Cap Bon Peninsula that is simply labelled an *oppidum* by Pliny.[27] There are at least two other towns that have a reasonable claim to be Caesarean colonial foundations,

---

[22] Namely Zulil (*NH*, 5.22), Babba (5.5), Cartenna, Rusguniae, Rusazus and Saldae (5.20), and Sicca, east of the Amsaga (5.22).

[23] Simitthus (mod. Shamtû, Fr. Chemtou): *C.* 14612 = *ILS* 6823: Co[l(onia)] I[u]l(ia) / Aug(usta) Num[id]ica [Si]m[i]thensium; as an *oppidum civium Romanorum*, see Append. A, no. 6.

[24] Thabraca (mod. Tabarqa): *ILAlg.* I, 109 = *ILS* 5976a (with further references in no. 20.4 above): Col(onia) V. P. Iul(ia) Thabr/acenorum; cf. Mallon, *Libyca* (Arch.-épigr.) 3 (1955) 315f.; as an *oppidum civium Romanorum* see Append. A, no. 14.

[25] Assuras (mod. Zanfûr): *C.* 1798: Col(onia) Iul(ia) Assuras, and *AE* 1913: 40: [Coloniae] / Iuliae Assuritanae; cf. Teutsch, *Städtewesen*, 31, 175–76; as an *oppidum civium Romanorum* see Append. A, no. 1.

[26] Clupea (mod. Kelibia): *C.* X, 6104 = *ILS* 1945; Teutsch, *Städtewesen*, 112. Curubis (mod. Korba): *C.* 980: Col(onia) Iul(ia) Curubis; *C.* 977: C(aio) Caesare imp(eratore) co(n)s(ule) II[ii] /L. Pomponius L(ucii) l(ibertus) Malc[hio] / duovir (quinquennalis?) / murum oppidi totum ex saxo quadrato aedific(andum) coer(avit); cf. *C.* 978 (21 B.C.) and 24100.

[27] Carpis (mod. al-Mraïssa): *C.* 25417 = *ILS* 6782: Col(onia) Iulia Carpitana; of Octavian (?), see Teutsch, *Städtewesen*, 160, or of Caesar (?), see *ibid.*, 113; cf. *C.* 24106 = *ILS* 9367.

The Elder Pliny's African Geography 437

namely Thysdrus and Neapolis, but they too appear only as *oppida libera* in the appendix.[28] If only Clupea and Curubis are accepted, however, the point is made. Once again, *the compiler is ignorant of important Caesarean grants of colonial status in Africa and so one has good reason to suspect that the lists must date to some time before 44 B.C.* Closer analysis of the rest of the appendix provides further clues to date and composition that confirm this suspicion. Before advancing to this analysis, however, let us consider one further telling point.

In his survey of the region of Byzacium (c. 24 *fin.* to 25) that is, the southern regions of Africa province, Pliny depends on two sources: 1) the Map of Agrippa for the distances in Roman miles, and 2) the 'appendix' for the statuses of the towns and cities. Having listed numerous *oppida libera* in the region (*hic oppida libera Leptis . . . Sabrata*) Pliny completes the chapter by summarizing the status of the *provincial* administration in a passage that is also taken from the 'appendix' (probably from the end of it, after the list of *nationes*). He states (25 *fin.*):

Ea pars, quam Africam appellavimus, dividitur in duas provincias, veterem et novam, discretas fossa inter Africanum sequentem et reges Thenas usque perducta...

Now it is true that the internal division of *Africa proconsularis* into *vetus* and *nova* appears to have remained in force for some time; a *fossa* marked some important division *within* the province of Africa at least until Flavian times and probably well beyond.[29] Pliny's statement, however, is more explicit than any simple reference to an internal administrative division. The passage clearly states that the *region* (*not* the *province*) of Africa *is* divided (*n. b.* the present tense) into two *provinces* (*Africa vetus* and *Africa nova*). This situation certainly did not exist at the time Pliny was writing. In fact, the description of the administrative situation in Africa in the passage above could only refer to a

---

[28] Neapolis (mod. Nabûl): C. 968: Col(onia) Iul(ia) Neapolis, cf. Teutsch, *Städtewesen*, 88; Gsell, *HAAN* 8 (1929) 178; Vittinghoff, *Bürgerrechtspolitik*, 82, and Gascou, *Politique municipale*, 21. Thysdrus: C. 51 = *ILS* 5777; C. 2343, 2406, 22895, 22845; *ILTun.* 111; and *AE* 1947: 138. Gascou *Politique municipale*, 192–94 believes a Caesarean colony, but cf. the inscription from Arles: "... o[riundus / m]unicipio Septimia libe[ra .../ T]hysdritanus" – A. Beschaouch, *Latomus* 26 (1967) 405–08.

[29] On the Fossa Regia see Eumachos, *FHG*, III, 102, no. 2 = Jacoby, *FGrH* 2.B (no. 178, Eumachos von Neapel), fr. 2; Appian, *Lib.* (IV) 53; Dio 47.9. Modern commentary can be found in C. Tissot, *Géographie comparée de la province romaine de l'Afrique*, 2 vols., Paris, Imprimerie nationale, 1884–1888, vol. 2, 14f.; Gsell, *HAAN* 3³ (1928) 327f.; L. Poinssot, "Note sur la *Fossa Regia*", *CRAI* (1907) 466–81; Ch. Saumagne, "Observations sur la trace de la *Fossa Regia*", *RAL* 4.4 (1928) 451–59 = *CT* 10 (1962) *Mélanges Saumagne*, 509–16; and M. Leglay, "Les Flaviens et l'Afrique", *MEFR* 80 (1968) 201–46, at p. 222–29, "Le problème de la *Fossa Regia*", for the Flavian resurvey.

very brief time span when Africa existed as *two provinces*, namely some time between the creation of *Africa nova* by Caesar in 46 B.C. and the merging of the two provinces into a united Africa in 42 B.C.[30] Hence we have already narrowed the date for the lists to the period between 46 and 42 B. C., even before approaching the information in the lists themselves.

III.2. The Six Colonies

At the beginning of the appendix Pliny lists the cities of the highest official status, the *coloniae*. He states that they were six in all, 'praeter iam dictas, Uthinam, Thuburbi'. By saying 'praeter iam dictas' Pliny is alluding explicitly to the method of composition discussed above, namely, the excerpting of important known cities from the lists in the writing of the main narrative. The other *four* colonies that Pliny has 'already mentioned' in the region east of the River Amsaga are: Cirta (c. 22), Sicca (c. 22), Carthage (c. 24) and Maxula (c. 24). We should now look at each of these towns and their status in turn.

III.2.a. *Colonia Carthago Magnae in vestigiis Carthaginis*

The above six words are the only notice Pliny accords the Roman colony of Carthage (c. 24) which in his own time had become the great urban hub of all Africa and, after Rome, the second metropolis of the Western Mediterranean. It does seem odd that such an important colonial foundation made by Caesar and Augustus should receive only a passing reference of this type. 'The colony of Carthage founded on the ruins of Great (Punic) Carthage' is the way in which the official list recorded the town. For an official survey the appellation seems strange, even improper. The colony founded by Caesar had an official title that is well known from epigraphic records: *Colonia Concordia Iulia Karthago*.[31] Not even the brief epithet *Iulia* of the coin legends is recognized in spite of the fact that Pliny does list epithets such as *Iulia* and *Augusta* elsewhere in his geography of Africa in connection with colonial foundations. The point here is not just the omission of the formal epithet in the context of an official list of colonies (which could occur in the main geography, as in the case of Banasa in Mauretania) but the fact that the whole description of

---

[30] The date of the merging of the two provinces is established by D. Fishwick & B. D. Shaw, "The Formation of Africa Proconsularis", *Hermes* 105 (1977) 369–80; J. Desanges' statement in his "Le statut des municipes d'après les données africaines", *RHD* 50 (1972) 353–73, at p. 363–64, that the lists draw no distinction between *Africa vetus* and *Africa nova* is simply not true; cf. R. Cagnat, *BMIR* 1 (1930) 77–85.

[31] On the Julian colony see, most recently, C. van Nerom, "Colonia Iulia Concordia Karthago", (in) *Hommages à M. Renard*, ed. J. Bibauw, *Collection Latomus* 102, Berchem Bruxelles, vol. 2 (1962) 767–76, with references. On its plan see Ch. Saumagne, "Colonia Iulia Karthago", *BCTH* (1924) 131–40 = "Le plan de la Colonie Julienne de Carthage", *CT* 10 (1962) 463–71.

Carthage contains no inkling of either the Caesarean or Augustan foundations. If the list is post-Caesarean then the omission of one of Caesar's most fundamental actions in Africa, the re-establishment of Carthage as *the* urban centre of the new province and his belated renewal of the Gracchan vision, is truly startling. Such an omission must be considered decisive in evaluating a document of this type; and if the document was of late Augustan date then it should have been even more explicit about the action of Octavianus in continuing his father's work.[32]

The only alternative, and the logical solution to the problem, is that the reference must be to the *first* colony proposed by C. Gracchus for the site, the ill-fated *Colonia Iunonia*. Whereas it is true that the operation of the *Lex Rubria* of 123 to settle 6000 (or more) colonists on the former site of Punic Carthage was abolished by the terms of the *Lex Opimia* of 121, it is certain that the *triumviri agris iudicandis adsignandis* did manage to begin their task.[33] They began laying out the cadaster of *Colonia Iunonia* and the assignation of the allotments to the colonists.[34] Since it was two years before the programme came to an end, it is relatively certain that at least some settlers were established on their new 200 *iugera* allotments.[35] This much is confirmed by the terms of the *Lex Agraria* of 111 which state that, in spite of the abrogation of the founding legislation, all such colonists who were established at the site were to be guaranteed their original property rights (presumably as per the Gracchan *Lex Rubria*).[36]

The large numbers of Roman citizens settled in the territory of the former Punic metropolis could not be ignored by any subsequent administrator; they were a *de facto* colony. But this was not the only 'unofficial' colonial settlement recognized in the Plinian 'appendix' (see the cases of Cirta and Sicca, below). When the case of Carthage is connected with the other examples of such quasi-colonial settlements, it is clear that it fits the context of 46–42 B. C. very well. All these settlements have the same type of connection with the one man who desired to recognize the status of these 'colonies' temporarily

---

[32] Octavianus sent out settlers in 29 B.C. (App. *BC*, 1.24; Plut. *C. Gracch*. 9; App. *Lib*. (IV) 136) – 3000 of them with the intent of drafting more from the surrounding regions. For Carthage as part of Octavianus' continuation of Caesar's project, see S. Gsell, "Les premiers temps de la Carthage romaine", *RH* 156 (1927) 225–40 and *HAAN* 7 (1928) 58f.

[33] On the Gracchan colony see App. *BC*, 1.24.104; and Ch. Saumagne, "Notes de topographie carthaginoise, II: Vestiges de la colonie de C. Gracchus à Carthage", *BCTH* (1928–29) 648–64 = "Le plan de la colonie Gracchane de Carthage", *CT* 10 (1962) 483–87, esp. 487. The Gracchan plan was taken over by Caesar-Octavianus' cadastration of 29 B.C., which followed a different orientation, see fig. 3, p. 484.

[34] On their operations see *ILLrp*. 892 (120 B.C.) and Teutsch, *Städtewesen*, 2–4.

[35] Cf. Fronto, *ad Ver*. II.1, "Gracchus . . . Karthaginem viritim dividebat . . ."

[36] Lex Agraria, ss. 59–61 (*CIL*, I², 585, p. 455; *FIRA*, I², no. 8, 102–21, p. 117–18; E. G. Hardy, *Roman Laws and Charters*, Oxford, Clarendon Press, 1912, 35–90, p. 78).

until he could formalize them. That man is, of course, Caesar. An apocryphal story recorded in Appian reveals that Caesar, when camped near the site of Carthage in 46, dreamed of refounding the city and immediately made a memorandum to that effect.[37] Simplistic propaganda, but doubtless an accurate reflection of Caesar's decision, taken before his departure from African shores that summer, to re-establish the first city of Africa. Perhaps even more striking is the verbal similarity between the Plinian description of this Carthage as *colonia... magnae in vestigiis Carthaginis* with Livy's description of the Gracchan colony as *in solo dirutae Carthaginis*.[38] There can be little doubt as to which Carthaginian colony the notice in the appendix refers – not to the Caesarean refoundation, but to the earlier Gracchan attempt.

III.2.b. The Status of Cirta and Sicca

In the passage in Pliny dealing with the region of Cirta the text reads as follows:

Oppidum Chullu, Rusicade, et ab eo XLVIII in mediterraneo colonia Cirta Sittianorum cognomine...

Firstly, and most obviously, it is clear from this information that the official appendix did not know of the existence of the Cirtan Federation. The mention of a colony at Cirta is not linked in any special way with Chullu and Rusicade, and the third member of the federation, Milev, is not even noted. Chullu and Rusicade are mentioned for the obvious reason that they were included as coastal towns in the *periplous*; given this source, it is quite easy to understand why Pliny merely calls them *oppida* although in his time they were Augustan colonies. So, too, it explains why Milev, a city in the hinterland, is omitted altogether. Faced with the difficulty of no information about urban centres in the hinterland, Pliny had recourse to the 'appendix' to provide what detail he could; but the 'appendix' only contained a bare reference to Cirta, no more. Again, the significant fact to note is the name of the colony at Cirta as the lists specified it: simply *colonia Cirta Sittianorum cognomine*. That is of particular assistance in dating the list. The full name of the Augustan colony at Cirta is known: *Colonia Iulia Iuvenalis Honoris et Virtutis Cirta*.[39]

Based on epigraphic and literary data, the municipal development of Cirta has been separated into three distinct phases, beginning with its foundation in 46/44 B. C. as a near-independent principality by the Campanian mercenary captain P. Sittius of Nuceria. But this foundation was only a *de facto*

---

[37] App. *Lib.* (IV) 136.
[38] Livy, *Ep.* LX.
[39] *ILAlg.* II, 1, 626 = *ILS* 6857; *ILAlg.* II, 1, 1999 (Cirta); cf. C. 7041, 7071; for Mela, *de Chorogr.* 1.6.30: "Cirta procul mari; nunc Sittianorum colonia".

settlement of irregular soldiers on African soil – it had no formal recognition as a *colonia*. Then, at some point between 44 and 27, Sittius' foundation was recognized as a formal Roman *colonia* with the epithet *Iulia*. Finally, in 26 B.C. there was a formal *deductio* of new colonists by Augustus whereupon the city received the additional names *Iuvenalis, Honoris,* and *Virtutis*.[40] For our purposes it is sufficient to note that the description of Cirta in Pliny merely as 'Sittian' must antedate the second stage, the formation of the Julian colony. Further, it seems probable that Caesar would have attempted some regularization of affairs at Cirta after the completion of the war in Africa, though this is not necessary. All the epithet *Iulia* tells us is that some step must have been taken to make the colony 'official' after 46 but before 27 B.C.[41]

There is good reason to believe that the unofficial colony at Cirta may have been recognized finally by Augustus, though while he was still Octavianus. This much may be deduced from an analysis of the so-called 'other Cirta', namely Sicca Veneria. Sicca is one of the six colonies included in the 'appendix'. The reason for its excerption (as with Cirta) is the fact that it is an inland centre for which no *periplous* could give Pliny any information. But in Pliny's account it is interesting to note that Sicca follows *directly* upon the mention of Cirta itself: ... *et alia (sc. colonia) intus Sicca*. The close connection between Cirta and Sicca is not just fortuitous — we know that the full name of the Roman colony at Sicca was *Colonia Iulia Sicca Veneria Cirta Nova*.[42] But it is not just the fact that Sicca was called "Cirta Nova" that strikes. The Roman citizens of Sicca were enrolled in the same voting tribe as the Cirtans, the *Quirina*.[43] *Veneria* was also an epithet shared by Rusicade, one of the other colonies of the Cirtan Federation.[44] In the case of Sicca it is clear that the epithet *Iulia* in the official name of the town must refer to the raising of the city to the status of a colony by Octavianus.[45] Considering the very close link

---

[40] See esp. A. Piganiol & H.-G. Pflaum, "Borne de Ksar Mahidjiba", *RSAC* 68 (1953) 215–28 = *AE* 1955: 202; cf. A. Berthier, "*Colonia Cirta Sittianorum*", *RSAC* 70 (1957–59) 89–118.

[41] Cf. Teutsch, *Städtewesen*, 71 and 42 where he notes that the Cirtan colony of 'stage 2' is not noted and therefore the source 'um das Jahre 46 v. Chr. entstanden'.

[42] C. 1632, 15858, 15868, and 16258 (Sicca Veneria).

[43] See W. Kubitschek, *Imperium Romanum tributim descriptum*, Vienna, F. Tempsky, 1889, 141–44, 153ff. Both cities shared a special type of organization of their rural hinterlands through the device of attributed *castella* that appears to be unique amongst African municipalities, see U. Laffi, *Adtributio e contributio. Problemi del sistema politico amministrativo della stato Romano* (Studi di lettere, storia e filosofia, Scuola Normale di Pisa, no. 35), Pisa, Nistri-Lischi, 1966, and Broughton, *Romanization*, 76. There must in fact have existed a common bond and organization basis between the two cities already during the period of the African kingdoms, see G. Camps, *Aux origines de la Berbérie: Massinissa ou les débuts de l'histoire* = *Libyca* (Arch.-épigr.) 8 (1960) 191–96 (henceforth, *Massinissa*) and Sall. *Bell. Iug.* 56.

[44] See *ILAlg*. II, 1: 5, 8, 17, 24, 687, 702, 3610–11 (Skikda).

[45] C. 27568 = *ILS* 6773: Divo Augusto / conditori / Siccenses. The dedication is of late date and so naturally refers to the emperor as 'Augustus' rather than 'Octavianus', but the epithet *Iulia*

IV

between the two cities, it seems quite likely that the same must also apply to the epithet *Iulia* in Cirta's official colonial name.[46]
We are now able to understand the full meaning of the Pliny lists. At the time of the redaction of the original administrative document, both cities were indeed 'colonies' but only in a *de facto*, not a *de iure* sense; and both were connected with the actual settlement of veterans on the land by the same man, Publius Sittius.[47] It was only later, sometime between 44 and 27 B.C., that Octavianus formalized the status of both cities as *coloniae Iuliae*. The official list, being prior to this time in date, only registers a Cirta "Sittianorum cognomine" and another "colonia" Sicca. The lists definitely antedate 27 B.C., but probably reflect a much earlier situation when it would have been expedient for Octavianus to recognize the Sittian colonies, that is, during the period of the Civil Wars — certainly no later than 42 B.C. The information in the lists reflects accurately the status of the two cities after their foundation by P. Sittius in 46 but before their formal recognition as *coloniae Iuliae* sometime before 42 B.C.

III.2.c. Uthina and Thuburbo Minus

Two of the remaining colonies listed by Pliny in the appendix at first seem to provide difficulties. They are *Thuburbo* and *Uthina*. Uthina (mod. Oudna) is known from an inscription found at Rome as *Colonia Iulia Tertiadecim [anorum] Uthina*.[48] The Thuburbo to which Pliny refers is Thuburbo Minus (mod. Tébourba), known officially as *colonia VIII (Octavanorum)*

---

in Sicca's official name clearly shows that it was 'Octavianus' who was the *conditor coloniae* (pace Teutsch, *Städtewesen*, 173–74).

[46] The study of the immigrant nomenclature of Sicca Veneria by J. M. Lassère, *Ubique Populus: peuplement et mouvements de population dans l'Afrique romaine* . . . (henceforth *Ubique Populus*), Paris, Editions du C. N. R. S., 1977, 149–55 establishes many links with both Cirta and Campania that must be connected ultimately with the actions of P. Sittius; one should not, however, be led by these similarities to accept the arguments of R. Charlier, "La Numidie vue par Salluste. Cirta Regia, Constantine ou Le Kef?", *AC* 19 (1950) 289–307 on the identification with al-Kaf with the Cirta of Sallust.

[47] See Teutsch, *Städtewesen*, 173–74 for a refutation of F. Vittinghoff, *Römische Kolonisation und Bürgerrechtspolitik unter Caesar und Augustus* (Akademie der Wissenschaften und der Literatur in Mainz, Geistes- und sozialwissenschaftliche Klasse, Abhandlungen, no. 4), Wiesbaden, Steiner, 1951 (henceforth *Bürgerrechtspolitik*) 113, no. 2 and 126, no. 9 that the epithet Veneria is to be connected with Caesar; more probably it is to be linked with the cult of an African deity in the city who was identified with the Greco-Roman Venus-Aphrodite, see Val. Max. 2.6.15.

[48] *C*. VI, 36917 = *ILS* 6784 (Rome); cf. Romanelli, *Storia*, 197; Chevallier, *MEFR* 69 (1958) 89, and Teutsch, *Städtewesen*, 167–68, all of whom believe it to be an Augustan colony; the only dissenting voice is that of Brunt, *Italian Manpower*, 594, no. 44, ". . . *perhaps* Caesarian; Caesar had the 13th legion with him in Africa in 46." (*m. .i.*).

The Elder Pliny's African Geography 443

Thuburbi.[49] In our handbooks both cities are ordinarily listed as 'Augustan colonies' or, to be more precise, Octavian settlements.[50] But *are* they? The case is hardly closed. The Thirteenth Legion was one of Caesar's most seasoned units, and was transported to Africa to engage in combat during the last stages of his war with the Pompeian forces.[51] The colony at Uthina, therefore, is more probably a Caesarean viritim settlement of veterans from his 13th Legion following the close of the war in Africa. The same observation applies to the Eighth Legion. The fully revised text of the *Bellum Africum* (not, most unfortunately, used by modern historians who have studied this question) clearly shows that both the eighth and the thirteenth legions were with Caesar in Africa, whereas there is no evidence at all to connect them with Augustus.[52] The colonies noted by the Plinian lists at Thuburbo and Uthina, therefore, were *not* part of the Augustan settlement after Actium, but were viritim veteran settlements made by Caesar upon completion of the war in Africa in 46 B.C.

III.2.d. The Case of Maxula

All the six cities listed by Pliny are known colonies with the sole exception of the problem posed by *Maxula* (mod. Rhadès). An inscription from Largo Argentina in Rome seems to substantiate Pliny's claim of colonial status for the town.[53] Teutsch claimed that this epigraphic evidence was very tenuous, and that it was contradicted by other, better epigraphic data showing Maxula as only a *civitas*. In addition, the *Codex Parisinus* ('E') of the 10th century has preserved an alternative, more sensible reading of Pliny:[54]

... colonia Carthago Magnae in vestigiis Carthaginis, colonia, et Maxula...

[49] *ILAfr.* 414, 1. 6f.; see A. Héron de Villefosse, "Une inscription de Tébourba, "Colonia Octavanorum Thuburbo", *CRAI* (1913) 436–40; Teutsch, *Städtewesen*, 169–70; most believe it to be an Augustan foundation, see Romanelli, *Storia*, 195, and Broughton, *Romanization*, 68–69, no. 134; and even Brunt, *Italian Manpower*, 594, no. 45, "But the 8th legion was *not* with Caesar in 46 (Rice Holmes iii. 534f.) – at the earliest after Actium" (*m. i.*). A further argument is that Caesar left three legions in Africa in 46 (App. *BC*, 3.85; cf. Gsell, *HAAN* 8 (1928) 166; cf. *Bell. Afr.* 19.3; 54.1; App. *BC*, 2.92–94; Dio 43.14.1), and the Senate recalled two of these to Italy in November of 43 (App. *BC*, 3.91–92). One of these legions must be either the 8th or 13th, and so the *viritim* settlement was complete at least by 43, and probably much earlier.
[50] See Lassère, *Ubique Populus*, 202, no. 283; and Gascou, *Politique municipale*, 24, citing the earlier views of Vittinghoff, *Bürgerrechtspolitik*, 111; Teutsch, *Städtewesen*, 167–69.
[51] See the references in *Bell. Afr.*. 60.
[52] See the excellent note, p. 101 (on *Bell. Afr.* 56.1. 22) of A. Bouvet, *César, Guerre de l'Afrique*, Paris, "Les Belles Lettres", 1949 (éditions... Budé); cf. *Bell. Afr.* 62, no. 11 and introd. p. x, no. 4, and *app. crit., ad loc.* where VIII stands.
[53] *AE* 1948: 91, reading *col[onia Iulia] Ind(ustria),* or *-ulgentia) Max(ula)* as suggested by A. Degrassi, *Doxa* 2 (1949) 77–78 = *Scritti vari di Antichità*, 1962, 348 = *AE* 1949: 175.
[54] See Teutsch, *Städtewesen*, 44–46.

But there *are* additional epigraphic data in inscriptions recording the *origines* of serving soldiers in Africa that seem to substantiate Pliny's claim, and Teutsch's recourse to a secondary reading in the MSS. does not seem particularly compelling.[55] The point is that if Pliny had recognized Maxula as a peregrine *civitas* he would not have included it in his list of six colonies. To Pliny, Maxula was a colony, even if he was mistaken in this view. For our purposes, however, it is a mute point; since nothing is known about the putative municipal history of Maxula, it cannot be used for evidence for either side of the present debate.

To sum up: the statuses of five of the six colonies in the lists (little being known about the sixth, Maxula, at any time) confirm a date of 46–44 B.C. Two of Caesar's viritim veteran colonies are noted, but his establishment of Carthage is not, and Sicca and Cirta are still merely 'Sittian' foundations.

III.3. Oppidum Latinum Unum Uzalitanum

The case of Uzalis, like that of *Castra Cornelia* (see section III.4 below) is rather puzzling. Why should Pliny bother to mention only *one* city of this type? And what precisely is meant by the term *oppidum Latinum*? From the terms of the *Lex Agraria* of 111 B.C. we know that Uzalis was a *civitas libera* at that time.[56] Apparently, like one other city in the Plinian list of *oppida libera* (Utica) Uzalis had lost its 'free status' in the interim. It seems most probable that Uzalis, a town near Utica (less than 10 km to the north) lost its freedom at the same time as Utica and for the same reason: for supporting the Pompeiani too eagerly during the Civil War in 46. This still does not solve the problem of what is meant by the term *oppidum Latinum*. At no other time does Pliny use such a term to define either a city of the Latin right or a *municipium*. The closest analogous term used in his geography of Africa is that for Arsennaria in Mauretania, which he calls an *oppidum Latinorum* (c. 19). It is opposed in status to the nearby towns of Quiza Centana, an *oppidum peregrinorum*, and Cartenna (mod. Ténès), a *colonia Augusti*. It seems, by analogy with the *oppida civium Romanorum* (see below section V) that Pliny must mean that there were large numbers of Latins in Uzalis − a sufficient reason to justify its inclusion in the lists, even though it had lost its former privileged status of *oppidum liberum*. It seems equally certain that Uzalis finds a special place in the list because of its proximity to both Utica and Castra Cornelia − both of which were important sites during Caesar's campaigns in Africa.

[55] C. 2567, l. 38; 18067a, l. 3; and 18087, *dextr.* l. 41 (Lambaesis); Ptolemy 4.3.2 refers to the town as a colony, but the Antonine Itinerary calls both Maxula and Leptis Minus *civitates*; see Brunt, *Italian Manpower*, 581.

[56] For the *Lex Agraria*, see no. 60 below. For its location, see now, L. Maurin & J. Peyras, "Uzalitana: la région de l'Ansarine dans l'Antiquité", *CT* 19 (1971) 11–103.

III.4. Oppidum Stipendiarium Unum Castris Corneliis

Again, the suspicion is immediately aroused: why does Pliny mention this site at all? There was a plethora of stipendiary towns in the province of Africa, that is, all those peregrine communities that owed a tax (*stipendium*) to the Roman state. To mention only *one* of them is rather odd and, in fact, Pliny first notes the town in the main body of his text merely as a 'place' (*locus Castra Cornelia*, c. 24). The second mention in the 'appendix' adds nothing to this. Why then does the official appendix mention one insignificant stipendiary town out of all those in the province of Africa?[57] The place, only two kilometres east of Utica, was named after P. Cornelius Scipio who made his winter camp here in the autumn of 204 B.C.[58] Its only real significance after that date is its connection with Caesar's campaigns during the Civil Wars; it was at this place that his lieutenant C. Curio staged his abortive attack on the Pompeian forces in Africa.[59] Therefore one might conjecture without too much risk that the reason for the inclusion of Castra Cornelia in the 'appendix' is that the compiler was associated with Caesar's operations in Africa and attached special importance to it because of Curio's expedition.

IV. The Free Cities of Africa

Since the less problematic status of those cities that remain to be considered is that of the *oppida libera*, let us turn to them first. As of ca. 46 B.C. the official lists recognized thirty of these cities in Africa from Mateur northwest of Carthage to Sabratha on the Mediterranean coast of the Lesser Syrtis.[60] By definition, cities granted the status of 'free' were within 'provincial' boundaries. In this context, four of the cities mentioned by Pliny are of particular interest: Bulla Regia (no. 19), Macomades (no. 28), Tacape (no. 29), and Sabratha (no. 30), to which we might provisionally add Zama (no. 18). All these cities were outside the boundaries of the *old* province of Africa.[61] The *Lex Agraria* of 111 B.C. lists the cities granted the status of *civitates liberae et*

---

[57] As Cuntz, *op. cit.* 41 put it so aptly, "Nemo putabit unam solam Africae civitatem fuisse stipendiariam", citing *C.* 68 (12 B.C.) in proof, if proof was ever needed.
[58] Livy 29.35.12–15; Polyb. 14.6.7; and Oros. *Adv. pagan.* 4.22.1; cf. Tissot, *Géographie comparée*, II, 83.
[59] Caes. *BC*, 2.23–24; Mela, *de Chorogr.* 1.34; Ptolemy 4.3; and App. *BC*, 2.44; cf. A. Lézine, *Karthago* 7 (1956) 127–38.
[60] See the list in Appendix A.
[61] Macomades, Tacape, and Sabratha are all beyond the southern limits of the province of *Africa vetus* at Thaenae. Even on the most optimistic westward extension of the *Fossa Regia*, Bulla Regia is still further to the west. The only problem is Zama. Teutsch (endmap) swings the line of the *Fossa* far to the south purposefully to include Zama, but this appears highly artificial and, without any evidential basis, it must be abandoned.

immunes following the defeat of Carthage in 146: Utica, Hadrumetum, Thapsus, Leptis Minus, Acholla, Uzalis, and Theudalis.[62] Of these cities, in Pliny's list Uzalis has become a 'Latin town' and Utica a 'town of Roman citizens'. Thus, between 146 B.C. and 46 B.C. twenty-five new *oppida libera* had been created. The number is large, even surprising. What possible circumstances could have been similar in gravity to the crisis of the third Romano-Carthaginian war that would have led Rome to extend this privileged status to so many other towns? By extending the status of 'free city' to those towns that remained loyal during her third major conflict with Carthage, Rome sought to reward those who had benefited her cause. The obvious parallel cases would be the grave situation in the early phases of the war with Jugurtha, which threatened the very existence of the Roman province in Africa, and the period of Civil Wars that erupted between the forces of Pompey and Caesar in 49 B.C. In these cases a similar policy of guaranteeing and rewarding loyalty by extending the right of 'freedom' would have been a logical one to follow. An examination of the geographical distribution and type of cities involved will help in the identification of possible situations in which such grants might have been made.

1) One group of cities is located along the coastline between the Lesser Syrtis and the Gulf of Gabès (Thaenae, Macomades, Tacape, Sabratha).
2) A second group is located along the Cap Bon — Sahelian coastline (Avitta, Aggar, Clupea, Curubis, Neapolis, Ruspina, Thysdrus, Ulusubburita, and Vaga *aliud*).
3) A third group is located in the hinterland of Carthage, centred in the Upper Bagradas-Siliana Valley (Abbir Cella, Thizika, Thagaste, Zama, Bulla Regia).

These three categories embrace most of the 'free cities' mentioned by Pliny. Clearly the first two groups are connected with the circumstances of the Jugurthine War.[63] It is known that during the course of the war Lepcis sent ambassadors of high rank to Metellus after the capture of Thala with the mission to ask to be accepted as Roman allies (*socii*). Indeed, the Lepcitani had already sought this privilege at the beginning of the war, sending an embassy to the consul Bestia to request friendship and alliance (*amicitiam et societatem rogatum*). This time the request was granted and four cohorts of Ligurians were sent to the city (*Bell. Iug.* 77.1). So it seems likely that Macomades,

---

[62] *Lex Agraria*, ss. 79 (cf. refs. no. 36 above): "... populorum leiberorum Uticensium, H[adrumtinorum T]ampsitanorum, Leiptitanorum, Aquillitanorum, Usalitanorum, Teudalensium, quom in ameicitiam populei Romani proxumum / [venerunt, ..."

[63] See the following references in Sall. *Bell. Iug.*, for Thala Capsa: 75.1,2,6,9; 77.1; 80.1; 89.4,6; 91.3–4; 97.1; for the Syrtes and Lepcis: 77.1,2; 78; 79.1; for the River Muthul-Sicca Region: 48.3; 56.3–5; Theraei: 19.3; Thirmida: 12.3; Utica: 25.5; 63.1; 64.5; 86.4; 140.1; Vaga: 29.4; 47.1; 68.1–3; 66.2; 69.1–3; and Zama: 56.1; 57.1; 58.1; 60.1, and 61.1.

Tacape and Sabratha may have made similar arrangements at the same time and became *civitates foederatae* during the course of the war. Zama was another important centre in the war; the old African capital city was the scene of one of the major battles (*Bell. Iug.* 56–61). The other royal centres were inevitably involved in the conflict, notably Bulla Regia, Hippo Regius and Sicca Veneria.[64] The remaining cities are not specified in the Sallustian account, but must have been affected by operations extending up the River Muthul (*Bell. Iug.* 48.5) to the region of Béja (anc. Vaga, cf. *Bell. Iug.* 29.4, 47.1, 66.2, 68.1–3, and 69.1–3). Either during the war or shortly after these cities were probably offered special status as 'friends and allies' of the Roman people, just as Lepcis had been. As long as they remained beyond the frontiers of the old Roman province of Africa, they continued to have the status of allied cities. In the list Pliny used as his source, however, these same towns are recorded as *civitates liberae*. The change in status is easy to explain, and sheds further light on the dating of the document. The most economical explanation is that all these cities: Bulla Regia, Lepcis, Sabratha, and all the rest were now located *within* a provincial frontier, which would have to be that of the greater province of Africa (*post* 42 B.C.) or *Africa nova* (post 46 B.C.). They could no longer remain sovereign 'friends and allies' of the Roman state, but their special status within the province could be maintained by granting them the status of 'free cities'. Why then, one might ask, is Lepcis no longer included in Pliny's list as a 'free city'? It should have this status since it became a 'friend and ally' during the war with Jugurtha. Its privileged status should have been 'transformed' when it was encompassed within Roman provincial boundaries by a grant of 'freedom'. But the reason why it was not is apparent. Caesar took harsh measures against the city in 46 B.C. for its role in the Civil War in Africa; the massive fines and reprimands imposed on the city must have been accompanied by the removal of its status as *civitas foederata* and the loss of any opportunity of shifting this privileged status to that of 'free city'.[65] Former royal cities such as Zama and Bulla Regia, however, would have been permitted to retain a comparatively privileged status within the new province

---

[64] See Camps, *Massinissa*, 212–13, 257–58 on these royal centres.

[65] On the boundaries of the province see *Bell. Afr.* 97.1; the same passage states that Caesar reduced Juba's kingdom to a new province. That Lepcis was outside his kingdom and probably still a *civitas foederata* of Rome can be seen clearly from Caes. *BC*, 2.38.1 where Juba is *recalled* to his kingdom by wars on the frontiers and arguments with the Lepcitani; the nature of these arguments is made clear by *Bell. Afr.* 97: a dissension amongst the *principes* of the city over an alliance with Juba. Doubtless the king was pressing the city for support, which he eventually received (*armis militibus pecunia iuverant*). On the fines levied by Caesar, see S. Gsell, "L'huile de Leptis", *Riv. Trip.* 1 (1924–25) 41–46; R. M. Haywood, "The Oil of Lepcis", *CPh* 36 (1941) 246–56, and P. W. Townsend, "The Oil Tribute of Africa at the time of Julius Caesar", *CPh* 35 (1940) 274–83. As the boast by Caesar about the tribute from his new province in Africa (Plut. *Caes.* 55) makes clear, the oil tribute was from Lepcis Magna in *Africa nova*.

created by Caesar. Zama, in fact, was probably the new administrative centre of *Africa nova*.[66] Sabratha, the sister city of Lepcis, was allowed to make the transfer from *civitas foederata* to *civitas libera* presumably because, as usual, it supported the opposite faction to Lepcis in the Civil War.[67] Presumably this also accounts for the loss of 'free' status by Utica, a status it had held since the end of the third war with Carthage — and the same would apply to Uzalis.[68] Nevertheless, because of the large number of Roman citizens in the former town, and the large number of Latins in the latter, Caesar felt obliged to notice the special status of the large formal 'citizen' groups in them (see below, section V).

Caesar himself was probably responsible for some of these grants of 'free status'. The document fits rather well with some of the putative actions Caesar would have taken towards the coastal cities of the Sahel and Cap Bon Peninsula as military commander in 46 (*i. e.*, those towns listed in group two above). Obviously he sought to woo some cities by rewarding them with 'free status', just as we know that he punished others like Lepcis Magna for siding with the Pompeiani. Some of the obvious candidates are the city states along the Sahelian coast of Tunisia that figure prominently in the *Bellum Africum*. Prime amongst these are Thysdrus (*Bell. Afr.* 36.2, 76.1, 97.3), Ruspina (67.1), Aggar (67.1, 76.2, 79.1), the *Vagense aliud* (74.1), and Zama in the interior (91. 1). The case of Zama is illustrative of circumstances in which Caesar would have wished to reward a city with free status. First, the town was *not* (*pace* Teutsch) within the *Fossa Regia* that marked the boundary of the old Roman province. The royal tributes and taxes that had been collected at Zama up to 46 B.C. and which Caesar let out before leaving Africa prove that Zama had been the capital city of Juba I's kingdom up to the time of his defeat.[69] The same passage in the *Bellum Africum* reveals that there were Roman citizens resident in Zama who sided with Juba I and Scipio. These persons had their goods confiscated and sold at auction by Caesar for their traitorous actions. The African populace of Zama, on the other hand, were rewarded by a lightening of their tribute burden for their actions in refusing to open the gates of their town to the forces of Juba I. It would seem probable that the town ultimately also received *libertas* from Caesar in 46.[70]

[66] *Bell. Afr.* 97.1.

[67] M. Grant, *From Imperium to Auctoritas: A Historical Study of Aes Coinage in the Roman Empire, 49 B.C. - A.D. 14*, Cambridge, Cambridge University Press, 1946, 341, cites the numismatic evidence, but mistakenly attributes the *libertas* to 7–6 B.C. under Augustus; cf. Tac. *Hist.* 4.50 on the inveterate hostility between Sabratha and Oea.

[68] Cf. *Bell. Afr.* 90.1–3 for the fines levied on the *conventus* and city of Utica.

[69] *Bell. Afr.* 97.1, ". . . tributis, vectigalibusque regiis locatis."

[70] *Ibid.*, "Caesar interim Zamae auctione regia facta bonisque eorum venditis qui cives Romani contra populum Romanum arma tulerant praemiisque Zamensibus, qui de rege excludendo consilium ceperant . . ."

V. Oppida Civium Romanorum

The most vexatious and acerbically debated question emerging from the Plinian lists is the status of the fifteen towns which he designates *oppida civium Romanorum*, 'towns of Roman citizens'. The status of these communities seems to have defied any generally acceptable solution. Broadly speaking, there are two schools of interpretation on this question. One holds that these towns were centres of associations of Roman citizens (*conventus*) in peregrine *civitates*.[71] The other interpretation, equally dogmatic, holds that Pliny (or his source) used the term to refer to what were in reality *municipia*.[72] Most arguments, on either side, have been confused by the acceptance of a late Augustan date for the documents. If we follow our new date of ca. 46–44 B.C., the status of these towns and their place in administrative planning becomes much clearer.

The case for regarding these towns as *municipia* is long and complex; it need not be reviewed in all its detail here.[73] Whatever arguments proponents of this view put forth, however ingenious and convincing they might seem to be, they must come to terms with several hard facts concerning the *oppida civium Romanorum* actually listed by Pliny. First, there is the historical context of municipal development in North Africa. It is extremely improbable that in 46 B.C., or even later in the reign of Augustus for that matter, there were fifteen towns in Africa, many of them insignificant and otherwise totally unknown (*e. g.*, Canopicum, Thigibba, Assuras, Abora) that had the status of *municipium*. In fact, the very opposite is *known* to be true. *In every case that can be tested in the list, no known town ever advanced beyond the status of a peregrine civitas*. Chiniava, for example, remained a *civitas* until the reign of Antoninus Pius, and probably beyond.[74] Further, the use of the grant of municipal status to a provincial community in Africa finds its first possible instance in the time of Octavianus, and this is still the much debated case of Utica.[75] *There are no further known cases of municipal grants in Africa until Tipasa and Volubilis in the time of the emperor Claudius* and, in all likelihood, these are the *first* such grants ever made in Africa. Then there is a further gap of time until a few more known grants were made by the Flavian emperors (*e. g.*,

---

[71] Ch. Saumagne, *Le droit Latin et les cités romaines sous l'Empire: essais critiques* (in) Publications de l'Institut de Droit Romain de l'Université de Paris, no. 22), Paris, Sirey, 1965, p. 81f.; cf. Teutsch, *Städtewesen*, 234.35.

[72] Desanges, *art. cit.* (1972) is the most recent extended argument, but, as he notes (p. 353, no. 4) it goes back at least as far as Mommsen in the *Staatsrecht*.

[73] See the detailed arguments in Desanges *art. cit.* (1972) and J. Gascou, "*Municipia Civium Romanorum*", *Latomus* 30 (1971) 133–41.

[74] *AE* 1892: 12 = Cagnat, *BCTH* (1892) 197, no. 15 = *MEFR* (1893) 185, a dedication to a patron from Carthage by the *ordo Chini(a)vensium peregrinorum* in the reign of Antoninus Pius.

[75] Dio 49.16, see note 84 below.

Bulla Regia, Icosium, *perhaps* Cillium, Mascula and Sufetula).[76] Then only two such cases under Trajan (Sala, Thubursicu Numidarum).[77] It is only with Hadrian and the Antonines that the granting of municipal status becomes more commonplace. Even then, the fifteen cases mentioned by Pliny, if *municipia*, would be equal to all known grants of municipal status made by Hadrian and Antoninus Pius, and would more than surpass all known grants made by Septimius Severus.[78] So on historical grounds alone, it is most implausible that the *oppida civium Romanorum* are *municipia* no matter what theoretical possibilities are outlined by some scholars.

A more positive and sensible view was championed by Teutsch, namely, that the *oppida civium Romanorum* were simply towns in which a large number of Roman citizens happened to reside.[79] This interpretation, which seems to be pre-eminently logical and reasonable, nevertheless was attacked vigorously from several sides.[80] The main argument proffered by the critics against accepting the *oppida civium Romanorum* as towns in which *conventus* or associations of Roman citizens were present is that such associations did not have any formally recognized juridical status in Roman municipal government: they were only private organizations of citizens who happened to reside in peregrine cities.[81] But even this observation is no serious objection to

---

[76] Tipasa (*AE*. 1966: 149; cf. Pliny, *NH*, 5.4.20); Volubilis (*C*. 21837, 21841, 21843–44; *AE* 1916: 42; *AE* 1924: 66 = *ILMar* 16). For the Flavian *municipia* see no. 18 above.

[77] For Sala see S. Gsell & J. Carcopino, *MEFR* 48 (1931) 28: line 15 of the decree mentions the *municipium* in existence before 144, and since the local senate chamber was called the *Curia Ulpia*, the deduction seems reasonable. For Thubursicu Numidarum, see *ILAlg*. 1, 1240.

[78] All known grants of municipal status by Hadrian total 8–9 and all known grants by Antoninus Pius 6–7, for a total of 14–16 under the Antonines. Septimius Severus' total of about 12 is the greatest for a single imperial reign. See Gascou, *Politique municipale*.

[79] See Gascou, *art. cit.* (1971); Vittinghoff, *Bürgerrechtspolitik*, 115 and *art. cit.* (1966) 226–27 considered the identification certain, but Gascou, p. 136, no. 1 and *Politique municipale*, 25–26, rightly denies this, drawing attention to the title *municipium civium Romanorum* as used by Pliny with respect to towns in Spain (*NH*, 3.1.7; 4.22.117). On the latter see now B. Galsterer-Kröll, "Zu den spanischen Städtelisten des Plinius", *Archivo español de arqueologia* 48 (1975) 120–28. Gascou, *Politique municipale*, 18 also draws attention to the anomaly of *known municipia* (Chiniava, Uchi Maius) that are *not* included in the Plinian lists as *oppida civium Romanorum*; he thought, however, that Teutsch's identification of *oppida civium Romanorum* with centres of Roman *conventus* was controverted by the case of Thibaris, a known centre of Marian veteran settlement, which is not included in the lists as an *oppidum civium Romanorum*. That would be a cogent argument if we knew the whole history of Thibaris' municipal development; in any event, the name *might* be one of the otherwise apparently unidentifiable town names in the lists (see, e. g., nos. 9 and 10, Append. A).

[80] Teutsch, *Städtewesen*, 234–35; Saumagne, *Droit latin*, 81; for a study of these early centres of Roman and Italian settlement see now Lassère, *Ubique populus*, 78–103.

[81] Especially by Vittinghoff, *art. cit.* (1966) 226–27 and in *Gnomon* 40 (1968) 587–88; G. Ch. Picard, "Le *conventus civium* Romanorum de Mactar", *Africa* 1 (1966) 69–70; counter-arguments accepted by Desanges, *art. cit.* (1972) 355–58. Cf. Luzzato, *SDHI* 31 (1965) 418.

Teutsch's views. The claim of his critics reduces to the assertion that the *oppida civium Romanorum* recorded by Pliny must themselves have some formal juridical status. But there is nothing in the lists themselves that would support such an assumption, or that would support the idea that 'official' and 'juridical' must be construed on so narrow a plane. Apart from the *coloniae* and the *oppida libera*, none of the types of communities listed by Pliny would seem to have any formal juridical status in the sense of 'colony' or 'municipality'. For example, he lists only *one* stipendiary city, one *oppidum latinum*, and several *nationes* (ethnic groups). So the term *oppidum civium Romanorum* might be a simple descriptive term (much as it naturally appears to be) to designate towns where significant numbers of 'alien' Roman citizens happen to dwell.

Pliny's use of precisely analogous phrases elsewhere in his African geography confirm this hypothesis. In his survey of Mauretania Caesariensis he refers to three cities grouped closely together in the following words (*NH*, V, 19):

> Portus Magnus oppidum civium Romanorum, Quiza Cenitana peregrinorum oppidum, Arsennaria Latinorum (*sc.* oppidum).

Clearly the terms are only an informal way of describing these towns: Portus Magnus, 'a town inhabited by significant numbers of Roman citizens'; Quiza, 'a peregrine town'; and Arsennaria, 'a town where a significant number of Latins happen to live'. That is to say, Portus Magnus and Arsennaria are noted because there are significant enough communities of Roman citizens and Latins resident in them, whereas Quiza is merely 'foreign' and deserves no special appellation. In spite of the citizen element, however, we must note that Portus Magnus *never* became a *municipium* or colony throughout the entire period of the empire; it remained a peregrine *civitas* until the time of Septimius Severus and probably beyond.[82] Hence there is no empirical basis for claiming that the term *oppidum civium Romanorum* designates a *municipium* in Pliny, or that it was ever anything more than a purely descriptive phrase.

A secondary and much weaker counter-argument often resorted to by Teutsch's critics is the apparent fact that Pliny does not mention any of the known *conventus* of Roman citizens recorded in the *Bellum Africum*, namely those at Utica (68.4), Hadrumetum (97.2), Thapsus (97.2), and possibly at Thysdrus (36.2). The obvious explanation is that these cities already have an official status, that of *civitates liberae*, which *is* mentioned by Pliny and which in and of itself overrides the existence of groups of Roman citizens within them. Each town is mentioned *only once* in the lists and then with its highest official status. Utica, known to have a *conventus*, is recorded as such in the lists

---

[82] Its only official status ever recorded in the epigraphic data is that of *res publica* (= *civitas*), C. 21613.

452

(that is, as an 'oppidum civium Romanorum', no. 15). Utica had been a *civitas libera* in 111 B.C. (cf. the *Lex Agraria*) and had kept this status at least until 54 B.C.[83] But sometime between 54 and 46 B.C. it had lost this privileged position. The reason why is obvious: the city was heavily punished for its support of Caesar's enemies during the Civil War.[84] No longer a *civitas libera*, it could not be included by Pliny under that heading in the official lists and so its *conventus*, the remaining element of importance to the compiler, *is* recorded.

In listing the cities of note in Africa, the original compiler included all the towns of obvious importance (colonies, free cities) but did not care, quite naturally, to list all the remaining cities of no special status (*e. g.*, the *civitates stipendiariae*). Out of all these cities, however, he did wish to single out for notice those stipendiary towns in which there was an important Roman citizen or Latin element in the local population. Both for purposes of controlling these local towns and knowing the location of the citizen groups whose land-tax (administrative) status would be different from that of the local populace, it was important to record their presence. We are then able to accept Teutsch's proposal that the *oppida civium Romanorum* are indeed merely stipendiary towns that happened to have 'conventus' of Roman citizens in them. However, we need only construe the term 'conventus' to mean 'groups' of such citizens in a very general sense, without attributing any special juridical sense of organization to the word. Nor need we be as dogmatic as he was in contending that *all* such concentrations of Roman citizens in these towns were due to Marian settlements, or that *all pagi* must similarly be explained.[85] Probably

---

[83] This observation effectively undercuts the basic argument of Desanges, *art. cit.* (1972) 358. Cf. Cic. *Pro Scaur.* 44–45: "Utica ... amica populo Romano ac libera civitas".

[84] The status of Utica is a much discussed problem, but the pieces of evidence are few, clearly separable, and should not cause any great difficulty.

(a) The passage from Cicero *Pro Scauro* (see no. 83) clearly refers to the city as a *civitas libera* still in 54 B.C.

(b) Obviously, then, the *beneficium Legis Iuliae* of 59 B.C. (Caes. *BC*, 2.36) could *not* have been a grant of municipal status, as Teutsch and others have claimed. This is also borne out by the fact that the city is listed amongst the *oppida civium Romanorum* in the Plinian lists (see no. 15, Append. A).

(c) The town may have received the status of *municipium* in 30 B.C. *if* a passage in Dio is correctly interpreted to mean this (see no. 75 above). This would make sense of a coin legend reading *Mun(icipium) Iul(ium) Uti(cense)*, see L. Müller, *Numismatique de l'ancienne Afrique*, II, Copenhagen, 1861, 159–60. It would have been able to obtain the status through the influence of the large number of Roman citizens in the city and the residence of the Roman governor there until 10 B.C. (see *C.* 1180 = 14310; A. Lezine, *Utique*, Tunis, 1970, 31).

[85] Not all *conventus/oppida civium Romanorum* had to be *pagi*, though *some* might have been. The argument has been bedevilled by the equation 'all *conventus* must be *pagi*' or a corollary 'all *pagi* are Marian veteran settlements'. Neither is true. Whereas *pagi* and Marian settlers could be designated by the term *cives Romani*, not *all oppida civium Romanorum* were necessarily of one or

not. The *conventus* were simply informal groups of businessmen, farmers, settlers, cattlemen, tax-collectors and other such Romans who settled in African towns for a variety of reasons that included everything from *viritim* land settlement (Thuburnica), to petty commodity dealings (*e. g.*, in grain, Vaga), to large-scale involvement in land and tribute collection (the *equites* at Utica). Of course, there were such citizen groups in the other cities recognized by the lists, but they are not noted because it would be otiose to do so. For example, we may safely postulate that they existed in all the colonies (Carthage, Thuburbo, Uthina) but that it would be pleonastic for any administrative document to say that Roman colonies contained groups of Roman citizens. Then again, there were similar groups in the free cities (Hadrumetum, Thapsus) but the formal status of such towns as *civitates liberae* effectively placed them outside the direct concern of the Roman administrator. Once he had noted their status of 'free city' he was done with them.

VI. Political Significance of the Official Document

The main conclusions concerning the document's date might be summarized briefly:

1) A general date of composition of the lists can be set in the biennium between Caesar's arrival in Africa in the spring of 46 and his death in 44, preferably towards the beginning of this period.
2) The time of composition can be narrowed somewhat by the following observations. The list is ignorant of some of Caesar's foundations, notably his refoundation of Carthage, but it does take cognizance of *viritim* settlement of veterans from legions involved in his African campaign, both around Thuburbo Minus and Uthina. The re-establishment of Carthage can be dated to late 45 or early 44, and with it the grants of colonial status to the coastal cities of the Cap Bon Peninsula: Neapolis, Curubis, and Clupea. This narrows the date of the document to 46–45 B.C., in the immediate aftermath of his campaigns in Africa.

What then is the purpose of the document? The compiler was interested in the official status of all administrative units, whether *coloniae*, *civitates liberae* or even tribes (*nationes*) in the region between the River Amsaga in the west and the borders of Cyrenaica in the east. The precise situation in which concerns like that would be paramount is at once obvious. Following upon his victory at

the other category. Teutsch was clearly mistaken in arguing that this was the case; but his critics are also wrong when, having proved Teutsch mistaken, they leap to the conclusion that *oppida civium Romanorum* cannot be *conventus* in the broader sense of the term, *i. e.*, 'groups of Roman citizens'.

Thapsus, and the final dissolution of enemy forces at Utica and Zama, Caesar set about entirely reorganizing the Roman *provincia* in Africa. He created the new province of *Africa nova* that encompassed all the former lands of Juba I's kingdom from Calama (mod. Guelma) and Theveste (mod. Tébessa) in the west to the Arae Philaenorum on the Greater Syrtis in the east. He further envisaged a readjustment of government in the old province of *Africa*, and the inclusion of the 'baronial' principality of P. Sittius within the framework of the Roman provincial administration. The precise purpose of the administrative document drafted, probably in late 46, then, is made clearer by the summation that follows the list of *oppida libera* in chapter thirty (*NH*, V, 30):

> Ex reliquo numero non civitates tantum, sed plerique etiam nationes iure dici possunt, ut Nattabutes, Capsitani, Musulami, Sabarbares, Massyli, Nicives, Vacamures, Cinithii, Musuni, Marchubi et tota Gaetulia ad flumen Nigrim, qui Africam ab Aethiopia dirimit.

What the official who drafted the lists was attempting to do is this: to make clear that in Africa there are several different types of administrative units, that is, essentially land-tax statuses. These were:

a) *coloniae* (6)
b) *oppida libera* (30).

Although all the remaining towns are technically tributary subject cities (*civitates stipendiariae*), he wished to single out for Caesar's consideration those towns amongst them in which there were notable concentrations of Roman citizens, hence:

c) *oppida civium Romanorum* (15).

Then, having completed this initial part of the survey, he added some odd pieces of information regarding towns of which he had some personal knowledge (Castra Cornelia, Uzelis), and then proceeded to the two remaining categories that encompassed all the other communities in Africa:

d) *civitates* (i. e., *stipendiariae*)
e) *nationes.*

All the tribes actually named, however, seem to be located outside the bounds of the old province of Africa, in the region of *Africa nova* that Pliny calls *tota Gaetulia.*[86] So the document is essentially one that attempts to provide information on all *existing* units of local administration in Africa as of late 46 B.C.

---

[86] Which, interestingly, shows (if the expression is not one added as a gloss by Pliny himself) that there was not even at this time a clear conception of the southern frontiers of Africa. Rome claimed sovereignty over all tribes as far south as 'Gaetulia' might extend.

The document is, therefore, an administrative survey drawing up the land-tax statuses of communities in Africa in 46 B.C. as basic data to be used by Caesar in his provincial reorganization, a programme that he never had the opportunity to bring to a conclusion. It was probably drafted by someone on his staff prior to his departure from North Africa in late 46. It also seems quite probable that he was either at Zama or had access to the royal records of the kingdom of Juba I from his capital city. I postulate this for two reasons. We know that Caesar went to Zama and let the royal taxes and tributes, which had normally been auctioned at Zama for the entire African kingdom. Caesar also made Zama the new capital city of his newly formed province of *Africa nova*.[87] Secondly, the document contains very specific information about the organization of this earlier African tax system. A little further along in his text in another passage surely drawn from the same document, Pliny specifies that there were *precisely* 516 *nationes* or tribes in the region under consideration. If such a number has been preserved accurately in our MSS., it could only reflect an official source of some sort that would have taken such an accurate count of ethnic groups. Since all the tribal groups that Pliny specifically mentions (probably, again, drawn from this document) come from regions beyond the old Roman province of *Africa*, one must presume that such specific information was not filed in the offices of the proconsular governor in Utica, but rather in the archives of the African kingdom.

The entire document, then, gives us a valuable insight into one of the basic processes of Roman imperialism: the formation of a new *provincia*. As one might logically expect, one of the first steps in this process was the drafting of a document of the above type containing basic information on the existing units of local government upon which the Roman commander or administrative committee could formulate a new organizational framework. Basically, we would expect the Romans to attempt to work with what was given. But in this case, we can see the specific process at work. If the ordering of the statuses in the document is not purely fortuitous, primary importance was given in the administrator's view to those centres in the putative province where there were concentrations of Roman citizens – local settlements of known quality with and through which he could deal. In our case the colonies are listed first (even though half of them are not yet formal *coloniae*). After them, the *oppida civium Romanorum*, though possessing no formal juridical status, are listed in priority *before* the 'free cities'. Next in order of importance come the 'free cities', and after them all the ordinary tax-paying tribute cities of the province. Significantly, tribal groups (*nationes*) are separated from the tribute paying provincial communities in our list. There are several possible explanations for this. If I am correct in deducing that this piece of information derived from the tax records

[87] *Bell. Afr.* 97, see no. 69 above.

of the African kingdom, then the African kings may have placed 'tribes' in a different administrative category from 'towns', and the raw data of the Roman document merely reflect this division. In any event, the Roman administrator was faced with an entirely new category which was not to be found in the old province of *Africa* and for which Caesar may have made some provision in his organization of *Africa nova*. It would probably be wrong to suggest that the ethnic groups were 'ex-tax' simply because they are listed separately from the *civitates*. If anything, the fact that such a precise record was kept of their number in the tribute files of the African kingdom logically suggests that the African kings were already taxing them in some manner, and that the Roman administration intended to continue tradition. After establishing the new province in Africa, but before he was able to complete his colonial foundations and what seems to have been his obvious intent to incorporate the Cirtan Federation as part of the province, Caesar had at his disposal a document that enabled him to take some of the important initial steps in organizing the two Roman *provinciae* in Africa. And, most importantly, this included an already-formulated policy towards the *tribes* (*nationes*), their control and administration, that had been developed in a quite detailed way by the tax system of the African kingdoms. In this particular case at least *Quellenforschung* has not only solved a riddle of origins and reconstituted an original source, it has also revealed one of the few known administrative documents associated with the founding of a new Roman province.

APPENDIX A

Reconstruction of the Lists

Pliny, *Historia naturalis*, V, 29–30.
Area covered: Ad hunc finem (*i. e.*, the Arae Philaenorum) a fluvio Ampsaga.
Colonies: in his colonias sex, praeter iam dictas Uthinam, Thuburbi.

In list	Source	Ancient Name	Modern Name
1) Cirta	c. 22	Cirta	Constantine
2) Sicca	c. 22	Sicca Veneria	al-Kâf
3) Carthago	c. 24	Karthago	Carthage
4) Maxula	c. 24	Maxula	Rhadès
5) Uthina		Uthina	Oudna
6) Thuburbo		Thuburbo Minus	Tébourba

IV

Oppida civium Romanorum: oppida civium Romanorum XV, ex quibus in Mediterraneo dicenda,

In list	Source	Ancient Name	Modern Name
1) Assuritanum (Absuritanum)		Assuras (?)	Zanfûr
2) Abutucense		Aptuca (?) Abthugni (?)	Hr. Oudeka Hr. as-Sûar
3) Aboriense		Abora	unknown (nr. Thuburbo Maius)
4) Canopicum		Canopisi (?)	unknown
5) Chiniavense		Chiniava	Hr. Guenba
6) Simittuense		Simitthus	Shamtû
7) Thunusidense		Thunusida	Sidi Meskin
8) Thuburnicense		Thuburnica	Hr. Sidi 'Ali-bel-Kassem
9) Thinidrumense			Manzil al-Ghorshi (?)
10) Tibigense		civitas Thibicaensis Thigibba (?)	
11) Uchitana duo		Uchi Maius	Hr. Duamis
12)		Uchi Minus	
13) Vagense		Vaga	Béja

To these must be added the towns Pliny has omitted from the list since he has already mentioned them in the main text.

| 14) Tabarca | c. 22 | Thabraca | Tabarqa |
| 15) Utica | c. 23 | Utica | Borj bû-Shatûr |

A Latin Town: oppidum Latinum unum Uzalitanum

                              Uzalis   al-Alia

A Stipendiary Town: oppidum stipendiarium unum Castris Corneliis

                              Castra Cornelia

Oppida Libera: oppida libera XXX, ex quibus dicenda intus:

In list	Source	Ancient Name	Modern Name
1) Achollitanum		Acholla	Ras Botria
2) Aggaritanum		Aggar	al-Maklûba
3) Avittense		Avitta (?) Avitta Bibba (?)	Hr. Awitta Hr. bû-Ftis
4) Abziritanum		Abbir Cella (?)	Hr. en Naam
5) Canopitanum		Canopis (?)	unknown
6) Malizitanum		unknown	unknown

(followed on p. 466)

IV

458

Chart II: *The Status of African Communities between the Roman Conquest and Caesar's War*

Town	146[a]	111[b]	105[c]	46[d]	46–45[e]	45–43[f]	Later
Abziritanum oppidum	×	×	×	×	oppidum liberum	×	×
Abora	×	×	×	×	oppidum civium Romanorum	×	×
Abutucense oppidum	×	×	×	×	oppidum civium Romanorum	×	×
Acholla	Stipendiary to Carthage App. *Lib.* 94	oppidum liberum		oppidum liberum et immune *Bell. Afr.* 33.1; Strabo 7.3.12	oppidum liberum	×	×
Aggar	×	×	×	oppidum *Bell. Afr.* 67.1; 76.2; 79.1	oppidum liberum	×	×
Assuras	×	×	×	×	oppidum civium Romanorum	Colonia Iulia (?)	Colonia Iulia
Avittense oppidum	×	×	×	×	oppidum liberum	×	Hadrianic municipium
Bulla Regia	×	×	oppidum Oros. 5.21	×	oppidum liberum	×	Flavian municipium
Canopicum	×	×	×	×	oppidum liberum	×	×

The Elder Pliny's African Geography 459

Capsa	×	oppidum magnum *Bell. Iug.* 91; immune from taxation of African king, 89.4.		×	Hadrianic municipium
Carpis	×	×	oppidum Pliny, *NH*, 5	Colonia Iulia	Colonia Iulia
Castra Cornelia	×	×	locus Pliny, *NH*, 5.24	oppidum stipendiarium	×
Chiniava	×	×	×	oppidum civium Romanorum	Peregrine civitas
Chullu	×	×	oppidum Pliny, *NH*, 21	×	Municipium
Clupea	Destroyed by Romans, Strabo 17.3.16	×	oppidum *Bell. Afr.* 2.6; 3.1; *Bell. Civ.* 2.23.2	oppidum liberum	Colonia Iulia
Curubis	×	×	Fortified by Caesar's legates; C. 979, 977	oppidum liberum	Colonia Iulia

IV

Town	146[a]	111[b]	105[c]	46[d]	46–45[e]	45–43[f]	Later
Hadrumetum	Stipendiary to Carthage App. *Lib.* 141	oppidum liberum	×	oppidum *Bell. Afr.* 3.1; conventus fined by Caesar 97.	oppidum liberum	×	Trajanic colony
Hippo Diarrhytus	×	×	×	oppidum Pliny, *NH*, 5.23	×	×	×
Hippo Regius	×	×	×	oppidum Pliny, *NH*, 5.22	×	×	×
Karthago	×	Gracchan colony	×	×	'colony'	Colonia Iulia	Colonia Iulia
Lepcis Magna	Tributary city of Carthage, Livy 34.62	×	civitas foederata *Bell. Iug.* 19.1.3; 77	Fined by Caesar, *Bell. Afr.* 97; Plut. *Caes.* 55	×	×	Trajanic colony
Lepti Minus	Stipendiary to Carthage App. *Lib.* 94	oppidum liberum	×	oppidum liberum et immune, *Bell. Afr.* 7.1; 62. 4–5, 63.1	oppidum liberum	×	×
Macomades	×	×	×	×	oppidum liberum	×	×
Malizitanum oppidum	×	×	×	×	oppidum liberum	×	×

Matera	×	×		×		×
Maxula	×	×		×	×	×
Milevis	×	×		×	×	colony
Missua	×	×		×	×	
Neapolis	Destroyed by the Romans Strabo 17.3.16	×	oppidum Pliny, *NH*, 5.24.	oppidum liberum	Colonia Iulia	Colonia Iulia
Rusicade	×	×	oppidum *Bell. Afr.* 2.6	×		Augustan Colony
Ruspina	×	×	oppidum Pliny, *NH*, 5.21	oppidum liberum	×	×
Sabratha	×	×	×	oppidum liberum	×	×
Salaphitanum oppidum	×	×	×	oppidum liberum	×	×
Sicca Veneria	×	Royal oppidum *Bell. Iug.* 56.3–4	×	'colony'	Colonia Iulia	Colonia Iulia
Simitthus	×	×	×	oppidum civium Romanorum	×	Augustan colony

Town	146[a]	111[b]	105[c]	46[d]	46-45[e]	45-43[f]	Later
Tabarca	×	×	×	×	oppidum civium Romanorum	Colonia Iulia	Colonia Iulia
Tacape	×	×	×	×	oppidum liberum	×	×
Tacatua	×	×	×	oppidum Pliny, *NH*, 5.22	×	×	×
Thaenae	×	×	×	oppidum Strabo 17.3.12	oppidum liberum	×	×
Tagense oppidum	×	×	×	×	oppidum liberum	×	×
Thala	×	×	oppidum magnum et opulentum *Bell. Iug.* 75	oppidum Strabo 17.3.12	×	×	×
Thapsus	Stipendiary to Carthage App. *Lib.* 94	oppidum liberum	×	oppidum *Bell. Afr.* 28.1; conventus fined, 97.	oppidum liberum	×	×
Theudense oppidum	×	×	×	×	oppidum liberum	×	×
Theudalis	×	oppidum liberum	×	immune oppidum	oppidum liberum	×	×

IV

The Elder Pliny's African Geography

Tibigense oppidum	×	×	×		oppidum civium Romanorum	×	×	
Thinidrumense oppidum	×	×	×		oppidum civium Romanorum	×	×	
Thisicense oppidum	×	×	×		oppidum liberum	×	×	
Thuburbo Minus	×	×	×		'colony'	Colonia Iulia	Colonia Iulia	
Thuburnica	×	×	×		oppida civium Romanorum	×	×	
Thunusida	×	×	×		oppida civium Romanorum	×	×	
Thysdrus	×	×	×	Conventus fined by Caesar Bell. Afr. 97	oppidum liberum	×	colony	
Tigense oppidum	×	×	×		oppidum liberum	×	×	
Tunis	Attacked by Romans Strabo 17.3.16	×	×		oppidum liberum	×	×	
Uchi Maius	×	×	Marian settlement		oppidum civium Romanorum	×	×	

IV

464

Town	146[a]	111[b]	105[c]	46[d]	46–45[e]	45–43[f]	Later
Uchi Minus	×	×			oppidum civium Romanorum	×	×
Uthina	×	×	×	×	'colony'	Colonia Iulia	Colonia Iulia
Utica	Stipendiary to Carthage App. *Lib.* 94 Deserts to Romans, Livy, *Ep.* 49; Polyb. 36.1.	oppidum liberum cf. App. *BC*, 8.135	oppidum *Bell. Iug.* 63.1; 64.5 86.4 5, 104	conventus fined by Caesar *Bell. Afr.* 90.	oppidum civium Romanorum	×	Hadrianic colony
Ulusippira	×	×	×	×	oppidum liberum	×	×
Uzalis	×	oppidum liberum	×	oppidum liberum Strabo 17.3.12	oppidum Latinum	×	×
Vaga (Zeugitana)	×	×	Royal oppidum *Bell. Iug.* 29.4; 47.1; 65; 68–69 Italian residents	×	oppidum civium Romanorum	×	×

… IV

The Elder Pliny's African Geography   465

Vaga (Byzacena)	x	x		oppidum *Bell. Afr.* 74.1; Strabo 17.3.12	oppidum liberum	x	x
Visense oppidum	x	x		x		x	x
Zama	x	x	urbs magna *Bell. Iug.* 56.1; 57	oppidum *Bell. Afr.* 91.1; Strabo 17.3.12	oppidum liberum	x	x

[a] Status at or about the time of the formation of the province of *Africa* following the defeat of Punic Carthage.
[b] Status as reflected in the *Lex Agraria* of 111 B.C.
[c] Status at the time of the Jugurthine War, principally as reflected in Sallust's *Bellum Iugurthinum*.
[d] Status at the time of Caesar's campaigns in Africa in 46 B.C. as noted in the *Bellum Africum* and some ancilliary texts, including Strabo.
[e] Status as noted in the Plinian 'Appendix', *NH*, 5.29–30.
[f] Status as altered by Caesar's actions upon forming the province of *Africa nova* and after his departure from Africa in the summer of 46.

IV

7) Materense		Matera	Matûr
8) Salaphitanum		unknown	unknown
9) Thisdritanum		Thysdrus	al-Jem
10) Thisicense		Thizika	Hr. Tishga
11) Tunisense		Tunis	Tunis
12) Theudense	cf. c. 23	Theudalis	Hr. Awân
13) Tagesense		Thagaste (?)	Sûq-Ahhras
14) Tigense		Thiges (?)	Hr. Tejiûs
15) Ulusubburitanum		Ulusippira	Hr. Zembra
16) Vagense aliud		Vaga	unknown (nr. Thapsus)
17) Visense		unknown	unknown
18) Zamense		Zama	Seba Biâr

To these must be added the towns Pliny has omitted from the list since he has already mentioned them in the main text.

19) Bulla Regia	c. 22	Bulla Regia	Hammâm Darrajîi
20) Clupea	c. 24	Clupea	Kalibia
21) Curubis	c. 24	Curubis	Korba
22) Neapolis	c. 25	Neapolis	Nabûl
23) Lepti Minus	c. 25	Lepcis	Lamta
24) Hadrumetum	c. 25	Hadrumetum	Sûsa
25) Ruspina	c. 25	Ruspina	Hr. Tenir
26) Thapsus	c. 25	Thapsus	Rass Dimass
27) Thaenae	c. 25	Thaenae	Hr. Thina
28) Macomades	c. 25	Macomades	Borj Yonga
29) Tacape	c. 25	Tacape	Gabès
† "Aves" †	c. 25	see *Appendix B*	
30) Sabratha	c. 25	Sabratha	Sabrata

Civitates stipendiariae et nationes

Ex reliquo numero non civitates tantum, sed plerique etiam nationes iure dici possunt, ut Nattabutes, Capsitani, Musulami, Sabarbares, Massyli, Nicives, Vacamures, Cinithi, Musuni, Marchubi, et tota Gaetulia ad flumen Nigrim, qui Africam ab Aethiopia dirimit.

APPENDIX B

Oppidum Liberum 'Aves'

If the list of *oppida libera* in chapter thirty is reconstructed from the supplementary data available in the main text (see Append. A) and all the 'free cities' in the text are counted, the total comes to *thirty-one* rather than the thirty announced by Pliny at the head of the chapter. Teutsch sought to remedy this problem by deleting Sabratha (the last city mentioned in the main text) from the list, claiming that it was located outside the region of Byzacium which that survey purports to cover.[1] But the hypothesis is totally unacceptable. If we accepted this basis for rejecting cities on the list we would also have to delete Macomades, Tacape, and Aves from the lists since these towns were also outside the southern boundary of *Africa vetus* (and, *a fortiori*, Byzacium) which stopped at Thaenae.[2] One would then be left with only twenty-seven of Pliny's total of thirty. In addition, the heading of the official list clearly does include the Syrtic coastline: it is a survey 'ad hunc finem' (*i. e.*, the *Arae Philaenorum*) 'a fluvio Ampsaga', that is, all North Africa from the border of Mauretania in the west to that of Cyrenaica in the east.[3] Teutsch's second objection, that Sabratha is mentioned again in a later section of the geography that surveys the Syrtic coast (c. 27) under its Greek name 'Habrotonum' is not reason arbitrarily to delete it here.[4] It is quite clear that Pliny has used a Latin source for c. 25, but has resorted to a different Greek source for c. 27. In his usual relaxed approach to his work, Pliny has not bothered to edit the two sections to remove discrepancies and inconsistencies. Sabratha must therefore stand as one of the *oppida libera*. How then are we to reconcile the apparent total of thirtyone with the announced total of thirty?

Among the cities listed in the 'appendix' itself (cf. nos. 1–18), the identification or location of three towns provides special difficulties: Malizitanum (no. 6), Salaphitanum (no. 8) and Vigense (no. 17). There are no known identifications for these towns, and their municipal history remains a mystery. There are other problems: the MSS spelling of Molizitanum places the town out of alphabetical order, an easy copying error that is neatly rectified by changing the 'e' to an 'a' (as I have done). But there are no MSS. difficulties with Salaphitanum or its order in the list. Vigense, however, is another troublesome case. But, in spite of the MSS. difficulties, it is clear that the town's name must have begun with a 'v' if the alphabetical order of the list is to be preserved. We are therefore left with the choice between the MSS.

---

1 Teutsch, *Städtewesen*, 90, esp. no. 243.
2 Macomades, Tacape, Aves, south of Thaenae, which is the southern terminus of *Africa vetus*.
3 The 'Official Survey', our 'appendix' covered the whole region of greater proconsular Africa.
4 Teutsch, *Städtewesen*, 90; cf. *IRT*, p. 21 on the Greek name for Sabratha.

IV

468

Map 1
City Status at the Time of the Lex Agraria (111 B.C.)

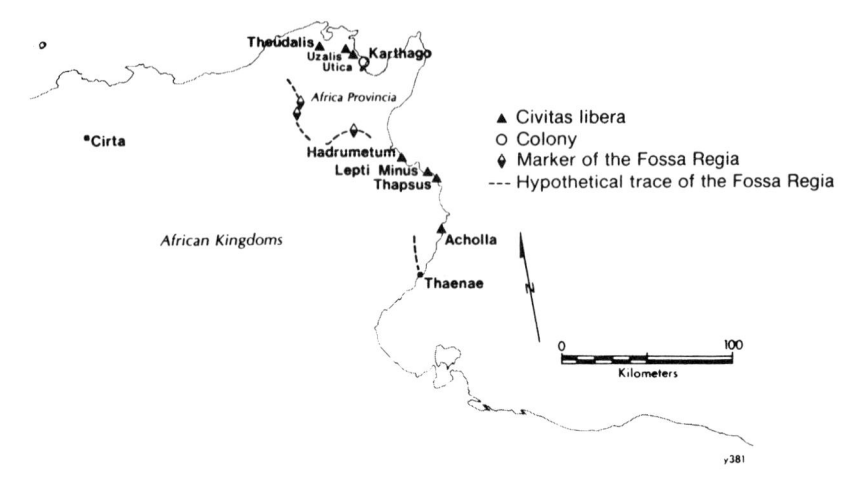

▲ Civitas libera
○ Colony
⚑ Marker of the Fossa Regia
--- Hypothetical trace of the Fossa Regia

Map 2
City Status at the Time of the Bellum Iugurthinum and Aftermath (ca. 110 - 100 B.C.)

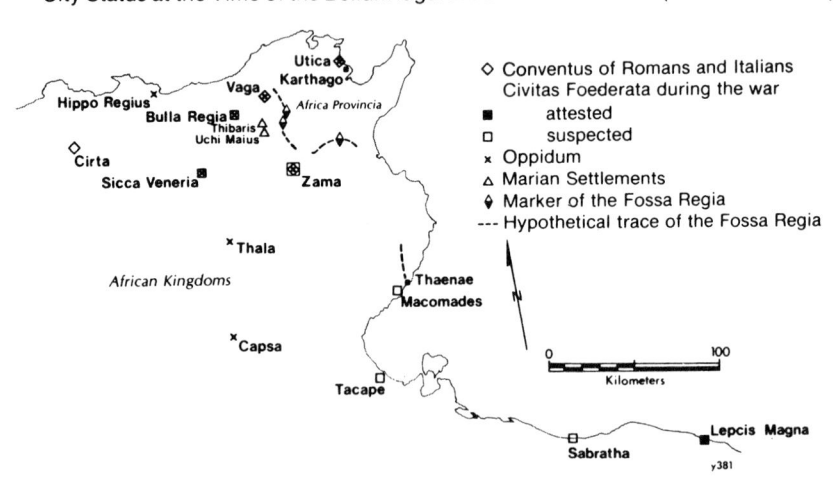

◇ Conventus of Romans and Italians
   Civitas Foederata during the war
■ attested
□ suspected
× Oppidum
△ Marian Settlements
⚑ Marker of the Fossa Regia
--- Hypothetical trace of the Fossa Regia

alternatives 'Vigense' and 'Visense'.[5] But nothing in the manuscripts themselves would otherwise cast any doubt on the actual existence of the above named towns; alphabetical order has been kept, and each city's name is intact, with only slight variations in spelling.

5 *vise* – H (D²); *vige* – E³, G *cum* B¹; Cuntz's proposal that the difficulties arose from a conflation of 'Vagense aliud, *Sigense*' is not probable since *Sigense* would not follow *Vagense* in alphabetical order. A conflation of 'Vagense aliud, Vigense' would be possible.

Map 3
City Status at the Time of the Bellum Africum (46 B.C.)

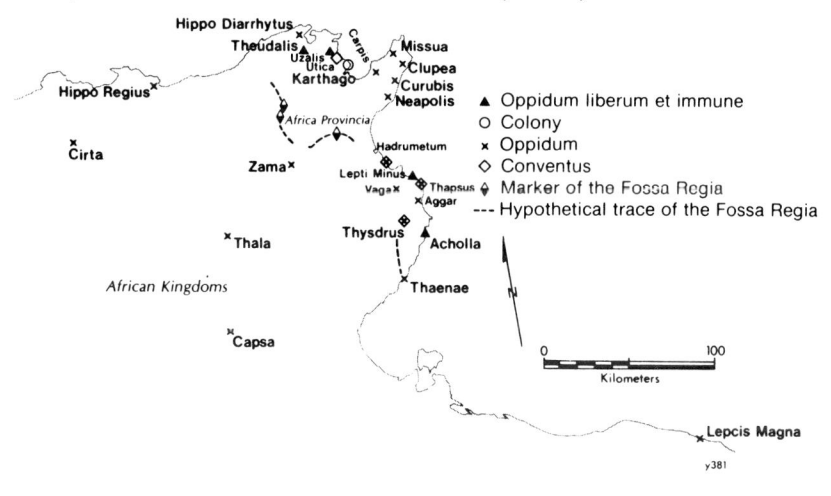

▲ Oppidum liberum et immune
○ Colony
× Oppidum
◇ Conventus
⚑ Marker of the Fossa Regia
--- Hypothetical trace of the Fossa Regia

Map 4
City Status under Caesar and Augustus (45/44 B.C. - A.D. 14)

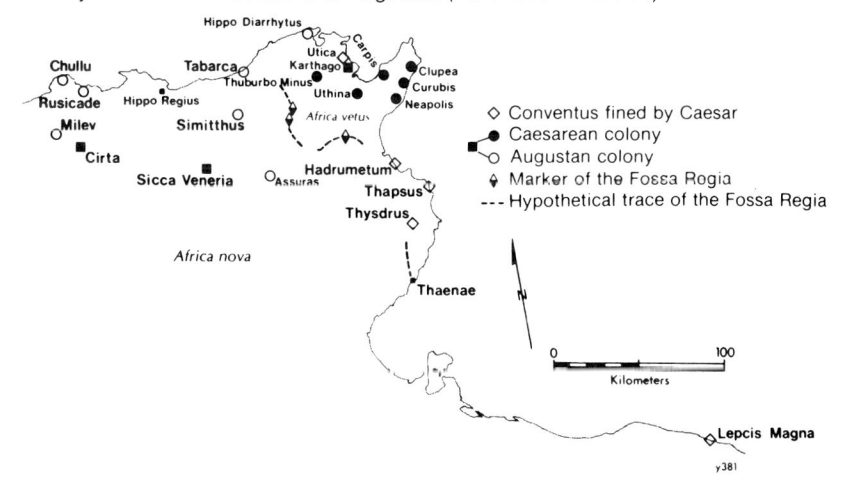

◇ Conventus fined by Caesar
● Caesarean colony
○ Augustan colony
⚑ Marker of the Fossa Regia
--- Hypothetical trace of the Fossa Regia

Of the *oppida libera* added to our list from passages in the main text, there is no difficulty with the first four (nos. 19–22). But this is not true of the last eight towns that complete the list (nos. 22–30), all taken from chapter twenty-eight of the main text, a mini-survey of Byzacium. That passage reads in full:

> Hic oppida libera Leptis, Hadrumetum, Ruspina, Thapsus. Inde Thenae, Aves, Macomades, Tacape, Sabrata contingens Syrtim minorem.

Map 5
City Status in the Elder Pliny's Geography (NH, V, 29 - 30, ca. 46/45 B.C.)

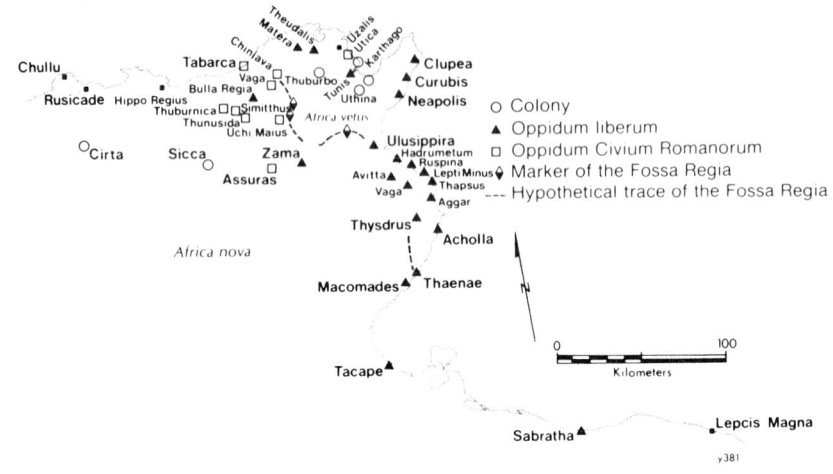

○ Colony
▲ Oppidum liberum
□ Oppidum Civium Romanorum
◊ Marker of the Fossa Regia
--- Hypothetical trace of the Fossa Regia

We are singularly fortunate in that this list, derived from the official list in the appendix, is preserved intact, *not* in the alphabetical order of the original document, but in a north-south geographical order. All the cities on this list can be identified easily, all that is except the curious 'Aves'. What is more significant is that 'Aves' presents the only MSS. difficulties in the whole passage, trouble that is especially apparent at the juncture THAENAE-AVES. There are at least six different MSS. readings for the ending of THAENAE.[6] 'AVES' is recorded in most MSS., but was deliberately omitted by at least one early editor.[7] Martianus Capella, an early fifth century compilor from Carthage quoted Pliny's geography extensively in his compendium of knowledge. In fact, he happens to quote this particular passage from Pliny *verbatim* but, once again, there is MSS. trouble. Instead of 'AVES', the MSS. have the readings 'ABES' and 'ABIES'.[8] Clearly, some difficulties had already arisen by the time Capella was copying Pliny.

Our suspicions about the existence of 'AVES' are deepened by the complete silence of any other evidence, literary, ephigraphic, or numismatic, about the

---

6 The readings in the *app. crit.* of the Teubner text (p. 370) are: *Thaenae* (a³ B e M Cap); *Thene* (f); *Thenco* (R¹); *Then* (R²); *Theana* (F); *Thena* (rv, J); cf. *C.* 22727; *AE* 1949: 38.
7 Omitted in the *editio* of Alexander Benedictus, published in Venice in 1507.
8 For Capella's background and date see W. H. Stahl & R. Johnson, *Martianus Capella and the Seven Liberal Arts*, 1, New York, Columbia University Press, 1971, 11-16 (on copying of the Elder Pliny, see 129-30, 138-39). For the readings see ss. 670 of the Teubner edition (ed. A. Dick, addit. J. Préaux, Leipzig, 1925).

presence of such a town. This silence is much more damning in this case than is the silence concerning the *oppida libera* mentioned above since there do not exist any good literary sources on the regions of the interior. This is not true for the region of the Kerkennah-Gulf of Gabès coastline which is well covered by most of the itineraries. But not one of these mentions an 'AVES'. All go directly from Thaenae to Macomades, and do not list any intervening towns.[9] Thus, there is no external corroboration for the existence of the town.

We might note too that many sources cite THAENAE in the plural form THENAS or THAENAS.[10] If this happened in the original lists, it is easy to understand how MSS. corruption led to the separate existence of a new town named 'AVES', since three of the elements of 'AVES', the 'a', 'e', and 's', are also present in the ending of THAENAS. When we note that the *only* MSS. difficulties in this passage occur precisely at the end of the word THAENAE we can conjecture that the individual letters AVES are, at best, 'palaeographically weak'. 'AVES', indeed, would seem to be an accident of writing, and probably should be the city deleted from the list of *oppida libera* to leave us with the correct total of thirty.

---

9 There is no mention of any 'Aves' in the Peutinger Table or in the *Itinerarium Antoninianum*; nor in Ptolemy, *Geographica*, 4.3.11: Θέαιναι, Μαχομάδα, Τρίτωνος ποταμοῦ ἐκβολαί, Ταχάπη. Anonymous of Ravenna, 3.5: 'Tacapas, ad Oleastrum, Macumades, Thenas, Patabura (= Taparura)' in north-south order; and the *Liber Guidonis*, ss. 89: 'Taparura, Themenas (= Thaenas), Macomades Minores, ad Oleastrum', in a south-north direction.

10 On the reasons for errors creeping into the Latin transliterations of these place names see L. Poinssot, "Macomades-Iunci", *MSAF* 81 (1944) 133–69, at 153, no. 3; the above argument is postulated on the basis of a unitary source for Pliny's 'appendix', an hypothesis not accepted by A. Luisi, "A proposito della regione Zeugitana in Plinio, *Nat. Hist.* V, 22–30. Considerazioni sulle fonti", *AFMB* 14 (1974–76) 83–102, but on the basis of traditional arguments I have rejected in this article.

V

THE FORMATION OF AFRICA PROCONSULARIS

Modern scholarship has accepted the convenient date of 27 B. C. for the formation of a unified province of Africa under a proconsular governor[1]. Evidence in support of this *communis opinio* turns out to be surprisingly slight. Of the two main literary passages usually called in aid that of Dio refers explicitly only to the division of the provinces between *princeps* and senate: καὶ ἐνομίσθη διὰ ταῦτα ἡ μὲν 'Αφρικὴ καὶ ἡ Νουμιδία ἥ τε Ἀσία καὶ ἡ Ἑλλὰς μετὰ τῆς Ἠπείρου, καὶ τὸ Δελματικὸν τό τε Μακεδονικὸν καὶ Σικελία, Κρήτη τε μετὰ Λιβύης τῆς περὶ Κυρήνην καὶ Βιθυνία μετὰ τοῦ προσκειμένου οἱ Πόντου, Σαρδώ τε καὶ Βαιτικὴ τοῦ τε δήμου καὶ τῆς γερουσίας εἶναι, τοῦ δὲ δὴ Καίσαρος . . . (53, 12, 4). It is true that Dio mentions 'Africa' and 'Numidia' separately — strictly speaking he should have said Africa Vetus and Africa Nova — but, if any significance is to be placed on this distinction *per se*, the proper conclusion is surely that the two provinces continued to be administered separately *after* 27 B. C. For Dio is clearly listing the various provinces in terms appropriate to the period after the settlement of that year: for example, Baetica, the district of Tarraco, Lusitania, Lugdunensis, Aquitania, Belgica. All that he is stating in effect is simply (and loosely[1a]) that the whole of Roman Africa was made a senatorial province in 27 B. C., nothing more. To infer that Africa Nova and Africa Vetus were merged at this particular juncture, thus bringing Proconsularis[2] into being, is a gratuitous assumption.

Precisely the same criticism applies to a passage of Strabo that has also been held to attest the formation of the proconsular province: ἀλλ' ἐν ἀρχαῖς γε διέθηκε ποιήσας ὑπατικὰς μὲν δύο, Λιβύην τε, ὅση ὑπὸ 'Ρωμαίοις ἔξω τῆς ὑπὸ 'Ιούβα μὲν πρότερον, νῦν δὲ Πτολεμαίῳ τῷ ἐκείνου παιδί, καὶ 'Ασίαν . . . (17, 3, 25). He then goes on to list ten praetorian provinces of the People, that is administered by the senate. As the opening sentence of the section confirms, Strabo is describing in his own terms the settlement of 27 B. C.:

---

[1] For example: S. Gsell, Histoire ancienne de l'Afrique du Nord (HAAN), VIII, 1928, 196, 209; T. R. S. Broughton, The Romanization of Africa Proconsularis, 1929, 71f.; Ch.-A. Julien, Histoire de l'Afrique du Nord (des origines à la conquête arabe) (rev. ed. by C. Courtois, 1966) 123; P. Romanelli, Storia delle Provincie Romane dell' Africa, 1959, 158; L. Teutsch, Das Städtewesen in Nordafrika in der Zeit von C. Gracchus bis zum Tode des Kaisers Augustus, 1962, 77f., 128f.; B. E. Thomasson, Die Statthalter der römischen Provinzen Nordafrikas von Augustus bis Diocletianus, I, 1960, 15f.; cf. RE Suppl. XIII, 1973, 1; J. Gascou, La Politique municipale de l'Empire romain en Afrique Proconsulaire de Trajan à Septime-Sévère, 1972, 20, n. 3; M. Rachet, Rome et les Berbères, Coll. Lat. 110, 1970, 59f.

[1a] Dio's information on Baetica(?) and Greece is similarly anachronistic.

[2] Romanelli notes ibid. that the term does not seem to have been applied to the province *ab initio*.

V

370

Αἱ δ'ἐπαρχίαι διήρηνται ἄλλοτε μὲν ἄλλως, ἐν δὲ τῷ παρόντι, ὡς Καῖσαρ ὁ Σεβαστὸς διέταξεν. The provinces mentioned make it abundantly clear that one cannot press Strabo's use of ποιέω to mean literally 'create'. Augustus did not 'make' Proconsular Africa any more than Asia or any of these provinces; he simply arranged which ones were to be 'senatorial' — whether consular or praetorian — and which should be administered directly by the princeps. In itself, therefore, the passage of Strabo tells no more about the unification of the two Roman provinces of Africa than does that of Dio[3]. Substantive testimony on when this was achieved must be sought elsewhere.

In his *Res Gestae*, the version of events by which he wished to be remembered, Augustus gives the following list of provinces swearing allegiance to his cause: *provi]nciae Galliae, Hispaniae, Africa, Sicilia, Sardinia* (25, 2). Unlike the Gauls or the Spains, Africa is in the singular and evidently not intended as a loose geographical expression; otherwise Augustus would have said 'Gaul', 'Spain'. Unless, then, one is to accuse him of oversight, negligence, or distortion (for reasons obscure), the implication is plainly that in 32 B. C. Africa was governed as one province. That this was the case is to all appearances confirmed by the circumstance that from 35 B. C. down to 27 B. C. the administration of Africa was in the hands of proconsuls, the sequence beginning with T. Statilius Taurus followed by L. Cornificius [?][4]. From this time onwards at least there are no known governors of Vetus and Nova independently, only what look to be single governors of both provinces combined. If so, all that the settlement of 27 B. C. did was to lay down that the proconsular governors of Africa should be appointed from the senate. Otherwise the administrative arrangement of Africa remained as before, and, if the two provinces were — at least from 35 B. C. — under one governor, they were in practice united[5].

If the *fasti* of the proconsular governors of Africa, to the extent that they are known, provide a rough *terminus ante* for the formation of the province, a *terminus post* is to be sought in the tangled history of the region itself following the Pompeian defeat at Thapsus (April, 46 B. C.). The most significant of Caesar's arrangements in Africa was to reorganize the eastern part of the former kingdom of Juba I as the province of Africa Nova[6]. Situated to the

[3] Suet. Aug. 47, which is sometimes quoted in this connection, is irrelevant to the origins of Proconsularis.

[4] T. Statilius Taurus: PIR[1] III, 615; BROUGHTON, MRR II, 409 & 413. L. Cornificius: PIR[2] C. 1503; MRR II, 412 & 416.

[5] Nothing seems to justify GSELL's view, l. c., that both were administered by one governor, yet continued to be juridically separate down to the division of the provinces; so also TEUTSCH, Städtewesen 129, cf. 77. One could equally well hold, particularly in view of Dio's wording, that this was as true of the period *after* 27 B. C. as before.

[6] Caesar Bell. Afr. 97, 1; Appian B. C. 2, 100; 4, 53; Dio 43, 9, 4. This seems not to have been an *ad hoc* plan taken in haste following Caesar's conquest of Africa but one

west of the Fossa Regia[7], the territory included the plains of Sūq Ahras and Sūq al-Arbā, an immensely fertile tract that could produce the agricultural surplus needed to meet the growing demands of Rome[8]. The new province was to be in the charge of a proconsular governor as distinct from the old praetorian province of Africa, now known as Africa Vetus; but in the confused aftermath of Caesar's assassination the precise status of either province is difficult to disengage from the often conflicting accounts of Dio and Appian. By the terms of the agreement at Bononia (ratified 27th November, 43 B. C.) both Africas fell under the control of Octavian, and, while nothing shows that Octavian intended at this stage to leave the two under a single governor, it is a fact that the actions taken by T. Sextius left him firmly in control of both provinces by the summer of 42 B. C. The following year Sextius continued to govern both as a single unit when Octavian's attempt to dislodge him (on suspicion of sympathising with Antony) misfired in the wake of the Perusine War[9]. De facto, then, both provinces of Africa were administered as one from 42 B. C. onward and no further governors of Nova are known after this date.

Following the triumviral agreement at Philippi (autumn 42 B. C.) the exact disposition of the African provinces is variously reported, but with Octavian receiving the West it seems more likely than not that he retained both Nova and Vetus[10]. Acting solely on his own authority, so it appears, Octavian subsequently gave Africa to Lepidus as a special province, an arrangement accepted by Antony at the council of Brundisium (autumn 40 B. C.)[11], though by Appian's account T. Sextius was still maintaining a position in

long considered on account of the region's fertility: cf. Caesar B. C. 2, 25, 4; Dio 41, 41, 3. The capital city probably remained Zama, as before, though GSELL, HAAN VIII, 166, followed by ROMANELLI, Storia 131, notes the alternative possibility of Thugga; cf. Dio 48, 21, 3. On Zama see G. PICARD, CRAI, 1948, 421—427.

[7] Pliny N. H. 5, 25; CH. SAUMAGNE, Observations sur le tracé de la »Fossa Regia«, RAL 4, 1928, 451—459 (= CT 10, 1962, 407—416). For the western boundary of Nova see GSELL, HAAN VIII, 158, 163; IlAlg. I, pp. ix—xii and end-map.

[8] A series of coins featuring on the obverse a portrait head of Ceres crowned with a wreath of corn appears to celebrate the significance of the new province: BABELON, MRR II, p. 14, n. 16; GRUEBER, CRRBM II, 576, nos. 21—25; and pl. cxxi, 13 & 14; SYDENHAM, CRR 170, nn.1023—1024. But see now M. H. CRAWFORD, Roman Republican Coinage, I, 1974, 93, n. 467, 1a (Pl. LV). For the propaganda value of his African conquests see Caesar's boasts; Plut. Caes. 55; cf. Caesar Bell. Afr. 97, 3.

[9] For details see GSELL, HAAN VIII, 183—194; ROMANELLI, Storia 142—146; BROUGHTON, MRR II, 360f. (Q. Cornificius); 363, 374, 383 (T. Sextius); 373, 382 (C. Fuficius Fango).

[10] Hinted at by Appian B. C. 5, 3, 12 & 46; cf. ROMANELLI, Storia 145. Little credence can be placed in Dio's statement (48, 1, 3; 22, 2) that Africa was now divided with Vetus going to Antony and Nova to Octavian. Nor is it likely that at this date Lepidus would have been promised 'Africa' (Dio's terminology would mean Vetus, Appian's both provinces) provided suspicions against him proved to be unjust. Both GSELL, HAAN, VIII 191 and TEUTSCH, Städtewesen 128, accept Dio at face value none the less.

[11] Appian B. C. 5, 12; cf. 53; 65; Dio 48, 20, 4; 28, 4; Plut. Ant. 30.

Africa down to late 39 B. C.[12]. By the end of that year, then, if not earlier, Lepidus will have been in uncontested control of both African provinces, having assumed formal control a year or more earlier. His arrival on the continent must presumably have taken place towards the end of 40 B. C., while the terminal date of his command can be placed about midsummer of 36 B. C. after his departure for Sicily to aid Octavian in the war against Sextus Pompeius[13]. Within this period tangible traces of his presence are extremely slight: a few *denarii* he apparently issued as governor and an honorific inscription from the port of Thabraca, set up to the triumvir Lepidus as patron *ex d(ecreto) d(ecurionum)*[14]. That Lepidus founded a Roman community here has been suggested but lacks positive proof[14a]. Otherwise the only explicit information we have is Dio's statement in 52, 43, 1, that Lepidus razed part of the city of Carthage, harsh measures characterized by Tertullian as *violenta ludibria* (de Pallio 1). What exactly he was about is quite obscure. GSELL conjectured that Lepidus removed parts of the colony which had impiously been placed on ground cursed by Scipio since he already knew he was to be made Pontifex Maximus[15]. The latter part of this view at any rate seems implausible, as there is nothing to show Lepidus had prior knowledge of his future appointment. No more convincing is TEUTSCH's view that some time before his departure Lepidus would have deliberately crushed supposed partisans of Octavian in Carthage: the two triumvirs remained nominal allies until after Naulochus.

A more fundamental explanation is possibly to be sought in the connection of these 'clearing operations' with the conversion of Carthage into the central city of 'proconsular' Africa — quite possibly on the lines suggested by GSELL[16].

[12] B. C. 5, 75. ROMANELLI, Storia 147, n. 5 treats the whole story as an error on Appian's part. [13] Appian B. C. 5, 98: cf. 104; Vell. Pat. 2, 80, 1.

[14] GSELL, HAAN, VIII, 194f.; TEUTSCH, Städtewesen 128. The coins were attributed to 40—37 B. C. by GRUEBER, CRRBM II, 568f., 579, nn. 29—31 (plates CXXII, fig. 2 and 3); doubted by ROMANELLI, Storia 147, n. 2, who notes that BABELON assigns them to 43 B. C. For the inscription see J. GUEY and A. PERNETTE, Karthago 9, 1958, 81—89 (= AEpig 1959, no. 77).

[14a] In the name *colonia V. P. Iulia Thabracenorum* (ILAlg. I, 109: second century) the letters *V. P.* might conceivably be expanded *Victrix Pontificalis:* J. GUEY and A. PERNETTE, ibid. 87, n. 40; GASCOU, Politique municipale (above, note 1) 23.

[15] HAAN, VIII, 195; followed by ROMANELLI, Storia 147.

[16] Previous discussion appears to have overlooked Appian's remark, Pun. 136, that the new Carthage was built not on the site of the old one but ἀγχοτάτω μάλιστα ἐκείνης, φυλαξάμενος τῆς πάλαι τὸ ἐπάρατον. This surely refers to the original foundation in 44 B. C. rather than to Octavian's reinforcement of the colony in 29 B. C.; see further below, note 30. If building had first got under way on the installment of the colony in the months following Caesar's death (below, note 29), it is quite possible that construction had spilled over onto cursed ground, where it was torn down a few years later by Lepidus. In Tertullian's eyes this violent activity could well have looked a mockery.

External pressures, both military and economic, lie at the root of this development. By 40 B. C. control of Sicily and the Straits of Messana had given Sextus Pompeius a stranglehold on the main supply-route by which grain was carried from Africa to Rome; famine and food riots in the capital are reported towards the close of the year[17]. Clearly the crisis in Rome's grain supply was directly related to the role of Roman Africa, a region of crucial importance to Octavian now that Antony held the alternative granary of Egypt. Under these conditions there was an obvious need to have a unified command in Africa, both to counter the threat from Pompeius and to organize the collection and shipping of African grain. And of course any new disposition in Africa that reckoned with the importance of Rome's food supply must have taken into consideration the vast fertile plains nominally in Africa Nova. Thus all the elements were at hand that might militate almost of necessity towards the unification of the two Roman provinces.

What is at any rate certain is that one later finds an extremely large *pertica* attributed to Carthage[18] — so large, in fact, that it included not only the middle and upper reaches of the Bagradas Valley but also places situated even further to the west within the territory Caesar had made the province of Africa Nova[19]. It would be a reasonable guess *a priori* that the origins of this vast administrative territory reach back at least to the time when Carthage was made metropolis of Roman Africa; but, as it happens, epigraphical evidence is to hand that may very well attest not only the existence of the *pertica Carthaginiensium* already under Lepidus but also the inclusion within it of Uchi Maius situated in the old territory of Africa Nova. Two well-known inscriptions reveal the activities of the freedman M. Caelius Phileros in Africa. The longer is from Formiae and gives the full cursus: *M(arcus) Caelius M(arci) l(ibertus) Phileros accens(us)/T(iti) Sexti imp(eratoris) in Africa, Carthag(ine) aed(ilis) praef(ectus)/i(ure) d(icundo) vectig(alibus) quinq(uennalibus) locand(is) in castell(is) LXXXIII/aedem Tell(uris) s(ua) p(ecunia) fec(it), IIvir Clupeae bis, Formis/August(alis) aedem Nept(unis) lapid(ibus) variis s(ua) p(ecunia) ornav(it) ... (CIL X 6104)*. A second stone, from Uchi Maius, reads on BROUGHTON's very probable restoration[20]: *M. C]ae[l(ius) Ph]ileros/castellum*

---

[17] Appian B. C. 5, 67f.; Dio 48, 31; Livy, Epit. 127. For the sequel see Appian 5, 71f., 77, 92; Dio 48, 36—38, 49, 2—3; Plut. Ant. 32.

[18] KORNEMANN's original theory, Die caesarische Kolonie Karthago und die Einführung römischer Gemeindeordnung in Africa, Philologus 60, 1901, 402—426. The term *pertica* can now legitimately be used since the discovery of a fragmentary inscription from Thugga, first published by C. POINSSOT, Immunitas perticae Carthaginiensium, CRAI 1962, 55—75.

[19] H. G. PFLAUM, La Romanisation de l'ancien territoire de la Carthage punique à la lumière des découvertes épigraphiques récentes, Ant. Afr. 4, 1970, 75—117. See further T. R. S. BROUGHTON, The Territory of Carthage, Mél. Durry (= REL 47, *bis*), 1970, 265—275.

[20] Romanization 64; AJ Phil 50, 1929, 278—285; above, note 19, 268, 270.

divisit/inter colonos et/Uchitanos termin(um)/que constituit (CIL VIII 26274 = ILTun 1370). Comparison between the two strongly suggests that the *castellum* of Uchi Maius was one of the eighty-three *castella* under the jurisdiction of Phileros[21], and, if one may judge from later examples of the office of *praef. i. d.*[22], he would appear to have been sent out from Carthage to administer the eighty-three *castella*, which presumably fall within the *pertica* of Carthage[23]. The number of the *castella* gives a clear indication of the early size of the *pertica*, while the activities of Phileros at Uchi Maius, where his division of land must be in connection with the juridical prefecture *vectigalibus quinquennalibus locandis*, prove its extension well to the west of the Fossa Regia. As Phileros was *accensus* to Titus Sextius, whose activities in Africa we have outlined above, it looks very much as though his aedileship at Carthage should be placed ca. 39 B. C.[24]. If so, the prefecture could very well have been served soon afterwards[25], when he will have been responsible for letting out five-year contracts for the local collection of rents at centres within the newly formed *pertica*. Taken together, then, the two inscriptions appear to mirror a situation arising from the recent assignment to Carthage of administrative territory and confirm that this overlapped into what had been Africa Nova as early as the administration of Lepidus.

Does, then, responsibility for the Carthaginian *pertica* rest squarely with Lepidus? The word *pertica* itself, now attested for the first time in African epigraphy by a recent inscription from Thugga[26], is helpful in this respect. The basic meaning of the word, as found in the vocabulary of the *gromatici*, is that of *territorium* formally assigned to a colony at the time of foundation as opposed to land taken from a neighbouring city and added later to this

---

[21] On the meaning of *castellum* see BROUGHTON, Romanization 62—64; POINSSOT o. c. 65, n. 2, 69, n. 3.

[22] For discussion and documentation see PFLAUM (above, note 19) 76 ff. The post was normally served at an early stage in the cursus.

[23] So KORNEMANN o. c. 418; POINSSOT o. c. (above, note 18) 69.

[24] This could be confirmed by the fact that he was a freedman in an important municipal office, a circumstance paralleled in other Caesarian colonies; cf. KORNEMANN, o. c. 415 with refs.; MOMMSEN *ad* CIL X 6104; Eph. Epig. II, 133 quoting *lex coloniae Genetivae* ch. CV (CIL II, p. 857). MOMMSEN notes in particular the case of L. Pomponius Malcius at Curubis (CIL VIII 977).

[25] POINSSOT, o. c. 69, objects that, if Phileros exercised his prefecture from or soon after his arrival in Africa, one cannot conclude that the Carthaginian *pertica* included Uchi Maius in the years immediately following 40 B. C. 'puisque la *praefectura* des *LXXXIII castella* pouvait n'être pas *encore* comprise dans la *pertica* et relever directement du gouverneur'. But surely the situation is that at the time of his prefecture Phileros was no longer aide-de-camp of Titus Sextius but answerable to the municipal senate at the colony of Carthage, from which he was sent out to administer the *castella*.

[26] Above, note 18 (= AEpig. 1963, no. 94).

original territory[27]. Only later does *pertica* come to have the looser connotation of a colony's territory in general. If the word is used in its original sense at Thugga[28], which certainly fell within Carthaginian jurisdiction in later times, it ought technically to mean land assigned to Carthage on its foundation — most probably in 44 B. C.[29]. This could be confirmed by Appian's account, if his report that περίοικοι were added to the colony applies to the Caesarian foundation, the 3,000 colonists being led out later early in the reign of Augustus[30]. Thugga itself, however, cannot have been included in the *pertica* at this point since Thugga is located in Africa Nova, not far from Uchi Maius, and Nova and Vetus were still governed independently in 44 B. C. That Carthage could have administered territory lying in two separate and distinct provinces is inconceivable. On the other hand Thugga may very well have found its place in the *pertica* by the time of Lepidus. This is indicated by the fact that Thugga, Uchi Maius, and the *pagus Suttuensis* look to have fallen within the same administrative district, all having (*ca.* A. D. 125—130?) the same *praefectus i. d.*[31]. If this arrangement was in force *ab initio*, the early appearance within the *pertica* of Uchi Maius (above, p. 373f.) would support the contemporary inclusion of nearby Thugga also. What the argument suggests

[27] See the discussion of the sources by P. VEYNE, MEFR 69, 1957, 9—97; Latomus 18, 1959, 576; cf. RE XIX, 1, 1937, 1059f. (SCHULTEN); BROUGHTON (above, note 19) 270f.

[28] The discovery of this inscription (dated between A. D. 102 and 144) finally explained a number of puzzling links with Carthage: the enrolment of *Thuggenses* in the tribe of Carthage, *Arnensis*; the intervention of magistrates from Carthage in the affairs of the *pagus*; the numerous priesthoods and municipal functions exercised at Carthage by members of the *pagus*. The explanation is that the *pagus* of Thugga was a subdivision of the Roman colony of Carthage, its members living in juxtaposition with the peregrine *civitas Thuggensis*: hence the cult of Concord and the word order *pagus et civitas* . . . found in the inscriptions. These particulars, however, are repeated at numerous other localities, a circumstance that has enabled PFLAUM to plot the extent and location of »Greater Carthage« (above, note 19). See further GASCOU, Politique municipale (throughout). Similarly at *Uchi Maius* (above, p. 374) the *coloni* of CIL VIII 26274 may be the Roman citizens of the *pagus* and the *Uchitani* the members of the *civitas*; cf. GASCOU 173f.

[29] So BROUGHTON (above, note 19) 271. KORNEMANN argued that Caesar himself assigned Carthage her *territorium* but this was because he thought the new foundation could be placed as early as 45 B. C.: above, note 18, 407, n. 21; 416, n. 58b; RE VII, 1900, 534f. s. v. *coloniae*. For the standard dating to 44 B. C. see GSELL, Rev. Hist. 161, 1927, 228—233; HAAN 174f.; BROUGHTON, Romanization 56; ROMANELLI, Storia 140; TEUTSCH, Städtewesen 101f.; C. VAN NEROM, Colonia Iulia Concordia Karthago, Hommages à M. Renard II, 1969, 767—776 with bibl.

[30] οἰκήτορας τε 'Ρωμαίους μὲν αὐτὸν τρισχιλίους μάλιστα πυνθάνομαι, τοὺς δὲ λοιποὺς ἐκ τῶν περιοίκων συναγαγεῖν (Pun. 136). KORNEMANN (above, note 18) 418 notes that this is a form of synoecism. Both BROUGHTON, Romanization 57, n. 73; 60, n. 85; above, note 19, 266 n. 2 and KORNEMANN, ibid. n. 59 understand Appian in the sense suggested. For the character of the colonists see further Strabo 17, 3, 15; Plut. Caes. 57, 5.

[31] Cf. CIL VIII 26615, 26267, 26419 (Sextus Pullaienus Florus Caecilianus); GASCOU 174 (quoting CIL VIII 26418).

therefore is that the *pertica Carthaginiensium* may have developed along either of two possible lines. *Either* Carthage was actually allotted territory within Africa Vetus in 44 B. C.[32] and this was later extended by Lepidus to include the Upper Bagradas basin west of the provincial boundary, *or* a *pertica* was formally assigned in 44 B. C. but not put into effect until the administration of Lepidus, who enlarged on the original plan by including territory formerly within Nova. Appian's statement[33] is sufficiently loose as not necessarily to conflict with the latter view, while the turmoil of the intervening years explains the delay. The word *pertica* could then legitimately be used at Thugga since *de facto* the town was included in the original assignation. Whichever reconstruction happens to be correct is in any case minor to the basic point that the *pertica* in the form we know it dates effectively from the time of Lepidus[34].

Confirmation of this conclusion could well be provided by the revival at Carthage of the traditional cult of the Cereres[35], the two goddesses of grain whose worship had spread sporadically through Africa, being particularly well attested in the eastern part of what was now Africa Nova[36]. A new foundation of the cult could in the first instance be linked with the rebirth of Carthage itself. But it might also be viewed as reflecting the inclusion within Carthaginian territory of the grain fields of the Upper Bagradas, particularly when holders of the cult priesthood were, at least in later years,

[32] No clear evidence exists for a preliminary assignation. The fact that the Caesarian colony of Curubis, for example, was enrolled in *Arnensis*, the tribe of Carthage (CIL VIII p. 127), does not necessarily mean that this was so from the time of its foundation.

[33] See note 30.

[34] POINSSOT's view, o. c. 69, is that the *pertica* was enlarged when Octavian strengthened the colony in 29 B. C. and that Appian's mention of περίοικοι relates to that event. He would therefore postpone the prefecture of Phileros until after 29 B. C. — this despite the fact that he would then be a freedman admitted to municipal honours in a colony of Octavian; cf. GSELL, Rev. Hist. 156, 1927, 229; DEBBASCH, R. D. 31, 1953, 335—377. While it is true that both Cirta and Beneventum, for example, had colonies and territory 'contributed' to them years after their foundation (cf. VEYNE, above, note 27), there is nothing to suggest two such stages of assignation within the Carthaginian *pertica*. But it is worth noting that, even if Thugga or Uchi Maius were added in 29 B. C. at a time when the *pertica* was supposedly enlarged, one would still have to suppose the amalgamation of Vetus with Nova several years before 27 B. C.; cf. POINSSOT 69, n. 6.

[35] On the Cereres see A. AUDOLLENT, Cereres, Mélanges Cagnat, 1912, 359—381 with bibl.; J. CARCOPINO, Salluste, le culte des Cereres, et les Numides, Rev. Hist. 158, 1928, 1—18; G. CH. PICARD, Les Religions de l'Afrique romaine, 1954, 182—190; LATTE, RRG 71 f. The plural may express two aspects of the composite divinity Ceres; cf. CL. POINSSOT, Suo et Sucubi, Karthago 10, 1959, 111 f. For criticism of the traditional origin of the cult (Diod. Sic. 14, 77, 5) see P. XELLA, Sull'introduzione del culto di Demetra e Kore a Cartagine, SMSR 40, 1969, 215—228 with refs. to earlier lit.; G. CH. PICARD, *Civitas Mactaritana*, Karthago 8, 1957, 56—58.

[36] G. CAMPS, Massinissa (= Libyca 8, 1960) 223—225 with map showing the distribution of cult places for the Cereres throughout Africa. POINSSOT (above, note 35) 127 f.

drawn not only from Carthage itself but from regions west as well as east of the Fossa Regia — thus showing that the office was also of interest to outlying *pagi*. The cult would be directly related to the emergence of Cathage as metropolis of Africa and administrative head of a large area under her control if it could be shown that its re-establishment goes back to the period under discussion. Fortunately the available evidence is so strong as to allow the date of institution to be assigned with some assurance to the first year or so of Lepidus's administration[36a].

Since the priests of the cult compute their year of office in terms of a peculiar era of the cult[37], the issue turns on the precise date to which one should assign *annus* I of the era. The key to the problem is an inscription from the base of an equestrian statue dedicated at Uchi Maius to Septimius Severus, whose titles give the year A. D. 197[38]. As C. Lucilius Athenaeus is recorded as *sacer. Cerer. c. I. K. anni CCXXXV, flam. p. p.*, it is clear that the 235th year must be either A. D. 197 or some earlier year. If the former, then *annus I* would be assignable to 38 B. C.; if not, it has usually been assumed that it must coincide with one of the years from 39 B. C. back to the foundation of Carthage in 44 B. C.[39]. Essentially the problem reduces to the question of which came first: the office of *flamen perpetuus* at Uchi Maius or of *sacerdos Cererum* at Carthage[40]. Nothing certain can be deduced from the inscription itself but examination of what comparative evidence is available is instructive. In a career served at Carthage the priesthood (or magistracy) of the Cereres was normally held at an early stage after the office of *praefectus iure dicundo* but before the duumvirate and therefore before the perpetual

---

[36a] Detailed discussion in D. FISHWICK and BRENT D. SHAW, The Era of the Cereres, Historia 27, 1978, forthcoming.

[37] For the list see L. TEUTSCH, Gnomon 33, 1961, 259, to which add CIL VIII 26,615. For a *sacerdos Cereris* of the year CXXVII, and a *sacerdos Cer.* of the year LXIIX (both unpublished) see Cl. Poinssot, BCTH 5, 1969, 255.

[38] *imp. Caes. L. Septimio Severo/Pio Pertenaci* (sic) *Aug. Parthico Arabico Par/thico Adiabenico trib. pot. V, imp. VIIII, cos. II,/p. p., divi M. fil., divi Commodi fratri, divi Anto/nini nep., divi Hadriani pronep., divi Traiani/abnep., divi Nervae adnepoti, res p. U.m.p.p.p./In quam rem/C. Lucilius C. f. Athenaeus sacer. Cerer. c. I. K. anni/CCXXXV, flam. p. p., depensis in curam s.s. quam ipse/gessit HS XII mil. n. summae suae honorariae, et am/plius pecunia publica erogata, basem cum orna/mentis suis sua pecunia fecit et epulo decurionib./dato dedicavit d(ecreto) d(ecurionum)* (C. 26,255 = ILS 9401).

[39] Above, note 29. M. GRANT, From Imperium to Auctoritas 1946, 51, 227, 231 argues improbably that Lepidus founded Carthage on Caesar's orders 42—40 B. C.; similarly J. CARCOPINO proposes 42 B. C. as the year of foundation, Aspects mystiques de la Rome païenne, 1941, 15, n. 1.

[40] For earlier discussion see TEUTSCH (above, note 37) 258; Städtewesen 105 f. with bibl.; R. GRÜNDEL, Anni Carthaginis = anni sacerdotii Cererum?, Klio 46, 1965,351—354.

flaminate, if held[41]. While an annual flaminate might on occasion precede[42], nothing supports the possibility that the *sacerdotium* of the Cereres would ever have succeeded the *perpetual* flaminate of the colony. A similar situation is observable in the case of careers served partly at Carthage, partly within a local *pagus* attributed to Carthage[43]. It follows, then, that the priesthoods of Athenaeus, who will have been a citizen of Carthage, are most probably listed in direct order and that A. D. 197 is the date of the perpetual flaminate. If so, the 235th year of the priesthood of the Cereres falls *before* A. D. 197. How long before cannot be said exactly, but a reasonable case can be made for preferring a date towards the end rather than the beginning of the quinquennium available[44]. The career of M. Vettius Latro[45] must have lasted

[41] CIL VIII 26615 = ILS 9404 (Sextus Pullaienus Florus Caecilianus: after full career at Carthage was chosen patron of both the *pagus* and the *civitas* of Thugga); ILAfr. 238 (L. Decianus Extricatus: no offices given beyond the priesthood of the Cereres); ILAfr. 384 (fragmentary: priesthood of the Cereres apparently held before the aedileship, quaestorship, and juridical prefecture); CIL VIII 25808c (Q. Paccius Victor Candidianus: *magister sacrorum Cererum*, then annual *flamen* of *divus Severus* at Carthage; subsequently *curator* and *patronus* at Furnos Minus).

[42] ILAfr. 390 = ILS 9406 (Q. Voltedius Optatus Aurelianus); CIL VIII 25808b = ILS 9403 (L. Octavius Felix Octavianus: decurion, annual *flamen* of *divus Pius*, *magister sacrorum Cerealium*, candidate for aedile at Carthage; subsequently *curator* [twice] and patron at Furnos Minus).

[43] ILTun. 720f. (M. Vettius Latro: annual flaminate of *divus Augustus* at Thuburbo Maius followed by the priesthood of the Cereres at Carthage). Apart from the inscription of Athenaeus, this seems to be the only example of a *sacerdos Cererum* who also held a local flaminate within the *pertica*. But numerous inscriptions attest an office or fuller career at Carthage followed by a high civil or religious post at some locality attributed to the city: CIL VIII 26519; cf. ILAfr. 520 (C. Caesetius Perpetuus); CIL VIII 26185 (L. Cornelius Maximus); CIL VIII 25450 (M. Iulius Probatus Sabinianus); CIL VIII 12370 (M. Fannius Vitalis); ILAfr. 247 (Fabius Victor Sestianus); ILTun. 1513; cf. 1391 (A. Gabinius Datus). For Sextus Pullaienus Florus Caecilianus, Q. Paccius Victor Candidianus, L. Octavius Felix Octavianus see above, notes 41f. The most telling example is the career of P. Marcius Quadratus, who after the annual flaminate of *divus Augustus* and the pontificate at Carthage was adlected to the five decuries, subsequently holding the perpetual flaminate in his *patria* of Thugga: ILTun. 1434f.; cf. the somewhat similar career of L. Marcius Simplex (CIL VIII 26609).

[44] The view that the cult of the Cereres would have been founded along with the colony itself is disputed by TEUTSCH, Städtewesen 106, noting that the Capitoline Triad ought normally to have been first in the field.

[45] *M(arco) Vettio C(ai) f(ilio) Quir(ina tribu) La|troni, flam(ini) divi Aug(usti), sa|cerd(oti) Cer(erum) an(ni) CXXXVII, equo pu|blico et in quinq(ue) dec(urias) adl(ecto), praef(ecto)|coh(ortis) I Alpin(orum) equit(atae), donis don(ato)|ab Imp(eratore) Caes(are) Ner(va) Trai(ano) Aug(usto) Ger(manico)|Dac(ico) bello Dac(ico) hasta pura coro|na murali vexillo arg(enteo), trib(uno)|mil(itum) leg(ionis) II Adiutr(icis) piae fidel(is),| praef(ecto) alae Silian(ae) c(ivium) R(omanorum) torquatae|armillat(ae), proc(uratori) annonae Ostiae|et in portu, proc(uratori) prov(inciae) Siciliae, pro|cur(atori) Alpium Cottiar(um), procur(atori)|Mauretaniae Caesariensis|M(arcus) Vettius Myrinus|lib(ertus)*

well over three decades since his final posting as procurator of Mauretania Caesariensis is dated by CIL VIII 8369 (Igilgili) about A. D. 128, whereas he served the first of his *militiae equestres* as prefect of the *cohors I Alpinorum equitata* during the 1st Dacian War (A. D. 101—102). He would then have been 30+, since the prefecture was preceded by adlection to the five decuries of jurors (minimum legal age 30; Suet. Aug. 32, 3), and will therefore have been at least 58 in *ca*. A. D. 128, already an advanced age to serve as procurator. Should this assumption be correct, his municipal flaminate at Thuburbo Maius (minimum legal age 25[46]) could hardly be earlier than A. D. 94—95 and the priesthood of the Cereres in the 137th year no earlier than 95—96. Of course if the local flaminate were held at a later age than 25 or were not immediately followed by the priesthood of the Cereres, then the latter office would be postponed by a corresponding length of time. Adlection to the board of jurors at a somewhat later age than 30 would certainly open up the possibility of an earlier date for the flaminate and thus for the priesthood of the Cereres — but suffer the corresponding disadvantage of a still later age for the governorship of Caesariensis. It would also mean that Latro will have served his *militiae equestres* in, say, his mid-thirties to mid-forties instead of in his thirties, as normally[47]. On the other hand, should he have been adlected to the five decuries *anno suo* — a justifiable assumption when adlection came so early in his career? — and the appointment made immediately before his first *militia*, then the priesthood of the Cereres is probably to be dated no earlier than A. D. 96. By any reckoning then it looks as though Latro served as priest of the Cereres in his late twenties and that the 137th year of the cult era falls somewhere in the period, say, A. D. 95—98. In that case *annus* I must be assigned to 42—39 B. C. With no historical grounds to support the two years or so preceding Lepidus's administration, the era of the cult would appear to date from 40—39 B. C.[48]

patrono opt(imo)/d(edit) d(edicavit) (II. Tun. 720f.) See PFLAUME basic commentary, Les Carrières Procuratoriennes Equestres sous le Haut-Empire romain, 1960, no. 104, pp. 240—243; further M. S. BASSIGNANO, Il Flaminato nelle Provincie Romane dell'Africa, 1974, 171.

[46] As with all municipal magistracies: R. ÉTIENNE, Le Culte Impérial dans la péninsule ibérique d'Auguste à Dioclétien, Bibl. des Écoles franç. d'Athènes et de Rome 191, 1958, 238. W. LIEBENAM, Städteverwaltung im römischen Kaiserreiche, 1900, (1967), 269 with n. 2; 345, n. 8 notes that priests of younger age are rarely attested.

[47] E. BIRLEY, The Equestrian Officers of the Roman Army, in Roman Britain and the Roman Army, 1961, 133—153. For the decorations received by Latro qua prefect of a cohort see D. FISHWICK, A Spanish Priest of Urbs Roma, Historia 24, 1975, 114—120.

[48] We would then have an additional indication of the approximate date when Phileros held his juridical prefecture since it was apparently during his tenure of this office that he constructed a temple of Tellus at his own expense. GSELL suggested (above, note 34) 229, n. 3 that this may have been the actual temple of the Cereres. Apart from the difficulty of the singular form *Tell(uris)*, one would have thought it unlikely that a freedman

What the discussion has attempted to show is that, whereas the 'governorship' of T. Sextius in both African provinces was clearly an *ad hoc* arrangement amid the confusion of the Civil Wars, everything points to the fact that a more permanent settlement of African affairs would have been sought under Lepidus. This was the time when the strategic importance of Africa was such as almost to compel the amalgamation of Vetus and Nova in a single unit; internally, there is evidence of violent, if obscure, activity by Lepidus at Carthage, which emerges at the end of his term with a vast *territorium* under her administration. That this dates essentially from the time of Lepidus is strongly implied both by the inscriptions and by the contemporary refounding of the cult of the Cereres, which must recognize, at least in part, the agricultural productivity of the *pertica*. If this reconstruction is correct, it holds a crucial implication for the establishment of Africa Proconsularis. The limits of 'Greater Carthage', which can be worked out on the basis of ties between the colony and outlying *pagi*, clearly overlapped the western boundary of Africa Vetus, reaching well into the territory that Caesar had made the province of Africa Nova. Thugga and Uchi Maius, for example, lie west of the old Fossa Regia. Such a situation surely precludes the existence of two separately administered provinces and can only mean that Vetus and Nova must have been united by or at the time Carthage received her dependent territory. Thus the westward extension of the *pertica Carthaginiensium*, which sealed the fusion of the two African provinces, provides a new *terminus* for the unification of Roman Africa under a single governor. It now appears that the formation of Proconsularis should be assigned not to 27 B. C., when the existing province was simply placed in the senatorial category, as Dio and Strabo report, but to the first year or so of Lepidus's appointment in Africa over a decade earlier. Proconsularis was on this view created a Roman province *ca.* 40—39 B. C.

---

praefectus i. d. would have been the founder of a new cult temple for so ancient and important a worship as that of the Cereres. The temple financed by Phileros could well have been a simple shrine *(aedes)* built at the period of the renaissance of the official cult, to which it doubltess owed its inspiration.

VI

«EATERS OF FLESH, DRINKERS OF MILK»:
THE ANCIENT MEDITERRANEAN IDEOLOGY
OF THE PASTORAL NOMAD*

«... the Menace is loose again, the Hell's Angels, the hundred carat headline, running fast and loud on the early morning freeway, low in the saddle, nobody smiles, jamming crazy through traffic and ninety miles an hour down the centre stripe, missing by inches ... like Genghis Khan on an iron horse, a monster steed with fiery anus, flat out through the eye of a beer can and up your daughter's leg with no quarter asked and none given ...»[1]

The quotation from Dr. Hunter Thompson is not intended to offend the reader's civilized sensibilities, but only to illustrate the obvious: that nomads, whether ancient or modern, have never had a 'good press'. Rarely have nomadic peoples bequeathed to us written records that detail their perception of the world, the function of their own society, or their relationships with sedentarist communities. This complete shortfall in recorded history of an entire sector of the human community is particularly true of Classical antiquity where we depend, with very few exceptions, on the written accounts of historians, geographers, military men, and administrators who had little sympathy with the pastoral nomad. In these written sources are found many types of prejudices commonly associated with mobile people even in our own society. But in the case of the ancient world there is the additional misfortune of not being able to check the written record against the oral history of the people concerned. Further, it is my contention that these written accounts, as we have them, contain more than mere prejudices — that the views in them about nomads are a more organized and structurally consistent set of ideas that I would label an 'ideology'.

---

* An earlier version of this paper was delivered to the *Canadian Learned Societies*, Anthropology Session, 4 June 1979. The author would like to record his gratitude to those who made comments at the session, and especially to Dr. D. Alan Aycock who read the paper in draft and made several valuable suggestions. He would also like to thank Joyce M. Reynolds (Newnham College, Cambridge) and Sir Moses Finley (Darwin College, Cambridge) for their comments on an earlier version.

[1] H.S. THOMPSON, *Hell's Angels*, Harmondsworth 1966, p. 13.

It is not surprising that the ideology of the pastoral nomad found in Greek and Roman ethnographers, geographers, and historians is so consistently hostile. The hostility, it seems, arises principally from the apparent separation of nomadic and sedentarist societies. The principal hallmarks of the ideology are two : first, a complete separation of nomads and sedentarists into two polarized and isolated taxonomic compartments wherein the two economies or 'human types' never merge or are perceived to have any dynamic interaction. And secondly, the nomad is seen as the ultimate barbaric human type who is directly opposed to the 'civilized' sedentary agriculturalist. This absolute separation and polarization of the two human types is not invariably found in all premodern analyses of pastoralist societies, but there are few exceptions in Classical antiquity (*e.g.* Poseidonios) to what can fairly be called the 'dominant' ideology.

Probably the most systematic exception to the rule in the social analyses of pre-modern writers is that of the fourteenth-century polymath Ibn-Khaldûn : soldier, politician, statesman, philosopher, historian and, some would say, the father of sociology[2]. In abbreviating his general historical schema, I obviously do great injustice to the subtlety of his ideas, but in general it can be maintained that Ibn-Khaldûn divided all human society into two camps and that the nature of this separation is reflected in his technical vocabulary. On the one hand, he writes of the 'primitive', in the sense of *prime* or elemental, level of culture (which he calls *'umran badawī*), and at the other end of this social spectrum he places what he calls 'civilized culture' (*'umran haḍarī* or simply *haḍara*)[3]. *Badawī* is an adjective derived from the Arabic verb *bada(w)* which means 'to begin, to appear, to initiate'. The verb also gives rise to such derivatives as *budā'ī* meaning 'primary, first' and by extension 'primitive', and the adjective *badw* meaning 'rural', 'desertic', or 'nomadic'[4]. The adjective *haḍarī*, on the other hand, is derived from the verb *haḍara* which means 'to be settled, sedentary, civilized', and yields the derivatives *haḍar^un* meaning 'a region

---

[2] For an excellent survey of his life, career and writings see Y. LACOSTE, *Ibn Kahldoun, naissance de l'histoire passé du tiers monde*, Paris 1978[4], ch. 2-3, p. 47-85; cf. *The Encyclopedia of Islam* III, Leiden 1968[2], *s.v.*

[3] M.M. MAHDI, *Ibn Khaldûn's Philosophy of History : A Study in the Philosophic Foundation of the Science of Culture*, Chicago 1964, p. 193f.

[4] Cf. H. WEHR-J.M. COWAN, *A Dictionary of Modern Written Arabic*, Wiesbaden 1971, *s.v.*, p. 47f.

with cities' and *hadarī* meaning 'settled, sedentary, urban', and hence 'civilized'[5]. What is unusual about Ibn-Khaldûn's thought is not that he separates the two worlds of nomad and sedentarist, but the manner in which he then systematically connects them. For Ibn-Khaldûn the pastoral nomad is the most basic representative of the world of the *'umran badawī*, and hence his name of 'bedouin'; he is the prime (*i.e.*, primordial) force from which the most fully developed social form of the 'civilized' world, the political state, is created. In assigning such a critical creative rôle to the pastoral nomad, Ibn-Khaldûn did not have an excessively rosy view of him as a human type. Quite the opposite. On a sliding scale from civilization to barbarism, nomads were placed decidedly at the extremes of barbarism. In his view they were even more primitive than wild mountain cave dwellers[6].

But Ibn-Khaldûn's interpretation also holds that nomads, by virtue of their position at the very base of human society in its 'natural' state (*i.e.* in the *'umran badawī*), are closer :

> «... to the original state of nature (*fitra*) [and hence] they are more prone to lead a virtuous life... Unlike city dwellers, they have not gone far in the practice of vice ... because they have never had the opportunity to practice [vice], their original nature remains pure and more receptive to the good. Their simple life leads them to form habits conducive to the practice of virtue, and these habits become a second nature with them and characterize their social action and psychological attitudes.»[7]

Ibn-Khaldûn then engages the pastoral nomad, as a primal force, in the very centre of the process of historical development by making him crucial to a cyclical pattern of the rise and fall of civilized states. He claims that pastoral nomadic societies are characterized by a type of social and political 'force' (called 'virtue' in the quotation above, *asabiyya* in Arabic) which enables them to topple, replace, and rejuvenate corrupt 'civilized' states. *Asabiyya* seems to be the collectivity of social forces, such as tribal unity, cohesion, cultural uniformity and purity, and political centralization, that are peculiar to nomads and which enable them to fuel the nascent steps in the evolutionary development

---

[5] *Ibid., s.v.*, p. 183f.
[6] M.M. MAHDI, *o.c.* (n. 3), p. 114f.
[7] M.M. MAHDI, *o.c.* (n. 3), p. 195; cf. A.J. TOYNBEE, *A Study of History* III, Oxford 1963, p. 321-328, 473-476; X, p. 84-87.

of the state[8]. Naturally, however, nomads who become sedentarized and civilized are 'corrupted' and in turn become prey for new primaeval forces pressing in from the desert frontier. Thus, for Ibn-Khaldûn, the nomad is a critical link in the process of history; at once creator and destroyer, he is culturally elemental and pure and represents the basic building material of states. Yet he is so removed from civilization by the stream of cultural evolution that he must pose a threat to the cultured life of town and country[9].

Although the dominant ancient Graeco-Roman ideology of the pastoral nomad does share the idea of the extreme polarization of the nomad and the sedentarist, it seems to lack the crucial link between the 'savage' and the 'civilized' provided by social analysts like Ibn-Khaldûn. If one considers the ethnography of the Greek historian Herodotos, the ideology of the pastoralist is immediately seen to be more brittle and uncompromising. Herodotos seems to apply a basic division to all human societies, a distinction that already appears fully developed in the early Greek ethnographers and historians, like Hellanikos and Hekataios, who preceded him. This division is the absolute separation of human societies, especially 'barbarian' ones, into ἀροτῆρες ('ploughmen' or 'farmers') on the one hand and νομάδες ('shepherds' or 'pastoralists') on the other[10]. Insofar as it attempted a rudimentary categorization of these peoples as either 'relatively civilized' or 'savage', this division merely reflected Greek prejudices about outsiders. But once it was integrated within the analytic-descriptive structure of ancient ethnography, the artificial dichotomy came to substitute for a more dynamic approach to research on the development of barbarian economies and societies[11].

For example, Herodotos, in enumerating the various tribal groups of Persia and India, rather than attempting to comprehend any observed diversity, invariably labels or categorizes them as either entirely 'agrarian' or 'pastoralist' in their economic régimes[12]. But perhaps nowhere in his writings are the undercurrents of an artificial structure marked by binary polarities so apparent as in his *Skythika*, his ethno-

---

[8] Y. LACOSTE, *o.c.* (n. 2), p. 134-147.
[9] Y. LACOSTE, *o.c.* (n. 2), p. 128-133.
[10] For some earlier examples see Hekataios, *FGrHist* 1 F 334-335, and Hellanikos, *FGrHist* 4 F 67. Cf. Pind., *Pyth.* 9.12.2-3.
[11] Cf. Hdt. I 125.4, III 98.3.
[12] E.g. Hdt. VII 50.4.

graphic survey of the peoples of the ancient Ukraine (see chart 1). Herodotos' 'research' must be viewed against actual knowledge of the region in antiquity, and on this point it has been acutely observed that hard factual information was difficult to obtain. «Frequent migration and conquest led to a great confusion in nationality, one which neither the Greeks nor the Romans were able to sort out...generally, 'Scythian' could mean everyone from the vast area north of the Black Sea»[13]. But Herodotos pretends to a rather precise knowledge. This precise knowledge, however, should not necessarily be tied to the question of whether he did or did not actually visit the Black Sea region, a question that might be largely irrelevant to our enquiry. A recent investigation of Herodotos' account of the peoples and geography of the Pontus concludes that he probably did traverse the region, but that the autopsy does not appear to have had any observable empirical effect on the composition of the histories themselves[14]. Nevertheless, his assertions about various ethnographic facts are rather definite. For example, in his survey of the Skythian tribes he is careful to specify whether or not each ethnic unit is agricultural or nomadic[15]. These two *a priori* categories divide and define ethnographic boundaries, and in his schema usually no mixed economic régime is permitted.

---

[13] M.I. FINLEY, *The Black Sea and Danubian Regions and the Slave Trade in Antiquity*, Klio 40 (1962), p. 51-59 (quotation p. 56-57).

[14] O.K. ARMAYOR, *Did Herodotus ever go to the Black Sea?*, HSPh 82 (1978), p. 45-62, citing the recent work by D. FEHLING, *Die Quellenangaben bei Herodot*, Berlin 1971. He concludes, despairingly: «But if we cannot take Herodotus' experience of the Black Sea at face value, we can only remain agnostic on the extent of it, and on such of Herodotus' historical authority as he attaches to it. For once we retreat from the face value of Herodotus' narrative, we hardly know where to stop. If we cannot believe that he saw the Pontus he talks about, we can hardly be sure that he went to the Pontus at all». And his 'solution' is equally confused: «It is difficult to understand how one of such wide and varied genius might have grown confused enough to set down in full earnest these impressions of the Pontus if he really went to see for himself. Either he did go and remained content to tell his readers what they wanted to hear in the first place even though it was not true, or he did not go at all. And, in either event, we cannot go on treating his stories as serious evidence of the fifth-century Black Sea». As I hope that my analysis indicates, while I would agree with the last statement (substituting 'empirical' for «serious»), I could not disagree more with the two simplistic assumptions that precede it (and are unnecessary to the conclusion in any event). Herodotos could very well have travelled in the Pontus without either reporting it empirically or engaging in telling false stories to an audience that demanded them. The reasons for this are not duplicity or stupidity on Herodotos' part, nor are they to be found, in any restricted sense, in a recourse to Greek historiographical tradition.

[15] Cf. Hdt. IV 3.1.

VI

CHART I — THE STRUCTURE OF THE HERODOTEAN SKYTHIKA

IV 17	IV 18	IV 19	IV 20	IV 21-22
Unknown lands ←	Uninhabited Desert ←			IURKAI: savage untamed hunters
NEUROI: customs like the Skythai, but they turn into wolves once a year, cf. IV 100, 105 ←	ANDROPHAGOI: cannibals, eaters of flesh, the most savage of all men, cf. IV 100, 106 ←			THUSSAGETAI: hunters and gatherers ←
SKYTHAI AROTERES: grow grain but do *not* eat it themselves; it is only grown for export	BARREN LANDS ←	SKYTHAI NOMADES	Marshes and uninhabited lands ←	Uninhabited Desert ←
ALIZONES: resemble Skythai, but they sow grain and eat bread	SKYTHAI GEORGOI ↑ GEORGOI (IV 54)		MELANCHLAINOI: «The Black Cloaks» cf. IV 100, 107 ↑	BUDINOI: nomadic Skythai; eaters of lice; distinct physical traits, cf. IV 109
KALLIPPIDAI: Helleno-Skythai, resemble Skythai but sow grains and eat bread	WOODLANDS		«ROYAL SKYTHAI»	GELONOI: Helleno-Skythai, tillers of soil and eaters of grain, cf. IV 108
				SAUROMATAI: Skytho-Amazonians inhabiting wild, uncultivated lands

River Turas (IV 51)
AGATHURSOI (customs *like* the Thracians: IV 48, 100, 104)
River Ister (IV 48)
THRACIANS
HELLENES — GREEKS

River Huparis (IV 52)
GEORGOI (IV 53)
River Borusthenes (IV 53)

River Pantikapes (IV 54)
River Hupakuris (IV 55)
SKYTHAI NOMADES (IV 55-56)
River Gerrhos (IV 56)

River Tanais (IV 57)

ARGIPPAIOI (milk and fruit mixed as cakes: IV 23)
Range of mountains beyond which: the Bald-Headed Men (IV 24)
The Goat-footed Men (IV 25)
ISSEDONES (devour dead human flesh and morsels of wild-sheep meat: IV 26)

THE BLACK SEA COAST

Take the case of two Skythian peoples, the Budinoi and the Gelonoi. Herodotos observes that the Budinoi are pastoralists (νομάδες) and that the Gelonoi are farmers (ἀροτῆρες). Therefore, he concludes, they must be two separate ethnic groups, and earlier Greek writers must be mistaken in claiming that they are a single tribe with the same name [16].

More importantly, however, the dichotomy not only separates individual ethnic units from each other, but also divides Skythia as a whole into two broad categories. Half the Skythians are classified as 'nomadic', the other half as 'agricultural'. The division is strictly moietic, with the dividing line between the two worlds being the River Pantikapes:

«To the east of the farmer Skythians, immediately beyond the Pantikapes, live the pastoralist Skythians who neither sow any grain nor plough the land...» [17]

This east-west polarity is matched by a north-south separation that marks each section of Herodotos' mental geography of Skythia. The vertical continuum passes from civilization in the south near the Black Sea coast to utter savagery in the interior to the north. Within this framework the identification of the human types νομάς (pastoralist) with barbarian, and ἀροτήρ (ploughman) with civilized man, provides Herodotos with an explanatory model for human customs and behaviour. Any barbaric trait he finds amongst the Skythians is explained quite naturally as a correlate of their pastoral nomadism [18]:

«... the Skythians blind all those prisoners whom they capture since, after all, they are not ploughmen (ἀροτῆρες) but pastoralists (νομάδες)».

Of course, even by Herodotos' own admission not *all* Skythians were pastoralists, yet the reversibility of the equation 'Skythian' equals 'barbarian' equals 'nomad' had an insidious effect. That is to say,

---

[16] Hdt. IV 109.1.
[17] Hdt. IV 19; cf. IV 56 where the division is repeated.
[18] Hdt. IV 2.2; cf. F. HARTOG, *Les Scythes imaginaires : espace et nomadisme*, Annales *(ESC)* 34 (1979), p. 1137-1154 at p. 1141 (he finds the attribution of this practice to their nomadism «curious»); since the submission of this article, his excellent analysis *Le miroir d'Hérodote. Essai sur la représentation de l'autre*, Paris 1980, was published, of which I have not been able to take account here.

12

since all Skythians were barbarians in Greek eyes, and since pastoralists were the quintessential 'barbarian type', by a sort of confused social syllogism all Skythians came to share the stigma of barbarism associated with pastoralists[19].

Further, any removal from the aura of civilization almost invariably brought in its train the stain of nomadic barbarism. In Herodotos' arrangement of Skythian tribes on his north-south axes (see chart 1), among those furthest removed from the southern base-line of civilization are the *Androphagoi* ('man-eaters', 'cannibals'). They are the most degraded human type in Skythia and the explanation for their barbarity, symbolized most vividly in their eating of *human flesh*, is the causal link between their customs and their type of society[20]:

> « The Androphagoi have the most savage customs of all men, not practicing any form of justice or using any laws, ... for they are pastoralists (νομάδες) ».

Indeed, almost any instance of 'barbaric' behaviour that surfaces in Greek society (*e.g.* the drinking of wine unmixed) is confidently ascribed by Herodotos to the evil influences of the *nomadic* Skythians upon the Greeks[21]. For in Herodotos' schema nomads are defined by characteristics which are the polar opposites of civilization (*e.g.* no laws or system of justice in the case of the *Androphagoi*). The nomad could not hope to attain to the habitation of urban centres (ἄστυ), much less its highest developed form amongst civilized men, the Greek *polis*[22]. Thus, by definition the nomad is removed from civilization (cf. the Latin *civis*, *civitas*) since he cannot form its central defining institution, the political city. Above all, however, it is his mode of consumption of the fruits of his labour that mark out the nomad. He is seen as the logical opposite of the farmer who *works* the land (γῆ ἔργεται), harvests crops (κήπους ἐκτημένοι), and eats grain (is a σιτοφάγος). Counterpunctually, the Skythian nomad is characterized by Herodotos as an 'eater of meat' (often *raw* flesh) and a 'drinker

---

[19] Cf. Strabo XI 8.7 (C 513); this functional reversibility of the ideology explains many of the features of the Skythian nomad-barbarian that seem so to puzzle Hartog. There seems to be no real substance to his apparent 'paradox' that Skythians are «nomads but not nomads».
[20] Hdt. IV 106.
[21] Hdt. VI 84.2.
[22] Hdt. VII 10.a².

of milk'[23]. The consumption of *raw human* flesh marks out the ultimate barbarity of the nomadic *Androphagoi* and, on his east-west continuum, it is perhaps interesting to note that Herodotos places a people called the Issedones at the extreme opposite of Greek civilization in the west. The Issedones, it might be added, consume dead human flesh mixed with morsels of wild sheep meat.

It is not necessary to review other Skythian ethnographies from antiquity; they all share the same stereotypical picture of the barbaric nomad. In fact, they do this to the extent that 'Skythian' came to be equated with any northern barbarian in general, the term being applied mistakenly even to the Huns in the fourth and fifth centuries A.D.[24]. Much the same structural absolutism can be found in Herodotos' ethnography of the North African tribes (IV 185-205, see chart 2). Herodotos' information has the apparent virtue, over other historical accounts of the region, of being contemporary and supposedly based on personal interviews and autopsy conducted by Herodotos himself when he visited the Greek colony of Cyrene in North Africa[25]. Indeed, when describing the lands of the nomads Herodotos claims to be reporting «what the Africans themselves say». But this same phrase recurs in other contexts where it is clear that Herodotos is dependent on verbal information from Cyrenaean Greeks and not on first-hand information given him by the Africans themselves[26]. What is more, Herodotos does not seem ever to have ventured beyond the city territory of the Greek colony to observe the lands of the indigenous Africans, and so he must have depended on second-hand oral informants for most of his ethnographic data[27]. One must then reasonably demand of Herodotos : how much of his ethnography reflects empirical realities, and how much is simply cast into an ideological framework traditional to Greek historians?

[23] Cf. Hdt. III 99.1; on the significance of the 'raw' in respect of civilization see Sir E. LEACH, *Oysters, Smoked Salmon and Stilton Cheese*, in *Lévi-Strauss*, London 1974², ch. 2, p. 21-35, esp. 29-34, an elucidation of more complex ideas in Cl. LEVI-STRAUSS, *The Raw and the Cooked* (transl. J. & D. Weightman), New York 1969 (vol. I of *Mythologiques*).

[24] O.J. MAENCHEN-HELFEN, *The World of the Huns : Studies in their History and Culture* (ed. M. Knight), Berkeley 1973, p. 6, though he is mistaken in the application to peasants.

[25] S. GSELL, *Hérodote*, Alger 1915, p. 55-67, is still unsurpassed on Herodotos' sources for North Africa.

[26] Hdt. IV 192; cf. IV 191.4, 192.3-193.1, as well as IV 173 and 187.

[27] Cf. Hdt. II 28, IV 187; S. GSELL, *Hérodote*, p. 67, and his *Histoire ancienne de l'Afrique du Nord* I, Paris 1913, p. 513 n. 2 and 455 n. 1.

CHART 2 — THE HERODOTEAN ETHNOGRAPHY OF NORTH AFRICA

				CYRENE			AMMŌNIOI (IV 181)
EAST	AFRICAN NOMADS (Λίβυης νομάδες): «DRINKERS OF MILK, EATERS OF FLESH»: IV 181, 186-188		ADURMACHIDAI (IV 186)		WILD BEAST LAND (IV 181)	NASAMŌNES (IV 182)	
			GILIGAMI (IV 169)				
			ASBUSTAI (IV 170)				
			AUSCHISAI (IV 170)			GARAMANTES (IV 174, 183)	
			NASAMŌNES (IV 172)				
			PSULLOI (IV 173)				
			MAKAI (IV 175)			ATARANTES (IV 184)	
			LOTOPHAGOI (IV 177)	GINDANES (IV 176)			
			MACHLUES (IV 178)	AUSEES (IV 180)			
LAKE TRITONIS (IV 179, 180, 186, 188-189) (or) THE RIVER TRITON (IV 191)							
WEST	TILLERS OF THE SOIL (ἀροτῆρες) AND FARMERS (γεωργοί): IV 187,191		MAXUES (IV 193)				
			ZAUĒKES (IV 193)				
			GYZANTES (IV 194)				
			CARTHAGE				

As in his Skythian ethnography, Herodotos enumerates the African peoples in a lateral east-west order, and the same absolute separation of the lands of the nomads from those of the farmers reappears. In North Africa the frontier between the two groups is marked, once again, by a body of water: the river (or lake) Triton. The river seems to be a consistent factor of 'liminality' in the ideology, and is no more amenable to identification in real geography than is the Pantikapes in Skythia[28]. After naming the first ten tribal groups who inhabit the coastal lands of North Africa west of Cyrene, Herodotos states that they are all 'nomadic' (IV 181). A few chapters later, upon the completion of the geographical outline of the 'nomads' country', Herodotos repeats the point explicitly[29]:

«Thus from Egypt as far as (lake) Triton, Africa is inhabited by pastoralist peoples, whose drink is milk and whose food is the flesh of wild animals.»

After a further disquisition on the food of the nomads, Herodotos emphasizes the fundamental geographical separation of the two worlds yet again[30]:

«This is the situation with the nomads, but to the west of Lake Tritonis the Africans are no longer nomads, and do not have any of the customs of the pastoralists...»

In order to stress the clean division between the 'eaters of flesh, drinkers of milk' and the γεωργοὶ σιτοφάγοι, Herodotos points out their geographical separation yet a third time[31]:

«To the west of the River Triton, and close to the Auseoi, are the Africans who are ploughmen (ἀροτῆρες) and who live in real houses...»

That Herodotos is unclear within these same passages as to whether or not the geographical dividing point is a river or a lake, and whether

---

[28] Hdt. IV 191, cf. 180; see E.H. MINNS, *Scythians and Greeks: A Survey of Ancient History and Archaeology of the North Coast of the Euxine Sea from the Danube to the Caucasus*, Cambridge 1913 (repr. New York 1971), p. 29: «The Panticapes is a puzzle», and the standard commentaries such as W.W. HOW-J. WELLS, *A Commentary on Herodotus* I, Oxford 1912 (= 1967), p. 324, for similar problems. Sir Edmund Leach has interpreted the river Jordan as having a similar structural rôle in the New Testament (unpublished lecture, Cambridge 1975).
[29] Hdt. IV 186.1.
[30] Hdt. IV 187.1.
[31] Hdt. IV 191.1.

CHART 3 — THE ARISTOTELIAN SYSTEM OF MODES OF SUBSISTENCE

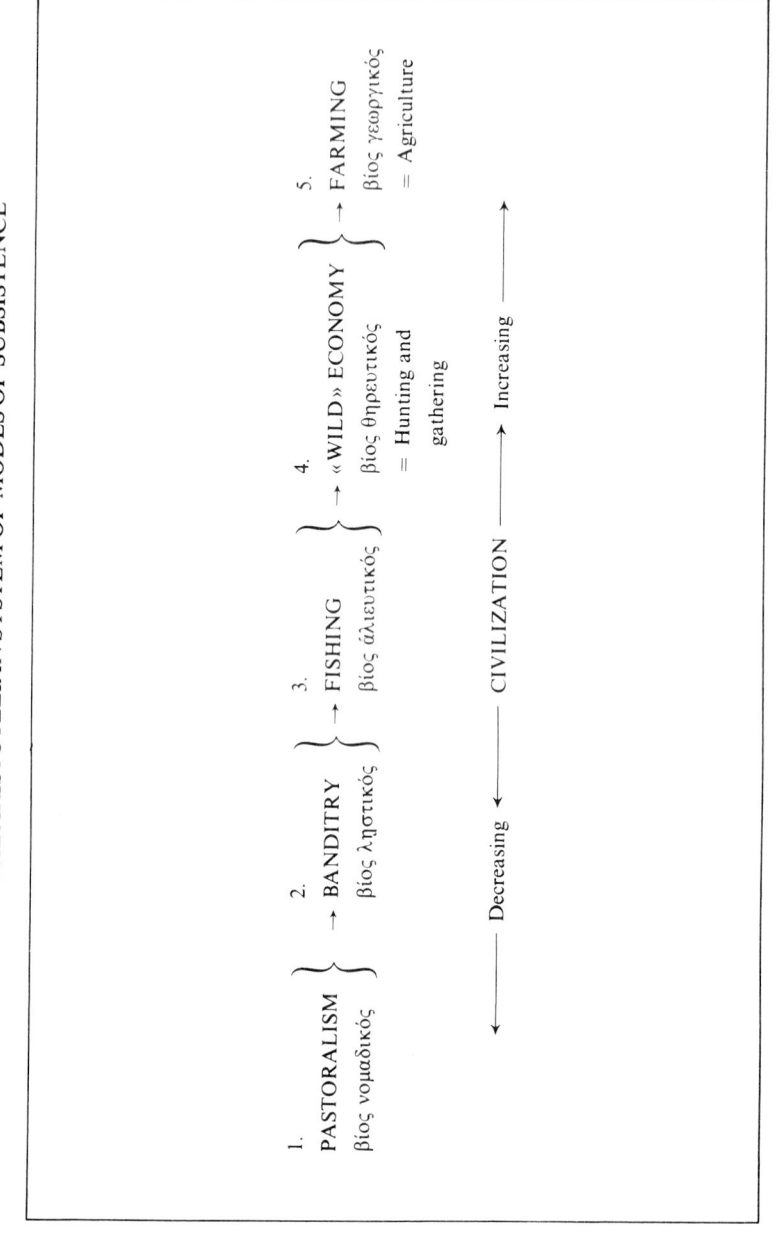

1. **PASTORALISM** βίος νομαδικός → 2. **BANDITRY** βίος λῃστικός → 3. **FISHING** βίος ἁλιευτικός → 4. **«WILD» ECONOMY** βίος θηρευτικός = Hunting and gathering → 5. **FARMING** βίος γεωργικός = Agriculture

← Decreasing ——— CIVILIZATION ——— Increasing →

it is called 'Triton' or 'Tritonis', is probably only a further indication of its ambiguous status as a real topographical feature. In both cases, that of the Skythians and that of the Africans, Herodotos' ethnography conforms to a fairly set pattern that arbitrarily separates nomads and sedentarists into isolated compartments, geographically and culturally, in which the barbarity of the nomad is highlighted by the manner of his food consumption.

A somewhat more complex and, to us, more satisfying theoretical model of the place of the pastoral nomad in the process of human development is to be found in the analysis of the various modes of human subsistence in the first book of Aristotle's *Politika*. Aristotle claims that there are several distinct modes of subsistence (βίος in the Greek) developed by Man[32]. Aristotle only countenances five 'pure types' of modes of subsistence. He admits that the modes of subsistence which he sees as a prime are, to a certain extent, theoretical constructs, since he has reduced them to those types where the application of human labour to its object is direct and self-sustaining (αὐτόφυτος, 'self-generating'), and hence autonomous[33]. The element of independent and directly productive human labour seems to be central to the Aristotelian system; thus he arbitrarily excludes all those types of economy which he considers 'dependent' or 'non-productive' in the sense of having no direct object of labour. In this latter category he discounts all those who earn their livelihood by barter and exchange (ἀλλαγή) or by business-like 'wheeling and dealing' (καπηλεία)[34].

---

[32] See *L & S*, s.v., for the correct definition of βίος in this case as «mode of subsistence»; cf. *AJA* 17 (1913), p. 29: ὁ ἴδιος βίος meaning «private property», and *Syll.*³ II 708 line 34 and 762 line 40 where the same element of property is present.

[33] Arist., *Pol.* 1256a 40-41; for ἐργασία see *L & S*, s.v.

[34] Arist., *Pol.* 1256a.40-1256b.1-7. For ἀλλαγή and καπηλεία see *L & S*, s.v., but for a more accurate appreciation of the significance of these terms see K. POLANYI, *Aristotle Discovers the Economy*, in *Trade and Market in Early Empire: Economies in History and Theory* (ed. K. Polanyi-C.M. Arensberg-H.W. Pearson), Glencoe 1957, p. 64-94, esp. 91f., and his *The Livelihood of Man* (ed. H.W. Pearson), New York 1977, ch. 12-14; and M.I. FINLEY, *Aristotle and Economic Analysis*, P & P 47 (1970), p. 3-25 = *Studies in Ancient Society* (ed. M.I. Finley), London 1974, p. 26-52, esp 39f. and 42f.; see now, in addition, the critique by S. MEIKLE, *Aristotle and the Political Economy of the Polis*, *JHS* 99 (1979), p. 57-73, esp. 62f.

The forms of production that remain are five; in order they are: 1. pastoralism (βίος νομαδικός); 2. banditry (βίος ληστικός); 3. fishing (βίος άλιευτικός); 4. hunting and gathering or, as Aristotle puts it, a 'wild' or 'natural' economy (βίος θηρευτικός); and lastly, 5. farming (βίος γεωργικός). It is perhaps interesting to note that Aristotle considered banditry an autonomous and productive form of labour, though there is not sufficient space here to pursue the interesting theoretical implications of this view[35]. Still, there are difficulties in discerning the basis on which Aristotle made these divisions. Some of the types appear to be teleological, *e.g.* fishing and farming appear to be defined with respect to their objects of labour, the sea in the one case, the land in the other. Other forms, however, such as banditry and the βίος θηρευτικός, seem to be defined on the basis of the dynamic function of the labour itself. The βίος θηρευτικός, for example, is 'wild' or 'natural' because Man does not exert any control over the environment by the application of his labour to transform it: he simply 'hunts' from it what he needs. This type would tend to subsume both our categories of 'hunting' and 'gathering' which is, in any event, an artificial distinction as is revealed by our constant merging of the two terms. Even so, it is difficult to understand the distinction between the βίος θηρευτικός and fishing since the latter is clearly based on the criterion 'natural' or 'wild' as well. Be that as it may, in theory Aristotle only conceived of the existence of these five basic types, though he admitted that in reality men often lived by combinations or admixtures of these forms.

If the Aristotelian system is thought of as a linear model (see chart 3), pastoralism is seen to be located at the distal end of the spectrum from agriculture, the civilized βίος, with the other types located in the intervening 'space'. Although Aristotle did admit the possibility of mixed βίοι, it is perhaps interesting to note that he actually *specifies* by example only pastoralism and brigandage, and farming and the 'wild' economy as the two mixable forms[36]. This would tend to suggest that pastoralism and agriculture, separated by the chasm of the intermediate forms, are not compatible types of subsistence. Pastoralism only merged with banditry, another savage

---

[35] Arist., *Pol.* 1256a.30-40, 1256b.1-2; cf. Thuc. I 5 and Strabo XVII 3.24 (C 839) on the βίος ληστικός.

[36] Arist., *Pol.* 1256b.1-6.

and uncivilized mode of subsistence, whereas agriculture could be assimiliated to hunting, a noble rather than a barbaric pursuit[37].

Further, Aristotle is quite emphatic on the reality of this continuum of modes of subsistence, and on the fact that the βίος νομαδικός is the least preferred of them all[38] :

> «Likewise (sc. as in the biological world of plants and animals) the modes of subsistence (βίοι) of Man are different in their type (γένος) The most inactive type (i.e. the least demanding of the application of human labour in altering the environment) is that engaged in by pastoral nomads since their means of subsistence is derived from domesticated animals and is gained *without any labour* and at their leisure. When their herds are forced to move, they themselves are compelled to move with them since they are, so to speak, cultivators of living fields. And there are some who live according to a 'natural' mode of subsistence, some in some ways, some in others, *according to their object*; just as some live from banditry, and others from fishing (that is, whoever lives by a bay, a lake, a river, or by the sea) and still others from hunting birds and wild animals. But the most common type of mode of subsistence is that derived from the exploitation of the land and domesticated plants.»

There are two fundamental criteria by which Aristotle assesses the value he places on any particular mode of subsistence. First, he considers the degree to which the mode is arbitrarily dependent on the forces or whims of nature. In the case of pastoral nomads this dependence is total primarily because they are 'lazy' and do not control the land with their labour. Quite the reverse : they are driven hither and thither by natural forces. What is immediately apparent in Aristotle's reasoning is that he castigates this mode of subsistence on *moral* grounds because it is *servile* in nature. This brings us to the second point, namely, that Aristotle's value judgement on economic forms is predicated on the degree to which human labour is exerted in a controlled fashion in the direct exploitation of the environment. This exertion extends from virtually nil amongst pastoralists, whom he blames for their indolence, to a maximum amongst sedentarist farmers. Labour, it seems, not only takes the environment, but also the man. On another level, however, *agricultural* labour was usually attributed the highest moral value in ancient Greek societies, not primarily because

[37] Cf. Xen., *Oec.* 6.11, esp. 5f.; *Mem.* II 1 18; *Cyr.*, *passim*; see also Polyb. XXXI 29 and Plato, *Leg.* VII 823d on the structurally important elements of the 'hunt'.

[38] Arist., *Pol.* 1256a.29-30 (Sir E. Barker's translation with slight modifications); cf. *Hist. An.* 682b.7.

of its economic productivity but because manly exertion in the farm fields was seen as the peacetime counterpart to virtuous exertion on the field of battle. It was the ultimate civilized *art*[39].

Thus, Herodotos and Aristotle offer, respectively, relatively simple and complex facets of the same ideology of the pastoral nomad. But the question must be posed: how 'ancient' is this mental structure? When attempting to answer the question one must bear in mind Professor Goody's critique of structuralist analyses of traditional societies. In his view such analyses face the danger of merely reproducing the artificial views of society engendered, in large part, by the advent of writing, literacy, and the impact and dictates of the written word such as the tendencies to list, grid, and polarize social phenomena[40]. This critique is of considerable importance to this investigation since we must know if our findings are to be restricted to the field of the *written* Classical text alone. I think not. In his pathbreaking work entitled *Polarity and Analogy: Two Types of Argumentation in Early Greek Thought*, G. E. R. Lloyd demonstrated the fundamental importance of a structural mode of thought and analysis in early Greek philosophy[41]. Only one of the more significant of the polarities to emerge in Greek thought between the sixth to fourth centuries B.C. is the dichotomy between 'nature' and 'culture' (φύσις and νόμος)[42]. There is not adequate space here to discuss the theoretical ramifications of this polarity for Greek ethnography; one can only note that the extreme polarization between the nomadic pastoralist as 'barbarian' and the agricultural sedentarist as 'civilized' must be placed within this mode of thought. But I think that it would be false to correlate this structural polarity with the impact of *written* philosophy alone; indeed, everything in Lloyd's argument points in the opposite

---

[39] See J. P. VERNANT, *Travail et nature dans la Grèce ancienne*, in *Mythe et pensée chez les Grecs* II: *Etudes de psychologie historique*, Paris 1974, p. 16-36, and *Aspects psychologiques du travail dans la Grèce ancienne*, ibid., p. 37-43.

[40] J. GOODY, *The Domestication of the Savage Mind*, Cambridge 1977, esp. ch. 4, p. 52-53, 68-70; ch. 5, p. 74, 105-108; ch. 8, p. 146-148.

[41] G. E. R. LLOYD, *Polarity and Analogy: Two Types of Argumentation in Early Greek Thought*, Cambridge 1966.

[42] For a convenient summary in English see W. K. C. GUTHRIE, *A History of Greek Philosophy* III: *The Fifth Century Enlightenment*, Cambridge 1969, ch. 4 («The 'Nomos-Phusis' Antithesis in Morals and Politics»), p. 55-134, which is, however, mainly descriptive; see too G. E. R. LLOYD, o.c. (n. 41), p. 124f. and 225f., and the classic work by F. HEINIMANN, *Nomos und Physis: Herkunft und Bedeutung einer Antithese im griechischen Denken des 5. Jahrhunderts*, Basel 1945 (repr. 1965).

«EATERS OF FLESH, DRINKERS OF MILK» 21

direction — that is, to the great antiquity of the mode of analysis to the point where it merges with 'myth'[43]. If one merely considers some early Near Eastern mythologies, such as the so-called Gilgamesh Epic or the stories of the book of Genesis in the Hebraic Bible, one is driven to the same conclusion[44]. Within the Greek tradition one can point to the Homeric epic poetry of the ninth and eighth centuries B.C., poems which, for the sake of my argument, I accept to be oral compositions produced by a non-literate society[45]. Again, I do not propose to consider all the strongly structural elements of thought in the Homeric poems; I only wish to point out that there is more than an occasional classification of nomads by their consumptive habits as 'eaters of flesh' and 'drinkers of milk', and that this small sign is a clue to more profound structural lineaments in the compositions[46].

For brevity's sake I shall concentrate on the myth of the Cyclopes as told in the ninth book of the *Odyssey*, if only because the Homeric account of these strange beasts has already been analyzed in some detail by Professor G. S. Kirk in his book on the meaning and function of myth[47]. In their wanderings after the fall of Troy, Odysseus and his men came upon an island inhabited by a savage race of being called Cyclopes[48]. Homer is quite explicit on the point that the Cyclopes are νομάδες (*i.e.* pastoralists) and, in his detailed description of their

---

[43] G. E. R. LLOYD, *o.c.* (n. 41), p. 15f. and 121f.
[44] Consult any standard translation of Genesis, and then the analysis by Sir E. LEACH, *Genesis as Myth, and Other Essays*, London 1971, esp. ch. 1; and a text of the Gilgamesh Epic (or the English version by N K Sandars) and the excellent analysis of its deep structure by G. S. KIRK, *Myth: its Meaning and Function in Ancient and Other Cultures*, Cambridge 1973, p. 113f.; for a guide to the Near Eastern data see my *Fear and Loathing: the Nomad Menace in Roman Africa*, in *Roman Africa-L'Afrique Romaine* (*The 1980 Governor General Vanier Lectures*), Ottawa 1980, esp. notes 1 and 2.
[45] The debate over the oral composition of the Homeric poems as we have them cannot yet be regarded as finally settled; for a good discussion see A. PARRY, *Have we Homer's 'Iliad'?*, *YClS* 20 (1966), p. 177-216, and his introduction to *The Making of Homeric Verse: the Collected Papers of Milman Parry*, Oxford 1971. See too W. F. HANSEN, *Heroic Epic and Saga: an Introduction to the World's Great Folk Epics*, London-Bloomington 1978, ch. 1, p. 7-26, and esp. the views of A. LESKY, *Homeros*, Stuttgart 1967. I accept the Parry-Lord views on the composition and will not engage in any special pleading that the particular case that I am considering (the Cyclopes episode in the *Odyssey*) is a later literary addition.
[46] Cf. *Od.* IV 85; *Il.* XIII 4-6, etc.
[47] G. S. KIRK, *o.c.* (n. 44), p. 152-161 («The Centaurs») and 162f. («The Cyclopes»).
[48] Hom., *Od.* IX 105f. (at least as far as line 465 for our purposes). Cf. Eur., *Cycl.* 120.

society, he gives us a clear picture of what he understood the salient characteristics of their economy to be. These are:

1) The Cyclopes have consciously rejected ploughing the soil and putting the ground to seed. They have no farms, no ships, or any other forms of economic development[49].
2) The Cyclopes live in a sort of *natural* utopia in which everything is provided for them by nature so that they are not compelled to *work* to exploit their environment[50].
3) They have no settlements and no social institutions, no laws or systems of justice; they live in a type of *individualistic anarchy*[51].
4) They are characterized by their mode of consumption. They are not like civilized men who eat grain; instead they consume *wild flesh* (in the most extreme case, that of Polyphemos, the raw human flesh of Odysseus' own men), *drink milk*, and sometimes eat a crude form of cheese[52].

Clearly then, all the salient features of the pastoralist ideology are to be found embedded in an oral epic poem of the eighth century B.C. Further, it is quite certain that *all* the Cyclopes are pastoralists and that all are equally tainted with the stigma of nomadism. Thus they must, *as a whole*, represent a contrast with civilization, implicitly present in Odysseus and his men. Therefore, Kirk's attempt to find a 'nature-culture' dichotomy *within* the community of the Cyclopes must be firmly rejected. For Kirk, Polyphemos represents 'savagery' as against the rest of the Cyclopes' 'culture'[53]. But such a view is untenable on closer examination, and Kirk himself realizes that there are problems with his interpretation. For example, he is puzzled by Polyphemos' devouring of *meat* which he sees as a contradiction of the Cyclopes' basically *vegetarian* diet[54]. The problem with this interpretation is that we are never informed of the specific contents or ordinary diet of

---

[49] *Od.* IX 108, 122-129.
[50] *Od.* IX 109-110, 131f.
[51] *Od.* IX 106, 111-115, 130, 189, 215, 272-280, 428.
[52] *Od.* IX 190-191, 219-225, 244-249; Polyphemos: IX 296f., 307-311, 336f., 341-344, and 373-374.
[53] G.S. KIRK, *o.c.* (n. 44), p. 162-163; the chapter on the structural interpretation of the Gilgamesh Epic, as I have stated above, I find particularly successful and have little quarrel there with his mode of analysis — but in the case of the Centaurs and the Cyclopes, I find the analysis strained beyond the point of conviction.
[54] G.S. KIRK, *o.c.* (n. 44), p. 166-167, and chart, p. 169.

«EATERS OF FLESH, DRINKERS OF MILK»

the Cyclopes other than Polyphemos; least of all do we have any certain knowledge that it was vegetarian. Rather it seems most plausible from the general context of the poem that their diet was much the same as Polyphemos' (*i.e.* meat, milk, and cheese). Then again, contrary to what Kirk states, there is no evidence (other than on one extraordinary occasion, which proves the point) that Polyphemos or any of the other Cyclopes drank wine. It is true that the fertile utopia in which they live automatically produces wheat, barley, and grapes in profusion, but there is utterly no evidence to suggest that the Cyclopes ever took advantage of the considerable natural resources of the island [55]. Significantly, it is the fact that they do *not* exploit the island and their *laziness* in not doing so that is the prime basis for Odysseus', and Homer's, denunciation of them as 'savage' and 'uncivilized'. In fact, the whole story in Homer would lack meaning if all the Cyclopes did not adhere to the pastoralist ideology; in this respect Homer's remarks on the *laziness* of the Cyclopes are an eerie foreshadowing of modern colonialist apologetics [56]. The Cyclopes, being nomadic, are *lazy* and *indolent*; they do not *labour* actively to produce from the land. As Odysseus himself is at pains to point out [57] :

«... they *could* have made this island a strong settlement for themselves, for it is not a bad place at all; it *could* bear all the crops in season ... there *could* be grapes grown there endlessly, and there is smooth land for ploughing, men *could* reap a full harvest ... etc.»

Clearly the land of the Cyclopes is *not* being exploited for agrarian produce; like any latter-day European colonist, Odysseus can only speak longingly of its *potential*. What makes Polyphemos a *more* savage being than his fellow Cyclopes is not the fact that he is a pastoralist (they *all* are), but that his *manners* are even more barbaric than theirs. Polyphemos is a real wild man : he drinks his milk *straight* [58].

---

[55] Cf. note 49 above and *Od.* IX 107-110 and 190-191.

[56] See S. H. ALAIAS, *The Myth of the Lazy Native*, London 1977; see further on the significance of the structural properties of ancient ethnographies to the contact with and control of 'barbarian' peoples the fundamental essay by M. CLAVEL-LÉVÊQUE, *Les Gaules et les Gaulois : pour une analyse du fontionnement de la 'Géographie' de Strabon*, *DHA* 1 (1974), p. 75-93, esp. on the 'then-now' temporal structure.

[57] The quotations are *Od.* IX 130-132, 133-134, but the whole passage, IX 130-139, should be considered.

[58] *Od.* IX 296-297; although it is an obvious structural play on the *civilized* practice of drinking *wine* mixed, some commentators have taken the idea 'seriously' (i.e. as

When he is induced to sip a little wine, provided by the civilized outsider Odysseus, it has a catastrophic effect on his senses[59].

The domination of the pastoralist ideology over other ideologies of the 'barbarian' remained a constant theme in Classical literary texts on nomads. It also seems to have overridden any empirical investigation of barbarian peoples; the real world was made to conform to a neat mentalistic polarity. Nomads are characterized by traits that are at the distal end of those that mark civilized men. Their νόμοι are barbaric, they are city-less, worse yet polis-less, without the established homes (οἶκοι) that were the very base of civilized society. Quite logically, then, they are also stateless, with no properly constituted rulers, no system of justice or code of laws. Above all, however, it seems that it is their mode of food consumption, which appears with greatest consistency in Classical authors, that is *the* stigma of barbarism. Mobility, or enforced movement, is noted by many authors as an epiphenomenal aspect of the nomadic economy, but only Aristotle attributes any economic importance to it. For the rest, the factor of movement is simply reduced to yet another pejorative element in their prejudices against the nomad[60]. Revealing of the prejudice against 'movers' in ancient society are the critical remarks made about early mobile craftsmen (δημιουργοί), and the fact that the prostitutes who wandered the streets of Athens were dubbed 'nomads' in popular parlance[61].

Indicative of the strength of the ideology is the fact that even those Classical authors who had direct, first-hand experience with pastoral nomads, such as the historian Sallust who served a term as Roman governor in North Africa, repeat the ideology rather than any empirical observations. Sallust's picture of the North African nomad conforms in almost every detail to the orthodox view outlined above[62]. And, quite literally, by dictionary definition the pastoral nomad remained till the end of antiquity a synonym for barbarism, savagery, and utter alienation from the world of civilized men[63]. In all the inter-

---

empirically true) and have engaged in some delightful scholarly gymnastics to find parallels in the real world; see e.g. W. B. STANFORD, *The Odyssey of Homer* I, London 1967, p. 358.
[59] *Od.* IX 347f.
[60] J. P. VERNANT, *o.c.* (n. 39), p. 26f.
[61] Photios II 327 = Naber IV (1864), l. 448; cf. Schol. Ar. *Nub.* 249.
[62] Sallust, *Bell. Iug.* 17-19.
[63] Suda, ed. Adler (*Lexicographi Graeci* I.3 : *Suidae Lexicon*) III 474-475.

vening period the same bleak picture is drawn time and again, in the most diverse of contexts — such as the stereotyped portrait of the so-called 'Herakles of Herodes', a wild man vividly described in Philostratos' life of the great philanthropist written in the early third century A.D.[64].

Finally, we see the picture in the last writings of ancient historiography, perhaps most explicitly in the caricature of 'Life amongst the Huns' as portrayed by Ammianus Marcellinus[65]. The account is so detailed and specific, and credible, that it has persuaded many modern scholars of repute in spite of the fact that it flies in the face of known archaeological data about the culture of the Huns[66]. In his description Ammianus claims that the Huns have no houses or settled homes, no political assemblies, no laws or system of justice, and no established political rulers. Further, they refuse to move a hand to grasp a plough or sow seed. In short, they lack every rudiment of civilization. Ammianus also lays stress on the mode of the Hun's consumption of their food. It is, he says, wild and uncooked flesh, since the Huns do not even have fire to cook their meat or even smoke to cure it. They only consume the roots of wild plants and the half-raw meat of whatever animal they happen to capture. The meat is at best half-raw, states Ammianus, since the most the nomads are able to do is to warm the meat up a little by placing it between the hind quarters of their horses before swallowing it whole![67] Maenchen-Helfen quite correctly pointed out that many of these features of the culture of the Huns, which were completely fictional, were literary *topoi* that could have been drawn upon by Ammianus[68]. That is true. But it is only a very small part of the truth. The consistency and manner in which the holistic picture of nomadism is embedded in larger mental structures of the ancient world argues for a deeper and more en-

---

[64] Philostratos, *VS* II 1.7 (552-554); cf. Aul. Gell., *Noct. Att.* 19.9.
[65] Amm. Marc. XXXI 2.
[66] O.J. MAENCHEN-HELFEN, *o.c.* (n. 24), p. 9f., compares Ammianus' account very favourably with other ethnologies of the Huns; M. ROSTOVTZEFF, *Skythien und der Bosporus*, Berlin 1931, p. 103, hailed it as «eine ganz realistische Sittenschilderung»; and E.A. THOMPSON, *A History of Attila and the Huns*, Oxford 1948, p. 41-43, was able on this basis to categorize the Huns as being «in the lower stage of pastoralism» in spite of the fact that archaeological data had shown them to have a metallurgical technology of some complexity. Still, Thompson claims that «the productive methods available to the Huns were primitive beyond what is now easy to imagine».
[67] Amm. Marc. XXXI 2.3.
[68] O.J. MAENCHEN-HELFEN, *o.c.* (n. 24), p. 13-15.

compassing explanation for the tradition from Herodotos to Ammianus than the mere copying of literary *topoi*. Recourse to a philological explanation does not reach beneath the surface of the text, and leaves room for the piecemeal acceptance or rejection of this or that particular *topos* instead of a comprehension of the dynamic of the whole mental structure behind it [69].

The ancient Mediterranean ideology of the pastoral nomad, which placed the pastoralist at the very base of society as its ultimate barbaric type, might be restricted to the academic interests of ancient historians alone were it not for the fact that it far outlasted the decease of ancient society. As a model for the process of the civilizing of Man it remained in dominance until the late eighteenth century, when it was still very much in vogue. I select only one exponent of it, the writer best known to us all for his authorship of *The History of the Decline and Fall of the Roman Empire*. Edward Gibbon entitled chapter 26 of his monumental work «Manners of the Pastoral Nations». For reasons of brevity, I shall not review Gibbon's ideas in all their complexity but will only draw attention to some of their more significant aspects [70].

1) He notes that what distinguishes civilized men from savages is the faculty of reason which forms men's opinions and *manners*; the latter are critically influenced by the exogenous factors of *food* and climate.

2) He notes that the *most extreme form of savagery* on the earth is represented by the *pastoral nomad*, whose *laziness* («indolence» is his word) causes him to refuse to cultivate the earth.

---

[69] For example, it does not prevent Maenchen-Helfen (*o.c.*, p. 15) from attempting a modern parallel for the 'meat-warmed-under-the-saddle'-story (cf. note 67 above). More seriously, it must be noted that other authors make the Huns, *as pastoralists*, the *most savage* of all mankind (Amm. Marc. XXXI 2.31: the headhunting Alans were more civilized; cf. Claud., *In Ruf.* 1.324-325 and Jord., *Get.* 12) and structure their ethnographies accordingly. In this sense, in spite of the promising titles, neither A. N. SHERWIN-WHITE, *Racial Prejudice in Imperial Rome*, Cambridge 1967, nor G. WALSER, *Rom, das Reich und die fremde Völker in der Geschichtsschreibung der frühen Kaiserzeit*, Basel 1951 or his *Caesar und die Germanen*, Wiesbaden 1956, have much to offer, since neither seems to recognize the structural peculiarities of the literary text upon which their analyses depend. Even Ammianus is not internally consistent on the Huns, since much of what he does tell us about their political organization (e.g. XXXI 2.10) contradicts his ideological view of pastoral anarchism (e.g. XXXI 2.7).

[70] E. GIBBON, *The History of the Decline and Fall of the Roman Empire* (*Everyman's Library*) London-New York 1910 (= 1966), III, p. 4-5.

3) He wishes to analyze pastoral society by three articles, the very *first* of which is *diet*.

To quote briefly from the first article[71]:

«The *corn*, or even rice [Gibbon's magnanimous concession to Chinese culture], which constitutes the ordinary and wholesome food of a civilized people, *can be obtained only by the patient toil* of the husbandman... The skilful practititioners of the medical art will determine ... how far the temper of the human mind may be affected by the use of animal or vegetable food, and whether the common association of the carnivorous and cruel deserves to be considered in any other light than that of an innocent, perhaps salutory, prejudice of humanity. Yet, if it be true that the sentiment of compassion is imperceptibly weakened by the sight and practice of domestic cruelty, we may observe that the horrid objects which are disguised by the arts of European refinement are exhibited in naked and most disgusting simplicity in the tent of the Tartarian shepherd. The ox or the sheep are slaughtered by the same hand from which they were accustomed to receive their daily food, and the *bleeding limbs* are served, *with very little preparation*, on the table of their unfeeling murderer.»

Gibbon then emphasizes that nomads always have on hand a 'sure and increasing supply of flesh and milk'. Under his second 'article' of *habitation*, he points out that it is 'the progress of *manufactures* and *commerce*' that 'insensibly' leads to the creation of civilized (*i.e.* citified) man[72]. Finally, under the third 'article' of his analysis, *Exercise*, Gibbon claims that[73]:

«The pastoral life, compared with the *labours of agriculture* and manufactures, is undoubtedly *a life of idleness...*»

The italicized phrases and words in the two passages are sufficient, I think, to establish the vitality of the ancient ideology. Of the two factors seen by Gibbon as central to the civilizing process, agricultural labour and the 'progress of manufactures and commerce', only the latter is a novel development in the ideology of civilization, added by the thinkers of seventeenth and eighteenth-century Europe[74].

---

[71] E. GIBBON, *o.c.*, p. 4-5.
[72] E. GIBBON, *o.c.*, p. 6.
[73] E. GIBBON, *o.c.*, p. 8.
[74] See J.G.A. POCOCK, *Gibbon as Civic Humanist*, in *Edward Gibbon and the Decline and Fall of the Roman Empire* (ed. G. W. Bowersock-J. Clive-S. R. Graubard), Cambridge

But Gibbon was one of the last proponents of the ancient ideology. The old tripartite schema of an historical evolution leading from primaeval pastoralism through agriculture to civilization[75] was gradually being replaced by a new 'four stage' theory in which the pastoralist was being deprived of his 'pride of place' as the world's quintessential barbarian. The critical factor in this ideological shift was the prolonged contact between European settlers and the indigenous inhabitants of the New World[76]. As a result of the new knowledge gained from this contact, it was impressed upon the Europeans with great force that the ancient ideology would have to be modified in order to accommodate an even more savage, primaeval Man than the pastoral nomad. The 'hunter-gatherer' of the New World and Africa began to replace the nomadic pastoralist as the most elementary form of human being, as the ultimate representative of Man in the state of nature. The view was first propagated with force by John Locke in his *Two Treatises of Government* (1690) whence it passed, by way of the French Physiocrats, to the Scottish academicians of the late eighteenth century[77]. Adam Smith, who moved from the Chair of Logic to the Chair of Moral Philosophy at the University of Glasgow in April 1752, propounded the new 'four stage' theory with great vigour in *The Theory of Moral Sentiments* published in 1759. In the new schema, the pastoral nomad, having been elevated by one step in human progress, acquired a little civilization: he was now thought to possess the rudiments of government, customs and law, as well as the manners of civilized men. Now it was the turn of the 'hunter-gatherer' to shoulder all the nihilistic-anarchic characteristics once attributed to

---

(Mass.) 1977, p. 103-120, esp. p. 116f. Cf. N. ELIAS, *The Civilizing Process* I: *The History of Manners* (transl. E. Jephcott), New York 1978, and the review by K. THOMAS, *The Rise of the Fork*, New York Review of Books 25 (1978), p. 28-31 for context; C. LEVI-STRAUSS, *The Origin of Table Manners* (transl. J. & D. Weightman), New York 1978. F. FURET, *Civilization and Barbarism in Gibbon's History*, in *Edward Gibbon and the Decline and Fall of the Roman Empire*, p. 159-166, is misleading and even incorrect on the rôle of barbarism and civilization in Gibbon; much better, though not specifically on Gibbon, is Meek (note 76 below) on the process of commerce and industry as new factors in the civilizing of Man. The idea that commerce *in itself* was a civilizing process was new, though not the rôle of commerce as an agent in the transmission of civilizing values; see e.g. Caes., *Bell. Gall.* I 1.

[75] See Varro, *RR* II 1.4-5.
[76] R.L. MEEK, *Social Science and the Ignoble Savage*, Cambridge 1976, esp. ch. 1, p. 5-36.
[77] R.L. MEEK, *o.c.*, p. 20-22 and 37-67.

the nomad. Less than two decades later Smith enshrined these views in a work on political economy that was to herald the New Age. And it is perhaps not entirely without significance that *An Inquiry into the Nature and Causes of the Wealth of Nations* was published in 1776, the very year that also saw Gibbon's *Decline and Fall*. Ideologically speaking, Gibbon was at the end of an ancient tradition concerning the relationship between barbaric and civilized men, just as Adam Smith was at the beginning of ours[78].

The universality of the ancient mode of thought before the emergence of the novel 'four stage' theory is indicated by its ubiquity in both written and oral traditions of the Classical and Near Eastern worlds as far back as such traditions can be traced. Within this pattern *diet* plays a conspicuously central rôle as a defining element. In ancient literary texts, such as that of the geographer Strabo, food consumption often demarcates an elaborate series of definitions of culture, extending along a fine continuum from the quasi-civilized (the Spanish in Strabo) to the utterly savage (the Irish)[79]. So too, Strabo's geography of Arabia is replete with an elaborate culinary frame of various φάγοι or 'eaters' (*e.g.* of elephants, fish, lice, eels, locusts, humans and ostriches)[80]. And within each of the individual categories, there are permanent consistencies between authors distant from each other in time and place, and who treat different ethnic groups. For example, in both Herodotos and Strabo 'lice-eaters' and 'fish eaters' have the curious tendency to alter the raw state of the food (usually forming it into cakes) before consuming it[81]. This artifical cultural 'map' of food consumption is much broader than the 'drinking of milk and eating of flesh' that characterizes pastoral nomads; indeed, it seems to embrace the definition of many cultural groups and provides a general framework in which specific ethnographies are embedded. Thus in Strabo mountain men are categorized as 'eaters of flesh and drinkers of

---

[78] R.L. MEEK, *o.c.*, ch. 3, p. 68-98 (cf. p. 91-92, 132-133 and 182-184) and ch. 4, p. 99-130.
[79] Strabo, books III and IV. Further on κρεοφάγοι see Diod. Sic. III 31-32 and 53.5; Strabo XVI 4.17-19; Polyb. II 17.10. On γαλακτοπόται/-φάγοι see Hdt. I 216; Diod. Sic. III 53.5; Strabo VII 4.6; Nic. Dam., *FGrHist* 90 F 104. For further analysis see P. BRIANT, '*Brigandage', dissidence et conquête en Asie achéménide et hellénistique*, DHA 2 (1976), p. 163-258 (section IIb, «Le cru et le cuit», p. 170-172).
[80] Strabo XVI.
[81] See Strabo XV 2.2 (C 721), XVI 4.9 (C 771), XVI 4.12 (C 772), XVI 4.13 (C 773), and my *Some Structural Elements in Strabonian Ethnography* (forthcoming).

water. This is an equally improbable empirical 'fact' or observation to that of the pastoral nomad, though it does serve quite neatly by a single change in the algebraic formula (*i.e.* 'milk' becomes 'water') to achieve a fine lateral distinction between transhumants and full nomads[82].

The conclusions of this brief investigation may now be formulated more properly as a number of general propositions. Firstly, autopsy and detailed field investigation of the so-called barbarian peoples of Graeco-Roman antiquity were rare practices. This proposition holds true even for the best existing literary sources where we know that personal ethnographic research was engaged in by the historian or geographer himself (*e.g.* Herodotos or Poseidonios). Secondly, in lieu of any accurate direct knowledge of 'barbarian' societies, the views held by civilized men of the outsiders in the world were a type of *a priori* mental construct that did not necessarily reflect any empirical evaluation of the socities concerned. Within the ideology concerning the pastoral nomad there are a number of 'fixed' points in the mental structure that are repeated by most ancient ethnographers and historians, and the nature of the barbaric food consumption or diet appears to be one of the more important of these constants. Lastly, we can see now how this ideology continued to function as a part of European thought concerning outsiders to the end of the early modern period, and how it was inherited and modified by Europeans according to the utilitarian dictates of colonialism. Even careful scholars whose principal concern it was to investigate 'primitive' mentalities in Graeco-Roman civilization were not always aware of its presence and the way in which its subtle working led even them to accept the ideology as empirical fact[83]. Such conclusions may seem to be bold and somewhat overstated for the purpose of argument, though I hope that in doing so I will not become the target of the sort of criticism directed by Mary Douglas against the old masters of Classical mythological thought and modern structuralist analysis. In levying her judgement she concludes[84]:

---

[82] Strabo III 3.7.

[83] See e.g. Jane HARRISON, *Prolegomena to the Study of Greek Religion*, Cambridge 1922³ (repr. Cleveland 1959), p. 487, who cites almost all the tenets of the pastoralist ideology as reiterated by St. Nilus (Migne, *PL* 79, *Nili Opera*) in his account of the camel herders of the Sinai, and then gives as her own considered observation that «... civilized man, as a rule, shrinks from raw meat».

[84] M. DOUGLAS, *Judgements on James Frazer*, Daedalus 107.4 (1978), p. 151-164 (quotation p. 162).

VI

«Frazer and Lévi-Strauss, both using a tone of voice that suggests the awe and splendour of their subject, diminish the meaning it holds. Frazer belittles the faculties of the primitive mind. Lévi-Strauss uses heavy equipment for dredging up nearly vacuous thoughts.»

Somewhere in between, I think, lies the meaning of the primitive mind of literate civilized man from Herodotos to Gibbon.

VII

Fear and Loathing: The Nomad Menace and Roman Africa*

> *In other parts, the land is strewn with rocks, and no seeds or herbs grow at all. There, the inhabitants have a very hard time. Examples of such people are the inhabitants of the Hijaz and the Yemen, or the veiled Sinhajah who live in the desert of the Maghrib on the fringes of the sandy deserts which lie between the Berbers and the Blacks. All of them lack grain and herbs. Their nourishment and food is milk and meat.*
>
> IBN KHALDÛN, *al-Muqaddimah*

...the Menace is loose again...

HUNTER THOMPSON

In ancient Mesopotamia, about 2000 B.C., a beautiful young girl, the daughter of a farmer, was contemplating marriage to a shepherd, Martu by name. Wishing to stop the marriage, her relatives attempted to impress upon the bride-to-be the crude barbarity of her prospective husband. "Martu", they said, "is a tent-dweller, blown here and there by wind and rain, he does not know prayer, he does not know grain..., Martu knows no house or town, he is a mountain dweller, who roots for truffles like a pig..., who does not bend his knees to cultivate the land, he is an eater of raw meat, he has no house in his lifetime, and is

---

* While writing this paper I received a copy of P. TROUSSET's paper entitled, "Rome et le nomadisme: mythe et réalité", by the kind attention of the author. This paper, presented to the *XIIth International Congress of Frontier Studies* (Sterling, Scotland, September 1979) contains many areas of full agreement with my approach in this lecture. Although there remain some areas where we interpret matters differently (e.g., the function of the *fossatum*, tribal reserve lands, etc.), it is heartening to record what appears to be a growing consensus on a new approach to old problems that is shared by both Professor Trousset and myself.

26

not brought to burial when he dies."[1] This Martu, of course, was not so much an individual character, whether man or god, as he was a personification of all nomads — in this case the *Mar.tu* as the Sumerians called them, the *Amurrû* of Akkadian texts, but perhaps better know to us as the Amorites of biblical sources.[2] The one thing any self-respecting Mesopotamian knew about these western Semitic nomads was that they were utterly savage; the hallmarks of the nomad's barbarity were firmly fixed in the mind of every farmer in the Tigris and Euphrates river valleys. The nomad was a wanderer, a mover without a home, without religion or social customs, ignorant of cultivated cereals, and a devourer of raw flesh. In short, he was a sort of human-animal. We might turn now, from the Near East and distant antiquity, to a period some two millennia later and to the region of North Africa. The following words are from the account of the war waged by the Roman state against the African king Iugurtha (111-105 B.C.) that was written more than half a century after the event by a Roman governor of Africa, the historian Sallust. "From the beginning, Africa was inhabited by the Gaetulian Africans, harsh and uncivilized men who, like animals, ate raw flesh and the natural produce of the earth. They were not ruled by customs or laws, nor were they subject to the rule of any man; wandering, moving, they made their homes wherever nightfall happened to find them", ..."Africans in the southern regions today endure conditions of aridity and rainlessness most easily, for they live, for the most part, on milk, and raw flesh".[3] From this point in time and place, we might move quickly to a period some four centuries later and read the account in the historian Ammianus Marcellinus of life amongst the Huns, the dangerous nomads of the Roman Empire's northern frontiers. "Although they have the *form* of men, however ugly, they are so harsh in their mode of life that they have no need of fire or cooked food, but devour the roots of wild plants and the raw flesh of any kind of animal whatever. They place this raw flesh between the thighs and back ends of their horses, and thus warm it up a little... No one in their country ever ploughs a

---

[1] The bibliography on this passage is staggering: generally, see G. ROUX, *Ancient Iraq* (Harmondsworth, 1966), p. 161; A. L. OPPENHEIM, *Ancient Mesopotamia: Portrait of a Dead Civilization*[2] (Chicago, 1977), p. 103 and no. 32; J. OATES, *Babylon* (London, 1979), p. 55; and S. N. KRAMER, *The Sumerians: their History, Culture and Character* (Chicago, Press, 1963), pp. 164, 253-54. More specifically: J. BOTTÉRO, "Relations with Mesopotamia: Syria during the Third Dynasty of Ur" *CAH*[3]; i. 2 (1971), pp. 559-66, pp. 563-64, and D. O. EDZARD, *Die 'Zweite Zwischenzeit' Babyloniens* (Wiesbaden, (1957), pp. 31 ff. (texts d-g). For the text see: E. CHIERA, *Sumerian Religious Texts* (Crozer Theological Seminary, Babylonian publications: (Upland, Pa., 1924), pp. 14-23; *Sumerian Epics and Myths* (Chicago, 1934), nos. 58 & 111; *Sumerian Texts of Various Contents* (Chicago, 1934), no. 3, on nomads' total ignorance of grains. See also S. N. KRAMER, *Sumerian Mythology: A Study of Spiritual and Literary Achievement in the Third Millennium*, rev. ed. (London-New York, (1961), pp. 98-101 for commentary on the mythological context.

[2] See C. J. GADD, "The Amorite Invasion", chap. 22.5, *CAH*[3], i .2 (1971), pp. 625-28; G. BUCELLATI, *The Amorites of the Ur III Period* (Naples, 1966); and the works by Kupper, Klengel, Luke and Tracy cited below.

[3] SALL., *Bell. Iug.* xviii. 1-2; lxxxix.7.

field or touches a plough handle. They are without fixed homes, without fire, without law, or a settled way of life, and keep roaming from place to place, like fugitives...".[4]

I have quoted these three passages, widely separated in time and space, merely to illustrate *one* aspect of a consistent ideology held by certain men — that is, the cultured men of the Mediterranean and the Near East — about other men who were foreign to their society, namely pastoral nomads. It is a highly prejudicial picture, marked by all the polar opposites of civilized society; it portrays the ultimate savage who has no habitation, no laws or customs, who knows nothing at all of agriculture, who is constantly on the move, and who is characterized, above all, by his mode of consumption: of undiluted milk and raw animal flesh. This synchronic ideology of the pastoral nomad, which changed very little over the millennia, was then embedded in a diachronic, evolutionary pattern in which the nomad was placed at the very bottom of the scale of human social development or, as in the somewhat more generous view of Varro, barely one step above the state of nature.[5] The nomad represented a particularly fearsome spectre in the minds of civilized men, embodying, as he seemed to, all the qualities antithetical to the cultivated ideals shared by the town-centred culture of the Mediterranean. In their writings there is a clear fear of the immanent threat of the anarchic forces 'out there' that might sweep suddenly out of the wastelands of the Syrian or Saharan deserts, or the Eurasian steppe, to bring death and chaos to organized society. The view finds its counterpart in modern scholarship in the hypothesis of wave-like invasions of nomads cresting out of the arid lands and across the vulnerable bands of farm land in the Near East. A particular favourite of exegetes of Semiticism and Mongol hordes, the idea dies a hard and bitter death.[6] We can only surmise that there must have existed some tremendous gap between two types of society and their ideals that permitted and encouraged the continued existence and strength of this ideology in the face of empirical experience to the contrary. But the vicious effect of the pattern of thought was not so much in the black, uncomplimentary picture of pastoral nomads fostered by it, as in the total explanation the myth

---

[4] AMM. MARC., *RG*, xxxi. 2.3, 2.10.
[5] VARRO, *RR* ii 1.3 ff.; cf. A.O. LOVEJOY & G. BOAS, *Primitivism and Related Ideas in Antiquity* (Baltimore, 1935) pp. 368-69. On the ideology see the pertinent remarks by J.G. TEXIER, "Polybe géographe", in *DdHA*, 2 (1976), pp. 395-412, and by P. BRIANT, "'Brigandage', dissidence et conquête en Asie Achémenide et Hellénistique", *DdHA*, 2 (1976), pp. 163-258, pt. II b, "'Le cru et le cuit'", pp. 170-72; and my forthcoming paper entitled, "'Eaters of Flesh, Drinkers of Milk': the Ancient Mediterranean Ideology of the Pastoral Nomad", *Ancient Society*, 13(1982).
[6] See S. MOSCATI, *The Semites in Ancient History: An Inquiry into the Settlement of the Beduin and their Political Establishment* (Cardiff, 1959); and J.R. KUPPER, *Les nomades en Mésopotamie au temps des rois de Mari* (Paris, 1957) — refuted, *in extenso*, by J.T. LUKE, "Pastoralism and Politics in the Mari Period: A Re-examination of the Character and Political Significance of the Major West Semitic Tribal Groups in the Middle Euphrates, ca. 1828-1758 B.C.", PhD. diss., University of Michigan, 1965 (esp. chaps. 2-3).

offered of a whole segment of human society. Since we all knew what nasty people pastoral nomads were, and in what precise ways, we could fit them neatly into our historical explanations, and otherwise conveniently forget them.

Counterpoised to this hostile stereotype of the nomad and its unquestioned acceptance in scholarly guise by many modern writers, is the acute realization by some perceptive historians that pastoral nomads formed the neglected 'other half' of ancient society. "Classical scholars", Momigliano points out, "too often forget that Greek and Roman civilizations were precarious, though glorious, achievements at the fringes of a well-developed world of nomadic or semi-nomadic tribes. It was the business of the Hellenistic kingdoms and of the Roman Empire to contain the nomads and enlarge the fringe of the cities".[7] By using an evocative word like 'fringe' of classical civilization, Momigliano achieves a sort of Braudelian insight, an inversion of the normal order of analysis. In writing these words, however, he himself was not embarking on any new analysis of the 'other half', but was merely reviewing the work of another giant of modern scholarship, Mikhail Ivanovich Rostovtzeff, on the Skythian and Sarmatian nomads of the Eurasian steppe.[8] More recently, there have been other calls for the reconsideration of the importance of pastoral nomadism in the history of the ancient world. From a Marxist perspective, Perry Anderson has placed the Eurasian nomad at the epicentre of the major historical developments that separated East from West in the course of the transition from the ancient to the mediaeval world.[9] But the causal relationship between the forces of pastoral nomadism and the great historical watersheds of south Mediterranean history has, of course, been prominent in our written history every since Pirenne.[10] What is perhaps surprising then is *not* the critical rôle assigned to pastoral nomadism in our histories, but our breathtaking ignorance of the peoples and economic form to which we readily concede such great causal significance. Even a casual consideration of the common meaning we give to 'nomad' and 'nomadic' in our vocabulary shows an easy acceptance of superficial aspects of a complex phenomenon — mainly the factor of movement — as satisfying our curiosity on the subject.[11]

---

[7] A. MOMIGLIANO, *Studies in Historiography* (London, 1966), p. 96.
[8] Cf. M. ROSTOVTZEFF, *Iranians and Greeks in South Russia* (Oxford, 1922), and *Skythien und der Bosporus*, i (Berlin, 1931).
[9] P. ANDERSON, *Passages from Antiquity to Feudalism* (London, 1974), pp. 217-18.
[10] H. PIRENNE, *Mahomet et Charlemagne* (Paris, 1928) (10th ed., 1937, Engl. trans. B. MIALL, New York, 1939); see P. BROWN, "*Mohammed and Charlemagne* by H. PIRENNE", *Daedalus*, 103 (1974), pp. 25-33.
[11] See e.g., *The Oxford English Dictionary*, vol. 7 (Oxford, 1933), pp. 182-83 and *Supplement*, vol. 2 (Oxford, 1976), p. 122; and *The American Heritage Dictionary of the English Language*, ed. W. MORRIS (New York, 1970), pp. 871 s. vv. 'nomad', 'nomadic' for some interesting examples.

FEAR AND LOATHING: THE NOMAD MENACE AND ROMAN AFRICA

What is also quite apparent is the certainty and consistency with which the hostile view of the nomad, bequeathed to us by antiquity, is reiterated and given credence by modern academic writers. In this regard, we might consider the views of one well-known scholar in the English-speaking world, one of whose principal fields of research is Roman North Africa. His opinions, as revealed in the following excerpts, are fairly typical of ideas held more generally about the rôle of pastoral nomadic groups in North African, and indeed, Roman history.[12]

> In the writer's view, the main factor in this process (*sc.* the historical separation of the Maghrib from Europe), and *one which has previously been underestimated* [my emphasis], was the impetus which the Arab victories gave to nomadism. The nomad and the transhumant gradually replaced the farmer... The most persistent threat which Rome... had to face along the southern and south-eastern *limes* of the empire had been confederations of nomadic tribes... (they) destroyed the uneasy balance which had existed in favour of the farmer during the five centuries of Roman and Byzantine rule. Henceforth, for more than a thousand years, the nomad with his destructive flocks of sheep and goats was lord of the arid but once richly cultivated plains... The desert returned. The farmer was pushed on to the defensive whence he did not emerge until the assertion of European influences during the last century.

That was in 1955. Our *ignotus* felt confident enough two decades later to pen the following words, in much the same vein, in 1975.[13]

> The nomads... represented a complete break with the settled Romano-African civilization that had survived both Vandal occupation and native Berber razzias..., their objective were plunder and pasturage... they were a major threat to ordered life in North Africa, which they succeeded in overturning... When the Romans came to this land, it was a home of semi-nomadic tribes, moving from plain to mountain with their meagre possessions according to the season. Rome's administrators ended this way of life. The tribes were settled within closely defined limits and encouraged to farm.

I have quoted these two passages at length not in order to engage in any *ad hominem* criticism, but merely to note the persistence of the picture of the hostile, destructive nomad in North African historiography, and also to point out the complete lack of *any* aspects of nomad-sedentarist relations in this analysis other than entirely negative ones. Our problem, then, is to ask how much of this stereotypical picture is true. How much is myth and how much is reality?

The difficulties involved in answering this basic question are further compounded by a problem that has alternately inspired and bedevilled the writing of North African history, namely, the interplay between ancient and modern. The various problems that have faced the countries of the so-called 'Third World' in the course of this century have come to take a central place in the historical analyses of the Roman past: *les*

---

[12] W. H. C. FREND, "North Africa and Europe in the Early Middle Ages", *Transactions of the Royal Historical Society* (ser. 5), 5 (1955), pp. 61-80, at pp. 63-64.
[13] W. H. C. FREND, "Nomads and Christianity in the Middle Ages", *JEH*, 26 (1975), pp. 209-21, at pp. 211-12.

VII

30

évolués, acculturation ('Romanisation'), *économies de sous-développement, colonialisme, impérialisme, problèmes militaires*, and *résistance des indigènes*.[14] On one plane, these approaches to the African past are simplistic byproducts (conscious or otherwise) of modern colonial experience in the Maghrib. On another level, however, they remain legitimate categories of inquiry, whatever their origin. Even the men of classical culture considered Africa to be their 'third world', although, juxtaposed with Asia and Europe, the appellation was conceded more by default than by any positive recognition of Africa as the third and equal partner in the ancient Mediterranean.[15]

The real problem with such an intimate confrontation of ancient and modern, when the moderns have so much at stake, is the need to read history to suit our needs and the subsequent generation of much mystification and myth-making. The ancient history of the Maghrib is strewn with such *mirages*, and the central difficulty has become one of separating ancient facts from what we moderns have made them say. The pastoral nomad is but one figure from the past whose significance is pervaded more by mystique than by analytical comprehension. The nomad has been caught in a 'Catch-22' vise of the long range interpretation of North African history that posited the experience of the Roman period as a direct analogue of modern colonial success in the Maghrib, and which perceived the intervening non-colonial period as one of general decline and impoverishment. The putative chaos of the Middle Ages was then simply attributed to the bogeyman conveniently at hand, the pastoral nomad — specifically to the Arab invasions of the seventh and eleventh centuries (or, sometimes, to a combination of this and other mythic causes such as the reintroduction of the camel or climatic change). Yet, no matter how important the nomad has been thought in causing catastrophic changes in history, with few exceptions the historical study of pastoralists has remained, like the nomad himself, peripheral and subliminal. The nomad has been *assumed* to be hostile, *thought* to be a dangerous threat, *considered* to be rootless and unpredictable in his wanderings, *felt* to be removed totally from the world of sedentary agriculture, and *believed* to be a primitive human type, low on the ladder of social evolution. Clearly, the factual bases for such assumptions, as we have already seen them in operation in the two passages I have quoted above, are rarely made explicit. The same lack of attention to the phe-

---

[14] T. R. S. BROUGHTON, *The Romanization of Africa Proconsularis* (Baltimore, 1929); M. RACHET, *Rome et les Berbères: un problème militaire d'Auguste à Dioclétien* (Collection Latomus no. 110) (Bruxelles, 1970); M. BÉNABOU, *La résistance africaine à la romanisation* (Paris, 1976); and A. DEMAN, "Matériaux et réflexions pour servir à une étude de développement et de sous-développement dans les provinces de l'Empire romain", *ANRW*, ii. ˆ (1975), pp. 3-97 are some examples of large works whose very titles proclaim such modern influences.
[15] Cf. HDT., ii.16; VARRO, *LL*, v,31; SALL., *Bell. Iug.* xvii.3; STRABO, xvii.1.1; MELA, *de Chorogr.*, i.2.9-4.2; LUC., *BC*, xi.411-13; PLINY, *NH*, iii.1.3, and AGENN. URB., *de controv. agror.*, B.90-91.

nomenon itself, with very few exceptions, characterizes modern writing on Roman history in general. If an imaginary diagonal line were drawn from the Iberian Mesta in the west to the steppelands of the Ukraine in the east, it is a reasonable certainty that in all lands lying to the south of that axis, including southern Italy and Sicily, some form of pastoral nomadism was an important aspect of the ancient economy. And yet no major synoptic work on the economy of the Roman Empire, from Rostovtzeff to Jones, devotes so much as a word to the subject, much less a concerted chapter of analysis.[16]

This state of assumed ignorance makes it imperative that we examine all the assumptions about pastoral nomads that pervade present studies on Roman North Africa, with attention to the few pieces of data we have from antiquity, and to comparative evidence on the subject, both ancient and modern. In performing this examination I shall concentrate on a very limited number of problems that specifically involve pastoral nomads, both in the process of the expansion of Mediterranean states (African, Carthaginian and Roman) over the African hinterland, very approximately down to A.D. 100, and in the phase of relative 'equilibrium' enforced by the Roman state after that date. Given the assumptions that historians have made about nomads, such as those outlined above, it is not surprising that the effects and results of nomad-sedentarist relations in ancient North Africa as interpreted by them have a considerable degree of sameness. These include: (1) the military repression of nomadic threats to sedentary life, especially that of farming communities, (2) the seizure of lands used by pastoral nomads and their *mise en valeur* by colonists introduced from outside by the state, (3) the exclusion of the pastoralists from lands with agricultural potential, and the use of military force to compel nomads to live on tribal 'reservations', that is, on a more restricted land area and on poorer land than they had used hitherto; and lastly, (4) where possible, the enforced sedentarization of pastoralists: their conversion to peasant farmers who could be controlled more easily by the state and who were generally more peaceful and beneficial for society as a whole.[17] It is the core of these specific propositions that I wish to investigate.

There can be no doubt that whenever the Carthaginians moved into the African hinterland, and whenever the forces of the Roman state

---

[16] There are a few tangential references in M.I. ROSTOVTZEFF, *The Social and Economic History of the Roman Empire*[2], ed. P.M. FRASER (Oxford, 1957), in some of the chapters dealing with the eastern frontiers, and some informative pictorial representations discussed by him; but there is really no discussion of nomads, their society or economy, as such (none at all in the chapters on North Africa). I could find no treatment of the pastoral economy at all in A.H.M. JONES, *The Later Roman Empire, 284-602: A Social, Economic and Administrative Survey* (Oxford, 1964).

[17] These theses are found in all the standard works on the subject; for a convenient, though overstated, summary of them, see Rachet, op. cit.; the classic paper is that by L. LESCHI, "Rome et les nomades du Sahara central", *Trav. IRS*, 1 (1942), pp. 47-83; his *Études d'épigraphie, d'archéologie et d'histoire africaines* (Paris, 1957, pp. 65-74).

32

intruded into these same regions, there was considerable violence. Our problem, as always, is in specifying the involvement of nomads in the larger context of violent conflict. Our ancient literary sources, and they are very few, only refer vaguely to *Gaetuli*, a term that would seem to have the connotation of 'southerner'. Some of these southern populations, or *Gaetuli*, certainly were pastoral nomads, but there is evidence to show that our sources understood Gaetulians to include people who farmed and who lived in villages as well as those who were herders.[18] Nor do our Greek and Latin sources give us many specific data on the social structure or economy of the pastoral nomadic groups in North Africa. I have stressed the paucity of the ancient evidence in order to argue that we are compelled to depend on modern comparative data in order to establish *some* limitations on the inferences that might reasonably be drawn from the scraps and shreds left to us in classical literary texts. Fortunately, modern studies have succeeded in delineating a number of characteristics of pastoral nomadic economies in the arid zone that are constant for a sufficiently large number of instances so as to give us some confidence of their general applicability. I would like to emphasize only a few of these characteristics here, those which I judge vital as a groundwork for any analysis of nomad-sedentarist relations.

I would like to emphasize further that these characteristics are meant to apply *only* to *pastoral nomads* in the *arid zone*. They do not necessarily apply to all economic groups in movement (e.g. hunter-gatherers), nor all nomads (e.g. those of the Eurasian steppe), nor indeed all pastoralists (e.g. ranchers and shepherds).

(1) Pastoral nomads engage in a distinct type of *economic régime*. They do *not*, however, produce any novel types of social organization that are not also known amongst sedentarists. On the other hand, they are incapable of generating (*pace* Krader) the more complex types of social organizations necessary to state formation.[19]

(2) The economic structure in which pastoral nomads are usually involved (i.e. private ownership of animals with communal access to common pasture lands), when combined with ecological forces, usually produces a constant flux within their society which compels not only physical displacement but also social displacement (i.e. the movement of the richest and poorest elements of the economy towards a sedentarist existence).

---

[18] Cf. the reference to the *duo oppida Gaetulorum* in the Ps.CAES. *Bell.Afr.*, xxv.2. Also, the account of the expedition of Cornelius Balbus through the southern regions of Africa in c. 20 B.C. (see PLINY, *NH*, v.35-38) clearly designates village settlements as the normal locus of resistance.

[19] See, e.g., P.C. SALZMAN, "Political Organization among Nomadic Peoples", *American Philosophical Society, Proceedings*, 111 (1967), pp. 115-31, and E. GELLNER, "Approaches to Nomadism", in C. Nelson (ed.), *The Desert and the Sown: Nomads in the Wider Society*, (Berkeley, 1973), pp. 1-9; the work of L. KRADER, e.g., "The Origin of the State among Nomads of Asia", chap. 14, in *Pastoral Production and Society*, (Cambridge and Paris, 1979), pp. 221-34, would apply, if at all, only to the peculiar situation of the Eurasian nomad.

Both forms of movement, however, are quasi-periodic and of a rather predictable nature.[20]

(3) Not only is their economic base weak, but nomads are demographically weak as well. That is to say, pastoral nomads are always fewer in number than the sedentarists with whom they must relate. Indeed, it may come as a surprise to some to learn that nomads are even outnumbered in the heart of the Sahara by oasis dwellers.[21]

(4) Whatever their ideological claims or self-perceptions, pure nomads hardly exist at all; most pastoral nomads have an important agricultural sector in their economy without which they cannot function. Pastoral nomadism is a symbiotic or parasitic economic form that developed in tandem with sedentary agriculture.[22]

(5) Pastoral nomads can only be said to be that segment or part of an ethnic group that practices the *economic* form as defined above (with the possible additional factor of production for autoconsumption alone). Therefore, one can rarely speak of pastoral nomadic *tribes* as a whole since tribal groups are often dimorphic — that is, they obtain an agricultural sector in their economy by 'half' the tribe being sedentary (sometimes this relationship is purely fictive).[23]

There are many other factors that could be mentioned, but these are a sufficient starting point for analysis. Given these inherent weaknesses and limitations of pastoral nomadism, it is understandable that the history of interaction between pastoral nomads and sedentarist states has been of a precise and limited type, characterized above all by specific modes of interdependence and exchange.

The form of relationship typical of a phase of expansion by a central state, but one that becomes routinized during a period of 'equilibrium',

---

[20] The classic study is by F. BARTH, *Nomads of South Persia: the Basseri Tribe of the Khamseh Confederacy* (Oslo, 1961), who is not, however, without his critics; see T. ASAD, "Equality in Nomadic Social Systems? Notes towards the Dissolution of an Anthropological Category", *Critique of Anthropology*, 3 (1978), pp. 57-65: chap. 25 in *Pastoral Production and Society* (note 19), pp. 419-28.

[21] See, e.g., J. BISSON, "Les nomades des départements sahariens en 1959», *Trav. IRS*, 21 (1962), pp. 199-206, and the relevant sections in R. CAPOT REY, *Le Sahara français* (Paris, 1953), for Earlier decades.

[22] On the question of ideology versus reality, see R. DYSON-HUDSON, "Pastoralism: Self-Image and Behavioural Reality", in W. IRONS & N. DYSON-HUDSON, *Perspectives on Nomadism* (Leiden, 1972), pp. 30-47, and especially, E. MARX, "The Tribe as a Unit of Subsistence: Nomadic Pastoralism in the Middle East", *American Anthropologist*, 79 (1977), pp. 343-63; on the question of the symbiotic relationship between the genesis of pastoral nomadism and agriculture see S.L. LEES & D.G. BATES, "The Origins of Specialized Nomadic Pastoralism: A Systemic Model", *American Antiquity*, 39 (1974), pp. 187-93; and the general remarks in C.C. LAMBERT-KARLOVSKY & J. SABLOFF, *Ancient Civilizations: the Near East and Mesoamerica* (Menlo Park, Calif., & London, 1979), pp. 46-50 & 144.

[23] On this dimorphic strategy see, e.g., E. PETERS, "Patronage in Cyrenaica", in E. GELLNER & J. WATERBURY, *Patrons and Clients* (London, 1977), pp. 275-89 with references to his earlier work; for the importance of this structure to encapsulated nomadic groups and their relations with states see M.B. ROWTON, "Enclosed Nomadism", *JESHO*, 17 (1974), pp. 1-30 with references to his earlier work. For its evidence in some of the ancient records, see V.H. MATTHEWS, "Pastoral Nomadism in the Mari Kingdom (ca. 1830-1760 B.C.), Ph.D. diss., Brandeis University, 1977, pp. 170 ff.

is the absorption of potentially violent nomadic elements within the irregular military forces of the state. In the ancient world we know of this process in greatest detail from the records of the Mesopotamian kingdom of Mari on the upper Euphrates in the period between c. 1900-1700 B.C.[24] The highly detailed records of the state archives, transcribed and translated since the 1930s, reveal the regular employment of pastoral nomads, who otherwise might have been hostile to its interests, as auxiliary military units by the state. To this end the palace of Mari established a *census* (the *tebêbtum*) of the major nomadic tribal groups with which it had contact (mainly the Hanaeans, 'Benjaminites',[25] and Suteans), and held local tribal authorities, the *sugâgum*, responsible for the nomad's behaviour. The *sugâgum* had contact with the central government through military officers called *merhum* (*praefectus gentis* would be a quite acceptable Latin translation) who were responsible for organizing the census of the tribe, principally for reasons of taxation and recruitment.[26] The whole process of integration, however, depended on the power of the state, in this case Mari, to enforce its control and provide adequate enticements since, at the best of times, the tribesmen were rather ambiguous; merely engaging in the census was regarded as a mark of submission and hence was condemned by non-census nomadic groups as a betrayal of their ideals. On the other hand, the rewards of land and guarantees of pasture offered by the state were powerful incentives — along, of course, with a legitimation of their raiding activities under the rubric of military service.[27]

Precisely this same type of integration of Gaetulian peoples is found in North Africa from the late Carthaginian period (c. 250 B.C.) onward. The Carthaginian state attempted to control the nomadic populations of the south by a judicious blend of agreements with local chieftains, punitive raids, and the opportunity of service in the Carthaginian armed forces, usually as cavalry.[28] All these factors can be seen under stress during the invasion of Carthaginian territory in North Africa after 310 B.C. by the Syrakusan tyrant Agathokles. Carthage attempted to check wavering loyalties amongst local chieftains and nomad auxiliaries by the use of punitive raids; Agathokles tried the same tactic to tempt their loy-

---

[24] In addition to the works of Kupper, Luke and Tracy cited above, see J. R. KUPPER, "Le rôle des nomades dans l'histoire de la Mésopotamie ancienne", *JESHO*, 2 (1959), pp. 113-27; H. KLENGEL, "Halbnomaden am mittleren Euphrat", *Das Altertum*, 5 (1959), pp. 195-205; "Zu einigen Problemen des altvorderasiatischen Nomadentums", *Archiv Orientalni*, 30 (1962), pp. 585-96; "Halbnomadischer Bodenbau im Königreich von Mari", *Das Verhältnis von Bodenbauern und Viehzüchtern in historischer Sicht* (Berlin, 1968), pp. 75-81.
[25] The name of the Benjaminites is in some doubt. There is no certain identification of this pastoral tribe with the Hebrew tribe of the same name. See LUKE, *op. cit.*, chap. 1.
[26] MATTHEWS, *op. cit.*, pp. 91-92, 148-58 and 228 ff.; J. R. KUPPER, "Le recensement dans les textes de Mari", in A. PAROT, *Studia Mariana* (Leiden, 1950), pp. 99-110.
[27] *Archives Royales de Mari*; no. 6, 7; see KUPPER, *op. cit.* (1950), pp. 108-09; MATTHEWS, *op. cit.*, pp. 10, 73-74, 91-92, and 216-35.
[28] Cf. DIOD. SIC., xix.106.2, 108.3, 109.4, 110.1; xx.3.3; cf. xiii.8.3.

alties in his direction. In circumstances such as these, where the authority of the central state has fallen into doubt, nomadic groups of the interior can be seen siding with both camps, or even remaining resolutely neutral, waiting to attach themselves to the eventual winner.[29] In other words, even in a moment of weakness of the Carthaginian state, when its control over the hinterland was temporarily challenged, there is no sign that the nomads posed a direct military threat to its existence. Rather, exactly as in the texts from Mari, there is every suggestion that they were merely parasitic on the actions of the contending central states and only reacted 'passively' to their primary moves. The nomads were 'beyond the pale' insofar as the Hellenistic states of Carthage, Syrakuse and the African Kingdoms were concerned, so that the nomads were left with the effective autonomy to accept or to reject the overtures made by them. Mere punitive raiding, and this is all that the Hellenistic states seemed willing and able to do, was not sufficient to encapsulate the nomadic groups within the state and to control them more completely.[30]

This type of relationship does not appear to have changed appreciably during the first decades, even century, of Roman rule in Africa after 146 B.C. The Roman authorities simply continued the traditional practice of the Carthaginian and African states of integrating potentially violent nomadic elements into their armies in an auxiliary rôle. The African king Iugurtha himself followed this policy in imitation of the actions of Massinissa, the 'George Washington' figure of early African history, who was renowned in the legend of state building for having turned nomads into farmers and brigands into regular soldiers.[31] The Gaetulians employed by the Roman commander Gaius Marius during the latter phases of the Iugurthine War (c. 107-5 B.C.) received land grants in recognition and legitimation of their services. The ultimate beneficiary of this particular act of co-operation on the Roman side was Julius Caesar, to whom numbers of Gaetuli defected in 46 B.C., transferring their loyalties to the apparent victor in a Roman civil war waged on African soil.[32] Although couched, probably falsely, in the language of Roman clientship, their desertion of one state for another in this case is precisely the same sort of ambivalent reaction seen earlier under Agathokles. Being parasitic on state organizations, the nomad, if he wished to have relations with them, was compelled to switch his allegiance in direct proportion to the perceived influence of the shifting configuration of state powers with which he was confronted.

---

[29] DIOD. SIC., xx.38.1-5.
[30] F. BRAUDEL, *The Mediterranean and the Mediterranean World in the Age of Philip II*, trans. S. REYNOLDS (London-New York, 1972) i., p. 175 f. on the inefficacy of this mode of control.
[31] Cf. SALL., *Bell.Iug.* lxxx.1-3; on Massinissa see STRABO, xvii.3.15.
[32] *Vir.Ill.*, 73.1, to be read with two important papers by J. GASCOU, "Inscriptions de Tébessa, 4: Marius et les Gétules", *MEFR*, 81 (1969), pp. 537-99; "Le cognomen *Gaetulus, Gaetulicus* en Afrique romaine", *MEFR*, 82 (1970), pp. 723-36, with the earlier bibliography city by him; Psj-CAES., *Bell.Afr.*, xxii.1-5; xxv.2-6.

There is no perceptible break in the type of these relations until the close of the internecine Roman state conflict between the forces of M. Antonius and C. Octavianus in North Africa in the late 40s B.C. It is precisely at this point, and the fact can hardly be coincidental, that the newly established hegemony of the single Roman state turned its violence onto the arid lands of the southern Maghrib in a series of military operations lasting from 37 B.C. to A.D. 8/9.[33] Again, hardly by accident, there erupts another different episode of violence involving these selfsame Gaetulians not long after the conclusion of this first phase of Roman military intervention in the south. This single episode has been claimed by modern scholarship as the example *par excellence* of the massive armed resistance of pastoral nomads to Roman rule.[34] The standard account of this violence portrays a seven to eight year war of resistance between A.D. 17 and A.D. 24 spearheaded by an African chieftain named Tacfarinas. He and his bands of raiders pillaged the Roman province, defied the combined military efforts of four proconsular governors, and forced the addition of another legion (*IX Hispana* in A.D. 20) to the Roman garrison in North Africa.[35] The cause has been specified by modern historians as indigenous resistance by nomads to the seizure of their pasturelands by Roman authorities and colonists, and the cutting of the north-south routes of transhumance by the Roman military. The latter policy is said to be marked specifically by the construction of a road by the legion from the military centre at Ammaedara to the Tunisian coast at Tacape.[36]

I would like to argue that there are better contexts for understanding this particular violent episode in North African history. Firstly, it must been seen as related to, and deriving from, the long period of Roman military activity in the south that ended about A.D. 8/9 and which admittedly resulted in the encapsulation of previously autonomous nomadic groups.[37] But it must also be based on a coldly critical evaluation of the reliability of the one basic account we have of these events, that of the Roman historian Tacitus.[38] Once these two fundamental adjustments are made to the contextual picture, the interpretation of the Tacfarinas revolt as an example of the armed resistance of pastoral nomads to the incursions of the Roman state on their lands simply collapses. To begin. It

---

[33] A convenient, though not always reliable, account of these campaigns can be found in Rachet, op. cit., pp. 57-84; much better, BÉNABOU, op. cit., pp. 43-73.
[34] The bibliography is too immense to cite in detail here; see Rachet, op. cit., pp. 82-126, and Bénabou, op. cit., pp. 75-84 with the earlier works cited by them. Add now, M. BÉNABOU, "Tacfarinas: insurgé berbère contre la colonisation", in *Les africaines* (Paris, 1978), vol. 7, pp. 297-313, for an optimistic view.
[35] The main passages in TACITUS are *Ann.*, ii.52, iii.20-21, 32, 73-74; iv.23-26.
[36] *CIL*, viii. 10018, 10023 (cf. 21915) = *ILS* 151. See, e.g., BROUGHTON, op. cit., p. 90; RACHET, op. cit., p. 75 etc.
[37] For the process of encapsulation see ROWTON et al. (note 23).
[38] See no. 35 above; later sources are clearly dependent on the Tacitean account, and although epigraphic and numismatic data are a valuable aid to the interpretation of Tacitus, they do not substantially add to or alter his reports.

can be demonstrated easily, even within the framework of Tacitus' own remarks, that no *war (bellum)* suddenly broke out in A.D. 17; rather there was a gradual, though perceptible, rise in the level of violence in the southern lands of the Maghrib in which Tacfarinas himself is known to have been involved, at least by A.D. 13 though probably even a bit earlier than this date. Secondly, Tacitus himself, rather unusually, does not tell us anything about the causes of the provincial revolt that supposedly broke out in A.D. 17 (certainly nothing about the putative objections of pastoral nomads; that is all modern hypothesis). Not at least until the year A.D. 22 when he mentions that Tacfarinas demanded *land (sedes, concessio agrorum)* from the Roman state for himself and for his men.[39] But such demands for *land* can be shown to function in numerous contexts (for example, in Roman Spain of the late Republic) where Roman military expansion and local violence merge to cause severe social disruption and often a symptomatic flight to banditry.[40] On the other hand, the resistance, such as it was, was rather easily brought to an end by the Roman governor of Africa, Q. Iunius Blaesus, in A.D. 22-23, merely by pressing an already developing Roman strategy of a more permanent occupation of the semi-arid zone. On a tactical level most support for the bandit-chief evaporated when the governor announced a general amnesty for the brigands.[41]

The principal cause of these events, nowhere spelled out in detail in Tacitus, does not seem to originate with pastoral nomads, but elsewhere. The actual development of Tacfarinas' raiding activities as outlined in Tacitus does provide some clues. Before his career as an insurgent, Tacfarinas had served in the *auxilia* of the Roman army in Africa for a sufficient duration to acquire a thorough working knowledge of Roman military organization. Nor was he alone since all his followers are characterized as deserters and men who had considerable experience in fighting in the Roman style. In the light of these facts, it seems only reasonable to postulate that Tacfarinas and his men were simply part of the long-standing tradition of central states in North Africa to recruit Gaetulian elements for service in their armies. We may also reasonably postulate that there must have been an interval of some years between the time of the mass desertions of Tacfarinas and other Gaetuli, and the year (A.D. 13) when their raiding became an important concern of the Roman governor. That points to an obvious conclusion: the coincidence

---

[39] TAC., *Ann.*, iii.73.1-2.
[40] Cf. S.L. DYSON, "Native Revolt Patterns in the Roman Empire", *ANRW*, II.3 (1975), pp. 146-51, compare the *Hâpirû* problem in the ancient Near East: in addition to the studies by Luke and Tracy cited above, see the convenient English summary by M.P. GRAY, "The *Hâpirû*-Hebrew Problem in the Light of the Source Material available at present", *Hebrew Union College Annual*, 29 (1958)-, pp. 135-202, and especially the interesting thesis on 'withdrawal' of marginal elements from organized society proposed by G.E. MENDENHALL, "The Hebrew Conquest of Palestine", *The Biblical Archaeologist*, 25 (1962), pp. 66-86 (cf. LUKE, *op. cit.*, pp. 272-77).
[41] TAC., *Ann.*, iii.73.

of large numbers of Gaetuli who had been co-opted as auxiliaries to Roman military forces and kept active (and out of trouble) down to c. A.D. 8/9, and their subsequent large-scale desertion. In this case, *desertion* seems to be a bad term since it is more likely that when the Roman state no longer had active use for these men after c. A.D. 10, they began to drift into a life of banditry. That is to say, they continued to do what they had always done, but no longer in the employ and under the umbrella of legitimacy provided by the state. Naturally these men and their leaders demanded land as recompense for their services — that had been the traditional reward. But there is no indication in that demand, or indeed elsewhere, that pastoral rights of access were being denied or abrogated by the Roman state or by any putative colonists.

I have written 'putative' colonists because I believe that we must reject firmly the idea of a large-scale European style colonization of North Africa by the Romans. There are, of course, no statistics to support such a notion, nor is there any substantial indicative evidence to suggest it. Hence it is unlikely that any of the hypothetical ill effects of an ancient colonial movement ever actually happened in the way in which is often intimated. Insofar as pastoral nomads are concerned, colonial land seizures are supposed to have sparked the Tacfarinas revolt and to have led to the enforced confiscation of the nomads' lands for agricultural development. The nomads themselves supposedly were either forced to move southwards away from the Roman advance, or were compelled to live on 'reservation lands' of much poorer quality than those they had once inhabited. In fact, there are only a small number of delimitations of such tribal lands, marked by stone stelai, that are actually known to us from Latin inscriptions (perhaps c. 20-25) as opposed to the total known number of ethnic groups (several hundreds).[42] But since at least half of these concern one tribal group, the Musulamii, it is possible to check some of the perimetres of the argument. At least in this one case there is no evidence of any enforced southward movement, nor any delineation of less favourable lands or a lesser extent of land, or indeed of any encroachment of urban settlements on pasture. On the other hand, the boundary stones do concede an immense formal *territorium* to the Musulamii. On the face of it this would *seem* to betoken a special treatment of a *favourable* kind rather than a harsh containment policy. In fact, I believe that these tribal *territoria* in strictly legal terms were not much different in kind from any other type of land that required definition, whether of towns, cities, farmsteads, or large agricultural estates. Was the status of such tribal lands, *qua* property, especially prejudicial? Again, I do not *believe* so, although the point is difficult to prove. It seems that these lands were conceived in law as being communal non-private property that belonged, in a general sense, to the tribe as a whole. Here one might add a possible negative argument to the balances. There do not seem to be any discernable traces of centuriation or a Roman land survey of these

---

[42] See BÉNABOU, *op. cit.*, pp. 429-45 and tables.

tribal *territoria*, and in the sense that this was the essential physical operation that was associated with taxation one might argue for a privileged status. I have claimed elsewhere in more detailed argument that the legal status of ownership of tribal lands was that of *usus* (an umbrella term covering *ususfructus* and/or *habitatio*, though somewhat less than each) and that the land could not be held as private property by members of the tribe but only as a 'habitation' or a bundle of access rights.[43] But, given our knowledge of the régime of the *ager compascuus* (common pasture) in Roman Italy, not even this aspect of tribal lands was all that revolutionary. Let me make it quite clear that in arguing this interpretation of the so-called reserves I am not advocating a compassionate Roman imperialism. I view the policy as one which, quite consistent with our comparative example of the state of Mari, was efficiently advantageous to the expansion of the state and its continued control of the land.[44] Of course the nice legalities of this control as they are reflected in our documents (and it is on this basis alone that I have argued the case) may indeed mask real behaviour that was repressive and exploitative; of this, however, we have no evidence in our sources.

The Roman state also responded, as I have indicated above, in the time leading up to the equilibrium phase, by the implementation of more formalized arrangements for the recruiting of African *auxilia* within the Roman army, and the regularization of the system of rewards. The system seems to have hinged on the work of officers known as *praefecti gentis* ('tribal commissioners') who had as their chief responsibilities, as did the *merhum* at Mari, the legitimation of the power of local chieftains, the taking of the census, and the registration and recruitment of men for the army. In effect, they were liaison officers between the provincial government on the one hand and the tribal chieftains *(principes)* and elders *(seniores)* on the other. As in Mesopotamia we can trace an evolutionary pattern (or better, constant oscillation) of recruitment and rank of tribal commissioners, from military officers, central bureaucrats, and local powerful (municipal) men to members of the ethnic group itself who act in concert with the provincial governor.[45]

Did the problems connected with nomad-sedentarist relations in my so-called 'equilibrium' phase change very much? Firstly, in military terms the nomad problem has traditionally reduced to one question: the function of the *limes* system, or frontier defences, constructed under Roman aegis, and more specifically the function of the so-called *Fossatum Africae*.

---

[43] Dissertation, pp. 217-19, admittedly on the tenuous evidence of *CIL*, viii. 8369.
[44] See C. TRAPENARD, *L'Ager Scripturarius. Contribution à l'histoire de la propriété collective* (Paris, 1908); for Mari, see MATTHEWS, *op. cit.*, pp. 73-86.
[45] See BÉNABOU, *op. cit.*, pp. 446-57; P. LEVEAU, "L'Aile II des Thraces, la tribu des Mazices et les *Praefecti Gentis* en Afrique du Nord (À propos d'une inscription nouvelle d'Oppidum Novum et de la pénétration romaine dans la partie orientale des plaines du Chélif)", *AntAfr.*, 7 (1973), pp. 153-92, at pp. 175-86; and C. LEPELLEY, La préfecture de tribu dans l'Afrique du Bas-Empire", in *Mélanges d'histoire ancienne offerts à W. Seston* (Paris 1974), pp. 285-95.

VII

40

By this term we mean the system of defensive fortifications along the Saharan frontier of Africa which included (though not always in a single combination) stone walls, ditches, earthen ramparts, forts and garrisons, watch towers, and the accompanying road system. When this *system* is traced on a map, however, one fact becomes apparent at once: that it is very limited in scope and specific in location. Continuous defensive systems of the type just described represent only a small fraction of the c. 2500 kilometre Saharan frontier of present day Algeria, Tunisia and western Libya. The total frontal length of the frontier covered by the *fossatum Africae* is only about 210-20 km; the remaining *clausurae* or valley cross-walls found in southern Tunisia and western Libya might account for another 40-50 km of such defences.[46] One of the more recent synoptic interpretations of the 'Grand Strategy' of the Roman Empire offers us, in the place of the concept of 'defence in depth' as first elaborated by Jean Baradez, the most famous student of the *fossatum*, a more subtle idea of static frontiers serving as a 'trip wire' device to signal the location and intensity of frontier threats, and finally their isolation and suppression by mobile units of the army.[47] The problem with this latest thesis, quite apart from its ill conceived notion of 'grand strategy', is that it still accepts the strategic aim of the system, the unity of the system, and the potential intensity of the threat.

So we must re-ask the question: why were these fortified lines constructed and what conceivable function did they have? Perhaps we should consider first a number of problematic questions concerning the ideological function of walls, not just in symbolic terms but in what they were *believed* to achieve by their builders. Wall-building was a characteristic activity wherever a 'civilized' society faced a 'barbaric' one. The frontiers between the two worlds, from the Antonine and Hadrianic walls in Roman Britain in the west to the Great Wall of China of the Ch'in Dynasty in the east, have often been marked by such constructions.[48] But none of these societies was faced with a nomad problem of

---

[46] The classic work is by J. BARADEZ, *Vue aérienne de l'organisation romaine de le Sud-Algérien*. *Fossatum Africae* (Paris, 1949); see now, in addition, P. TROUSSET, *Recherches sur le Limes Tripolitanus du Chott el-Djerid à la frontière Tuniso-Libyenne* (Paris, 1974), and his important papers, "Connaissances archéologiques sur la frontière saharienne de l'empire romain dans le sud ouest de la Tunisie", *101ᵉ Congres national des Sociétés savantes, Lille*, section d'archéologie (1976), pp. 21-33, and "Les bornes du Bled Segui: nouveaux aperçus sur la centuriation romaine du Sud Tunisien", *AntAfr.* 12 (1978), pp. 125-55; and the survey of recent work in southern Tunisia by M. EUZENNAT, "Quatres années de recherches sur la frontière romaine en Tunisie méridionale", *CRAI*, 1972, pp. 7-27.

[47] E.N. LUTTWAK, *The Grand Strategy of the Roman Empire from the First Century A.D. to the Third* (Baltimore & London, 1976), esp. pp. 60-80 (Ph.D. diss., "Force and Diplomacy in Roman Strategies of Imperial Security", Johns Hopkins, 1975).

[48] On the Hadrianic and Antonine Walls, see the introduction by D.J. BREEZE & B. DOBSON, *Hadrian's Wall*, rev. ed. (Harmondsworth, 1978), pp. 37-40; on the Great Wall see O. LATTIMORE, *The Inner Asian Frontiers of China* (London, 1940), pp. 440-43. Like the *fossatum*, the Great Wall was never constructed as a system at one point in time but became, under the Ch'in Dynasty, an amalgam of previously existing local constructions.

the type envisaged for North Africa. Our best parallels and more specific information derive from Mesopotamia of c. 2100-2000 B.C. In one of the earliest periods of human history for which we have considerable documentation, the Third Dynasty of Ur, we find the disintegrating conglomerate of small city-states under the tutelage of Ur facing considerable pressure from nomadic peoples whom they identified as the *Mar.tu*. In the fourth year of Shu-Sin, the last ruler of the dynasty, this threat became so great that the unusual, probably panicky, step was taken of constructing a great wall. Called the 'Wall of Amurrû' (or the 'Fender of Tidnum') the earthen wall and accompanying ditch ran for a length of 270 km, bridging the gap between the Tigris and Euphrates river valleys some distance just north of their closest approach to each other. Fortunately, there is a letter from the chief engineer in charge of the project, one Sharrüm-barri, in which it is explicitly stated that the wall was intended to bar the approach of nomads.[49] Similar projects, known as the 'King's Walls', are known to have been built in the Sinai under the Pharaohs with the conscious intent of barring pastoral nomads from access to the country.[50] There can be no doubt, then, that great walls were built with the intent and expectation that they would contain nomadic raids; that none of them seem to have been very successful in this aim never prevented the attempt from being made. Therefore it is quite possible that the Roman administration in North Africa *might* have attempted a similar construction. In this case, however, we might reasonably expect some indication of the objective in the bare archaeological record itself — i.e. the orientation and plan of the system should betray its intent. But it is precisely in this respect that the traditional explanations of the *fossatum* are most suspect. The plain fact is that there are large 'gaps' sometimes of 60-70 km in width between neighbouring sections of the *fossatum*, and *its is precisely through these gaps that the major routes of nomadic pastoralists to the north must have been located*. This is a singularly odd way of providing strategic protection 'in-depth' for the grain-producing regions to the north. That interpretation must be rejected. So too must be a more subtle interpretation which attempts to take into account the fact of the 'gaps' in the system. This view holds that the walls and defences were only intended as devices 'to direct traffic', so to speak, to compel nomads to take specific routes in and out of the *tell*.[51] But such compulsion was not needed in the first place. Geographical and ecological restraints overwhelmingly restricted the movements of

---

[49] EDZARD, *op. cit.*, p. 47, no. 207; GADD, *op. cit.*, pp. 609-11, 615, 625-28; A. GOETZE, "Sakkanakkus of the Ur III Empire", *JCS* 17 (1963), pp. 1 ff.; T. JAKOBSEN, "The Reign of Ibbi-Suen", *JCS*, 7 (1953), pp. 36-47, at p. 39; on the structure of the wall and ditch see J. READE, "El-Mutabbaq and Umm Rus", *Sumer*, 20 (1963), pp. 83-89, and R. D. BARNETT, "Xenophon and the Wall of Media", *JHS*, 83 (1963), pp. 1-26.
[50] See *ANET*², i, pp. 19, cf. 231; and Sir A. GARDINER, *Egypt of the Pharaohs* (Oxford, 1961), pp. 36, 131, cf. *JEA*, 1, p. 105: "'Walls of the Ruler, meant to repel the Setyu and to crush the Sand Crossers".
[51] E.g. E. FENTRESS, *Numidia and the Roman Army: Social, Military and Economic Aspects of the Frontier Zone* (Bar Int. S. 53), (Oxford, 1979), p. 112 f.

nomads out of the Sahara to very well defined routes. There could not have been any reasonable concern on the part of the Roman authorities on this score.[52] Is there *any* possible explanation? I believe so. It was noted, long ago, by Jean Despois, the *doyen* of geographers of the Maghrib, that there exist in the arid zone uniquely exploitable bands or 'belts' (Arab. *dîr*) of land running along the bases of the Saharan mountain massifs; agricultural communities can and have flourished in these narrow zones of soil which are watered by runoff from the highlands above them.[53] The problem is that these thin lines of settlements were extremely vulnerable and isolated; in Roman times they were open to attack and raiding in a way that the denser and better connected agricultural settlements of the northern plains were not. And often they had to face a double danger: not only raids from pastoral tribesmen or neighbouring communities, but also sudden descents from the inhabitants of the mountains above. It is within this context that I would argue that the defences associated with these settlements (e.g. the *fossatum* system *that completely surrounds* the Hodna massif *at its base*) were of a purely local nature and were intended to deal with 'low intensity' threats directed against them alone.[54] If this interpretation is correct it means that there was never a perception of a strategic or 'high intensity' threat of nomadic peoples emanating from the Sahara, and that the defences were never intended to deal with nomadic pastoralists as such.

What then were 'normal' relationships between sedentarists and nomads like in an area and period of maximum state power? We know, from a wealth of comparative data, that such relationships tend to be ones of symbiosis, founded on a bilateral exchange of goods and services.[55] The same would seem to be true of the Roman period. One pice of evidence that can be adduced in support of this view is a well known Latin inscription found at Aïn Zraïa (ancient *Zarai*) in Algeria.[56] The inscription, set up in A.D. 202, lists a number of commodities on which *portoria* (fees assessed on goods crossing Roman frontiers) were to be levied. Over half (22) of the nearly forty commodities listed on the tariff at *Zarai* are a direct reflection of a pastoral economy, being either animals or animal by-products. This fact, combined with the total absence of produce typical of a sedentarist dry-farming economy and the location

---

[52] See, e.g., J. DESPOIS, *Le Hodna (Algérie)* (Paris, 1953), p. 289 f. and map, fig. 30.

[53] See his seminal paper, "La bordure saharienne de l'Algérie orientale", *RAf*, 86 (1942), pp. 197-219.

[54] As is literally proclaimed in some of the few pieces of contemporary literary evidence from the system itself; cf., e.g., *CIL*, viii. 2494-95.

[55] For North Africa the facts were outlined clearly by A. BERNARD & N. LACROIX, *L'évolution du nomadisme en Algérie* (Alger and Paris, 1906); e.g., pp. 49-62, 207-93 — and in a host of subsequent anthropological works; see, e.g., BARTH, *op. cit.*, and Abbas MOHAMMED, "The Nomadic and the Sedentary: Polar Complementaries — not Polar Opposites", in C. NELSON, *The Desert and the Sown* (1973), pp. 97-112.

[56] *CIL*, viii. 4508, cf. 18643 (Zraïa, Algeria); cf. J.P. DARMON, "Note sur le Tarif de Zaraï", *CT*, 12 (1964), pp. 6-23.

of the post on one of the major routes used by pastoral nomads from the Sahara even to the present day, is a considerable argument in favour of interpreting the tariff as directed to the taxation of pastoral nomads on their annual journey to summer pastures in the north. The tariff seems to indicate two principal aspects of nomad-sedentarist relations. First, it shows that nomads brought north not only their animals for pasture, only *some* of which were to be offered for sale in rural periodic markets in the *tell*, but also a wide range of other commodities for trade. Listed on the tariff are a number of animal by-products: rough, cleaned and tanned leathers; cattle, sheep and goat hides; suede leathers, and glue. Also listed are a range of household manufactures derived from animal produce (mainly wool): five different types of African cloaks, bulk cloth, riding equipment, and other unspecified items of clothing. Beyond this, there are certain commodities on the tariff that point to the involvement of the nomads as middlemen in transporting the produce from the oases along the Saharan periphery to northern markets: dates, figs and alum. Second, and perhaps more important, is the attitude of the Roman authorities to the annual trek of the nomads. Whereas the trade commodities are tariffed at 'normal' rates (c. 2-2 1/2% *ad valorem*), the animals are taxed at less than 1/3 to 1/5 of 1%. At six to twelve times less than the normal rates for all other commodities, the *portorium* levied on the animals is obviously a fixed token charge. In that case, they are not like *portoria* at all, but more like the *scriptura* or fixed head tax *(certum aes)* assessed by the state for the use of public pasture lands *(pascua publica)* in Italy.[57] In lieu of any other concrete evidence, this text would seem to be indicative of the attitude of the Roman administration during the 'equilibrium period' to the movement of the pastoralists to and from summer pastures (note, also, that the stone was set up *after* the departure of the Roman military unit from Zarai). To charge full *portoria* or 'border fees' on the very basis of a household economy when a cyclical movement of a rather predictable nature was enforced on it would have been nonsensical and needlessly provocative. There is no indication that the Roman authorities ever acted in such a harsh way, whereas there is some suggestion of the opposite, namely, a special response in an attempt to accommodate the nomad, not to eliminate or exclude him.

Given some of the specific ways in which nomads and sedentarists managed to engage each other's services, there is no reason to believe that an administration would not attempt to live with the 'normal situation'. Nomads came north, not only with their animals and a wide range of trade commodities, but also with one commodity that would not find any mention in a document like the Zarai tariff, that is, their own labour. Modern observations have shown how the nomads usually arrive in the northern plains at about the same time as the local farmers need extra labour to carry the grain to harvest their crops and additional animal transport to carry the grain to storage areas. Traditionally, both needs

---

[57] TRAPENARD, *op. cit.*, pp. 209 ff., and FESTUS, s.v. 'Scripturarius Ager'.

44

have been met by bands of nomad-labourers and their animals.[58] The phenomenon is attested for North Africa of the Roman period from the example of the famous 'Maktar Harvester' who managed gangs of labourers each year in the 'Nomadic Plains' south of Cirta (modern Constantine), to the so-called *circumcelliones* of the late fourth century.[59] But this labour could take other specific forms. Because of the constraints of space, I shall mention only one of them. As outsiders to the society they entered each summer nomads could perform vital 'observer' functions for which outsiders to the local community are normally required (e.g. police work). A letter from Augustine to a certain Publicola, a Roman landlord in the Jabal Nafûssa region of Tripolitania, reveals that tribesmen from the nomadic Arzuges were recruited to take harvests off his lands. In some years, however, the supply of such nomad-labour was deficient, but Publicola still sent his *conductores* (managers) south to recruit a few of the tribesmen to perform the vital function of *custodes fructuum* ('guardians of the harvest') on his estates.[60] From other African and Italian evidence we know that these 'guards' were not simply innocuous watchmen; in fact, they were present to make certain that the local peasantry, who were not likely to be very co-operative in this regard, handed over *all* the portions of the crop which they owed to the landlord.[61] But, once again, the nomad was useful to sedentarists *precisely because he was an outsider* to settled society and could therefore have a peculiar function within it, just as slaves, women, and other 'external' or outcaste groups could.

All the above argument, plus a host of comparative data, places the burden of proof for the claim of an ancient policy directed to the conscious sedentarization of nomads squarely on the shoulders of those who make such claims. It seems unlikely that any planned policy would have been attempted or would have succeeded; sedentarization is largely another bogeyman of modern historians.[62] I cannot refrain from retelling a story first recounted in Bernard and Lacroix's classic work on nomadism in Algeria published in 1906. A nameless French general, involved in the 'pacification' of the south, when passing through a region where he spotted some nomads, decided that the pastoralists would have to be

---

[58] BERNARD & LACROIX, *op. cit.*, pp. 209 ff., and many subsequent studies.

[59] *CIL*, viii. 11824 *ILS* 7457 (Mactar, Tunisia); on the *circumcelliones* there is, as yet, no satisfactory treatment; there is a reasonably good synoptic discussion of the evidence, with earlier theories, in J.-P. BRISSON, *Autonomisme et Christianisme dans l'Afrique romaine* (Paris, 1958), iv.1, pp. 325-59. I strongly disagree with any attempt to make sectarian 'storm troopers' or any other sort of religious phenomenon of a social and economic group whose connexions with the religious struggles of fourth century Africa were secondary to the principal causes of existence. But there is not the space, or the reasons, to discuss the matter in detail here.

[60] AUG., *Ep.*, 46.1-6; cf. *Ep.*, 93.

[61] For one Italian example, see PLINY, *Ep.*, ix.37.3; for one African example, see *CIL*, viii. 25902.

[62] A. BERNARD & N. LACROIX, "L'évolution du nomadisme en Algérie", *Annales de géographie*, 15 (1906), pp. 152-65, pp. 161-62.

sedentarized. When ordered to construct houses according to a model provided for them, the nomads set about the task with great zeal and vigour. Upon his return from an expedition to the further south, the general and his men, viewing the collection of new houses from afar, were filled with pride at their successful experiment. On a closer approach, however, they were dismayed; the nomads were encamped in their tents next to the settlement while the new residents of the houses, goats and sheep, poked their heads out of the windows. Apocryphal or not, the story neatly illustrates the real hurdle in attempting to change a whole economy merely by fixing abodes. Such programmes have rarely met with success in modern times, and the evidence for their implementation in antiquity is meagre and perhaps of more ideological than practical value.[63]

If, in reconsidering the military and economic relationships between nomads and sedentarists in the ancient Maghrib, I have persuaded you to rethink some of your prejudices against 'movers', even in our own society, then I have succeeded. Pastoral nomads, I think, are in dire need of some advocacy, compared, as they often have been, to some of the most fearsome and loathsome animals man knows. In the fourteenth century Ibn Khaldûn wrote fearfully of the nomadic raiders, who had attacked parts of North Africa some three centuries before his own time, as having destroyed the finest flower of Arabic civilization in the Maghrib "like a cloud of locusts".[64] That compelling simile has impressed itself on the minds of more historians than one would care to mention, and has been repeated as historical fact. What they have failed to note is that the simile is an ancient Semitic literary topos, found as early as the book of Judges in the biblical tradition when fearful Israelites recorded their first encounter with camel-borne nomads.[65] In spite of this, Ibn Khaldûn's highly prejudicial views on pastoral nomads became the founding stone of long-accepted modern theories on the wholesale destruction of the brilliant society of Fatimid Ifriqiyya by the Banû-Hillâl and the Banû-Solaïm in the eleventh century. That has proved one of the most difficult of facile historical interpretations to eradicate.[66] It is not my purpose to

---

[63] Not that large-scale attempts to sedentarize were not made, in very special circumstances they were — see Plut., *Pomp.* 28 for one example, though one has only to read that passage to feel the profound ideological rationale for the programme, and we have no measure of its success.

[64] Ibn KHALDÛN, *Histoire des Berbères* (from the *Kitab al- Ibâr*), trans. M. DE SLANE, (Algiers, 1852-56), vol. 1, p. 34, cf. C.-A. JULIEN, *History of North Africa (Tunisia, Algeria, Morocco): From the Arab Conquest to 1830*, trans. J. PETRIE (London, 1970), pp. 72 ff.

[65] Judges, vi.4-7, cf. vii.12-13, reflecting numerous biblical passages attesting 'clouds of locusts' as destructive agents. Ibn Khaldûn's passages (*op. cit.*, 3, p. 179) on the 'destructive nomad' in much the same vein are quoted by Frend (1955), p. 74, and (1975), p. 213, as fact.

[66] For traditional interpretations see G. MARÇAIS, *La Berbérie musulmane et l'orient au Moyen Age* (Aubier, 1946) ii, "L'invasion hilâlienne et ses conséquences immédiates", pp. 195-228, and X. DE PLANHOL, "La ruine de Maghrib, 2: Les invasions hilâliennes et

deny that man can actually cause the materialization of his own worst fears. The colonial encroachment on African soil in modern times and the widespread institution of private property by its colonists did precisely this. Although many sincere attempts were made, such as in the *Senate-consulte* of 1863, to avoid encroachment on the sensitive military lands of southern Algeria, and to provide 'corridors' of access to summer pastures, the insidious effect of the widespread appropriation of the northern lands under a régime of private property had the ultimate effect of upsetting whatever nomad-sedentarist balance had been struck in the pre-colonial period. At least, this much was *perceived* to be the case in the eyes of the actors themselves. In the reported words of a *qaïd* of the Awlâd-Reshaïsh:[67]

> Les Français nous ont battu dans la plaine de Sbikha... ils nous ont tué nous jeunes hommes, ils nous ont imposé des contributions de guerre. Tout cela n'était rien... Mais la constitution de la propriété individuelle et l'autorisation donnée à chacun de vendre les terres qui lui seront échues en partage, c'est l'arrêt de mort de la tribu, vingt ans après l'exécution de ces mesures, les Ouled Rechaïch auront cessé d'exister.

It is no wonder, then, in the context of a situation such as this that a group of *colons* who founded a small settlement at Shellala in the Adûra of the Hodna Basin in the 1930s named their new village, not inappropriately, Maginot.[68] What I will insist upon as being the historian's purpose, then, is the explanation of the precise forms that relations between nomads and sedentarists have taken in history, not merely the mindless repetition of ideological perceptions of them.

Wishing to end this story on a more positive note, however, I return to our poor shepherd, Martu, whom I mentioned at the beginning. You might be interested to learn that, in spite of the many unkind remarks made by her in-laws, the Sumerian girl decided to marry him and, to the best of our knowledge, they lived happily ever after. A real triumph of love over ideology.

---

leurs conséquences", in *Les fondements géographiques de l'histoire de l'Islam*, (Paris, 1968), pp. 134-55. Now contradicted by a host of studies: H. DJAIT, "L'Afrique arabe au VIIIe siècle (86-184/705-800)", *Annales (E.C.S.)*, 28 (1973), pp. 601-21; C. VANACKER, "Géographie économique de l'Afrique du Nord selon les auteurs arabes du XIe siècle au milieu du XIIe siècle", *Annales (E.S.C.)*, 28 (1973), pp. 659-80; see especially the debate, J. PONCET, "Le mythe de la 'Catastrophe Hilâlienne'", *Annales (E.S.C.)*, 22 (1967), pp. 1099-1120, "Encore à propos des Hilâliens: la 'mise au point' de R. Idris", *Annales (E.S.C.)* 23 (1968), pp. 660-62; H.R. IDRIS, "L'invasion hilâliene et ses conséquences", *Cahiers de civilisation médiévale* 11 (1968), pp. 353-69, and "De la réalité de la catastrophe hilâlienne", *Annales (E.S.C.)*, 23 (1968), pp. 390-96; and the judgement of C. CAHEN, "Quelques mots sur les Hilâliens et le nomadisme", *JESHO*, 11 (1968), pp. 130-33; in any event, the hypothesis is founded on a mistaken reading of Ibn Khaldûn's intent, see Y. LACOSTE, "Le mythe de l'"invasion arabe"", in *Ibn Khaldoun: naissance de l'histoire passé du tiers monde*[4], (Paris, 1978), pp. 87-105.

[67] BERNARD & LACROIX, *op. cit.*, p. 293.
[68] J. BERQUE, *French North Africa: the Maghrib between the Two World Wars*, trans. J. STEWART (London, 1967), p. 139 (*Le Maghrib entre deux guerres*, Paris, 1962), one of the most perceptive works of colonial history.

VIII

AUTONOMY AND TRIBUTE : MOUNTAIN AND PLAIN IN MAURETANIA TINGITANA

« L'âpreté du relief, l'isolement, le manque de contact avec les techniques progressives, l'administration et la police des États naissants font des montagnes méditerranéennes un réservoir abondant de bandits et de héros. L'autorité de Philippe II était bravée dès la médiocre Sierra Morena, et si les États modernes croyaient avoir éliminé définitivement les zones insoumises, les troubles qui ont suivi la deuxième guerre mondiale ont bien montré que ce n'était qu'une illusion et que les brigands de Calabre, les rois des montagnes grecques ne sont pas morts. »[1]

The geographical theatre that is the domain of the modern historian of antiquity extends, in its widest sense, over the whole of the Mediterranean and the Near-East, and adjacent regions. For the historian of Classical antiquity in particular, however, it is the lands more immediately around the Mediterranean itself that still form the chief focus of his problem. Whatever internal differences are found within this region, including rather distinct north-south and east-west geopolitical frontiers, it is arguable that the Mediterranean forms a distinct unit of study. In more recent times, the cultural diversity of the rural inhabitants of its vast geographic expanses has become the object of a burgeoning subfield of anthropology and sociology. One of the apparent faults in this new disciplinary approach to the Mediterranean, noted in a perceptive survey made at the end of the 1970s, has been its tendency to reflect all too well the fact of diversity in the fragmentation of its own analyses and descriptions; few attempts have been made at systematic comparisons between different regions, social structures, and historical developments[2]. The observation is perhaps a little ironic, since it was in the Mediterranean that the modern discipline of historical geography, with its great emphasis on comparative structures, was born. It was Fernand Braudel who first drew one of the comparative constants of Mediterranean life, that of the dichotomy between mountain and plain, to the centre of historical analysis of events in the region[3]. It was he who tried to emphasize the dominant impact of the mountains in the role of the environment in the historical process. But behind Braudel, and acknowledged by him, lay an earlier and parallel achievement, that of the revolution in thinking about geography forged by Vidal de la Blache and his students, including the pathbreaking contribution of Lucien Febvre.The genesis of a genuine cultural geography for the Mediterranean was signalled by the culmination of a multitude of microstudies of the Mediterranean produced by the "new geography" in the perspectives offered by Jean Dresch in the synoptic work co-authored by himself and Pierre Birot in the early 1950s[4]. In *La Méditerranée et le Moyen-Orient* the dichotomy of mountain and plain once again emerged as one of the historical verities of the Mediterranean world.

This essay proposes to consider the political relationships between mountain and plain in the ancient Maghrib by a study of the particular case of Mauretania Tingitana, and to advance the cause of comparison a little by contrasting this north African instance with similar problematic situations involving mountain and plain in the broader context of the Roman Empire. More specifically, a comparison will be made with modes of relationships between central states and highland peoples as known from the much better documented case of the mountains of Cilicia-Isauria in the southeastern quadrant of Anatolia. The comparison is admissible on at least one basis : both regions had mountain highlands that were eventually incorporated (at least nominally) within the frontiers of the Roman empire. Both facts, that of their analogous topography and that of their formal subjugation to the same imperial power, afford the possibility of a comparative analysis. Conversely, the comparison is extended by polar contrasts between the two regions : the one land is northern Mediterranean, the other is southern; one is western, the other eastern. One of these mountain highlands, Isauria, was located in the "more developed" (i.e. urbanized) zone of the east, and had been the object of numerous attempts by imperial states to incorporate it within their political structures; western Mauretania, on the other hand, had not been the object of few (if any) such attempts before its annexation by the Roman state in the early 40s AD. Comparisons may also be made over time, since the mountain-plain relationship in late mediaeval and modern Morocco surely offers the historian a set of conditions that more closely approach those that obtained during Roman antiquity than for most other areas of the Mediterranean.

No geographical facts stand alone. Some of the salient topographical factors involved in this case might nevertheless bear brief mention as a precursor to analysis. The Roman province of *Mauretania Tingitana* was formed of a small enclave of terrain at the northwestern tip of the modern state of Morocco in the far west of the Maghrib. Its precise political boundaries are very uncertainly known today, and were probably only vaguely defined by the Roman state itself. Rather than delineating the unit in terms of precise boundaries, it is perhaps better to conceive of the northwestern part of Morocco as consisting of a number of rather distinct geographic zones. These include, first of all, the principal area of lowland settlement, today called the *Rharb*, which is a large alluvial basin drained by wadis Loukkos in the north and Sebou (with its tributaries wadis Beth and Werrha) in the south. To the north of this plain rises the mountain highland of the Rif, bordered on its northern edge by a Mediterranean coastal strip from Tanger in the west to Melilla in the east. To the south the Rharb plain is blocked at its fringes by the forests of the Mamora, and beyond that by the harsh plateaus of the Meseta. Finally, there looms the huge mountain curtain blocking the hinterland to the east and southeast of the plain formed by the ranges of the Middle Atlas. A very generous estimate of the lowlands in these sectors that came under Roman aegis, including some of the piedmont zones, and so on, could not produce an area much in excess of 9,000 km².[5] By almost any measure this leaves Mauretania Tingitana as one of the smallest territorial provinces of the high Roman empire, smaller even than tiny Judaea; in fact it is only matched in scale by the three diminutive Alpine provinces of the empire (see Table 1). It might seem rather paradoxical, given the small size and apparent remote location of Tingitana, to discover that it was one of the most heavily armed of Roman provinces, with a standing army composed of auxiliary units of the army that neared or exceeded 10,000 men in strength. In terms of the garrison of any one province of the empire that number is perhaps not excessively impressive, but it is rather large if one considers the ratio of the commitment in manpower to the territorial area covered.

Table 1
Areas of selected imperial provinces

The figures offered here are only gross estimates of the planar or "flat-map" areas of the provinces. They are not true surface areas. The boundaries of many of the provinces are only approximately known, and many of them were not well established in antiquity.

Province	Approximate area (km²)
Italy	260,000
Britannia	170,000
Africa Proconsularis*	140,000
Mauretania Caesariensis	110,000
Noricum	55,000
Raetia	45,000
Sicilia	25,000
Cilicia/Isauria**	25,000
Numidia*	25,000
Judaea	12,500
Alpes Poeninae et Graeae	10,000
Mauretania Tingitana	9,000
Alpes Cottiae	7,000
Alpes Maritimae	6,200

* Not including the "Cirtan Federation".
** Mountain province of "Tracheia" as of the mid-second century AD.

VIII

Autonomy and tribute in Mauretania

Given the relatively great input of military manpower, the Roman presence in Mauretania could hardly be categorized as one of the great success stories of imperial rule. Roman type cities remained few in number, adumbrated in size and extent, and isolated from each other. This was one of the two salient characteristics that Mauretania Tingitana shared with provinces of the empire in the west that lay beyond the narrower circum-Mediterranean boundaries of the inner empire, areas like the three northern Gallic provinces or Britain. In those regions one also finds a continued domination of rural structures of economic exploitation and power over the city. Concomitant with this strong separation between administrative centre-places and the countryside is the apparent lack of integration of local élites with the institutions of the central state. Just as in the case of the northern Gauls and Britain, Mauretania Tingitana shows little or no production of senior military officers (at the rank of centurion or above), equestrian officials in state posts, or any local men who attained the rank of senator[6]. Then there is another simple fact : it is now generally conceded that Mauretania Tingitana was one of the few areas of the empire in which the central state conceded "defeat", and from which it retreated at some point in the third century, probably early in Diocletian's reign[7]. That is to say, in spite of whatever cultural and economic commitments, and successes, the Roman state had in western Mauretania, it decided in effect to "cut its losses" and to retreat. Part of that decision must have been the inability, or reluctance, of the state to pay the military price involved in maintaining its hegemony of violence in the region. The costs, whatever they may have been, were simply too great. No small part of this process, it is evident, was played by bare topography and the technological limitations of ancient states, like Rome, to impose an adequate control over mountain frontiers. The fact that the main area of civil settlement, the Rharb plain and its adjacent areas, was encircled by high and rugged mountain ranges, set effective limits on the state's power — as did the more general, strategic location of Mauretania Tingitana within the geopolitical structure of the Roman state[8].

In attempting to study the process of the relationship between mountain and plain in Mauretania Tingitana, however, we are stymied by the almost complete lack of the requisite historical data and sources. The paltry literary sources shed almost no light on the problem; these include, for the most part, the standard imperial geographies and scattered tangential references in the usual histories. The only way in which this deficit can be closed a little is by recourse to the sources provided by the modern disciplines of archaeology and epigraphy. The latter has indeed provided some important clues. In this paper I shall concentrate on one such set of epigraphical data that record actions taken by representatives of the Roman state in the region towards the highland peoples of the Middle Atlas. The documents inscribed on stone monuments are records of the agreements reached between the Roman governors of Mauretania Tingitana and the representatives of certain of the mountain peoples[9]. They all come from the centre of *Volubilis* (Qsar Farasûn/Sidi Moulay-Idriss), which we must assume to have been the *de facto* "capital" city of the Roman province[10]. These records at least have the advantage of forming a quasi serial set, and so offer some hope of interpreting change over time. To them may be added a singularly important document discovered in June of 1957 at *Banasa* (Sûq Tleta ar-Rharb, on the lower wadi Sebou) which has received the appellation *Tabula Banasitana*, and which has been much studied, though mostly from the perspective of the *Staatsrecht* of the Roman government[11]

The eleven inscriptions which record the agreements reached by the Roman governors and the heads of various peoples of the Mauretanian highlands deserve attention first of all because they are unique — no comparable set of epigraphical records of verbal negotiations between Roman officials and "barbarian" men of power exists from any other part of the empire[12]. This uniqueness itself requires some explanation and produces problems of interpretation; it also gives us the opportunity to see a process through a first-hand and immediate record that is elsewhere available to us only through secondary literary and historical accounts. The inscriptions cover a period of slightly more than a century, from the first instance in the early AD 170s to the last in AD 280 (see Table 2)[13]. That is to say, they are strategically located in that time period between the establishment of a military equilibrium of a sorts over the lowlands of Tingitana by the Roman state, and its final withdrawal from those same plains regions. It can be no coincidence, therefore, that this series of inscriptions begins almost precisely where the series of inscriptions known as "military diplomas" ends. Military *diplomata* were small bronze tablets issued to retiring veterans from the auxiliary formations of the Roman army (including those in Mauretania) in order to attest to their receipt of special privileges or *beneficia* granted to them by the Roman emperor, including the grants of citizenship to themselves, their wives and children[14]. In the whole empire generally there is a remarkable break in the issuance of these diplomas in the decade after AD 170, a pattern which is also reflected in the Mauretanian *diplomata*. In Tingitana the granting of military diplomas ceases suddenly in the early 160s AD. In all likelihood the Roman state decided to discontinue issuing such records because they had become a redundant formality. The auxiliary military units that were required to maintain the balance of force were in place, and by the mid-second century most of the manpower needed to fill them was provided overwhelmingly from the pool of sons of existing soldiers (i.e. by men who therefore already possessed Roman citizenship). It is right at this juncture, with the consolidation of lowland control, that the first evidence emerges of a serious negotiation between the two spheres of mountain and plain.

The archaeological and epigraphic record also indicates an earlier phase of equilibrium, one which took about a century to achieve but which is palpable by the decades following the reign of Trajan. By this period, the towns of the Rharbian lowland were experiencing continuing and stable development. During this initial equilibrium phase the first contacts between the Baquates and the Roman government are signalled, though not in the form of negotiations. In AD 140, at Volubilis, a *princeps* of the Baquates, one Aelius Tuccuda, set up a dedication to the Roman emperor Antoninus Pius[15] Three decades before the first attested formal negotiations, therefore, the *principes* of the Baquates were already engaged in dealings with the Roman government, and were presumably involved in an exchange of services of the sort that would lead the Roman governor to recommend the *beneficium* of citizenship. This equilibrium took as long as a century to establish, no doubt in part because of the physical domination of the mountain environment over an ecologically weak and disjointed lowland. Not only did the mountains have more solidity and unity than did the plains of the Rharb, hampered as they were by marshes, flood-basing, bush-land and forest cover, they probably also harboured a denser and larger population [16]. The geopolitical and ecological function of Volubilis within the Rharb was then, as more recently, as a center-place that served both as a market and as an ideal administrative and military control point; its relationship to the local massif of Jabal Zerhûn/Moulay Idriss made it part of an ecological island that was strategically located as the nodal communications point in the western Rharb [17].

Table 2
Elements of the Negotiation Dedications from Mauretania Tingitana

N°	IAM	Date	God(s)	Empe-ror(s)	Gover-nor	Collo-quium	Ethnic Head	Ethnic Group(s)	Pax	Altar	Date
1	348	169/76	×	1 (a)	2	3 (a)	4	5 (1)	(×?)	(×?)	(6?)
2	384	173/75	×	1 (b)	2	3 (a)	4	5 (2)	×	×	(6?)
3	349	180	×	1 (a)	2	3 (a)	4	5 (1)	×	×	6
4	350	200	×	1 (a)	2	3 (a)	4	5 (1)	×	×	6
5	356	226	1 (a)	2 (b)	3	4 (a)	5	(6×)	7	8	9
6	402	223/34	(1a?)	2 (b)	(3)	(4)	5	6 (2)	(7)	8	9
7	357	239/41	1 (a)	2 (b)	3	4 (a)	(5)	6 (1)	7	8	9
8	358	241	1 (a)	2 (b)	3	4 (a)	(5)	6 (1)	7	(8)	9
9	359	245	1 (a)	2 (b)	3	4 (b)	5	6 (1)	7	8	9
10	360	277	1 (a)	2 (a/b)	3	4 (c)	5	6 (1)	7	8	9
11	361	280	1 (a)	2 (a)	7	4 (c)	5	6 (1)	8	9	10

Gods : (a) I.O.M. ceterisque diis deabusque immortalibus.
Emperor(s) : (a) genio imperatoris *vel sim.*
(b) pro salute et incolumitate et victoriae *vel sim.*
Colloquium : (a) conlocutus cum
(b) conloquium cum
(c) conloquio habito cum
Ethnic Group(s) : (x) number in brackets indicates the number of such groups mentioned.

The inscriptions from Volubilis that record and publicize the Roman-Baquatian relations are of a highly formulaic nature (see Table 2). Though spanning over a century in time, and eleven provincial governors and ethnic chief men, their composition remains surprisingly consistent. With some minor exceptions, most of the inscriptions consist of the following elements : 1) a dedication to/invocation of the gods, beginning with Iuppiter Optimus Maximus, 2) a dedication to the emperor, his *genius*, his well-being and safety, 3) the name of the Roman governor of Mauretania Tingitana, 4) the mention of the negotiation or *colloquium* he conducted, 5) the name of the ethnic head man and 6) the name of the ethnic group(s) with whom the governor conducted the negotiation, 7) the designation of the settlement or *pax*, 8) the mention of the altar that consecrates the settlement, the *ara pacis*, and, finally 9) the precise consular date of the agreement. The only significant departures from this formulaic expression are in nos 1-4 and no. 11 in the set. In the first four items of the set, the invocation to the gods at the beginning (1), the elements of the mention of the *pax* (7), and the altar (8) are missing. I do not think that the absence of these elements in the early items of the series is significant. The very fact that these inscriptions (i.e. nos. 1-4) were also inscribed on altars that are no different in their physical design from the later examples surely shows that these formulae were also understood to be part of the procedure, even if they were not referred to explicitly in the dedication[18]. Since the altar was an assumed part of the ceremonial of the *pax*, it seems best to assume that there was also some divine sanction for the whole series from the beginning, and that this divine sanction was provided by Jupiter and all the other gods and goddesses. Numbers 5-11 in the series, therefore, only make more explicit in the written record what was already present in fact in the earlier cases. The last item in the series, no. 11, has small, but perhaps important, divergences from the rigid formula, including the insertion of a new third element, the significance of which will be discussed later.

The process of contact between the Roman governors of Tingitana and the chief men of the ethnic groups in the Middle Atlas is therefore reflected in a five stage movement : (a) party A; (b) contacts; (c) party B; (d) there is a result; which is (e) confirmed. The two critical junctures in this process are therefore the meeting, or contact, which is specified as a *colloquium* in the inscriptions, and the result, or agreement, which is designated a *pax*. Our inquiry might therefore begin by investigating what might be meant by these terms within the context of a meeting between representatives of mountain and plain. The Roman representative was the provincial governor; there is no problem here — he was simply the agent of the Roman emperor. On the other side are found a series of *principes* or «first men» (maintaining a sort of balance, the term was also used of the Roman emperor) of the highland peoples[19]. In all except two instances there is only one such group concerned : the *gens Baquatium*. In the other cases (no. 2, AD 174/75; and no. 6, AD 223/34) an additional group is associated with the *Baquates*; in the former case the *Macennitae* and in the latter the *Bavares*. In both instances, however, it is still a single chief man with whom the Roman governor deals[20]. The highland peoples involved, therefore, were principally those of the Baquates, with the addition of one other group on two separate occasions. The following chiefs or first men of the Baquates are listed in the inscriptions as having conducted negotiations with the Roman governor (Table 3).

Table 3.
Principes of the Baquates in the colloquia

Name	Date	Title
1. (....o)	169/76	*princeps gentium [...]*
2. Ucmetius	174/75	*princeps gentium Macennitum et Baquatium*
3. Canart(h)a	180	*princeps constitutus genti Baquatium*
4. Ililasen	200	*princeps gentis Baquatium*
5. U[r]elius or Uret (?)	226	*(princeps gentis Baquatium?)*
6. (name missing)	223/34	*[princeps] gentis Bavarum et Baquatum*
7. (name missing)	239/41	*princeps g[enti]s Baquatiu[m]*
8. (name missing)	241	*[princeps gentis Baqua]tium*
9. Sepemazin	245	*p(rinceps) g(entis) Baquatium*
10. Iulius Nuffuzi	277	*rex g(entis) Baq(uatium)*
11. Iulius Mirzi	280	*p(rinceps) g(entis) Baquatium*

In addition to the eight headmen whose names are known from these inscriptions as having conducted *colloquia* with the Roman governor, there are two others to whom reference is made in the negotiation inscriptions. In no. 4, one Uret, the father of Ililasen the *princeps* who made the agreement, is mentioned. Uret himself had also been princeps of the Baquates. In no. 10, Iulius Matif, who was the father of Iulius Nuffuzi is noted. His position is unknown, though he too may have been a *princeps* of the group. The only other relationship explicitly attested among all these men is between nos. 10 & 11, it being specified in the latter inscription that Iulius Mirzi was the brother *(frater)* of Iulius Nuffuzi. All that these names can tell us is that the selection of heads of the Baquates could pass either to sons or to brothers of existing *principes*.

The formal term *colloquium* is used to designate these encounters. An historical study of its use reveals that the term was usually employed in political contexts of this type for the sphere of relationships that fell outside the domain of a given state — where one had to enter a realm of contact between autonomous groups which therefore had no overriding institutional frame. Let us consider two exemplary cases, and then attempt to draw some preliminary generalisations. The first comes from north Africa at the time of the Jugurthine War. The incident took place in the final year of the war, 106-05 BC, when the African king *(rex)* Bocchus was preparing to abandon his support of Jugurtha. Bocchus initiated the contact with Marius by sending two «most faithful» *legati* to him to begin discussion on a matter of common concern. Marius eventually agreed to deal though his legate Sulla. Bocchus sent one Dabar, a man of *fides* and a holy-man *(sanctus vir)*, as a go-between *(internuntiatus)* to tell Sulla what he should set the terms for the conference *(colloquio diem, locum, tempus ipse deligeret)*[21]. Bocchus was desirous of establishing the precise conditions of war and peace between the two sides. A *colloquium* with an exact time and place was therefore set so that the agreement or *pax* could be confirmed[22]. It was at another *colloquium*, to which Jugurtha and Bocchus were supposed to come to meet each other unarmed, that Jugurtha himself was finally captured and handed over to the Romans[23].

The second exemplary incident comes from another time and place : Caesar on campaign in Gaul in 58 BC, facing the independent German king *(rex)* Ariovistus. Once again, contact between the two sides proceeded through a series of ritualistic steps. It was initated by *legati* acting as intermediaries; a request was made for a *colloquium* and the appropriate *condiciones* were established. When Caesar accepted the terms, a *dies colloquio dictus est*. Each side was to come unarmed to the meeting. A *locus colloquendi* was established on a mound in a plain equidistant from the two camps. At the meeting each of the leaders ritualistically recounted his mutual *beneficia* and *munera*. Ariovistus asserted his independence in terms of his legitimate right to demand hostages and tribute of the peoples whom he controlled. When it appeared that no negotiated settlement was possible, Caesar *loquendi finem facit*[24]. Two days later, Ariovistus once again sent *legati* to Caesar to announce that he wished to re-set a day for another *colloquium*, or, in lieu of that, to arrange some alternative means of communication. The surrogate personal actions which then substituted for the formal parlay make clear the general framework in which a *colloquium* was meant to function. Instead of engaging in a formal meeting, Caesar sent one C. Valerius Procillus, a Gaul whose father had received Roman citizenship, and M. Mettius, who had relationships of *hospitium* with Ariovistus, to act as go-betweens. Procillus was also selected because of his *fides* and his knowledge of the Gallic language[25].

The *colloquium* was therefore a ritualistic mode of contact between two autonomous groups. The contact was struck on the only grounds that existed outside the organized structures available to either society, namely direct personal ones. Contact was initiated and maintained by personal means, if possible by those who had some prior relationship of trust with the two parties[26]. The rationale for the meeting was usually expressed as a «common concern» that had to be negotiated[27]. The *condiciones* of the meeting were then established, which included a definite time and place for the *colloquium*; the *locus colloquendi* had to be on neutral ground, a *locus medius*[28]. The parties could come to the meeting armed or unarmed as per the prior agreements set for the *colloquium*[29]. The aim of the meeting was to achieve a negotiated settlement, a *pax*. Finally, the personal nature of the *colloquium*, a face-to-face meeting between men representing the two sides, was at the same time the means by which it took place and the guarantee used to confirm the agreement. The *pax* was often sealed by ritualistic gestures such as an embrace, a kiss, or a handshake[31].

The nature of the *colloquium* therefore confirms another argument already noted by others concerning the *colloquia* inscriptions from Volubilis, namely that their unusual periodicity and, in some cases, extraordinary close-bunching in time, rules out any mechanical interpretation of them as formal «peace negotiations» following a war or similar conflict[32]. As Romanelli has pointed out, we must think of them instead as ritualistic means by which normal relations of «friendship» were consolidated by meetings between the two sides. The appearance of each new leader in the highlands would necessitate a ritualistic renewal of the pact, since its validity reposed on the basis of personal links between the two men : «A mio parere è da credere che la rinnovazione del *conloquium* a così pochi anni di distanza da un altro precedente non sia tanto da mettere in relazione con la necessità una pace stata turbata nel frattempo, quanto piuttosto con quella di riconfermare i rapporti di amicizia dopo l'avvenuto di un nuovo princeps. Tali rapporti avevano sempre un carattere per così dire personale, cioè erano legati alla persona che li conraeva : da une parte l'imperatore, attraverso il suo rappresentante, il governatore dalla province, dall'altra il *princeps*, direttamente o a mezzo per esso di un suo rappresentante : quando l'uno o l'altro mutava pur, il rapporto doveva venire rinnovato»[33].

The details of the *Tabula Banasitana* also contribute to a better understanding of the context of the Volubilis negotiation inscriptions. The acts recorded in the *tabula* relate to a people or peoples known collectively as the *Zegrenses* who probably inhabited the foothills regions of the pre-Rif to the north and east of Banasa[34]. From the contents of the document, which refer to dealings between the central Roman government, the governor in Tingitana, and certain headmen of the Zegrenses between AD 168 and 177, we may make some of following generalisations about the context of the contact between the two sides. First, the social structure of the Zegrenses was the instrument through which the Roman state had to work in order to control the pre-Rif zone north of Banasa. There is no indication in this document, or in any other source, of the presence of concrete and depersonalized political structures (e.g. administrative towns) that could have mediated Roman power; rather, we find only a pyramidal set of interwoven kinship, ethnic and household units — *domus, familiae, gentes* — as the sole available conduits of communication. The terms indicate a direct and personal type of social structure that was by this time an alien artefact of the past for most lowland societies elsewhere in the empire, indeed elsewhere in north Africa itself[35]. Power in this social structure seems to have peaked, perhaps occasionally, in the hands of *primores* or «leading men», one of whom might be *the* leading man or *princeps*. It is through these leading men that the agents of the Roman state had to attempt somehow to exert influence that would lead by a process of osmosis, or sequential action, to a sympathetic response in the successive ethnic units that constituted local society.

It is equally clear from the document that few of the Zegrensian groups displayed any active obedience *(obsequium)* to, or performed favourable services *beneficia* for, the Roman state. It was hoped that the reward of citizenship given to the family of Julianus for its meritorious services to Rome would incite other Zegrensians to emulate its behaviour. Since these are the polite diplomatic terms in which the document casts relations between the Zegrensians and the Romans, we would surely not be far wrong in presuming that the opposite was the case — that latent hostility, dissidence, and even forceful interference in the affairs of the lowlands constituted the norm of contumacious behaviour in the region[36]. The Graeco-Roman nomenclature of members of the family of the *princeps* Julianus, far from betokening any move to Roman models, is revealed in context to be wholly exceptional. Few, if any, of the Zegrensian peoples outside the Julianus *familia* had bothered to add Roman-style names to their African ones. Every marriage attested outside the family is to a woman bearing a distinctly non-Latin name (a Ziddina and a Faggura), and citizenship had to be granted to the wives and children of the son and grandson of the first Julianus who was himself made a Roman citizen. The latter action shows that both the women, and by default their children, were not Roman citizens, and that whenever the Julianus men moved to marry outside their family it was to women from groups that had not experienced any change in their citizenship status.

In spite of this pervasively local and ethnic nature of the groups of Zegrenses, it is equally clear that the Roman state asserted its nominal control over them. Whatever their *de facto* ability to assert military and administrative power over these Africans, the manner in which Roman officials extended citizenship to some of the leading Zegrenses makes clear the precise limits of their claim. The grant was made on each occasion with the rider that it was *salvo iure gentis* («with no detriment to the validity of local ethnic law»). But it was also to be *sine diminutione tributorum et vectigalium populi et fisci* («not to diminish the tributes and revenues of the Roman people and the imperial treasury»). That is to say, whatever the force of the (normal?) legal exceptions made with this grant of Roman citizenship that allowed for the continued and parallel validity of the local system of «law» of the ethnic group, these peoples were assumed to be permanent tributaries of the Roman state. This observation raises the question of where the boundaries of tribute ended in Mauretania Tingitana. Did they also encompass the Baquates? Euzennat has argued, ingeniously and perhaps correctly, that the whole gamut of peoples to the south of the province were labelled *autoteleis* («self-tributary peoples») precisely because they were in control of their own «taxation» and hence beyond the realm of the Roman treasury. A demarcated frontier of sorts does indeed seem to have been recognized to the south[37]. To the east, however, we are on considerably less certain ground — but these very conditions of uncertainty may have encouraged the tentative series of responses that would have created the precise type of situation in which we find the Volubilis inscriptions.

Linked to tribute, though not explicity mentioned in the *Tabula Banasitana*, was the factor of military service — presumably one of the *beneficia* that local ethnic groups could perform for the Roman state [38]. Indeed, the avenue of recruitment into the auxiliary formations of the Roman army was one of the major ways in which violent elements in local societies were integrated into the civil networks of the central state, and could actually be made useful in maintaining its peace, usually at some point on the imperial frontiers distant from their home terrain. This means of siphoning off potential threats seems to have had some success elsewhere in north Africa, as evidenced by the office of *praefectus gentis*, a man who served as an intermediary between the state and the ethnic group, principally in matters of tribute and military service [39]. The consistent record of activity by *praefecti gentis* during the whole period of Roman rule in the other north African provinces indicates a type of state-tribe interaction in those cases that seems wholly absent in Tingitana [40]. The presence of groups such as the *Afri, Gaetuli, Maures, Musulamii* and *Numidae* amongst the auxiliary and ethnic units stationed in garrisons on distant frontiers of the empire attests to the viability of this tactic. Such a policy, however, does not seem to have been pursued with any success in further Mauretania; no known auxiliary unit bears the name of any of the ethnic groups of *Tingitana*, and there few signs of the recruiting of ethnic peoples into the auxiliary units stationed in the province itself [41].

Perhaps one of the better sets of comparative evidence to which we can have recourse in order to understand better the import of the negotiations in Mauretania Tingitana is the record of dealings between Roman officials, sometimes the emperor himself, and «barbarians» on the northern frontiers of the empire. The paradigmatic episodes we shall employ come from the reign of Marcus Aurelius, negotiations which cover the temporal mid-range of the Volubilis inscriptions from Tingitana. By the time of Marcus Aurelius, the norms of contacts between the Romans and external ethnic groups tended to fall into regular patterns, with much the same steps as seen in the case of the Baquates in Mauretania. These included contacts initially struck through intermediaries, the conference or *colloquium*, and conditions of «peace» as established by either side, often sealed by an exchange of hostages [42]. Two cases will suffice to illustrate the range of actions normally taken. In AD 175 the Marcomanni sent go-betweens to strike contact with Marcus. He agreed that they had fulfilled all the conditions of the relationships that had been set for them (albeit grudgingly and reluctantly). Their actions called for a *quid pro quo* on the part of the Romans. Marcus therefore restored to them one-half of a DMZ along the Danube frontier, allowed them new places to settle within that zone, and established controlled periodic markets for their use. The whole deal was then sealed with an exchange of hostages [43]. The second episode comes from AD 179-80, when Marcus was arranging affairs with the Iazyges. Once again the contact was initiated by a series of go-betweens, and the point of the conference was to request an alteration of some of the agreements previously made by the Romans and Iazyges. Concessions were made so that the ethnic groups would not become alienated from Roman interests. The Iazyges (and Buri), however, refused to seal the agreement until they received the requisite *pisteis* from the Romans.

The actions and attitudes of the emperor as representative of the Roman state in both cases is made clear by an aetiological schema appended to the latter case. Dio explains that the negotiations with external ethnic groups, and the reactions engendered by them, extended over a range of possibilities that was defined by tribute and status (Table 4). Dio's words suggest a series of potential responses determined by an assessment of whether or not the peoples concerned were thought to be worthy and capable of : a) receiving citizenship, b) being granted freedom from tax imposts *(ateleia)*, c) being granted exemption from tribute that was tied to a time limit, or d) such an exemption that was without time limitation; or, finally, e) being in a position to retroject conditions a-d, to reverse the tax-tribute flow, and to be in receipt of payments or support from the Roman state[44]. Which one of those possibilities was made operative depended on the success with which violent force could be applied by either side. Negotiation of an agreement, or *pax*, and use of violence were two parts of the same continuum. In the events of AD 179-80 described above, the emperor brought into play a force of 20,000 Roman soldiers who attempted systematically to block access to the traditional pasture lands of the Iazyges and to create a situation of insecurity that would prevent the Iazyges from cultivating their lands. These moves were then followed by the construction of a system of forts and outposts in their terrain to act as permanent points of observation and surveillance[45]. Doubtless, both options were also used in Tingitana, and in much the same way[46]. In addition to the use of force, and the negotiated settlement that bridged the two worlds, marked by an «altar of peace», we must assume that all the other ritualistic elements that Dio refers to in the case the Marcomanni and Iazyges, were also present in the meeting between the Roman governor and the *princeps* of the Baquates in Mauretania Tingitana. These elements included ritualistic gestures, and the exchange of objects of trust *(pisteis)* and of hostages to seal the agreement[47]. There is a probable record of one of the hostages that has survived in the tombstone of a young man called Memor (?) who was the son of Aurelius Canartha, the *princeps* of the Baquates noted in the *colloquium* of AD 180 (see Table 3.3). He died in Rome at age sixteen[48].

Table 4
The Tribute-Autonomy Continuum

Citizenship	Internal imposts	Permanent tribute	Temporary tribute	No tribute	Reverse tribute

are to be correlated with :

Full domination	Full domination	Full domination	Partial domination	Full autonomy	Full autonomy

Whatever the role played by ethnic social structure and entrepreneurial violence in local autonomy, there can be little doubt about the determinate role played by mountain topography in dictating the form relationships between various ethnic groups and the Roman state took in Tingitana. Of particular importance are the mountains of the pre-Rif to the north and northeast of the Rharb, and the ranges of the Middle Atlas to the east and southeast. The peaks of the Middle Atlas, rising to 2500-3000 metre heights to the south and east of Volubilis-Meknès-Fès are well endowed with natural resources of rain and ground cover that provide a good environment for a habitational retreat. At the same time, the rugged mountain terrain presents a formidable obstacle to penetration from the outside. In modern times the Middle Atlas have been one of the core areas of the Land of Dissidence (the *Bilad As-Siba*) that lay beyond the effective domination of the lowland state's Treasury (the *Bilad al-Makhzan*)[49]. The consequences of the existence of this mountain world for the structure of Moroccan politics and history are well known. The first of these has been the *de facto* autonomy of the mountain dwellers, their freedom from any sort of direct physical control, above all in matters of administration and taxation, by the states of the lowland[50]. This default left the lowland inhabitants exposed, not so much to purposeful wars or deliberate raids from the highlands as to an uneasy situation that could be punctated unpredictably by violent irruptions which they could not control, and by a threatening atmosphere created by a dominant highland society that hemmed in the plain of the Rharb on all sides. It is precisely this type of local violence, that was related by degrees and steps to the full war that highland peoples might threaten, with which the Roman military officer Sulpicius Felix had to deal at Sala and in its rural territory in the AD 140s[51]. It is not surprising, therefore, to find that agricultural settlement and development in the Roman period seems to have been limited to concentric circles of occupation spreading outwards from the few urban centres in the plain where the forces of the local communities and of the Roman army could patrol and provide surveillance[52]. There are hardly any remains of agricultural settlements of the Roman period to be found east or south of the radius of surveillance that was centered on Volubilis. That is to say, there is no evidence of any Roman-type centres of agricultural exploitation in the plains regions east of Volubilis in the lowland zone of the Saïs between Fès and Sefrou, or southwards in the plains and piedmont between Meknès and al-Hajab[53]. Notably, it is in the southeastern quadrant of Volubilis's rural territory, facing the Middle Atlas, that remains of defensive *castella* are to be found scattered throughout the countryside, whereas evidence for them is lacking in the quadrant facing to the north and northeast[54].

An ethnic group of the early-modern period that was found in precisely the same physical location in the Middle Atlas as the *Baquates* of Roman times were the Aït Ndhir, whose territory dominated the northern parts of the Middle Atlas around al-Hajab, south of the Meknès-Fès-Sefrou line, beginning with the line of foothills about 40-50 km southeast of Volubilis. That is why they were called a *qaba'il at-taraf*, «a people of the edge« : they were located at the edge of the effective limits of the *makhzan's* power. What is known of the relationships between the Aït Ndhir and the *makhzan*? Their independence from central control was guaranteed, in their eyes, by three critical factors : an economy that allowed them to withdraw from the sphere of *makhzan* power for a good part of each year; the control of their own lands in the mountains; and the maintenance of their own customary law *(izref)*. The critical links that signified control by the *makhzan* over them were taxation and provision of armed service (or, at least, forms of pacific behaviour that did not threaten the *makhzan*). The *makhzan* attempted to extend its control into the social struture of the Aït Ndhir by forging personal linkages in the form of «pacts» or agreements and by the appointment or recognition of local men of power as «representatives» of the interests of the *makhzan* (the *qaïds*) whose main responsibilities were to insure payment of tribute and provision of military services[55]. The breakdown of this relationship, which was in a state of continual flux, was signalled by the reversion of the Aït Ndhir to their favourite occupation : banditry and highway robbery[56]. In almost every respect, therefore, the record of the relationships between the Aït Ndhir and the central state or *Makhzan* offers a model of parts of the relationships between the Baquates and Zegrenses and the Roman government that are preserved for us in the epigraphical record. These include the nature of the negotiation and pact struck between the two sides, the role of violence, and its precise location in the whole matrix of tribute, military service, and the preservation of local ethnic law. Further, the timing of the agreements struck between the group and the *makhzan* of the Sultanate or the French colonial power tended to coincide with the periods when the tribe was most exposed to external pressures during its twice annual transhumant movement down from and up into the mountains. And those are precisely the periods to which the Volubilis inscriptions date the *colloquia* : to March-April or to September-October[57].

But the delineation of these relationships in the « Far West » of the ancient Maghrib still begs the question of just how determinant mountains themselves were in the wider context of the Roman Empire. There is no straightforward answer to this question, as the examination of comparable instances in north Africa itself readily shows. The argument has convincingly been made that some montane regions were more penetrable by the low-level agrarian technologies of antiquity than they are by the powerful, but more restricted, techniques of our age[58]. A detailed archaeological survey of the mountainous zone inland of Caesarea in the neighbouring province of Mauretania Caesariensis bears out the claim; the economic penetration of Roman forms of rural economic exploitation was thorough and surely had political consequences for the local autonomy of the region[59]. Perhaps a starker and (historically) better-documented example from outside north Africa would help clarify the problem. A consideration of the parallels offered by the mountains of Isauria-Cilicia may offer some useful insights[60]. Physiographically the region presents a rough analogy to Mauretania Tingitana. A large mountain mass, that of the western Taurus and the anti-Taurus to the east, surrounds and overshadows the enclosed alluvial plain of Cilicia. The plains zone, as in Tingitana, formed by the drainage basin of two rivers, was known as Level or Flat Cilicia *(Cilicia Pedias)* in antiquity, whereas the highlands dominating it were known as Rough or Harsh Cilicia *(Cilicia Tracheia)*. The major urban centres of the region, including Tarsus and Adana, were located in the plain of Flat Cilicia. But this urban milieu was only able to flourish in conditions where the weak and vulnerable plains region was attached to a strong central state. Otherwise the cities were under continual threat, and, as in Mauretania Tingitana, were weak and had a tendency to diminish in size and importance. They were therefore in constant need of replenishment and, sometimes, even refoundation by the central state. This was so in part because of the demographic domination of the mountains over the plains — in the political, technological and ecological conditions obtaining in antiquity the Taurus mountains harboured a larger and denser population than did the plains below. During, and before, the period of Roman control of the region (roughly from the end of the second century BC onward) most of the same repertoire of relationships is found as that documented for Mauretania Tingitana. The various ethnic groups in the mountains, collectively known as the *Kietai*, maintained a long-running cultural and political autonomy, above all from any tribute control by the Roman state or its surrogate in the region. Tribute payment was repeatedly rejected by the Kietan highlanders as an acceptable mode of relationship with the lowland states that attempted to dominate them. The lowland states, including Rome, used a bifurcated approach to the region, a combination of violent force and diplomatic negotiation, as the only means of controlling it. Negotiation, whether in the Roman or pre-Roman periods, proceeded via the channels of power and communication provided by local «big men» in the mountain highlands.

Highland chieftains (such as Datames, Tarkondimotos, or Flavius Zenon, in different eras) were attached to representatives of lowland states by links of friendship *(philia, amicitia)*, thereby becoming their formal «friends» *(philoi)*. This friendship was mediated by go-betweens, who co-opted the highlands chiefs by a judicious mixture of appeals to friendship and kinship, and the use of violence. Negotiation and violent force were ever-present parts of a unified dichotomy of power. The negotiated agreement or *pax* struck between the two sides was formalized at a *colloquium* set up by *legati* from either side; *fides* or «trust» was the moral force used to operate the contact. The *pax* or final agreement was then sealed by an exchange of *pisteis* or *pistia* (objects of good faith), by ritualistic gestures (such as the exchange of «right hands»), and by the trading of hostages[61]. Throughout the seven to eight centuries that this relationship can be documented for Isauria, it was the singular fact of the imposition of tribute that was felt to be the critical stigma of political domination and subjugation, and one that was resisted from beginning to end by the highlanders[62]. In all other spheres of interaction, however, exchanges were mostly left open to whatever course they might take (e.g. in the areas of economic or cultural influence). The one consistent link with lowland society that the Isaurians had over the whole of the Roman imperial period was that of violence, either in the form of forced extraction from the lowland communities by means of brigandage, or in terms of a more formal exchange of labour where the Isaurians provided mercenary soldiers, violent enforcers for hire on the private market, or soldiers that were formally integrated into the regular army, often in its so-called auxiliary formations.

Given the long term co-existence of these two worlds, one of which (the central state) subscribed to a claim of total domination of the other, the not-too-surprising result was a pronounced schizophrenia in Roman attitudes towards Isauria. On the one hand, from the very beginning the Roman state, and its representative who governed the region, claimed all the mountain zones as within the notional orbit of Roman control. Although no armies or administrators established a permanent presence in them, the very existence of the Kietan highlanders was regarded as an affront to the Roman name, as contumacious and rebellious behaviour. The Kietai were recognized as Free Cilicians, but at the same time were regarded as persons who ought to be tributaries of the Roman state. But the historical record is fairly clear on the fact that Roman arms never succeeded in establishing a permanent domination in the mountains of Isauria. Even during the high-point of Roman power in the region, roughly between the AD 120s and 220s, there is no indication of anything other than local policing emanating from the various Greek and Roman cities of the Cilician plains and coastal regions as the best that could be attained in the way of forceful control of the region. In real terms, then, the Kietai were left to sort out their own internal hierarchies of domination based on various forms of personal armed competition; and the units of attack and defence that the violent entrepreneurs of Isauria created remained beyond the effective long-term reach of the Roman state.

The mountains of Isauria therefore offer similarities to the case of Mauretania Tingitana. But there are considerable differences as well. It seems that the prolonged exposure of the Kietai to the types of social and political force brought to bear on them by lowland states of the region, and the repeated attempts at incorporation of the region by means of violent confrontation, provoked a commensurate reaction in the montane communities in their own organization of violence. That is to say, the types of violent force we find in Isauria seem to be better organized, and more centralized, than those in Mauretania Tingitana. The Isaurians therefore represented a more virulent form of reaction to lowland pressures. Part of this virulence was due to another distinction between the two montane regions, namely their strategic location within the networks of power in the empire as a whole. Whereas Mauretania Tingitana was peripheral and remote, Isauria was central and more fully integrated into the Roman imperial system; communications to the whole eastern part of the empire had to run through or around Isauria (a situation that was exacerbated with the shift of central power to Constantinople after the end of the fourth century AD)[63]. The more powerful form of «banditry» found in Isauria was also more deeply enmeshed into the structure of east Roman society, and was therefore capable of achieving fuller reversals of power. What happened in Mauretania Tingitana when the central state began to experience pressures on its resources was a withdrawal of its forces[64]. In a comparative sense, the Roman *Maroc utile* had yielded to *Maroc indispensable*, and finally to *Maroc dispensable*[65]. During this same period the Roman state reacted in precisely the opposite way to the problem posed by the mountains of Isauria. Instead of withdrawing, Roman armies pushed back forcefully against Isaurian violence and established a more concrete *limes* around the region; and central state claims of tributary power over the region were asserted even more strongly after the Diocletianic-Constantinian retrenchment. The result, instead of political withdrawal, was the eruption of classical episodes of «banditry» marked by movements of internal secessionism that were labelled as *latrocinium* by the central state. Mauretania Tingitana and Isauria therefore represent (though in different ways) an internal secessionist *étatisme* that typified the political structure of the Roman empire[66].

The two ancient cases can be unified through the comparative materials provided by the study of the fluctuating relationships between the *siba* and the *makhzan* in early modern Morocco[67]. It can hardly be accidental that, just as with the Free Cilicians, the modern highlanders of the Middle Atlas thought of their own language, the core of their cultural communication, as «free» *(tamazight)*, and identified themselves as the *imazighin* or the Free Men[68]. But what was the content of this freedom? In a world where the alternatives of autonomy and subjugation were not widely separated by a range of other political choices, the simple facts of tribute payment and obligations of violent service represented the irreducible minimum of domination. When two previously autonomous peoples came into contact, the choices along that spectrum were further reduced, and usually some decision was forced on one of the two parties. The modes of contact, in situations where one people was not able to dominate the other by arms, were reduced to various forms of personal negotiation. The modes found in Mauretania Tingitana are not much different from those used by once-autonomous groups who became fully or partially subject to Roman domination along the northern frontiers of the empire. Whatever the result of the endless debate over the precise juridical status of the Baquates, therefore, the simple fact of these negotiations guarantees their *de facto* autonomy of Roman control[69]. That is the sort of situation reflected in the so-called Verona List, which divides the Roman world into the regular provincial areas, appropriately listed, and «the barbaric peoples who swarm under the rule of our emperors», amongst whom are listed «the peoples that are in Mauretania», including the Quinquegentiani, Mazices, Bavares and Baquates[70]. The point is not so much whether they were inside or outside «the frontiers» of the Roman state — obviously so since even at this late date, after the abandonment of Mauretania Tingitana (it is no longer in the list of provinces), these peoples were still considered to be «under our emperors» — as it is the division between «civilized» provincial areas and the «barbarians»[71]. It is therefore probably more fruitful to think of an ongoing situation that contrasted provinces and their urban networks with rural ethnic regions dominated by free peoples. What permitted the Baquates and the Isaurians to enforce this long-term autonomy was simply the determinant force of montane topography which they had on their side.

We therefore find both in Mauretania Tingitana and Isauria forms of ethnic autonomy that were powerfully aided by the geopolitical force of a montane topography. In both cases the impact of mountain terrain was decisive in a premodern world where the technological forces of domination were inadequate to the task of controlling this type of topography[72]. What is more, the mountains made the violent ethnicity of the highlands an immediate threat to the lowlands below, and, in some cases, even beyond that horizon. Which fact provoked Maréchal Lyautey, in summarizing the problem from the vantage point of the lowlands of the Moroccan Rharb, to remark that if the French did not occupy the mountains, the mountains would occupy them[73]. The statement was already an anachronism at the moment the great colonial marshal uttered it; but it is an adequate gnomic assessment of the problem of mountain and plain faced in the Far West by those Romans whom Lyautey knew so well.

NOTES

1. Birot & Dresch (1953-56), I, 109.
2. Davis (1977) 5, cf. 14 f.
3. Braudel (1966) pt. I, i (1).
4. Birot & Dresch (1953-56); Jean Dresch provided all the north African materials for the first volume of this study.
5. The lands actually occupied and exploited within the Rharb were even more restricted than this; they consisted of «islands» of defended fertile terrain dependent on close networks of military posts. They were further isolated by the inroads of hostile environments such as swamps and dense woodlands; the remaining *zone utile* was much more limited than the whole area. Of the 150,000 ha. of the Rharb in the Volubilis region, 80 % of the known agricultural sites of the Roman period are located within a constricted defensive triangle about the town that covered only 15,000 ha. or about one-tenth of the whole; see Euzennat (1969) 198.
6. See Sherwin-White (1967) 52-54; the problem is that Sherwin-White still assumes a dominant model of the upward mobility of *local* elites into the highest ranks of the Roman state (i.e. as senators) as the normal paradigm of provincial integration into the Roman system. The model, however, is surely in need of some iconoclastic revision.

7. The point, originally proffered by Carcopino (1943) 244-54, is still a matter of some dispute, but certain types of evidence seem to indicate a deliberate withdrawal of Roman military and administrative forces from the whole southern zone of the province in the latter part of the third century. A frontier beachhead in Africa was maintained opposite the Straits of Gibraltar, as well as some ports-of-call on the western coast, including Sala, as indicated by the *Notitia Dignitatum* (Seeck (1876) 177 = *Occ*. xxvi, «Comes Tingitaniae», 7; and now confirmed by *AE* 1963 : 65); see Marion (1967) 112-14, and (1978) 210 ff.

8. Of which three facts may be noted : 1) its location at the extreme southwestern periphery of the whole geopolitical body of the empire, 2) its far-western frontier position with respect to the rest of Africa, in which case it was effectively cut off from the rest of Africa to the east by any readily usable land communications; it had to be reached, in terms of practical travel, by the sea routes via the Straits of Gibraltar, and 3) its strongest local ties were as a southern frontier for the Spanish provinces.

9. For earlier studies of these documents see Frézouls (1957) and Romanelli (1962).

10. Following the geopolitical dictates of the Roman state, the *de iure* capital of the province must have been *Tingi* (as the name of the province itself indicates), located at the interface between the general land mass of the province and its Mediterranean seacoast. But the governor could hardly have governed the whole isolated southern plain of the Rharb, which constituted the main *local* part of the province, without physically going to the major urban centre of the region, which was Volubilis. There was therefore a sort of dichotomy in the geopolitical structure of the province. This schism was reflected after the Roman retreat of the late third century, when Tingi continued to have an imperial function long after the rest of the province had been abandoned. One could usefully compare the parallel case of *Caesarea* and Jerusalem in the province of Judaea.

11. Seston & Euzennat (1961); Schönbauer (1963); Seston & Euzennat (1971); Oliver (1972); Sherwin-White (1973); Volterra (1974); Williams (1975); and Corbier (1977), quite apart from numerous other uses of the inscription as a standard reference, are sufficient to demonstrate the general direction which studies of the text have taken.

12. A point emphasized by Romanelli (1962) 1347-48.

13. All the epigraphical materials employed in this analysis, including this set, will be referred to by their catalogue number in M. Euzennat, J. Marion & J. Gascou, *Inscriptions antiques du Maroc, 2 : Inscriptions Latines*, Paris, 1982; henceforth abbreviated as *IAM*, 2; for the *IAM* numbers of this set, see Table 2.

14. For a general outline of their intent, content, and social-geographic-chronological distribution, see Roxan (1981); for auxiliary diplomas see section 3, p. 273 f.; for the temporal distribution of the whole set see fig. 3, p. 274; for Mauretania Tingitana in particular, see her earlier analysis Roxan (1973).

15. *IAM*, 2, 376; given his *nomen* one must suspect a grant of citizenship perhaps dating to Hadrian.

16. On the ecological conditions of the Rharb see Le Coz (1964) esp. vol. I, pt. i. pp. 19-132; 181-222; and Euzennat (1984), with the implications for Roman control of the region. The demographic differential can only be a matter of speculation for the Roman period, but it has been true of comparable modern conditions, see Le Coz (1964) 317 ff. and Célérier (1938) 110-13.

17. See especially Dresch (1930) 503-04.

18. On the altars see *IAM*, 2, 349 and 350 photographs; items 348 and 356 are unknown because the inscriptions are so fragmentary, but since they lie just before and just after the known items in the series, it seems a reasonable deduction that their formal presentation was no different from the rest.

19. The Roman emperor was habitually referred to as *princeps*, even in these same inscriptions, see *IAM*, 2, 349.

20. This is perhaps doubtful in the case of no. 6 (*IAM*, 2, 402) because of the fragmentary state of the inscription, but is probable and seems to be confirmed by no. 2, *IAM*, 2, 384.

21. Sall. *Bell.Iug.* 102 2.-3.; 108.1-109.4. The matter is always a *res communis*; and the grounds set so that no one need fear *insidia*.

22. Sall. *Bell.Iug.* 112.3 for the *condiciones belli* and *pax*; further, «Ceterum Bocchus si ambobus

consultum et ratam pacem vellet, daret operam, ut una ab omnibus quasi de pace in conloquium veniretur...»; and 113.2 «Postea tempore et loco constituto, in conloquium uti de pace veniretur».
23. Sall. *Bell.Iug.* 113.6, «Eodem Numida cum plerisque necessariis suis inermis, uti dictum erat, adcedit...», etc.
24. Caes. *Bell. Gall.* 1.42.1-46.2.
25. Caes. *Bell. Gall.* 1.47.1-47.4, «et propter fidem et propter linguae Gallicae scientiam... ad eum mittere, et M. Mettium, qui hospitio Ariovisti utebatur.» Procillus was no ordinary interpreter; he had earlier served Caesar in a *colloquium* with Diviciacus, see *Bell.Gall.* 1.19.3; «Cotidianis interpretibus remotis, per C. Valerium Procillum, principem Galliae provinciae, familiarem suum, cui summam omnium rerum fidem habebat, cum eo colloquitur».
26. Compare Livy 25.18.15 (Campania, 212 BC) for *hospitium*; Livy 32.32. (Philip-T. Quinctius Flamininus, 197 BC) for *fides*; the examples are too numerous to cite in full. For the definition of the institution involved here see Herman (1986) ch. 2.
27. For *communis res* see Caes. *Bell.Gall.* 1.35.2. (Ariovistus-Caesar, 58 BC) in addition to the exemplary cases cited in the text above.
28. Caes. *Bell. Gall.* 1.34.1. (Ariovistus-Caesar, 58 BC); Livy 28.35 (Massinissa-Scipio, 206 BC), 33.12.1-13.1 (Philip-T. Quinctius Flamininus, 197 BC), 38.25 (M. Fulvius-chief of Tectosagi, 189 BC; Tac. *Ann.* 13.38 (Tiridates-Corbulo, AD 58), 15.28 (Vologaeses-Corbulo, AD 63). See Varro, *LL*, 6.57 for a general definition of the institution.
29. Tac. *Ann.* 13.38 (Tiridates-Corbulo, AD 58).
30. Livy 32.33 (Philip-T. Quinctius Flamininus, 197 BC), 33.12.1-13.1 (Philip-T. Quinctius Flamininus, 197 BC), 38.25 (M. Fulvius-chief of Tectosagi, 189 BC).
31. See, e.g., Livy 28.35, handshake and pledges, «eius dextra fidem sancire»; Tac. *Ann.* 15.28, «tali pignore... et viso Corbulone rex prior equo desiluit; nec cunctatus Corbulo, sed pedes uterque dexteras miscuere». For comparative material from Isauria, see nn. 60-61 below. On these gestures and their significance see Herman (1986) chs. 3.2-3.
32. Still the interpretation offered by Sigman (1976) 119 f., 128 ff.; the significance of the irregular time-gaps was deduced by Romanelli (1962) 1349.
33. Romanelli (1962) 1349 and 1351.
34. On the location of the *Zegrenses* see Euzennat (1974).
35. Compare Tertullian, a contemporary African, whose understanding of these terms is wholly different from the social structure implied in the *Tabula Banasitana*. Indeed, his only parallel usage, a reference to interlocking social units of *gentes, populi* and *familiae*, is found in a reference to Patriarchal Hebrew society, which he clearly regards as an archaic type of social structure that has no analogue in his own experience; see *Adv. Marc.* 4.36.18 = *CCL*, 1, 450 = *PL*, 1, 645.
36. The significance of this generalized situation of insecurity is rather difficult to specify. In any event, it cannot be used in some crude sense to produce repeated episodes of armed crisis that can readily be perceived in the historical record. The views of Sigman (1976), and the subsequent synopsis of the same in Sigman (1977), must be firmly rejected; for some of the reasons see Frézouls (1980).
37. Euzennat (184) 376-79. The line of the frontier to the south was marked, in part, by a *fossa*, probably built under the aegis of Sulpicius Felix in the AD 140s (see n. 51 below), between Sala and W. Bou Regreg. East of the latter point, the «frontier» was probably understood to lie along a line south of, and parallel to, the bed of W. Bou Regreg.
38. It was also a tactic employed by the *Makhzan* in more modern times; the obligations and benefits of tribute and armed service were integrally linked such that those ethnic groups that provided armed service (the so-called *jaish* or «army» tribes) received tribute exemption in compensation, thereby becoming doubly knit into the service of the Sultan.
39. Lepelley (1974) and Leveau (1973) 175-87; compare the function and role of the *officiers des affaires indigènes* on whom see Bidwell (1973) ch. 9, 155-98, esp. p. 183.
40. For the comparative data see Shaw (1982) 38.
41. The ethnic units or *numeri* bearing the name of *Mauri/Maurorum* are clearly derived from

African peoples in central *Proconsularis*; otherwise no auxiliary units of the army bear names of peoples from *Tingitana*, not even the purely «ethnic» units of the army, see Speidel (1975), largely devoted to the *Mauri*, see pt. iii, pp. 208-21.
42. See Dio 67.7.2 (Decebalus and Domitian) and 67.5.1 (Chariomerus, king of the Cherusci).
43. Dio 72.15. Control of periodic markets was surely enforced in Mauretania Tingitana, despite the absence of evidence for such a policy from the province itself; there is clear evidence of their manipulation by Roman authorities elsewhere in north Africa, see Shaw (1971) pt. 4, pp. 46-49 and pt. 8, pp. 67-71. For market control as part of modern-day colonial policy with respect to the mountain peoples in Morocco see Bidwell (1973) 14-15, 44-46, in addition to the comparative material cited in Shaw.
44. Dio 72.18-19.
45. Dio 72.20.1.
46. The comparison with Maréchal Lyautey's policies in Morocco in the early decades of this century needs no emphasis; see Bidwell (1973) chs. 2-3, pp. 12-47; and Porch (1983) ch. 11, 122-36.
47. As in more recent times, see Bruno & Bousquet (1946) who show the great diversity in type of these agreements (none of which can be recovered adequately from our ancient evidence); the *tagmat* and *tada* types, which most closely approximate ours, were struck by a clasping of right hands, the sharing of a communal meal, and the swearing of an oath (all usually with the mediation of an *agurram*), see pp. 365 ff. For comparative evidence on the same type of institution from antiquity, see Herman (1986) ch 3.
48. *CIL*, VI, 1800 = *ILS*, 855 (Rome), on its probable reading : «D(is) M(anibus) / Memoris / fili(i) / Aureli(i) / Canarthae / principis gentium / Baquatium / qui vixit / ann(is) XVI.» For comparative instances from modern-day Morocco see Bidwell (1973) 36.
49. Célérier (1938) 110 f., 143 f., and 169 f.; cf. Bernard (1915) 25-27; in 1915 Bernard was able to characterize the region thus : «Le Moyen Atlas est vraiment le pôle de divergence du Maroc, le réduit de la résistance berbère. Il est même, à cet égard, beaucoup plus important que le Haut-Atlas ou le Rif... Les tribus de cette région sont les plus sauvages et les plus belliqueuses de tout le Maroc, ce qui s'explique fort bien, car ce sont les plus isolées et les plus éloignées de tout contact avec les influences du dehors.» (p. 27). A military survey made in English at the beginning of the Second World War made the same point, see Admiralty (1941), «The Middle Atlas», 49-43, at p. 41 : «The Middle Atlas is the least known part of Morocco, and the last considerable area to be pacified.»
50. The theme is so well known as not to require elaboration here. See Gellner & Micaud (1973), especially the contributions by Hart, Seddon and Burke; cf. Bidwell (1973) passim.
51. *IAM*, 2, 307 (28 October 144); his police actions, undertaken to protect the herds and fields of the (wealthy?) inhabitants of Sala from «the usual sort of raiding» finds structural parallels with actions in the same region documented in more modern times, see Biarnay (1917).
52. R. Rebuffat, *ANRW*, II.10.2 (1982) map, fig. 9, p. 487 = *BAM*, 9 (1973-75), fig. 2 p. 380, for the 25 km radius patrol circles, and correlate them with the topographical distribution of Roman-type agricultural centres known from archaeological surveys—see Luquet (1964) and (1966); and Ponsich (1966).
53. Euzennat (1976) 312-15, with full bibliographical references to all known work in nn31-32, p. 314. As he points out, the ruins at Bou Hellou, whatever once were, are not evidence of a permanent Roman presence at this site, some 90 km east of Volubilis; nor are the ruins at Annoceur, as was once thought, evidence of a Roman outpost well to the south of Fès in the foothills of the Middle Atlas; see Euzennat (1960).
54. Luquet (1964) 300.
55. Bidwell (1973) 73 ff.
56. Vinogradov (1974) 2-3; and ch. 3 by Vinogradov (in) Gellner & Micaud (1973) 67-83.
57. Vinogradov (1974) 45 f. and 71 f.; and Sigman (1976) 150; the pattern is not contradicted by those inscriptions where the precise date of the *colloquium* survives, see *IAM*, 2, 350 (March) 359, 361 (April); 356 (September); and 344 (October). For control of access to pasture lands, see the case of the lazyges cited above and Bidwell (1973) 35 f. for colonial Morocco.
58. See especially Leveau (1977).

59. Leveau (1984) 487 ff., with references to his earlier work.
60. For what follows, see Shaw (1986).
61. See Shaw (1986) esp. pt. ii, «The Story of Datames».
62. As was also the case in colonial Morocco; cf. Bidwell (1973) 46, «The final mark of civilization arrived after pacification : taxation was introduced. Berriau regarded this as the proof and guarantee of submission.» As did the Aït Ndhir of the Middle Atlas, and, most probably their distant ancestors of Roman times—hence the critical provisions of the *Tabula Banasitana* regarding tax.
63. The peripheral nature of Tingitana was recognized in antiquity and reflected in its nomenclature as *Mauretania extuma* (Pliny, *NH*, 5.1.19); or, more officially, upon its first becoming a Roman Province as *provincia nova Mauretania ulterior tingitana*, Desanges (1960). The same feeling of geopolitical remoteness is also reflected in the Arabic term for the region, *al-Maghrib al-Aksa*, «the furthest West».
64. There are several indicators that the retreat came as a decisive step, about AD 280 : 1) the numismatic evidence, especially from hoards, indicates a rather dramatic absence of new coinage from that date onwards (see n6 above); 2) there are no signs of official building in the south after that date as evidenced by both archaeology and epigraphy; 3) the last of the *colloquia* with the Baquates took place in AD 280, at which time the heads of the Baquates were beginning to assume the title *rex* for themselves; and 4) the last attested Roman governor of Tingitana is also dated to this time : Clementius Valerius Marcellinus, AD 277-80 (Thomasson, *RE, supplbd.* 13 (1973) 315=(1960) II, 310). The singular post held Lucilius Constantius (*PLRE*, I, «Constantius», 9, p. 227) in c. AD 350/60 as *praeses Mauretaniae et Tingitanae* (*CIL*, XI, 6958=*ILS*, 1252; Luna, Etruria) must have been a special *ad hoc* command of Caesariensis and what remained of Tingitana to the west; cf. Seeck (1876) for the «Comes Tingitaniae», *Not. Dig. occ.* xxvi, who may be the precursor to Constantius' fossil post.
65. Lyautey (1927) 349; cf. Catroux (1952) 159 f.
66. Romanelli (1962) 1354 long ago saw that the situation in Mauretania Tingitana was a case at the height of the empire of what we see happening much more clearly in the later empire : the rise of nascent indigenous states. For the relationship of this problematic to that of banditry see Shaw (1984) 24 f. and 49 f.
67. The two must not be understood to be different territories, but rather as competing claims to loyalty, principally in terms of tribute and armed service, as defined by the successful marshalling of the resources of violence and personal obligation. See Gellner (1962) and Rabinow (1975) esp. ch. 3.
68. The same was true in antiquity where the general identification of individuals above and beyond their particular ethnic group (e.g. *Baquates*) was as *Mazikes*, surely a cognate or root of the modern Berber term.
69. Lemosse (1967) 27 f., 31 f., and 44; one must reject the contention that Rome's control of the men of power in the mountains of Tingitana and Isauria rested on their prior surrender to Roman power, for which there is no evidence; cf. Lemosse (1969) where the fundamental point is made that such ethnic groups, which could *on occasion* become linked to the Roman state by more formal treaty agreements, were in an ambiguous situation as to whether they were or were not within the «frontiers» of the empire.
70. *Laterculus Veronensis*, xiv.2-5 (in) Seeck (1876) 252 : «Gentes barbarae, quae pullulaverunt sub imperatoribus».
71. For example, the Verona list also includes as «barbarians», in a category separate from the provinces, peoples like the Celiberi, Carpetani and other Iberians who were clearly within the imperial frontiers.
72. Note that various forms of resurgent ethnicity in the modern world, from the Assamese and Kurds in Asia to the Basques (on whom see Heiberg, 1975) Scots and Welsh in Europe, have been powerfully aided by mountain refuges; see Smith (1981) who does not, however, note the the geopolitical factor. It is precisely these mountain-based societies that have proven to be such irreducible nodes of ethnicity even inside the modern nation state, and which are basis for resurgent «subnationalisms» today, see Gellner (1983) 83 f.
73. Lyautey (1927) 329-32, 335; cf. Vinogradov (1974) 33.

BIBLIOGRAPHY

ADMIRALTY, British (1941), *Morocco*, 2 vols., Geographical Handbook Series B.R. 506. London, Naval Intelligence Division, 1941.
BERNARD, A. (1915), *Le Maroc*, 3ᵉ ed., Paris, Félix Alcan, 1915.
BIARNAY, E. (1917), «Voleurs, receleurs et complices dans les vallées inférieures du Sebou et de l'Ouargha», *Archives berbères*, 2 (1917) 135-48.
BIDWELL, R. (1973), *Morocco under Colonial Rule : French Administration of Tribal Areas, 1912-1956*, London, Frank Cass, 1973.
BIROT, P. & DRESCH, J. (1953-1956), *La Méditerranée et le Moyen-Orient*, 2 vols., Paris, Presses Universitaires de France, 1953 & 1956.
BRAUDEL, F. (1966), *La Méditerranée et le monde méditerranéen à l'époque de Philippe II*, Paris, Armand Colin, 1949; 2ᵉ ed., 1966; Engl. transl. Siân Reynolds, *The Mediterranean and the Mediterranean World in the Age of Philip II*, London, Collins, 1972.
BRUNO, H. & BOUSQUET, G.H. (1946), «Contributions à l'étude des pactes de protection et d'alliance chez les Berbères au Maroc central», *Hespéris*, 33 (1946) 353-70.
CARCOPINO, J. (1943), *Le Maroc antique*, Paris, Gallimard, 1943.
CATROUX, Gén. G. (1952), *Lyautey, le Marocain*, Paris, Hachette, 1952.
CÉLÉRIER, J. (1938),. «La montagne au Maroc (essai de définition et de classification)», *Hespéris*, 25 (1938) 109-80.
CORBIER, M. (1977), «Le discours du prince, d'après une inscription de *Banasa*», *Ktema*, 2 (1977) 211-32.
DAVIS, J. (1977), *People of the Mediterranean : An Essay in Comparative Social Anthropology*, London, RKP, 1977.
DESANGES, J. (1960), «Mauretania ulterior tingitana», *Bulletin d'archéologie marocaine*, 4 (1960) 437-41.
DRESCH, J. (1930), «Le massif de Moulay Idriss (Maroc septentrional) : étude de géographie humaine», *Annales de géographie*, 39 (1930) 496-510.
EUZENNAT, M. (1960), «Annocur (Kasba des Aït Khalifa), faux poste romain dans le Moyen Atlas», *Annales de géographie*, 39 (1930) 496-510.
EUZENNAT, M. (1969), «Le *limes* de Volubilis», (in) *Studien zu den Militärgrenzen Roms...*, Cologne-Graz, Böhlau (1969) 194-99.
EUZENNAT, M. (1974), «Les Zegrenses», (in) *Mélanges d'histoire ancienne offerts à William Seston*, Publications de la Sorbonne, série études n° 9, Paris, Boccard (1974) 175-86.
EUZENNAT, M. (1976), «Les ruines antiques du Bou Hellou (Maroc)», (in) *101ᵉ Congrès national des sociétés savantes*, Lille, 1976, archéologie (1976), 295-329.
EUZENNAT, M. (1981), «Le *limes* du Sebou (Maroc)», *Bulletin archéologique du comité des travaux historiques*, n.s. 17b (1981) 377-80.
EUZENNAT, M. (1984), «Les troubles de Maurétanie», *Comptes Rendus de l'Académie des Inscriptions et Belles-Lettres* (1984) 372-93.
FRÉZOULS, E. (1957), «Les *Baquates* et la province romaine de Tingitane», *Bulletin d'archéologie marocaine*, 2 (1957) 65—115.
FRÉZOULS, (1980), «Rome et la Maurétanie Tingitane : un constat d'échec?», *Antiquités africaines*, 16 (1980) 65-93.
GELLNER, E. (1962), «Patterns of Rural Rebellion in Morocco during the Early Years of Independence», *Archives européennes de sociologie*, 3 (1962) 297-311 = ch. 3 (in) *Muslim Society*, Cambridge, Cambridge University Press (1983) 194-206.
GELLNER, E. (1983), *Nations and Nationalism*, Oxford, Blackwell, 1983.
GELLNER, E. & MICAUD, C (eds.) (1973), *Arabs and Berbers : From Tribe to Nation in North Africa*, London, Duckworth, 1973.
HEIBERG, M. (1975), «Insiders/Outsiders : Basque nationalism», *Archives européennes de sociologie*, 16 (1975) 169-93.
HERMAN, G. (1986), *Ritualized Friendship and the Greek City*, Cambridge, Cambridge University Press, 1986.
LE COZ, J. (1964), *Le Rharb, fellahs et colons : étude de géographie régionale*, 2 vols. Rabat, Inframar, 1964.

LEMOSSE, M. (1967), *Le régime des relations internationales dans le Haut-Empire romain*, Paris, Sirey, 1967.
LEMOSSE, M. (1969), «La position des *Foederati*», (in) *Studi in onore di Edoardo Volterra*, 2, Milan, Giuffrè (1969) 147-55.
LEPELLEY, C. (1974), «La préfecture de tribu dans l'Afrique du Bas-Empire», (in) *Mélanges d'histoire ancienne offerts à William Seston*, Publications de la Sorbonne, séries études no. 9, Paris, Boccard (1974) 175-86.
LEVEAU, P. (1974), «L'aile II des Thraces, la tribu des Mazices et les *praefecti gentis* en Afrique du Nord...», *Antiquités africaines*, 7 (1973) 153-92.
LEVEAU, P. (1977), «L'opposition de la montagne et de la plaine dans l'historiographie de l'Afrique du Nord antique», *Annales de géographie*, 86 (1977) 201-05.
LEVEAU, P. (1984), *Caesarea de Maurétanie : une ville romaine et ses compagnes*, Rome, Ecole française de Rome, 1984.
LUQUET, A. (1964), «Contribution à l'Atlas archéologique du Maroc. Région de Volubilis», *Bulletin d'archéologie marocaine*, 5 (1964) 291-300.
LUQUET, A. (1966), «Contribution à l'Atlas archéologique du Maroc. Région du Rharb», *Bulletin d'archéologie marocaine*, 6 (1966) 365-75.
LYAUTEY, Maréchal L.H.G. (1927), *Paroles d'action, Madagascar-Sud-Oranais-Oran-Maroc : 1900-1926*, 2ᵉ éd., Paris, Armand Colin, 1927.
MARION, J. (1967), «Note sur la contribution de la numismatique à la connaissance de la Maurétanie Tingitane», *Antiquités africaines*, 1 (1967) 99-118.
MARION, J. (1978), «Les trésors monétaires de Volubilis et de Banasa», *Antiquités africaines*, 12 (1978) 179-215.
OLIVER, J.H. (1972), «Text of the *Tabula Banasitana*», *American Journal of Philology*, 93 (1972) 336-40.
PONSICH, M. (1966), «Contribution à l'Atlas archéologique du Maroc. Région de Lixus», *Bulletin d'archéologie marocaine*, 6 (1966) 377-423.
PORCH, D. (1983), *The Conquest of Morocco*, New York, Knopf, 1983.
REBUFFAT, R. (1979-80), «Le fossé romain de Sala», *Bulletin d'archéologie marocaine*, 12 (1979-80) 238-60.
RABINOW, P. (1975), *Symbolic Domination : Cultural Form and Historical Change in Morocco*, Chicago, University of Chicago Press, 1975.
ROMANELLI, P. (1962), «Le iscrizione Volubilitane dei Baquati e i rapporti di Roma con le tribù indigene dell'Africa», (in) *Hommages à A. Grenier*, ed. M. Renard, Collection Latomus no. 58, Berchem-Bruxelles (1962) 1347-66.
ROXAN, M. (1973), «The *Auxilia* of Mauretania Tingitana», *Latomus*, 32 (1973) 838-55.
ROXAN, M. (1978), *Roman Military Diplomas, 1954-1977*, London, Institute of Archaeology, Occasional Publications no. 2, 1978.
ROXAN, M. (1981), «The Distribution of Roman Military Diplomas», *Epigraphische Studien*, 12 (1981) 265-87.
SCHÖNBAUER, E. (1963), «Eine wichtige Inschrift zum Problem der *Constitutio Antoniniana*», *Iura*, 14 (1963) 71-108.
SEECK O., ed. (1876) *Notitia Dignitatum, accedunt Notitia Urbis Constantinopolitanae et Laterculi Provinciarum*, Berlin, Weidmann, 1876, (reprint : Frankfurt, Minerva, 1962).
SESTON, W. & EUZENNAT, M. (1961), «La citoyenneté romaine au temps de Marc-Aurèle et de Commode d'après la *Tabula Banasitana*», *Comptes rendus de l'Académie des Inscriptions et Belles-Lettres* (1961) 317-23.
SESTON, W. (1971), «Un dossier de la Chancellerie romaine, la *Tabula Banasitana*», *Comptes rendus de l'Académie des Inscriptions et Belles-Lettres* (1971) 468-90.
SHAW, B.D. (1971), «Rural Markets in North Africa and the Political Economy of the Roman Empire», *Antiquités africaines*, 17 (1971) 37-83.
SHAW, B.D. (1982), «Fear and Loathing : The Nomad Menace and Roman Africa» (in) C.M. Wells ed., *L'Afrique romaine/Roman Africa*, Ottawa, University of Ottawa Press (1982) 29-50.
SHAW B.D. (1984), «Bandits in the Roman Empire», *Past & Present*, 105 (1984) 3-52.
SHAW, B.D. (1986), «Bandit Highlands and Lowland Peace : the Mountains of Isauria-Cilicia» (in) *IX International Economic History Congress, Proceedings*, Berne, 1986.

SHERWIN-WHITE, A.N. (1967), *Radical Prejudice in Imperial Rome*, Cambridge, Cambridge University Press, 1967.
SHERWIN-WHITE, A.N. (1973), «The *Tabula* of Banasa and the *Constitutio Antoniniana*», *Journal of Roman Studies*, 63 (1973) 86-98.
SIGMAN, M. (1976), *The Role of the Indigenous Tribes in the Roman Occupation of Mauretania Tingitana*, PhD dissertation, New York University, 1976.
SIGMAN, M. (1977), «The Romans and the Indigenous Tribes of Mauretania Tingitana», *Historia*, 26 (1977) 415-39.
SMITH, A.D. (1981), *The Ethnic Revival in the Modern World*, Cambridge, Cambridge University Press, 1981.
SPEIDEL, M. (1975), «The Rise of Ethnic Units in the Roman Army», *Aufstieg und Niedergang der römischen Welt*, 2.3. (1975) 202-31.
THOMASSON. B.E. (1960), *Die Statthalter der römischen Provinzen Nordafrikas von Augustus bis Diocletianus*, 2 vols., Lund, Gleerup, 1960.
VINOGRADOV, Amal Rassam (1974), *The Ait Ndhir of Morocco : A Study of the Social Transformation of a Berber Tribe*, Ann Arbor, The University of Michigan, Museum of Anthropology, Anthropological Papers no. 55, 1974.
VOLTERRA, E. (1974), «La *Tabula Banasitana*. A proposito di una recente pubblicazione», *Bolletino dell'Istituto di Diritto romano*, 77 (1974) 407-41.
WILLIAMS, W. (1975), «Formal and Historical Aspects of Two New Documents of Marcus Aurelius, 2 : The *Tabula Banasitana*», *Zeitschrift für Papyrologie und Epigraphik*, 17 (1975) 56-78.

IX

SOLDIERS AND SOCIETY: THE ARMY IN NUMIDIA

The relationship between armed force and political control is an important one that is already widely recognized in our standard histories of the Roman empire. In the last two decades or so the 'other half' of that relationship, that of the army as a 'social instrument', has come to be equally widely recognized and studied (1). Although studies of the defensive frontier systems in North Africa as physical constructions have been prolific, holistic studies of the army as an institution *in itself* – that is to say, of the individual men who manned the forts and their relationships with the local population – have not been anywhere near as abundant. It is therefore a welcome sign that studies of 'the frontier' in other than a technical-military sense have appeared in recent years, with the promise of more to come (2). It is the purpose of this paper to consider two of these new syntheses in order to understand better the type of problem they are attempting to formulate and to answer. *Numidia and the Roman Army* by Elizabeth Fentress is an important book precisely because it seeks to review the *history* of the Roman army in a region in which it was undeniably a major factor in the political integration of that same region into the Roman empire (3). What is more, it seeks to demonstrate the complex set of economic and social relationships in which the army and the soldiers were involved in the scope of a book-length treatment which the subject has not received since René Cagnat published his series of monographs entitled *L'Armée romaine d'Afrique* around the turn of the century (4). The work of Michel Janon on the army and Numidia, on the other hand, although it has not yet taken the form of a monograph, has also consistently attempted to employ new approaches and methods in tackling these same problems (5). Both scholars, therefore, are striving to broaden the scope of 'frontier studies' and to provide novel insights into the process of becoming part of the Roman empire on its periphery. And both consciously deploy new methodologies in the exploration of hitherto unstudied aspects of this problem.

As Fentress emphasizes in the introduction to her study, Numidia is an ideal territorial unit for the analysis of a frontier society and the impact of the Roman army upon it since the province was, she contends, 'liminal' in the Van Gennepian sense. If her introduction to the problem may be summarized fairly, if briefly, it is that Numidia is to be viewed as a frontier that was a threshold in every major sense: geographical, political, economic, and military (6). Within this conception of the frontier, the army, she claims, was also liminal in two precise senses. Firstly, by the use of force it *defined* the 'horizontal' or geopolitical boundaries between 'barbarians' outside the Roman province and 'civilized' men within it. Secondly, within provincial society the army was the critical interstitial element in the vertical mosaic of Numidian social relations, halfway between the governor and the ruling elite at the top and the subject peoples at the bottom.

Having thus outlined a framework for the problem of the army in this frontier province, Fentress then proceeds to develop the groundwork for her study in the following chapters in her work which are devoted to the ecological factors of the region, and the social and economic development of pre-Roman Numidia. Everyone would agree that these two facets are a necessary prerequisite to the central problematique. The critical question that must be posed in regard to 'factors' like geography, however, is the extent to which they may justifiably be viewed as independent variables which can be extracted and isolated from the problem itself. Traditionally 'geography' has been regarded as precisely such an independent factor that can be abstracted from the problem to which it is eventually to be applied; the result is the introductory chapter on 'geographical background' to events, a 'geography' which once dispensed with in this manner rarely re-appears in the events themselves. But the study of geography cannot simply be reduced to this sort of preliminary positivistic outline of major topographical features perceived as neutral and without bearing on the social relations of the people living in the environment (7). But that is, most unfortunately, what one tends to get, even in this recent study of Numidia: a geographical survey, prefixed to the whole, that tends either to the jejeune or to matters that might well seem obscure or exotic to those who are not already *aficionados* of *res africanae*. The collection of facts, therefore, necessarily lacks point and direction, and tends to skirt critical questions of historical changes in the environment over the long term (8). The approach also tends to allow 'facts' about the environment to be stated baldly as 'facts' (to be noted) but without their significance for the political process involved (i.e. Roman imperialism) being drawn out. For instance, Fentress states that there was no greater forest cover on the high plains regions of Algeria in antiquity than there is at present. Although there seems to be insufficient data to prove the point, she may well be correct (9). Yet, even if the 'fact' were only a working hypothesis, its implications for the early economic history of Numidia as a geographical zone do not seem to be pursued systematically. For example, there is a tendency already observable in our earliest literary evidence pertaining to the period of the African kingdoms, to exploit the plains regions through centralized systems of political control and to base this economic exploitation on a systematic organization of a cerealculture that was able to provide, even at this early period, 'surpluses' of grain (politically defined, of course) for Mediterranean political allies, clients, and friends. By contrast, Janon's work seems to attempt a synthesis of geographical fact and hypothesis by deploying both empirical data and theoretical argument in order to demonstrate the *level* and *type* of agrarian development in the region before the advent of the Roman army (10). That is to say, 'geography' is not perceived as a neutral and independent element, to be studied in isolation from the precise historical and social formations that are part of geography itself.

Given the presumption of a purely neutral historical ecology it might seem possible, even beneficial, for the historian to emphasize factors that appear, isolated and in themselves, as 'good' or 'bad'. Hence one might be led to evaluate positively an apparently optimistic factor such as 'greater forest cover', though ironically the obvious might not be that pertinent to an accurate historical assessment of determinant factors in the development of Numidian society. Indeed, the very aridity and lack of heavy vegetal cover might suggest a developmental advantage of the region: that of open agricultural land unhampered by the need for large-scale clearing operations. If so, Numidia (and the Constantine plains areas further to the north and east, and the Sétif plains to the west) offered a comparative advantage in dryness and aridity, and lack of forest cover, that favoured, perhaps even impelled, their development by the specific type of cerealculture in evidence for the pre-Roman period. Some of these aspects, when viewed from the particularistic perspective of the northern Mediterranean, may seem terribly negative, but their natural advantage for ancient farmers working with a rather limited agricultural technology is manifest. It can therefore be no coincidence that such lands tended to become 'developed' in certain economic forms that are stereotypical of ancient Mediterranean cities and the political control of their agrarian hinterlands. The pattern is often repeated, as for example in the Greek colonization of Sicily where one finds an initial avoidance of the damp and malarial lowland coastal plains in favour of an attempt to establish permanent settlement in the high, flat, and dry open plateaux of the interior. A simple historical observation like this is important because it begins to question how much of the cerealculture and arid-zone development of a region like Numidia is necessarily to be tied to any aspect of Roman imperialism (11). The results of close field survey work in Numidia has convinced Janon that the pattern most typical of agricultural exploitation in the region — an arid-zone exploitation of runoff zones based on an intense parcellation of the land — is a local response to regional ecological conditions, and that such systems functioned primarily by local customary regulation as exemplified in the irrigation arrangements attested at Lamasba (12). The questions raised by 'geography' and by 'economic development' in the region are, however, integrally connected with a third problem: the degree and type of social development in Numidia before the advent of the Roman army.

The method the historian may employ here, as in the case of ' geographical background', is that of a separate introduction to the subject — and this is, indeed, the approach that Fentress has decided to use. But to a critical historian such an approach may seem to suffer from much the same defect as the 'geography': too many discrete details of unequal or unrelated value assail the reader. The problem, as with the geography, is that a positivistic collection of data in the sense of a vulgar grab-bag of givens will not suffice. The historian of antiquity, no less than the one of more contemporary societies, must place his or her theoretical framework first — even in matters as apparently innocuous as geography or historical background. Limited as it is to a discussion of 'evidence' and 'sources', this section of her work does not seem an altogether successful approach to the central problem of regional economic development. Much space is devoted to regions other than Numidia, and to a simple listing of data. There is a *catalogue* of *known* 'pre-Roman' sites, and a detailed consideration of Marion's work in the Oujda region of eastern Morocco. A preliminary problem concerning the latter is that the Oujda region is some five hundred kilometres, or more, west of Numidia. The patterns discernable in the highland hills of this small ecological niche in eastern Morocco may or may not have relevance to the central geographical and economic problems of development in Numidia. It is difficult to know because Fentress does not consistently demonstrate such connections by the use of an argument employing *types* of environments for the purpose of constructing a comparative historical geography of the ancient Maghrib that would be able to shed some light on the particular case of Numidia. In lieu of such a consistent comparative historical geography, we lack sufficient specific focus on the data from Numidia to illustrate clearly its regional peculiarities. Janon's studies, though seemingly more parochial and narrowly circumscribed in territorial terms, appear to be more sensitive to the micro-environmental niches found in the region, particularly to the south and southwest (13). His approach would seem to provide a better guide for future studies, based, as it is, on a two-tiered model of analysis of local geography: 1) the establishment of the macro-environmental *areas* of the whole region (i.e. its geopolitics), and 2) the establishment of micro-environmental *types* within each of the geopolitical zones. This sort of approach has the merit of avoiding vast catalogues of discrete data on the one hand, and on the other of attempting to establish a typology which can then be used both comparatively and analytically. *Types* of urban development, of rural development, and the linkages between them can be more satisfactorily demonstrated (14).

In discussing 'pre-Roman' African political structures as a precursor to her problem, Fentress begins with a number of good premises, amongst them the realization of the opaqueness of terms used by ancient writers in their description of 'barbarian' societies (*e.g. gens, natio, princeps*) and, as a result, some much needed correctives are introduced to the treatment of 'tribal' societies by historians of antiquity (15). But the recognition of the problem tends to remain at the level of a mere observation of the difficulty, with no use of comparative anthropological data (other than brief recourse to Gellner) and no *systematic* employment of work by other students of the ancient Mediterranean (16). Both comparisons can and should be used at least in order to proffer possible solutions or to indicate the limited range of possible anwers. The absence of such an alternative schema, however hypothetical, leaves the modern student of Roman Numidia uncertain and unprepared to assess the degree or type of change in *local* society after the arrival of the Roman army. Much the same criticism must apply to her treatment of the conquest period (17). A good beginning, which must now be shared by all historians of the region, is the rejection of much that has appeared under the rubric of *résistance* in the interpretation of the ancient history of the Maghrib. She rightly suggests, for example, that there must be a more convincing explanation of the Tacfarinas episode than either as a 'provincial rebellion' or as a 'tribal (nomadic) revolt'. And in the oft-repeated catechism about the so-called 'tribal reserves', there is the beginning of a refutation, a sweeping aside of much scholarly nonsense about the subject (e.g. the 'pushing back' of Africans/nomads onto poorer quality lands). In making the *limitatio* of tribal lands part of the larger process of the organization and centuriation of rural lands and urban centres, she is surely correct, although the full implications and the details of a Roman policy to tribal lands is never fully developed. Both her rejection of simplistic models of the organization of local (e.g. 'tribal') society and of related ideas on the Roman treatment of locals (e.g. 'L'hypothèse du refoulement systématique des indigènes vers les régions désertiques...') are also shared by Janon (18).

The central theme of the new interpretations offered by both Janon and Fentress is, quite naturally, the function of the Roman military-defensive systems around the Hodna, Aurès, and Mememsha mountain ranges. Fentress' survey of the *Limes Numidiae* recognizes the pioneering work of Baradez but, justifiably, criticizes the inconsistency of his research methods and his presentation of the results. After a survey and catalogue of the forty major fortified sites on the *limes*, however, she seems to arrive at the conclusion that little more can be wrung out of the data than a general typology of forts based, ultimately, on epigraphical rather than archaeological data (19). There is the firm realization that traditional explanations of the function of the *fossatum* are untenable, and an alternative is proposed: the *fossatum* and the road and fort system which it is connected were designed 'to control and to direct the flow of traffic into and out of occupied areas' (20). It is a possible answer-one of those already suggested by Trousset for the *clausurae* of the *Limes Tripolitanus* further to the east (21). As the ostraca from Bu Njem (ancient *Golas*) have shown, surveillance was indeed one of the prime duties of the advance forts of that frontier system (22). But there are certain peculiarities of the *fossatum* line (e.g. the near complete encirclement of the Hodna Mountains on both the north and south flanks) that seem difficult to explain within this monocausal model. Yet another shibboleth (already questioned by others) that both Fentress and Janon dispute is Baradez' conception of 'defence in depth'. Fentress, in particular, questions the validity of the concept given that the system as a whole is somewhat of an illusion. Its various component parts were actually constructed at different times and for different purposes (23). Both in this matter and in that of the function of the *fossatum*, however, much recent work, such as that of Luttwack, that is suggestive of the long-range impetus and directional function of these discrete regional systems as part of an overall defensive system in the empire has not been fully integrated into the analysis of the regional system in Numidia. As his longer range interpretation shows, a defensive system' may indeed be constructed at different times and in a fragmented manner, but may still have been part of a slow working towards a final long term aim. However much one might disagree with his analysis, it at least deserves more serious consideration by regional historians of the Roman frontiers (24).

The whole interpretation of systems like the *fossatum* as directed towards the massive control of *external* enemies, however, often seems to run the risk of inventing such threats in order to explain the rationale of the system in modern terms. Hence there is too ready an acceptance of questionable interpretations of the evidence, such as the commonplace assertion that an epigraphical reference to *Bavares* 'Transtagnenses' must suggest the incursion of Saharan nomads from south of Shatt al-Hodna (the *stagna*) deep into the hinterland of the *tell* some five-hundred kilometres far to the northwest, to the Mediterranean coast near modern Oran (25). Given the extreme unlikelihood of such a movement (and given both ancient and modern control data) one can only see the determinant factor in such interpretations as the impulsion to see *Saharan nomads* as particularly dangerous and as the sole *point d'interpretation* for explaining the building of military systems in the region and for the massive presence of the Roman army. This view is quite favourable to the Roman state — it emphasizes beneficent protection. But what if one were to remove that viewpoint — or at least scale it down so that 'Saharan nomads' become no greater a threat that any other particular sector of local society? One would then be left only with local repression, a view Syme is quite willing to contemplate as a real function of the Roman armies on the Rhine in a situation where there was arguably even a genuine external threat (26). Janon, on the other hand, seems to be calling for a much more profound revolution in our conceptualization of Numidia as a frontier or frontier zone (27):

Il ne paraît pas raisonnable de voir, dans la densité et l'étendue de l'occupation militaire ou para-militaire romaine, un dispositif tourné uniquement vers un ennemi extérieur. On prend le risque en ce cas d'étendre la zone arrière du *limes* jusqu'aux rivages méditerraneens. Abandonnons les images d'épinal: celle du Berbère sur son piton contemplant avec haine et concupiscence la prosperité romaine, comme celle du centurion scrutant la ligne jaune des dunes d'où vont tout à l'heure surgir les hordes barbares prêtes à assassiner la présence romaine.

Given this new view one can still ask what the function of the *limes* system in Numidia was. Janon offers us a comparison with the Rhine frontier — a hard unbroken line contrasted with the broken, episodic 'mini-limites' of Numidia, apparently lacking any coherent strategy. Clearly the answer may be that the system was multifunctional, and was directed as much to highly local, and internal, threats, as to any 'grand design'.

In Fentress' work on the subject of the army and settlement we begin to approach the core importance of the study of the army and local society. One must be somewhat disappointed, however, by the repeated insistence on the peasant-soldier-settler hypothesis, even if it still seems to have rather wide currency, because there is probably no other region where it ought to have been exposed to more critical scrutin than Numidia. Firstly, there is the simple question of numbers. Surely it is too optimistic to claim that 800 men were retiring from the legion and auxiliaries every two years (or, more specifically, an unspecified figure over 700 every four years from the legion alone, indicating about 200 a year). Even though, as I shall argue elsewhere, the strength of the Roman army in Africa has been greatly underestimated (a fact which Fentress does not, in any event, question), the total strength of the legion plus auxiliaries in the region of Numidia could not have exceeded a figure of 7,000-8,000 men by very much, and that on the optimistic assumption that most legionary forces remained in the region. The latter assumption may indeed not be tenable, given the number of *vexillationes* of the legion posted to other areas of Africa (e.g. Tripolitania), the cohort dispatched each year to the governor at Carthage, and the large number of *stationes* or military guard posts located all throughout the older part of the province. Even so, the postulated high number of soldiers in Numidia itself will still yield only about 650 men every two years as *veterani*. But this figure is far too theoretical for practical historical interpretation. It can only be reached on the assumption that the legion and the auxiliary units were at full strength at all times (a fact which does not hold where we have good information on unit manpower), that all men lived to retirement age, that others were not forced to retire early for reasons of ill health, and that still others did not remain under colours long after twenty-five years' service (as was often the case with centurions, for example). The factor of living to retirement age is but one element that must be taken into serious consideration, based on what we can assume to be true of ancient demographic patterns (28). To take the legion alone, and a postulated generation of about 200 veterans a year, let us for the sake of argument make the following assumptions: 1) a legion of about 5,000 men, and 2) an 'ideal' age-set (cohort) distribution of 200 men per year over a 25 year span, from recruitment at about age 20 to retirement at about age 45. We may then work with a set of model lifetables for populations whose main characteristics reflect those of populations of the ancient Mediterranean (29).

Table 1 *Survival Rate of Recruits to the Legion*

1. South Population, Level 3, Males (e° = 24.7) Out of 435 alive at age 20 there are 291 alive at 45 = 134 survivors of an original cohort of 200 = 67%
2. South Population, Level 4, Males (e° = 27.0) Out of 470 alive at age 20 there are 324 alive at 45 – 138 survivors of an original cohort of 200 – 69%
3. South Population, Level 5, Males (e° = 29.3) Out of 503 alive at age 20 there are 338 alive at 45 = 142 survivors of an original cohort of 200 = 71%

So, at best, given demographic limitations alone of a population where, say, life expectancy at birth was 25 (perhaps too high for the Roman world) only about 135 men would even survive to retirement age (or about 130 if e° was indeed in the low 20s). But this factor is not even considered by Fentress; nor are any of the others contributing to a further diminution of this number (e.g. debilitating diseases, alone accounting for 10-20% attrition in pre-modern armies). Clearly one must substract a substantial number from the c. 135 *per annum* optimum to arrive at a reasonably realistic guess of the level of veteran retirements. In spite of Frebtress unsubstantiated protestations, the figure of about 100 men *per annum* for a legion offered by Mann must be closer to the truth. But a further question remains: How many of these 100 men, or so, having received their *honesta missio*, would turn to farming in their old age? One can only recall the acerbic remarks of Cicero on the Rullan land bill in 63 BC, to the effect that no land redistribution programme was going to solve the problem posed by the urban poor who had long ago lost the desire or the skill to farm, and his remarks on the failure of Sullan veterans to adjust to and to make a success of their farming ventures (30). The Sullan *veterani* had almost assuredly not spent twenty-five consecutive years of their life in the isolating environment of an imperial army, so one must suppose that indisposition to peasant farming must have even more deeply ingrained in men who spent all their adult life in a professional army. Those who survived to old age would have lived every waking hour of their life in one of the two large institutional apparatuses known in the ancient world, one which at once conduced to their isolation from local society and to a position of considerable social privilege. Were these men to engage, at the end of such a life-long experience, in the degradation and poor rewards of manual labour on the soil? Given such an hypothetical postulate, one cannot then be surprised at the extreme paucity of evidence for supposed veteran farmers. In fact, empirical evidence does not support the concept of large numbers of *veterani* demanding or choosing the farming life, either in the late Roman Republic (a wrong-headed and misleading theme constructed by modern historians) or in Africa of the Roman empire. An even more questionable thesis, one integrally allied to this idea of the large-scale settlement of veteran soldiers on the land, is the hypothesis of *veterani* playing a critical role in the agricultural and economic development of the frontier by turning to farming *and* introducing new 'Roman' farming technologies. Apart from the problems already mentioned above, one must ask in what possible circumstances they would be taught these 'new techniques'. Surely not in the army base at Lambaesis.

Hence I believe that Fentress is mistaken to make most of her succeeding arguments hinge on the supposed effect of large numbers of veteran soldiers turning into peasant farmers. At the town of Lamasba, for example, a Roman-style *municipium* close to the army camps and on the main routes of communication in southwestern Numidia (therefore a good test case) direct evidence for soldier settlers is most meagre, and one cannot see any direct effect of this small number on the local economy of the town and territory (31). This questionable thesis is then linked to another: the contention that there were a large number of *imperial* estates in southern Numidia — in fact that 'a large amount of the land in the northern Aurès formed part of the *res privata*, and veteran settlement on this was encouraged with a view to development or *mise en valeur* of these properties'. The problem is that there is no empirical evidence for such a contention. One must therefore question any such list of imperial estates wherein only one instance, that of the *vicus Augustorum*, might be justified (though even in this case it may merely signify the foundation of the village under the aegis of the emperors) (32). Further, the attempted correlation between veteran settlement and imperial estates fails. A map produced to substantiate the claim (Fentress, no. 10) reveals that, out of nineteen putative imperial estates, only three or four have any coincidence with areas of veteran settlement, and that such estates are conspicuously absent near the major camps. To this is added the highly dubious method of extrapolating the land-property relations and managerial regimes of estates and imperial domains of the Upper Bagrada valley (Tunisia) to conditions obtaining in southern Numidia. In the complete absence of a similar *type* of estate organization and land regime in Numidia, what possible argument in there to claim that when veterans did obtain land in the region they only held conditional tenure? Or, most strange of all, that the terms *colonus* and *possessor* must invariably refer to *imperial tenants* when simple farmers and owners need be neither 'imperial' nor 'tenants'? In fact we know they often were *not* elsewhere so one simply must demand *some* supportive data from Numidia to justify the postulation of such an unusual proprietorial regime for this region alone. By contrast, Janon seems to understand the economic *type* of agrarian development typical of the region to be characterized by a dense indigenous rural population and an equally intense subdivision of the land into thousands of small parcellations worked by small (probably independent) peasant communities, with no clear evidence of even any administrative control of these in the form of 'imperial domains'. The intensive subdivision and working of the land is abundantly confirmed by aerial surveys of the region. A further claim about the precise proprietorial regime connected to this physical pattern of development must, of course, remain somewhat speculative But given the complete lack of epigraphical evidence for 'imperial estates' and some evidence that points to other proprietorial regimes (e.g. as at Lamasba), Janon's option must seem the more probable of the two (33).

Also necessary to any clear evaluation of the role of the army in the region is a coherent idea of what types of administrative frameworks (both public and private) were characteristic of Numidia. There is, indeed, too narrow an association of the whole economy of the region with a few specific forms of Roman exploitation (e.g. the imperial domain) simply because these loom so large in our modern academic literature and in the surviving ancient literary data. What this overemphasis leads to is a rather fragmentary approach that separates and treats each historical 'fact' in isolation, producing, ultimately, an incoherent analysis of the *whole* of the local Numidian economy in the Roman period. Janon at least attempts to avoid this methodological pitfall by building on a local 'base', as suggested by the broad spectrum of archaeological data, and then placing the 'Roman facts' in context. There are many problems with this approach, but they are mainly technical, not theoretical. That is to say, the method produces sound results, as far as it goes — the principal limitations are imposed by the lack of archaeological data or present difficulties in interpreting their meaning. Perhaps more serious than this default, however, are basic misconceptions Fentress seems to share about the nature of Roman public administration in the region of Numidia. Indeed, in her zealous pursuit of the thesis that Numidia was in some sense ruled directly by the emperor and his agent, that is to say directly by the crown, she is led into an aberrant conception of Numidia's status as a territorial and governmental unit. In claiming that Numidia was administered by the army and legate alone, she contends that the Numidians escaped at least one level of Roman taxation beyond that of the legate, namely the exactions of the imperial procurator. Tacitus (*Agricola*, 15.2) is quoted in support. But that is a Tacitean fantasy, as anyone who has studied the archaic states of Gaul and Britain knows (34). The same applies to Numidia of the African kings and under Roman rule. Pflaum's study of the procurator *ad fusa per Numidiam* (not even mentioned by Fentress) proves the point (35). But since there seems to be so much general confusion about the governmental status of Numidia, let us briefly review it here.

One simple fact must not be lost from sight amidst the welter of complex administrative texts: *Numidia* was fully part of the province of *Africa* from the inception of the greater province around 40 BC until *Numidia* itself achieved autonomy as a province in its own right soon after AD 200. Of course, *Numidia* was somewhat peculiar as a region within *Africa proconsularis* but in every other respect it was simply part of an existing province. What gave *Numidia* its peculiar status was the inbuilt potential for conflict between the commander of the legion and the provincial governor. Until about AD 40 the commander of the legion was wholly subordinate to the provincial governor of *Africa* — properly so since 'Numidia' was only a region within the province. Nevertheless, there did exist the ever-present potential for conflict between the two men since commanders of Roman legions, being direct appointees of the Roman emperor (*legati Augusti*) were not normally subordinate to provincial governors selected by the Senate. Because of this conflict in power and status, and for other reasons that need not be elaborated upon here, about AD 40 the emperor Gaius moved to separate the two men in terms of their mutual spheres of authority. Henceforth the legate was to have command of all imperial army forces in the province of *Africa*, whereas the proconsular governor was to be restricted to matters of civil administration only (37). But the emperor did not create two 'provinces' at the time in any formal territorial sense - be merely divided spheres of power *within* the province of *Africa*. In other words, *Numidia* remained a district fully within the province of *Africa* one where the proconsular governor of *Africa* retained all full powers over it in matters of civil administration (e.g. jurisdiction, taxation). On the other hand, the commander of the legion now obtained full authority in all military matters (e.g. roads, boundaries, military units other than the urban cohort) in the whole of the province of *Africa*, including region far outside *Numidia* itself where the legion had units stationed (e.g. southern Byzacena and Tripolitania). The situation remained in effect until the creation of an autonomous province of *Numidia* soon after AD 200. From that date onwards the proconsular governor no longer had authority in matters of civil administration within *Numidia*, though the legionary legate still retained his power to 'interfere' in military affairs within the province of *Africa*. This 'one way' extension and restriction of powers only reflected the importance placed by the emperor on his personal appointee and on the local power of the military, neither of which were to be curtailed in any way.

Hence it is egregious to suggest that *Numidia* somehow managed to escape the powers of taxation of imperial procurators simply because of the presence of the legionary commander. It is also mistaken in a *de iure* sense to maintain that the legionary legate 'governed' *Numidia*.

He did not. He only commanded the legion and all other military forces in the province of *Africa*. This is not to deny that the legionary legate must have acquired a *de facto* practical governance over the region of Numidia, even in some civil matters, if only because of his presence in the region and the proximity of the forces he commanded. That is probably the major reason why the region was eventually turned into a separate province. But the governor of *Africa* did continue the civil administration of *Numidia* as a district of the proconsular province up to AD 200; the mere presence of the legate did not save *Numidia* from the full force of imperial exactions. There was a regional office of the procurators at *Thamugadi* precisely like the other ones in the province of *Africa* (at *Hadrumetum*, *Hippo Regius*, and *Theveste*) staffed, as they were, by a servile administrative service. There was a regional representative of the *advocati fisci*, and a regional office of the *annona* (38).

The external administrative structure, however, only provided a framework within which the actual relations between the soldiers and local society took place. Fentress' treatment of this critical problem is subsumed under the title 'The Army *and* Civilians'. The heading is somewhat misleading, however, since her analysis deals less with the real problem of relations between the army *and* the local populace that it does with the *civilian functions* of the soldiers. The trouble with this approach is that a study of the various roles of soldiers as administrators, farmers, herders, tax-collectors, and builders does *not* add up to an analysis of the effect of the army on the local populace. But even a cursory glance over the lists of soldiers' 'civilian' activities is revelatory, As 'builders' they built almost wholly for themselves — forts, roads, temples (for their cults), baths (for themselves), amphitheatres (for themselves) and so on. It is in this context that Fentress' studied evasion of the long lists of (veteran) soldiers from Lambaesis seems absolutely inexplicable, since even the most superficial study of them would reveal *patterns* of recruiting that have considerable implications for the relations between the army garrisons and local society (39). The fundamental fact is that entrance to the ranks of the legion was mainly determined by the possession of Roman citizenship. For regions of the empire where there was a high level of demand for legionary troops combined with low levels of municipal development (e.g. the Rhine and Danube frontiers) Brunt and others have been quite correct to stress that Roman authorities often had to resort to press-gang tactics (or at least some sort of forced conscription) in order to fill the ranks with suitable candidates (40). But this observation cannot be applied without discrimination as an iron-clad rule to all the regions of the empire.

Numidia and *Africa* were clear exceptions. Within the latitude of meaning the word had in antiquity, peace was the rule in these regions — there was no great threat from external enemies to place high demands on military manpower, nor was there any lack of municipal development to provide manpower with the requisite legal status for entry into the legion. On the contrary, Africa of the mid-first to early third century represented one of the most successful and intensive areas of municipal development in the Roman empire. Supply and demand converged neatly to produce a distinctive pattern of recruitment clearly discernable in the record (see Table 2a).The tide of municipal development in the eastern parts of the province of *Africa* produced the raw material (i.e. men with Roman citizenship) for army recruitment on the frontier to the west. The cumulative data on the municipal origins of recruits for the legion clearly reveals this (remembering, as Forni indicated long ago, that this type of evidence is greater for north Africa than for all other provinces of the empire combined). All the soldiers' *origines* (except for those born *in castris*, in itself part of the pattern) are found in the developed urban centres to the east, with the most significant centres (by far) being Carthage and the urban conglomerate of the Sahel (Hadrumetum, Leptis Minus, Thysdrus etc.). These and recruits from the area of the old army bases of the first century (Ammaedara, Thelepte, Theveste, Cillium) provide the bulk of the army recruits along, of course, with the men born in the camp itself. The degree to which recruiting for the legion was 'inbred' becomes even clearer when the pattern of recruiting for army units (principally for legions) outside north Africa is studied separately (see Table 3). The highly urbanized areas of Carthage-Utica and the Sahelian coast remain dominant — what has entirely disappeared from the recruiting base is the group born *in castris*. They are entirely retained by *III Augusta*. This brief and inadequate glance at this one source on the make-up of the legionary forces in Numidia is sufficient to provide a fine, but necessary, qualification to the overly general commonplace assertion that recruiting in the army had become 'local' by the end of the first century AD. Certainly all the recruits are 'African', but what sort of African is the question. The point is that not one of them is local in the sense of being from *Numidia*, and their 'foreign' derivation when combined with the fact of the continued absence of any local municipal development (i.e. apart from the sites of the army camps themselves) fuelled a terrible estrangement between the body of the soldiery and the local populace.

This estrangement was further emphasized by the *internal* institutions of the legion, institutions which Fentress seems to regard as of little account in determining the real social relations of the soldiers with the local populace. The legion was, to use Goffman's terminology, a 'total institution'. Upon entering it and swearing the *sacramentum* a man passed, so far as be and outsiders were concerned, out of the normal relations of civil society (41). Not only did the legion itself encompass the men totally in their habits and in their economic support during their whole adult lifetime, determining by discipline and rewards their daily routine, it also provided sets of subinstitutions within the legionary body (e.g. the *collegia* that flourish openly after AD 198, presumably because

Table 2a *Origines of Recruits of Legio Tertia Angusta*
DATES (AD)

	0-40	40-70	70-115	115-235	Total
Abthugni	0	0	0	1	1
Ammaedara	0	0	0	23	23
Assuras	0	0	0	3	3
Bagai	0	0	0	6	6
Banasa	0	0	0	1	1
Bisica	0	0	0	1	1
Bulla Regia	0	0	0	2	2
Calama	0	0	0	4	4
Capsa	0	0	0	3	3
Carthago	4	1	7	108	120
Casae	0	0	0	1	1
Castra (Lambaesis)	0	0	0	221	221
Chusira	0	0	0	1	1
Cillium	0	0	0	13	13
Cirta	1	0	2	45	48
Cuicul	0	0	0	7	7
Diana Veteranorum	0	0	0	2	2
Furnos (Maius)	0	0	0	1	1
Gusira (?)	0	0	0	1	1
Hadrumetum	0	0	1	26	27
Hippo Regius	0	0	2	3	5
Lamasba	0	0	0	1	1
Lambaesis (Municipium)	0	0	0	101	101
Lambiridi	0	0	0	1	1
Lamigigga	0	0	0	5	5
Lepcis Magna	0	0	0	1	1
Leptis Minus	0	1	0	5	6
Mactaris	0	0	0	1	1
Madauros	0	0	0	3	3
Manliana	0	0	0	1	1
Mascula	0	0	0	5	5
Maxula	0	0	0	3	3
Milevis	0	0	0	4	4
Mina	0	0	0	1	1
Mustis	0	0	0	1	1
Naragarra	0	0	0	3	3
Oea	0	0	0	5	5
Phua	0	1	0	0	1
Rusicade	0	0	0	1	1
Rusucurru	0	0	0	1	1

IX

	0-40	40-70	70-115	115-235	Total
Sabratha	0	0	0	1	1
Segermes	0	0	0	1	1
Sicca Veneria	0	0	0	13	13
Simitthus	0	0	0	7	7
Sufes	0	0	0	2	2
Sufetula	0	0	0	1	1
Tacape	0	0	1	2	3
Thabraca	0	0	0	1	1
Thaenae	0	0	0	2	2
Thagora	0	0	0	1	1
Thamugadi	0	0	0	31	31
Thelepte	0	0	0	12	12
Theveste	0	0	7	33	40
Thibica	0	0	0	3	3
Thigibba (Bure)	0	0	0	1	1
Thuburbo (Maius)	0	0	0	4	4
Thuburnica	0	0	0	1	1
Thubursicu (Bure? Numidarum?)	0	0	0	2	2
Thugga	0	0	0	1	1
Thunusida	1	0	0	0	1
Thysdrus	0	0	0	11	11
Tipasa	0	0	0	5	5
Uthina	0	0	0	3	3
Utica	0	1	2	9	12
Vaga	0	0	0	4	4
Verecunda	0	0	0	5	5
Vicus Augusti (?)	0	0	0	1	1
Vina	0	0	0	1	1
Zabi	0	0	0	1	1
Zama	0	0	0	1	1
Zarai	0	0	0	2	2
Total N =					811

Sources: Forni, *Reclutamento*; Forni (1974); AE 1970-1978

Table 2b *Regional Sources of Legionary Recruits in North Africa*

Region	N =	% (of total)
1. Lambaesis (municipium and castra) - Thamugadi	336	41
2. Carthage-Utica	132	16
3. Ammaedara-Cillium-Thelepte-Theveste	88	11
4. Cirta	48	6
5. Hadrumetum-Thysdrus	38	5
subtotal	642	79
6. All other centres	169	21

Table 3 *African Recruits for Army Units outside North Africa*

Acholla	1	Oea	1
Ammaedara	5	Rusicade	1
Assuras	1	Sicca Veneria	1
Bararus	1	Sufetula	1
Caesarea	8	Tacape	1
Carthage	51	Thaenae	1
Cirta	4	Thambe	2
Cuicul	1	Thamugadi	2
Gales	1	Theveste	8
Hadrumetum	11	Thuburbo Maius	2
Hippo Regius	1	Thysdrus	8
Lamiggiga	1	Ulisippira	1
Lepcis Magna	4	Uthina	3
Leptis Minus	9	Utica	19
Maxula	1	Uzalis	1
Melzitana	1	Total N =	163

Sources: Forni, *Reclutamento*; Forni (1974); Lassère, *Ubique Populus*, 636-43; AE 1970-1978.

For Units:
Legio II Traiana (Laterculum, AE 1969-70: 633)   Egypt   94
Legio II Adiutrix   Pannonia Inferior   15
Legio III Cyrenaica   Arabia   3
Legio III Adiutrix   Pannonia inferior   2
Legio II Parthica   Italy   2
Legio VII Gemina   Spain   2
Legio VI Victrix   Britain   1
Legio XXII Deiotauriana   Egypt   1
Legio I Italica   Moesia Inferior   1
Praetorians
Vigiles   Rome   40
Urban Cohorts

of the lifting of legal prohibitions) which at once provided for the group solidarity of different 'ranks' and yet also tied them into the vertical system of patronage and promotion. Vertical loyalties were further reinforced by the cult of the standards and by the imperial cult which focussed the attention of the soldiery directly on the emperor himself as their immediate patron and benefactor (42). As outsiders to local Numidian society and as members of a 'total institution', the soldiers were doubly removed from the concerns of the inhabitants of the region. There are few signs that this isolation was in any way mitigated by other normal modes of interrelation within civil society (e.g. intermarriage — all *discernable* patterns at Lambaesis point to a strong element of marriage between soldiers and other soldiers' daughters). Given this inward-looking ethos and customary behaviour, one cannot be surprised at the actions of the legionaries in the events of AD 238 (not mentioned by Fentress). The events of that year represented an acid test of soldiers' loyalties, and so it is not without significance that they identified themselves wholly with the interests of their commanding officers and of a militaristic central government against any local interests, even broader upper-class ones (43).

In 238 a regional revolt against the central government was led by groups of upper class landowners in north Africa. The revolt was directed against what they perceived as unjust and exorbitant tax demands made by an emperor in Rome in support of warfare on the Rhine and Danube frontiers far to the north. There was a real separation of interests between the new soldier-emperors who, like Maximinus Thrax, had risen from the ranks of the army on that frontier and the senatorial and equestrian landowners in north Africa. The latter, therefore, attempted a 'coup' against the new government in Rome by arming their peasants and their violent gangs of aristocratic youths to kill the emperor's procurator while he was directing his tax-collectors in the region of Thysdrus. Their next action was to try to establish the governor of the province, M. Antonius Gordianus Sempronianus, himself an African, as the new emperor. Gordian just 'happened' to be in Thysdrus at the time. In fact, this landowners rebellion did succeed in most of its initial objectives. But the reaction of the wholly African recruited legion, which had been stationed in Numidia for about two centuries by this time, was to side immediately and without question with the military emperor Maximinus. In a surprisingly swift reaction, the soldiers followed the legionary legate in an invasion of the province. There, following upon the defeat of Gordian and his son outside Carthage, they conducted a veritable blood bath of local municipal aristocrats and of the landowning elite, a purge in which, it seems, many ordinary Africans suffered as well. This action alone is but a small measure of the degree of attachment of the soldiers to their own centres of loyalty, entirely regardless of their nominal derivation from African society (44).

In the face of this isolated and in-bred nature of the local army contingents, therefore, the actions of soldiers in 'civilian' roles are of peripheral interest since these roles only tended to reinforce the inner solidarity of the military community in Numidia rather than to connect it with the local Numidian population. Hence the legate as patron (principally for the sake of army promotions and for the municipal advancement of army towns), the army's involvement in construction projects, and *veterani* filling municipal posts in their own army settlements need provoke no surprise. It is the insidious implications of these actions that Fentress seems to miss entirely. The only concrete advantage of the legion's presence that she is able to suggest lies in such hypothetical economic 'introductions' such as the *foggara* (a system of underground channels designed to tap subsurface water), in this case supposedly introduced by Syrian units brought in from the east. The hypothesis reminds one very much of other 'introductionist' arguments involving eastern importers, such as the 'introduction' of the camel (dromedary), still accepted by some. As Fentress herself admits, the *foggara* is found in the Fezzan in early Roman contexts, and may well have diffused from a Near Eastern source at a rather early date, if it cannot be shown to be a local innovation (45). As for other, more subtle, types of influences that soldiers might might have brought with themselves to the region, such as new patterns of belief that are evidenced in stelai containing dedications to Jupiter Dolichenos or in the Mithraeum at Lambaesis (the *only* one in Africa) Fentress has not a word — though here too the record would seem to support the idea of an enclosed army community that did not connect with or influence local beliefs. The so-called cult of Saturn, for example, is rife in the region of Numidia (and to the southwest, as at *Nicivibus*) and yet not one serving soldier in the region ever so much as made a dedication to the god (46). Indeed, the whole ethos of the soldiery as shown in their construction of their own amphitheatre, or in the adherence to the cult of Mithra (again emphasizing their membership in a hierarchical organization that set them apart from ordinary society), is at the heart of their social relations with Africans who were not 'army' (47).

The culmination of Fentress' analysis of the army in *Numidia* is an attempt to construct a general model to explain the impact of the army on the development of an 'inland economy'. Her two basic assumptions are: 1) that the army diffused a money economy throughout the region, and 2) that the army remained the principal source of (coined) money throughout the period under study. Both propositions are often asserted and are probably true for Numidia (48). But the argument which Fentress then develops is a fiscal variant of the Chayanovian 'tax preassure-peasant production' thesis. The problem with the indiscriminate application of this theory is that it is not always valid. In the ancient world tax pressure led as often to *agri deserti* and *anachoresis* (Pharaonic, Ptolemaic and Hellenistic Egypt, Sicily of the *Verrines*, and the later Roman empire generally) as it did to greater agricultural productivity. Just as often, from Cicero's Sicily to Le Roy Ladurie's Languedoc, surtaxation simply meant peasant starvation (49). Be that as it may, Fentress postulates that during the hypothetical period when the input of coined money was above the level of taxation the army acted as a focus of consumption and stimulated the production of specific produce (primarily cereal grains). But later, when taxes putatively rose above the level of coin input, the local economy had to acquire the surplus capital to pay taxes. This surplus, she claims, was obtained by developing cash crops, mainly the olive, for sale on Mediterranean markets. This is a sketchily developed variant of the 'central tax-peripheral production' argument that appears to be gaining in popularity (as, e.g., in the work of Hopkins). In this case, olive oil, unlike cereal grains, is supposed to be a more economically profitable export for an 'inland economy' because of the cost-benefit balance (Fentress provides the appropriate calculations).

But there are many, many problems with this sort of pure model. For that is *all* that it is: a pure model of *one possible* type of economic framework for economic relations in Roman Numidia — one that must be tested against the available data. One of these is her own assertion that there is no way of quantifying the wage-equivalencies of peasant labour, nor indeed any validity in applying the concept of wage labour to the rural economy of ancient Numidia. Another is her admission that the late date usually ascribed to olive mills and presses found on archaeological sites in the region is the result of impressionistic observations. It has turned out to be a false impression in cases where the rural economy has been investigated in detail (e.g. in Tripolitania and in the Tangiers region) (50). And it is one that is severely questioned by the work of Janon. He, on the contrary, postulates a well-developed indigenous agriculture in the countless wadi valleys, small plains, and miniature plateaux of the Aurès mountains — an agriculture founded on the careful control of wadi waters, runoff, and the development of parcellations planted to cerealculture crops and arboricultural plants, principally fruit trees and the olive (51). But there are even theoretical problems with the model. In effect it is a classic 'input-output' analysis in which virtually every factor in the input and output equations are real variables. That is to say, everything from the natural productivity of the soil to the mental disposition of the producers must be considered as parts of the general equation. Hence thare is no *one* economic model that will explain the facts of all sets of situation (e.g. that of Roman Numidia). Increased central state taxation will not invariably lead to increased production or productivity because there are too many variables that affect the input and output. Firstly, the central state would actually have to increase the level of taxation over any previous local level, would probably have to demand its payment in coin (thereby impelling production for markets), producers would have to be required *from their own perspective* to produce more to meet either type of demand, and so on. But Fentress discusses *none* of these other variables (except for her contention that Numidia 'escaped one level of imperial exactions' which, as I have shown above, is untrue) — i.e. how much was the level of Roman central state taxation in excess of that of the previous African kingdoms? Was it mandatory to pay in coin or were most exactions paid in kind (as *seems* to have been the case in Africa generally)? And, were local Numidian farmers and herders required to dig that much deeper into their stores to pay the 'extra' tax? (52)

It may indeed seem like gratuitous carping, but there is so much that seems obviously to be missing from Fentress' treatment, matters that would seem important to any consideration of the level of economic development, concentration and organization of resources, in the pre-Roman period. Massive cemeteries of megalithic construction, and great individual projects like the Medrasen (only c. 25 km north of the Lambaesis-Thamugadi line) in the heart of Numidia surely attest to a degree of concentration of wealth in the hands of local African *principes* in the pre-Roman period, including some form of 'tribute' (53). At the other end of the temporal scale, work by the Morizots in the Aurès has produced a clearer view not only of local types of social and political organization, but also of the 'normal' operations of the army up and down the countless mountain defiles of the region (54). Naturally any historical work must make a choice between what is admitted and what in excluded from consideration, but the lack of any clear theoretical groundwork in advance of the process of sifting the data leaves the prospective student of Roman Numidia grasping for the criteria upon which apparently relevant material is excluded from consideration. The theoretical weakness, unfortunately, is also revealed in other other contexts, such as the analytical conclusions drawn from the data themselves. Dubious statements emerge, made without any external substantiation — such as the contention that 'A prosperous territory is unlikely to revolt' — a proposition likely to be questioned on the basis of historical experience (55).

To give Fentress' new approach to Roman Numidia its due, the work does include a number of fresh insights and commonsensical views that allow her to escape the obvious pitfalls of past historiography on the subject. But too often they remain at the level of intuitive rejections of past absurdities, and are not thoroughly developed into a coherent new understanding of the subject. It is to be hoped that her present work will form a sort of prolegomena to a more careful and detailed research project of the type hinted at in her brief survey of the *Diana Veteranorum* region (append. 4). But to return to Van Gennep. He used the concept of liminality as a tool to analyze *rites de passage* in 'primitive' societies. To apply the concept to a quite separate historical situation is a metaphor. The problem is that the historian must be very cautious of such metaphorical usage lest it become confused with reality. Van Gennep's idea is indeed suggestive when applied to frontier societies, but not so literally. The Roman army was *not* halfway between the ruler and the ruled; it was *the* instrument of violent force wielded by the central power structure of the empire. No metaphor should be allowed to obscure that naked fact. And Numidia was not on the threshhold between the civilized and the barbaric — that is an ancient idea paraded as modern historical analysis.

The army was in *Numidia* for a reason, and it would seem thet a more empirically based approach linked to a *consistent* theoretical base, such as that offered by Janon, offer some prospect of comprehending both that reason and the 'secondary' effects of the army's presence in the regions in which it was stationed. If I may quote at length from one indicative passage (56):

Point n'était besoin d'employer d'importants effectifs: l'organisation tribale, telle que nous l'avons entrevue, est celle d'une société en équilibre précaire. Une nouvelle force militaire et économique, même réduite mais pouvant compter sur de gros bataillons en reserve, était à même de s'attribuer le rôle arbitre et de regler les échanges et les mouvements, qui du reste ne l'avaient pas attendu pour s'organiser. Par leur presence même, les garnisons introduisaient un élément perturbateur et si elles ne rompaient pas l'équilibre, elles devaient à coup sûr favoriser le glissement sur une pente favorable à Rome, ou plutôt favoriser ce qui, de l'organisation traditionnelle, était en accord avec une vision romaine du monde.

'Favoriser le glissement sur une pente favorable a Rome'. That must be our starting point. Though we must be careful to remember in our use of metaphors like 'favoriser' and 'pente' that the encouragement and the inclination were fraught with violence and the threat of violence.

NOTES

(1) R. MacMullen, *Soldier and Civilian in the Later Roman Empire*, Cambridge, Mass., Harvard University Press, 1967; R.W. Davies, *The Daily Life of the Roman Soldier under the Principate*, ANRW 2, 1, 1974, 299-338, are two good examples of an approach now becoming integrated into regional histories such as P. Salway, *Roman Britain*, Clarendon Press, Oxford 1981.

(2) In the African context I am thinking especially of the work by Pol Trousset on another frontier, that of the *Limes Tripolitanus* (see n below). His paper, *L'idée de frontière au Sahara d'après les données archéologiques*, in *Le Sahara dans les taches d'édification nationale des états maghrebins*, CNRS, Centre de Recherches et d'Études sur les sociétés méditerraneennes (Table Ronde, Aix-en-Provence, 19-21 novembre 1981) epitomizes this new approach to frontier studies. To the comparative studies cited by him there might be added three others of some utility: D. Gerhard, *The Frontier in Comparative View*, 'CSSH' 1, 1958, 59, 205-29; D.H. Miller & J.D. Steffen (eds.), *The Frontier: Comparative Studies*, Norman, University of Oklahoma Press, 1977; and, more recently, H. Lamar & L. Thompson (eds.), *The Frontier in History: North America and South Africa Compared*, Yale University Press, New Haven 1981. Other studies of Mediterranean frontiers such as the Ottoman (McNeil) and the Hispano-Arabic (Glick, McKay) also add perspective to the general problem. For the Roman world in general one should consult S.L. Dyson, *The Role of Comparative Frontier Studies in Understanding the Roman Frontier*, in D.M. Pippidi (ed.), *Actes du IXe Congrès international d'études sur les frontières romaines, Mamaia, 6-13 septembre 1972*, Editura Acedemiei, Bucarest; Röhlau, Vienna-Cologne 1974, 277-83. It may be remarked here that a rigorous comparative view of the frontier, even within the Roman empire, is still a desideratum for north Africa.

(3) Elizabeth W.B. Fentress, *Numidia and the Roman Army: Social, Military and Economic Aspects of the Frontier Zone*, BAR International Series no. 53, Oxford 1979. This slim volume presents the substance of an Oxford doctoral dissertation. It must be remarked here that there are severe reservations about the production quality of the book which, most unfortunately, detracts from an appreciation of its contents. BAR are capable of high production standards (compare J. Bintliff's book, also derived from a dissertation) so what possible excuse is there for the nearly 1000 spelling and typographical errors, mistaken cross-references, and missing items of bibliography? This is not to mention the more serious item of Latin inscriptions that are incorrectly resolved or ancient texts that are misprinted or incorrectly translated (see, e.g., p. 128 (*CIL* VIII, 2392) and Append. 2, *passim*). These may be typographical, but they do almost vitiate the value of reprinting the inscriptions and literary sources for the sake of reference. This article, however, will eschew further reference to these problems in order to concentrate on the ideas expressed by the author.

(4) R. Cagnat, *L'Armée romaine d'Afrique et l'occupation militaire de l'Afrique sous les empereurs*, 1. ed., Imprimerie nationale, Paris 1892; 2. ed., 1913 (reprint: Arno Press, New York 1975). The work is less a 'book' than at first appears since it includes as a substantial part a series of monographs written by Cagnat in the 1880s. The second 'edition' incorporated few changes over the first.

(5) M. Janon, "Recherches à Lambèse", *Ant Afr* 7, 1973, 194-254; *Lambèse et l'occupation militaire de la Numidie méridionale*, in *Studien zu den Militärgrenzen Roms*, 2, *Vorträge der 10. Internationalen Limeskongressus*, Böhlau, Bonn-Cologne 1977, 475-85; cf.

his work on use of computers in epigraphical analysis, *Ant Afr* 9, 1975, 127-44, and 63-96, his work with J.C. Golvin on the amphitheatre at Lambaesis in 'BCTH' 12-14B, 1976-78, 169-93, and his general synopsis in *AW* 8.2, 1977, 7-20. But here I shall concentrate on his synthetic analysis *Paysans et soldats*, in C.M. Wells (ed.), *Les Conférences Vanier 1980: L'Afrique romaine* = *Revue de l'Université d'Ottawa* 52.1, 1982, 47-63.
(6) Fentress, *op. cit.*, 12.
(7) See M. Foucault, *Questions on Geography*, ch. 4, in C. Gordon (ed.), *Power/Knowledge: Selected Interviews and other Writings, 1972-1977*, Pantheon, New York 1980, 63-77; for an excellent explication and application of the method to north African circumstances see C. & H. Geertz, and L. Rosen, *Meaning and Order in Moroccan Society: Three Essays in Cultural Analysis*, Cambridge University Press, Cambridge 1979, 8-12.
(8) See, for example, C. Vita-Finzi, *The Mediterranean Valleys: Geological Changes in Historical Times*, Cambridge University Press, Cambridge 1969; the work by M. Couvert on the proto-historical environments of the Aurès in 'Libyca' (APE) 17, 1969, 213-6, 20, 1972, 45-8, and 24, 1976, 9-20; and the work by C. Roubet on protohistorical pastoralist communities in the same region: *Economie pastorale préagricole en Algérie orientale. Le néolithique de tradition capsienne, exemple: Aurès*, CNRS, Paris 1981, with reference to her earlier published work — all of these having implications for the difference between the environment of Numidia, then and now.
(9) See my *Climate, environment and history: the case of Roman North Africa*, ch. 16 in T.M.L. Wigley et al. (eds.), *Climate and History: Studies in Past Climates and their Impact on Man*, Cambridge University Press, Cambridge 1981, 379-403, at 391-3.
(10) Cf. Janon (1982), 52-3.
(11) The point can be argued at greater length; see my *Water and Society in the Ancient Maghrib: Technology, Property and Development*, 'Ant Afr', forthcoming, where comparative and theoretical arguments are adduced, in addition to empirical data, to demonstrate the point.
(12) Janon (1982), 57-8.
(13) Janon (1982), 53-4, an excellent example of his careful treatment of one micro environment in Numidia.
(14) Janon (1982), 53-4.
(15) Fentress, *op. cit.*, 49 ff.
(16) For but one example of an ethnologist who has worked on both ancient and modern data in the Mediterranean see J. Caro Baroja, *Organización social de los pueblos del norte de la península Iberica en la antigüedad*, in A. Viñayo Gonzalez (ed.), *Legio VII Ge mina* (Coloquio internacional, Leon, 16 al 21 septiembre de 1968), Instituto Leonés de Estudios Romano-Visigoticos, Leon 1970, 12-62.
(17) Fentress, *op. cit.*, ch. 5.
(18) As against M. Rachet, *Rome et les Berbères: un problème militaire d'Auguste à Dioclétien*, Collection Latomus no. 110, Brussels 1970, and M. Bénabou, *La résistance africaine à la romanisation*, F. Maspero, Paris 1976; cf. Janon (1977), 476-7.
(19) Fentress, *op. cit.*, 111 ff.
(20) *Ibid.*, 112.
(21) P. Trousset, *Recherches sur le Limes Tripolitanus du Chott el-Djerid à la frontière Tuniso-Libyenne*, CNRS, Paris 1974, 139 ff., and in subsequent work, e.g. 'Ant Afr' 15 1980, 135-54, cfr. 12, 1978, 125-77.
(22) R. Marichal, *Les Ostraca du Bu Njem*, 'CRAI', 1979, 436-52.
(23) Fentress, *op. cit.*, 117.
(24) E.N. Luttwack, *The Grand Strategy of the Roman Empire, from the First Century AD to the Third*, Johns Hopkins University Press, Baltimore-London 1976, — based on his doctoral dissertation, *Force and Diplomacy in Roman Strategies of Imperial Security*, Johns Hopkins University, Baltimore 1975.
(25) Fentress, *op. cit.*, 110; there are other alternatives — shatts or salt lakes (*stagna*) ring the Oran Plain to the southwest.

(26) Sir R. Syme, *Tacitus*, 2 vols., Oxford, Clarendon Press, 1958, 1, 454.
(27) Janon (1977), 477 & 479.
(28) See K. Hopkins, *On the Probable Age Structure of the Roman Population*, 'Population Studies' 20, 1966, 245-64. In the article by Brunt cited in n 40 below (1974) 107, n. 81, he refers to his assumption that 'a recruit of 17 had only a 50% chance of surviving till discharge'. But he notes that this estimate was based on Burns' demographic figures in which he no longer has confidence. He states that he now argues that 'legionaries in Augustus' time had a 60% chance of survival, *Italian Manpower*, 132 f., 332-41'. As our tables in the text show, Brunt's suspicions seem well-founded, and a survival rate of c. 65-70% (even higher than which he now postulates) seems entirely possible.

(29) The data base is J. Coale & P. Demeny, *Regional Model Life Tables and Stable Populations*, Princeton University Press, Princeton 1966, 658-60. B. Frier, *Roman Life Expectancy: Ulpian's Evidence*, 'HSCPh' 86, 1982, 213-51, has constructed a coherent life table for Roman populations yielding e° of about 21, lower than any of the life expectancies at birth postulated here.

(30) Cic. *De Lege Agraria*, 2.27 (71) and *passim*; cf. his remarks on the Sullan veterans in the *Catilinarians* where they are, of course, singled out for comment for purely political reasons; but there is no reason to believe that other 'settled veterans' fared any better.

(31) B.D. Shaw, *Lamasba: An Ancient Irrigation Community*, 'Ant Afr' 18, 1982, 61-103; for a full list of known veterans settled in the region see J.M. Lassère, *Ubique Populus: peuplement et mouvements de population dans l'Afrique romaine...*, CNRS, Paris 174-89. The evidence for areas outside the army camps is not impressive: Mascula (2), Theveste (7), Aquae Caesaris (2?), Ad Maiores (1), Calceus Herculis (1), Casae (6, or 7?), Lamasba (4), Lambiridi (1), Lamiggiga (9), Zarai (7), and Diana Veteranorum (5). In addition, many of these were army posts or former sites of camps (e.g. Theveste) where soldiers may have settled in urban contexts. As the last-named example shows, however, specific attestation of *veterani* by individual epigraphical mention may be no sure guide to actual levels of settlement, if the name of the town is any indication. But the very low numbers of *veterani* attested in areas outside the urban setting of large army camps must at least raise the question of the real impact of veteran settlement on the rural economy of the region.

(32) Fentress, *op. cit.*, 138.
(33) Janon (1977) 477, (1982) 57-8; cf. J. Soyer, *Les cadastres anciens de la région de Saint-Donat*, 'Ant Afr' 7, 1973, 257-96, and *Les centuriations romaines en Algérie orientale*, ibid. 10 (1976) 107-80.

(34) *Singulos sibi olim reges fuisse, nunc binos imponi, e quibus legatus in sanguinem, procurator in bona saeviret*. This colourful literary passage must be interpreted in context. Tacitus is trying to provide, by imagination, reasons for an impending ethnic rebellion; in consequence he lapses into a stereotypical self-critique of Roman rule. In fact, both Gallic and British 'chieftains' had taxes and tax-collecting agencies, *and* made demands on military manpower: see E.A. Thompson, *The Early Germans*, Clarendon Press, Oxford 1965; D. Nash, *The Celts of Central Gaul...*, DPhil Thesis, Oxford 1975; and S. Lewuillon, *Histoire, société et lutte des classes en Gaule: une féodalité à la fin de la république et au début de l'empire*, ANRW 2, 4, 1975, 425-583. In any event, Tacitus, to be precise in interpreting him, only says that *one* king was replaced by *two* new masters, not that the exactions either changed in kind or rose in level.

(35) H.G. Pflaum, *At fusa per Numidiam*, 'RAf' 100, 1976, 315-18; cf. his *Les carrières procuratoriennes équestres sous le Haut-Empire romain*, 3 vols., Institut français d'archéologie de Beyrouth, Bibliothèque d'archéologie et d'histoire no. 57, Beirut 1960-61, nos. 274-75; cf. no. 331 bis for the later *procurator provinciae*.

(36) H.G. Pflaum, *A propos de la date de la création de la province de Numidie*, 'Libyca' Arch.-épigr.) 5, 1957, 61-75, and M.P. Speidel, *The singulares of Africa and the Establishment of Numidia as a Province*, 'Historia' 22, 1973, 125-27. I believe that a date of AD 202 can be established for the creation of the province.

(37) Tac. *Ann.* 4.48; Dio 59.20.7; cf. M. Bénabou, *Proconsul et legat. Le témoignage*

de Tacite, Ant Afr' 6, 1972, 129-36, though I disagree with some of the details of Bénabou's interpretation.

(38) See CIL VIII, 18909 = ILS 9070 (Thibilis) = Pflaum, Carrières, no. 274, cf. no 275; CIL VIII, 2757 (Lambaesis): an advocatus fisci who was shifted, consecutively, through the procuratorial districts of Theveste, Hadrumetum, and Numidia, cf. J. David in 'Ant Afr 11, 1977, 149-60; for the regional office of the annona at Thamugadi see AE 1948: 18.

(39) The major inscriptions are CIL VIII, 2564-69, 18068, 18084-87; the first studies of them were done by CIL VIII eds. and by Cagnat, Armée[2], pt. 6, ch. 1, Recruitement de l'armée d'occupation, 287-308, subsequently by G. Forni, Il reclutamento delle legioni da Augusto a Diocleziano, Fratelli Bocca, Milan-Rome 1953, and his supplemental study, Estra zione etnica e sociale dei soldati delle legioni nei primi tre secoli dell'impero, ANRW 2, 1 1974, 339-91.

(40) P.A. Brunt, Conscription and Volunteering in the Roman Imperial army, 'Scripta Classica Israelica' 1, 1974, 90-115.

(41) See, for example, the indicative remarks by Tertullian in De corona militis and De Idol. 19.1; however coloured by Christian belief, they reveal a most serious separation bet ween soldier and society.

(42) Cagnat, Armée[2], pt. 6, ch. 3, 342-55, and ch. 6, 386-408, on the collegia. This early study is complemented by M. Besnier, Les scholae de sous-officiers dans le camp romain de Lambèse, 'MEFR' 19, 1899, 198-258 (demonstrating the importance of orientation to emperor worship); H. Battifol, Les règlements des collèges de musiciens de la Legion IIIe Auguste, 'RAf' 67, 1926, 179-200; and H. Schulz-Falkenthal, Die Unterstützungstätigkeit ir einem Militärkollegium der Legio III Augusta in Lambaesis und das Problem der Sozial leistungen im römischen Vereinswesen, in H.J. Diesner et al. (eds.), Afrika und Rom in der Antike, Wissenschaftliche Beiträge der Martin-Luther-Universität, Halle 1968, 115-71.

(43) On the revolt and the place of the legion in it see now F. Kolb, Der Aufstand der Provinz Afrika Proconsularis im Jahr 238 n. Chr.: Die wirtschaftlichen und sozialen Hinter gründe, 'Historia' 26, 1977, 440-70, and F. Jacques, Humbles et Notables: la place de humiliores dans les collèges de jeunes et leur rôle dans la révolte africaine de 238, 'Ant Afr 15, 1980 217-30, who cite all the relevant earlier literature.

(44) Cf. P. Romanelli, Storia della province romane dell'Africa, L'Erma, Rome 1959 445-65.

(45) On the camel see B.D. Shaw, The Camel in Roman North Africa and the Sahara History, Biology, and Human Economy, 'Bull. IFAN' 41, ser. B, 1979, 663-721, and compare Fentress, op. cit., 119; for foggara see Fentress, op. cit., 38.

(46) On Saturn see M. Leglay, Saturne africain, histoire, Boccard, Paris 1966, 402-03 of serving soldiers he can find two officers (one centurion, a questionable instance, at Lam baesis, and the prefect of a cohort at Volubilis; and one ex-soldier at Tébessa — that is all) cf. his references to his catalogues. For Mithra see the references in Leglay, art. cit. in the following note, and add AE 1973: 633 and AE 1973: 642-3.

(47) See L. Leschi, Autour de l'amphithéâtre de Lambèse, 'Libyca' (Arch.-épigr.) 2 1954, 171-86, and M. Leglay, Le Mithraeum de Lambèse, 'CRAI' 1954, 269-77. For the social significance of adherence to Mithraism see R.L. Gordon, Mithraism and Roman Society Social Factors in the Explanation of Religious Change in the Roman Empire, 'Religion' 1 1972, 92-121; for Dolichenos see M.P. Speidel, The Religion of Iuppiter Dolichenos in the Roman Army, Leiden, Brill, 1978 (EPRO, no. 63), esp. 66 ff.

(48) In all this one must overlook economic absurdities, such as the claim that the legion could be supported by the surplus product of 651 households (with appropriate calcu lations, see Fentress, op. cit., 125). On the model see K. Hopkins, Economic Growth o, Towns in Classical Antiquity, ch. 2, in P. Adams & E.A. Wrigley eds., Towns in Societies Essays in Economic History and Historical Sociology, Cambridge University Press, Cambrid ge 1978, 35-77; cf. R. MacMullen, Rural Romanization, 'Phoenix' 22, 1978, 337-41, but one must also heed warnings by Crawford about the actual extent to which coined money would have been used for exchange in and around the major army camps, see M. Crawford, Money

and *Exchange in the Roman World,* 'JRS' 60, 1970, 40-8, at 44-5.

(49) On the question of *agri deserti* and their relation to taxation see C.R. Whittaker, *Agri Deserti,* ch. 8, in M.I. Finley (ed.), *Studies in Roman Property,* Cambridge University Press, Cambridge 1976, 137-207; cf. E. Le Roy Ladurie, *The Peasants of Languedoc,* transl. J. Day (of *Les Paysans de Languedoc,* S.E.V.P.E.N., Paris 1966) University of Illinois Press, Chicago-London 1976, 263 ff.

(50) M. Ponsich, *Recherches archéologiques à Tanger et dans sa région,* CNRS, Paris *1970, 204-18, 273-82; and* A. di Vita, *Il˜limes romano di Tripolitania nella sua concretezza archeologica e nella sua realtà storica,* 'Lib Ant' 1, 1964, 65-98.

(51) Janon (1982), 52 ff.

(52) See G. Ardant, *Théorie sociologique de l'impôt,* 2 vols., S.E.V.P.E.N., Paris 1965 for some of the complexities of the question. Note too that a 'higher level' of taxation might not require higher taxes. It may result, for example, simply from more efficient administration of formal taxes 'on the books'. The more efficient British administration of existing taxes in post-Mughal Bihar and Uttar Pradesh led to a priod of agrarian crisis – that is to say, the taxes 'on the books' had never been rigorously exacted in full by previous administrations, even though they are generally believed to have been relatively efficient by contemporary European standards; see P. Robb in 'EcHR' 34, 1981 and J.F. Richards in 'CSSH' 23, 1981, 285-308 on Mughal state finances.

(53) A point made by A. Deman, *Matériaux et réflexions pour servir à une étude de developpement et de sous-developpement dans les provinces de l'Empire romain,* ANRW 2, 3, 1975, 3-97, at 19 f.

(54) J. Morizot, *Vues nouvelles sur l'Aurès antique,* 'CRAI', 1979, 309-37, with reference to earlier publications.

(55) Fentress, *op. cit.*, 124; the tendency is not helped by a questionable use of jargon. I am not denying a proper place for sociological terminology, but too often the needless use of abstractions where simple English would suffice serves only to confuse – e.g., "These may be seen as concrete manifestations of the complementarity of the two unities." (p. 132) referring to rather simple connections between Timgad and Lambaesis.

(56) Janon (1982), 55-6.

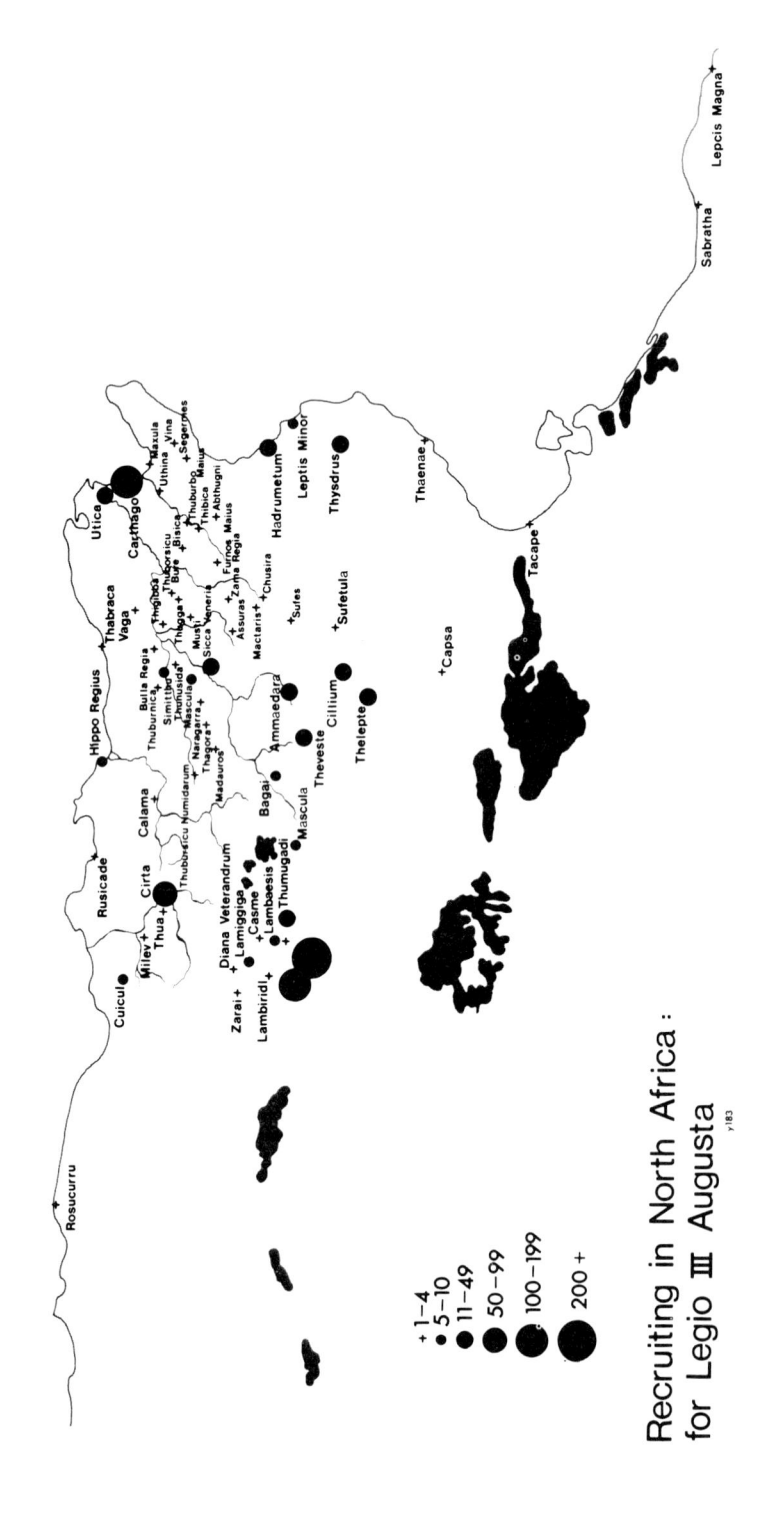

Recruiting in North Africa: for Legio III Augusta

IX

Recruiting in North Africa:
for Army Units outside the Region

X

THE ELDERS OF CHRISTIAN AFRICA*

Elders, that is persons designated by the epithet *seniores*, were an apparently powerful yet obscure part of the lower echelons of Christian and pagan society in North African antiquity. Their very obscurity and humbleness prompt recourse to the Brownian metaphor of the scholar as a "deep sea diver" who descends the murky depths of ancient Mediterranean society to see what strange life forms lurk there. The metaphor, once issued, was promptly and correctly rejected. The "depths" of ancient society are in fact not the world of the bizarre or the unusual: they are the common foundation of the hierarchy raised above, and the daily experience of the vast majority of men of the time. The evidence on the institution of the "elders" in African Christianity, therefore, offers another opportunity to observe one of those great continuities in the social structure of the ancient Mediterranean. As a most important precursor to that discussion, however, one must note that *seniores* are also attested as the fundamental political institution in the society of the myriad hamlets and villages of Africa in the pre-Christian period.[1] Furthermore, just as elders (*seniores*) as village councillors in the pagan period are attested solely in the epigraphic records of North Africa, so the literary sources reveal that elders (also called *seniores*) who functioned as an integral part of the structure of the Christian Church are to be found in North Africa alone. The coincidence is surely not fortuitous, though the argument for the continuity of the two institutions has been overlooked, deliberately ignored, contested, or simply denied.[2]

Given the simple fact that the Christianization of the African countryside signalled a religious revolution of considerable significance to individual attitudes, but not necessarily a radical change in social institutions, the argument for continuity in structure and function (though circumstantial) is more persuasive than is usually admitted. Acceptance of Christianity did involve a fundamental realignment of the individual's world view, but the reorientation often meant no more than continued participation in traditional institutional life but now "as a Christian". Frequently social institutions, it seems, were only 'Christianized' insofar as their collective membership was Christian. Beyond the fact that the existence of *seniores* within the Church of the third and fourth centuries, and later, is attested in North Africa alone, one must also seek some explanation for the presence of "elders" in the African Church over a number of centuries, and

---

* I would like to record a debt of thanks to Dr. E.G. Hardy (Faculty of Divinity, University of Cambridge) for his extensive remarks on an earlier version of this paper. Although I have not agreed with him in all that I have written, his comments were a rich store of *consilia probata*. I would also like to thank the anonymous referee of this collection for his perceptive observations. And I must thank Dr. R. G. Abrahams (Churchill College, Cambridge) for reading a draft of this paper and for his anthropological observations.

[1] For village elders in the pagan centuries, see B. D. SHAW, "The Structure of Local Society in the Ancient Maghrib: the Elders" (forthcoming).

[2] All examples cited in the standard studies of *seniores* in the early Christian Church come from Africa; e.g., P.-G. CARON, *I poteri giuridici del laicato nella Chiesa primitiva*, Milan, 1948, p. 208-12, at p. 9: "Les sources où l'on parle des *seniores laici* sont principalement les écrits des Pères de l'Église africaine..." where the "principalement" suggests a body of evidence on *seniores* apart from that provided by Africa, which there is *not*. The treatments of the subject by P. MONCEAUX, *BSAF*, 1903, 283-85 and by H. LECLERCQ, "Laïques", *DACL*, 8, 1, 1928, p. 1053-64, at p. 1053 f., and "Seniores Laici", *DACL*, 15, 1, 1950, p. 1198-1200, suggest that the institution was peculiar to Africa, a view reiterated by W.H.C. FREND, "The *Seniores Laici* and the Origins of the Church in North Africa", *JThS*, 12, 1961, p. 280-84, at p. 282. P. MONCEAUX, in his monumental *Histoire littéraire de l'Afrique chrétienne*, 7 vols., Paris, 1901-23 (reprint: Brussels, 1966), v. 3 (1905), p. 83-84, made a fleeting reference to pagan magistrates in Africa with the same title (i.e. *seniores*), but did not develop the case for continuity. He calls the Christian elders in Africa "une institution curieuse"; cf. T.D. BARNES, *Tertullian: A Historical and Literary Study*, Oxford, The Clarendon Press, 1971, p. 274, "a remarkable phenomenon". Cf. J. GAUDEMET, *L'Église dans l'empire romain (IVe-Ve siècles)*, Paris, Sirey, 1958, p. 191, who only claims that, "C'est en Afrique que la participation laïque à l'administration ecclésiastique semble avoir pris la forme la plus nette..."

for the unusual power wielded by them in Africa long after they had disappeared as an institution in the Church elsewhere.[3]

Evidence on the origins and development of elders in the primitive Church reveals much of relevance to the emergence of the priesthood (πρεσβύτερος) and the office of the bishop (ἐπίσκοπος) but provides no antecedent to the peculiar African practice of investing considerable power in elders who were not part of the clergy but who were quite distinct from the general body of the laity. Elders, as distinct from presbyters (priests), may have existed in the Latin West at some time, though there is no positive evidence for this.[4] In a commentary on a passage in First Timothy mentioning problems concerning the respect to be shown to *seniores*, a late fourth century exegete, the anonymous personality commonly identified as "Ambrosiaster", explains that age itself is honoured among all peoples: hence the Jewish Synagogue and later the Apostolic Church had elders without whose advice no action was taken (*ecclesia seniores habuit, quorum sine consilio nihil agebatur in ecclesia*).[5] "Ambrosiaster" admits that *seniores*, as an institution, no longer exist in the Church of his own time, though he does not know the reason for their disappearance. Probably he had no information at his disposal other than the passage that he was explaining and so made the error of equating *presbuteroi* with *seniores*, not realising that the former had simply made the transition to the institution of the priesthood, whereas the latter had never actually existed as an institution in the Apostolic Church. However correct "Ambrosiaster" may be with regard to the early existence of a formal body of *seniores* within the Synagogue and early Church is not at issue here. All we need assume is that he was conversant enough with the orthodox ecclesiastical institutions of his own time to be certain that such *seniores* had not been part of them within living memory. This would eliminate the possibility of *seniores* as an integral institution within the structure of the Church in Italy (and probably Spain and Gaul as well) by the mid-fourth century. Certainly the complete absence of corroborating evidence for elders in the Church in Italy and other western provinces at this time does seem to substantiate "Ambrosiaster's" claim. And yet, during these same centuries, the *seniores* were a living and institution in Christian churches in Africa. Not only that, they were an integral part of the Church hierarchy (in a more general sense of "hierarchy", as shall be explained below) and a council that wielded considerable influence in local Church affairs — men who authority, if not real power, could not be easily ignored by priests, deacons, and bishops.

There is one other rather significant point in the words of "Ambrosiaster" to which attention should be drawn. In explaining the position of the elders in the primitive Church "Ambrosiaster" uses the following phrase: *quorum sine consilio nihil agebatur in ecclesia*. It does not occur in the Biblical passage he is explaining — yet precisely this same phraseology appears in the early fourth century *Gesta apud Zenophilum* from Africa (A. D. 320). In a letter written by the bishop Purpurius of Limata addressed to the clergy and elders of Cirta (a city in Africa; the particular case will be discussed below, p. 214) he declares: "*Clamat Moyses ad omnem senatum filiorum Israel dixitque illis, quae dominus iubeat fieri... sine consilio seniorum nihil agebatur.*" In spite of the suggestion of Purpurius' statement, however, there does not appear to be any *scriptural* authority or source behind it. Hence it seems improbable that "Ambrosiaster" derived his statement about the *seniores* independently from a Biblical source, but rather that he depended on a tradition known *in Africa* about half a century before his own time. The passage is doubly significant since Augustine, another African, chose to write an exegetical piece on the very passage in Leviticus about the *seniores Israel* which Purpurius surely had in mind when he made his remarks to the elders at Cirta (see below). "Ambrosiaster", therefore, is surely conversant with a peculiar African tradition not known elsewhere in the Christian West, a fact which not only sheds light on the identity of "Ambrosiaster" himself, but also adds substance to the peculiarity of the African ecclesiastical institution we are about to discuss.

---

[3] There is one possible reference to an elder in the epigraphy outside Africa: *CIL* ix, 2079 = *ILCV* 386a, "Hic requi/escit Acho/litus se/nior qui viscit an. (*vac.*)"; cf. *ILCV* 386b, "Hic requi/escat Fausti/nus seni/or, qui viscit annis (*vac.*)". But even the names have an African flavour (*viz.*, Acholitanus = "inhabitant of Acholla"?).

[4] BARNES, *Tertullian*, p. 274, briskly rejects Frend's hypothesis (derived from CARON, "Les 'seniores laici'...", *art. cit.*, p. 9) that the elders in North Africa were in some way the result of Judaic influence on African Christianity. H. VON CAMPENHAUSEN, *Ecclesiastical Authority and Spiritual Power in the Church of the First Three Centuries*, London, Adam & Charles Black, 1969 (= *Kirchliches Amt und geistliche Vollmacht*, Tübingen, 1953), chap. 5, "The System of Elders and the Beginnings of Official Authority", p. 76-123, and A. E. HARVEY, "Elders", *JThS*, n.s. 25, 1974, p. 318-32, may be consulted on the position of elders (*presbuteroi*) in the early Church.

[5] "AMBROSIASTER", *Comm. in ep. I Timoth.* 5.1.1. (*PL*, 17, 475-76 = *CSEL* 81.3 (1969) 277-78). The passage glossed is *Seniorem ne increpaveris, sed exhortate ut patrem, iuniores ut fratres.* Commentary: *Nam apud omnes utique gentes honorabilis est senectus; unde et synagoga et postea ecclesia seniores habuit, quorum sine consilio nihil agebatur in ecclesia. Quod qua neglegentia obsolverit, nescio, nisi forte doctorum desidia* (PL, desideria), *aut magis superbia, dum soli volunt aliquid videri.*

The earliest mention that seems to relate to *seniores* as part of the functional organization of the Christian Church in Africa is found in Tertullian's acerbic defence of the faith, the *Apologeticum*. The passage in question describes a typical meeting of Christians, and is intended to contrast the high morality and purpose of the Christian assembly with its pagan counterparts. Over these Christian assemblies preside certain elders whom Tertullian briefly describes as follows:[6]

> *Praesident probati quique seniores, honorem istum non pretio, sed testimonio adepti, neque enim pretio ulla res Dei constat.*

Over these meetings of Christians preside "elders" of proven good character, who have gained their *office (honor)* not by bribery but by their witness and reputation — for no matter of God's is agreeable to bribery.

The question is: are these *seniores* "elders" in the sense in which the term was later understood in African ecclesiastical documents, or is Tertullian simply referring to priests (i.e. *seniores* = πρεσβύτεροι)? The argument in support of the latter interpretation has been clearly put: that the Christians of Tertullian's time would have been affronted if mere laymen were to perform such *sacerdotalia munera* as outlined in the passage.[7] But the argument pends on two tenuous assumptions. First, that Tertullian actually speaks of the *seniores* undertaking duties appropriate to priests, which he does not. He simply states that at Christian meetings elders who are of proven good character preside over the proceedings and further that these men have gained their office (*honor*) not by payment of a sum of money but by personal approval as voiced by Church members (*non pretio, sed testimonio*). The obvious reference is to the distinction between the probity of an office in the Christian Church and the pecuniary requirements for an office in local Roman municipal government. The latter was obtained, Tertullian intimates, not simply at the legally established entrance fee (*summum honorarium*) but in an atmosphere which verged on bribery (no doubt he was well aware of the practice of *pollicitatio* in Roman municipal elections). Secondly, Tertullian merely states that the elders preside or direct these Christian assemblies. He does not attribute any priestly *munera* to them, such as that of the offering of the Eucharist. As for the elders being laymen, that is also an assumption. Nowhere in our extant records are the elders called *seniores laici* — the latter epithet is a modernism. Admittedly the elders did emerge from the general church congregation (the *plebs*) and were integrally connected with it in a way in which the clergy were not. But this does not reduce them to the status of the ordinary *laicus*. They were, as Tertullian himself states, in possession of a sort of office (*honor*) acquired through *testimonium*, that is, as a result of a consensus among the *plebs* as to their character, ability, and inherent worth to fill the post. The position of the priest was presumably much more "official" and Tertullian could have referred to them as *presbyteri* using the common designation then current, rather than using the term *seniores*.[8] Of course, at this early date in the history of the African Church (the *Apologeticum* probably dates to 197-198) the distinction between the imposed authority of the presbyters (priests) and the local practice of placing authority in a council of elders (*seniores*) would have become blurred in our sources, if only because the terminology for the priesthood was not entirely set by this date. Since the latter institution, which had evolved out of a system of elders in the East (πρεσβύτεροι, hence the title presbyter), still retained an ambiguous appellation not "translated" into Latin, confusion between the two was bound to occur.[9]

A document contemporary with Tertullian and often closely associated with him, the *Passio Sanctae Perpetuae*, also contains references to *seniores*. The account of the martyrdom of Perpetua and her

---

[6] TERTULLIAN, *Apol*. 39.4-5 (*CSEL* 69 (1939) 92 = *CCL* 1.1, 150). The chapter is generally devoted to an explanation to pagans of what a Christian assembly is like. It begins: *Nam et iudicatur magno cum pondere, ut apud certos de dei conspectu, summumque fidei futuri ludicii praeiudicium est, si quis ita deliquerit, ut a communicatione orationis et conventus et omnis sancti commercii relegetur.*

[7] Cf. BARNES, *Tertullian*, p. 273-75, comparing *Cor mil*. 3,3 on the attitudes of orthodox Christians at Carthage towards the *eucharistiae sacramentum*. The latter could not be received correctly except from the hands of *praesidentes* (... *nec de aliorum manu quam praesidentium sumimus*). MONCEAUX, *op. cit.*, v. 2, p. 283, was certain that the elders were priests. *Seniores laici*, it should be noted, is a modern Latinism without any ancient authority. Although the elders did emerge from the *plebs* or *populus*, it would be misleading to represent them as mere "senior laymen".

[8] Tertullian certainly knew the proper terminology for presbyters (*e.g., Cast*. 7.6 bis, where the distinction is drawn quite clearly; *de Paen*. 9.3, and *de Pud*. 13.7 etc.). Cf. *de Praescr. Haer.* 41.8, *Itaque alius hodie episcopus, cras alius; hodie diaconus, qui cras lector; hodie presbyter qui cras laicus. Nam et laicis sacerdotalia munera iniungunt*, a searing passage ridiculing the "church organization" of "heretical sects". The whole terminology for the priesthood and attendent *officia* is in any case in some doubt and flux during the period; see M. BÉVENOT, "*Sacerdos* as understood by Cyprian", *JThS*, 30, 1979, p. 413-429.

[9] See esp. HARVEY, *art. cit.*, p. 310-320, 327-329, the reply by C. H. ROBERTS "Elders, A Note", *JThS*, 26, 1975, p. 402-405, and CAMPENHAUSEN, *Ecclesiastical Authority*, p. 84-85, on the confusion in meaning within the Greek-speaking Christian communities on πρεσβύτερος as both "old man, elder" and "priest".

companions at Carthage is to be dated to about A.D. 203.[10] In a dream sequence related by the catechumen Saturus in which a journey by the martyrs to celestial paradise is recounted, the Lord (*hominem canum, niveos habentem capillos et vultu iuvenili*) is flanked by four elders to his right and to his left (*et in dextra et in sinistra seniores quattuor*) behind whom stand a coterie of other elders (*et post illos ceteri seniores conplures stabant*). The dream is surely a reflection of the earthly assembly of Christians translated to a celestial context. The everyday Christian world must lie at the basis of the African martyrs' preception of the structural organization of the heavenly kingdom. God, the celestial equivalent of the priest or bishop, is flanked by his council of elders. What is significant for us is the fact that the elders about the central figure appear to conduct the Christian "service" in heaven in which the martyrs themselves figure as the counterpart to the earthly congregation. The elders announce the actions to be performed by the martyrs: *et ceteri seniores dixerunt nobis "Stemus" ... et dixerunt nobis seniores "Ite et laudate"*, and so on.[11] From other sources we know that the elders performed minor duties in the church service, such as those reflected in this passion account. These functions, such as leading singing and choruses of praises, and others, mark the elders out as men who had an important *popular* rôle to play in leading and directing the common people, or congregation, in formal assemblies, as well as in the broader "political" networks of the Church. Throughout the whole account of the *Passio* the parallel Greek text employs the word "πρεσβύτερος" since the Greek is incapable of making the distinction "elder/priest". But the Latin text *does* note the difference: whereas the elders are called *seniores*, the priests are called *presbyteri*. One such example occurs immediately after the above passage in the dream sequence recorded by the same Saturus, a reference to Aspasius the presbyter who is not a *senior* but a *presbyter*.[12] Thus from a document contemporary with Tertullian we gain some support for the claim that a distinction was drawn between elders and priests, and that the former were called *seniores*, the latter *presbyteri*.

There is considerable gap in the literary evidence during the entire mid-third century before elders are mentioned again in an African context. The year is A.D. 303, and the document the *Passio sancti Felicis episcopi*.[13] Diocletian's edict against the Christians, issued on 24 February 303, was implemented in an African village not far from Carthage by the *curator rei publicae* of the town, Magnilianus, who demanded that the elders hand over the sacred writings of the local Church.[14] The curator Magnilianus, who enforced the decree in the town under his supervision on the 5th of June 303, ordered the elders of the Church to be brought before him in lieu of the bishop Felix, who was then at Carthage:

> *Tunc Magnilianus curator iussit ad se perduci seniores plebis, quoniam eadem die Felix episcopus Carthaginem fuerat profectus, sed et Aprum presbyterum ad se iussit perduci et Cyrillum et Vitalem lectores.*
>
> Then the *curator* Magnilianus ordered the *seniores plebis* to be brought to him, since on the very same day the bishop Felix had gone to Carthage. He also ordered the priest Aper to be brought before him, as well as the readers Cyrillus and Vitalis.

First, note the priority accorded by the *curator* to the various levels of the local church hierarchy in the absence of the bishop. The summons is directed in the first instance to the *seniores*, then to the priest Aper, and finally to the readers Cyril and Vitalis. In the mind of the official charged with the town administration, a man probably not unacquainted with the organization of the local church, the elders and not the other clergy were the figures of authority to be dealt with in the absence of the bishop. It might be possible that the elders refused to comply with the orders issued by Magnilianus as did the bishop Felix. Subsequently, the *curator* then summoned the priest and the *lectores* since the latter were usually in charge of the sacred writings.

---

[10] For the date see BARNES, *Tertullian*, p. 263-265.

[11] The basic text is R. KNOPF, G. KRÜGER, G. RUHBACH, *Ausgewählte Mätyrakten* (Sammlung Ausgewählter kirchen- und dogmengeschichtlicher Quellenschriften, n.f., no. 3), Tübingen, 1965, no. 8, p. 35-44, cf. J. A. ROBINSON, *The Passion of S. Perpetua* (in) *Texts and Studies*, 2, Cambridge, Cambridge University Press, 1891, 11.12 (p. 80) = C.I.M.I. VAN BEEK, *Passio Sanctarum Perpetuae et Felicis* (in) *Florilegium Patristicum*, Bonn, Hanstein, vol. 43, 1938, 40-43 = H. MUSURILLO, *The Acts of the Christian Martyrs*, Oxford, The Clarendon Press, 1972, p. 120-21.

[12] *Passio*, s. 13.1; cf. the *Apoc* 4.4, 4.10, 5.5, 6.8, 11, 14, 7.11-14, 11.16, 14.4, and 19.4 on the twenty-four elders about the throne of God.

[13] KNOPF-KRÜGER-RUHBACH, *Ausgewählte Märtyrakten*, 1965, no. 22, p. 90-91, cf. T. RUINART, *Acta martyrum*[2], Amsterdam, 1713, p. 390-91 = H. DELEHAYE, "La passion de S. Félix de Thibiuca", *Anal. Boll.*, 39, 1921, p. 241-76, at p. 268 = MUSURILLO, *Acts*, no. 20, p. 266-71.

[14] MONCEAUX, *op. cit.*, v. 3, p. 93-96; R.P. DUNCAN-JONES, "An African Saint and His Interrogator", *JThS*, n.s. 25, 1974, p. 106-10, identifies the *curator rei publicae* Magnilianus in the *passio* with Q. Vetulanius Urbanus Herennianus *signo* Magnilianus, the *curator* of Hr. bû-Scha (*Municipium Aurelium C[ommodianum]*) mentioned in a double inscription from that town (*CIL* viii, 23964-965) and hence disputes the identification of the site as Thibiuca. There are numerous mss. variants (see his n. 2, p. 109).

The *seniores* continue to figure prominently in later conflicts which found their roots in the events of 303. In the village of *Abthugni* (modern Hr. Assūar) the town's chief magistrate, the *duumvir* Alfius Caecilianus, was involved in the enforcement of the imperial edict. But his dealings with the local bishop Felix were later supposed not to have been entirely as hostile as the atmosphere of persecution would demand. In fact, it was intimated that the two men had been on rather too friendly terms with one another. Compromise and even collaboration were alleged. Since the same Felix was one of the three bishops who later consecrated Caecilianus as primate of Africa in 312, the incident which lay bare the schism within the African Church, the probity of his conduct in the Church's time of trial became a matter of more than local interest. Consequently, in 314, the emperor had Felix placed on trial to determine whether or not he had indeed been a *traditor* (a "traitor", one who "handed over" the scriptures to the authorities). At the trial a document was read out damming Felix's behaviours in 303. Once again, the elders were at the pivotal point of the prosecution:[15]

> *Volusiano et Anniano consulibus, XIII Kal. Sept. in iure apud Aurelium Didymum Speretium, sacerdotem Iovis Optimi Maximi, duovirum splendidae Coloniae Carthaginiensium, Maximus dixit: loquor nomine seniorum Christiani populi catholicae legis.*
>
> On the 19th of August A.D. 314, in court before the governor Aurelius Didymus Speretus, the priest of Jupiter the Greatest and the Best and co-mayor of the glorious Colony of Carthage, Maximus said: "I speak in the name of the elders of the Christian people of the 'Catholic' practice."

That is, Maximus formulated the charge and the case against Felix in the name of the elders of the Christian congregation. The power of the *seniores* to initiate such proceedings seems to be connected directly to their position as a quasi-judicial *concilium* within the local church.

Early fourth-century documents, such as those just cited, attest the central role played by the council of elders (*seniores*) in the local church, even though the elders themselves were not a formal part of the clergy. The potential power wielded by the elders seems to have become especially prominent in the aftermath of the Great Persecution when internecine conflict in the Church was marked by the convenient device of accusations of misconduct during the period 303-304, notably the accusation of having been one who surrendered the scriptures (a *traditor*). But what was the ordinary position of the elders within the structure of the Church and what were their nominal powers? Even in correspondence of the early fifth century, Augustine was still careful to take cognizance of their importance in formal address, such as the following:[16]

> *Dilectissimis fratribus, clero, senioribus, et universae plebi ecclesiae Hipponiensis...*
> To my dearest brothers, clergy, elders, and all the people of the Church at Hippo...

The form of the greeting implicitly recognizes the existence of the *seniores* as a corporate body with a status distinct from that of the *plebs*. A council which was from the laity and yet quite separate from it — that was the ambiguous position of the elders.

The manner in which the council of elders functioned as an integral part of the African Church is perhaps best illustrated by the sordid events recorded in the proceedings of a trial held before Zenophilus, the governor of Numida, in December 320.[17] In order to understand the significance of the hearings at which it was established that Silvanus, the bishop of *Cirta* (by then called Constantine), was a *traditor*, it is necessary to examine the situation in the church at Cirta at an earlier date, during the time of the persecution. We are able to study these earlier events in some detail since an accurate record of them has been preserved within the account of the later trial of 320. One of the principal witnesses at the trial, a certain

---

[15] *CSEL* 26, 1893, p. 198 (ed. C. Ziwsa).
[16] Aug., *Ep.* 78 (*PL*, 33, 267 = *CSEL*, 34, 1898, p. 331, ed. A. Goldbacher), A.D. 404. Cf. a similar address in a disputed letter attributed to Augustine: *Auctoribus ac principibus vel senioribus Coloniae Sufetanae* (*Ep.* 50; *PL*, 33, 190).
[17] For the text, see *CSEL*, 26, 1893, p. 185-97 (ed. C. Ziwsa). For analysis, see O. Seeck, "Quellen und Urkunden über die Anfänge des Donatismus", *ZKG*, 10, 1889, p. 505-68, pp. 545-47; much superior, however, is the treatment by Monceaux, *op. cit.*, v. 4, p. 228-39. The text, as edited by Ziwsa, is full of faults and uncorrected errors. A better collation of the mss. and a new edition are certainly a desideratum. Many criticisms of the text were already noted by C. H. Turner, "*Adversaria critica*: Notes on the Anti-Donatist Dossier and on Optatus, Books I-II", *JThS*, 27, 1925-26, p. 283-96. T. D. Barnes, "The Beginnings of Donatism", *JThS*, n.s. 26, 1975, p. 13-22, has questioned the veracity of the trial record but, on closer examination, I believe it to be both genuine and original. Doubts, it seems, have arisen primarily because of a basic misunderstanding of the context of the document both in relation to its time of writing and to its later use as a series of documents in a so-called "Anti-Donatist dossier". The relationship of the central character, Nundinarius, to the principal *personae* of the trial has also been misunderstood, adding further confusion to an accurate assessment of the document's validity.

Victor, a *grammaticus*, continued to deny emphatically that he knew Silvanus to be a *traditor* and claimed that he himself had not been present in Cirta when scriptures in his house were seized by the civil authorities. In order to prove that Victor was lying, the prosecutor, one Nundinarius, had the municipal records of Cirta that related to the day when the terms of Diocletian's edict were enforced read aloud to the court.

The municipal records revealed that the *flamen perpetuus* and *curator rei publicae* of the colony of Cirta, Munatius Felix, had been putting the terms of the edict into effect by the 19th of May, 303 — the day the documents read out recall in detail. Leaving aside some other interesting details of this document, let us concentrate on the passage which outlines the hierarchy of the local church on that date.[18]

> *Sedente Paulo episcopo, Montano et Victore Deusatelio et Memorio presbyteris, adstante Marte cum Helio diaconis, Marcuclio, Catullino, Silvano, et Caroso subdiaconis, Ianuario, Meraclo, Fructuoso, Miggine, Saturnino, Victore et ceteris †fossoribus†...*
>
> The bishop Paul was seated there, as were Montanus, Victor Deusatelius, and Memorius the priests; standing alongside were Martis and Helius the deacons; then Marcuclius, Catullinus, Silvanus, and Carosus the subdeacons; finally Januarius, Meraclus, Fructuosus, Miggin, Saturninus, Victor and other †gravediggers†...

The hierarchy of the clergy and others who were part of the Cirtan Church at the moment of the persecution might be represented schematically as follows:

Bishop	Paulus
Episcopus	
Priests	Montanus
Presbyteri	Victor Deusatelius
	Memorius
Deacons	Martis
Diacones	Helius
Subdeacons	Marcuclius
Subdiacones	Catullinus
	Silvanus
	Carosus
Gravediggers	Ianuarius
†*Fossores*†	Meraclus
	Fructuosus
	Miggin
	Saturninus
	Victor
	and others

There are no problems with the ranking of the clergy: one bishop, three priests, two deacons, and four subdeacons. But who are the enigmatic "fossores" at the end of the list? Though *fossor* or gravedigger did exist in the early Church as a sort of low ranking office, it seems strange, if not totally incongruous, to find them listed as an ordinary part of the Church hierarchy, grouped together with the highest officers of the Christian community at Cirta. Their presence is noted, but not that of other Church officers who surely ranked far above them — as for example the *lectores* who were surely of greater importance in a situation involving the seizure of the holy scriptures than were a group of gravediggers.[19] The best edition of the mss. we have at our disposal is certainly in error; the reading in the court transcript must have been "senioribus", *not* "fossoribus". The error is easy to explain on two counts. In the script copied by the scribes of the surviving mss., the distinction between *senior* (dat) and *fossor* (dat) could have been mistaken. Both words have the same number of letters and the confusion between the initial "s" and "f" quite

---

[18] *CSEL*, 26, 1893, p. 186-87.
[19] For *fossores*, see *ThLL*, 6, 1, p. 1215; they are present in the epigraphy of Rome from the beginning of the fifth century onwards, *e.g.*, *CIL* vi, 7543, 9655; *ICRR*, I, 1429 (A.D. 337-57), 1554 (A.D. 365-445), 448 (A.D. 400), 517 (A.D. 400), and 653 (A.D. 426). Cf. J. GUYON, "La vente des tombes à travers l'épigraphie de la Rome chrétienne (IIIe-VIIe siècles): le rôle des *fossores, mansionarii, praepositi* et prêtres", *MEFRA*, 86, 1974, pp. 549-96, at p. 551-80; p. 574 our case is cited; cf. LACT., *Div. Inst.*, 6.12 (*CSEL*, 19, 1890, p. 529) for their rank: *ultimum illud et maximum pietatis officium est peregrinorum et pauperorum sepultura...* cf. JEROME, *Ep.* 1 (*CSEL*, 54, 1910, p. 7, ed. HILBERG).

possible. *Fossores* did exist as a Church office outside Africa (they are *not* attested in Africa except for this document) and the scribe probably did know of them, but *not* of *seniores* (cf. discussion of the Ambrosiaster passage, p. 208, above). Once this emendation is made, some technical obscurities in the *Gesta* are clarified.[20]

Munatius Felix was not able to force the bishop Paulus to reveal the names or whereabouts of the *lectores* who were in charge of the scriptures, so he brought pressure to bear on the subdeacons, especially Silvanus and Carosus, to identify the readers. With the help of these men and the town clerks, Edusius and Iunius, who were able to consult official records, Felix was able to ferret out the readers one by one and demand that they hand over the writings in their possession. The *lectores* so named in the record are:

Readers	Eugenius
Lectores	Felix, the *sarsor*
	Victorinus
	Proiectus
	Victor, the *grammaticus*
	Euticius (Caesariensis)
	Goddeus (MS. Coddeus)[21]

From the municipal records concerning the actions taken by Munatius Felix on 19 May 303, the court was able to demonstrate that both Silvanus the subdeacon and Victor the *grammaticus* (the *lector*) were involved in the surrender of Church property and the holy scriptures.[22] We might also deduce from the record that the one man who resolutely refused to compromise or collaborate, the bishop Paulus, was arrested, sent before the provincial governor, and executed.[23] His death led to a power struggle within the Church at Cirta for the position of bishop, a fight from which Silvanus, then a subdeacon, emerged victorious. Silvanus' "election" at Cirta during the years of the persecution was a particularly violent and vicious affair, so that he had to wait for confirmation till the time when the forces of the persecution had abated. This took place on 5 March 305 when Secundus, the bishop of Tigisis and primate of Numidia, called a synod at Cirta for the purpose.[24] The election of Silvanus as bishop of Cirta was later to become the *cause célèbre* about which dispute and disagreement were to erupt.

In 320, long after the end of the persecution and after Silvanus' formal confirmation, a deacon named Nundinarius at the Church at Constantine (as Cirta was now called) fell into dispute with the bishop. The

---

[20] For example, *fossoribus* should be excised completely from 187, line 11, since Marcuclius, Silvanus and Carosus were *subdeacons*; there can be no doubt about their position in the account.

[21] Goddeus, cf. *CIL* viii, 18851 (J. Taya sanctuary near *Thibilis*), 12378 (*Giufi*, Hr. Bir M'scherga); Coddeus, 8520 (*Sitifis*, Setif), 18410 (*Lambaesis*), and 19627 (*Cirta*, Constantine). See F.L. BENZ, *Personal Names in Phoenician and Punic Inscriptions*, Rome, Biblical Institute Press, 1972 (Studia Pohl, 8) 102, 294-95, probably the precursor of the frequently used Afro-Latin name "Fortunatus". For *Miggin* in this same list (cf. p. 212, above), see BENZ, pp. 133-37 and 338-39.

[22] For Silvanus:
F(elix) to M(arcuclius), S(ilvanus) and C(arosus): *Proferte hoc, quod habetis.*
S & C: *Quod hic fuit, totum hoc eiecimus.*
F: *Responsio vestra actis haeret.*
(Postea quam in bibliothecis inventa sunt ibi armaria inania, ibi protulit Silvanus capitulatam argenteam et lucernam argenteam, quod diceret se post orcam eas invenisse.)
Victor Aufidius to S: *Mortuus fueras, si non illas invenisses.*
(*CSEL*, 26, 187, cf. his actions at 187-88)
For Victor:
(*Et cum ad grammatici domum ventu fuisset*)
F. *Profer scripturas quas habes ut praecepto parere possis!*
(*Victor grammaticus optulit codices II et quiniones quattuor*)
F: *Profer scripturas; plus habes!*
V: *Si plus habuissem, dedissem.*
(*CSEL*, 26, 188)

[23] Paulus must have died well before 5 March 305 since Silvanus' confirmation on that date by the Synod of Cirta was made at the first possible opportunity after the persecution was over. Thus, it is clear that Paulus died during the persecution. In all probability because of his refusal to compromise at the time Felix was enforcing Diocletian's edict on 19 May 303. He would have been arrested and sent to the provincial governor for trial and execution, probably by the summer of 303.

[24] For the events, see W.H.C. FREND, *The Donatist Church: A Movement of Protest in Roman North Africa*, Oxford, The Clarendon Press, 1952 (reprint: 1971) p. 11-13; for the date, see AUG., *Brev. collat.*, 3.17.22 (*PL*, 43, 644 = *Oeuvres*, ser. 4, t. 5, 214-15); for Secundus' rank, see 3.13.25 (*PL*, 43, 638 = *Oeuvres*, sér. 4, t. 5, 192-93): *Secundum Tigisianum... qui tunc habebat primatum episcoporum Numidarum*.

conflict between the two became bitter, then violent. Nundinarius seems to have had evidence of corruption involving both Silvanus and his cohort Purpurius, bishop of Limata. Not surprisingly he faced the organized violence of the bishop; indeed Nundinarius alleged that Silvanus had tried to have him stoned to death. No doubt in fear for his own life, Nundinarius decided to bring pressure to bear on his enemies. He sent notice to Purpurius, bishop of Limata, in the form of a petition (a *libellus*) outlining his case against Silvanus and, by implication, against Purpurius himself. He demanded that Purpurius should intercede with Silvanus.[25] To judge from the tone of Purpurius' subsequent correspondence with Silvanus, it is clear that Nundinarius intimated to Purpurius that, if he did not obtain satisfaction within the Church, the matter would end up in the civil courts — and that was an eventuality which neither Purpurius nor Silvanus would want.[26]

The letters written by Purpurius and other ecclesiastical officials (a certain Fortis and a Sabinus) concerning this matter were read into the court record, all of which urged that the affair be settled *quietly* within the Christian community before it came to the attention of the civil authorities.[27] This correspondence is very revealing of the manner in which the African Church hierarchy functioned under stress. First, two of the principal correspondents, Purpurius and Fortis, each sent a *pair* of letters to the Church at Cirta: one to Silvanus the bishop and a separate one to the clergy and the *elders*. That action in itself is instructive, and even more so is the different text of each of the pair of letters. Of the two letters written by Purpurius, the one addressed to Silvanus has the air of a private, confidential communication to a fellow bishop:

> *Purpurius episcopus Silvano coepiscopo in domino salutem.*
> Purpurius the bishop to Silvanus, his cobishop in the Lord, greetings.

After referring to Nundinarius' knowledge of their questionable activities and the danger this could present to them both, Purpurius presses Silvanus to reconsider his position. He makes clear the way in which he should handle this delicate matter:

> *Quaere remedium, quo modo poterit ibi malignitas ista extingui, antequam flamma exsurgat, quae post demum extingui non poterit sine sanguine spiritali, adhibete conclericos et seniores plebis ecclesiasticos viros et inquirant diligenter, quae sunt istae dissensiones, ut ea, quae fiunt, secundum fidei praecepta fiant. non declinabis ad dexteram vel ad sinistram, libenter autem aurem conmodare nolis malis instructoribus, qui nolunt pacem.*
>
> Find a solution, whereby this terrible business can be stamped out there (*i.e.* at Cirta) before a fire breaks out that will not be able to be extinguished without the shedding of Christian blood. Summon together your fellow clergy *and* the elders of the common parishioners (both of whom are of the Church) and seek diligently that these conflicts are resolved in such a way that whatever happens, happens according to the rules of the Faith. Don't bend to "the right" or "the left" in this matter, don't give ear to bad advisors — men who do not wish peace in the Church.

That is, the conflict is to be resolved by the mediation of the clergy on the one hand and the *seniores plebis* on the other (both being designated, significantly, *ecclesiastici viri*). The elders seem to have been the ordinary "court" by which such disputes among Christians were dealt with inside the Church. That the *seniores* did, in effect, function as a quasi-legal council within the Church is confirmed by the contents of a letter which Purpurius wrote to *them*:

> *Purpurius episcopus clericis et senioribus Cirtensium in domino aeternam salutem! clamat Moyses ad omnem senatum filiorum Israel dixitque illis, quae dominus iubeat fieri. sine consilio seniorum nihil agebatur. itaque et vos, carissimi, quos scio omnem sapientiam caelestem et spiritalem habere, omni vestra virtute cognoscite, quae sit dissensio haec, et perducite ad pacem.*

---

[25] This much can be inferred from the letter of Purpurius to Silvanus: *Venit ad me Nundiniarius diaconus filius noster et petiit, has litteras deprecatorias a me ad te, sanctissime, dirigerem, ut, si fieri posset, pax inter te et ipsum sit. Hoc enim volo fieri, ut nemo sciat, quid inter nos agatur, si volveris scripto tuo, ut et ego solus ibi in re praesenti veniam et dissensionem ipsam de inter vos amputem, manu sua enim mihi tradidit libellum rei gestae, pro qua causa tuo praecepto fuerit lapidatus. Non est verum, ut pater castiget filium contra veritatem, et scio quia vera sunt, quae in libello mihi tradito sunt conscripta.*

[26] Note the constant exhortations to secrecy under the pretence that the Christian community's reputation in the eyes of the local pagans should not be tarnished. Whereas in Purpurius' letter to Silvanus this is reduced to *ut nemo sciat, quid inter nos agatur*, in his letter to the clergy and elders it is covered by an elaborate excuse about the affairs of the Christian community remaining within the Church: *Elaborate, nemo sciat, quae sit coniuratio haec*. Fortis' letter to Silvanus also develops the idea of Christian unity to support a case of having the matter decided within the Church and ends with *Nemo sciat*. On precise parallels of local communities to keep affairs like these within the bounds of local decision making without appeal to formal external governmental authority, see J. BEATTIE, *Bunyoro: An African Kingdom*, New York, Holt, Rinehart & Winston, 1960, p. 66-69, and R. G. ABRAHAMS, *The Political Organization of the Unyamwezi*, Cambridge, Cambridge University Press, 1967, ch. 8, esp. p. 167 ff.

[27] Fortis and Sabinus cannot be identified with certainty; they would appear to be bishops.

X

THE ELDERS OF CHRISTIAN AFRICA

Purpurius the bishop to the clergy and elders of the Cirtan church, in the name of the Lord greetings! Moses cries out to all the senate of the sons of Israel and told them what the Lord ordered to be done. "Nothing is to be done without the advice of the elders." Thus even you, my dearest brethren, whom I know have all heavenly and spiritual wisdom, judge with all your powers what sort of conflict this is, and bring it to a peaceful conclusion.

The letter is patently directed to the *elders*, the address to the *clerici* being a mere formality. The terms in which he speaks to the elders draws a clear analogy between them and a deliberative court or senate (*e.g. omnis senatus*) and emphasizes their important role as a council: "Nothing was done without the advice of the elders." Purpurius then lauds them as men who possess all heavenly and spiritual wisdom, again laying stress on the qualities most characteristic of a *concilium* of men who wielded real powers of decision within the Church. The use of the verb *cognosco* (with its derivative *cognitio*) once again implies that the *seniores* formed a judicial court capable of hearing cases.

The involvement of elders in the social and ecclesiastical problem of "accusation" is further made evident by a canon of the African Church (*Cod. can.*, 8, A.D. 419, but derived from a Carthaginian synod of 387 or 390) wherein a certain Numidius, a bishop of *Maxula* (modern Rhadès, just southeast of Carthage) states that "there are *very many*, not of good character, who think their elders (*seniores*) or bishops would be the object of accusations." That not only places the elders directly on the level of the bishops in the perspective of the members of the laity involved in the accusations, but also admits, implicitly, the equal importance of the *seniores* in the power structure of the local Church. As such they must have been involved in the same remedies to accusation (*i.e.* ecclesiastical court actions) as were the bishops, priests, and deacons. And further, as noted above (p. 209), there is also the implicit recognition in the Greek translation of the African canons of the *seniores* as a veritable γερουσία, even though Augustine went far out of his way to deny this interpretation of their powers and function (see p. 222, below). This quasi-judicial aspect of the elders becomes more apparent in the second half of Purpurius' letter:

Bonum quaerite remedium, quomodo extinguatur haec res cum *in iudicio* veniatis. *Istum iudicium* inter partes *iudicate secundum gravitatem vestram et iustitiam*. cavete vobis, ne declinetis in dexteram neque in sinistram: dei res agitur, qui scrutatur *cognitiones* singulorum. elaborate, nemo sciat, quae sit coniuratio haec.

Seek a good solution (when you go into *court session*) by which this matter may be extinguished. Made a *fair judgement in your court* between the opposing sides, according *to your serious bearing* and *justice*. Beware — bend neither to the right nor to the left. A matter of God is being dealt with, who critically reviews *the trials* of individual men. Act in such a way that no one will know what this conspiracy was.

The italicized phrases need not be elaborated upon. By themselves they indicate that Purpurius regarded the elders as having an authority analogous to that of a Roman court of law. His main concern is that the *seniores* should exercise this power in the quarrel between Silvanus and Nundinarius so that the matter could be "hushed up" and not have to go before the civil courts.

In the trial record of 320 there is also a pair of letters from a certain Fortis whom Nundinarius had also approached with his case. Fortis wrote to Silvanus to urge that the bishop should take care to see that the matter did not become public, but remained within the confines of the Church. The second letter addressed "*Fratribus et filiis, clero et senioribus*" emphasizes this same concern, but reproaches the *concilium* with a Pauline stricture:[28]

Et scriptum est: Non est sapiens quisquam inter vos, qui possit iudicare inter fratres? Sed et frater cum fratre iudicatur, sed apud infideles, sicuti vos cum in iudicio non intenditis.

And it is written: "Is there not a wise man among you who is able *to make a judgement* between brothers? But let brother be judged by brother, not amongst those of no faith," just as you do not intend to *when in your court*.

The point of the letter cannot be misunderstood: the *seniores* are a *iudicium* who should take this case more seriously and reach a decision quickly to prevent the matter from becoming public.

Another letter follows, this time from a certain Sabinus to Silvanus, urging the latter to relent so that the Church might celebrate the approaching Easter in peace. This was not to be. The last letter in the collection, from Sabinus to Fortis, reveals that the matter was to be in deliberation up till Easter, if not beyond. Silvanus was adamant and the *seniores* could not compel him to back down.

Since Nundinarius did not obtain satisfaction from the council of elders, he took his charges, including the fact that Silvanus was a *traditor*, before the court of the provincial governor Zenophilus in December 320. The trial records begin with the interrogation of a Victor, *professor Romanarum litterarum, grammaticus*

---

[28] *CSEL*, 26, 191; cf. I *Cor.* 6.5 f.

latinus, who was also a *lector* in the Christian Church at Cirta. Victor's father was a decurion in the municipal government at Constantine and his grandfather had been a soldier who had served at the governor's headquarters. His family was of African ethnic descent.[29] Why was this Victor the central witness called by Nundinarius? His importance is apparently crucial since his denial of any knowledge that Silvanus was a *traditor* has to be proven as false by Nundinarius. So too, Victor also denies that he had surrendered writings in his possession as a *lector*. Instead he claims that he fled the town at the time of the persecution with two officers of the Church, the deacon Martis and the priest Victor Deusatelius. While they were in a safe retreat on Mt. Bellona, the scriptures at his home were seized by the civil authorities. To controvert this testimony Nundinarius had the municipal records from the time of the persecution read to the court (above, p. 212), but Victor still steadfastly denied that he was ever present when the scriptures were removed from his home. Nundinarius then had an episcopal letter drafted by Fortis read to the court (probably a document from the synod called by Secundus of Tigisis to confirm Silvanus in 305). It is a statement by the dissenting bishops who opposed the ordination of Silvanus:

> *Testis est Christus et angeli eius quoniam tradiderunt, quibus communicastis, id est Silvanus a Cirta traditor est et fur rerum pauperum; quod omnes vos episcopi, presbyteri, diacones, seniores scitis de quadringentis follibus Lucillae, clarissimae feminae, etc.*
>
> Christ and his angels are witness to the fact that they were *traditores* (i.e., men who had handed the Scriptures over to the authorities) with whom you communicated and that Silvanus from Cirta is a *traditor* and a thief of poor people's property. Because all you bishops, priests, deacons, and elders know about the 400 *folles* of Lucilla, the woman of senatorial rank who...

In other words, those who knew that Silvanus was a *traditor* and a common thief were the members of the Church at Cirta, the clergy (*episcopi, presbyteri, diacones*) and the elders (*seniores*). Since the evidence is meant to controvert Victor's testimony and we know that he was not a member of the ecclesiastical hierarchy (*i.e.* that he was a *lector*), the conclusion emerges that Victor must have been one of the *seniores*. It was in this capacity that he knew Silvanus to be a *traditor*. We may then safely identify Victor with the man of the same name mentioned among the "*fossores*" at Cirta, whom we have postulated to be the "*seniores*". What follows in the trial then makes sense. Nundinarius then has the correspondence concerning the quarrel between himself and Silvanus read to the court (above p. 212). The whole point of the letter was, as we have demonstrated, to ensure that Silvanus and especially the *elders* as a judicial *concilium* reached the appropriate solution. That is why Nundinarius has the letters read to *Victor* and not to other witnesses whom he calls — because Victor was a member of the *seniores*, indeed probably one of the most influential amongst their number.

After this barrage of evidence Victor breaks down and confesses that he does in fact know that Silvanus was a *traditor*, but he continues to insist that he was not present when scriptures were seized from his house. Nundinarius, however, as prosecutor, is permitted by Zenophilus to press the original line of his enquiry in cross-examining Victor:

> N *(to Victor)*: *"Vos seniores clamabatis: exaudi, deus, civem nostrum volumus, ille (sc. Silvanus) traditor est."*
> Z *(to V.)*: *"Clamasti ergo cum populo, quod traditor esset Silvanus et non deberet fieri episcopus?"*
> V: *"Clamavi et ego et populus. Nos enim civem nostrum petebamus, integrum virum."*
>
> N (to Victor): You elders shouted out: "Hear us God, we want you to know that our fellow townsman, that man (*i.e.* Silvanus) is a *traditor*."
> Z (to V.): "Did you shout with the people that Silvanus was a *traditor* and ought not to be made bishop?"
> V: "Yes, I shouted it — I and the people. For we wanted (another) fellow citizen of ours to be bishop, a good and upright man."

From this exchange, it can be established beyond unreasonable doubt that Victor was one of the *seniores*. In fact, he was probably the member of the council of elders who incited the *populus*; hence his importance to Nundinarius' case.

---

[29] *CSEL*, 26, 185:
Z: *Quis vocaris?*
V: *Victor.*
Z: *Cuius condicionis es?*
V: *Professor sum Romanarum litterarum, grammaticus Latinus.*
Z: *Cuius dignitas es?*
V: *Patre decurione Constantiniensium; avo milite, in comitatu militaverat; nam origo nostra de sanguine Mauro descendit.*

The whole episode at Cirta reveals with great clarity several facts about the *seniores'* functional place within the Church. First, they represented a council that ranked immediately after the officers of the Church (*i.e.* the bishops, priests and deacons) and they wielded a considerable power that was quite separate from that of the bishop and his clergy. As a power base distinct from the bishops, the elders directed and represented the interests of the congregation in the local church, variously referred to as the *plebs* or *populus*.[30] Their effective control of the *plebs* meant that the elders figured very prominently in the "secular" affairs of the Church, that is to say its "political" as opposed to its theological concerns. Whenever disputes of a political or structural nature arose, the *seniores'* influence with the *plebs* and their own power as a deliberative *concilium* had to be taken into account. They represented an alternative locus of power in the organization of the Church which, in case of a dispute, could become a counterbalance to the bishop. As a council the elders wielded quasi-judicial powers and, being removed from the bishop and his subordinates, could even initiate proceedings within the local church or take independent action against the bishop. Naturally, as in the case of Silvanus' election as bishop of Cirta, the *seniores* could be a decisive force in any internal conflict.

A notice in *Optatus* of Milev would seem to indicate that when the bishop left his see the position of the elders was considerably enhanced, even to the point where they might be considered the temporary directors of the local church. In late 311 or early 312, a priest at Carthage named Felix had written certain pamphlets that were critical of the usurper Maxentius.[31] As a result, his arrest was demanded by an order from the "persecutor" emperor (*epistula de tyranno imperatore*). In fear for his life, he hid with Mensurius, the bishop of Carthage. The authorities demanded that Mensurius surrender Felix, but met with an outright refusal. The officials then dispatched a *relatio* to the imperial court; the reply (*rescriptum*) stated that, if Mensurius did not hand Felix over to the authorities, he should be sent to the imperial court for trial (*ad palatium dirigeretur*). Mensurius did refuse and so was arrested and sent away under escort. Before he left his see, Mensurius placed the possessions of the church in the hands of trusted elders. There could hardly be a more graphic example of the fact that *seniores* were the repository of power in the local church in the absence of the bishop:[32]

> *Conventus non leves patiebatur angustias; erant enim ecclesiae ex auro et argento quam plurima ornamenta, quae nec defodere terrae, nec secum portare (sc. Mensurius). Quae quasi fidelibus senioribus commendavit...*

The congregation did not take these hardships lightly. For the church had very many ornaments of gold and silver which he was not able to bury underground or to carry with himself. These things he entrusted to some faithful elders...

The goods were entrusted to the elders and were to be handed over to his successor if Mensurius did not return. The *seniores* were thus the medium by which continuity in the administrative hierarchy of the local church could be ensured in lieu of the formal authority of the bishop and his subordinates.

Another incident in the Church at Carthage towards the end of the fourth century, the so-called Maximianist-Primianist struggle, illustrates the same exercise of power by the elders within the Christian community. This time the struggle was within the so-called "Donatist" or African Christian church in the metropolis. The main outlines of the Maximianus *affaire* may be summarized briefly as follows. Upon the death of Parmenianus, the African bishop of Carthage, probably in 392, a successor was appointed in somewhat dubious circumstances. The new bishop, Primianus, was a man of rigorous views whose actions and elevation to the post of Primate of Africa did not meet with the approval of certain sections of the people at Carthage; opposition to him began to coalesce around one of the deacons called Maximianus.[33] It is the structure of the conflict which ensued between these two parties that is of prime interest. The

---

[30] On the conception in Augustine, see J.D. ADAMS, *The Populus of Augustine and Jerome*, London-New Haven, Yale University Press, 1971, p. 17-69. The work suffers from an exceedingly narrow philological approach that limits its concern to the very word *populus* alone. Thus, all other references to congregation, whether under other headings (*e.g.*, *plebs*) or by oblique reference, are simply omitted from consideration.

[31] For the events, see FREND, *The Donatist Church*, p. 15-17. and W.H.C. FREND & K. CLANCY, "When Did the Donatist Schism Begin?", *JThS*, n.s. 28, 1977, p. 104-09 (without, however, accepting the specific conclusions reached by them on the origins of the "schism").

The texts are:
CSEL, 26, 1893, p. 189. The document is quoted later by Augustine, *Contra Cresc.* 3.29.33 (*PL*, 43, 514 = *CSEL* 52.2 (1909) 440-41 = *Oeuvres*, sér. 4, t. 4, 334-35).

[32] *Optatus*, 1.17 (*PL*, 11, 918 = *CSEL*, 26, 1893, p. 19. ed. C. ZIWSA).

[33] Cf. the accounts in MONCEAUX, *op. cit.*, v. 4, p. 57 f.; 299 f.; v. 6, p. 111 f., and FREND, *The Donatist Church*, p. 213 f. C. PALLU DE LESSERT, "Le conflit entre Primianus et Maximianus, Donatistes en 392", *BSAF*, 1917, p. 143-46.

opposition to Primianus, welling out of the common people (*plebs sancta Carthaginiensis ecclesiae*) was directed by the *elders*, the leaders of the *plebs*. Primianus moved against their nominee, Maximianus, first by attempting to have priests from his faction "frame" Maximianus and three of his deacons on trumped-up charges. When this ploy failed, ostensibly because of the refusal of the priests to cooperate, Primianus had Maximianus excommunicated when the latter happened to be ill and powerless to resist. Whether or not all the "atrocities" committed by Primianus are to be believed (including the dumping of one of his own priests into the sewers of Carthage, and the admission of "Claudianists", a sect accused of practicing incest, into the Church) is not at stake here. What *is* significant is the manner in which the opposition to the Primate of Africa was directed. The resistance was led by the *seniores* ; as a result of pressure brought to bear by them, a conference was held at Carthage towards the end of 392 or the beginning of 393. The elders were so enraged by Primianus' actions that they dispatched letters to all the churches in the ecclesiastical province of Africa: [34]

> *His itaque permoti seniores ecclesiae supradictae, ad universum chorum litteras legatosque miserunt, quibus non sine lacrimis deprecati sunt ad se ferventius veniremus, quo perpenso libramine, intentionibus exploratis, existimatio ecclesiae purgaretur.*
>
> Thoroughly upset by these acts, the elders of this church sent letters and representatives throughout the whole rural territory (*i.e.* of Carthage) to whom they had pleaded tearfully to return to them as quickly as possible, so that the scales might be weighed, motives investigated, and the public estimation of the Church be cleansed.

In response, forty-three bishops from churches in the immediate vicinity of Carthage met in the metropolis to discuss the situation.[35] Primianus, however, had the civil authorities on his side, as well as organised bands of men. From this position of strength, he could easily resist the demands of the council to appear before it. Primianus sent his gangs after the councillors, drove the local bishops and clergy from their homes, and had them stoned. The *seniores* who were holding out in the basilica were killed or maimed in an attack on their stronghold.[36] Although Primianus succeeded in quashing the resistance led by the *seniores*, before the Council adjourned it passed a preliminary judgement (*praeiudicium*) against him. The *seniores* pressed for further action. This time they sent letters to all the churches in Africa asking for a larger council to be held on the matter, preferably outside Carthage. The council was convened on 24 June 393 at Cabarsussa in Byzacium and was presided over by Victorinus, the primate (*senex*) of the ecclesiastical province. The preamble read out to the assembled bishops makes it quite clear that the conference was meeting at the request of the *seniores* at Carthage:[37]

> *Hoc igitur edicto legis admoniti, necesse nos fuerat Primiani causam, quem plebs sancta Carthaginiensis ecclesiae episcopum fuerat in ovile Dei sortita, seniorum litteris eiusdem ecclesiae postulantibus audire atque discutere sub eo...*
>
> Therefore, warned by this edict of Law, it was necessary that we hear the case of Primianus whom the sacred congregation of the Carthaginian Church had as bishop of God's flock, as the elders of this same church demanded in their letter to us...

The council issued its judgement against the Primate Primianus and set dates by which his clergy and followers were to abandon communion with him. The document was signed by fifty-three of the bishops who attended. The importance of this whole incident lies in the central role played by the *seniores*. It was they who led the battle against the Primate of the African Church and they who initiated the contacts with other bishops and demanded that a Church council be held to deal with the problem. Even though Primianus commanded support among some of the laity and clergy, and had the power of the civil authorities on his side, it was the crucial decision of *seniores* to dissent from his election which completely undermined his position. The *seniores* remained a powerful force independent of the bishop and clergy even, as in this case, when the bishop was the duely elected Primate of Africa.

Despite the decision of the Council of Cabarsussa, there was a backlash in the greater African Church. Many bishops who were not represented at Cabarsussa felt that Primianus had been properly elected as Primate and that his position ought to be respected. On 24 April 394, a much larger council

---

[34] AUG., *Enarr. in Psalm.* 36.2.20 (*PL*, 36, 378 = *CCL*, 38, 363).
[35] The Council of Carthage, A.D. 393, see J.L. MAIER, *L'Épiscopat de l'Afrique romaine, vandale et byzantine*, Neuchâtel, Attinger, 1973, p. 33, with full sources.
[36] AUG., *Enarr. in Psalm.*, 36.2.20 (*PL*. 36, 379-80 = *CCL*, 38, 364) *quod supra dictus Primianus multitudinem miserit; quae Christianorum domos everteret; quod obsessi sint episcopi simul et clerici, et postea ab eius satellitibus lapidati; quod in basilica caesi sint seniores, quod indigne ferrent ad communionem Claudianistas admitti...*
[37] AUG., *Enarr. in Psalm.*, 36.2.30 (*PL*, 36, 377 = *CCL*, 38, 362).

assembled at Bagai in southeastern Numidia.[38] Primianus was confirmed as the rightful Primate of Africa and the supporters of Maximianus condemned as heretics. Consequently, Primianus was now able to turn on the bishops in the Carthaginian hinterland who had responded to the appeal of the *seniores* and to replace them with his own men. Since the authorities recognized the decision of the Council of Bagaï as binding, they openly supported the purge directed by Primianus.[39] Salvius, the bishop of Membressa (modern Mejez al-Bāb) in the upper Bagradas Valley, was to be replaced after the case against him was heard by Flavius Herodes, the Proconsul of Africa. On 2 March 395, Herodes heard similar cases brought against Praetextus, the bishop of Assuras (modern Hr. Zanfūr), and Felicianus, bishop of Musti (modern Hr. Mest). Note that the official record shows that the charges were lodged by the *seniores* of the local church:[40]

> Post consulatum dominorum nostrorum Arcadii ter et Honorii iterum Augustorum VI Nonas Mart. Carthagine in secretario praetorii Titianus dixit: Peregrinus presbyter et seniores ecclesiae Mustitanae et Adsuritanae regionis tale desiderium prosequuntur...

> After the third consulship of our Lord Emperor Arcadius and the second of our Lord Emperor Honorius, on the 2nd of March, at Carthage, in the governor's office, Titianus declared: Peregrinus the priest and the elders of the Church of Mustis and of the region of Assuras are pursuing their aim of...

There had been more than a two-month delay between the decision of the Council of Bagaï (24 December 394) and the day the charges were brought to Carthage (2 March 395), but the affair was prolonged for more than a year and a half with no satisfactory decision being reached. In late 396, despite the appointment of at least one new bishop (Rogatus at Assuras), the Maximianist bishops, Felicianus and Praetextus, still held their sees. The local *seniores* once again took their case before the Proconsul of Africa, Flavius Mallius Theodorus, on 22 December 396, in order to get him to enforce the ruling already made by his predecessor Herodes:[41]

> Producitur autem iste conflictus, quantum ex gestis proconsularibus et municipalibus indagare potuimus. Usque ad Theodorum proconsulem, hoc est usque anni alterius XI Kal. Ian. quo die clerici et seniores agentes sub Rogato episcopo, qui in locum damnati Praetexti Adsuritani fuerat subrogatus, allegaverunt memorati proconsulis iussionem...

> That conflict erupted, which we are able to follow from the provincial and municipal records, up to the governorship of Theodorus, that is, up to the year before last, on the 22nd of December. On that day the clergy and the *seniores* who were under the bishop Rogatus (who had been summoned to Assuras in place of the condemned Praetextus) recalled the order of the former governor...

That the *seniores* did in fact represent an institution set in counterpoise to the bishop and clergy and that, as a council, they had the power to resist these officials on their own accord is further revealed by an incident from 407 involving the elders of a rural hamlet. The precise reasons for the dispute are unknown. The incident is only preserved as part of the canons of the African Church, a collection of documents assembled about 419 that often contains excerpts from proceedings and rulings of earlier councils. At the council held at Carthage on 13 June 407, a bishop of Madauros, Placentius, acting in a representative capacity for the African inhabitants (*legatus... Numidarum*) of a village called Nova Germania, read out a charge levelled by the *seniores* of this small village against Maurentius, the bishop of Thubursicu Numidarum.[42] Nova Germania seems to have been a hamlet close to Thubursicu Numidarum, which was under Maurentius' jurisdiction. In spite of a second and third attempt to summon them, the *seniores* could not be made to come to Carthage to place their charges against Maurentius in person.[43] Maurentius then

---

[38] For the Council of Bagaï, see MAIER, *op. cit.*, p. 36-37, with full sources. It is difficult to see the basis for Frend's contention (*The Donatist Church*, p. 216 f.) that the bishops attending the conference were Numidian-Mauretanian as opposed to the proconsular-Tripolitanian bias of the Cabarsussa Conference. Many, like Maier, assume *a priori* that all the bishops at Cabarsussa were Maximianists and identify them as such. But only 16 bishops (of the 310 present) are named. Of these, the origin of 10 is not known, 3 can be identified as from *Africa*, 3 from *Numidia*. Six of the 10 were also at Cabarsussa.
[39] FREND, *The Donatist Church*, p. 219. Cf. esp. AUG., *Contra Cresc.*, 4.4.4 (*PL*, 43, 549 = *Oeuvres*, sér. 4, t. 4, 470-73 = *SEL*, 52, 501-03, ed. PETSCHENIG).
[40] AUG., *Contra Cresc.*, 3.46.62 (*PL*, 43, 529 = *Oeuvres*, sér. 4, t. 4, 396-97 = *CSEL* 52.2 (1909) 467-68, ed. M. PETSCHENIG).
[41] AUG., *Contra Cresc.*, 3.56.62 (*PL*, 43, 530-31 = *Oeuvres*, sér. 4, t. 4, 398-99 = *CSEL* 52.2 (1909) 468-69, ed. M. PETSCHENIG). The passage finishes with, *cum a foris erant a communione vestra et eiusdem communionis vestrae inimici in iudicis publicis arguebantur et expellendi de locis Deo summo consecratis tamquam sacrilegi petebantur*, showing again the tension between courts within the Church and recourse to the public courts outside it.
[42] *Cod. can.*, 100 (*De suggestione Maurentii episcopi*) = *Concilia Africae*, a. 345- a. 525, *CCL*, 149 (1974) 217 (ed. C. MUNIER).
[43] I accept the reading Nova Germania rather than Munier's odd Nova Germaniensis (A.D. 484), see J. MESNAGE, *L'Afrique chrétienne. Évêchés et ruines antiques...*, Paris, Leroux, 1912, p. 426, and MAIER, *op. cit.*, p. 181. So too, I retain the reading Xantippus rather than Maier's Sanctippus. Xantippus was probably from Taoura, *Thagora municipium*, see AUG., *Exp.*, 59.1-2. Nova Germania was probably situated in the valley of W. Tifesh, roughly midway between *Thubursicu Numidarum* (Khamissa) and *Madauros* (M'daurush).

demanded that the council should not judge him in the absence of his accusors and that, as the innocent party, he should be given the benefit of the doubt. In order to preserve ecclesiastical custom and procedure in the matter, however, the council decided that a letter should be sent to Xantippus, the Primate (*senex*) of Numidia, to let him know that the council was appointing judges (*iudices*) who were to go to Thubursicu to hold court on the dispute. Maurentius was permitted to select some of the men who were to sit on the *concilium*. Xantippus was to see that the remaining judges required to fill out the number needed to form the *concilium* were to be chosen from the *seniores* of Nova Germania.

The power and influence wielded by the elders of Nova Germania is manifest. They were able to initiate charges against the bishop of a rather important nearby town and make certain that their complaints were voiced at a council of the whole Church through the medium of the bishop of another nearby centre, Madauros. The local bishop, Maurentius, despite his power and presence among an assembly of his peers, was able to achieve no more than a selection of peers as half the number of judges who would be assessing his case. More importantly, the elders chose not to make the journey to Carthage, despite having been requested to do so three times by the Church hierarchy. The principal reasons for their hesitation would seem to be obvious. Elders who were part of these small, face-to-face village communities would be very reluctant to leave their self-enclosed world, to undertake an arduous journey to a strange city in order to face a conference on foreign territory and a large assembly of men who were of a status quite unlike their own. Although the *seniores* persistently refused to budge from their village, the council could not ignore them. Instead, it decided to hold the hearing at Thubursicu Numidarum, Maurentius' see, where the elders could easily attend. Beyond this, the inclusion of the *seniores* as the jurors on the panel of *iudices* sitting in judgement on Maurentius clearly shows that Catholic Church councils recognized the elders' competence and right to assume such juridical functions. Indeed, in this particular case, the bishops assembled at Carthage seem to have taken extraordinary measures to ensure that the elders of a rather insignificant hamlet near Thubursicu would be included as members of the *iudicium*.

Indeed, in reference to elders in the Church at Hippo Regius, Augustine suggests that *seniores* were representatives of the people who had emerged as natural leaders because of their manifest qualification for this role in the eyes of the congregation.[44] In one particular incident, the Christian people at Hippo (*plebs*, *populus* in the account) had been moved to uproar over their demand that Pinianus, husband of the wealthy lady Melania (who owned vast estates near Thagaste), be appointed to the rank of priest (*presbyter*). But Pinianus had extracted a promise from Augustine that he would *not* make the appointment. As the crowd became more violent and assertive, Augustine met with the notable and venerable men from among them in the apse of the church where they held an impromptu conference over the issues at stake (*Dicebam ego quibus poteram, qui ad nos in absidem honoratiores et graviores ascenderant*). Their power manifestly derived from their *honestas* and *gravitas*, that is, from non-official "charismatic" qualities. The issue was simple: Pinianus, as a wealthy man, would be a valuable catch for the *plebs* who liked to exploit ecclesiastical office as a method of enrolling patrons. Augustine characteristically reports that he was not to be moved from his promise to Pinianus. For their part, the *plebs* massed on the steps of the basilica and roared their disapproval to the elders who were consulting with Augustine in the apse. Thus the delicate negotiations were carried on by the representatives of the *plebs* who were most anxious to see that Pinianus did not escape their clutches.

If the structural position of the elders is considered in the three different contexts we have just studied — in the hamlet or village (Abthugni, Municipium Commodianum), in the city (Cirta, Hippo Regius), and in the metropolis and capital city (Carthage) — the gradations and variations in their authority and power that one would expect from the concomitant level of development of other ecclesiastical institutions in these same urban settings is clearly perceptible. In the commonest and most widespread urban milieu, that of the village, the elders retain a very high level of authority and power with respect to the local bishop and priest. In the setting of the larger town or city, where the external ecclesiastical hierarchy was much better established, the elders retain a respectable position, but their power is noticeably attenuated. If the situation at Hippo under Augustine could be judged as "normal", then the elders certainly had to be consulted, but the bishop and other church officials were definitely in a superior formal position. The relationship between the two appears to have been a "negotiated one". Finally, the situation at Carthage

---

[44] AUG., *Ep.*, 126; cf. P. BROWN, *Augustine of Hippo: A Biography*, London, Faber & Faber, 1967, p. 197; events as in A.D. 411. And F. VAN DER MEER, *Augustine the Bishop*, transl. B. Battershaw & G.R. Lamb, London, Sheed & Ward, 1961 1978, pp. 140-48.

at the extreme end of the spectrum, seems to be the most abnormal for Africa. Being a large Mediterranean metropolis and by far the largest city in Africa (indeed, unique in size and administrative importance), Carthage more readily reflects the "orthodox" structure of the non-African world. But size and importance alone would almost have guaranteed that the principal ecclesiastical centre of the whole region would reveal a clear dominance of the formal and orthodox structures of the Church. And this does indeed appear to be the case. Although "elders" do appear as a part of the Church in Carthage, their authority is severely diminished and they appear not to be a significant part of the church structure. Even by the time of our earliest sources (Tertullian, the *Passio Perpetua et Felicitas*), the *seniores* at Carthage never had the authority, power, or position they did elsewhere in Africa. Their position appears even further diminished by the fourth century, only suddenly to increase in power and importance (as in the case of the *seniores* at Cirta) in times of extreme trouble and stress. This observation should only warn us to be aware of the obvious — that the relationship between the various elements of local and external authority in the ecclesiastical hierarchy was bound to be exceptional at Carthage (and other very large urban centres), and therefore the Carthaginian situation cannot be taken to mirror accurately the general truth for the vast regions of the African countryside.

Thus, the *seniores* formed a well defined body within Christian communities in Africa, whether in towns and cities such as Carthage and Cirta, medium-sized villages like Assuras or Mustis, or hamlets like Nova Germania. In all cases, they were the direct representatives of the *plebs* or *populus* out of whom they had emerged as informal leaders. The influence and patronage that they controlled meant that the elders had power to be reckoned with in the secular affairs of local churches. This residual or potential power vested in the elders became especially apparent in internal conflicts or during the absence of the bishop. From the cumulative evidence, the position of the elders within the local church hierarchy might be represented schematically (see fig. 1). The *seniores* and people can thus be seen as one half of a dichotomy which divided the structure of the local church in which the bishop and clergy were balanced against a council of elders who acted as a check on the power of the clergy. In fact, it seems as though the *plebs* and *seniores* represent a natural local unit on which the ecclesiastical hierarchy has been juxtaposed, or better, superimposed. This does not mean that there was no upward mobility from the *plebs* to the minor ranks of the clergy (recall that Victor at Cirta was both *lector* and *senior*), or that there was no continuous contact between all three elements of the church (the clergy, elders and people) in everyday affairs. It merely suggests that the two systems were structurally different and distinct. One might also note that as opposed to the strict hierarchy of the clergy there is no internal structural differentiation of the elders. Hence the "informal" and "official" elements are opposed: it would be very unusual to find a man who was at once an elder *and* the holder of a high office in the clergy.

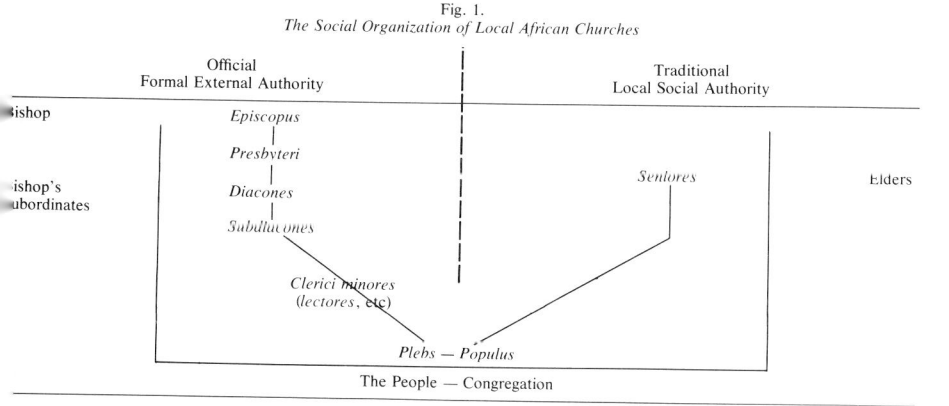

Fig. 1.
The Social Organization of Local African Churches

	Official Formal External Authority		Traditional Local Social Authority	
Bishop	*Episcopus*			
	Presbyteri		*Seniores*	Elders
Bishop's subordinates	*Diacones*			
	Subdiacones			
	Clerici minores (*lectores*, etc)			
		Plebs — Populus		
		The People — Congregation		

How did the peculiar situation arise in Africa? There are, in fact, simple historical reasons rooted in the sociology of rural villages and the subsequent appearance of Christianity, that is the Church, in them.

Traditional village society and its administration was functionally divided into the local leadership based on "non-official", customary procedure and the general populace or *plebs* from which the leadership emerged. This social system continued to function in the countryside of North Africa, but with the advent of Christianity these communities donned a new framework within which all social relationships within the village took place. The Christianization of the countryside did not require structural changes in the indigenous institutions, but rather a reorientation or transformation of them within the context of the Christian Church. What, in concrete terms, did this reorientation mean? The coming of Christianity signalled not only a change in individual religious values, but also the arrival of a totally new corporate institution within which that religious life was to function — the Church. Yet, in these small, inwardly-directed communities were personal relationships and interdependence were already determined by traditional patterns, the conversion of individuals merely legitimized established social institutions and only meant that the institution became "Christian" as its membership adopted the new faith. The metamorphosis cut both ways: the Church succeeded in Christianizing pre-existing village hierarchy, but the village was unlikely radically to alter its structure upon the Christianization of its members. The "Christian" elders (*seniores*) would tend to maintain their previous relationship with respect to the "Christian" commoners (*plebs, populus*). The old patterns of social relationships were in no way to be broken by the advent of the new faith. This situation posed considerable problems for the functioning of the Church in Africa — whether Catholic or African ("Donatist").

With the introduction of an externally developed hierarchy into the village society, conflict within the local system was always a potential threat. More often than not, however, some sort of *modus vivendi* would emerge between the two systems — after all, the people involved on both sides did have a common faith. The local bishop would tend to take account of the Christianized village hierarchy (the *seniores*) and the elders would *not* invariably see the bishop as their antagonist, but rather the spiritual leader of the community. Cooperation and mutual consultation would have been the usual relationship between clergy and elders. But the structural split within the Christian community still persisted and it could always be expressed in terms of hostility, especially in situations where the bishop ignored the elders or where the two sides drifted apart, for example, in internal disputes or under external pressure of persecution. The Christianized traditional power structure of the village could not simply be ignored, so the *seniores* had to be integrated into the structure of the local church. But not being fully part of the ecclesiastical hierarchy, or even capable of being fully integrated into it, the elders always represented a potential alternative source of power, a potential threat to the local bishop who had to deal with them. The traditional interdependence and close ties between *seniores* and the *plebs* in secular matters would have remained much the same as before. The bishop, on the other hand, being either an outsider or a man who was effectively isolated from local village society by the very fact that he occupied a position which was not encompassed by traditional social institutions, would be compelled to come to terms with the leaders of the local society, the elders. Hence the *seniores* presented an ambiguous and well nigh insoluble problem for the African Church. There was no real place for them within its structure and yet they could not be ignored; they were apart but had to be included.

In this context we may now understand the formulaic sense of addresses such as "*clero, senioribus et plebi*" (or some such phrase). The inclusion of the *elders* gives no real clue to their status. They are included because some recognition must be made of their *de facto* importance in the Church even though they were not part of the official structure of the clergy as developed by Mediterranean orthodoxy that is, bishops, priests, deacons, subdeacons, etc. Since the elders were an integral part of the local village society, both diachronically and socially, in a way in which the bishop and his subordinates were not they continued to exercise very real powers which could not be overridden by the bishop. Thus, if a dispute involving the official clergy arose, there was an alternative power structure in the village *within the Christian community* to which an outsider could appeal or which he could exploit. Since the elders did represent a local continuity with the past and were closely enmeshed in the social structure of the village their powers in the temporal affairs of the church were probably more effective than those of the bishop in many instances. The conciliar nature and powers of the *seniores* were of course clearly recognized by the bishop. For example, in a piece of exegetical writing designed to explain to his African audience a passage from the Book of Leviticus concerning the *senatus Israhel*, Augustine was careful to explain the phrase "*senatus Israhel*" in terms which the Africans would comprehend, that is as a group of *seniores* though he cautions against the normal interpretation which some would put on *senatus* as an *ordo seniorum*

That indeed would be the conclusion which many Africans who heard the words would reach based on their own experience.[45]

But it is possible to be more specific about the conciliar character of the *seniores*. Most African hamlets and villages (generally designated by the appropriate but bland term *"locus"* or simply "place") were so small and their social horizons so limited that the same circle of "more powerful" men would fill all positions of a hierarchical nature in the local society. In the mean world of these isolated rural settlements, "big men" would be distinguished by the narrowest of margins: a few more cattle or sheep, a few more *iugera* of land, a bit more prestige or learning. Once these men became Christians, they would be the same men identified in our sources as the *seniores* within the small Christian communities. There would be no juxtaposition of separate bodies of *seniores* within the Church and as part of the village administration; the two functions would be filled by the same group of men. Indeed, no such overlap is attested in any instance; in all villages where *seniores* are known to have existed as village administrators (*i.e.* from the epigraphical data), no parallel and *separate* body of Christian elders is ever attested. The one institution simply continued to function as before, only now in a Christian milieu. In the larger towns and villages, of course, there might exist a separate Roman government (Carthage to cite an extreme example; Mustis, Abthungi, Hippo Regius, and Cirta would be others). In these cases, "Christian" elders would be limited to the Christian community. Even so, their existence in towns which possessed Roman municipal governments reveals the tendency for African society to create "subofficial" levels of leadership along traditional lines. Even in towns with a long history of municipal institutions, there is the same propensity to throw up small distinct "district" or village "quarter" councils. Note at Cirta, long a city of Roman colonial status, the names of the *seniores*: Ianuarius, Meraclus (Punic), Saturninus and Victor. By nomenclature alone these men can be identified as derived from those levels of society within a "Roman" town where village and ethnic traditions persisted and flourished again at the first opportunity. The Church, as a corporate organization, offered the ideal milieu in which traditional institutions could be resurrected and legitimized.

External civil authorities, when dealing with Roman municipalities, had a regular and definite alternative to village elders, that is to say the local Roman *ordo*. But when it came to forming links and communicating official action to the mass of villages and hamlets in the countryside, they had to deal with the ordinary institutional governments of these communities, usually councils of elders. That they would also happen to be Christian was beside the point. A number of edicts issued in connection with the great Council of Carthage in 411 illustrate this process. The first is an order issued by the commissioner Flavius Marcellinus who had been appointed by Honorius to preside over the great conference of African and Catholic bishops.[46] The edict was issued at Carthage on 19 January 411:[47]

> *Et quoniam libenter assensum tribuit clementia principalis et concilium fieri intra Africam universale decrevit, utriusque partis iuxta poscentibus episcopis, huic me disputationi principis loco iudicem voluit residere.*
>
> *Unde cunctos per Africam tam catholicae quam donatianae partis episcopos huius edicti tenore commoneo ut intra tempus lege praescriptum, id est, intra quattuor menses, qui dies intra diem kalendarum Iunarium sine dubio concludetur, ad civitatem splendidam Carthaginiensem concilii faciendi gratia convenire non differant, ne eam partem de merito propriae fidei appareat iudicasse quam defuisse constiterit. Universos etiam cunctarum provinciarum curatores, magistratus et ordinis viros, necnon et actores, procuratores, vel seniores singulorum locorum pari admonitione convenio, sub propriae existimationis dignitatis reatu salutisque periculo, quatenus in civitatibus locisque in quibus consistunt utriusque partis episcopos convenire, vel sub gestorum confectione vel sub cuiuslibet scripturae, documento exstante, festinent; ita ut, si ipso in tempore in civitatibus non potuerint inveniri, per rura etiam perquisitis tam imperialis praecepti forma quam tenor huius innotescat edicti, quatenus intra hos quattuor menses ordinum relatione cognoscam singularum partium voluntatem.*

---

[45] AUG., *Quaest. in Hept.* (Lib. III, Quaest. Leyldel) 3.23 (*PL*, 34, 686 = *CCL*, 33, 192 = *CSEL* 28.2 (1895) 256 57, ed. I. ZYCHA), A.D. 419.
Quem quidam nostri "senatum" interpretati sunt, γερουσίαν *graecus habet; hoc est ergo secutus interpres, quia et senatus a senio videtur dictus. Non autem apte in latino diceretur: vocavit senectutem Israhel pro senibus vel senioribus. Quamvis eadem locutio esset, si diceretur: vocavit iuventutem Israhel pro iuvenibus. Sed hoc usitatum est in lingua latina, illud autem non est. Non hoc proprie diceretur, si diceretur: vocavit senectutem Israhel. Unde quidam insolenter putantes etiam 'senatum' dici interpretati sunt 'ordinem seniorum'. Conpendio tamen forsitan melius diceretur: vocavit seniores Israhel.*
Leviticus 9.1 as Augustine read it: *Et factum est die octavo vocavit Moyses, Aaron et filios eius et senatum Israhel*, though the *Vulgate* reads, *Facto autem octavo die vocavit Moses, Aaron et filios eius ac maiores natu Israhel.*

[46] For the Conference of Carthage, A.D. 411, see MAIER, *op. cit.*, p. 44-63, with full references. On the person of Flavius Marcellinus, see LANCEL, *op. cit.*, no. 45, p. 61-65: "Le juge Marcellinus", where he contests FREND's view, *The Donatist Church*, p. 273-75, that he was either a "Count" or indeed a close associate of Augustine's.

[47] *Gesta Conlationis Carthaginiensis, anno 411* (ed. S. LANCEL, *CCL* 149a (1974) I.5.56-57 (= *PL*, 11, 1262).

The passage has been quoted at length so that the full context and extent of the *notarius*' order can be easily perceived. It is also important to note the very close similarity between the terminology employed by the official of the Roman government in this document and a partisan Catholic decree issued over seven years earlier. This was the demand for a council issued by the Catholic party at their Conference of Carthage held on 24 August 403 and presided over by Aurelius, the Catholic bishop of Carthage and Primate of Africa:[48]

> *Aurelius episcopus dixit: Quod in tractatum venit caritatis vestrae, puto hoc ecclesiasticis gestis esse firmandum. Professio enim vestra omnium hoc deprompsit, debere unumquemque nostrum in civitate sua per se convenire Donatistarum praepositos, aut adiungere sibi vicinum collegam, ut pariter eos in singulis quibusque civitatibus vel locis per magistratus vel seniores locorum conveniant. Hoc si omnibus placet, educatur.*

The similarity in phraseology would seem to indicate that Marcellinus modelled his edict on his earlier Catholic decree and that it was not quite the impartial official document it has been made out to be. After the completion of the Great Conference, on 26 June 411, in his official *sententia cognitionis* against the African Christians, Marcellinus issued the following decree in favour of the Catholic Church:[49]

> *Unde universos ordinis viros, dominos etiam fundorum, actores, conductores tam domus divinae quam etiam privatarum possessionum, senioresque omnium locorum, huius edicti auctoritate commoneo quatenus memores legum, dignitatum, aestimationis salutisque propriae, donatistarum conventicula in omnibus civitatibus et locis prohibere contendant, ita ut ecclesias quas eis humanitate mea absque imperiali praecepto usque ad diem sententiae constat indultas Catholicis tradere sine ullo dilatione festinent, ni malunt tot sanctionum laqueis irretiri: quas quidem, si unitati catholicae consentire voluerint, eorum esse sat certum est.*

It is abundantly clear from the very format of these three decrees that the officials called upon to implement their terms are listed in order of their official rank. First are the city and town officers. The *curatores* are the *curatores rei publicae* who at this time held supreme jurisdiction over many municipalities and were empowered to directly implement decrees and edicts of this type (compare the actions of the *curator* Magnilianus, above, p. 210). In municipalities where *curatores* were not present, the *duumviri*, the chief magistrates, and the decurions were held responsible (*magistratus et universi ordinis viri*). Then follow the rural regions administered under the aegis of the great landed domains. The landlords of great private estates (*domini fundorum*) or, if they were not present, the managers of *both* private and imperial domains (*actores, procuratores*; *conductores tam domus divinae quam etiam privatarum possessionum*) were to enforce the terms of edict.[50] These officials effectively covered all autonomous urban communities and all the rural regions which could be reached through the control exercised by landlords or their agents. This still left the majority of villages and hamlets which had no formal Roman *ordines* and not coming under any domanial administration. In the edict these are the numerous *castella, vici, oppida* and *civitates* which only merit the general appeliation of *loci*. For all these settlements *seniores* were held responsible (designated *seniores singulorum/omnium locorum*). Thus, although the *seniores* are last on the official lists of 411, they were the most common form of government found in the myriad hamlets and villages which lay beyond the compass of the great landowners and the sphere of towns which had adopted Roman municipal governments. At the very base of an ascending pyramid of types of governmental administrations the elders were probably the most common sort of polity found in the rural regions of Africa. Here is the very nexus of indigenous village administration in Africa, the lowest common denominator, upon which all other levels and types of government were superimposed. Although these edicts treat the *seniores* as a secular administrative body, there can be little doubt that they were Christian as well. Once this premise is accepted, it seems improbable that they would be distinguishable from the Christian *seniores* who were also the "big men" in the local village church.

---

[48] Catholic Conference of Carthage, A.D. 403; see MAIER, *op. cit.*, p. 41, with references. *Cod. can.*, 91 (*Concilia Africae CCL*, 249 (1974) 210, ed. C. MUNIER = J.D. MANSI, *Sacrorum conciliorum nova et amplissima collectio*, Florence, 1759, III. p. 791 = H.T. BRUNS, *Canones Apostolorum et Conciliorum veterum selecti*, Berlin, 1839, I. 180). Cf. *Cod. can.*, 93 (*CCL*, 249, 210: *Notitia de concilio Carthaginiensi*, 16 Iunii 404):
Quale commonitorium acceperunt legati contra Donatistas... Litterae enim ad iudices mittendae sunt, ut donec Dominus legatos nos redire permittat, tuitonem per ordines civitatem et possessores praediorum ecclesiae catholicae impertiant. (Issued again under Aurelius' aegis; cf. J.P. BRISSON, *Autonomisme et Christianisme dans l'Afrique romaine de Septime-Sévère à l'invasion vandale*, Paris, E. de Boccard, 1958, p. 270.)

[49] *Edictum cognitoris* (*PL*, 11, 1419 = *CCL* 249, 1974, 178).

[50] For the position of *actores*, see *DE*, 1, 1895, p. 66-70, *s.v.* "actor" and P. HABEL, 'Actores (2)', *RE*, 1, 1894, p. 329-30. They were roughly equivalent to *vilici* or *procuratores* (in the case of imperial estates). The *seniores* were held responsible for seeing that the great number of bishops from the rural regions would be present. On rural bishoprics in general, see S. LANCEL *Actes de la Conférence de Carthage en 411*, Paris, Éditions du Cerf, 1972 (= *SC*, 194), I, p. 134-43, and R.A. MARKUS, "Christian Bishops in Byzantine Africa," chap. 1 (in) D. BAKER, ed., *The Church in Town and Countryside*, Oxford, Blackwell, 1979, p. 1-15.

Unfortunately, little can be said about the internal structure or definition of the elders in Christian Africa, except that, as in the secular context, they do not display any internal differentiation as compared to the official Church hierarchy. It can only be assumed that the elders emerged from the *plebs*/*populus* on much the same basis as they had in pre-Christian times. Such a view supposes the simple continuation of the old customary, traditional elements of marginal wealth, charisma, kinship ties, patronage, and other such criteria. It has been claimed that an electoral system analogous to the municipal system existed for the Christian *seniores*. This view is based on a funerary inscription from the hinterland of Hippo Regius (modern Annāba):[51]

D.M.S. / (crux magna in circulo) / Maritis (?) senator de nu/mera (sic) bis elect(or)um fide/lis visit in pace ann(is) LX / quiebit sub d(iebus) non(orum) Au/[gus(ti) ind(ictione) t(emporis) C(aesarum) XV

The inscription, dating to the early decades of the sixth century, does not appear to say anything of the sort. Not even the man's name is certain, much less the significance of "*Senator*". So too the sense of the *electi* of which Maritis (?) was a member might suggest some sort of religious community, through not necessarily even Christian.[52] That the "elders" were opposed to the "youth" among the *plebs*, as may be inferred from a passage in Augustine, and may also be suggested by the evidence of a triple burial at the town of Putput (modern Sūq al-Abiod), though it seems more probable that the latter is merely a family group in which "seniors" are distinguished from "juniors"[53] But the existence of *senior* as a title is attested in the Church at Carthage.[54] Thus, although the position of *senior* may have carried a title of respect, that is to say the congregation clearly gave recognition to who was an elder and who was not, there are no indications that it was even an elective post analogous to Roman municipal *honores*.

The functional role of the elders within the Church in Africa highlights the continuity in structure and social fabric of the strands in the society which gave rise to the institution of the secular elders. The functional norms of African society which determined the conservative make-up of the *seniores* (with emphasis, as their title suggests, on respect for age) were so powerful that they permeated the whole formal structure of the Church. One example of this conservatism and the way in which it affected the official ranks of the Church is reflected in the African practice followed in the appointment of primates in each of the ecclesiastical provinces. It was normal practice outside Africa to appoint the bishop who had earned his way to the top; that is, the man who held the position of bishop in the capital city of each province since the see in the metropolis was considered to be the highest in rank. In Africa only the ecclesiastical province of "Africa" with its metropolis at Carthage followed this rule. All the other ecclesiastical provinces allowed an unusual practice not paralleled or condoned in the Church elsewhere in the Mediterranean. In this local system, followed by *both* the African and Catholic churches in Africa, the bishops were ranked according to a system of seniority based on the date of their consecration. In Christian terms, the "elder" bishop according to this criterion was appointed primate and styled himself *senex*, literally "the old man". From the letters of Gregory the Great, we know that this practice, though officially condemned by the Church, was still in force in the very last years of the sixth century and, in all probability, remained in

---

[51] *ILAlg* I, 82 (new reading: cf. C. 17414 = *ILCV* 495 = *Eph. epigr.* vii, 329, Mokta al-Hadid); A. PAPIER, "Sur dix-huit inscriptions nouvelles communiquées à l'Académie d'Hippone", *BAH*, 21, 1886, p. 81-112, p. 88-90, no. 10. If the interpretation of the fifteenth *indictio* is correct, the date should be the 520s or 530s (i.e., 522 37). On the rank of "*senator*" in the Church, see JEROME, *Contra Iohannem Hierosolymitanum*, 19 (PL, 23, 370); EUCHER., *Pass St. Maur.* (PL, 50, 829); *Nov. Theod.* 21.1; *CIL* iii, 14188 and *ILS* 8883; *Notiz. Scav.* (1890) 170; with HIRSCHFELD in *SPAW* (1893) p. 432, no. 2. Mentions of a *numerus electorum* at Thamugadi and Caesarea are very much earlier in date, see USELL, *BCTH* (1901), p. 313.

[52] His name may be Maritus (*C.* 22740, Gigthis; 22783, Sidi bu-Babas, near Gabès) or Martialis, an extremely common name in Africa, see *CIL* viii, *indices*, p. 99. On *electi* in African Manichaeism, see F. DECRET, "Aspects du Manichéisme dans l'Afrique romaine" (in) *Études Augustiniennes*, Paris, CNRS, 1970, p. 58, no. 5. *Electi*, however, were also found in the conceptual framework of "normal" Christian communities. I reject out of hand the interpretation of *numerus electorum* as a military unit.

[53] *ILTun.* 1702 (Tabarqa, anc. *Thabraca*): see Capt. BENET, "Les fouilles de Tabarka en 1904", *BCTH* (1905) 378-94, no. 16; P. GAUCKLER, *BSAF* (1905) 246; *Quod dev(s)/Senior i/n pace si / sero sed cu/m domino*. *CIL* viii, 24097 = *ILCV* 385, cf. P. GAUCKLER, *BCTH* (1901) 146-47, no. 77 (*Putput*, Sūq al-Abiod): *Nardus senior, / Turassus iunior, / Restitutus iunior / recessit pridie Idus / Maias, fideles in pace.* Cf. AUG., *De nat. et orig. animae*, 2.5.9 (*CSEL* 60, 1913, 342-43, ed. C. F. URBA & I. ZYCHA), AD 415, which mentions *seniores* and *iuniores* in the Christian community, but only in a general sense; cf. E. ARMANI, "L'uso di 'senior' e 'iunior' nelle iscrizioni" *RAL* 31, 1976, p. 9-34.

[54] *CIL* viii, 25040 = *ILCV* 384, cf. P. GAUCKLER, *BCTH* (1897) 447, no. 295 (Carthage): *Flavius / Valens, senior / sodalici memo/ria hac fecit / sic semper / A ☧ Ω.*

use until the Islamization of North Africa.[55] Until the last years of Roman domination in Africa, the primacy of age was thus the decisive factor in the appointment of officers of the Church at the very pinnacle of its hierarchy.[56]

So engrained was the concept and practice of rule by councils of elders, in both sacred and secular contexts, that we should not be surprised at their continuity. But the persistence of the elders within the framework of the Church was a truly remarkable phenomenon, as an epitaph discovered at Qairwân was to reveal:[57]

> In no(mine) d(omi)ni. In hoc [tumulo iacet cor]pus Pe[t]ri senioris [qui vixit annos---] et qui[ev]it die sabb(atorum) i[n anno VI millmo D] XXXXIII ind(ictione) cou[arta]

The text of this stone (and another like it from Qairwân) was at first misinterpreted by Gauckler and Monceaux who believed it to be of Byzantine date. Subsequent analysis, however, points to a date in the *mid-eleventh century*: to be precise, 1050-1051.[58] The *senior* Peter at Qairwân attests the presence of a Christian community in the capital city established by Sidi Oqba in A.D. 670 and regarded as forbidden to infidels. Whether this community was monastic (Saumagne) or a regular church (Seston) is not possible to answer from the bare record of the inscription alone. A contemporary epitaph (A.D. 1048) from Qairwân, however, marked the grave of a Sisinnus, son of Firmus, the *lector*.[59] Though both *seniores* and *lectores* were present in monastic communities in Africa during the Romano-Byzantine period, examples are very rare and monasticism was never so highly developed in Africa as to make probable its survival four centuries after the fall of the Byzantine hegemony south of the Mediterranean. Is it not, rather, the continuity of a formidable and basic institution of African society in a Christian *context* even in the last years of its existence? If so, our metaphoric "deep sea diver" has discovered at least one social life form that can be traced over a millennium and more of African and Roman culture in the Maghrib. It was, however, one that was to lose much of its religious power and meaning with the advent of Islam, a religion lacking the formal external structure that could absorb and incorporate the local political authority of village elders. The *shaykh* and the *shiyukh* returned, once again, to the secular world of their distant pre-Christian ancestors.

---

[55] In their general surveys of the period, neither W. SESTON, "Sur les derniers temps du Christianisme en Afrique", *MEFR*, 53, 1936, p. 101-24, nor R. A. MARKUS, "Donatism: the Last Phase", in *Studies in Church History*, ed. C.W. DUGMORE & C. DUGGAN vol. 1, 1964, p. 118-26, emphasize this peculiarity. Yet it is specifically attested in the letters of Gregory the Great, *e.g. Epp.* 72 and 75 (AD 591, *MGHepist*, 1, 1887, 92-93, 95). For the Catholic Primate of Numidia as *senex*, see note 42 above.

[56] For an earlier example, see the testimony of Crescentianus in the *Gesta apud Zenophilum* which refers to the bishop of Cirta as *senex*, *CSEL* 26 (1893) 196.

[57] *CIL* viii, 23128a = *ILTun* 269a. See SESTON, *art. cit.*, p. 106 f, pl. 1, fig. 2; SAUMAGNE, *BCTH* (1930-1931) 164; L. POINSSOT & R. LANTIER, *Atti del III° Congresso internazionale di archeologia cristiana* (1932) 401 (Qairawân, AD 1050-51).

[58] P. MONCEAUX, *RA* (1903) 244-45, and P. GAUCKLER, *NAMS* 15 (1907) 359-60, no. 141, pl. IX.

[59] *ILTun* 271, cf. SAUMAGNE, *BCTH* (1928-1929) 371 and SESTON (1936) 110-11, fig. 3 (Qairawân, AD 1048).

XI

African Christianity: Disputes, Definitions, and 'Donatists'

> *Nobis hoc non salvum sit quod non debuimus reticere*
> It would not be good for us to pass this way in silence
> (Petilianus, African bishop of Cirta/Constantine: *GCC*, 1.167)

> Drama is anything you can get away with.
> (Abbie Hoffman, *Revolution for the Hell of It*)

The important texts for understanding the following essay are two. First of all, *Alice in Wonderland*. In that wonderful piece of childish profundity there is the following bit of repartee between a dubious young girl and a hashish-smoking Caterpillar: 'Who are you?,' said the Caterpillar. (This was not an encouraging opening for a conversation). Alice replied, rather shyly, 'I—I hardly know, Sir, just at present—at least I know who I was when I got up this morning, but I think I must have changed several times since then.' The Caterpillar persisted. 'You!,' said the Caterpillar contemptuously, 'Who are you?' Which brought them back to the beginning of the conversation. Alice...drew herself up and said, very gravely, 'I think you ought to tell me who you are, first.' The second text is from *Through the Looking-Glass*. This time a confrontation between the young girl and a rather large Egg. Exasperated after so much apparent prevarication on the part of the Egg, she objected: 'The question is,' said Alice, 'whether you can make words mean so many different things.' 'The answer is,' said Humpty Dumpty, 'which is to be master—that's all.' Identity and some old-fashioned nominalism. Power and drawing lines. Here you will stand. There you will not. Such problems were to confront Christians, with especial force, in the early decades of the fourth century. And, let's face it, there is probably no better way of finally settling a matter of difference than fighting it out. Face to face. Nothing like an old-fashioned standoff.

In the summer heat of the first day of June, in the year 411, in the center of Carthage, the magnificent metropolis of north Africa—a city second only to Rome itself in importance—two bitterly hostile groups of Christians met in precisely such a great confrontation finally to settle the differences between them.[1] To the heat of controversy was added the fact that the only public venue large enough to contain the numbers on either side were the monumental Baths of Gargilius (*Thermae Gargilianiae*).[2] So they met, hundreds of them from either party. Ranged on one side of the bath were about 285 'Catholic' bishops. Glaring at them from across the aisle were about the same number of 'Donatist' bishops. 'Catholics' and 'Donatists.' Thus Christians in north Africa had been divided ever since a minor crisis in the

---

[1] The primary source for this conference has received a masterful edition by Serge Lancel: *Actes de la Conférence de Carthage en 411, t. I: Introduction générale*, Paris, 1972 [= Sources chrétiennes, no. 194]; *t. II: Texte et traduction de la capitulation générale et des actes de la première séance*, Paris, 1972 [= Sources chrétiennes, no. 195]; *t. III: Texte et traduction de la deuxième et de la troisième séance*, Paris, 1975 [= Sources chrétiennes, no. 224]. These will be referred to as Lancel, *Actes*. The final edition by Serge Lancel, *Gesta Conlationis Carthaginiensis, anno 411; accedit Sancti Augustini Breviculus Conlationis cum Donatistis*, Turnhout, 1974 [= Corpus Christianorum, Series Latina, no. 149A] will be used to provide the basic in-text references to the proceedings [as *GCC*]. Alas, the version we have is not a direct and unmediated report. It is actually derived from a copy kept by one Marcellus (an otherwise unknown personality who held the rank of *memorialis*)—there are no blatant signs of any deliberate tampering with the MSS as he had it, with the obvious exception of the 'table of contents' with which he prefaced the whole (see Lancel, *Actes*, 1, 357-63, and n16 below). Important supplementary historical data, principally the writings of Augustine directly relevant to the Conference and its aftermath, will be cited from the edition of Emilien Lamirande, *Oeuvres de Saint Augustin, t. 32: ser. 4: Traités anti-Donatistes, 5: Breviculus Collationis cum Donatistis; Ad Donatistas post Collationem*, trans. G. Finaert, Bruges 1965 [= Lamirande, *Oeuvres de Saint Augustin*]; additional technical materials will be cited from J.R. Martindale, ed., *The Prosopography of the Later Roman Empire, 2: A.D. 395-527*, Cambridge, 1980 [= *PLRE*, 2]; and A. Mandouze, ed., *Prosopographie chrétienne du Bas-Empire, 1: Afrique (303-533)*, Paris, 1982 [= *PCBE*, 1].

[2] They have not been located at the modern site; cf. Augustine, *Breviculus Collationis*, 1.14, and *Ad Donatistas post Collationem*, 25.43 who places them *in urbe media*; cf. Lancel, *Actes*, 1, 50-53, reviews the literature.

election of a bishop at Carthage in 311/312 had careered vertiginously into a colossal battle over what Christianity was, and was not, to be.[3] In this conflict the 'Catholics' had been, in a sense, 'the winners' (or at least had the upper hand), supported, as they were, by all the power and might of the Roman state. The 'Donatists,' on the other hand, were portrayed as schismatics, a querulous faction of trouble-makers, disturbing the peace of the universal Church, deserving of brutal repression. The seizure of their basilicas, churches, and other material assets, and the driving of their priests and bishops from legitimate places, was justified in the name of establishing the 'true' or Catholic church.

The history of this north African Christianity, or 'Donatism' as it has consistently been called (by modern-day historians, who ought to know, and do, better) is especially bedevilled by being the history of a lost cause. There is also the manifest fact of the virtual disappearance of Christianity, of whatever type, from north Africa, and its replacement by Islam (again, of various types) from the mid-seventh century onward. The problems represented by 'Donatism,' however, were revived because of their living relevance during the period of the so-called European Reformation. The battle of an earlier form of rigorist Christianity against a 'corrupt' and 'authoritarian' Catholic Church, a conflict preserved in considerable detail in the early Christian records and writers, struck a responsive chord. So Protestant theologians and historians, especially, had a model and a subject to hand, and, in the latter half of the seventeenth century, poured forth numerous treatises on the subject. But historians should have their own agenda. They are called upon to understand a whole situation—not to exploit the past for present ideological purposes, not to accept existing labels simply for sake of convenience. This primary task of simple understanding and reportage, however banal and obvious its demands, has largely been abandoned by those whose specific duty it is.[4]

---

[3] As it was put in the Catholic *mandatum* of 30 May: the *ecclesia qualis nunc est* as opposed to the *ecclesia qualis futura est*. Other, very important, aspects of this conflict, such as the identification of the so-called *circumcelliones*, the attendant problems of social revolution, mass peasant mobilization, and the connection of these with 'millenarian' aspects of north African Christianity, cannot be dealt with within the scope of this paper (though I do hope to do so elsewhere).

[4] Take just two examples (others will be referred to as circumstances

8

An attendant problem that has much afflicted research is the simple fact that historians are lazy. In the existing records (as obviously biased as they are) 'those' people are called 'Donatists.' They are so-called, almost without exception, but then the record itself is, almost without exception, written by the 'winners.' So what else are *we* to call them but 'Donatists'? Even presuming that modern-day historians did expend some energy on behalf of impartiality, however, and correctly rejected the label 'Donatist' for these north African Christians, they would still run head on into the very ideological success and hegemonic domination of the labelling process itself.[5] For, if we are not to call them 'Donatists,' what then? After all, we, as historians, need a label for 'them.' They, as we shall see, just wanted to be called 'Christians,' but how are we to distinguish them from the Catholics who successfully swept the field of definitions? We cannot call them simply 'Christians' (as the Catholics also properly were) or negatively 'non-Catholics' (that rings, and is, false). What then? An arbitrary choice has to be made and defended, and my choice is to add the adjective 'African' to the noun 'Christian.' The defence is somewhat as follows. It is not that the Catholic Christians in north Africa were not also 'Africans.'

---

permit): the classic, and standard, history of north African Christianity by Paul Monceaux treats the conference in some detail: *Histoire littéraire de l'Afrique chrétienne depuis les origines jusqu'à l'invasion arabe*, vol. 4, *Le donatisme*, Paris, 1912, (reprint: Brussels, 1966), ch. 2.4, pp. 388-425, and is characterized by gross types of bias: the African Christians are constantly labelled 'Donatists' or 'les schismatiques' (repeatedly), and are marked by 'leur imprudence'; their declarations 'trahissent la mauvaise humeur, l'intention de se dérober par des faux-fuyants et des chicanes'; 'les schismatiques veulent le désordre,' 'l'on ne peut prendre au sérieux les motifs invoquées dans leur Notaria,' and so on. Similarly, Monceaux wholly buys into the Catholic view that what 'the Donatists' were doing at the conference was nothing but 'les obstructions,' 'une perpétuelle obstruction,' 'toute d'obstructions et de chicanes,' in which 'ils commettaient une grosse imprudence,' and their refusal to be seated can be grouped amongst 'les scruples bouffons des Donatistes' and can be judged to be 'un intermède héroï-comique.' The standard history in English by W.H.C. Frend (see fn. 7 below) does not do much better: the African Christians continue to be labelled as 'Donatists'

[5] It is, for example, somewhat depressing to see that an excellent historian like Robert Markus, whose own work has contributed directly to a clear understanding of the insidious nature of this labelling process, himself falls back on the convenient labels in subsequent work—R.A. Markus, *The End of Ancient Christianity*, Cambridge (1990) 51-53, 79, 85, 92-93, 148.

They were. But from the critical perspectives of power, perception and definition, the Catholics were, as their label suggested, less tied to African traditions and roots than were their opponents. If anything, the critical hallmark of the Christians who so bitterly opposed the Catholic intrusion into their lives was that of being local and derived from north African traditions to the exclusion of outside influences. It was the opposite characteristic that defined the Catholics—they ultimately anchored their legitimacy to a 'universal' orthodoxy. These differences were fundamental, despite the repeated claim that the dispute was 'amongst us Africans.'[6] The label 'African Christians,' therefore, though not exclusive to the so-called 'Donatists' is at least a more objective descriptor that distances the historian somewhat from the manifestly pejorative labels used at the time, and is a more neutral term, which one suspects the north African Christians of the time might have accepted as a reasonable, if somewhat bland, description of who they were.

The bitter conflicts the historian is called upon to understand, however, were not the result of any ill-health in African Christianity itself. In terms of wealth, numbers, power, size, and resources, the Church in north Africa represented one of the greater, if not greatest, parts of all western Christendom in the first three to four centuries after Christ. The earliest history of the spread of Christian belief and organization in the Maghrib is, however, a hidden book. When Christian churches first appear in our surviving written records, around AD 200, they are already fully developed communities. The courageous obstinacy of African martyrs from small towns like Scillium (in 180) and large ones like Carthage (Perpetua and others, in the years right after 200) attest a strong, multitudinous, and firmly entrenched Christian tradition. Voluminous writers like Tertullian (in the early 200s) and the actions of strong bishops like Cyprian of Carthage (at mid-century) gave African Christians a leading ideological role in western Mediterranean Christian communities of the period. Throughout the third century, African Christianity, so far as can be measured by any docu-

---

[6] E. Lamirande, *Oeuvres de Saint Augustin*, notes complémentaires, no. 12, "Le Donatisme, une affaire d'Africains," 703-04; at least, that is what Augustine reported of the African Christians' feelings on the matter: it was a *disputatio inter Afros* (*Breviculus Collationis*, 3.3.3).

mentation, went from strength to strength. The great problems of division and definition that were to afflict African Christians in the early to mid-decades of the fourth century were simply not of their own making. They were made by the emperor Constantine. The creation of a state-bound orthodoxy in 312/313 raised at a single stroke the problem of 'incorrect' views held by various brands of Christianity that had evolved in different regional and cultural contexts around the Mediterranean.

The final spate of official violence directed by the Roman State, and local non-Christian communities, against Christians (the so-called 'Great Persecution' of 303-05) had created certain internal problems of identification within the African church. When the persecution finally subsided, the critical question, the litmus test of acceptability, concerned the extent to which those who had collaborated with the forces of repression were to be reconciled following the return of official toleration. In north African Christianity a firm line had traditionally been drawn to exclude those who were being considered for church offices: bishops and those who consecrated them in office could not be 'traitors' (*traditores*) who bowed to the forces of persecution. That traditional stance had provoked battles here and there over assignment of positions of power, especially in 312-13 in the election to the most prestigious ecclesiastical position in Africa, the bishopric of Carthage. A substantial part, if not a majority, of bishops at that time refused to accept the ordination of a certain Caecilianus as bishop of Carthage on the grounds that he had been ordained by a 'traitor' (*traditor*). Instead they supported his opponent, Majorinus. On the latter's death they then consecrated a certain Donatus, a former bishop from the village of 'Dark Houses' (*Casae Nigrae*) in Numidia, as his successor. The incident, replete with the sordid machinations and violence usual to such ecclesiastical *affaires*, would have had little further meaning had it not become implicated in the emperor Constantine's drive for the institutionalization of a secular Mediterranean-wide Christian church, and the attendant push for ideological uniformity. In 313 an official commission under Miltiades, the bishop of Rome (therefore, one must believe, already committed to the government's position in the matter) decided for Caecilianus and against the supporters of Donatus.[7] After all, that was what was required, politically speaking, for the formation of a universal church. Reconciliation and consensus had to be the order of the day. The dubious actions of Christian leaders in the preceding period of state repression had to be overlooked—and for good reasons. The new hegemonic power of a central and unified church demanded agreement, hierarchical solidarity, and obedience. These needs provoked overpowering secular motives to institute a structural amnesia, and to side with the powers that be. In this case, that was rather easy. It was the Caecilianuses of this world that the new Church wanted, not ideological diversity and the open questioning of each authority's performance in the past. Judgment was given in favour of him and against the 'side of Donatus.'

New or restored authoritarian orders display a lamentable preference for old collaborators over the old resistance. The former may well be repellent creatures, but they have the sort of character (a tendency to support 'present realities') that any new régime finds more comfortable. Caecilianus was found to be in agreement with the new consensus, the 'right thinking' or orthodoxy established by the center. He was acceptable and in line with 'universal' (catholic) thinking on the matter. Those who opposed him, and, implicitly, the new secular powers of the central Church, were branded as the strange followers of a quirkish personal guru. No longer Christians, therefore, they found themselves labelled, almost overnight, as 'followers of Donatus' or 'Donatists.'[8] Over a five-year period, from 316-321, the Roman state moved with official coercion against the renegades. But even with the resources of

---

[7] For the details, see W.H.C. Frend, *The Donatist Church: A Movement of Protest in Roman North Africa*, Oxford, 1952 (reprint: 1971; rev. ed. 1983) [= *Donatist Church*], chs. 1 & 11; the whole 'dossier' of documents relating to the origins of the conflict, and its subsequent history, is now readily available in J.-C. Maier, *Le dossier du Donatisme*, Berlin, Akademie Verlag, 1987 (= *Texte und Untersuchungen zur Geschichte der Altchristlichen Literatur*, Bd. 134 & 135)

[8] To be technically accurate, and the fine point of detail is worth making, not quite 'overnight.' They were in fact at first labelled 'the party of Majorinus' or 'Majorians' after the first bishop put up in opposition to Caecilianus. It was only Majorinus' death (in the fall of 313?) and the longevity in a position of power of Donatus, his successor, which meant that the Africans came to be labelled 'Donatists' (as we know them today in all our books) rather than Majorians, or such. Which only serves to underscore the contingent nature of the label and the labelling process.

the state at its disposal, the new 'catholic' or 'orthodox' church that supported the faction of Caecilianus was not able to enforce any final claim over its legitimacy to be considered the Christian church in north Africa. The so-called 'Donatists' in fact represented the main-line of regional or local 'orthodoxy' within the north African tradition. In terms of simple belief and action they were nothing other than the continuous line of Christians and Christianity that had been the Church for centuries of the African past.[9] It must have been a most rude awakening to find themselves labelled, in effect, as non-Christian.

Disoriented and distressed, though naturally disinclined to accept such a situation, they could only be driven from it by the use of force and violence against them. That meant that by end of the fourth century African Christian communities, so-called 'Donatists,' had been largely driven by official persecution, by the use of violence, by confiscation of their goods and other such devices, from the major urban communities where the Catholic church could effectively draw upon the repressive instruments of power of the Roman state. In wide areas of the countryside outside those towns, however, where the mandate of the state could not be effectively enforced, African rather than Catholic Christianity retained its traditional strength.[10] African Chris-

---

[9] R.A. Markus, "Christianity and Dissent in Roman North Africa: Changing Perspectives in Recent Work," (in) D. Baker ed., *Schism, Heresy and Religious Protest = Studies in Church History* 9, Cambridge (1972) 21-36, at pp. 28-29: "Donatism was no new creation. It was the representative in the fourth century of an older African theological tradition with deep roots in its characteristic religious mentality...[therefore] it would be less misleading to speak of a 'catholic' than of a 'Donatist' schism...Donatism was, quite simply, the continuation of the old African Christian tradition in the post-Constantinian world. It was that world that had changed, not African Christianity." Markus credits the blind scholar Jean-Paul Brisson for these insights—see the latter's, *Autonomisme et christianisme dans l'Afrique romaine de Septime-Sévère à l'invasion vandale*, Paris, 1958, and critique by A. Mandouze, "Encore le Donatisme. Problèmes de méthode posés par la thèse de J.P. Brisson," *L'Antiquité classique* 29 (1960) 61-107.

[10] The work of Emin Tengström, *Donatisten und Katholiken: Soziale, wirtschaftliche und politische Aspekte einer nordafrikanischen Kirchenspaltung*, Göteborg, 1964, is largely responsable for 'inverting' the 'Frend thesis' (see Frend, *Donatist Church*, esp. chs. 3, 'Town and Country in Roman Africa,' and 4, 'The Geographical Distribution of Donatism'). Frend took the recorded 'Donatist' bishoprics, and their geographical distribution, to be proof of a 'nativistic' and rural (even Numidian) base and origin for the 'schism.' This now seems improbable.

tianity probably remained strong in the large cities too, but that strength remains hidden from our view by the systematic official/Catholic ability to remove the institutional supports of their opponents (e.g., basilicas, churches, seats for bishops, formal church organizations) and thereby the signs by which later historians might be able to recognize a 'Donatist' presence in any given town or city. One cannot underestimate violence as the core cause of the definitions that we see in the surviving records. Violence and force were fundamental. They were the very foundation of the later edifice of Christianity in north Africa.[11] If they had not been exercised, and, one must suspect, exercised with some success (especially in the urban foyers of Roman power), the peculiar 'remnant' distribution of 'Donatism' would not be there for us to read on our maps.

The labelling of an out-group as something odd and unacceptable was therefore at the heart of the historical process. Hence the paradox that 'Donatists' were artificially created by definitions issued by a central power and that 'they' never existed as such. And, simultaneously, that there were large numbers of humans who were treated as if they were 'Donatists' and who were made to live the sort of experiences that the definition demanded. Thus, the label 'Donatist' was systematically applied to north African Christians who continued to insist on the legitimacy and validity of their own beliefs, practices, and traditions. The label derogated from their legitimacy, as in almost all other such labelling processes—consider the various Carpocratians, Pelagians,

---

That distribution is actually the result of the African Christian churches being systematically expelled from the urban milieux where the Catholic Church was able to exert force against them. African Christianity, therefore, was Christianity in Africa till the beginning of the fourth century, and was every bit as 'urbane' and 'Latin' as 'Catholicism' was later to appear; see P.A. Février, "Toujours le Donatisme. A quand l'Afrique? Remarques sur l'Afrique à la fin de l'Antiquité. A propos du livre de E. Tengström," *Rivista di storia e letteratura religiosa* 2 (1966) 228-40

[11] The work of Peter Brown remains fundamental: "Religious Dissent in the Later Roman Empire: the Case of North Africa," *History* 46 (1961) 83-101 = *Religion and Society in the Age of Saint Augustine*, London (1972) 237-59; and, "St. Augustine's Attitude to Religious Coercion," *Journal of Roman Studies* 54 (1964) 107-16 = *Religion and Society in the Age of Saint Augustine*, London (1972) 260-78, wherein it is made clear that Augustine accepted as an 'unfortunate necessity' the use of 'persuasion' on the 'Donatists,' also accepting that this persuasion was of the bicycle-chain and lead-pipe variety.

14

Priscillianists, Maximianists, Rogatianists, Valentianists, Arians, and many other such 'personal followings' that marked the theological landscape of early Christianity. By suggesting that the beliefs and practices had no universal aura to them, that they were simply an aberration perpetrated by a solitary human individual to whom they could be attributed—in this case the bishop Donatus—centralist orthodoxy achieved its tactical goal of marginalizing the prey, usually before moving in for the kill. Donatus of *Casae Nigrae* is, in any event, such a shadowy figure that very little is known about him. Neither labelers nor adherents could agree on who he was (or how many of him there were).[12] But labeling is indeed the core of what was happening here. Who could make words, and the attendant concepts, mean what they meant? Who had the power to make those meanings stick? Obviously, Catholic orthodoxy wished to usurp the title of 'Christian' *tout court*, and to sweep the ideological field by allowing no competing claims to the name. What was at stake, however, was not just the fate of aberrant versions of Christianity in any particular social setting in the Mediterranean. It was, rather, a colossal battle over secular power. Who, finally, was to control all the local communities, their peoples, and their material resources, would be determined, to a large extent, by who won the regional battles.

But did the north African Christians who asserted the legitimacy and validity of their traditional beliefs and practices see matters this way? Did they accede at the beginning to being labelled in this way, to seeing themselves as 'Donatists'? Or, in the case that they perhaps did not, did they, over a century or so of persecution and repression, finally relent under the cumulative pressures, overt and insidious, directed against them and come to accept that they were in fact 'Donatists'? Did they come to appropriate or interiorize the external definition?[13] Precisely a century after the dispute over 'right thinking'

---

[12] *GCC*, 3, 539-40 (from the 'Capitula' only; the original transcript does not survive for this passage); cf. Augustine, *Breviculus Collationis*, 3.20.38 (= Lamirande, 230-33, with his note no. 31, 'L'attitude de saint Augustin à l'égard de Donat,' pp. 727-28). The entry "Donatus (5)" in *PCBE*, 1, 292-303, is instructive: the evidence is so confused that rigorous modern analysis cannot separate the two men (if duality ever existed).

[13] There are varying degrees of acceptance here, from, say, the examples offered by the early modern cases of the 'Methodists' or, perhaps, even more to

first erupted the two sides met in a monumental confrontation, one of the largest of its type ever to take place in the history of the early Church. In the year 411, in the Gargilian Baths, in the heart of Carthage, the great metropolis of all north Africa, there assembled hundreds of bishops of the two Christian churches to debate precisely that issue: Who was finally to define what would mean what, and who would have the force to make those definitions stick? It was, of course, as we shall see, a 'set-up' job in which the so-called 'Donatists' were not to be allowed a whisper of a chance of succeeding. But that is not the point here. There are, first of all, some rather interesting preliminary matters about this great meeting that are, how shall we put it, of 'historical' interest.

Historians are by nature much 'taken' by the simple existence of evidence, but even more so by the sort of direct evidence of speech and action that allows them to breathe their prey, to set their fangs into human flesh. In this particular case, quite rightly so. The number of extensive verbatim reports we have of any collective encounter in the world of Graeco-Roman antiquity, including its later Christian periods, are so few as to be derisory. It is not that assemblies were not a normal part of the collective life of Mediterranean communities. For the tens of thousands of meetings of that august governing body, the Senate of imperial Rome (whose proceedings were indeed recorded), however, there survives not one complete (or indeed partial) verbatim transcript.[14] And only scrappy portions survive of the tens, if not hundreds of thousands of council meetings held in the hundreds of municipalities scattered over the length and breadth of the Mediterranean during the first four or five centuries after Christ.[15] Similarly, the actual words

---

the point (given the element of personal labelling) that of the 'Lutherans.' Both were able successfully to appropriate and defuse the derogatory connotation of the labels foisted upon them by those hostile to them.

[14] R.J.A. Talbert, "Records and their Use," ch. 9 (in) *The Senate of Imperial Rome*, Princeton (1984) 303-37; R.A. Coles, *Reports of Proceedings in Papyri*, Brussels, 1966 (Papyrologica Bruxellensia, no. 4, pp. 55-61); cf. B. Baldwin, "The *acta diurna*," *Chiron* 9 (1979) 189-203, and A. Lintott, "*Acta Antiquissima*: A Week in the History of the Roman Republic," *Papers of the British School at Rome* 54 (1986) 213-28.

[15] E. Posner, *Archives in the Ancient World*, Cambridge, Mass. (1972) 203-04, 219-21; reference to such in north Africa in *GCC*, 1.177-80 (*gesta municipalia*).

uttered in the debates that took place in almost all of the great Church conferences have also been lost (most often, if there were any formal declarations or rules issued, it is those that we happen to have).[16]

Set against these losses, the conference held at Carthage in the summer of 411 is a great exception—the explicit verbal content of its participants has survived in startling detail. Because of the minute notarial precautions taken and because of the historical importance of the debates for the ecclesiastical battles being waged at the time, the word-by-word record of what the participants said over the days between first and eighth of June of that year has survived, mostly intact.[17] In fact, the detailed description of the painstaking scribal and notarial provisions made for the conference have given us one of the clearest pictures of how such records were kept in the Roman world.[18] The great efforts exerted by both sides to ensure the preservation of a

---

[16] The Council of Chalcedon (AD 451) is a striking exception, and so provides an interesting historiographical parallel to our document (with attendant potential for exploitation by historians—a great opportunity that, to the best of my knowledge, has not yet been taken up).

[17] Even for this almost-complete document, alas, it is clear that part of the proceedings of the third session (of 8 June) is missing (i.e., the 'Capitula' at the head of the document indicate that chapters 282-585—303 chapters—or a little more than the last half of the original have been lost). What remains, however, is a detailed verbatim record of what was said for all of the first and second sessions, and a substantial portion of the third—at any rate, more than enough for our purposes.

[18] The study of Emin Tengström, *Die Protokollierung der Collatio Carthaginiensis. Beiträge zur Kenntnis der römischen Kurzschrift nebst einem Exkurs über das Wort scheda (schedula)*, Göteborg, 1962, is fundamental; for a synopsis of his findings, see Lancel, *Actes*, 1, 342-53. First of all, heading the 'secretarial team' were six secretaries (*scribae, exceptores*) of various ranks attached to the *officia* of various imperial officials in Carthage, who were assisted by two secretaries (*notarii*) from each church. The actual note-taking was assigned to four stenographers (*exceptores*) from official sources, plus four stenographers assigned by each church. The final ecclesiastical stenographic teams were deliberately 'mixed' and were composed of four persons, two selected from each side. These teams were then rotated through the day, recording the day's proceedings. Since each team had both 'Donatists' and 'Catholics' on it, the opposing members acted as a check on each other's versions. When each scribal team left the Conference hall, its notes were counterchecked by a team of *custodes codicum/ chartarum/tabularum* (guardians of the documents) as they were variously called, again composed of both 'Catholics' and 'Donatists,' who placed their seal on the documents (*tabulae, codices*) in the presence of Marcellinus.

verbatim record, not only succeeded at the time, but have succeeded historically. This record is not without its peculiar technical problems and biases (which I shall attempt to make clear at any point of relevance). But the transcript was systematically checked by both sides in the debate, and it is extensive and highly detailed. Each speaker had his words recorded. There was a team of scrutineers from either side who checked that record. Each speaker was then asked to authenticate, to sign and notarize that his words had been accurately taken down. He did so by writing in his own hand the word 'Recognovi' ('I have reviewed, inspected' and therefore have 'authenticated, accepted, certified') at the end of transcript of his words. Moreover, a study of the syntax and grammar of the Latin reveals that, whatever subsequent subediting took place, that the document bears vestiges of the original oral character of the proceedings. Men who were otherwise renowned as complex and artful writers and highly skilled rhetoricians fell back on a limited real-time speech vocabulary, full of repetitions, rhetorical interjections, and the sudden lapses and shortcuts of actual talk.[19] Therefore, an almost unprecedented quality of recording. A real gem of hard reportage. What does it tell us?

The conference is an interesting historical laboratory. The position of the participants in it broadly reflected the main powers and forces on either side. The meeting was, not to 'mince words,' a kangaroo court. The prefabricated directives under which it operated reflected in miniature the power situation of either side. The Catholics entered it with all of the force of the Roman state behind them. The man whom the emperor Honorius appointed to preside over the conference, and to direct it to its end, the *tribunus et notarius* Flavius Marcellinus, was a faithful orthodox Catholic and a close friend of the man who was arguably the most prestigious of the Catholic bishops in north Africa, Aurelius Augustinus.[20] Augustine had an intimate correspondence

---

[19] Lancel, "Etude linguistique," ch. 4 (in) *Actes*, 1, 289-335, esp. 309 ff.

[20] There seems no good reason to doubt Marcellinus' inclinations in this matter—though, given both his behaviour in the matter, and the chronology of Augustine's dealings with him, we might be very cautious in accepting too 'total' a pre-commitment on his part. Augustine's correspondence with him does not begin until the time of the Conference itself, and much follows in the aftermath (including the dedication of *The City of God*). It would seem to me that an equally convincing case could be made that Marcellinus was heavily

18

with Marcellinus, and was later to dedicate the grandest of all his writings, *The City of God (De Civitate Dei)*, to him.[21] The imperial mandate given to Marcellinus, and the wording of his own decrees regarding the setting up of the conference, guaranteed that it was to be a puppet trial, the conclusion of which was already decided in advance of the debates themselves. The emperor Honorius had ordered the holding of the conference, under force of compulsion if necessary. The 'Donatists' were to come whether they liked it or not. If they decided not to come, they were to be judged as guilty for reasons of contumacious behaviour (because of their refusal to attend). Once they attended, the sole declared purpose of the conference was to find them guilty, to stamp out 'this seditious superstition' as the emperor put it in his directive to Marcellinus.[22] A monumental Catch-22 faced the local African church leaders. If they refused to attend, they were guilty; if they did attend, they were still guilty. The Catholics already knew as much. It was precisely for reasons of show that they wanted the conference, not for any decision to be arrived at as the result of free debate. It was the ceremonial display of power, the witness and seeing of it, that mattered. 'So,' as Augustine puts it with his characteristic harsh realism, 'in seeking this conference with you, we are not looking

---

'lobbied' by Augustine from the inception of the Conference, and that much that followed between them is better read in the light of his successes in that regard. Marcellinus' behaviour, therefore, must be read in a more narratological manner— his attempts at moderation and 'impartiality' were, no doubt, a response in part to his recognition of the 'realities' of the situation he faced when he got to north Africa (when he surely realized he could not crudely impose the mission in the stark terms presented in the imperial edict). Madeleine Moreau, "Le Dossier Marcellinus dans la correspondance de saint Augustin," *Recherches Augustiniennes* 9 (1973) 3-181, has the full record—of which the chronological sequence is rather significant.

[21] See "Fl. Marcellinus (10)" in PLRE, 2, 711-12; and the extensive notice, "Flavius Marcellinus (2)," in *PCBE*, 1, 671-88. Augustine dedicated the first three books of *De Civitate Dei*, which he composed and published in the immediate aftermath of the Conference, to Marcellinus by summer of 413; he temporarily discontinued the rest when Marcellinus was executed: T.D. Barnes, "Aspects of the Background of the *City of God*," (in) C. Wells ed., *L'Afrique romaine/Roman Africa*, Ottawa (1982) 69-85, at pp. 70-71.

[22] *C(odex) Th(eodosianus)* 16.11.3 (Honorius' edict of 14 October 410): 'Emperors Honorius and Theodosius Augustuses to their dear friend, Marcellinus, Greetings. We abolish the new superstition, and We command that those regulations in regard to the Catholic law shall be preserved unimpaired and inviolate...'

for yet another 'final decision' on this matter, but to have what has already been settled (in our minds) made known, especially to those who seem to be unaware that it is so.'[23]

The 'laws' or regulations by which meeting was to be conducted were a series of ground-rules dictating the constraints within which the game was to be played. The African Christians' expectations and desires, their assumed model of what a Church conference should be like (which they expressed for the record) meant that they saw these rules as unfair. Their natural expectation of a church conference was one of more democratic and egalitarian dimensions—a meeting in which each and every bishop would be allowed to speak and to have his say in turn.[24] Instead, the elaborate rules established by Marcellinus for the confrontation, apparently according to the prior wishes of the Catholic side, were intended to restrict both discussion and membership. Each side was to select only seven representatives or agents who were to be empowered to speak on behalf of all the bishops of their party. Each group of seven was to have access to a further group of seven who were to act as advisers, but who were not to be allowed to speak. In addition to these fourteen persons, each side was to be permitted to appoint a team of four persons who were to act as invigilators of the verbatim transcript of the proceedings.

To the Catholics, this was the long-awaited (and demanded) final verbal confrontation. The local African church leaders, however, had no reason to see this as but one more battle in a century-long fight against attempts to outlaw and belittle their view of Christianity, and the defence of the centuries-old African traditions. They came knowing full well the purpose of the conference and its avowed aim. But they could ignore the pre-set end, and join the battle in the trenches over symbols and display, over the assertion of labels and words, and what they were to mean. The Catholics could be confident that the final judgement of Marcellinus, their man, was 'in the bag,' but it would be a hollow victory indeed if it was perceived by north Africans in general as imposed by force, the coercive act of an imperial and secular power, and just another in the long line of attempts by 'the Catholic side' to impose its illegitimate views on local society. What would

---

[23] Augustine, *Ep.*, 88.10
[24] Frend, *Donatist Church*, 280-81

happen between the opening and the finale of the Conference, was, therefore, grand theater of some importance. The dramaturgical aspects were not lost (at least in retrospect) on the foremost of the Catholic bishops, Augustine of Hippo. As he vividly remembers: "Bishops are assembled from all of Africa...The orators charged with speaking on behalf of all of them are selected. The site worthy of such a great event is located in the city-center. The two sides assemble. The judge is present. The books are opened. Every heart is in suspense, waiting on the finale of such a great confrontation."[25] Flavius Marcellinus, the president of the conference, was surrounded by a resplendent *officium* of twenty-three persons. The struggle was to be a great public contest, a battle between the finest and most eloquent on both sides. It is in these acts and words that the historian might properly seek the self-definition of the African Christians.

When the bishops of either side assembled in the Baths of Gargilius on 1 June, the presiding officer Marcellinus had the edict of the emperors Honorius and Theodosius of 14 October 410 read aloud to them all. The imperial edict repeatedly emphasized the emperor's concern with the maintenance of 'Catholic law.' He thought it good that 'terror and dire warnings' had been used against 'the Donatists' whose 'hollow error and sterile disagreements have polluted Africa, the greatest part of our empire.' The words of the edict labelled the opposition as 'Donatist bishops,' and foresaw the only possible result of the arguments at the conference as being 'a refutation of superstition by manifest reason' [1.4]. There followed a reading of Marcellinus' own edict, again with the identification of the two sides as 'Catholic' and 'Donatist' [1.5]. Although the end was set, the Africans could assert their identity in words and acts that could demonstrate their power separate of the terms imposed by the imperial power.[26]

The extensive and detailed 'table of contents' (*capitula gestorum*) that prefaces the current manuscript identifies the two sides quite clearly the Catholics (*catholici, pars catholicorum*) on the one side and 'Donatists' (*donatistae, pars donatistarum*) on the other.[27] The problem is that the table is a later addition to the main account and is

---

[25] Augustine, *Ad Donatistas post Collationem*, 25.43 (= Lamirande, 352-53)
[26] P. Connerton, *How Societies Remember*, Cambridge, 1989
[27] Lancel, *Actes*, 2, 420-557

clearly an official or Catholic gloss or guide to the contents of the original transcript. It cannot therefore be used for any other purpose than to demonstrate the obvious—that the Catholic church and the imperial power identified their opponents as 'Donatists' and used that label as the means of marking them. In the text itself, however, the individual speakers on either side are not so identified. Whereas the Catholic bishops are clearly marked as such (e.g., 'Augustinus, episcopus ecclesiae catholicae, dixit,' 'Aurelius, episcopus ecclesiae catholicae, dixit,' or 'Alypius, episcopus ecclesiae catholicae, dixit'), their opponents never identified themselves as 'Donatists,' 'of the Donatist Church' or anything of the sort, but merely as a 'bishop' (e.g., 'Emeritus, episcopus, dixit' or 'Petilianus, episcopus, dixit'). The only thing the African bishops assented to being called, therefore, was 'bishop' (that is, of the Christian church). They did not recognize, or accept, any more specific designation, least of all that of being a 'Donatist.' However this was done (and there are clear indications of how), the African bishops managed to enforce this perception of themselves throughout the entirety of the official transcript.

The matter of who was being identified as whom became a critical center of dispute on the opening of the second day's proceedings (5 June) in the Baths—probably because by then the African bishops had had the opportunity to read the identification foisted on them in the official record. The descriptive introduction to those days in the proceedings specifies the two men, Ianuarius and Vitalis, who were the secretarial team of the 'Catholic church' (*notarii ecclesiae Catholicorum /Catholicae*) and those, Victor and Crescens, who were those of 'the Donatist Church' (*notarii ecclesiae donatistarum*) [2.1]. The introduction of the debating teams assigned by either side is marked by a similar identification: from one side enter the bishops of the Catholic Church (*episcopi ecclesiae catholicae*) and from the other, those of 'the Donatist side' (*episcopi partis Donati*) [2.2]. The conference secretary (*exceptor*), Martialis, informed the president Flavius Marcellinus of the notification which 'the Donatist bishops' had presented to 'your Nobility' on the previous day [2.8]. These very words provoked an immediate response from Petilianus, the leading African spokesman, in which he made it about as clear as he could, that he and his fellow bishops were not at all prepared to accept this identification: "We are simply bishops of the truth of Christ, our Lord—so we call ourselves and so it is usually noted in the public records. As for Donatus of holy memory, a man of a martyr's glory—although he is our predecessor and an embellishment of the Church of this city, we (only) accord him the sort of honor and status he deserves." [2.10] The correction obviously hit at the heart of the Catholic attempt to label the African Christians, and so provoked a carping response from the Catholic bishop Possidius: "Bishops of the truth! That's something for them to prove and not simply to assert" [2.11]. The objection was all the more powerful, however, in that the Africans apparently made it stick. The president of the court Marcellinus accepted that the statements 'of either party' were to be recorded (*Utrarumque partium prosecutiones gesta retinebunt*) [2.12]. From that point on in the record the so-called 'Donatists' are never so-called again. Henceforth, when Marcellinus referred to the two groups he was careful to refer to 'either side' in the dispute (e.g., 2.19 & 24). Martialis, the court notary who had made the reference to 'the Donatists' that provoked the objections by Petilianus in the first place, now corrected the record to read 'bishops and defenders of the church of the truth' (*episcopi et defensores ecclesiae veritatis*) [2.12]. It is probably with this particular episode in mind that the African bishops insisted on their legal right to reread and correct the transcripts of the first day's proceedings [2.25]

What is the significance in this brief encounter over definition for a better historian's understanding? It is still a puzzle why a minimum of impartiality in the writing of history, of a subject technically so remote in time and place, seems so difficult for historians to achieve. Simple reportage of what happened has been, and continues to be, one of the basic requirements of writing history. But there still seems to be an overwhelming tendency to write the history of the period from the perspective of the 'winners.' Strange 'winners' indeed—they lost the great game (the fate of Christianity in Africa), but won the game of historical records. Paradoxically, the Catholic labelling process won where it actually lost. Even simple technical entries of an encyclopaedic type, the supposed reportage of mere fact, are full of primary bias. Take the following entry on Marcellinus, the tribune and notary appointed to head the conference: 'He presided over the Council of Carthage, 411 June 1-26, at which the catholic and Donatist bishops of Africa met to discuss their differences. He restored order to the African church, both by his decisions at the Council in favour of the catholics, and also by subsequent disciplinary measures against the recalcitrant Donatists.'[28] On the other hand, if we begin with the rejection of this identification, we can begin to make sense of what has otherwise been portrayed as a 'lost cause.' The behaviour of the African bishops summoned to the confrontation in the summer of 411 is a pedagogy for the persecuted. Their actions were far from those who regarded themselves as amongst the defeated. Improvisation, the gaining of space, the insistence on the meaning of words, the refusal to concede automatic obedience—all of these tactics, and more, worked, and worked against legitimizing the 'final verdict' of the court because they contested precisely the grounds for which Augustine, and the Catholics, wanted the conference—the legitimation of their cause through ceremonial public advertisement.[29] The African bishops, it must be remembered, still had very great numbers of the local people with them—so their audience was more than worth the effort.

One stratagem was to win the battle of 'public opinion.' To make a decisive visual impact on the great numbers of people who would be in Carthage to witness the 'exterior' effects of the conference (but who could not participate in its inner workings—a distribution of

---

[28] So *PLRE*, 2, 'Marcellinus (10),' p. 711 [1980]

[29] The same approach was utilized, for example, by defendants in the trial of the 'Chicago Eight' in 1969, where the charges of 'conspiracy' were manifestly casuistic means used by the formal powers of the time which were guaranteed (so they thought) to rid them of political undesirables. The reaction of certain of the defendants was to reject the basic legitimacy of the court itself by turning it into countertheater: 'For Abbie [Hoffman] and Jerry [Rubin]... the courtroom was a new theater, perhaps a purer kind of theater than anything in previous Yippie history. More than any of the other defendants, they wanted to create the image of a courtroom shambles.' The proponents of such tactics accepted that the final verdict would go against them (as it did): '...as Abbie said, the trial would be "a victory every day until the last".' Tom Hayden disagreed with these tactics ('Then we would be sentenced for contempt. We could strip away the authority of the judge and prosecution but not their power.'), but he was finally constrained to admit that they worked: 'In the end, Dave [Dellinger] and Abbie were right in their argument that a symbolic stand would move people.' (T. Hayden, *Trial*, New York (1970) 69-72). These tactics were castigated by supporters of the powers of the *status quo* at the time as 'silly,' 'a waste of court time,' 'absurd,' 'needless delaying tactics,' 'comic,' 'childish antics,' 'nihilistic,' and so on—that is to say, much the same sort of formal charges levelled by Augustine against the actions of the African bishops.

24

power that would be to the advantage of whoever could manipulate their desire, and need, to know). That could be achieved by some sort of public demonstration of power outside the confines of the conference proper. There were many potential spectators in Carthage, the metropolis of all Africa and one of the largest cities of the empire. Such a great event must naturally have had a popular audience.[30] The Catholic bishops therefore resolutely resisted their opponents' demand for a full conference for fear of the popular tumult that might result.[31] The African Christians, however, turned this popular element to their advantage by staging an ostentatious parade of their bishops and priests, and their attendants, into Carthage and through its streets, on 18 May.[32] The parade by which the bishops entered Carthage was so impressive that Augustine later remarked on it with a sarcasm that betrays the clear impact it made: "So many bishops were gathered from all of Africa. They entered Carthage with the great pomp and ceremony of a magnificent parade, so that they turned the eyes and attention of the inhabitants of the great city on themselves."[33] In other words, the plan to affect public sentiment worked. Even before the first formal words of the conference had been uttered, the African bishops had struck their first collective blow.

The problem for historians in evaluating events like the parade is that they tend to lock themselves within the highly artificially defined world of the conference itself—not to raise their eyes outside the retaining walls of the Baths of Gargilius. That means that the views of the bishops, mostly rather elderly males, are taken to define the limits of power.[34] But that is a clear mistake. There was an enormous

---

[30] The presence of crowds and the possible 'tumult' that they might cause are occasionally referred to: e.g., *GCC*, 2.72

[31] Augustine, *Breviculus Collationis*, 1.7

[32] *GCC*, 1.14.7-11; 1.29.2-4; cf. Augustine, *Breviculus Collationis*, 1.4; for the utility of parade-like demonstrations of power (and why this one might have had such effect) see E.E. Rice, *The Grand Procession of Ptolemy Philadelphus*, Oxford, 1988; S. MacCormack, *Art and Ceremony in Late Antiquity*, Berkeley-Los Angeles, 1981; and M. McCormick, *Eternal Victory: Triumphal Rulership in late Antiquity, Byzantium, and the Early Medieval West*, Cambridge, 1987, on 'adventus' ceremonial with which the bishops must have been familiar.

[33] Augustine, *Ad Donatistas post Collationem*, 25.43 (= Lamirande, 352-53)

[34] Just how 'old' and decrepit is difficult to say, but probably older in

'audience' outside, and whether or not they were persuaded by the highly defined proceedings inside was precisely what was at issue. That audience included vast numbers of Christians, young and old, male and female, who were not at the conference itself. We cannot overlook them—they and their actions could be as decisive as anything that happened within the confines of the baths.

After all, the whole thing began with a kiss and a woman. A kiss is something, the sheer power of which historians, such as the one writing these words, have not always fully recognized. The woman was named Lucilla. She was a very wealthy person of senatorial rank resident at Carthage in the early fourth century. A woman of independent disposition, even in matters religious, she had carried on her devotions in a manner that seemed appropriate to her—which, on one occasion, included bestowing a kiss on a holy relic.[35] For this act of 'excessive' devotion she was harshly disciplined by Caecilianus, the (then) archdeacon of Carthage. Angered by his unwanted interference in what she deemed to be her own affairs, she aligned herself and her resources with one Majorinus whom she encouraged in his opposition to Caecilianus in the forthcoming election to the bishopric of Carthage in 311. Her encouragement did not require any extraordinary exertions on her part since Majorinus, though a man, was directly in her power—he was, in fact, a servant in her own household.[36] So it was her power,

---

north Africa than elsewhere: see B.D. Shaw, "The Elders of Christian Africa," (in) P. Brind'Amour ed., *Mélanges offerts à R.P. Etienne Gareau*, Ottawa, Editions de l'Université d'Ottawa = numéro spéciale de *Cahiers des études anciennes* (1982) 207-226; and "Latin Funerary Epigraphy and Family Life in the Later Roman Empire," *Historia* 33 (1984) 457-97, on the factor of patriarchy and seniority in north African society in general, and in the church in particular. The roll call of the bishops seems to guarantee as much—extraordinary numbers, up to about a third from either side, were absent because of sickness, other weaknesses of old age, or death itself (not a few of the latter occurring *en route*).

[35] F. Dölger, "Das Kultvergehen der Donatistin Lucilla von Karthago. Reliquienkuss vor dem Kuss der Eucharistie," (in) *Antike und Christentum*, 3 (1932/1950) 245-52: that she is pre-emptively designated 'a Donatist' by Dölger says a lot about the haste with which historians rush to accept *ex post facto* labels; see Frend, *Donatist Church*, 18-21 for context.

[36] Optatus, 1.19: 'Majorinus, qui lector in diaconio Caeciliani fuerat, domesticus Lucillae, ipsa suffragante episcopus ordinatus erat' ['Majorinus, who was a reader under the deacon Caecilianus, a household servant (or even slave) of Lucilla's, was ordained bishop because of her support']. Of course, the historian

XI

26

her wealth, and her force of personality that provided the basic resources that organized and financed the dissident conference of seventy bishops at Carthage that elected Majorinus primate of Africa and, in effect, created the 'Donatist' schism.[37] Hence an absolutely critical historical actress, whose actions were a crucial determining element in what happened to the course of north African Christianity. Analyses of the conference of 411 that remain within the defined walls of the conference halls simply miss all of those who, like Lucilla, were 'defined out' of its proceedings.[38] And yet it is precisely all of the Lucillas of that world whose voice and power must be restored if one is to begin to understand what the verbal battles within the walls of the baths were all about, and, perhaps more important, about their probability of success in persuading those on the outside.

The question of which side deserved recognition as the Christian Church in Africa also hinged, for example, on a clear demonstration that neither was just some fringe sect, but had a numerous and widespread representation from all parts of Africa. The importance of numbers was recognized by both sides. Following the first long roll-call (of the Catholic bishops), Marcellinus wished to get out of repeating the lengthy and time-consuming procedure for the Africans. But, since the compelling of an impartial count could be used to dramatic effect by them, they insisted on the duplication. Petilianus objected that the whole purpose was to give each bishop a chance to make his own

---

must make due allowance for the exploitation of the female image in the hostile male rhetoric; such 'bad women' seen at the heart of black conspiracies and evil machinations had a long history in Latin writing. Livy's account of the Bacchanalian conspiracy of 186 BC, Cicero's portrait of Sassia in the *Pro Cluentio* or his Clodia of the mid 50s BC, and Sallust's Sempronia in his *Bellum Catilinum*, are some amongst many predecessors of a common theme that heavily marked imperial historiography as well (e.g., the 'bad wives' of emperors).

[37] The sources are outlined in *PCBE*, 1, 'Lucilla (1),' p. 649; cf. *PLRE*, 1, 'Lucilla,' p. 517; note their open hostility: Optatus, 1.16 'potens et factiosa femina.'

[38] Such powerful and wealthy women were still wielding decisive rôles in the era of the Conference itself. If any evidence has to be adduced in support of an obvious continuity, then it is provided by Augustine (*Ep.* 43.9.26 and *Sermo in Ps.* 36.19 = *PL*, 36, 377) who refers to another woman (unnamed, as usual) who was 'a second Lucilla' involved in conflicts within the church at Carthage in the 390s, being central to the creation of yet another division within the African church, that of the 'Maximianists.'

declaration (e.g., making quite clear publicly where there existed no Catholic bishop opposite them) and thereby to demonstrate, for example, the absolute numerical superiority of the African Christians in Numidia. Further, Petilianus argued, the distribution revealed by such a roll-call would be a manifest way of demonstrating that they had maintained their numbers by peaceful means, whereas the Catholics had achieved theirs by force (*GCC*, 1.165). Such public demonstration of quantity was, in part, the purpose of the great parade of bishops that preceded the conference itself, as Augustine later recognized.[39] That is why the African Christians had persevered with the tactic from the beginning. Thus, when the Catholic bishops, in obedience to the orders of Marcellinus turned up at the Baths on the morning of 1 June with their full complement of 18 bishops to represent them, the African Christian bishops turned up *en masse*.

The president could have demanded that all except the deputized speakers and their assistants should leave the Baths venue. But he was trapped by the ensuing arguments which led to demands from both sides to check, by way of public declaration, the presence of the bishops who had signed the mandate empowering their respective deputies (*GCC*, 1, 186). The Africans declared 279 signatories—exclusive of six of their representatives, which brought their full total to 285. The Catholics, on the other hand, objected to absent bishops, and even one dead one, on the list. The Catholics then declared 266 subscribers. That left them in an apparent minority. The bishop Alypius was sent out to drum up another twenty Catholic bishops who were at least capable of walking into the Baths. Once recognized, they brought the Catholic total to 286—one more than the Africans a critical, even if the smallest, margin of difference.[40] The African bishop from Cirta, Petilianus, began by challenging the veracity of the Catholic signatories. He wanted to see each Catholic bishop in person. He was able to cite cases from personal experience of the Catholic creation of shadow bishoprics (*GCC*, 1.59, 61). Moreover, by forcing an in-person parade of bishops of either side, the Africans could demonstrate that they too had the numbers, and were no trivial sect (*GCC*, 1, 89-93).

---

[39] Augustine, *Ad Donatistas post Collationem*, 24.41

[40] The best discussion of the numbers is to be found in Lancel, *Actes*, 1, 110-18; each side claimed about 400+ bishoprics in total in north Africa.

But the challenges issued by either side ultimately played into the hands of the Africans because it provoked another bit of drama: a second parade of bishops. In order to match names against signatures, claims of bishoprics against actual bishops, the president agreed to a roll-call of all bishops on either side. The agreed procedure was that the name of the Catholic bishop was read out first (if he existed)—he declared his presence ('Present'). Then the African bishop from the same see would declare his presence (normally by saying 'I recognize him'—i.e. his opposing number).

The interest in this one-on-one confrontation lies less in the checking of numbers and identities of bishops on either side, than in the dramatic way in which each bishop walked forward to the center of the Baths, made a declaration of his identity, and placed that identification within the context of his relationship to an opponent. Each confrontation became a mini-drama of self-assertion. Bishops who had driven all contesters from their see (mostly Catholics) could vaunt the fact when they came forward to identify themselves, as in the case of Aptus, Catholic bishop of Tigias: 'Present. I have not had, and do not have, any Donatist bishop in my place' (*GCC*, 1.120). Or, Innocentius, Catholic bishop of Germania: 'Present. I have no adversary' (*GCC*, 1, 121). Urbicosus, Catholic bishop of Igilgili, could declare, belligerently: 'Present. My town has been entirely Catholic for a very long time' (*GCC*, 1.121). Compare similar expectorations such as 'Totally Catholic,' 'My community has been Catholic from its beginning,' or 'I have no competitors, no heretics' (*GCC*, 1.126). Denigrating the status of the opponent was another favourite tactic: Privatus, Catholic bishop of Usula: 'Present. I don't have any bishop against me—just a priest' (*GCC*, 1.126). Or frank admissions meant to frighten, as made by Trifolius, Catholic bishop of Abora: 'Present. Anyone known as one of them in my see is stoned' (GCC, 1.133.84-85). Naturally, the African bishops could also use the parade to make their point. So, Honorius, African bishop from Vartani identifying his Catholic counterpart Victor: 'I have had the pleasure of making his acquaintance recently because of the harm he has done me' (*GCC*, 1, 126). Or one could combine denigration and a jab of personal betrayal: so Donatus, African bishop of Vamacurra, of his opposite number: 'I recognize him. He was once my priest' (1.128). Another African bishop claimed to have been driven from his seat by violence. 'He's just lying,' replied the Catholic. 'It's simple terror and nothing else that's driven everyone out,' retorted the African. 'He's lying' (1.134.1-13). One could rub in an insult: 'I have Felix opposite me—but he only has one parishioner!' (1.135. 1-6). Or, to play a final card, one could deny the very existence of the other. Asterius, the Catholic bishop of Vicus: 'In this place there is no other bishop but me.' Urbanus, his opposite number, could trump that: 'With God as my witness, I don't even recognize this man' (1.143.56-61). Others put the matter more bluntly: 'I don't know him any more than he knows me!' (1.133.13). Such game-playing could finally exasperate the judge. Following on another such standoff, Marcellinus finally blurted out: 'Well, do you at least recognize his face?' (1.177-179).

Such repartee could exploit familiar Mediterranean themes, like threats of vengeance. When, in one of usually feisty retorts, Petilianus drew to the Catholics' attention that one day there would be revenge for the hurt they had done the Africans (1.169), that too was another part of getting the matter 'on the record.' Earlier, in his personal 'identification routine' with his Catholic opposite, Fortunatus of Constantine, Petilianus had made the point in an angry exchange about the violence that had been vented on him and his followers. He ended: 'Let the transcript of these proceedings record that you are a persecutor. In the right time and place you will hear what you deserve' (1.139). Such pointed references to future times and places of reckoning were intended to make the adversary realize that, although he might have the upper hand now, there would be vengeance one day. So Dativus the African bishop of Petra, northwest of Diana Veteranorum: 'And I don't have any adversary, because it is there where our 'Lord' (i.e., the martyr) Marculus lies, for whose blood God will exact vengeance on the day of judgment' (1.187.73-76).

The identification parade also opened up other possibilities for labelling the opposition, such as the deployment of the collective slur. If a dispute was to be made over numbers, then the quality of those numbers could be drawn into question. Halfway through the African Christians' declarations of their bishoprics, Alypius, the Catholic bishop from Thagaste (Augustine's old home-town) objected that most of them were mere rural estates (*villae*) or farms (*fundi*). In raising this point, Alypius was not just making some technical point about the location of these bishoprics, but was playing on a deeply rooted prejudice of the time amongst cultured men against the countryside and a near-racial bias against those who lived in it as somehow distinctly and permanently inferior to city-dwellers. Given the pervasive nature of those assumptions, the moral stain of having most of your bishops derived from a context of rural idiocy was a near-impossible one to refute. Petilianus did his best: the Catholics, he said, had many rural bishops as well. They shouldn't talk too much. Too bad, too, that *they* had almost no parishioners in theirs (*GCC*, 1.181-182).

Of course, it is only the written record we have. Hence, certain caveats. It catches very little of the world of gesture and expression (especially facial) that must have marked these confrontations. Only a very small part of this world of movement and appearance is available to us through chance remarks in the record. And the act of refusal to recognize could be publicly signalled in such small acts. For example, the simple ritual of making the body obey implicit orders. Rational people will sit down together to discuss their differences. The mere act of sitting down together, as the African bishops recognized, was already a surrender to the organization of space by their opponents. But in their *guerrilla,* the Africans were to begin by challenging the minutiae of the organization of space itself. Early in the course of the first day's proceedings, the presiding judge Marcellinus issued what must have seemed to him an innocuous invitation: to be seated [*GCC*, 1.144]. The African bishops objected. They would not sit. They would stand.[41] There was good historical precedent. Christ had stood before his persecutors. So would they (*GCC*, 1.145). The meeting of the second day brought another invitation from the court president for the participants to be seated (GCC, 2.3). Once again, the Africans ostentatiously refused. They would stand. After all, they had biblical authority on their side. The righteous should not sit down with sinners (*GCC*, 2.4). Did not the Psalmist say, 'I have not sat among worthless men, nor do I mix with hypocrites; I hate the company of evil men, I refuse to sit down with the wicked' (*Ps.* 26.4-5). What was the presiding officer, Marcellinus, to do? To get proceedings under way, he conceded. The Africans literally stood their ground.

---

[41] Again, a political management of space. Just as, on the twenty-fourth day of their trial, the Chicago Eight ostentatiously refused to stand, and so, with their bodies, denied the legitimacy of the court.

All the rhetorical and behavioural microrebellions clearly had the disruption of the 'normal course' of the conference as part of their objective. Theirs was a 'little war' meant to challenge the legitimacy of the proceedings. In this they succeeded.[42] They proved to be a source of immense frustration, both to the civil authorities charged with conducting the trial, above all Flavius Marcellinus, and to the Catholic bishops who had hoped for a quick and decisive final confrontation. Marcellinus finally had to use his superior force simply to declare a sudden end to the conference, bringing proceedings to an abrupt halt on the third day, and calling the bishops back together later the same evening to hear his 'final sentence' in the candle-lit darkness of the baths. That matters did not proceed smoothly to their foreordained end was something that had a great impact on the participants. Augustine, who has given the most extensive set of *ex post facto* 'debriefings' in his subsequent writings relevant to the conference, repeatedly labels the actions of the African Christians as nothing more than purposeful and perverse 'delays' (*delationes* and *morae*, repeatedly), obstructions, roadblocks, actions intended to do nothing other than waste time and deviate proceedings from their proper course.[43] That modern-day historians have so consistently bought into this one-sided interpretation of what the African Christians were trying to do is a condemnation of their science as historians, and has added nothing to our understanding of what those human beings were doing in the June days of 411. 'Delays' and 'deliberate obfuscations,' to be sure—but to what end? Were the African Christians summoned merely to play the imperial State/Church's game? Under the assumption that they too were human, are historians not to grant a rationality to their resistance?

Augustine had declared the purpose of the Conference: it was a blatant propagandistic machine designed even before it started to achieve two ends: persuasion and legitimation. That the African Christians

---

[42] So the contempt charges issued by Judge Julius Hoffman in the trial of the Chicago Eight for having brought the court into disrepute were a confession that the 'contumacious' tactics of the defendants had in fact succeeded in de-legitimizing the authority of the court.

[43] For example, Augustine's recapitulation of his view of matters in the *Breviculus Collationis*, 1.9, 2.3 (twice), 3.2, 3.3, 6.7, 8.10; a point he frequently reiterates elsewhere, e.g., *Ad Donatistas post Collationem*, 24.42

would do everything possible to delegitimize the proceedings in the Baths of Gargilius is surely both rational and understandable. From their point of view, the more the 'debates' were reduced to a chaos and a shambles, the better. It appears that far from being 'beaten' in this aim, they largely succeeded.[44] That was why the court president Marcellinus was constrained to bring the whole show to a sudden halt. If anything, the response by the leading Catholic bishops afterwards, above all that of Augustine, is surely to be read as a type of 'damage control.' His 'little and brief account of the Conference' (the *Breviculus Collationis*), produced hastily in the aftermath of the assembly for widespread distribution, is therefore noteworthy not so much for its outright lying (of which there is some) as for its slanted and selective reportage. Augustine rapidly synopsizes the first two days of the proceedings so that he can concentrate on what he wishes to be accepted as the substance of the Conference—the extended theological debate of the third session. Gone are any references to the calculated embarrassments caused by the African Christians—above all, their clear and pointed demand that they *not* be labelled 'Donatists' (a self-identification which Augustine, of course, cavalierly disregards throughout his 'summary'). Augustine's much vaunted insight—to have foreseen the importance of entering the fray at a popular level in order to persuade ordinary people by readable 'digest' versions of the conference, by the composition of simple 'ABC' folk songs, and other such 'pop' media—is rather significant. It does indeed impart a distinctive modern character to the propaganda battles.[45] But the recourse to these radical new tactics was not so much a marvel of

---

[44] Again, the words of William Kunstler, the defence attorney in the Trial of the Chicago Eight: 'The significance of the trial is that it showed...for the first time how ingenious defendants can use a courtroom to get their point across and not to be afraid of authority.' Which is all true, except for the claim about 'the first time.'

[45] This unusual 'modern' element in the struggle, *une chose avant son temps*, so to speak, has been noted by several scholars; see Lamirande, *Oeuvres de Saint Augustine*, 'Le caractère populaire de la lutte anti-donatiste," 217-20; and Monceaux, *Histoire littéraire*, 7, 193-199; the references to earlier concerns with popular persuasion that precede the conference (e.g., *Contra litt. Petil.* 1.1.1, or *Contra Crescionum*, 1.3.4-5.7) are not very persuasive on that score; his great concern with entering the battle at a popular level seems to date from the year of the Conference.

prescience as it was a response compelled from the bishop by the failure of the Conference to achieve its set end.

The conference's consequence? It is ordinarily portrayed by historians as a great Catholic victory. The final death blow to 'Donatism.' After 411 it was all downhill and decline for the African Christians.[46] A decline not without its own ironies. Flavius Marcellinus, a direct party to the 'defeat,' the judge appointed to assess the African's deviations, was himself executed on 13 September 413, about two years after delivering his final judgement, in Carthage, the very city in which he had given it.[47] The problem is, once again, one of definition, power, and the sorts of evidence left for historians to interpret. If, as has been argued, the so-called 'Donatists' never existed except insofar as a Catholic Church, backed by the power of the Roman state, was able to label and to define them, then, logically, when the latter no longer had the authority and the sheer force to keep that definition alive, no more 'Donatists' would exist. Rather, the traditional Christians of north Africa would continue to exist as *they* always had. The precipitate collapse of the political and military structures of the Roman state in the west, first in 410 and then, finally, in 476, meant that the critical conditions for the existence of 'Donatism' simply no longer existed. That, in turn, will produce a problem with the evidence—drastically affecting the ability of historians, like us, to sight 'Donatists.' There is, of course, the additional problem of the extreme paucity of evidence for the period (especially following the death of Augustine, and the Vandal presence in north Africa after AD 430). Even so, there is enough evidence to refute both easy theories about the decline of traditional north African Christianity or the 'sudden and great' victory

---

[46] Implicit in the account of Frend, *Donatist Church*, throughout, but especially in his chs. 17, 'The Aftermath of the Conference, 412-29,' and 18, 'The Last Phase: Donatism in Vandal and Byzantine Africa'; his final judgment is an outrage both against the canons of historical research and common sense: 'The Donatists had come to a conference, been out-argued, and proscribed by the due process of the law' (p. 289).

[47] *Plus ça change*...it was not the first or last time that irony was to happen—compare the fate of Jean de Coras, the investigating judge in the Martin Guerre case (Natalie Zemon Davis, *The Return of Martin Guerre*, Cambridge, Mass., 1983, 114-15, 154n2). There is some speculation that the African bishops condemned by him in 411 were involved in Marcellinus' denunciation for treason and his execution—a sweet revenge for them, if true.

of orthodox Catholicism.[48]

Of course, the conference at Carthage was also part of a long battle not just over some notorious ecclesiastical *causes célèbres* in north Africa, but also over the larger problem of what Christianity was to be. Perhaps lost in the minutiae and heat of individual exchanges, it is itself a matter worth brief recapitulation, and some reconsideration. The Catholic position was clear and coherent. There was one world, one Church, one belief, and hence only a single unity. And that clearly meant that there could be only one Christian path to the future. Hence all had to be compelled to it. To think otherwise was to accede to becoming lost, and damned, in the process. The African vision was significantly different, even if not as coherently elaborated as the Catholic view—after all, the Africans, as part of their natural history, had never really considered the Catholic position to be a necessary one. It was one that they had consciously to face only following their being labelled 'heretics' after 311/312. Their counter-vision ran something like this. Each region, each culture, had developed its own Christianity. What is 'universal' in the Christian message, its moral center, is to be found in each peculiar expression given to it. That meant that each local tradition, each individual view, had its own legitimacy, and did not require instruments of repression and persecution to enforce a universal uniformity. As I've said, a rather different view of Christianity from Catholic orthodoxy, but, given our current circumstances (maybe especially because of them) perhaps every bit as compelling. It was certainly a perspective that had strikingly different implications for definition and identity.

Who are you? 'The answer is which is to be master—that's all.' Well, as the African Christians at Carthage in the summer of 411 knew, not quite 'all.'

---

[48] The evidence is assembled, almost against his own conclusions, by R.A. Markus, "Reflections on Religious Dissent in North Africa in the Byzantine Period," (in) G.J. Cuming ed., *Studies in Church History*, 3, Leiden (1966) 140-49, and his, "Donatism: the Last Phase," (in) C.W. Dugmore & C. Duggan eds., *Studies in Church History*, 1, London (1964) 118-26.

CRITICAL BIBLIOGRAPHICAL ADDENDA

The following notes are intended to guide the reader through some of the recent research pertinent to my essays on the history of the ancient Maghrib collected in the two volumes of the Variorum Reprint series. They are not meant to be comprehensive bibliographic guides or updates to the subjects concerned, but rather are intended to draw the reader's attention to debates and controversies in the field where they traverse subjects dealt with in the collected studies. I have tried, where possible, to highlight alternative interpretations or analyses that have questioned hypotheses for which I argued in the reprinted articles. The addenda move in sequential order through the subject matter of the articles as reproduced, with the volume number (Arabic numeral) and chapter sequence (Roman numeral) in the volume referred to at the head of each section in bold (e.g., 1.III = Volume 1, article 3 of the reprint edition) to cue the reader to the original publication that is being discussed.

In referring to periodical and serial publications, as well as to corpora of primary data (principally epigraphical) the following conventional abbreviations have been used:

AAR	African Archaeological Review
AAT	Atlas archéologique de la Tunisie, ed. René Cagnat and Alfred Merlin (Paris, 1914-1926)
AE	L'Année épigraphique
AntAfr	Antiquités africaines
Atl.arch.	Atlas Archéologique de l'Algérie, ed. Stéphane Gsell (Paris, 1911)
BAA	Bulletin d'Archéologie Algérienne
BASOR	Bulletin of the American Schools of Oriental Research
BCTH	Bulletin Archéologique du Comité des Travaux Historiques
CIL	Corpus Inscriptionum Latinarum
CRAI	Comptes Rendus de l'Académie des Inscriptions et Belles-Lettres
ILAfr	Inscriptions Latines d'Afrique: Tripolitaine, Tunisie, Maroc, ed. René Cagnat, Alfred Merlin, and Louis Chatelain (Paris, 1923)

2 CRITICAL BIBLIOGRAPHICAL ADDENDA

IAM   Inscriptions Antiques du Maroc, 2: Inscriptions Latines, ed. Maurice Euzennat, Jean Marion, and Jacques Gascou (Paris, 1982)
JRA   Journal of Roman Archaeology
LibStud   Libyan Studies (Report of the Society for Libyan Studies to vol. 9, 1977-1978; Libyan Studies from vol. 10, 1979)
PA   Palaeoecology of Africa
RMM   Revue de l'Occident Musulman et de la Méditerranée (to vol. 47, 1988; Revue du Monde Musulman et de la Méditerranée from vol. 48, 1989)
RSAC   Receuil des Notices et Mémoires de la Société Archéologique de Constantine
SEG   Supplementum Epigraphicum Graecum
ThLL   Thesaurus Linguae Latinae

On **theory and archaeology** (1.I) there has emerged a vast bibliography in the last decade. A good recent exemplar that discusses the specific contribution reprinted here is John Bintliffe ed., *The Annales School and Archaeology* (Leicester, 1991). See also the comments by Bruce Hitchner, "The Merits and Challenges of an *Annaliste* Approach to Archaeology," *JRA* 7 (1994) 408-17, with particular reference to evidence adduced in the North African case studies reprinted in this collection.

On the subject of the **long-term environmental and climatic changes** that have affected North Africa and the Sahara (1.II and 1.III) there is a substantial but sometimes forbiddingly technical bibliography. In selecting a few items from this long list, I have borne in mind the relevance of the findings to the historian's main concern with these changes as they affected the historical ecology of the Maghrib. For synoptic views of the problem of long-term climatic change in the region, résumés of recent research can be found in Erhard Schulz, "Trends of Pleistocene and Holocene Research on the Sahara," *PA* 16 (1984), pp. 193-201; William Laver and Peter Frankenberg, "Modelling of Climate and Plant Cover in the Sahara for 5500 BP and 18000 BP," *PA* 12 (1980), pp. 307-14, and his *Zur Landschaftsdegradation in Südestunisien* (Wiesbaden, 1983); H.J. Pachur and G. Braun, "The Palaeoclimate of the Central Sahara, Libya and the Libyan Desert," *PA* 12 (1980), pp. 351-63; Alfred Muzzolini, "Climats au Sahara et sur ses bordures, du Pleistocène final à l'aride actuel,"*Empuries* 47 (1985), pp. 8-27; and Martin Williams, "Late Quaternary Prehistoric Environments in the Sahara," (in) J. Desmond Clark & Steven A. Brandt eds., *From Hunters to Farmers* (Berkeley, 1984), pp. 71-83. On the relationship between endogenous and strictly climatic causes of environmental change in the region, see Pierre Rognon, "Pluvial and Arid Phases in the Sahara: the Role of Non-Climatic Factors," *PA* 12 (1980), pp. 45-62; and Daniel Stiles, "Desertification in Prehistory: the Sahara," *Sahara* 1 (1988), pp. 85-92. General synopses for the eastern sector of the Sahara are provided by Fred Wendorf and Romuald Schild, *Prehistory of the Eastern Sahara* (New York, 1980), and by Angela Close ed., *Prehistory of Arid North Africa: Essays in Honor of Fred Wendorf* (Dallas, 1987).

Baldur Gabriel, "Palaeoecological Evidence from Neolithic Fireplaces in the Sahara," *AAR* 5 (1987), pp. 93-103 offers a synopsis of his work on the subject, and concludes that the neolithic environment of the Sahara was close in type to that of the contemporary Sudanese Sahel, but that after 5000 BP conditions became much more arid. The same conclusions are reached by Katharina Neumann, "Holocene Vegetation of the Eastern Sahara: Charcoal from Prehistoric Sties," *AAR* 7 (1989), pp. 97-116. The general tendency of these works (as confirmed by Aumassip and Barich, cited below, for zones close to the Maghrib proper) still seems to substantiate the general pattern of relationship between climate and environment argued in 1.II—namely that the environment of the Sahara and environs after 8000 BP was already very arid, although it was slightly better compared to present-day conditions through 5000 BP, but that thereafter the Saharan environment further degraded to its present state. The evidence accumulated to date certainly does not indicate any macro-level changes in climate from the protohistoric period through the end of the Roman era in the Maghrib. Two studies on the palaeobotanical environment of the Sahara by Erhard Schulz, "Die Holozäne Vegetation der Zentralen Sahara (N-Mali, N-Niger, SW-Libyen)," *PA* 18 (1987), pp. 143-61, and "Paléoenvironment dans le Sahara central pendent l'Holocène," *PA* 22 (1991), pp. 191-201, demonstrate that from 6000 BP onwards there was a gradual impoverishment and reduction of plant cover, a general retreat of the savannah-desert boundary northwards, and a transitional 'plateau' phase down to 4000 BP, after which the desert vegetal cover of the Sahara became established in much its present form.

With regard to the relationship of the changing environment to patterns of economic subsistence, and specifically **the development of nomadic pastoralism**, on evidence of the Saharan rock art see Alfred Muzzolini, *L'arte rupestre préhistorique des massifs centraux sahariens* (Oxford, 1986), who, in an iconoclastic and revisionist work derived from his 1983 'thèse du 3e cycle' at the Université de Provence, questions the basic stylistic and chronological categories that have been used to derive historical conclusions about the environment and pastoralism. Similar critiques of his that appeared subsequently include: "Premier moutons sahariens d'après les figurations rupestres," *Archaeozoologia* 1 (1987), pp. 129-47; "Sheep in Saharan Rock Art," *Rock Art Research* 7 (1990), pp. 93-109; and "'Bovidien' dans l'art rupestre saharien: un re-examen critique," *Anthropologie* 96 (1992), pp. 737-57. A relevant series of studies on the relationship between the Saharan environment and the emergence of pastoralism have been offered by Andrew B. Smith, "Environmental Limitations on Prehistoric Pastoralism in Africa," *AAR* 2 (1984), pp. 99-111; "Origins of the Neolithic in the Sahara," (in) J. Desmond Clark & Steven A. Brandt eds., *From Hunters to Farmers* (Berkeley, 1984), pp. 84-92; and "The Neolithic Tradition in the Sahara," (in) Martin Williams and Hugues Faure eds., *The Sahara and the Nile: Quaternary Environments and Prehistoric Occupation in North Africa* (Rotterdam, 1980), pp. 451-65, with specific discussion of our studies. Alfred Muzzolini, "Emergence of a Food-Producing Economy in the Sahara," (in) *Archaeology of Africa: Food, Metals and Towns* (London, 1993), pp. 227-39, offers a synoptic view of his many contributions. More specific to the regions of the eastern Sahara is the work by Kimball M. Banks, *Climates, Cultures and Cattle: the Holocene Archaeology of the Eastern Sahara* (Dallas, 1984), especially the consideration of the problems of the origins of animal domestication and pastoral nomadism. Finally, the overview by Achilles Gautier, "Prehistoric Men and Cattle in North Africa: A Dearth of Data and a Surfeit of Models," ch. 9 (in) Angela Close ed., *Prehistory of Arid North Africa* (Dallas, 1987), pp. 163-87, is a salutary caution against an over-reading of the existing data which, though large in number, are still not of the quality or type necessary to produce viable interpretive models.

For the **Saharan borderlands of the Maghrib**, the essential work is Ginette Aumassip, *Le Bas-Sahara dans la préhistoire* (Paris, 1986), especially her general conclusions in ch. 13, "La vie des populations Néolithiques," pp. 485-556. A convenient summary of her conclusions can be found in the "Neolithic of the Basin of the Great Erg," ch. 12 (in) Angela Close ed., *Prehistory of Arid North Africa* (Dallas, 1987), pp. 235-58. For the Tadrart Acacus region that was part of my arguments in 1.II, Barbara E. Barich ed., *Archaeology and Environment in the Libyan Sahara: the Excavations in the Tadrart Acacus, 1978-1983* (Oxford, 1987) is important; a convenient synopsis of her book is available in her paper "Adaptation in Archaeology: An Example from the Libyan Sahara," ch. 10 (in) Angela Close ed., *Prehistory of Arid North Africa* (Dallas, 1987), pp. 189-210. Barich's interpretations are part of a general trend to date the appearance of domesticated cattle rather late and to accept the possibility of their introduction from eastern foci. Achilles Gautier, "New Data Concerning the Prehistoric Fauna and Domestic Cattle from Ti-n-Torha (Acacus, Libya)," *PA* 16 (1984), pp. 305-09, argues that even the meliorist environmental phase of a combined pastoral and hunting economy in the region in the second millennium BC existed in a desiccated environment of a maximum of 150 mm rainfall per annum—that is, not much better than the hyper-arid conditions of the present day. An excellent historical comparison of environmental degradation on the other side of the Sahara is offered by James Webb, *Desert Frontier: Ecological and Economic Change along the Western Sahel, 1600-1850* (Madison, Wisconsin, 1995).

For the **protohistoric and historic periods**, see the studies by Madeleine Rouvillois-Brigol, "La steppisation en Tunisie depuis l'époque punique: déterminisme humain ou climatique?" *BCTH* n.s. 19B (1983 [1985]), pp. 215-24, and her "Quelques remarques sur les variations de l'occupation du sol dans le Sud-Est Algérien," (in) *Histoire et archéologie de l'Afrique du Nord: Actes du IIIe Colloque international, Montpellier, 1-5 avril 1985* (Paris, 1986), pp. 35-53. Both articles are specifically concerned with interpretations developed in 1.III. She believes that a dry phase set in after the fifth-century (A.D.) and reached a peak of intensity in the fourteenth. As part of this same series of historical studies on the environment, Pol Trousset, "*Limes* et 'frontière climatique'" (pp. 55-84) offers an estimate of the effect of the climate and ecological régime of the historic period on setting the 'frontier' of Roman occupation in North Africa. For the historical environment in general, the panoramic perspective offered by Robert Sallares, *The Ecology of the Ancient Greek World* (London, 1991) offers a good synopsis of the modern studies on the eastern Mediterranean that provide a context within which the ancient environment of the Maghrib can be better understood. More broadly ranging with specific reference to **1.II & III**, is J. Donald Hughes, *Pan's Travail: Environmental Problems of the Ancient Greeks and Romans* (Baltimore, 1994), esp. at pp. 185 ff. where he accepts my general arguments concerning the respective impacts of climatic change and human action on the degradation of the North African environment in historical times.

On the historical ecology of the **dromedary** (1.IV), Richard W. Bulliet, "Le chameau et la roue au Moyen-Orient," *Annales (ESC)* 24 (1969), pp. 1092-1103, and then in a full-length monograph *The Camel and the Wheel* (Cambridge, Mass; 1975), essayed the speculative thesis that the presence and increased use of the camel was one of the principal reasons for the inhibition to the development of roads and wheeled vehicular transportation in large areas of the Near East and North Africa. For the latter region (*The Camel and the Wheel*, pp. 136-40 and pp. 190-201), however, the thesis is rather improbable because he still argues for a late introduction of the camel to North Africa (this time from a southerly source) and the need for such an hypothesis is rejected in the specific arguments set forth in my chapter on the subject (**1.IV**). Ilse Köhler, *Zur Domestikation des Kamels* (Hannover, Inaugural-Dissertation, Tierärztliche Hochschule Hannover, 1981) outlines the basic historical data for the Near East and North Africa. Reuven Yagil, *The Desert Camel: Comparative Physiological Adaptation* (Basel-New York, 1985) provides an up-to-date summation that modifies some of the physiological traits covered in my historical survey. It is, however, the magisterial treatment by Hilde Gauthier-Pilters and Anne Innis Dagg, *The Camel: Its Evolution, Ecology, Behavior, and Relationship to Man* (Chicago, 1981), that remains the classic synopsis that links both the physiology and the historical ecology of the animal, and should be the work to be consulted to gain more specific data on any of the general points on the physiology of the dromedary alluded to in my analysis.

On the prehistoric evidence, Vanni Bettrami, "Introduzione, ecologia, impieghi e rappresentazioni rupestri del dromedario nel Sahara in età protostorica," (in) A. Mastino ed., *L'Africa romana 8.1* (Sassari, 1991), pp. 313-15, affirms the interpretative position taken by myself regarding the significance of the prehistoric rock-art evidence for the (false) thesis concerning the late historical 'introduction' of the camel to North Africa. On the context of the domestication of the camel amongst the range of other domesticated animals of the protohistoric period, see Gabriel Camps, "Origines de la domestication en Afrique du Nord et au Sahara," (in) *Le sol, la parole et l'écrit: 2000 ans d'histoire africaine = Mélanges en hommage à Raymond Mauny* (Paris, 1981) 547-60. Of the material evidence from the historical period, the reliefs at Ghirza are best consulted in Olwen Brogan and David J. Smith, *Ghirza: A Libyan Settlement in the Roman Period* (Tripoli, 1984): my no. 3 = pl. 67b (commentary, p. 138, no. 10); my no. 4 = pl. 77a (commentary, p. 152); my no. 5 - pl. 64a (commentary, p. 127, no. 4 [although their plates and commentary are confused at this point]); my no. 6 = pl. 110b (commentary, p. 191, no. 6).

The general subject of the **arid-zone farming practices (1.V)** found in North Africa in the Roman period and their relationship to traditional agricultural techniques in the same region now has a vast and substantial bibliography, primarily centered on large scale archaeological surveys such as the *UNESCO Libyan Valleys Survey*—for *ULVS* Report #1 through *ULVS* Report #26, see *LibStud* 11 (1979-1980) through *LibStud* 24 (1993); and the *Kasserine Archaeological Survey* (directed by Bruce Hitchner)—see his reports in *AntAfr* 24 (1988), pp. 7-41 and *AntAfr* 26 (1990), pp. 231-60. Philippe Leveau, "Une vallée agricole des Némenchas dans l'Antiquité romaine: l'oued Hallaïl entre Djeurf et Aïn Mdila," *BCTH* n.s. 10-11B (1974-1975 [1977]), pp. 103-21, provides a detailed survey of a valley in the eastern Aurès which, like the surveys of Oued Guechtane and Oued al-Arab done by the Morizots and Jean Birebent to which I refer in my study, shows that exactly the same developmental processes and types of arid-zone farming techniques were found in these similar ecological zones. Pierre Morizot, "Economie et société en Numidie méridionale: l'exemple de l'Aurès," (in) A. Mastino ed., *L'Africa romana*, 8.1 (Sassari, 1991), pp. 429-46 gives a synoptic overview of arid-zone culture and society in the arid-zone of southern Algeria. Jean Peyras, "Les campagnes de l'Afrique du Nord antique d'après les anciens *gromatici*," (in) *Histoire et archéologie de l'Afrique du Nord: Actes du IIIe Colloque international, Montpellier, 1-5 avril 1985* (Paris, 1986), pp. 257-72, considers the use of the texts of the Roman land surveyors for a better understanding of the land-water use in the ancient Maghrib (see especially [i] 'hydrologie', pp. 258-60, where he analyzes the texts that I used in my analysis and suggests ways in which my interpretation might be refined).

For regions of north Africa further to the east, Pol Trousset, "De la montagne au désert: 'Limes' et maîtrise de l'eau," *RMM* 41-

42 (1986), pp. 90-115, at pp. 97-98 applies the general schemata that I developed concerning rainfall and *impluvia* to the region of southern Tunisia and western Libya during the Roman period, and at pp. 99-100 he offers a broader context in which to place my interpretation of the irrigation system at Lamasba. David J. Mattingly, "New Perspectives on the Agricultural Development of Gebel and Pre-Desert in Roman Tripolitania," *RMM* 41-42 (1986), pp. 45-65, connects the general principles of rural water use that I have developed (1.V) with the specific historical situation in Tripolitania, especially in the light of the data acquired from the *ULVS* surveys (see above). Much the same type of application of the general water control principles developed in my article to the wadis inland of the Syrtic coasts of eastern Libya is used by Michel Reddé, *Prospection des Vallées du Nord de la Libye (1979-1980): La région de Syrte à l'époque romaine* = *Cahiers du groupe de recherches sur l'armée romaine et les provinces*, no. 4, Paris (1988), especially at pp. 73-80, where he discusses the nature of water control schemes and their relationship to Roman influences on the local economy.

The irrigation scheme at **Lamasba (1.VI)** and my interpretation of it, has received attention from Richard Duncan-Jones, "Land and Landed Wealth," ch. 8 (in) *Structure and Scale in the Roman Economy* (Cambridge, 1990), pp. 121-42, at pp. 135-36 and fig. 36. David J. Mattingly, "Regional Variation in Roman Oleoculture: Some Problems of Comparability," (in) Jesper Carlsen *et al.* eds., *Landuse in the Roman Empire* (Rome, 1994) 91-106, at pp. 96-97, accepts my proposed solution for the 'k' unit of irrigation, but objects that I have underestimated the area covered by such units of irrigation by a factor of three or four. The specifics of irrigation in terrace-culture as attested in a later set of documents which I used to illuminate the Lamasba scheme is well analyzed by David J. Mattingly, "Olive Cultivation and the Albertini Tablettes," (in) A Mastino ed., *L'Africa romana*, 6.1 (Sassari, 1989), pp. 403-15. My claim that the archaeological record of arid-zone farming practices and water distribution systems were precisely those described in the texts of these late fifth-century property documents found near Djebel Mrata in southeastern Algeria (the so-called *Tablettes Albertini*) is substantiated by the research of R. Bruce Hitchner, "Historical Text and Archaeological Context in Roman North Africa: the Albertini Tablets and the Kasserine Survey," (in) David B. Small ed., *Methods in the Mediterranean: Historical and Archaeological Views on Texts and Archaeology*, Leiden-New York (1995), pp. 124-

42. He argues from what 'is perhaps the most detailed archaeological record presently available of a Roman period landscape in the Maghreb,' his survey of the Kasserine region of southern Tunisia, that one can see the material record of the arid-zone farming techniques reflected in the texts of the wooden tablets from Djebel Mrata. The terraces, water-channels, wells, cisterns, and wadi cross-dams from his Kasserine survey, and the agricultural crops sustained by them, can be closely correlated with the *gemiones*, *aquaria*, *aqua putei*, and the specific arid-zone crops described in the tablets. In this way, the archaeological record can be linked to a written one where the ownership and property régimes are described in detail.

Regarding the important subject of the nature of water as property and the modes of its allocation to proprietors, there is an important revision by Pol Trousset, "Les oasis présahariennes dans l'Antiquité: partage de l'eau et division du temps," *AntAfr* 22 (1986), pp. 163-93. Trousset forcefully argues that such schemes were always communal in organization, and that some early historians, like Stéphane Gsell, explicitly recognized the significance of this fact for the history of the Roman period (p. 164). He further proposes that the 'k' of the Lamasba scheme should be understood as *k(adus)* rather than *k(aput)*, and that what was involved was a time measurement of water allotted from a constant source (and also that the former term lies at the base of the current Arabic term *gadus* used for time-unit measurement of water in oasis environments in North Africa). He further emphasizes that a division between 'water' and 'soil' based systems of irrigation is rather artificial and that the two types of measurement are not separated in practice. Like the *gemiones* of the *Tablettes Albertini* and their later Berber equivalent *gemoun*, meaning 'an irrigable square,' there is a unitary 'hydrospatial' conception in which the two modes of measurement are integrally linked. Legal aspects of the control of water as property is specified in a new inscription on water rights: Zeïnab ben Abdallah, "La mention des servitudes prèdiales dans une dédicace à *Ammaedara* personifiée faite par un légat d'Afrique proconsulaire," *CRAI* (1988), pp. 236-51 (= *AE* 1988: 1119).

On the subject of **urban aqueduct systems** and their place in the general context of Roman water control schemes and devices (**1.VII**) see A. Trevor Hodge, *Roman Aqueducts and Water Supply* (London, 1992), especially ch. 3, "Wells and Cisterns," pp. 48-66. At pp. 251 ff. he explains the rural use of flood zone agriculture, largely accepting the positions for which I argued (see pp. 404-05 for my evaluation of the historiographical tradition; and pp. 447-50 on my analysis of the Lamasba inscription). Relevant materials can also be found in A. Trevor Hodge ed., *Future Currents in Aqueduct Studies* (Leeds, 1991). Especially applicable are two important papers in this collection: John Peter Oleson, "Aqueducts, Cisterns, and the Strategy of Water Supply at Nabataean and Roman Auara (Jordan)," pp. 45-62; and an excellent guide to research on North African water-works in the context of recent studies is offered by Philippe Leveau, "Research on Roman Aqueducts in the Past Ten Years," pp. 149-62. Concerning the relationship between urban development and permanent water supply by cistern and aqueduct, see Hédi Slim, "Le modèle urbain romain et le problème de l'eau dans les confins du Sahel et de la Basse Steppe," (in) *L'Afrique dans l'Occident romain (Ier siècle av. J.-C.—IVe siècle ap. J.-C.* (Rome, 1990), pp. 169-201; and Sadok ben Baaziz, "Le problème de l'eau dans l'Antiquité dans la région de Bizerte," in *ibid.*, pp. 203-12.

Periodic markets were so much at the heart of the day-to-day economic interactions of North Africans (**2.I**) that the novelist Apuleius could vividly describe a crowded periodic market place encountered in the course of quotidian travels through the countryside (*Metamorphoses*, 3.29.6) and in a studied aside in an oration at Carthage he itemized the common cosmetic utensils for the baths which he himself had purchased at such 'weekly' markets (*Florida*, 9.81). The history of these periodic and fixed markets in Roman Italy has been well surveyed by Joan M. Frayn, *Markets and Fairs in Roman Italy: Their Social and Economic Importance from the Second Century BC to the Third Century AD* (Oxford, 1993), especially ch. 1, "From the *Fora* to the *Macella*,' pp. 1-11; and ch. 8, "Fairs and Festivals," pp. 133-44. On the nature of the permanent urban marketplaces in the empire, see Claire de Ruyt, *Macellum: Marché alimentaire des romains*, (Louvain-la Neuve, 1983); and the useful study by Manuel Martín-Bueno, "The *Macellum* in the Economy of Gerasa," (in) *Studies in the History and Archaeology of Jordan*, vol. 4 (1992), pp. 315-19. With specific reference to North Africa, Sabina Sechi, "Razionalizzazione degli spazi commerciali: *fora e macella* nell'*Africa Proconsularis*," (in) A. Mastino ed., *L'Africa romana*, 8.1 (Sassari, 1991), pp. 345-63, places the marketplace in the context of the political design of the city.

The nature of the larger, longer duration periodic fairs (*panêgyreis*) has been analyzed by Luuk de Ligt and Pieter Willem de

Neeve, "Ancient Periodic Markets. Festivals and Fairs," *Athenaeum* 66 (1988), pp. 391-416, who assert (p. 395) that I mistakenly claimed that *nundinae* were exactly equivalent to *panêgyreis*. This is untrue. I only held that *panêgyreis* and *nundinae* were similar in the sense that both types of markets were periodic or were held at recurrent intervals as opposed to the *mercatus* in towns (such as *macella* or *fora*) that were, by contrast, usually fixed and permanent. Their views are given fuller development in Luuk de Ligt, *Fairs and Markets in the Roman Empire: Economic and Social Aspects of Periodic Trade in Pre-Industrial Society* (Amsterdam, 1993). A specific analysis of the rationality of the location of periodic markets and the competing interests of large-landowners and local communities is offered by Luuk de Ligt, "The *Nundinae* of L. Bellicius Sollers," (in) Heleen Sancisi-Weerdenburg, R.J. van der Spek, H.C. Teitler and H.T. Wallinga eds., *De Agricultura: In Memoriam Pieter Willem de Neeve (1945-1990)*, Amsterdam (1993), pp. 238-62. De Ligt also considers the potential conflicts provoked by the involvement of periodic market fairs in provincial and local community taxation systems. With specific regard to the late imperial inscription from Utica (**2.I**, p. 58, note 6) that contains evidence bearing on the involvement of periodic markets in taxation, see Jean-Pierre Callu, "*Pensa* et *follis* sur une inscription d'Afrique," *AntAfr* 15 (1980), pp. 273-83 (= *AE* 1980: 903).

Several of the specific cases alluded to in my paper are also treated by Johannes Nollé, *Nundinas instituere et habere: Epigraphische Zeugnisse zur Einrichtung und Gestaltung von ländlichen Märkten in Afrika und in der Provinz Asia* (Hildesheim-Zurich-New York, 1982). He offers (pp. 11-58) a general interpretation of periodic markets in the light of the new inscription on the thrice-monthly markets held at Mandragoreis in Asia Minor (*SEG* 32 (1982), no. 1149, pp. 313-15). In the course of his analysis of the new Greek inscription he considers the North African markets on the domains of Lucilius Africanus (pp. 89-117), Munatius Flavianus (pp. 119-29), and Antonia Saturnina (pp. 131-34), at the vicus of Phosphorus (pp. 145-43), at Castellum Mastarense and Castellum Tidditanorum (pp. 145-51), and at Vanisnesis (pp. 153-55). Jean Andreau, "Mercati e mercato," (in) *Storia di Roma*, vol. 2: *L'Impero mediterraneo*, 2: *I principi e il mondo* (Turin, 1991), pp. 367-85, sets periodic markets within the context of the wider imperial economy and networks of commercial exchange. He accepts my analysis of the modular nature and periodicity of the specific north African cases (p.

368), but he disputes the proposed connections between the 'micro' and 'macro' levels of economic activity suggested in my article (p. 376). The general recapitulation of some of the primary evidence by Henriette Pavis d'Escurac, "Nundinae et vie rurale dans l'Afrique romaine," *BCTH* n.s. 17B (1981 [1984]), pp. 251-59, unfortunately adds nothing new to the discussion.

To the dossier of primary materials in my study of periodic markets should be added the inscription from Ras al-Aiûn (near Borj Sabath) concerning the *Saltus Poctanensis P(h)osphorianus* published by Jean Lassus: *RSAC* 71 [1969-1971], pp. 62-66 = *AE* 1972: 697. The economic, political, and cultic associations attested in the inscription are well within the interpretive framework that I outlined for the period markets on this domain. The association of the god Saturn with the genius of the domain is a pattern found elsewhere, as at Ksar al-Ahmar where Saturn is the genius of the *Saltus Sorothensis* (Marcel Le Glay, *Saturne africain, Monuments*, vol. 1, pp. 416-17 = *AE* 1898: 36); and there is the dedication at al-Aria to the *Genus Salti Bagatensis* on behalf of the health of the *dominus* of the *saltus* (*AE* 1902: 223). The freedman servitor who made the dedication at Ras al-Aiûn, Q. Antistius Agathopus, is known from several other inscriptions from the Thibilis region (*CIL*, 8, 18893, 18898-99), all of them votive dedications on behalf of the health of his masters, Q. Antistius Adventus and L. Antistius Burrus, who were senators and large landowners in the region. The last named was a relative of Marcus Aurelius and was *consul ordinarius* in 181 with his half-brother Commodus as colleague. The same freedman is also found in a new inscription also published by Jean Lassus (Lassus, *op.cit.*, pp. 66-67 =*AE* 1972: 698).

The connection between the *vicus Phosphorianus* and periodic markets has received a full study by Jehan Desanges, "*Saltus* et *vicus P(h)osphorianus* en Numidie," (in) A. Mastino ed., *L'Africa romana*, 6.1 (Sassari, 1989), pp. 283-91. Desanges argues (p. 91) that my interpretation (2.I, p. 62) of the market inscription is 'perverse' because I take the *ipsius* to refer to a person other than the grammatical subject of the inscription. The objection is mistaken on both grounds. In explication of claims made by *another* scholar (i.e., Elena Schtaerman), I clearly stated that this was a *possible* interpretation. My precise claim was that *if* one argued that the freedman agent named the *vicus* after his master (the *ipse* therefore referring rather grandly to the master as 'Himself'), then *ipsius could* be interpreted in this manner. This was not, however, the interpretation that I myself sustained. That *ipse* can have the sense of referring to a 'third person' is not 'perverse' but is affirmed by many citations as one of the possible commonplace uses of the word: see *ThLL*, vol. 7.2 (Leipzig, 1962), s.v. 'ipse' at p. 344, lines 13 ff.

Finally, to the list of Africans who bore the cognomen 'Nundinarius'and allied forms should be added the case of a woman named 'Nundina' from Iomnium (Tigzirt) reported by Jacques Martin, "Extrait du catalogue des inscriptions latines du Bassin de l'Isser et de l'Oued Sebaou," *BAA* 7.1 (1977-1979), pp. 69-85. He notes that while the masculine form 'Nundinus' was previously known (*CIL* VIII, 25734), this is the first attestation of the feminine form of the name.

The indigenous institution of the **XIprimi** (2.II) has received further attention from Jean Peyras, "Recherches nouvelles sur les *Undecimprimi* de l'Afrique romaine," (in) *Résumés: 118e congrès national des sociétés historiques et scientifiques* (Pau, 25-29 octobre 1993), p. 186. A newly discovered inscription from Sutunurca that casts light on the function of the *XIprimi* is to be published by Louis Maurin and Jean Peyras as part of their study, "Romanisation et tradition africaine dans la région de Bir M'cherga," *Cahiers de Tunisie* (1993), forthcoming. Peyras argues that the *XIprimi* are not to be equated to the functional position of *flamines* in a Roman municipal context, nor, as a group, are they equivalent in function to a Roman municipal council or *ordo decurionum*.

A significant new piece of information has been added to our knowledge of the indigenous institution of the **elders or seniores** in North Africa (**2.III**) by Pierre Morizot, "Les inscriptions de Tazembout (Aurès): aperçu sur un village romain de haute montagne au IIIe siècle," *BCTH* n.s. 20-21 (1984-1985 [1989]), pp. 69-100 = *AE* 1989: 895. Tazembout is located in the foothills of the Aurès, about 18 kilometres southwest of Lambaesis. At this site was found a dedication to Jupiter Optimus Maximus made on behalf of the health of the emperors and the whole imperial family, and also on behalf of the well-being of the governor, Marcus Aurelius Cominius Cassianus (A.D. 246-47). It was made by two *magistri* of the town, Caius Julius Martialis and Titus Alfius Messor, and by the *seniores loci* (the 'elders of the place'). As Morizot argues, the *seniores* have such a prominent position in the running of village affairs because of the very smallness and remoteness of the settlement—as compared, for example, with *Tfilzi*, a wealthier and somewhat larger town in the Aurès where the *magistri* act on their own: see Pierre Morizot,

"Le génie Auguste de *Tfilzi* (nouveaux témoignages de la présence romaine dans l'Aurès)," *BCTH* n.s. 10-11B (1974-1975 [1977]), pp. 45-61, at p. 47 (= AE 1976: 710). The terms of the new inscription support my suggestion concerning the consistent association of *seniores* and *magistri* as chief 'executive' officials in the context of the small villages of the ancient Maghrib.

Controversy over the origins and sources of the 'official documents' in the **Elder Pliny's geography of North Africa (2.IV)** remains as lively as ever. There has appeared the fundamental commentary of Jehan Desanges: *Pline L'Ancien, Histoire naturelle, Livre V, 1-46: L'Afrique du Nord* (Paris, 1980) done for the Budé series, which considers not only various hypotheses on the nature of the three basic administrative sources used by Pliny (introduction, pp. 11-27; and commentary, pp. 276-349) but also my thesis regarding the nature and timing of the creation of the proconsular province (p. 276). He assigns the Plinean mention of a colony at Carthage (see below) to the colonial foundation made by Octavian (pp. 218-19). A detailed study of the Augustan settlement of the Mauretanias by Nicola Mackie, "Augustan Colonies in Mauretania," *Historia* 32 (1983), pp. 332-58, confirms that these Roman colonies were 'an otherwise unexampled use of colonisation in royal territory...an exception which proves the rule,' and a status that 'they acquired only by accident of their novel location.' Their oddness is yet another indication of the 'ad hoc' manner in which imperial solutions to African problems proceeded during in this period. A. Luisi, "A proposito della regione Zeugitana in Plinio, *Nat.Hist.* V, 22-30. Considerazioni sulle fonti," *Annali della Facoltà di Magistero dell'Università di Bari* 14 (1974-75/1975-76 [1977]), pp. 83-102, argues that it is mistaken to think that Pliny was dependant on a single administrative source. Instead, he hold that Pliny drew on a potpourri of official and non-official documents of various dates, and that he edited these sources rather erratically and thereby created a confused final text. He also claims that it is probable that Pliny had knowledge of a law passed by Curio in 50 B.C. which intended to declare the territory of the African kingdom property of the Roman people. Whereas the latter is possible, Luisi's model for Pliny's treatment of the source materials for the formal lists of provincial communities seems improbable.

The relationship of the delineation of the so-called *Fossa Regia* to the later provincial boundaries has received near comprehensive treatment by Ginette di Vita Evrard, "La *Fossa Regia* et les diocèses d'Afrique proconsulaire," (in) A. Mastino ed., *L'Africa romana*, 3 (Sassari, 1986) 31-58, who canvasses all the received views and reproduces the various suggested routes on a set of useful maps. The problem has been compounded by the discovery of a new stretch of a *fossa* immediately south of Zama and to the east of Limisa (Qsar Lemsa) which may or may not be linked to the *Fossa Regia*: see Naïdè Ferchiou, "Nouvelles données sur un fossé inconnu en Afrique proconsulaire et sur la *Fossa Regia*," (in) *Histoire et archéologie de l'Afrique du Nord: Actes du IIIe Colloque international, Montpellier, 1-5 avril 1985* (Paris, 1986), pp. 351-65.

On the status of **the colony at Carthage** mentioned by Pliny, Alessandro Cristofori, "*Colonia Carthago Magnae in vestigiis Carthaginis* (Plin. *Nat.Hist.*, V.24)," *AntAfr* 25 (1989), pp. 83-93, argues, directly against my reconstruction of the problem, that the reference must be to the later Caesarean *Colonia Iulia Concordia Karthago* because only it would actually have been literally *magnae in vestigiis Carthaginis*, that the Gracchan settlers who remained *in situ* would not have sufficed to evoke the Plinean description, and that the parallels that I see between its status and those of Cirta and Sicca will not stand close scrutiny. He gives a fair summary of my main arguments (pp. 84-85), but I am not persuaded by his objections to them. The reasons he proffers to support his argument that most of the Gracchan settlers must have sold or abandoned their lands are purely hypothetical (p. 87), and he has to admit that the large and complex text of the *Lex Agraria* of 111 B.C. hardly makes any sense if the colonial settlement was on such a small and negligible scale (and this a decade after the supposed formal abrogation of the colony). His claim that those who remained turned into businessmen (*negotiatores*) at Utica or Hadrumetum seems even more far-fetched. Finally, I believe that he reads the phrase *magnae in vestigiis Carthaginis* too literally—the Punic city had an urban core (which was indeed ritualistically cursed) and an enormous rural *territorium*. Most of the Roman colonial settlement was in the latter zone, and was just as much 'in the traces' of great Carthage as were any urban bidonvilles. It is true that I claim that the colonies noted at Sicca Veneria and Cirta were informal colonial settlements, later recognized by Caesar and Augustus. I therefore do not understand Cristofori's objections to this description of them—they were *de facto* settlements made by a freebooting quasi-autonomous 'soldier of fortune' in the midst of a major civil war in lands well beyond the formal borders of the Roman province in Africa. But the settlements nevertheless had been founded, were organized along formal Roman lines, and had to be described by a terminology that would suit their status and existence. They were 'colonies' in effect, and that is all that Pliny's description of them suggests.

That my reconstruction of the **official lists of cities in Pliny's geography** of Africa is correct is substantiated by information relating to the list of the thirty *oppida libera* which shows that both the order and the number of cities included on that list (excluding the spurious case of Aves) is indeed as I have suggested. The sixth city on that list, given as Malzita (*oppidum liberum Malzitanum*) in the manuscripts, is probably to be identified with the town called Melz(ita) attested on a list of African soldiers serving with the *Legio II Traiana* in Egypt (G. Forni and D. Manini, "La base eretta a Nicopoli in onore di Antonino Pio dai veterani della legione II Traiana," (in) *Studi di storia antica in memoria di Luca de Regibus*, Genoa (1969), pp. 177-210, pl. iv-vii = *AE* 1969-1970: 633: col. iv, line 22). That these particular towns were noted because they were tribute-administrative centres of either the African or Punic state and were being confirmed in that status and rôle in the context of the new Roman provincial administration is shown by the fact that even a small and otherwise unattested locale called *oppidum liberum Canopitanum* on the lists and more simply as the town of Canopis is attested as the *mensa* or local collection office of imperial freedman procurators of the imperial administration of the high Roman empire. For the inscription found at Thuburbo Maius (Hr. Qasbat) that mentions the *mensa* of the *regio Thuburb. Maius et Canopitan.* manned by an imperial slave (*Aug. vern.*) and treasurer (*dispensator*), see *ILAfr.* 246; cf. A. Merlin, *BCTH* (1915) cxxxiv. The precise location of Canopis, which must always have been in the vicinity of Thuburbo Maius, has been confirmed by the discovery of a boundary stone of the *territorium* of the *Col(onia) Canopitana* of Hadrianic date: see Azedine Beschaouch, "Eléments celtiques dans la population du pays de Carthage," *CRAI* (1979), pp. 394-409, at pp. 403-07; the location is found at *AAT*, f. xxi, 'La Goulette,' in the Plain of Mornag, near the former Créteville (= *AE* 1979: 658).

There has also been continuing and lively debate on the precise **origin of the Roman proconsular province** in North Africa (**2.V**) and on the political significance and historical circumstances of its creation. Both the dating and context proposed by myself and Duncan Fishwick have been questioned, especially by Jacques Gascou in "La carrière de Marcus Caelius Phileros," *AntAfr* 20 (1984), pp.

105-20 (= *AE* 1988: 1105), and "Les *Sacerdotes Cererum* de Carthage," *AntAfr* 23 (1987), pp. 95-128. A series of in-depth studies by Duncan Fishwick have defended the interpretation we proffered of the Roman state's provincialization of North Africa, as well as the dating and cadence of those changes as proposed in our original article: "On the Origins of *Africa Proconsularis* I: the Amalgamation of *Africa Vetus* and *Africa Nova*," *AntAfr* 29 (1993), pp. 53-62; "On the Origins of *Africa Proconsularis*, II: The Administration of Lepidus and the Commission of M. Caelius Phileros," *AntAfr* 30 (1994), pp. 57-80; "On the Origins of *Africa Proconsularis*, III: the Era of the *Cereres* Again," *AntAfr* 31 (1995) forthcoming; and his "Dio and the Provinces," (in) *Mélanges Marcel Le Glay* (forthcoming). Marcel Le Glay, "Les premiers temps de Carthage romaine: pour une révision des dates," (in) *BCTH* n.s. 19B (1983 [1985]), pp. 235-48, accepts the main lines of the arguments proposed by Fishwick and Shaw, but adds some additional specific data on terminal dates and phases of the process (at pp. 238-39, he assigns the Plinean mention of Carthage to the colony founded by Caesar).

A major revisionist work on the nature of **the Roman frontiers (2.VI-VII)** is now available in a more developed version in English: C.R. Whittaker, *The Frontiers of the Roman Empire* (Baltimore, 1994). It is a work with particular significance for the North African frontiers since they are set in perspective by a scholar who has specific expertise in the history of the region; a briefer synoptic overview can also be found in his "Le frontiere imperiali," (in) *Storia di Roma*, vol. 3: *L'Età tardoantica*, 1: *Crisi e trasformazioni* (Turin, 1993), pp. 369-423. A general analysis of the problem of nomads and frontiers in North Africa, with specific reference to the papers reprinted in these volumes, is found in David J. Mattingly, "War and Peace in Roman Africa: Observations and Models of State-Tribe Interaction," (in) R.B. Ferguson and N.L. Whitehead eds., *War in the Tribal Zone: Expanding States and Indigenous Warfare* (Santa Fe, New Mexico, 1992), pp. 31-60. Maurice Euzennat, "La frontière romaine d'Afrique," *CRAI* (1990), pp. 565-80, presents a lucid *état de question*, and sets the interpretations argued by myself in the wider context of current views on the North African frontiers in general; and the theme of the difference between ideology and 'real conditions' (2.VI) is developed by R. Bruce Hitchner, "Image and Reality: the Changing Face of Pastoralism in the Tunisian High Steppe," (in) Jesper Carlsen *et al*. eds., *Landuse in the Roman Empire* (Rome, 1994), pp. 27-43. My interpretation of the relationship between nomads and frontiers has, for the most part, received critical assent. A persuasive general analysis is offered by Andreas Gutsfeld, *Römische Herrschaft und einheimischer Widerstand in Nordafrika. Militärische Auseinandersetzungen Roms mit den Nomaden* (Stuttgart, 1989). A more specialized study by Arnaldo Marcone, "Note sulla sedentarizzazione forzata delle tribù nomadi in Africa alla luce di alcune iscrizioni," (in) A. Mastino ed., *L'Africa romana*, 9.1 (Sassari, 1992), pp. 104-14, analyzes the demarcations of 'tribal' territories by Roman authorities that are supposed to be one of the main causes of insurrections involving pastoral nomads.

For an assessment of the significance of the **Tacfarinas** episodes (2.VII) that differs substantially from mine, see Marcel Bénabou, "Tacfarinas," (in) *Les Africaines*, vol. 8 (Paris, 1982), pp. 293-313, and his "L'Afrique," (in) Michael H. Crawford ed., *L'Impero Romano e le strutture economiche e sociali delle province* (Como, 1986), pp. 127-41, where he takes specific issue with my interpretation of the revolt and of the frontiers. His views are modified somewhat by Jean-Marie Lassère, "Un conflit 'routier': observations sur les causes de la guerre de Tacfarinas," *AntAfr* 18 (1992), pp. 11-25. The basic literary source is re-investigated in Olivier Devillers, "Le rôle des passages relatifs à Tacfarinas dans les *Annales* de Tacite," (in) A. Mastino ed., *L'Africa romana*, 8.1 (Sassari, 1991), pp. 203-11.

Philippe Leveau, "Le pastoralisme dans l'Afrique antique," (in) C.R. Whittaker ed., *Pastoral Economies in Classical Antiquity* (Cambridge, 1988), pp. 177-95, at pp. 187-88 tends to accept Marcel Bénabou's critique of my theses on the integration of **pastoral nomads** within the social and economic networks of North African society, though (p. 189) he does accept my arguments on the history of the camel as having been demonstrated. For further critique of the positions argued in my papers, see Philippe Leveau, "Occupation du sol, géosystèmes et systèmes sociaux. Rome et ses ennemis des montagnes et du désert dans le Maghreb antique," *Annales (ESC)* 41 (1986), pp. 1345-58, with reference to his many other excellent studies on the subject. Dennis Kehoe, "Pastoralism and Agriculture," *JRA* 3 (1990), pp. 386-98, at pp. 397-98, argues for the acceptance of my 'integrative' model of pastoral nomadism, as opposed to the more polarized view of an inveterate antipathy between desert and sown, and supports my general interpretation of the frontier defence systems.

CRITICAL BIBLIOGRAPHICAL ADDENDA 19

The general situation of the frontier in North Africa, and the 'menaces' threatening it (2.VII), should offer a good point of comparison with the outpouring of studies on the desert frontier along the eastern borders of the Roman empire—where there has developed at least one school of thought which holds that the pastoral nomads themselves did not constitute the major threat to Roman frontier defences. Exemplary of these new interpretations of nomads on the Eastern Frontiers of the empire are S. Thomas Parker, *Romans and Saracens: A History of the Arabian Frontier* (Winona Lake, Indiana, 1986), and his "Peasants, Pastoralists and *Pax Romana*: A Different View," *BASOR* 265 (1987), pp. 35-51; David Graf, "Rome and the Saracens: Reassessing the Nomadic Menace," (in) T. Fahd ed., *L'Arabie préislamique et son environnement historique et culturel* (Leiden, 1989), pp. 341-400; and Benjamin Isaac, *The Limits of Empire* (rev. ed., Oxford, 1992). All are subjected to points of criticism made by Michael MacDonald, "Nomads and the Hawrân in the Late Hellenistic and Roman Periods: A Reassessment of the Epigraphic Evidence," *Syria* 70 (1993), pp. 303-403. A note of caution must be sounded, therefore, that some of the revisionist interpretations of the 'nomad threat' are still hotly contested. For an initial foray in the direction of comparison between the eastern and southern frontiers of the empire, see Ariel Lewin, "La difesa dal deserto: osservazioni preliminari per uno studio conparato delle frontiere," (in) A. Mastino ed., *L'Africa romana*, 6.1 (Sassari, 1989), pp. 197-209. New evidence on the role of the office of *praefectus gentis* or 'colonial supervisor' of indigenous peoples in the semi-arid zone of southern Africa Proconsularis has been published by Z. Benzina ben Abdallah, "Du coté d'*Ammaedara* (Haïdra): *Musulamii et Musunii Regiani*," *AntAfr* 28 (1992), pp. 139-45.

The frontier in **Mauretania Tingitana** (2.VIII) has received much recent attention, of which the following are especially noteworthy. The fundamental study that provides the exacting and precise reading of the archaeological data so necessary as context for the historical interpretation of the epigraphical evidence is Maurice Euzennat, *Le Limes de Tingitane: La frontière méridionale* (Paris, 1989), especially "Le Limes de Volubilis," pp. 274-92. In its exacting record of the material record, its command of the geographical factors affecting the disposition of Roman forces and settlement, and its lavish presentation of the findings, this study will remain the essential point of departure for all subsequent investigations of frontier problems in the region. In an earlier synoptic view of the problem of defence and threats in the region, "Les troubles de Maurétanie," *CRAI* (1984), pp. 372-93, Maurice Euzennat provided a valuable analysis set in the context of the abundant literature on indigenous 'resistance' to Roman rule (see especially pp. 372-73, nos. 3-5 for full reference to the antecedent bibliography). René Rebuffat, "L'implantation militaire romaine en Maurétanie Tingitane," (in) A. Mastino ed., *L'Africa romana* 4.1 (Sassari, 1987) 31-78, offers an exhaustive register of all known Roman military units in the province, along with the geographic location and the temporal duration of their postings. A synoptic overview is offered by René Rebuffat, Eliane Lenoir, and Aomar Akerraz, "Plaine et montagne en Tingitane méridionale," (in) *Actes du 3e Colloque d'histoire et d'archéologie de l'Afrique du Nord, Montpellier, 1-5 avril 1985* (Paris, 1986), pp. 215-52. On the tribute-domination spectrum proposed in the essay, one might also consider the arguments proffered by Jacques Gascou, "*Vici* et *provinciae* d'après une inscription de Banasa," *AntAfr* 28 (1992), pp. 161-72 who analyzes the terms an edict of Caracalla (*IAM*, 2, 100, lines 12-14) and who argues that *vici* were rural lands inhabited by indigenous peoples who, even though they were not a *de facto* part of the province, were still subordinate to Rome in the precise sense that they were subject to tribute.

Further evidence on the use of Roman officials who supervised indigenous 'tribes' (*praefecti gentis*) and possible linkages that the actions of such officials might have had with the parallel actions of the governors of Mauretania Tingitana is provided by Jacques Martin, "Extrait du catalogue des inscriptions latines du Bassin d'Isser et de l'Oued Sebaou," *BAA* 7.1 (1977-1979), pp. 69-85. Two Africans with names similar to those borne by the headmen of the Baquates in Mauretania Tingitana were found in a region well to the east in Mauretania Caesariensis. An Aurelius Illilasen at Iaggachen (no. 11, pp. 78-80; *Atl.arch.*, f. 6, no. 64) and a M(arcus) Aurelius Imten, an *ex prefectus gentis Milidiorum*, noted in an inscription dated to A.D. 241 found at Mechtras (no. 14, pp. 81-83; *Atl.arch.*, f. 6, no. 160). In his collection of inscriptions from the region, Martin records finding five inscriptions of *ex praefecti gentis*, four of whose names are known: M. Aurelius Masilsilen (no. 101), M. Aurelius Vindex (no. 102); the M. Aurelius Illilasen (no. 121) and the M. Aurelius Imten (no. 14) already mentioned above; and one, whose name is lost, who was *ex pref(ectus gentis) Nabuxorum*. Their nomenclature and position bear a resemblance to the heads of the

Baquates in Mauretania Tingitana, save for the fact that the title of 'prefect of the tribe' shows that they were regarded as fully within the Roman system of governance. Martin further speculated that the *Nabuxi* and *Milidi*, along with the other three (unnamed) *gentes* were perhaps the same five tribal groups that constituted the *Quinquegentanei*, a 'confederation' attested in this same region at the end of the third century.

On the subject of **recruiting to the legion** in Africa (**2.IX**), and the nature of the integration of the army with the local society of Roman Numidia, the comprehensive collation of evidence by Yann Le Bohec, "L'apport de l'Afrique à l'armée romaine," pt. 3, ch. 1 (in) *La troisième légion Auguste* (Paris, 1989), pp. 491-530, is now the best point of departure. For further analysis of the problems raised by Elizabeth Fentress's interpretation of the economic rôle of the legionary settlements in Numidia (one of the principal objects of my criticism in the chapter on 'soldiers and society' reprinted here), see Yann Le Bohec, "Timgad, la Numidie et l'armée romaine: à propos du livre d'E. Fentress," *BCTH* n.s. 15-16B (1979-1980 [1984]), pp. 105-20. One should also consult Elizabeth Fentress's replies to my criticisms in the same issue of the journal in which **2.IX** appeared: "Forever Berber?" *Opus* 2 (1983), pp. 161-75.

On the role of **elders or seniores in Christian North Africa** (**2.X**), I would now eschew my somewhat elaborate argument by which I wished to find an error in the manuscripts and to argue that the *fossores* at Cirta were a copyist's error for *seniores*. I do not now think that this error was likely, and believe that some other solution must be sought to explain the apparent confusion in identities of the persons attested in the record. For the rest, however, the argument stands—and is, in fact, substantiated by research done subsequently on a completely separate field of Roman cultural history, that of family and gender relationships, in which I demonstrated the peculiar cultural valuation placed on seniority or 'elders' by North Africans, as opposed to other population groups in the Roman empire, see: Brent D. Shaw, "Latin Funerary Epigraphy and Family Life in the Later Roman Empire," *Historia* 33 (1984), pp. 457-97; and "The Cultural Meaning of Death: Age and Gender in the Roman Family," ch. 4 (in) David I. Kertzer & Richard P. Saller eds., *The Family in Italy from Antiquity to the Present* (New Haven-London, 1991), pp. 66-90.

Finally, on the subject of **'Donatists'** and the problem of identity in the social and religious struggles of the fourth and fifth centuries (2.XI), it should be noted that prosopographical research also substantiates the interpretation, championed by Jean-Paul Brisson, that the so-called 'Donatists' were strongly inter-mixed with Catholic communities in both urban and rural contexts, and that the peculiar rural distribution of 'Donatist' ecclesiastical sees is surely the end result of political repression: see André Mandouze, "Les Donatistes entre ville et campagne," (in) *Histoire et archéologie de l'Afrique du Nord: Actes du IIIe Colloque international, Montpellier, 1-5 avril 1985* (Paris, 1986), pp. 193-217. An earlier study of the technical composition of the acts of the conference that should be noted is James S. Alexander, "Methodology in the *Capitula Gestorum Conlationis Carthaginiensis*," in Elizabeth A. Livingstone ed., *Studia Patristica* 17.1 (1982), pp. 3-8, especially his argument that the *capitula*, though they might seem somewhat haphazard in organization at first glance, bear a consistent relationship to the original minutes of the conference proceedings. Even they, however, reveal a consistent bias against the 'Donatist' participants. On the tactics engaged in by the 'Donatists' and the charges made against them, see Maureen A. Tilley, "Dilatory Donatists or Procrastinating Catholics: The Trial at the Conference of Carthage," *Church History* 60 (1991), pp. 7-19, who reaches some of the same conclusions emphasized by myself. She first notes that the the conference record is a rather 'under-used' valuable historical source, and then makes the substantial point that the 'Donatist legal manoeuvres at the Conference of Carthage in 411 in no way merit the description "dilatory".' For the fate of 'Donatists' in the aftermath of the conference, see Serge Lancel, "Le sort des évêques et des communautés donatistes après la Conférence de Carthage en 411," (in) Cornelius Mayer and Karl Heinz Chelius eds., *Internationales Symposion über den Stand der Augustinus-Forschung* (Würzburg, 1989), pp. 149-65, who is perhaps slightly more sanguine about the success of the Catholic repression than I am, but who agrees that the lack of primary sources on the question after the 430s explains much of the historians' relative lack of interest in the problem.

INDEX

Abonius Secundus (Q.): II 7
Abthugni (mod. Hr. Assûar): X 211
Acholla: IV 446
advocatus fisci: IX 143
Aelius Tuccuda: VIII 70
Africa nova: IV 437-8, 448, 454; V 369-70
Africa vetus: IV 437; V 369, 371
Afri (ethnic): VIII 76
Agathokles: VII 34
ager compascuus: VII 39
agri deserti: IX 149
'Aïn Meshira (Algeria): I 60-61, 74
'Aïn Mclûk (Algeria): I 62; III 35
'Aïn Qsar (Algeria): III 41-2
Aït Ndhir (ethnic): VIII 78-9
Alfius Caecilianus: X 211
Alice in Wonderland: XI 5
Altava (mod. Hajar Rûm): III 23
Alypius (bishop of Thagaste): XI 29
Ambrosiaster: X 208
Ammaedara (mod. Haïdra): III 35; VII 36
Ammianus Marcellinus: VI 25-6, VII 26
Amorites: VII 26
Amsaga (river): see Wadi al-Kebir
Amurrû (ethnic): VII 26
Anderson, P.: VII 28
Androphagoi (ethnic): VI 12-13
annona: IX 143
Antonia Saturnina: I 60-61, 74
Antoninus Pius: III 31, 44
Appian: III 25; V 375
Aquae Iasae (Pannonia): I 45
ara pacis: VIII 71-2, 77
Arae Philaenorum: IV 434-5
Arabia: VI 29
Ariovistus: VIII 73

Aristotle: VI 16-20
Arrius Antoninus (C.): I 62-3
Arrius Pacatus (C.): I 61
Arsennaria: IV 444, 451
Arzuges (ethnic): VII 44
asabiyya: VI 7
Assuras (mod. Hr. Zanfûr): X 219
Astrices (ethnic): III 21
At fusa per Numidiam: IX 142
Atlas Mountains: VIII 68
Augustine (Aurelius Augustinus): VII 44; X 220, 222-3; XI 17-18
Augustus:
 - *Res Gestae*: V 370
Aurelius Canartha: VIII 72, 77
Aurelius Cominius Cassianus (M.): I 66
Aurelius Diogenes (M.): I 59
Aurelius Honoratianus (M.): I 63
Aures Mountains: IX 137, 150
Austuri (ethnic): III 21
auxiliaries: VII 37; VIII 76
Aves: IV 467-71
Awlâd Fraïshish (ethnic): III 35
 - Majûr (ethnic): III 35
 - Reshaïsh (ethnic): VII 46

Bagaï: I 70; X 218-19
Bagrada (river): III 37
Baitokaikê (Syria): I 46
Banasa (mod. Sûq Telta ar-Rharb): VIII 69, 74
Banû Hillâl (ethnic): VII 45
Banû Solaïm (ethnic): VII 45
Baquates (ethnic): VIII 70, 72, 75, 77, 82
Baradez, J.: VII 40; IX 137
Barthel, W.: IV 427
baths: I 61
        Balineum Pacatianum (Cirta): I 61

- Thermae Gargilianae (Carthage): XI 6
Bavares (ethnic): VIII 72, 82; IX 138
Benjaminites (ethnic): VII 34
Bilad al-Makhzan: VIII 78, 81
Bilad as-Siba: VIII 78, 81
Biracsaccar (mod. Sidi Bou Medien): II 5
Birot, J.: VIII 67
bishop(s): I 70; X 208, 212
Bisica Lucana (mod. Henshir Bijga): II 5; III 37, 56
Bocchus: VIII 73
Braudel, F.: VII 28; VIII 67
Broughton, T.R.S.: II 6
Brunt, P.A.: IX 143
Budinoi (ethnic): VI 11
Bulla Regia: IV 445-7
Bu Njem: see 'Golas'
Buri (ethnic): VIII 76
Byzacium: IV 437; X 218

Caecilianus (bishop of Carthage): XI 10, 25
Caecilius Metellus (Q.): IV 446
Caelestis: I 63; III 35
Caelius Phileros (M.): V 373
Caesar, C. Iulius: III 25-6
Cagnat, R.: IX 133
Caius Curio: IV 445
Caledius Maximus: II 8
Calpurnius Bestia (L.): IV 446
Campanian 'B' Ware: I 49
Candidus, son of Balsamon: II 6
Caracalla: III 32-3
Carcopino, J.: III 25
Carpis: IV 436
Cartenna (mod. Ténès): IV 444
Carthage: III 37; IV 438-40
Casae (mod. Hr. Begwâr): I 54, 74
Casae Nigrae: XI 10
Castellum Biracsaccarensium: see 'Biracsaccar'
Castellum Mastarense (mod. Rûffash): I 66, 75
Castellum Tidditanorum (mod. al-Kheneg): I 66, 75
Castra Cornelia: IV 444-5
Cato the Elder: I 57
cerealculture: IX 134
Cereres: see 'Ceres'
Ceres: III 25; V 376
- sacerdos Cererum: III 27, 37
Chayanov, A.V.: IX 149
Chidibbia (mod. Henshir Sluguia): II 8; III 56
Chiniava: IV 449
Chullu: IV 440
Church Councils:
- Bagaï, A.D. 394: X 218-19
- Cabarsussa, A.D. 393: X 218
- Carthage, A.D. 387 [or] 390: X 215
- Carthage, A.D. 392-93: X 218
- Carthage, A.D. 396: X 219
- Carthage, A.D. 411: X 223-4
- Carthage, A.D. 419: X 215
- Elvira, A.D. 305: I 69
Cinithii (ethnic): I 56; III 43-4
circumcelliones: VII 44
Cirta (mod. Constantine): I 59, 61; II 3; III 25, 37; IV 433, 438, 440-41; X 211; XI 5
citizenship, Roman: VIII 70, 75
Claudianists: X 218
Claudius Sollers (Ti.): I 48, 64
clausurae: VII 40; IX 137
Clupea: IV 436
Coculnius Quintillianus (M.): II 3
collegia: I 47, 55-6
colloquium: III 25; VIII 71-4, 77
colonization: VII 38
colonus: I 63; IX 141
comparative method: VIII 67
conductor(es): VII 44; X 224
Corippus: III 21
Cornelius Nepos: IV 431
Cornificius (L.): V 370

INDEX

Cuntz, O.: IV 426, 429
curator(es) rei publicae: III 33-4; X 210, 212, 224
Curubis: IV 436
custodes fructuum: VII 44
Cyclopes: VI 21-4
Cyrene: VI 13

Danube: VIII 76-7
deacon(s): X 212-13, 216
decurio(nes): X 216
defensor gentis: I 63
Despois, J.: VII 42
Detlefsen, D.: IV 426-9
Diana Veteranorum: I 61; IX 151; XI 29
Dii Ingirozoglezim: I 51
Diocletian: VIII 69
Diodorus Siculus: III 24
diplomas, military: VIII 70
dir: VII 42
Domitius Rufus: I 46, 48
domus: III 20, 22, 42-3; VIII 75
Donatus (of Casae Nigrae): XI 10, 14
Douglas, Mary: VI 30
dreams: I 52-3
Dresch, J.: VIII 67
duumvir: III 33; X 211, 224
   - *quinquennalis*: III 32

elders: see 'seniores'
Emadaucapensis (mod. 'Aïn Kerma): I 59, 74
Euzennat, M.: VIII 75

familia: III 20, 22, 43; VIII 75
Febvre, L.: VIII 67
Felicianus (bishop of Musti): X 219
Fentress, E.: IX 133
Fezzan (Libya): IX 149
fides: VIII 73-4, 80
Finley, M.I.: I 72
flamen perpetuus: II 6-7; III 33; V 377; X 212

Flavius Herodes (governor of Africa): X 219
Flavius Mallius Theodorus (governor of Africa): X 219
Flavius Marcellinus (*tribunus et notarius*): X 223; XI 17-20
Florus, son of Labaeo: II 3
Fogg, W.: I 39
foggara: IX 149
forests: IX 133-5
Forni, G.: IX 144
Fossa Regia: III 37; IV 448; V 371, 374, 377
Fossatum Africae: VII 39-40; IX 137
fossor(es): X 212
Frazer, Sir James: VI 31
Fundus Verrona: III 27
Furnos Minus (mod. Henshir Msaadîn): II 6; III 56

Gaetuli (ethnic): VII 26, 32, 37; VIII 76
Garamantes (ethnic): I 56
Gellner, E.: IX 136
Gelonoi (ethnic): VI 11
Genius Vanisnesi: I 50-52
gens: III 43; VIII 75
Gens Bacchuiana (mod. Bû Jelida): II 5; III 37, 56
Gesta apud Zenophilum: X 208, 215-17
Gibbon, E.: VI 26-7, 29
Gigthis (mod. Bû Ghara): III 42-4
Goffman, E.: IX 144
Golas (mod. Bu Njem): IX 137
Goody, J.: VI 20
Gordian (M. Antonius Gordianus Sempronianus-emperor): IX 148
Gracchus, Gaius: IV 439
grammaticus: X 213, 215
Gregory the Great: X 225
Gsell, S.: V 372
Guert-Guessès Plain (Algeria): I 58

Hadrumetum (mod. Sûsa): III 26; IV 446, 451
Hamilcar: III 24
Hanaeans (ethnic): VII 34
handshake: VIII 74
Hanno: III 24
Hasebroek, J.: I 72
Hassawana: I 50
Heichelheim, F.: I 72
Henshir 'Aïn Kedim: III 27
- 'Aïn Tella: III 36
- el-Aluin: II 7
- Debbik: II 6; III 56
- Sidi Merzûg: III 32-4
Herennius Felix (P.): II 8
Herodotus: III 23; VI 8-13
Hippo Regius (mod. Annâba): IV 447; X 220, 225
Hodna (Algeria): I 59, 61, 63; VII 42-3, 46; IX 137-8
Hoffman, A.: XI 5
holy man: I 53, 69-70; VIII 73
Homer: VI 21-4
Honorius (emperor): X 223; XI 17
Hopkins, K.: IX 150
hospitium: VIII 73
hostage(s): VIII 73, 76-7, 80
Huns: VI 13, 25-6
hydraulic works:
- canals: III 27-8
- cisterns: III 27-8
- reservoirs: III 28

Iazyges (ethnic): VIII 76-7
Ibn Khaldûn: VI 6-7
Igilgili (mod. Jijil): III 40
Ilaguatan (ethnic): III 21
Ililasen: VIII 72
Isauria: VIII 67, 79-81
Issedones (ethnic): VI 13
Iulia Domna: III 33
Iunius Blaesus (Q.): VII 37
Iunius Faustinus Postumianus (C.): III 27
Iunius Martialianus (P.): I 66
ius coeundi: I 56

ius commercii: I 43
ius nundinandi: I 48, 54

Jabal Buenó (Tunisia): III 35
- M'zila (Tunisia): III 27
- Nafûssa (Libya): VII 44
- Zaghalma (Tunisia): III 27
- Zerhûn (Morocco): VIII 71
jama'a: I 56
Janon, M.: IX 133-5
Juba I: IV 429-31, 448; V 370
Juba II: I 51-2
Jugurtha: III 25, 35; IV 446; VII 26
Jugurthine War: III 25; IV 446-7; VII 35; VIII 73
Julius Caesar (C.): IV 445, 455-6; V 370; VIII 73
Julius Mirzi: VIII 72-3
Julius Nuffuzi: VIII 72-3
Jupiter: I 50; VIII 72
- Dolichenos: IX 149
- Optimus Maximus: II 8; VIII 71

Kala'at as-Senâm: III 27
Kef Smaar (Algeria): I 49
Khoumirie (Tunisia): III 36
Kietai (ethnic): VIII 79-80
king(s): III 40-41 (see also: 'Juba' 'Jugurtha,' 'Massinissa,' 'Syphax')
Kirk, G.S.: VI 21-2
kiss: VIII 74; XI 25
Kornemann, E.: IV 427-8
Koulê (Lydia): I 46

Lamasba: IX 140
Lambaesis: IX 149
Largius Numidicus (P.):
Laws (*leges*);
- *Lex Agraria*, 111 B.C.: IV 439, 444-5, 451
- *Lex Opimia*, 121 B.C.: IV 439
- *Lex Rubria*: IV 439
Leach, Sir Edmund: VI 13

lector(es): X 210, 213, 216, 226
legati: VIII 73
Legions:
- *Legio VIII*: IV 443
- *Legio XII*: IV 443
- *Legio III Augusta*: I 59, 68; IX 144
- *Legio IX Hispana*: VII 36

Lepcis Magna: IV 446-8
Leptis Minus: IV 446
Le Roy Ladurie, E.: IX 149
Lesser Qabiliyya (Algeria): III 40-41
Lévi-Strauss, C.: VI 13, 31
Libanius: I 64
Ligurians: IV 446
Limes Tripolitanus: IX 137
liminality: I 40; IX 133
Lloyd, G.E.R.: VI 20
Locke, John: VI 28
Locus Octavensis: I 71
Lucilius Africanus: I 54-5, 74
Lucilius Athenaeus (C.): V 377
Lucilla: XI 25
Luttwack, E.: IX 137
Lyautey, Maréchal Hubert: VIII 82

macellum: I 43
Macennitae (ethnic): VIII 72
Macomades: IV 445-6
Mactar: II 7
- 'Harvester': VII 44
Madauros (mod. M'daûrûsh): X 219-20
Maenchen-Helfen, O.J.: VI 25
Maginot Line: VII 46
magister/magistri: III 30, 36, 41
Majorinus (bishop of Carthage): XI 10, 25
Mann, E.: IX 140
map of Agrippa: IV 426-9, 431
Marcomanni (ethnic): VIII 76
Marcus Aurelius: III 31-2; VIII 76
Mari: VII 34
Marion, J.: IX 136
Marius, Gaius: VII 35
Masqueray, E.: III 39

Massinissa: III 25, 39; VII 35
Maurentius (bishop of Thubursicum Numidarum): X 219-20
Mauri (ethnic): I 56; III 21
Maximianus (contender Primate of Africa): X 217-19
Maximinus Thrax: IX 148
Maxula (mod. Rhadès): IV 438, 443-4
Mazices (ethnic): VIII 82
Medrasen: IX 151
Mejâna Plain: I 50
Melania (Iunior): X 220
Membressa (mod. Mejez el-Bab): X 219
Memmius Pacatus (L.): III 43
Mensurius (bishop of Carthage): X 217
mercatus: I 43
Mercury: II 7; III 36
merhum: VII 34
Mesopotamia: VII 25-6, 34, 41, 46
Messius Pacatus (C.): III 43
Meyer, E.: I 72
Milev: IV 440
Miltiades (bishop of Rome): XI 10
Mithras: IX 149
Momigliano, A.: VII 28
Morizot, J.: IX 151
Munatius Felix: X 212
Munatius Flavianus: I 59, 74
municipalities: IV 425; III 43-4; IX 144, 149
Municipium Septimium ... (see: 'Henshir Debbik')
Musti (mod. Hr. Mest): X 219
Musulamii (ethnic): I 56; III 27, 35; VII 38; VIII 76

Nasamones (ethnic): III 23
nationes: IV 434, 451, 455-6
Nattabutes (ethnic): I 63
Neapolis: IV 437
Nememsha Mountains: IX 137
Neptune: III 28

Nicibes (ethnic): I 59, 63
Nicivibus (mod. N'gaûs): IX 149
Nicomedia: I 47
nomads, pastoral: I 61; IX 137
Nova Germania: X 219
Numerius Caesius: II 5
Numidia: IX 133 f.
Numidae (ethnic): I 50; VIII 76
nundinae: I 44
Nundinarius: I 68, 76-9; X 213

olives:
    - mills: IX 150
    - presses: IX 150
oppida civium Romanorum: IV 449-53
oppida libera: IV 429, 445-8
oppidum Latinum: IV 444
oppidum peregrinorum: IV 444
Opstorius Saturninus (P.): II 7
Optatus (bishop of Milev): I 71; X 217
Orosius: III 24

Paccius Rogatus (C.): III 33
pagus: III 28-9
Pagus Suttuensis: V 375
panêgyris: I 43
Pantikapes (river): VI 11, 15
Parmenianus (bishop of Carthage): X 217
patronage: III 42-4; VIII 75-6; IX 149
Paulus (bishop of Cirta): X 212-13
pax: VIII 71-2, 74, 77, 80
Perpetua: X 209
Petilianus (bishop of Cirta): XI 5, 26-7
Petronius Celer (C.): I 50
Pflaum, H.G.: IX 142
Pinianus: X 220
Pirenne, H.: VII 28
pisteis: VIII 76-7, 80
Placentius (bishop of Madauros): X 219
Pliny the Elder: IV 425

Polanyi, K.: I 72
Polybius: III 24; IV 431
Pomponius Mela: III 20, 23
portae: III 39-40
portoria: VII 42-3
Portus Magnus: IV 451
possessor: IX 141
praeco: I 71
praefectus gentis: VII 34, 39; VIII 76
    - *iure dicundo*: V 375, 377-8
    - *kastelli*: III 33
Praetextus (bishop of Assuras): X 219
priest(s): X 208-10, 212, 216-17, 220
Primianus (bishop of Carthage and Primate of Africa): X 217-19
primores: III 20
principes: I 52; II 3; III 20; VII 39; VIII 72-3, 77; IX 151
Probus (emperor): I 59
Purpurius (bishop of Limata): X 208, 214-15
Putput (mod. Sûq al-Abiod): X 225

Qabiliyya (Algeria): I 39
Qairwân: X 226
Quinquegentiani: VIII 82
Quiza Centana: IV 444, 451

reader(s): see 'lector(es)'
recruiting: IX 144-7
resistance: IX 136
Rharb (Morocco): VIII 68-9, 77
Rif (Morocco): I 39
Rogatus (bishop of Assuras): X 219
Roll, E.: I 72
Romanelli, P.: VIII 74
Rostovtzeff, M.I.: I 72; VII 28
Rusicade: IV 440-41

Saboides (ethnic): II 3; III 56
Sabratha: IV 445-8
Sallman, K.: IV 431-2

INDEX

Sallust: I 49; III 25, 35; VI 24; VII 26
Saltus Massipianus: III 27
Saltus Pacatensis: I 62
Salvius (bishop of Membressa): X 219
Sanctippus: see 'Xantippus'
Saturn: I 52, 69; II 5; III 35-6; IX 149
Scipio, P. Cornelius: 445, 448
scriptura: VII 43
Scythians: VI 9-13
Secundus (bishop of Tigisis): X 213, 216
Senatus Consultum de Nundinis Saltus Beguensis. I 54
seniores: VII 39; X 219
Sentius Felix Repostus: II 6
Sentius Felix Respostianus (L.): II 6
Sepemazin: VIII 72
Septimius Severus: III 35
Sertei (mod. Kherbet Guidra): I 52
Servilia Serena: II 42-3
Servilius Draco Albucianus (M.): III 44
Servilius Serenus (C.): III 43
Seston, W.: III 39
Sextius (T.): V 371, 374, 380
Sextus Pompeius: V 373
Sicca Veneria (mod. el-Kef): III 27; IV 438, 441-2, 447
Sicilibba (mod. Henshir el-Aluîn): II 7; III 56
Silvanus (bishop of Cirta): X 211, 214
Simitthus (mod. Shamtû): IV 436
Sittius (P.): IV 440-42
slave(s): VII 44
Smith, Adam: VI 28
Sol Invictus: I 45
Statilius Taurus (T.): V 370
Strabo: V 369; VI 29
subdeacon(s): X 212
Suburbures (ethnic): I 61, 63
Suburbures Regiani (ethnic): I 63
sufetes: II 5; III 37

sugâgum: VII 34
Sulpicius Felix: VIII 78
summum honorarium: II 7-8; III 37; X 209
surveying: IX 141
- *limitatio*: IX 137
Sutaeans (ethnic): VII 34
Syme, R.: IX 138
Syphax: III 25

Tabula Banasitana: III 43; VIII 69, 74-6
Tacape: IV 445-7; VII 36
Tacfarinas: I 56; III 35; VII 36-7; IX 137
Tacitus: VII 36; IX 142
Taurinus (*Comes Africae*): I 71
taxation: I 58-60; V 374; VIII 73; IX 148-50
Tellus: III 25
Tertullian: X 209
Tetrapyrgia (Asia): I 46
Teutsch, L.: IV 424, 429-30; V 372
Thabraca: IV 435-6; V 372
Thagaste: X 220; XI 29
Thala: III 34; IV 446
Thalai (ethnic): III 35
Thamugadi (mod. Timgad): IX 143
Thapsus: IV 446, 451; V 370
Theudalis: IV 446
Thompson, Dr. Hunter: VI 6
Thuburbo Minus (mod. Tébourba): IV 442-3
Thubursicum Numidarum (mod. Khamissa): X 219-20
Thugga (mod. Dougga): II 5; III 39-40; V 374-5
Thysdrus (mod. el-Jem): IV 437, 448, 451; IX 148
Tiaret (Algeria): I 49
Tituli (mod. 'Aïn Majûba): III 27-31
traditor(es): X 211, 216; XI 10
'tribes': see *nationes*
Triton (lake, river): VI 15-17

Uchi Maius: V 373-4, 376-7
Ucmetius: VIII 72
Ucubi (mod. Hr. Kaussât): III 31
Ucutamani (ethnic): III 40-41
'umran badawi: VI 6
'umran hadari: VI 6
undecimprimi: II; III 37-9
Uret: VIII 72-3
Usufruct: VII 39
Usus: VII 39
Uthina (mod. Oudna): IV 442-3
Utica: IV 435, 444-6, 449, 451
Uzalis: IV 444, 448

Vaga (mod. Béja): I 49; III 25; IV 429-30, 447
Valerius Catullinus: I 45
Valerius Procillus (C.): VIII 73
Van Gennep, A.: IX 133, 151
Varro: IV 429, 431; VII 27
Vazi Sarra (mod. Henshir Bez): II 7; III 37, 56
Verona List: VIII 82
veteran(s): IX 139-40, 149
Vettius Latro (M.): V 378
Vicetia (Italy): I 48, 64
Victor Deusatelius: X 216
Victorinus (primate of Byzacium): X 218
Vicus Augustorum: IX 140
Vidal de la Blache, P.: VIII 67
Volubilis (mod. Qsar Farasûn/Sidi Moulay Idriss): VIII 69-71, 78

Wadi al-Kebir (Algeria): III 36; IV 433
- Beth (Morocco): VIII 68
- Enja (Algeria): III 40
- Haïdra (Tunisia): III 27
- Jinejîn (Algeria): III 40
- Loukkos (Morocco): VIII 68
- Mina (Algeria): I 49
- Sarrath (Tunisia): III 27
- Sebou (Morocco): VIII 68
- Siliana (Tunisia): III 37
- Tinguigest (Algeria): I 49
- Werrha (Morocco): VIII 68
Weber, M.: I 72
week: I 67
Westermarck, E.: I 39
Women: I 60-61, 68; III 42-3; VII 44; VIII 70, 75; IX 148; X 220; XI 25

Xantippus (Primate of Numidia): X 220

Zama: IV 445-8, 456
Zarai (mod. 'Aïn Zraïa): I 60; VII 42-3
Zegrenses (ethnic): III 43; VIII 74
Zenophilus (governor of Numidia): X 211
Zopyrus, son of Tiro: II 5